CLASSICS OF PHILOSOPHY

VOLUME I

Ancient and Medieval

CLASSICS OF PHILOSOPHY

VOLUME I
Ancient and Medieval

Louis P. Pojman

New York   Oxford
OXFORD UNIVERSITY PRESS
1998

OXFORD UNIVERSITY PRESS

Oxford   New York

Athens   Auckland   Bangkok   Bogotá   Bombay   Buenos Aires
Calcutta   Cape Town   Dar es Salaam   Delhi   Florence   Hong Kong
Istanbul   Karachi   Kuala Lumpur   Madras   Madrid   Melbourne
Mexico City   Nairobi   Paris   Singapore   Taipei   Tokyo   Toronto

and associated companies in

Berlin   Ibadan

Library of Congress Cataloging–in–Publication Data
Philosophy: the classics/[edited by] Louis P. Pojman.
p.   cm.
Includes bibliographical references.
Contents: v. 1. Ancient and medieval—v. 2. Modern and contemporary
ISBN 978-0-19-511645-8 (v. 1) —ISBN 978-0-19-511646-5 (v. 2)

1. Philosophy.   I. Pojman, Louis P.
BD21.P476   1997
100–dc21   97-1134
                                                                CIP

Printed in the United States of America
on acid-free paper

Dedicated to
WILLIAM LAWHEAD AND WALLACE MATSON
whose love of the classics
has inspired me

Contents

* Selection reprinted in its entirety

Preface

This volume contains the first two parts, "The Ancient Period" and "The Medieval Period", of the four-part volume *Classics of Philosophy*. It includes major works from Pre-Socratics (beginning with Thales in 585 B.C. to William of Ockham (1280–1349). The major portion consists of the work of Plato and Aristotle, the two greatest philosophers of Ancient Greece. In contrast to most works of this sort I begin with the Pre-Socratics, for, although their writings are enigmatic, they provide invaluable understanding of the genius that launched philosophical inquiry two and one half millennia ago. To exclude them would be tantamount to excluding the book of Genesis from the Bible. Four complete works of Plato and large parts of two more are included. I have used the whole of Waterfield's recent translation of *Republic*. Selections from seven works of Aristotle are contained herein. The classic works of Epicurus, Epictetus, Sextus Empiricus, and Plotinus round out the first part of the work.

In Part II, "The Medieval Period," we begin with Augustine's work on freedom of the will and the nature of time. Next comes Boethius's discussion of free will and foreknowledge, Avicenna's "Essay on the Secret of Destiny," Anselm's ontological argument, Maimonides's "Guide for the Perplexed," selections from Thomas Aquinas, and William of Ockham.

Brief introductions on each philosopher, including a bibliography, precede his works.

Because the Pre-Socratic philosophers are difficult to understand, I have included a brief commentary on their selections.

I have included complete works or, at least, complete sections of works, wherever possible, given the constraints on a book like this. With regard to works in other languages, I have chosen the best translations in terms of accuracy and accessibility.

Beginning on page xi I have included a time line in order to place the philosophers in this collection in chronological context with other major figures and events.

Several people gave me constructive advice on this project: Brian Magee, James Allard, Daniel Frank, Stanley Obitts, and Wayne Pomerleau. I especially want to thank Wallace Matson who provided special help, allowing me to use his translation of Epictetus's *Encheiridion* and correcting an earlier draft of my introductions. To him and my long time friend and former colleague Bill Lawhead, both of whom have contributed to my knowledge of the history of philosophy, this work is dedicated. My editor, Robert Miller, was a strong support, providing encouragement at every step of the way. My wife, Trudy, with her love and devotion, as always was the force that enabled me to accomplish this task with exhilarating joy.

United States Military Academy L.P.P.
West Point, N.Y.

Time Line

Philosophers		Major Figures and Events

THE ANCIENT PERIOD

Thales*	c. 624–545 B.C.	Thales predicts solar eclipse, 585 B.C.
Anaximander	c. 610–545 B.C.	Lao-tzu, c. 575 B.C.
Anaximenes	c. 580–500 B.C.	Buddha, c. 563–483 B.C.
Pythagoras	c. 570–495 B.C.	Confucius, c. 551–479 B.C.
Xenophanes	c. 570–478 B.C.	
Heraclitus	c. 540–480 B.C.	Republic of Rome established, c. 508 B.C.
Parmenides	c. 515–450 B.C.	Sophocles, c. 495–406 B.C.
Anaxagoras	500–428 B.C.	Battle of Marathon, 490 B.C.
Empedocles	c. 495–435 B.C.	
Zeno the Eleatic	c. 490–430 B.C.	Parthenon built in Athens, 438 B.C.
Portagoras	c. 490–420 B.C.	
Gorgias	c. 483–375 B.C.	Peloponnesian War, 431–404 B.C.
Socrates	c. 470–399 B.C.	Trial & death of Socrates, 399 B.C.
Democritus	c. 460–360 B.C.	
Plato	c. 428–348 B.C.	Plato founds the Academy, c. 388 B.C.
Aristotle	384–322 B.C.	Aristotle found the Lyceum, 334 B.C.
Pyrrho	c. 360–270 B.C.	Death of Alexander the Great, 323 B.C.
Epicurus	341–270 B.C.	Epicurus opens school in Athens, 306 B.C.
Zeno the Stoic	c. 336–264 B.C.	Zeno opens his school at the Stoa, 301 B.C.
		Rome conquers the Greek world, 200–128 B.C.
		Caesar is Dictator of Rome, 49–44 B.C.
		Jesus Christ, c. 4 B.C.–A.D. 30
Epictetus	c. 50–138	Romans destroy Temple in Jerusalem, 70
Marcus Aurelius	121–180	
Plotinus	205–270	

* Philosophers whose names appear in **boldface** appear in this volume.

THE MEDIEVAL PERIOD

Constantine grants tolerance to Christianity

Saint Augustine	354–430	Theodosius I makes Christianity the state religion of Rome, 392
Boethius	c. 480–524	Fall of the Roman Empire in the West, 476
John Scotus Erigena	c. 810–877	Muhammad, c. 570–632
Anselm	1033–1109	
Avicenna	980–1037	
Al-Ghazali	1058–1111	
Peter Abelard	1079–1142	William the Conqueror conquers England, 1066 Start of the Crusades, 1096
Averroës	1126–1198	University of Paris founded, 1160
Moses Maimonides	1135–1204	Oxford University founded, 1167 Cambridge University founded, 1209
St. Thomas Aquinas	1225–1274	
Meister Eckhart	c. 1260–1327	Dante Alighieri, 1265–1321
John Duns Scotus	c. 1266–1308	The Black Death ravages Europe, 1347–1351
William of Ockham	c. 1280–1349	

CLASSICS OF PHILOSOPHY

VOLUME I

Ancient and Medieval

PART I

THE ANCIENT PERIOD

Chapter 1
THE PRE-SOCRATICS

INTRODUCTION

Philosophy begins with wonder, and even now it is wonder that causes philosophers to philosophize. At first they wondered about the obvious difficulties and
then they gradually progressed to puzzle about the greater ones, for example, the
behavior of the moon and sun and stars and the coming to be of the universe.
Whoever is puzzled and in a state of wonder believes he is ignorant (this is why
the lover of myths is also in a way a philosopher, since myths are made up of
wonders). And so, if indeed they pursued philosophy to escape ignorance, they
were obviously pursuing scientific knowledge in order to know and not for the
sake of any practical need.[1]

(ARISTOTLE)

They looked into the heavens and wondered how the universe had come about. They pondered
the structure of the world. Is there one fundamental substance that underlies all of reality or are
there many substances? What is the really *real*, and not just a matter of appearance?

The first philosophers were Greeks of the sixth century B.C. living on the Ionian coast of the
Aegean Sea, in Miletus, Colophon, Samos, and Ephesus. Other people in other cultures had wondered about these questions, but usually religious authority or myth had imposed an answer. Typically, as in the Hebrews' Genesis 1 or the Greek Hesiod's *Theogony* the world order was said
to have arisen from God or the gods. Now a break occurred. Here for the first time a pure philosophical and scientific inquiry was allowed to flourish. The Great Civilizations of Egypt, China,
Assyria, Babylon, Israel, and Persia, not to mention those of the Incas, Mayans, and Africans,
had produced art and artifacts and government of advanced sorts, but nowhere, with the possible
exception of India, was anything like philosophy or science developed. Ancient India was the
closest civilization to produce philosophy, but it was always connected with religion, with the
question for salvation or the escape from suffering, Ancient Chinese thought, led by Confucius
(551–475 B.C.), had a deep ethical dimension. But no epistemology or formulated logic. Now
Greek philosophy, especially from Socrates on, also had a practical bent and was concerned with
ethics, but it went deeper and further than ethics, asking for the nature of all things, aiming at
knowledge and understanding for its own sake, seeking systematic understanding of metaphysics,
and using experiment and logical argument, rather than religion or intuition alone, to reach its
conclusions. Indeed, Socrates was the first to develop dialectical argument (the "Socratic Method")
and Aristotle invented formal logic, the system of syllogisms.

---

1. Aristotle, *Metaphysics* 1.2 982b.

3

The first Greek philosophers were materialists and naturalists, sometimes called *Hylicists* (from the Greek *hulé*, which means matter), for they rejected spiritual and religious causes and sought naturalistic explanations of reality. The standard date for the beginning of philosophy is May 23, 585 B.C., when, according to Herodotus, Thales of Miletus (625–545 B.C.) on the coast of Asia Minor (then called Ionia, now Turkey) predicted a solar eclipse.[2] What has the prediction of an eclipse to do with philosophy? Thales used mathematical and astronomical investigation to make his prediction. In this sense he may have been the first scientist, and since at this early stage of development science cannot be separated from philosophy, the prediction of the solar eclipse serves as a clothespin holding one end of the long sheet of the history of philosophy to the clothesline of world history.

Thales, who was an engineer by training, asked, "What is the nature of reality? What is the ultimate explanation of all that is?" and speculated and experimented in order to come up with the answer. What was his answer? "Water." Water is necessary for the production and sustenance of life. Water is everywhere, look past the coastline and you'll find a sea of water, dig under the ground and you're bound to find water. It rises as mist from the sea and falls down to earth as rain. Heat water and it becomes a gas like air, freeze it and it becomes solid. So Thales concluded that earth was just especially solid water, a hard flat cork which floated in a sea of liquid of the same substance. It is the first recorded attempt to give a naturalistic answer to the question "What is reality?"

A simple beginning? No doubt, but it is worth quoting Friedrich Nietzsche here.

> Greek philosophy seems to begin with a preposterous fancy, with the proposition that water is the origin and mother-womb of all things. Is it really necessary to stop there and become serious? Yes, and for three reasons: Firstly, because the proposition does enunciate something about the origin of things; secondly, because it does so without figure and fable; thirdly, because in it is contained, although only in the chrysalis state, the idea—Everything is one. The first-mentioned reason leaves Thales still in the company of religious and superstitious people; the second, however, takes him out of this company and shows him to us as a natural philosopher; but by virtue of the third, Thales becomes the first Greek philosopher.[3]

After Thales his fellow Ionian Anaximander (ca. 612–545 B.C.) rejected the idea that water was the root substance and hypothesized that ultimate reality could not be equated with any one material substance, but was neutral between them, yet underlying all matter. It was an unknown boundless material substance, the *Infinite* or *Boundless*.

> Anaximander asserted that the source and elements of existing things is the *infinite*. He was the first to introduce this name for the source. He says that it is neither water nor any of the other so-called "elements," but of another nature which is infinite, from which all the heavens and the world-order in them arise.

No mention is made of the gods, nor of a beginning nor end of reality.

> Everything either is a beginning or has a beginning. But there is no beginning of the infinite; for if there were, it would limit it. Moreover, since it is a beginning, it is unbegotten and indestructible. For there must be a point at which what has come into

---

2. Discussed and quoted in G. S. Kirk and J. E. Raven, *The Presocratic Philosophers* (Cambridge: Cambridge University Press, 1957), pp. 74–81.

3. Friedrich Nietzsche quoted in Ed L. Miller, *Questions That Matter* (New York: McGraw-Hill, 1987), p. 61.

being reaches completion, and a point at which all perishing ceases. Hence, as we say, there is no source of *the Infinite*, but it appears to be the source of all the rest and "encompasses all things" and "steers all things," as those assert who do not recognize other causes besides the infinite. And this, they say, is divine; for it is "deathless" and "imperishable" as Anaximander puts it, and most of the physicists agree with him.

The Infinite is externally in motion and the source of time, space, matter and mind. An opposition of forces keeps the world in its revolving place. These opposites "make reparation to one another for their injustice," creating an exterior homeostasis or equilibrium of forces.

> Into those things from which existing things have their coming into being, their passing away, too, takes place, according to what must be; for they make reparation to one another for their injustice according to the ordinance of time.[4]

Analogously, health is an inner homeostasis, an equilibrium of opposing forces within us. Our world is only one of many worlds produced by the Infinite in its eternal motion, a motion which is perpetually whirling. This Whirl separates as in a vortex or whirlpool in which heavy objects move to the bottom and light to the top. Hence the colder elements, earth and water, move downward and the lighter ones, fire and air, upward. This seems to be the beginning of the idea of Natural Law in which natural causes, blind and impersonal, replace the gods. Wind, not Zeus, causes lightning. He rejected Thales notion of a stationary flat earth and suggested that the earth was a revolving, cylindrical body, whose flat top was our home.[5]

Rejecting the anthropocentric notions of the religious and mythological explanations and anticipating Darwin by 2500 years, Anaximander put forth a theory of evolution based on the need for species to adapt to their environment. Human beings evolved from fish or fishlike creatures who had to adapt to land and so developed the characteristics we now have.

Anaximander's disciple Anaximenes (585–528 B.C.) accepted his teacher's notion that reality is infinite, but observing evaporation and condensation and how breath animated both humans and animals, he posited air as the ultimate substance. "Just as our soul, being air, keeps us together in order, so also breath and air encompass the whole cosmos."

One other philosopher from the Ionian coast deserves mention. Xenophanes (ca. 570–ca. 478 B.C.) noted the anthropomorphic nature of the gods, their immorality, their stealings, adulteries, and deceivings, their ethnic qualities, suggesting that each culture creates its gods in its own image.

> The Ethiopians make their gods black and snub-nosed. The Thracians make theirs have grey-eyes and red-hair. And if oxen and horses and lions had hands and could paint with their hands, and produce works of art as men do, horses would paint the forms of the gods like horses, and oxen like oxen, and make their bodies in the image of their own.[6]

He argued that there was one God beyond all these mythological and anthropomorphic counterfeits, who seeks, hears and thinks all over. "He remains forever in the same place, without mov-

---

4. Quoted by Simplicius in his *Physics*. Quoted in John Mansley Robinson, *An Introduction to Early Greek Philosophy* (New York: Houghton Mifflin Company, 1968), p. 34.

5. Alcameon developed this thought, applying it to health: The essence of health lies in the "equality" of the powers—moist, dry, cold, hot, bitter, sweet, and the rest—whereas the cause of sickness is the "supremacy of one" among these. For the rule of any one of them is a cause of destruction . . . while health is the proportionate mixture of the qualities. Quoted in Robinson, op. cit., p. 35.

6. Quoted in Robinson, op. cit., p. 52.

ing; nor is it fitting for him to go about from one place to another. But without labor he sets all things in motion by his intelligent willpower."

PYTHAGORAS

The first philosopher of which we have substantial information is Pythagoras of Samos (580–496 B.C.), who settled in Croton in southern Italy, where he founded the first community of philosophers. Pythagoras either visited Egypt himself or learned from those who did, since the Greek historian Herodotus points to similarities between his ideas and the Egyptians (religious customs forbidding people to wear wool in temples and belief in an afterlife).[7] It could be argued that not Thales but Pythagoras was the father of philosophy, for with him a comprehensive study of the fundamental questions of philosophy first takes place: What is reality? How does one come to know the truth? How shall I live my life? Here is an early document on what he taught:

> First he said that the soul is immortal; second, that it migrates into other kinds of animals; third, that the same events are repeated in cycles, nothing being new in the strict sense; and finally, that all things with souls should be regarded as related to each other. Pythagoras seems to have been the first to introduce these ideas into Greece.[8]

Pythagoras rejected the Hylicist's materialism and opted for a refined spiritualism, a mathematical mysticism, aiming at the purification of the whole person, body and soul. Knowledge (or Science) and Music would purify the soul and Gymnastics and Medicine, the body. All living things (including plant life) had souls and were related to one another and involved in the transmigration of souls. Pythagoreans generally despised the body as inferior to the soul, which they sought to purify by ascetic practices. They were vegetarians, eating neither meat nor eggs nor beans, nor drinking wine. A story circulated in the ancient world that when Pythagoras noticed a man beating a dog, he cried to him to desist, claiming that he recognized in the dog the "voice of a dear friend."

Pythagoras related morality to the harmony of the soul. A good soul has a proper order of standards and impulses within itself like beautiful music and the sublime system of the heavens. Pythagoreans were renowned for their mutual friendship, altruism, integrity, devotion to duty. At the end of each day they asked themselves what wrongs they had committed, what duties they had neglected, what good they had done.

Pythagoras is the first person on record to hold the doctrine of universal brotherhood, which led him to provide equal opportunity for men and women. Two centuries before Plato's famous declaration of this doctrine in the *Republic* Pythagoros accepted women on an equal basis with men, admitting them into his school. He also called for, and himself practiced, humane treatment of slaves. He was reputed to have never chastised a slave.

Under the government of the Pythagoreans, Croton succeeded in establishing an intellectual aristocracy over a territory about four times the size of Attica, which was destroyed by the democratic party in the second half of the fifth century B.C. The democrats massacred the Pythagoreans, surrounding their assembly house, in which the leadership was lodged, and burning it to the ground.

Pythagoras's fundamental doctrine was that the world is really not material but made up of numbers. Numbers are things and constitute the essence of reality. The original "one," being fire, sets the surrounding cold air in motion, drawing it upon itself and limiting it. From numbers the world is created:

---

7. See Richard McKirahan Jr. *Philosophy Before Socrates* (82–87) for a lucid discussion of this point.

8. Diogenes Laertius viii.5 quoted in Robinson, p. 57.

From numbers points, from points lines, from lines plane figures, from plane figures solid figures, from these sensible bodies, of which the elements are four: fire, water, earth, and air. These change and are wholly transformed; and from them arises a cosmos animate, intelligent, and spherical, embracing earth (itself spherical and inhabited all around) as its center.

Pythagoras was led to this doctrine by his musical studies. He recognized that the pitch of tones depends on the length of the strings on musical instruments and that musical harmony is determined by definite mathematical propositions. The recognition of this fact led the Pythagoreans to the soul, which was not contained in matter itself but was suprasensual. Thus the anthropological dualism of body and soul was extended to the cosmic dualism of matter and form, or, as they expressed it, of the unlimited and the limit. Hence number was for them something essentially different from water for Thales, or the Apeiron for Anaximander or air for Anaximenes; it was something opposed to matter and distinguished from it although closely connected with it, something which limits it and gives it shape. Matter, as such, was presupposed by the Pythagoreans, and they seem to have imagined it in a way that combined Anaximander's Unbounded and Anaximene's air. Matter is unlimited breath, that is, the endless expanse of air beyond the cosmos from which the world draws its breath.

Now that number was established as a world-principle, they proceeded to make remarkable speculations on its nature. They drew distinctions between straight and not-straight, unity and duality, and thus derived two further pairs of opposites, whose number was later rather arbitrarily extended up to ten. Individual numbers were considered particularly sacred. One (1) is the paradoxical point, both the limited and the unlimited, 2 is the line, 3 the plane, 4 the solid, 5 physical qualities, 6 animation, 7 intelligence, 8 health, 9 love and wisdom, 10 the sacred Decad, by which they were accustomed to take oaths. From their experiments with numbers they were led to the discovery of the "Pythagorean Theorem," (the sum of the squares of the sides of a right angle triangle are equal to the square of the hypotenuse). Theophrastus tells us that the Pythagoreans were the first to speak of the spherical shape of the earth, the harmony of the spheres and planetary motion. Pythagoras supposed there to be a Central Fire around which the round earth revolved.

Mystic and mathematician, Pythagoras held that we are strangers and pilgrims in the world, that the body is the tomb of the soul, that the visible world of matter is appearance, which must be overcome if we are to know reality. In this life there are three types of people who come to the Olympic Games. The lowest class is made up of those who come to buy and sell, the next above them are those who compete. Best of all, however, are those who come simply to look on. These three types of people correspond to three parts of the soul: the love of gain, of honor, and of wisdom. We must aim at Purification from the world, which comes about through the disinterested pursuit of philosophy. We will meet all these ideas again in Plato, who seems have been influenced by Pythagoras.

Pythagoras apparently wrote nothing, so we cannot study his writings.

THE ELEATICS

With Parmenides (540–470 B.C.) a further advance in philosophical discourse took place. Parmenides observed that nature is constantly changing and noted that such flux was inimical to the idea of knowledge: to have knowledge there must be permanence, something which is unchanging. He theorized that the real world was unchanging on the order of Pythagoras's number, whereas the apparent, illusory world was the world of change. The senses grasped the changing world of unreality or *Non-being*, whereas reason alone could grasp the real world of *Being*. Being never comes into existence, nor does it cease to be, for it always is. It cannot be divided or added onto, for it is whole and complete in itself, one. It is unmoved and undisturbed, for motion and disturbance are forms of becoming. Being is. It doesn't become. It is self-identical and uncaused. This view is sometimes called Absolute Idealism: there is an Absolute Idea which makes up all there is, and all change is illusory. All is One and Permanently at Rest.

Three theses can be identified in Parmenides's work.

1. That which is, is and cannot not-be; that which is not, is not and cannot be. The real is and cannot be nonexistent).

2. That which is can be thought or known and truly named. That which is not, cannot. Thinking and the thought that it is are the same thing.

3. That which is, is one and cannot be many. The real is unique. There is no second thing besides it. It is also indivisible. It does not contain a plurality of distinct parts.

Being or Reality is one, immaterial, continuous, indivisible, motionless, beginningless, imperishable, and everywhere. It is wholly indeterminate and can only be described in negative terms. It cannot be created nor pass away. It cannot be created, for if it were, it would have to be created from Nothing, which is impossible. It cannot be destroyed, for if it could, then something could become nothing, which is impossible. When thought has negated all that can be negated, it is Being which remains, the unique, godlike One.

Parmenides's most famous disciple was Zeno of Elea (ca. 490–ca. 430 B.C.), who defended the Eleatic Idealism against those who claimed that there were both multiplicity and motion. Zeno is the first philosopher we know of who self-consciously makes use of the law of noncontradiction to argue against his opponents. Using universally acceptable premises, he develops a series of paradoxes which leads to the conclusion that there is no motion or multiplicity. One of his paradoxes, *The Line* (see Readings) attempts to show that motion does not exist.

The Eleatics held that a line was one, whereas their opponents held that it was divisible into parts, discrete units. Zeno argues that if a line was divisible into units, it must be divisible into an infinite number of discrete units, so that each unit must be infinitely small. But if there were an infinite number of these units, then if we multiplied them, we would get a line which was infinitely large, for the smallest magnitude multiplied by infinity becomes an infinite magnitude. So what started out as a finite line turns out to be infinitely long, which is a contradiction.

> A second paradox is his Arrow Paradox: the Argument Against Movement. If everything is at rest when it is in a place equal to itself, and if the moving object is always in the present and therefore in a place equal to itself, then the moving arrow is motionless.[9]

Consider an arrow flying from one place to another. Does it really move? No, movement is only an illusion. Consider.

1. The arrow could not move in the place in which it is not.

2. But neither could it move in the place where it is.

3. For this is "a place equal to itself."

4. Everything is always at Rest when it is "at a place equal to itself."

5. But the flying arrow is always at the place where it is.

6. Therefore the flying arrow is always at Rest and cannot move.

---

9. Aristotle, *Physics* 6.9, 239.

A body must either be moving in a place where it is or where it is not. It can't be moving in a place where it is not, for it is not there. But if it is in place, it cannot be moving. For the arrow is at rest at any point in the trajectory and what is at rest at any point cannot move. Therefore the flying arrow cannot be moving.

All of the paradoxes have the same form. Any quantity of space must either be indivisible or divisible ad infinitum. If it is composed of indivisible units, these must have magnitude which can't be divided. If it is composed of divisible units, it must be divisible ad infinitum and we are faced with the contradiction of supposing that an infinite number of parts can be added up to make a finite sum total.

Zeno's paradoxes were in part aimed at destroying Pythagorean doctrines that motion and plurality could be explained by mathematics and logic. He showed that logic led to paradoxes that undermined the notions of motion and plurality. In this he vindicated the Eleatic doctrine that Reality was One, immovable, eternal, and uncreated.

HERACLITUS

Heraclitus (535–475 B.C.) of Ephesus, a cynical, aloof, solitary aristocrat, sometimes called "the weeping philosopher," was contemptuous of democracy ("most men are bad") and scornful of the Pythagorean and Eleatic Idealism and set forth an opposing philosophy (Pythagoras claimed for his own wisdom what was but a knowledge of many things and an art of mischief"). Rejecting the notion that only Being is, he posited that only Becoming is ("nothing ever is, everything is becoming"). All things are in perpetual flux (Greek, *panta rhei*), and permanence is an illusion. There is a single principle at work in the universe. It is fire. "Mind is fire." Fire, an infinite mass of substance, uncreated and eternal, is identical with the universe.

> The world order was not made by a god or a man, but always was and is and will
> be an ever-living fire.[10]

Fire consumes fuel, thus changing all, but is in constant flux. Transforming all that it comes in contact with, fire replaces Anaximander's Unlimited. Reality is like a stream of fire in constant motion. Nothing is stable. All comes from fire and to fire it shall return. At the same time Heraclitus posited *logos* (reason) as the lawlike process which governed the world.

The world follows an orderly process, though one of conflict and survival of the fittest. Hence war is reason's way of justice in the world. It is the "father of all and the king of all."

The logos, as the rational principle of the universe, has independent existence and according to it all things come into existence. It perpetually confronts people, calling on them to awake from their sleep of illusion. "To those who are awake the world-order is one, common to all, but the sleeping turn aside each into a world of his own."

The logos is hidden in humanity. We become intelligent "by drawing in the divine logos when we breathe." In sleep we are separated from the source of our being and forget. Further, Heraclitus said that the laws of the city were but a reflection of the logos which runs through all things.

> It is necessary for men who speak with common sense to place reliance on what is
> common to all, as a city relies upon law, and even more firmly. For all human laws
> are nourished by the one divine law. For it governs as far as it will, and it is suffi-
> cient for all things and outlasts them.

---

10. This and the following quotations are from Diogenes Laertius ix.

THE PLURALISTS: EMPEDOCLES AND THE ATOMISTS

Three philosophers rejected both the absolute monism of the Eleatics and the spiritual dynamics of Heraclitus. The first was Empedocles (ca. 450 B.C.) who argued that the world was made up of different combinations of four basic elements, water, earth, air, and fire. At the center of the universe there are two forces: attraction and repulsion, called "Love" and "Hate," which are in constant strife. When Love prevails, all things tend toward unity. When Hate prevails, all things separate, individuate. An eternal cosmological battle is waged, so that as one seems to be winning, the other experiences a resurgence.

According to Empedocles it is literally the case that "Love makes the world go round." But, so does Hate.

The second reaction to the Eleatics was that of the materialists, who hearkened back to the Milesians. Leucippus (ca. 450 B.C.) and his more famous disciple, Democritus (460–370 B.C.) taught that the ultimate constituents of the world were atoms (from the Greek *a* for "not" and *tome* for "cut" or "separable"). They were simple, indestructible, internally solid, homogeneous particles which are perpetually in motion in the void of empty space. Their combination and interaction account for all that is. Materialists were hedonists who believed that the only thing that is good is pleasure and the only thing bad is pain. They did not believe in the gods or in immortality.

ANAXAGORAS OF CLAZOMENAE

Anaxagoras (500–428 B.C.) was the first philosopher to make his home in Athens. He retintroduced pluralism, going against the Eleatic stream of monism, but he also rejected Empedocles's notion of the four elements (earth, fire, air, and water) of which all things were composed. They failed to account for the infinite variety and differentiation of the world of experience. Instead Anaxagoras taught that all things contain a portion of everything else.

> In everything there is a portion of everything. For how else could hair come from what is not hair? or flesh from what is not flesh? unless hair and flesh as well as teeth, eyes, and bone, et cetera are contained in food?[11]

Nous is a material (airy) substance but it is the purest and most rarefied of things, having power over all else. As an efficient cause, Nous sets up a rotary motion in the undifferentiated mass of being and causes separation and differentiation.

Anaxagoras was accused of uttering blasphemy in saying that the sun was a red hot stone and the moon was made of earth, for the Athenians regarded the heavenly bodies as gods. He was condemned, tried, found guilty of blasphemy, but escaped Athens to another country.

Socrates heard someone reading from a book of Anaxagoras. He was struck by the phrase, "Mind orders all things," and got hold of the book. Although the book proved a disappointment, concerning itself mainly with mechanical causation, it was a catalyst in turning Socrates away from speculations about the physical world and toward the study of human existence.

FOR FURTHER READING

Copleston, Frederick. *A History of Philosophy* vol. 1. (Doubleday, 1962).
Freeman, Kathleen, ed. and trans. *Ancilla to the Pre-Socratic Philosophers*. (Harvard University Press, 1948).

---

11. Diels and Kranz *Fragments of the Presocratic Philosophers* (henceforth "DK") 59 B 11.

Furley, David and R. E. Allen, eds. *Studies in Presocratic Philosophy*, 2 vols. (Routledge & Kegan Paul, 1970).

Guthrie, W. K. C. *A History of Greek Philosophy*, 6 vols. (Cambridge University Press, 1962–1981).

Hussey, Edward. *The Presocratics*. (Scribners, 1972).

Irwin, Terrence. *A History of Western Philosophy: Classical Thought*. (Oxford University Press, 1989).

Jones, W. T. *Selections from Early Greek Philosophy*. (Harcourt Brace Jovanovich, 1970).

Matson, Wallace. *A New History of Philosophy*. (Harcourt Brace Jovanovich, 1987).

McKirahan, Richard D. *Philosophy Before Socrates: An Introduction with Texts and Commentary*. (Hackett Publishing Co., 1994).

Robinson, John Mansley. *An Introduction to Early Greek Philosophy*. (Houghton Mifflin, 1968).

Stace, W. T. *A Critical History of Greek Philosophy*. (Macmillan, 1920). Reprint St. Martin's Press, 1967.

Readings

Here are some of the major quotations either from the Pre-Socratics or from other Greek philosophers reporting on their doctrines. Because no complete texts of the Pre-Socratic philosophers exist, our knowledge of their views comes from testimonies and fragments in the works of later writers, especially Aristotle and Diogenes Laertius.

THALES

1. The first philosophers believed that the only principles of all things were various forms of matter.... Thales the founder of this type of philosophy, says the principle [underlying all reality] is water, for which reason he declared that the earth rests on water, getting the notion perhaps from seeing that the nutriment of all things is moist, and that heat itself is generated from the moist and kept alive by it (and that from which they come to be is a principle of all things). He got this notion from this fact, and from the fact that the seeds of all things have a moist nature, and that water is the origin of the nature of moist things.[12]

2. Some declare that the soul is mixed in the whole universe, and perhaps this is why Thales thought all things are full of gods.[13]

ANAXIMANDER

1. [Anaximander] held that the first animals arose in moisture, being enclosed in spiny "barks" but that as they grew older they emerged onto the drier land and there, as the bark ruptured, lived a different sort of life for a short time.

He says that in the beginning man was born from animals of a different sort, arguing from the fact that whereas animals are soon able to fend for themselves, the young of humans are dependent for a long period of time. Hence, if man had been in the beginning as he is now, he would never have been able to survive.

He held that there arose from warm water and earth creatures which were either fish or fish-like. Inside these human beings were formed, remaining there like fetuses until the time of puberty. At this time the creatures broke open, and men and women already capable of getting food for themselves emerged.[14]

ANAXIMENES

1. Anaximenes also says that the underlying nature of things is one and infinite. But he does not regard it as *indeterminate*, as Anaximander does, but as determinate, calling it *air*; and he says that

---

12. Aristotle, *Metaphysics I.3 983b* (DK 11A2, 12).

13. Aristotle, *On the Soul* 1.2 405a (DK 11A22).

14. Quoted in Robinson, op. cit., p. 33.

it differs in respect of thinness and thickness in different things. When dilated it becomes fire; when compressed, wind and then cloud. When it is compressed further it becomes water, then earth, then stone. The rest are produced from these. He too makes motion eternal, through which for him also change comes about.

2. Anaximenes says that the rainbow is produced when the rays of the sun fall on dense thick air. Hence the leading edge of it appears red, being burnt by the sun's rays, while the rest is dark where the rays have been overpowered by the moisture.

3. Anaximenes says that air is a god.[15]

PYTHAGORAS

1. The Pythagoreans construct the whole heaven out of numbers. Not, however, out of numbers considered as abstract units; for they suppose the units to have magnitude. But how the first "one" was constructed so as to have magnitude, they seem unable to say.[16]

2. First Pythagoras declared that the soul is immortal; then that it changes into other kinds of animals; in addition that things that happen recur at certain intervals, and nothing is absolutely new; and that all things that come to be alive must be thought as related to each other. Pythagoras seems to have been the first to introduce these ideas into Greece.[17]

PARMENIDES

1. "The Way of Truth."
Come now I will tell thee
What are the only ways of inquiry
That can be thought.
The one is the way of how it is,
And how it is impossible
For it not to be;
It attends the truth.
The other is the way of how it is not.
And how it is necessary for it not to be.
This is a way wholly unknowable.

Since you cannot know what is not.
Nor could you speak of it,
For thought and being are the same.
It makes no difference
At what point I begin,
For I shall always come back again to this.
Thinking and the thought that it is are the same;
For you will not find thought apart from what is,
In relation to which it is uttered.[18]

ZENO

1. *The Line:* A Demonstration that Motion Does Not Exist.
If there is motion, there will be something which has traversed an infinite series of distances in a finite time. For since the process of dichotomy has no limit, in any continuum there will be an infinite number of halves, since every part of it has a half. A body, therefore, which has traversed a finite distance will have traversed an infinite number of halves in a finite time, i.e., in the time which it actually took to traverse the finite distance in question. Zeno assumes that is is impossible to traverse an infinite distance in a finite time (because it is impossible to complete an infinite series), and thus does away with the existence of motion.[19]

HERACLITUS

1. Heraclitus describes change as a way up and down, and the world-order as coming into being in accordance with it. For fire, when it is contracted, becomes moist; when it is contracted still further it becomes water; and water, when it is contracted, turns to earth. This is the downward way. And earth liquefies again; and from it water arises; and from water the rest. For he refers nearly everything to the evaporation of the sea. And this is the upward way.

2. The way up and the way down are the same.

3. All things come into being through opposition, and all are in flux like a river.

4. You cannot step into the same river twice, for other and yet another waters are ever flowing on.

15. DK 13 A 5 quoted in Robinson, p. 41, 47.

16. Aristotle, *Metaphysics* 14.2 1091.

17. Porphry, *Life of Pythagoras* 19 (DK 14.8a).

18. DK 28 b2. Based on Kirk and Raven, op. cit., pp. 269–279.

19. Simplicius *Physics* 1289, 5. Quoted in Robinson, op. cit., p. 132.

5. The sun is new every day.

6. Wisdom is at once the unity of all things, the measure and harmony, but it is pure as well. . . . Mind is fire.

7. All comes from fire and to fire it shall return.

8. With this *Logos*, which is eternally valid, men keep on being out of contact, both before they heard it and when they first hear it. For although everything happens in accordance with this Logos, men are like novices when they are put to the test of such works and deeds as I present when I define each thing according to nature and tell what it is. But as for other men, such things as they do when they are awake escape their notice, just as when they go to sleep they forget what they are doing.

9. The sun will not overstep measures. If he does, the Furies, guardians of Justice, will find him out.

10. One thing is wise: to discern the rule whereby all things are piloted through all.

11. Those who speak with common sense must strengthen themselves with what is common to all, just as a city with its law, and much more strongly. For all human laws get sustenance from the one divine law.[20]

12. Good and bad are the same. . . . Upward, downward, the way is one and the same.

13. War is natural, justice is conflict, and everything that is is created through conflict, according to how things must be. For fire lives the death of earth, and air lives the death of fire; and water lives the death of air, and earth that of water. War is the father and king over all.

14. Though the logos is as I have said, men always fail to comprehend it, both before they hear it and when they hear it for the first time. For though all things come into being in accordance with this logos, they seem like men without experience, though in fact they do have experience both of words and deeds such as I have set forth, distinguishing each thing in accordance with its nature and declaring what it is. But other men are as unaware of what they do when awake as they are when they are asleep.

15. Though they are in daily contact with the Logos, they are at variance with it, and what they meet with appears alien to them.

16. Asses would rather have straw than gold.

17. Listen not to me but to the logos; it is wise to acknowledge that all things are one. Heraclitus sets forth the two moral principles of antiquity: "know thyself" and "In nothing too much."

18. It is hard to contend with passion; for whatever it desires to get it buys at the cost of soul. It is part of all men to know themselves and to be temperate. To be temperate is the greatest virtue; and it is wisdom to speak the truth and to act according to nature with understanding.

19. All men have the capacity of knowing themselves and acting with moderation.

20. To God, all things are beautiful, good and just; but men have assumed some things to be unjust and others just.

21. The thunderbolt steers the universe.

22. Much learning does not teach one to have intelligence.

23. Nature likes to hide.[21]

ANAXAGORAS

1. All things were together, infinite in number and in smallness, for the Small also was infinite. And since all were together, nothing was distinguishable because of its smallness. For Air and Ether dominated all things, both of them being infinite. For these are the most important [elements] in the total mixture, both in number and size.

2. Mind controls the whole rotation, so that it rotates in the beginning. And at first it began to rotate from a small beginning, but now it rotates over a larger area, and it will rotate over a still larger area. And Mind knows all things that are mingled and separated out and distinguished. And what sort of things were to be, and what sort of things were (which no longer are), and what now is, and what sort of things will be—all these Mind arranged, and the rotation in which now rotate the stars and the sun and the moon and the

---

20. DK 22 B. Translated by Wallace Matson and cited in his *A New History of Philosophy* vol. I (New York: Harcourt Brace Jovanovich, 1987), pp. 24–26.

21. DK 22 73 & 50. The quotations of Heraclitus are based on Robinson's translation, op. cit., pp. 94–95.

air and the ether that are being separated from the rare, and the hot from the cold, and the bright from the dark, and the dry from the moist.

3. There exist many portions of many things. Nothing is separated entirely, or distinguished one from another, except Mind. Mind is all alike, both the greater and the smaller, but nothing else is like anything else, but each individual thing is and was most manifestly whatever that of which it has the most portions.

4. Mind is godlike, homogeneous, omnipotent, omniscient, and orders all phenomena.

5. Anaxagoras held that *Nous* (Mind) is the cause of all motion.

6. Other things have a share of everything, but Mind is infinite and self-ruled and not mixed with anything, but is alone by itself. For if it were not by itself, but were mixed with anything else, it would, by virtue of being mixed with this, have a share of all things; for there is a portion of everything in everything. And the things that were mixed in it would hinder it, so that it could control nothing as it does now, being alone by itself. For Mind is the finest of all things and the purest, and it has all knowledge concerning all things and the greatest power; and over everything that has soul, large or small, Mind rules.[22]

EMPEDOCLES

1. Hear first the four roots of all things: bright Zeus, life-giving Hera (air), and Aidoneus (earth), and Nestis who moistens the springs of men with her tears.

2. And a second thing I will tell thee: There is no origination of anything that is mortal, nor yet any end in baneful death; but only mixture and separation of what is mixed, but men call this "origination."

3. But when light is mingled with air in human form, or in form like the race of wild beasts or of plants or of birds, then men say that these things have come into being; and when they are separated, they call them evil fate; this is the established practice, and I myself also call it so in accordance with custom.

4. For from what does not exist at all it is impossible that anything come into being, and it is neither possible nor perceivable that being should perish completely; for things will always stand wherever one is each case shall put them.

5. And these [elements] never cease changing place continually, now being all united by Love into one, now each borne apart by the hatred engendered of Strife, until they are brought together in the unity of the all, and become subject to it. Thus inasmuch as one has been wont to arise out of many and again with the separation of the one the many arise, so things are continually coming into being and there is no fixed age for them; and farther inasmuch as they [the elements] never cease changing place continually, so they always exist within an immovable circle.

6. Now I shall go back over the course of my verses, which I set out in order before, drawing my present discourse from that discourse. When Strife reached the lowest depth of the eddy and Love comes to be in the midst of the Whirl, then all these things come together at this point so as to be one alone, yet not immediately, but joining together at their pleasure, one from one place, another from another. And as they were joining together Strife departed to the utmost boundary. But many things remained unmixed, alternating with those that were mixed, even as many as Strife, remaining aloft, still retained; for not yet had it entirely departed to the utmost boundaries of the circle, but some of its members were remaining within, and others had gone outside. But, just as far as it is constantly rushing forth, just so far there ever kept coming in a gentle immortal stream of perfect Love; and all at once what before I learned were immortal were coming into being as mortal things, what before were unmixed as mixed, changing their courses. And as they [the elements] were mingled together there flowed forth the myriad species of mortal things, patterned in every sort of form, a wonder to behold.[23]

7. And Empedocles makes more use of causes than Anaxagoras, but not indeed sufficiently; nor does he find in them what has been agreed upon. At any rate Love for him is often a separating cause

22. DK (B 12)

23. All of the entries included in this section on Empedocles are from Milton Nahm, *Selections from Early Greek Philosophy* (Appleton-Century-Crofts, 1934), pp. 116–124.

and Strife a uniting cause. For whenever the all is separated into the elements by Strife, fire and each of the other elements are collected into one; and again, whenever they all are brought together into one by Love, parts are necessarily separated again from each other. Empedocles moreover differed from those who went before, in that he discriminated this cause and introduced it, not making the cause of motion one, but different and opposite. Further, he first described the four elements spoken of as in the form of matter; but he did not use them as four but only as two, fire by itself, and the rest opposed to fire as being one in nature, earth, and air and water.[24]

DEMOCRITUS

1. Man is a universe in small.
2. For all men the good and the true are the same, but what is pleasant varies.
3. The hope of evil gain is the beginning of ruin.[25]
4. Democritus considers the eternal objects to be small substances infinite in number. For these he posits a place infinite in magnitude, and he calls the place by such names as void, nothing, and infinite, but each of the substances he calls, something, solid, and existent. He thinks the substances are so small that we cannot perceive them, yet they have all sorts of forms and shapes, and differences in size. Accordingly from these as from elements he generates and combines visible objects and perceptible masses. And they are disturbed and move in the void because of their dissimilarity and the other differences mentioned, and as they move they collide and become entangled in such a fashion as to be near to and touch each other. However this does not in truth give rise to any one single nature, for it is altogether silly that two or more things may ever become one. The coherence up to a certain point of substances he explains by the gripping and intermingling of the bodies, for some of them are scalene in shape, some are barbed, some concave, some convex and others have countless other differences. Accordingly he thinks they cling to each other and cohere until some stronger necessity from the surroundings approaches, shakes and scatters them.[26]

24. From Aristotle's *Metaphysics* I.4.915a21.

25. The entries under Democritus are from DK (B 69 & 221).

26. From Aristotle *On Democritus* (quoted by Simplicus in *de Caelo*). Quoted in Nahm, op. cit., p. 156f.

Chapter 2
PLATO

The safest general characterization of the European philosophical tradition is that it consists of a series of footnotes to Plato.

(ALFRED NORTH WHITEHEAD)

Plato is Philosophy, and Philosophy is Plato. . . . Out of Plato comes all things that are still written and debated among men of thought.

(RALPH WALDO EMERSON)

Plato (427–347 B.C.) is generally recognized as the Father of Philosophy, the first systematic metaphysician and epistemologist, the first philosopher to set forth a comprehensive treatment of the entire domain of philosophy from ontology to ethics and aesthetics. He was born into an Athenian aristocratic family at the end of the Periclean Golden Age of Greek democracy.[1] During much of his life, Athens was at war with Sparta, the Greek city state to the south. He was Socrates' disciple, the developer of his teacher's ideas, the founder of the first university and school of philosophy (the Academy in Athens), Aristotle's teacher, and an advisor to kings, Dionysius and Dion. His goal may have been to found the ideal state, described in Book V of the *Republic*, where philosophers ruled with justice. Among his important works are the *Euthyphro*, *Apology*, *Crito*, *Phaedo*, *Meno*, and *Republic*, which are included in this part of our book. Most of his books are dialogues in which Socrates is the key spokesman and interlocutor, who seeks an understanding of difficult concepts.

Socrates (470–399 B.C.), the son of Sophroniscus, an Athenian stone cutter, and Phanenarete, a midwife, one of the most important yet enigmatic figures in philosophy, was the inspiration for Plato's thought. At one time a follower of the "Pre-Socratic" cosmologists (perhaps of Anaxagoras), he later turned from cosmological speculation about the heavens to consider ethics, how we ought to live. He wrote nothing, but his ideas are conveyed to us by Plato. In the early dialogues, such as the *Euthyphro*, *Apology*, and *Crito*, Plato may be reporting Socrates' own thoughts, if not his own words, but as Plato developed his own philosophy, he continued to use Socrates as his mouthpiece. After the infamous trial and execution of Socrates in 399 B.C., Plato, then twenty-eight, abandoned thoughts for a political career, traveled, and then began his career as a philosopher.

What were Plato's distinctive ideas? The most famous idea is the *Theory of Forms*, an instance of the idea of the *One and the Many*. What do the *many* similar things have in common? The *one* Form. All beautiful things have in common participation in the form of the Beautiful; all good things have in common participation in the Form of the Good.

---

1. Pericles (495–429 B.C.) was the great Athenian General and statesman under whose leadership Athens developed into a human democracy and prospered materially and culturally.

What do all triangles or green objects have in common? Triangles come in different shapes and sizes. It is true that all triangles are closed plain figures with three sides and three angles adding up to 180 degrees, but the sides may be different sizes and the shape of the triangle may be isosceles or scalene. Even before we can articulate the definition of a triangle we seem to know one when we see it. Regarding green objects, we cannot even define their common property—*green*. We cannot help a blind person understand what it is or even describe it to one who knows what green is. It is an unanalyzable simple property. All green things have this undefinable property in common. Now let us go from perceptual objects (triangles, colors, chairs, and tables) to abstract ideas: friendship, equality, justice, beauty, goodness. What do all exemplars of each of these properties have in common? Plato's *Theory of Forms* (sometimes referred to as his "Theory of Ideas") seeks to give us a satisfactory answer to this question.

Aristotle tells us how Plato first came upon this theory:

> The Theory of forms occurred to Plato because he was persuaded of the truth of Heraclitus' doctrine that all things accessible to the senses are always in a state of flux, so that if knowledge or thought is to have an object there must besides things accessible to the senses be certain other entities which persist; for there is no knowledge of things which are in a state of flux. Socrates occupied himself with the moral virtues, and was the first to look for general definitions in this area. There are two things which may fairly be ascribed to Socrates, arguments by analogy and general definitions, both of which are concerned with the starting point of knowledge. But whereas Socrates made neither the universal nor the definition exist separately, others gave them a separate existence and this was the sort of thing to which they gave the name of Forms. So for them it followed by almost the same argument that there are forms for everything to which general words apply.[2]

Whereas Socrates sought clear definitions of concepts in order to have a common basis for discussion (how can we even settle on an understanding of what a "just society" will be if we have different definitions of *justice*?), Plato went beyond *verbal* definitions and posited a comprehensive theory of reality.

According to Plato, every significant word (noun, adjective, and verb) and thing partakes of and derives its identity from a Form or Forms. The Forms are single, common to all objects and abstract terms, perfect as the particulars or exemplars are not, independent of any particulars and yet their cause, having objective existence (they are the truly real, while particulars are only apparently so). While independent of the human mind, they are intelligible and can be known by the mind alone and not by sense experience. The Forms are divine, eternal, simple, indissoluble, unchanging, self-subsisting reality, existing outside space and time. They are the cause of all that is.

We will encounter Plato's ideas of the Forms in his dialogues *Phaedo* and *Republic*.

Related to Plato's theory of the Forms in his doctrine of *Innate Ideas and the Theory of Recollection*. In the dialogue *Meno*, Plato, through his spokesman Socrates, seeks to prove that we are born with innate ideas of the Forms. The dialogue begins with Meno raising a puzzle about learning: how do you know when you have found the answer to a question you are asking? Either (1) you don't know the answer and so won't know when you've found it; or (2) you already know the answer, in which case why make an inquiry in the first place? Socrates sets about to solve this riddle about the impossibility of learning through the theory of recollection of knowledge. The specific question Meno raises is whether virtue can be taught. He calls one of Meno's slaves, an uneducated boy, who will be the test case as to whether learning takes place through

---

2. Aristotle, *Metaphysics*, 1078.

recollecting knowledge learned in a previous existence. He will argue that in provoking the correct answers from the slave he demonstrates that we have innate ideas which must have been learned in a previous existence. This method of evoking implicit knowledge from the student is now referred to as the "Socratic method" of teaching, though it need not include a theory of innate ideas.

Our first reading, the *Euthyphro*, deals with the question "What is piety?" and raises the issue of whether the god or gods love the good because it is good or whether the good is good because the god loves it.

FOR FURTHER READING

By Plato

Plato: The Collected Dialogues, ed. Edith Hamilton and Huntington Cairns. (Princeton University Press, 1982). This complete set of Plato's dialogues is the best single-volume collection of his works. The translations are typically excellent.

The Dialogues of Plato, 4 ed., revised by D. J. Allan and H. E. Dale. (Oxford University Press, 1953). Jowett's translation is still among the best, literary and accurate.

Plato's Republic, trans. G. M. A. Grube. (Hackett, 1980). This is an accessible, accurate translation.

About Socrates

Benson, Hugh, ed. *Essays on the Philosophy of Socrates*. (Oxford University Press, 1992).

Guthrie, W. K. C. *The History of Greek Philosophy*, vol III. (Cambridge University Press, 1969).

Kraut, Richard. *Socrates and the State*. (Princeton University Press, 1984).

Taylor, A. E. *Socrates*. (Methuen, 1933).

Vlastos, Gregory. *Socrates, Ironist and Moral Philosopher*. (Cornell University Press, 1991).

Vlastos, Gregory, ed. *The Philosophy of Socrates*. (Doubleday, 1971).

About Plato

Annas, Julia. *An Introduction to Plato's Republic*. (Oxford University Press, 1981).

Crombie, I. M. *An Examination of Plato's Doctrines*, 2 vols. (Humanities Press, 1963, 1969).

Grube, G. M. A. *Plato's Thought*. (Methuen, 1935). An insightful discussion of Plato's thought, especially of the Forms.

Guthrie, W. K. C. *The History of Greek Philosophy*, vol IV & V. (Cambridge University Press, 1975, 1978).

Irwin, Terrance. *Plato's Moral Theory. Early and Middle Dialogues*. (Clarendon Press, 1977). A complex, advanced but rich scholarly work.

Kraut, Richard, ed. *The Cambridge Companion to Plato*. (Cambridge University Press, 1992).

Ross, W. D. *Plato's Theory of Ideas*. (Oxford University Press, 1951). This book traces the theory of the Forms from the early dialogues to the Laws. A brilliant analysis.

Taylor, A. E. *Plato: The Man and His Work*. (Methuen, 1950). A splendid exposition of the entire Platonic corpus.

Vlastos, Gregory, ed. *Plato: A Collection of Critical Essays*, 2 vols. (Doubleday, 1970, 1971).

About the Period

Jones, W. T. *The Classical Mind*. (Harcourt, Brace, 1952). A helpful overview of the Ancient Greeks and their culture.

Renault, Mary. *The Last of the Wine*. (Pantheon, 1956). A novel depicting Athens in the days of Socrates.

Euthyphro

Socrates and Euthyphro meet at the entrance to the law courts, and to Euthyphro's surprised question—"What has taken you from your haunts in the Lyceum?"—Socrates answers that a charge has been brought against him which is rather a grand one, that of corrupting the youth of Athens, and that the prosecutor knows just how it is done and how Socrates is doing it. But why, he asks in turn, is Euthyphro here? The reason, the latter answers, is that he is prosecuting his own father on a charge of murder. Socrates' astonishment at this does not disturb him. He is by profession an interpreter of religion, a theologian, and he tells Socrates that with his special insight into what is right and wrong he knows that he is acting in the spirit of true piety. When Socrates asks what then is piety, he gives the answer characteristic of the orthodox everywhere—in effect, "Piety is thinking as I do." His sincerity is as patent as his conceit. He really believes that he ought to prosecute his father who though certainly not a murderer is not free from blame.

The conversation that follows is chiefly an attempt to define piety, and comes to nothing, but in the course of it Socrates makes a distinction fundamental in reasoning and often disregarded, that the good is not good because the gods approve it, but the gods approve it because it is good.

The real interest of the dialogue, however, is the picture of Socrates just before his trial. There is no question that he realized the danger he was in, but Plato, who knew him best of all, shows him engaging humorously and ironically and keenly in a discussion completely removed from his own situation. Just at the end he says that if only Euthyphro will instruct him in what true piety is he will tell his accuser that he has become the pupil of a great theologian and is going to lead a better life. But Euthyphro, by this time in no mood to define anything, gives up. "Another time, then, Socrates," he says and hurries away.

2   EUTHYPHRO: This, Socrates, is something new? What has taken you from your haunts in the Lyceum, and makes you spend your time at the royal porch? You surely cannot have a case at law, as I have, before the Archon-King.

SOCRATES: My business, Euthyphro, is not what is known at Athens as a case at law; it is a criminal prosecution.

b   EUTHYPHRO: How is that? You mean that somebody is prosecuting you? I never would believe that you were prosecuting anybody else.

SOCRATES: No indeed.

EUTHYPHRO: Then somebody is prosecuting you?

SOCRATES: Most certainly.

EUTHYPHRO: Who is it?

SOCRATES: I am not too clear about the man myself, Euthyphro. He appears to me to be a young man, and unknown. I think, however, that they call him Meletus, and his deme is Pitthos, if you happen to know anyone named Meletus of that deme—a hook-nosed man with long straight hair, and not much beard.

EUTHYPHRO: I don't recall him, Socrates. But tell me, of what does he accuse you?

SOCRATES: His accusation? It is no mean charge. For a man of his age it is no small thing to have settled a question of so much importance. He says, in fact, that he knows the method by which young people are corrupted, and knows who the persons are that do it. He is, quite possibly, a wise man, and, observing that my ignorance has led me to corrupt his generation, comes like a child to his mother to accuse me to the city. And to me he appears to be the d only one who begins his political activity aright, for the right way to begin is to pay attention to the young, and make them just as good as possible—precisely as the able farmer will give his attention to the young plants first, and afterward care for the rest. And so Meletus no doubt begins by clearing us away, the ones who ruin, as he says, the tender

Reprinted from *Plato on the Trial and Death of Socrates: Euthyphro, Apology, Crito, Phaedo*, translated by Lane Cooper. Copyright © 1941 by Lane Cooper. Used by permission of the publisher, Cornell University Press.

shoots of the young. That done, he obviously will care for the older generation, and will thus become the cause, in the highest and widest measure, of benefit to the state. With such a notable beginning, his chances of success look good.

EUTHYPHRO: I hope so, Socrates, but I'm very much afraid it will go the other way. When he starts to injure you, it simply looks to me like the beginning at the hearth to hurt the state. But tell me what he says you do to corrupt the young.

b SOCRATES: It sounds very queer, my friend, when first you hear it. He says I am a maker of gods; he charges me with making new gods, and not believing in the old ones. These are his grounds for prosecuting me, he says.

EUTHYPHRO: I see it, Socrates. It is because you say that ever and anon you have the spiritual sign! So he charges you in this indictment with introducing novelties in religion, and that is the reason why he comes to court with this slanderous complaint, well knowing how easily such matters can be misrepresented to the crowd. For my own part, when I c speak in the Assembly about matters of religion, and tell them in advance what will occur, they laugh at me as if I were a madman, and yet I never have made a prediction that did not come true. But the truth is, they are jealous of all such people as ourselves. No, we must not worry over them, but go to meet them.

SOCRATES: Dear Euthyphro, if we were only laughed at, it would be no serious matter. The Athenians, as it seems to me, are not very much disturbed if they think that so-and-so is clever, so long as he does not impart his knowledge to anybody else. But the moment they suspect that he is giving his ability to others, they get angry, whether out of jealousy, d as you say, or, it may be, for some other reason.

EUTHYPHRO: With regard to that, I am not very eager to test their attitude to me.

SOCRATES: Quite possibly you strike them as a man who is chary of himself, and is unwilling to impart his wisdom; as for me, I fear I am so kindly they will think that I pour out all I have to everyone, and not merely without pay—nay, rather, glad to offer something if it would induce someone to hear me. Well then, as I said just now, if they were going to laugh at me, as you say they do at you, it wouldn't be at all unpleasant to spend the time laughing and joking in court. But if they take the e matter seriously, then there is no knowing how it will turn out. Only you prophets can tell!

EUTHYPHRO: Well, Socrates, perhaps no harm will come of it at all, but you will carry your case as you desire, and I think that I shall carry mine.

SOCRATES: Your case, Euthyphro? What is it? Are you prosecuting, or defending?

EUTHYPHRO: Prosecuting.

SOCRATES: Whom?

EUTHYPHRO: One whom I am thought a maniac to 4 be attacking.

SOCRATES: How so? Is it someone who has wings to fly away with?

EUTHYPHRO: He is far from being able to do that; he happens to be old, a very old man.

SOCRATES: Who is it, then?

EUTHYPHRO: It is my father.

SOCRATES: Your father, my good friend?

EUTHYPHRO: Just so.

SOCRATES: What is the complaint? Of what do you accuse him?

EUTHYPHRO: Of murder, Socrates.

SOCRATES: Good heavens, Euthyphro! Surely the crowd is ignorant of the way things ought to go. I fancy it is not correct for any ordinary person to do that [to prosecute his father on this charge], but only for a man already far advanced in point of wisdom. b

EUTHYPHRO: Yes, Socrates, by heaven! Far advanced!

SOCRATES: And the man your father killed, was he a relative of yours? Of course he was? You never would prosecute your father, would you, for the death of anybody who was not related to you?

EUTHYPHRO: You amuse me, Socrates. You think it makes a difference whether the victim was a member of the family, or not related, when the only thing to watch is whether it was right or not for the man who did the deed to kill him. If he was justified, then let him go; if not, you have to prosecute him, no matter if the man who killed him shares your hearth, and sits at table with you. The pollution is the same c if, knowingly, you associate with such a man, and do not cleanse yourself, and him as well, by bringing him to justice. The victim in this case was a laborer of mine, and when we were cultivating land in Naxos, we employed him on our farm. One day he had been drinking, and became enraged at one of our domestics, and cut his throat; whereupon my father bound him hand and foot, and threw him into a ditch. Then he sent a man to Athens to find out from the seer what ought to be done—meanwhile paying no attention to the man who had been bound, neglecting him because he was a murderer and it d would be no great matter even if he died. And that was just what happened. Hunger, cold, and the shackles finished him before the messenger got back from visiting the seer. That is why my father and my other kin are bitter at me when I prosecute my father as a murderer. They say he did not kill the man, and had he actually done it, the victim was himself a murderer, and for such a man one need have no consideration. They say that for a son to e prosecute his father as a murderer is unholy. How ill they know divinity in its relation, Socrates, to what is holy or unholy!

SOCRATES: But you, by heaven! Euthyphro, you think that you have such an accurate knowledge of things divine, and what is holy and unholy, that, in circumstances such as you describe, you can accuse your father? You are not afraid that you yourself are doing an unholy deed?

EUTHYPHRO: Why, Socrates, if I did not have an 5 accurate knowledge of all, I should be good for nothing, and Euthyphro would be no different from the general run of men.

SOCRATES: Well then, admirable Euthyphro, the best thing I can do is to become your pupil, and challenge Meletus before the trial comes on. Let me tell him that in the past I have considered it of great importance to know about things divine, and that now, when he asserts that I erroneously put forward my own notions and inventions on this head, I have be-b come your pupil. I could say, Come Meletus, if you agree that Euthyphro has wisdom in such matters, you must admit as well that I hold the true belief, and must not prosecute. If you do not, you must lodge your complaint, not against me, but against my aforesaid master; accuse him of corrupting the elder generation, me and his own father—me by his instruction, his father by correcting and chastising him.

And if he would not yield, would neither quit the suit nor yet indict you rather than myself, then I would say the same in court as when I challenged him!

EUTHYPHRO: Yes, Socrates, by heaven! If he undertook to bring me into court, I guess I would find c out his rotten spot, and our talk there would concern him sooner by a long shot than ever it would me!

SOCRATES: Yes, my dear friend, that I know, and so I wish to be your pupil. This Meletus, I perceive, along presumably with everybody else, appears to overlook you, but sees into me so easily and keenly that he has attacked me for impiety. So, in the name of heaven, tell me now about the matter you just felt sure you knew quite thoroughly. State what you take piety and impiety to be with reference to murder and

all other cases. Is not the holy always one and the d same thing in every action, and, again, is not the unholy always opposite to the holy, and like itself? And as unholiness does it not always have its one essential form, which will be found in everything that is unholy?

EUTHYPHRO: Yes, surely, Socrates.

SOCRATES: Then tell me. How do you define the holy and the unholy?

EUTHYPHRO: Well then, I say that the holy is what I am now doing, prosecuting the wrongdoer who commits a murder or a sacrilegious robbery, or sins in any point like that, whether it be your father, or your mother, or whoever it may be. And not to pros- e ecute would be that such is the law. It is one I have already given to others; I tell them that the right procedure must be not to tolerate the impious man, no matter who. Does not mankind believe that Zeus is the most excellent and just among the gods? And these same men admit that Zeus shackled his own 6 father [Cronus] for swallowing his [other] sons unjustly, and that Cronus in turn had gelded his father [Uranus] for like reasons. But now they are enraged at me when I proceed against my father for wrongdoing, and so they contradict themselves in what they say about the gods and what they say of me.

SOCRATES: There, Euthyphro, you have the reason why the charge is brought against me. It is because, whenever people tell such stories about the gods, I am prone to take it ill, and, so it seems, that is why they will maintain that I am sinful. Well, now, if you who are so well versed in matters of the sort b entertain the same beliefs, then necessarily, it would seem, I must give in, for what could we urge who admit that, for our own part, we are quite ignorant about these matters? But, in the name of friendship, tell me! Do you actually believe that these things happened so?

EUTHYPHRO: Yes, Socrates, and things even more amazing, of which the multitude does not know.

SOCRATES: And you actually believe that war occurred among the gods, and there were dreadful hatreds, battles, and all sorts of fearful things like that? Such things as the poets tell of, and good artists represent in sacred places; yes, and at the great Pana- c thenaic festival the robe that is carried up to the Acropolis is all inwrought with such embellishments? What is our position, Euthyphro? Do we say that these things are true?

EUTHYPHRO: Not these things only, Socrates, but, as I just now said, I will, if you wish, relate to you many other stories about the gods, which I am certain will astonish you when you hear them.

SOCRATES: I shouldn't wonder. You shall tell me all about them when we have the leisure at some other time. At present try to tell me more clearly what I asked you a little while ago, for, my friend, d you were not explicit enough before when I put the question. What is holiness? You merely said that what you are now doing is a holy deed—namely, prosecuting your father on a charge of murder.

EUTHYPHRO: And, Socrates, I told the truth.

SOCRATES: Possibly. But, Euthyphro, there are many other things that you will say are holy.

EUTHYPHRO: Because they are.

SOCRATES: Well, bear in mind that what I asked of you was not to tell me one or two out of all the numerous actions that are holy; I wanted you to tell me what is the essential form of holiness which makes all holy actions holy. I believe you held that there is one ideal form by which unholy things are e all unholy, and by which all holy things are holy. Do you remember that?

EUTHYPHRO: I do.

SOCRATES: Well then, show me what, precisely, this ideal is, so that, with my eye on it, and using it as a standard, I can say that any action done by you or anybody else is holy if it resembles this ideal, or, if it does not, can deny that it is holy.

EUTHYPHRO: Well, Socrates, if that is what you want, I certainly can tell you.

SOCRATES: It is precisely what I want.

EUTHYPHRO: Well then, what is pleasing to the 7 gods is holy, and what is not pleasing to them is unholy.

SOCRATES: Perfect, Euthyphro! Now you give me just the answer that I asked for. Meanwhile, whether it is right I do not know, but obviously you will go on to prove your statement true.

EUTHYPHRO: Indeed I will.

SOCRATES: Come now, let us scrutinize what we are saying. What is pleasing to the gods, and the man that pleases them, are holy; what is hateful to the gods, and the man they hate, unholy. But the holy and unholy are not the same; the holy is directly opposite to the unholy. Isn't it so?

EUTHYPHRO: It is.

SOCRATES: And the matter clearly was well stated.

EUTHYPHRO: I accept it, Socrates; that was stated.

SOCRATES: Was it not also stated, Euthyphro, that the gods revolt and differ with each other, and that hatreds come between them?

EUTHYPHRO: That was stated.

SOCRATES: Hatred and wrath, my friend—what kind of disagreement will produce them? Look at the matter thus. If you and I were to differ about numbers, on the question which of two was the greater, would a disagreement about that make us angry at each other, and make enemies of us? Should we not settle things by calculation, and so come to c an agreement quickly on any point like that?

EUTHYPHRO: Yes, certainly.

SOCRATES: And similarly if we differed on a question of greater length or less, we would take a measurement, and quickly put an end to the dispute?

EUTHYPHRO: Just that.

SOCRATES: And so, I fancy, we should have recourse to scales, and settle any question about a heavier or lighter weight?

EUTHYPHRO: Of course.

SOCRATES: What sort of thing, then, is it about which we differ, till, unable to arrive at a decision, we might get angry and be enemies to one another? Perhaps you have no answer ready, but listen to me. d See if it is not the following—right and wrong, the noble and the base, and good and bad. Are not these the things about which we differ, till, unable to arrive at a decision, we grow hostile, when we do grow hostile, to each other, you and I and everybody else?

EUTHYPHRO: Yes, Socrates, that is where we differ, on these subjects.

SOCRATES: What about the gods, then, Euthyphro? If, indeed, they have dissensions, must it not be on these subjects?

EUTHYPHRO: Quite necessarily.

SOCRATES: Accordingly, my noble Euthyphro, by e your account some gods take one thing to be right, and others take another, and similarly with the honorable and the base, and good and bad. They would hardly be at variance with each other, if they did not differ on these questions. Would they?

EUTHYPHRO: You are right.

SOCRATES: And what each one of them thinks noble, good, and just, is what he loves, and the opposite is what he hates?

EUTHYPHRO: Yes, certainly.

SOCRATES: But it is the same things, so you say, 8 that some of them think right, and others wrong, and through disputing about these they are at variance, and make war on one another. Isn't it so?

EUTHYPHRO: It is.

SOCRATES: Accordingly, so it would seem, the same things will be hated by the gods and loved by them; the same things would alike displease and please them.

EUTHYPHRO: It would seem so.

SOCRATES: And so, according to this argument, the same things, Euthyphro, will be holy and unholy.

EUTHYPHRO: That may be.

SOCRATES: In that case, admirable friend, you have not answered what I asked you. I did not ask you to tell me what at once is holy and unholy, but it seems that what is pleasing to the gods is also hate-b ful to them. Thus, Euthyphro, it would not be strange at all if what you now are doing in punishing your father were pleasing to Zeus, but hateful to Cronus and Uranus, and welcome to Hephaestus, but odious to Hera, and if any other of the gods disagree about the matter, satisfactory to some of them, and odious to others.

EUTHYPHRO: But, Socrates, my notion is that, on this point, there is no difference of opinion among the gods—not one of them but thinks that if a person kills another wrongfully, he ought to pay for it.

SOCRATES: And what of men? Have you never c heard a man contending that someone who has killed a person wrongfully, or done some other unjust deed, ought not to pay the penalty?

EUTHYPHRO: Why! There is never any end to their disputes about these matters; it goes on everywhere, above all in the courts. People do all kinds of wrong, and then there is nothing they will not do or say in order to escape the penalty.

SOCRATES: Do they admit wrongdoing, Euthyphro, and, while admitting it, deny that they ought to pay the penalty?

EUTHYPHRO: No, not that, by any means.

SOCRATES: Then they will not do and say quite everything. Unless I am mistaken, they dare not say or argue that if they do wrong they should not pay d the penalty. No, I think that they deny wrongdoing. How about it?

EUTHYPHRO: It is true.

SOCRATES: Therefore they do not dispute that anybody who does wrong should pay the penalty. No, the thing that they dispute about is likely to be who is the wrongdoer, what he did, and when.

EUTHYPHRO: That is true.

SOCRATES: Well then, isn't that precisely what goes on among the gods, if they really do have quarrels about right and wrong, as you say they do? One set will hold that some others do wrong, and the other set deny it? For that other thing, my friend, I take it no one, whether god or man, will dare to say—that the wrongdoer should not pay the penalty! e

EUTHYPHRO: Yes, Socrates, what you say is true—in the main.

SOCRATES: It is the individual act, I fancy, Euthyphro, that the disputants dispute about, both men and gods, if gods ever do dispute. They differ on a certain act; some hold that it was rightly done, the others that it was wrong. Isn't it so?

EUTHYPHRO: Yes, certainly.

SOCRATES: Then come, dear Euthyphro, teach me 9 as well, and let me grow more wise. What proof have you that all the gods think that your servant died unjustly, your hireling, who, when he had killed a man, was shackled by the master of the victim, and perished, dying because of his shackles before the man who shackled him could learn from the seers what ought to be done with him? What proof have you that for a man like him it is right for a son to prosecute his father, and indict him on a charge of murder? Come on. Try to make it clear to me beyond all doubt that under these conditions the gods must all consider this action to be right. If you can adequately prove it to me, I will never cease from b praising you for your wisdom.

EUTHYPHRO: But, Socrates, that, very likely, would be no small task, although I could indeed make it very clear to you.

SOCRATES: I understand. You think that I am duller than the judges; obviously you will demonstrate to them that what your father did was wrong, and that the gods all hate such deeds.

EUTHYPHRO: I shall prove it absolutely, Socrates, if they will listen to me.

SOCRATES: They are sure to listen if they think c that you speak well. But while you were talking, a notion came into my head, and I asked myself, Suppose that Euthyphro proved to me quite clearly that all the gods consider such a death unjust; would I have come one whit the nearer for him to knowing what the holy is, and what is the unholy? The act in question, seemingly, might be displeasing to the gods, but then we have just seen that you cannot define the holy and unholy in that way, for we have seen that a given thing may be displeasing, and also pleasing, to gods. So on this point, Euthyphro, I will let you off; if you like, the gods shall all consider the act unjust, and they all shall hate it. But suppose that we now correct our definition, and say what the d gods all hate is unholy, and what they love is holy, whereas what some of them love, and others hate, is either both or neither. Are you willing that we now define the holy and unholy in this way?

EUTHYPHRO: What is there to prevent us, Socrates?

SOCRATES: Nothing to prevent me, Euthyphro. As for you, see whether when you take this definition you can quite readily instruct me, as you promised.

e EUTHYPHRO: Yes, I would indeed affirm that holiness is what the gods all love, and its opposite is what the gods all hate, unholiness.

SOCRATES: Are we to examine this position also, Euthyphro, to see if it is sound? Or shall we let it through, and thus accept our own and others' statement, and agree to an assertion simply when somebody says that a thing is so? Must we not look into what the speaker says?

EUTHYPHRO: We must. And yet, for my part, I regard the present statement as correct.

10 SOCRATES: We shall soon know better about that, my friend. Now think of this. Is what is holy holy because the gods approve it, or do they approve it because it is holy?

EUTHYPHRO: I do not get your meaning.

SOCRATES: Well, I will try to make it clearer. We speak of what is carried and the carrier, do we not, of led and leader, of the seen and that which sees? And you understand that in all such cases the things are different, and how they differ?

EUTHYPHRO: Yes, I think I understand.

SOCRATES: In the same way what is loved is one thing, and what loves is another?

EUTHYPHRO: Of course.

b SOCRATES: Tell me now, is what is carried 'carried' because something carries it, or is it for some other reason?

EUTHYPHRO: No, but for that reason.

SOCRATES: And what is led, because something leads it? And what is seen, because something sees it?

EUTHYPHRO: Yes, certainly.

SOCRATES: Then it is not because a thing is seen that something sees it, but just the opposite—because something sees it, therefore it is seen. Nor because it is led, that something leads it, but because something leads it, therefore it is led. Nor because it is carried, that something carries it, but because something carries it, therefore it is carried. Do you c see what I wish to say, Euthyphro? It is this. Whenever an effect occurs, or something is effected, it is not the thing effected that gives rise to the effect; no, there is a cause, and then comes this effect. Nor

is it because a thing is acted on that there is this effect; no, there is a cause for what it undergoes, and then comes this effect. Don't you agree?

EUTHYPHRO: I do.

SOCRATES: Well then, when a thing is loved, is it not in process of becoming something, or of undergoing something, by some other thing?

EUTHYPHRO: Yes, certainly.

SOCRATES: Then the same is true here as in the previous cases. It is not because a thing is loved that they who love it love it, but it is loved because they love it.

EUTHYPHRO: Necessarily.

SOCRATES: Then what are we to say about the d holy, Euthyphro? According to your argument, is it not loved by all the gods?

EUTHYPHRO: Yes.

SOCRATES: Because it is holy, or for some other reason?

EUTHYPHRO: No, it is for that reason.

SOCRATES: And so it is because it is holy that it is loved; it is not holy because it is loved.

EUTHYPHRO: So it seems.

SOCRATES: On the other hand, it is beloved and pleasing to the gods just because they love it?

EUTHYPHRO: No doubt of that.

SOCRATES: So what is pleasing to the gods is not the same as what is holy, Euthyphro, nor, according to your statement, is the holy the same as what is pleasing to the gods. They are two different things.

EUTHYPHRO: How may that be, Socrates?   e

SOCRATES: Because we are agreed that the holy is loved because it is holy, and is not holy because it is loved. Isn't it so?

EUTHYPHRO: Yes.

SOCRATES: Whereas what is pleasing to the gods is pleasing to them just because they love it, such being its nature and its cause. Its being loved of the gods is not the reason of its being loved.

EUTHYPHRO: You are right.

SOCRATES: But suppose, dear Euthyphro, that what is pleasing to the gods and what is holy were not two separate things. In that case if holiness were loved because it was holy, then also what was pleas- 11 ing to the gods would be loved because it pleased them. And on the other hand, if what was pleasing to them pleased because they loved it, then also the holy would be holy because they loved it. But now you see that it is just the opposite, because the two are absolutely different from each other, for the one [what is pleasing to the gods] is of a sort to be loved because it is loved, whereas the other [what is holy] is loved because it is of a sort to be loved. Consequently, Euthyphro, it looks as if you had not given me my answer—as if when you were asked to tell the nature of the holy, you did not wish to explain the essence of it. You merely tell an attribute of it, namely, that it appertains to holiness to be loved by all the gods. What it *is*, as yet you have not said. So, b if you please, do not conceal this from me. No, begin again. Say what the holy is, and never mind if gods do love it, nor if it has some other attribute; on that we shall not split. Come, speak out. Explain the nature of the holy and unholy.

EUTHYPHRO: Now, Socrates, I simply don't know how to tell you what I think. Somehow everything that we put forward keeps moving about us in a circle, and nothing will stay where we put it.

SOCRATES: Your statements, Euthyphro, look like c the work of Daedalus, founder of my line. If I had made them, and they were my positions, no doubt you would poke fun at me, and say that, being in his line, the figures I construct in words run off, as did his statues, and will not stay where they are put. Meanwhile, since they are your definitions, we need some other jest, for in fact, as you see yourself, they will not stand still.

EUTHYPHRO: But, Socrates, it seems to me that the jest is quite to the point. This tendency in our state- d ments to go in a circle, and not to stay in one place, it is not I who put it there. To my mind, it is you who are the Daedalus; so far as I am concerned, they would have held their place.

SOCRATES: If so, my friend, I must be more expert in his art than he, in that he merely made his own works capable of moving, whereas I give this power not merely to my own, but, seemingly, to the works of other men as well. And the rarest thing about my talent is that I am an unwilling artist, since e I would rather see our arguments stand fast and hold their ground than have the art of Daedalus plus all the wealth of Tantalus to boot. But enough of this. And since, to my mind, you are languid, I will myself make bold with you to show how you might teach me about holiness. Do not weaken. See if you do not think that of necessity all that is holy is just.

EUTHYPHRO: Yes, I do.

SOCRATES: Well then, is all justice holy too? Or, 12 granted that all holiness is just, is justice not all holy, but some part of it is holy, and some part of it is not?

EUTHYPHRO: I do not follow, Socrates.

SOCRATES: And yet you surpass me in your wisdom not less than by your youth. I repeat, you are languid through your affluence in wisdom. Come, lucky friend, exert yourself? What I have to say is not so hard to grasp. I mean the very opposite of what the poet wrote.

Zeus, who brought that all to pass, and made it all to grow,
You will not name, for where fear is, there too is b reverence.[1]

On that I differ from the poet. Shall I tell you why?

EUTHYPHRO: By all means.

SOCRATES: I do not think that 'where fear is, there too is reverence.' For it seems to me that there are many who fear sickness, poverty, and all the like, and so are afraid, but have no reverence whatever for the things they are afraid of. Does it not seem so to you?

EUTHYPHRO: Yes, certainly.

SOCRATES: Where, however, you have reverence, there you have fear as well. Is there anybody who has reverence and a sense of shame about an act, and does not at the same time dread and fear an evil c reputation?

EUTHYPHRO: Yes, he will be afraid of it.

SOCRATES: So it is not right to say that 'where fear is, there too is reverence.' No, you may say that where reverence is, there too is fear—not, however, that where fear is, there always you have reverence. Fear, I think, is wider in extent than reverence. Reverence is a part of fear, as the uneven is a part of number; thus you do not have the odd wherever you have number, but where you have the odd you must have number. I take it you are following me now?

EUTHYPHRO: Yes, indeed.

SOCRATES: Well then, what I asked you was like that. I asked you if wherever justice is, there is holiness as well; or, granted that wherever there is ho- d liness, there is justice too, if where justice is, the holy is not always to be found. Thus holiness would be a part of justice. Shall we say so, or have you a different view?

EUTHYPHRO: No, that is my opinion. I think that you are clearly right.

SOCRATES: Then see what follows. If holiness is a part of justice, it seems to me that we must find

1. Stasinus, fr. 20.

out what part of justice it is. Suppose, for instance, in our case just now, you had asked me what part of number is the even, and which the even number is. I would have said it is the one that corresponds to the isosceles, and not to the scalene. Does it not seem so to you?

EUTHYPHRO: It does.

SOCRATES: Then try to show me in this way what part of the just is holiness, so that we may tell Meletus to cease from wronging me, and to give up prosecuting me for irreligion, because we have adequately learned from you of piety and holiness, and the reverse.

EUTHYPHRO: Well then, Socrates, I think that the part of justice which is religious and is holy is the part that has to do with the service of the gods; the remainder is the part of justice that has to do with the service of mankind.

SOCRATES: And what you say there, Euthyphro, to me seems excellent. There is one little point, however, on which I need more light. I am not yet quite clear about the thing which you call 'service.' I suppose you do not mean the sort of care we give to other things. The 'service' of the gods is not like that—the sort of thing we have in mind when we assert that it is not everybody who knows how to care for horses. It is the horseman that knows, is it not?

EUTHYPHRO: Yes, certainly.

SOCRATES: I suppose it is the special care that appertains to horses?

EUTHYPHRO: Yes.

SOCRATES: In the same way, it is not everyone who knows about the care of dogs; it is the huntsman.

EUTHYPHRO: True.

SOCRATES: The art of the huntsman is the care of dogs.

EUTHYPHRO: Yes.

SOCRATES: And that of the herdsman is the care of cattle.

EUTHYPHRO: Yes, certainly.

SOCRATES: And in the same way, Euthyphro, holiness and piety mean caring for the gods? Do you say so?

EUTHYPHRO: I do.

SOCRATES: And so the aim of all this care and service is the same? I mean it thus. The care is given for the good and welfare of the object that is served. You see, for instance, how the horses that are cared for by the horseman's art are benefited and made better. Don't you think so?

EUTHYPHRO: Yes, I do.

SOCRATES: And so no doubt the dogs by the art of the huntsman, the cattle by that of the herdsman, and in like manner all the rest. Unless, perhaps, you think that the care may tend to injure the object that is cared for?

EUTHYPHRO: By heaven, not I!

SOCRATES: The care aims at its benefit?

EUTHYPHRO: Most certainly.

SOCRATES: Then holiness, which is the service of the gods, must likewise aim to benefit the gods and make them better? Are you prepared to say that when you do a holy thing you make some deity better?

EUTHYPHRO: By heaven, not I!

SOCRATES: Nor do I fancy, Euthyphro, that you mean it so—far from it. No, it was on this account that I asked just what you meant by service of the gods, supposing that, in fact, you did not mean that sort of care.

EUTHYPHRO: And, Socrates, you were right. I do not mean it so.

SOCRATES: Good. And now what kind of service of the gods will holiness be?

EUTHYPHRO: Socrates, it is the kind that slaves give to their masters.

SOCRATES: I understand. It seems to be a kind of waiting on the gods.

EUTHYPHRO: Just that.

SOCRATES: See if you can tell me this. The art which serves physicians, what results does it serve to produce? Don't you think that it is health?

EUTHYPHRO: I do.

SOCRATES: Further, what about the art that serves the shipwrights? What result does it serve to produce?

EUTHYPHRO: Obviously, Socrates, the making of a ship.

SOCRATES: And that which serves the builders serves the building of a house?

EUTHYPHRO: Yes.

SOCRATES: Now tell me, best of friends, about the service of the gods. What result will this art serve to produce? You obviously know, since you profess to be the best informed among mankind on things divine!

EUTHYPHRO: Yes, Socrates, I say so, and I tell the truth.

SOCRATES: Then tell me, I adjure you, what is that supreme result which the gods produce when they employ our services?

EUTHYPHRO: They do many things and noble, Socrates.

14 SOCRATES: Just as the generals do, my friend. All the same you would have no trouble in summing up what they produce, by saying it is victory in war. Isn't it so?

EUTHYPHRO: Of course.

SOCRATES: And the farmers too, I take it, produce many fine results, but the net result of their production is the food they get from the earth.

EUTHYPHRO: Yes, surely.

SOCRATES: Well now, of the many fine and noble things which the gods produce, what is the sum of their production?

EUTHYPHRO: Just a little while ago I told you, b Socrates, that the task is not a light one to learn precisely how all these matters stand. I will, however, simply tell you this. If anyone knows how to say and do things pleasing to the gods in prayer and sacrifice, that is holiness, and such behavior saves the family in private life together with the common interests of the state. To do the opposite of things pleasing to the gods is impious, and this it is that upsets all and ruins everything.

SOCRATES: Surely, Euthyphro, if you had wished, you could have summed up what I asked for much more briefly. But the fact is that you are not eager to instruct me. That is clear. But a moment since, c you were on the very point of telling me—and you slipped away. Had you given the answer, I would now have learned from you what holiness is, and would be content. As it is—for perforce the lover must follow the loved one wherever he leads the way—once more, how do you define the holy, and what is holiness? Don't you say that it is a science of sacrifice and prayer?

EUTHYPHRO: I do.

SOCRATES: Well, and is not sacrifice a giving to the gods, and prayer an asking them to give?

EUTHYPHRO: Precisely, Socrates.

d SOCRATES: By this reasoning, holiness would be the science of asking from the gods and giving to them.

EUTHYPHRO: Quite right, Socrates; you have caught my meaning perfectly.

SOCRATES: Yes, my friend, for I have my heart set on your wisdom, and give my mind to it, so that nothing you say shall be lost. No, tell me, what is this service to the gods? You say it is to ask of them and give to them?

EUTHYPHRO: I do.

SOCRATES: And hence to ask aright will be to ask them for those things of which we stand in need from them?

EUTHYPHRO: What else?

SOCRATES: And, on the other hand, to give aright e will be to give them in return those things which they may need to receive from us? I take it there would be no art in offering anyone a gift of something that he did not need.

EUTHYPHRO: True, Socrates.

SOCRATES: And therefore, Euthyphro, holiness will be a mutual art of commerce between gods and men.

EUTHYPHRO: An art of commerce, if you like to call it so.

SOCRATES: Well, I do not like it if it is not so. But tell me what advantage could come to the gods from the gifts which they receive from us? Everybody 15 sees what they give us. No good that we possess but is given by them. What advantage can they gain by what they get from us? Have we so much the better of them in this commerce that we get all good things from them, and they get nothing from us?

EUTHYPHRO: What! Socrates. Do you suppose that the gods gain anything by what they get from us?

SOCRATES: If not, then what would be the meaning, Euthyphro, of these gifts to the gods from us?

EUTHYPHRO: What do you think they ought to mean but worship, honor, and, as I just now said, good will?

SOCRATES: So, Euthyphro, the holy is what b pleases them, not what is useful to them, nor yet what the gods love?

EUTHYPHRO: I believe that what gives them pleasure is precisely what they love.

SOCRATES: And so once more, apparently the holy is that which the gods love.

EUTHYPHRO: Most certainly.

SOCRATES: After that, will you be amazed to find your statements walking off, and not staying where you put them? And will you accuse me as the Daedalus who makes them move, when you are yourself far more expert than Daedalus, and make them go round in a circle? Don't you see that our argument has come full circle to the point where it began? Surely you have not forgotten how in what was said before we found that holiness and what is pleasing to the gods were not the same, but different from each other. Do you not remember?

EUTHYPHRO: I do.

SOCRATES: And are you not aware now that you

say that what the gods love is holy? But is not what the gods love just the same as what is pleasing to the gods?

EUTHYPHRO: Yes, certainly.

SOCRATES: Well then, either we were wrong in our recent conclusion, or if that was right, our position now is wrong.

EUTHYPHRO: So it seems.

SOCRATES: And so we must go back again, and start from the beginning to find out what the holy is. As for me, I never will give up until I know. Ah!
d Do not spurn me, but give your mind with all your might now at length to tell me the absolute truth, for if anybody knows, of all mankind, it is you, and one must not let go of you, you Proteus, until you tell. If you did not know precisely what is holy and unholy, it is unthinkable that for a simple hireling you ever would have moved to prosecute your aged sire on a charge of murder. No, you would have feared to risk the wrath of the gods on the chance that you were not doing right, and would have been afraid of the talk of men. But now I am sure that you think you know exactly what is holy and what is not. So tell me, peerless Euthyphro, and do not hide from e me what you judge it to be.

EUTHYPHRO: Another time, then, Socrates, for I am in a hurry, and must be off this minute.

SOCRATES: What are you doing, my friend? Will you leave, and dash me down from the mighty expectation I had of learning from you what is holy and what is not, and so escaping from Meletus' indictment? I counted upon showing him that now I had gained wisdom about things divine from Eu- 16 thyphro, and no longer out of ignorance made rash assertions and forged innovations with regard to them, but would lead a better life in future.

The Apology

Characters
Socrates
Meletus
Scene—The Court of Justice

St. 1
p. 17 SOCRATES. I do not know what impression my accusers have made upon you, Athenians. But I do know that they nearly made me forget who I was, so persuasive were they. And yet they have scarcely spoken one single word of truth. Of all their many falsehoods, the one which astonished me most was their saying that I was a clever speaker, and that you must be careful not to let me deceive you. I thought that it was most shameless of them not to be ashamed to talk in that way. For as soon as I open my mouth they will be refuted, and I shall prove that I am not a clever speaker in any way at all—unless, indeed, by a clever speaker they mean someone who speaks the truth. If that is their meaning, I agree with them that I am an orator not to be compared with them.

My accusers, I repeat, have said little or nothing that is true, but from me you shall hear the whole truth. Certainly you will not hear a speech, Athenians, dressed up, like theirs, with fancy words and phrases. I will say to you what I have to say, without artifice, and I shall use the first words which come to mind, for I believe that what I have to say is just; so let none of you expect anything else. Indeed, my friends, it would hardly be right for me, at my age, to come before you like a schoolboy with his concocted phrases. But there is one thing, Athenians, which I do most earnestly beg and entreat of you. Do not be surprised and do not interrupt with shouts if in my defense I speak in the same way that I am accustomed to speak in the market place, at the tables of the money-changers, where many of you have heard me, and elsewhere. The truth is this: I am more than seventy, and this is the first time that I have ever come before a law court; thus your manner of speech here is quite strange to me. If I had really been a stranger, you would have forgiven me for speaking in the language and the manner of my 18

From **Apology:** *Plato: Euthyphro, Apology, Crito* by Church, F. J., © 1955. Reprinted by permission of Prentice-Hall, Inc., Upper Saddle River, NJ.

native country. And so now I ask you to grant me what I think I have a right to claim. Never mind the manner of my speech—it may be superior or it may be inferior to the usual manner. Give your whole attention to the question, whether what I say is just or not? That is what is required of a good judge, as speaking the truth is required of a good orator.

II   I have to defend myself, Athenians, first against the older false accusations of my old accusers, and then against the more recent ones of my present accusers. For many men have been accusing me to you, and for very many years, who have not spoken a word of truth; and I fear them more than I fear Anytus[1] and his associates, formidable as they are. But, my friends, the others are still more formidable, since they got hold of most of you when you were children and have been more persistent in accusing me untruthfully, persuading you that there is a certain Socrates, a wise man, who speculates about the heavens, who investigates things that are beneath the earth, and who can make the worse argument appear the stronger. These men, Athenians, who spread abroad this report are the accusers whom I fear; for their hearers think that persons who pursue such inquiries never believe in the gods. Besides they are many, their attacks have been going on for a long time, and they spoke to you when you were most ready to believe them, since you were all young, and some of you were children. And there was no one to answer them when they attacked me. The most preposterous thing of all is that I do not even know their names: I cannot tell you who they are except when one happens to be a comic poet. But all the rest who have persuaded you, from motives of resentment and prejudice, and sometimes, it may be, from conviction, are hardest to cope with. For I cannot call any one of them forward in court to cross-examine him. I have, as it were, simply to spar with shadows in my defense, and to put questions which there is no one to answer. I ask you, therefore, to believe that, as I say, I have been attacked by two kinds of accusers—first, by Meletus[2] and his asso-

ciates, and, then, by those older ones of whom I have spoken. And, with your leave, I will defend myself first against my old accusers, since you heard their accusations first, and they were much more compelling than my present accusers are.

Well, I must make my defense, Athenians, and try 19 in the short time allowed me to remove the prejudice which you have been so long a time acquiring. I hope that I may manage to do this, if it be best for you and for me, and that my defense may be successful; but I am quite aware of the nature of my task, and I know that it is a difficult one. Be the outcome, however, as is pleasing to god, I must obey the law and make my defense.

Let us begin from the beginning, then, and ask III what is the accusation that has given rise to the prejudice against me, on which Meletus relied when he brought his indictment. What is the prejudice which my enemies have been spreading about me? I must assume that they are formally accusing me, and read their indictment. It would run somewhat in this fashion: "Socrates is guilty of engaging in inquiries into things beneath the earth and in the heavens, of making the weaker argument appear the stronger, and of teaching others these same things." That is what they say. And in the comedy of Aristophanes[3] you yourselves saw a man called Socrates swinging around in a basket and saying that he walked on air, and sputtering a great deal of nonsense about matters of which I understand nothing at all. I do not mean to disparage that kind of knowledge if there is anyone who is wise about these matters. I trust Meletus may never be able to prosecute me for that. But the truth is, Athenians, I have nothing to do with these matters, and almost all of you are yourselves my witnesses of this. I beg all of you who have ever heard me discussing, and they are many, to inform your neighbors and tell them if any of you have ever heard me discussing such matters at all. That will show you that the other common statements about me are as false as this one.

But the fact is that not one of these is true. And IV if you have heard that I undertake to educate men, and make money by so doing, that is not true either, though I think that it would be a fine thing to be able 20 to educate men, as Gorgias of Leontini, and Prodicus of Ceos, and Hippias of Elis do. For each of

[1]Anytus is singled out as politically the most influential member of the prosecution. He had played a prominent part in the restoration of the democratic regime at Athens.—Ed.

[2]Apparently in order to obscure the political implications of the trial, the role of chief prosecutor was assigned to Meletus, a minor poet with fervent religious convictions. Anytus was evidently ready to make political use of Meletus' convictions without entirely sharing his fervor, for in the same year as this trial Meletus also prosecuted Andocides for impiety, but Anytus came to Andocides' defense.—Ed.

[3]The Clouds. The basket was satirically assumed to facilitate Socrates' inquiries into things in the heavens.—Ed.

them, my friends, can go into any city, and persuade the young men to leave the society of their fellow citizens, with any of whom they might associate for nothing, and to be only too glad to be allowed to pay money for the privilege of associating with themselves. And I believe that there is another wise man from Paros residing in Athens at this moment. I happened to meet Callias, the son of Hipponicus, a man who has spent more money on sophists than everyone else put together. So I said to him (he has two sons), "Callias, if your two sons had been foals or calves, we could have hired a trainer for them who would have trained them to excel in doing what they are naturally capable of. He would have been either a groom or a farmer. But whom do you intend to take to train them, seeing that they are men? Who understands the excellence which a man and citizen is capable of attaining? I suppose that you must have thought of this because you have sons. Is there such a person or not?" "Certainly there is," he replied. "Who is he," said I, "and where does he come from, and what is his fee?" "Evenus, Socrates," he replied, "from Paros, five minae." Then I thought that Evenus was a fortunate person if he really understood this art and could teach so cleverly. If I had possessed knowledge of that kind, I should have been conceited and disdainful. But, Athenians, the truth is that I do not possess it.

v   Perhaps some of you may reply: "But, Socrates, what is the trouble with you? What has given rise to these prejudices against you? You must have been doing something out of the ordinary. All these rumors and reports of you would never have arisen if you had not been doing something different from other men. So tell us what it is, that we may not give our verdict arbitrarily." I think that that is a fair question, and I will try to explain to you what it is that has raised these prejudices against me and given me this reputation. Listen, then. Some of you, perhaps, will think that I am joking, but I assure you that I will tell you the whole truth. I have gained this reputation, Athenians, simply by reason of a certain wisdom. But by what kind of wisdom? It is by just that wisdom which is perhaps human wisdom. In that, it may be, I am really wise. But the men of whom I was speaking just now must be wise in a wisdom which is greater than human wisdom, or else I cannot describe it, for certainly I know nothing of it myself, and if any man says that I do, he lies and speaks to arouse prejudice against me. Do not interrupt me with shouts, Athenians, even if you think

that I am boasting. What I am going to say is not my own statement. I will tell you who says it, and he is worthy of your respect. I will bring the god of Delphi to be the witness of my wisdom, if it is wisdom at all, and of its nature. You remember Chaerephon. From youth upwards he was my comrade; and also a partisan of your democracy, sharing your recent exile[4] and returning with you. You remember, too, Chaerephon's character—how impulsive he was in carrying through whatever he took in hand. Once he went to Delphi and ventured to put this question to the oracle—I entreat you again, my friends, not to interrupt me with your shouts—he asked if there was anyone who was wiser than I. The priestess answered that there was no one. Chaerephon himself is dead, but his brother here will witness to what I say.

Now see why I tell you this. I am going to explain to you how the prejudice against me has arisen. When I heard of the oracle I began to reflect: What can the god mean by this riddle? I know very well that I am not wise, even in the smallest degree. Then what can he mean by saying that I am the wisest of men? It cannot be that he is speaking falsely, for he is a god and cannot lie. For a long time I was at a loss to understand his meaning. Then, very reluctantly, I turned to investigate it in this manner: I went to a man who was reputed to be wise, thinking that there, if anywhere, I should prove the answer wrong, and meaning to point out to the oracle its mistake, and to say, "You said that I was the wisest of men, but this man is wiser than I am." So I examined the man—I need not tell you his name, he was a politician—but this was the result, Athenians. When I conversed with him I came to see that, though a great many persons, and most of all he himself, thought that he was wise, yet he was not wise. Then I tried to prove to him that he was not wise, though he fancied that he was. By so doing I made him indignant, and many of the bystanders. So when I went away, I thought to myself, "I am wiser than this man: neither of us knows anything that is really worth knowing, but he thinks that he has knowledge when he has not, while I, having no knowledge, do not think that I have. I seem, at any rate, to be a little wiser than he is on this point: I do not think that I know what I do not know." Next I went to another man who was reputed to be still wiser than the last, with

[4]During the totalitarian regime of The thirty which remained in power for eight months (404 B.C.), five years before the trial.—Ed.

exactly the same result. And there again I made him, and many other men, indignant.

VII Then I went on to one man after another, realizing that I was arousing indignation every day, which caused me much pain and anxiety. Still I thought that I must set the god's command above everything. So I had to go to every man who seemed to possess any knowledge, and investigate the meaning of the 22 oracle. Athenians, I must tell you the truth; I swear, this was the result of the investigation which I made at the god's command: I found that the men whose reputation for wisdom stood highest were nearly the most lacking in it, while others who were looked down on as common people were much more intelligent. Now I must describe to you the wanderings which I undertook, like Herculean labors, to prove the oracle irrefutable. After the politicians, I went to the poets, tragic, dithyrambic, and others, thinking that there I should find myself manifestly more ignorant than they. So I took up the poems on which I thought that they had spent most pains, and asked them what they meant, hoping at the same time to learn something from them. I am ashamed to tell you the truth, my friends, but I must say it. Almost any one of the bystanders could have talked about the works of these poets better than the poets themselves. So I soon found that it is not by wisdom that the poets create their works, but by a certain instinctive inspiration, like soothsayers and prophets, who say many fine things, but understand nothing of what they say. The poets seemed to me to be in a similar situation. And at the same time I perceived that, because of their poetry, they thought that they were the wisest of men in other matters too, which they were not. So I went away again, thinking that I had the same advantage over the poets that I had over the politicians.

VIII Finally, I went to the artisans, for I new very well that I possessed no knowledge at all worth speaking of, and I was sure that I should find that they knew many fine things. And in that I was not mistaken. They knew what I did not know, and so far they were wiser than I. But, Athenians, it seemed to me that the skilled artisans had the same failing as the poets. Each of them believed himself to be extremely wise in matters of the greatest importance because he was skillful in his own art: and this presumption of theirs obscured their real wisdom. So I asked myself, on behalf of the oracle, whether I would choose to remain as I was, without either their wisdom or their ignorance, or to possess both, as they did. And I answered to myself and to the oracle that it was better for me to remain as I was.

From this examination, Athenians, has arisen IX much fierce and bitter indignation, and as a result a 23 great many prejudices about me. People say that I am "a wise man." For the bystanders always think that I am wise myself in any matter wherein I refute another. But, gentlemen, I believe that the god is really wise, and that by this oracle he meant that human wisdom is worth little or nothing. I do not think that he meant that Socrates was wise. He only made use of my name, and took me as an example, as though he would say to men, "He among you is the wisest who, like Socrates, knows that his wisdom is really worth nothing at all." Therefore I still go about testing and examining every man whom I think wise, whether he be a citizen or a stranger, as the god has commanded me. Whenever I find that he is not wise, I point out to him, on the god's behalf, that he is not wise. I am so busy in this pursuit that I have never had leisure to take any part worth mentioning in public matters or to look after my private affairs. I am in great poverty as the result of my service to the god.

Besides this, the young men who follow me about, X who are the sons of wealthy persons and have the most leisure, take pleasure in hearing men cross-examined. They often imitate me among themselves; then they try their hands at cross-examining other people. And, I imagine, they find plenty of men who think that they know a great deal when in fact they know little or nothing. Then the persons who are cross-examined get angry with me instead of with themselves, and say that Socrates is an abomination and corrupts the young. When they are asked, "Why, what does he do? What does he teach?" they do not know what to say. Not to seem at a loss, they repeat the stock charges against all philosophers, and allege that he investigates things in the air and under the earth, and that he teaches people to disbelieve in the gods, and to make the worse argument appear the stronger. For, I suppose, they would not like to confess the truth, which is that they are shown up as ignorant pretenders to knowledge that they do not possess. So they have been filling your ears with their bitter prejudices for a long time, for they are ambitious, energetic, and numerous; and they speak vigorously and persuasively against me. Relying on this, Meletus, Anytus, and Lycon have attacked me. Meletus is indignant with me on behalf of the poets, Anytus on behalf of the artisans and politicians,

24 and Lycon on behalf of the orators. And so, as I said at the beginning, I shall be surprised if I am able, in the short time allowed me for my defense, to remove from your minds this prejudice which has grown so strong. What I have told you, Athenians, is the truth: I neither conceal nor do I suppress anything, trivial or important. Yet I know that it is just this outspokenness which rouses indignation. But that is only a proof that my words are true, and that the prejudice against me, and the causes of it, are what I have said. And whether you investigate them now or hereafter, you will find that they are so.

XI   What I have said must suffice as my defense against the charges of my first accusers. I will try next to defend myself against Meletus, that "good patriot," as he calls himself, and my later accusers. Let us assume that they are a new set of accusers, and read their indictment, as we did in the case of the others. It runs thus: Socrates is guilty of corrupting the youth, and of believing not in the gods whom the state believes in, but in other new divinities. Such is the accusation. Let us examine each point in it separately. Meletus says that I am guilty of playing a solemn joke by casually bringing men to trial, and pretending to have a solemn interest in matters to which he has never given a moment's thought. Now I will try to prove to you that this is so.

XII   Come here, Meletus. Is it not a fact that you think it very important that the young should be as good as possible?

MELETUS. It is.

SOCRATES. Come, then, tell the judges who improves them. You care so much,[5] you must know. You are accusing me, and bringing me to trial, because, as you say, you have discovered that I am the corrupter of the youth. Come now, reveal to the gentlemen who improves them. You see, Meletus, you have nothing to say; you are silent. But don't you think that this is shameful? Is not your silence a conclusive proof of what I say—that you have never cared? Come, tell us, my good man, who makes the young better?

MEL. The laws.

SOCR. That, my friend, is not my question. What man improves the young, who begins by knowing the laws?

MEL. The judges here, Socrates.

SOCR. What do you mean, Meletus? Can they educate the young and improve them?

MEL. Certainly.

SOCR. All of them? Or only some of them?

MEL. All of them.

SOCR. By Hera, that is good news! Such a large 25 supply of benefactors! And do the members of the audience here improve them, or not?

MEL. They do.

SOCR. And do the councilors?

MEL. Yes.

SOCR. Well, then, Meletus, do the members of the assembly corrupt the young or do they again all improve them?

MEL. They, too, improve them.

SOCR. Then all the Athenians, apparently, make the young into good men except me, and I alone corrupt them. Is that your meaning?

MEL. Certainly, that is my meaning.

SOCR. You have discovered me to be most unfortunate. Now tell me: do you think that the same holds good in the case of horses? Does one man do them harm and everyone else improve them? On the contrary, is it not one man only, or a very few—namely, those who are skilled with horses—who can improve them, while the majority of men harm them if they use them and have anything to do with them? Is it not so, Meletus, both with horses and with every other animal? Of course it is, whether you and Anytus say yes or no. The young would certainly be very fortunate if only one man corrupted them, and everyone else did them good. The truth is, Meletus, you prove conclusively that you have never thought about the young in your life. You exhibit your carelessness in not caring for the very matters about which you are prosecuting me.

Now be so good as to tell us, Meletus, is it better XIII to live among good citizens or bad ones? Answer, my friend. I am not asking you at all a difficult question. Do not the bad harm their associates and the good do them good?

MEL. Yes.

SOCR. Is there anyone who would rather be injured than benefited by his companions? Answer, my good man; you are obliged by the law to answer. Does anyone like to be injured?

MEL. Certainly not.

SOCR. Well, then, are you prosecuting me for corrupting the young and making them worse, voluntarily or involuntarily?

MEL. For doing it voluntarily.

---

[5]Throughout the following passage Socrates plays on the etymology of the name "Meletus" as meaning "the man who cares."—Ed.

SOCR. What, Meletus? Do you mean to say that you, who are so much younger than I, are yet so much wiser than I that you know that bad citizens always do evil, and that good citizens do good, to those with whom they come in contact, while I am so extraordinarily ignorant as not to know that, if I make any of my companions evil, he will probably injure me in some way? And you allege that I do this voluntarily? You will not make me believe that, nor anyone else either, I should think. Either I do not corrupt the young at all or, if I do, I do so involuntarily, so that you are lying in either case. And if I corrupt them involuntarily, the law does not call upon you to prosecute me for an error which is involuntary, but to take me aside privately and reprove and educate me. For, of course, I shall cease from doing wrong involuntarily, as soon as I know that I have been doing wrong. But you avoided associating with me and educating me; instead you bring me up before the court, where the law sends persons, not for education, but for punishment.

XIV The truth is, Athenians, as I said, it is quite clear that Meletus has never cared at all about these matters. However, now tell us, Meletus, how do you say that I corrupt the young? Clearly, according to your indictment, by teaching them not to believe in the gods the state believes in, but other new divinities instead. You mean that I corrupt the young by that teaching, do you not?

MEL. Yes, most certainly I mean that.

SOCR. Then in the name of these gods of whom we are speaking, explain yourself a little more clearly to me and to these gentlemen here. I cannot understand what you mean. Do you mean that I teach the young to believe in some gods, but not in the gods of the state? Do you accuse me of teaching them to believe in strange gods? If that is your meaning, I myself believe in some gods, and my crime is not that of complete atheism. Or do you mean that I do not believe in the gods at all myself, and that I teach other people not to believe in them either?

MEL. I mean that you do not believe in the gods in any way whatever.

SOCR. You amaze me, Meletus! Why do you say that? Do you mean that I believe neither the sun nor the moon to be gods, like other men?

MEL. I swear he does not, judges. He says that the sun is a stone, and the moon earth.

SOCR. My dear Meletus, do you think that you are prosecuting Anaxagoras? You must have a very poor opinion of these men, and think them illiterate, if you imagine that they do not know that the works of Anaxagoras of Clazomenae are full of these doctrines. And so young men learn these things from me, when they can often buy them in the theater for a drachma at most, and laugh at Socrates were he to pretend that these doctrines, which are very peculiar doctrines, too, were his own. But please tell me, do you really think that I do not believe in the gods at all?

MEL. Most certainly I do. You are a complete atheist.

SOCR. No one believes that, Meletus, not even you yourself. It seems to me, Athenians, that Meletus is very insolent and reckless, and that he is prosecuting me simply out of insolence, recklessness, and youthful bravado. For he seems to be testing me, by asking me a riddle that has no answer. "Will this wise Socrates," he says to himself, "see that I am joking and contradicting myself? Or shall I deceive him and everyone else who hears me?" Meletus seems to me to contradict himself in his indictment: it is as if he were to say, "Socrates is guilty of not believing in the gods, but believes in the gods." This is joking.

Now, my friends, let us see why I think that this is his meaning. You must answer me, Meletus, and you, Athenians, must remember the request which I made to you at the start, and not interrupt me with shouts if I talk in my usual manner.

Is there any man, Meletus, who believes in the existence of things pertaining to men and not in the existence of men? Make him answer the question, gentlemen, without these interruptions. Is there any man who believes in the existence of horsemanship and not in the existence of horses? Or in flute playing and not in flute players? There is not, my friend. If you will not answer, I will tell both you and the judges. But you must answer my next question. Is there any man who believes in the existence of divine things and not in the existence of divinities?

MEL. There is not.

SOCR. I am very glad that these gentlemen have managed to extract an answer from you. Well then, you say that I believe in divine things, whether they be old or new, and that I teach others to believe in them. At any rate, according to your statement, I believe in divine things. That you have sworn in your indictment. But if I believe in divine things, I suppose it follows necessarily that I believe in divinities. Is it not so? It is. I assume that you grant that, as you do not answer. But do we not believe that divinities are either gods themselves or the children of the gods? Do you admit that?

MEL. I do.

SOCR. Then you admit that I believe in divinities. Now, if these divinities are gods, then, as I say, you are joking and asking a riddle, and asserting that I do not believe in the gods, and at the same time that I do, since I believe in divinities. But if these divinities are the illegitimate children of the gods, either by the nymphs or by other mothers, as they are said to be, then, I ask, what man could believe in the existence of the children of the gods, and not in the existence of the gods? That would be as absurd as believing in the existence of the offspring of horses and asses, and not in the existence of horses and asses. You must have indicted me in this manner, Meletus, either to test me or because you could not find any act of injustice that you would accuse me of with truth. But you will never contrive to persuade any man with any sense at all that a belief in
28 divine things and things of the gods does not necessarily involve a belief in divinities, and in the gods.

XVI   But in truth, Athenians, I do not think that I need say very much to prove that I have not committed the act of injustice for which Meletus is prosecuting me. What I have said is enough to prove that. But be assured it is certainly true, as I have already told you, that I have aroused much indignation. That is what will cause my condemnation if I am condemned; not Meletus nor Anytus either, but that prejudice and resentment of the multitude which have been the destruction of many good men before me, and I think will be so again. There is no prospect that I shall be the last victim.

Perhaps someone will say: "Are you not ashamed, Socrates, of leading a life which is very likely now to cause your death? I should answer him with justice, and say: "My friend, if you think that a man of any worth at all ought to reckon the chances of life and death when he acts, or that he ought to think of anything but whether he is acting justly or unjustly, and as a good or a bad man would act, you are mistaken. According to you, the demigods who died at Troy would be foolish, and among them Achilles, who thought nothing of danger when the alternative was disgrace. For when his mother—and she was a goddess—addressed him, when he was resolved to slay Hector, in this fashion, 'My son, if you avenge the death of your comrade Patroclus and slay Hector, you will die yourself, for fate awaits you next after Hector.' When he heard this, he scorned dan-

ger and death; he feared much more to live a coward and not to avenge his friend. 'Let me punish the evildoer and afterwards die,' he said, 'that I may not remain here by the beaked ships jeered at, encumbering the earth.' "[6] Do you suppose that he thought of danger or of death? For this, Athenians, I believe to be the truth. Wherever a man's station is, whether he has chosen it of his own will, or whether he has been placed at it by his commander, there it is his duty to remain and face the danger without thinking of death or of any other thing except disgrace.

When the generals whom you chose to command XVII me, Athenians, assigned me my station during the battles of Potidaea, Amphipolis, and Delium, I remained where they stationed me and ran the risk of death, like other men. It would be very strange conduct on my part if I were to desert my station now from fear of death or of any other thing when the god has commanded me—as I am persuaded that he has done—to spend my life in searching for wisdom, 29 and in examining myself and others. That would indeed be a very strange thing. Then certainly I might with justice be brought to trial for not believing in the gods, for I should be disobeying the oracle, and fearing death and thinking myself wise when I was not wise. For to fear death, my friends, is only to think ourselves wise without really being wise, for it is to think that we know what we do not know. For no one knows whether death may not be the greatest good that can happen to man. But men fear it as if they knew quite well that it was the greatest of evils. And what is this but that shameful ignorance of thinking that we know what we do not know? In this matter, too, my friends, perhaps I am different from the multitude. And if I were to claim to be at all wiser than others, it would be because, not knowing very much about the other world, I do not think I know. But I do know very well that it is evil and disgraceful to do an unjust act, and to disobey my superior, whether man or god. I will never do what I know to be evil, and shrink in fear from what I do not know to be good or evil. Even if you acquit me now, and do not listen to Anytus' argument that, if I am to be acquitted, I ought never to have been brought to trial at all, and that, as it is, you are bound to put me to death because, as he said, if I escape, all your sons will be utterly corrupted by practicing what Socrates teaches. If you were therefore to say to me, "Socrates, this time we will

---

[6]Homer, *Iiliad*, xviii, 96, 98.—Ed.

not listen to Anytus. We will let you go, but on the condition that you give up this investigation of yours, and philosophy. If you are found following these pursuits again, you shall die." I say, if you offered to let me go on these terms, I should reply: "Athenians, I hold you in the highest regard and affection, but I will be persuaded by the god rather than you. As long as I have breath and strength I will not give up philosophy and exhorting you and declaring the truth to every one of you whom I meet, saying, as I am accustomed, 'My good friend, you are a citizen of Athens, a city which is very great and very famous for its wisdom and power—are you not ashamed of caring so much for the making of money and for fame and prestige, when you neither think nor care about wisdom and truth and the improvement of your soul?' " If he disputes my words and says that he does care about these things, I shall not at once release him and go away: I shall question him and cross-examine him and test him. If I think that he has not attained excellence, though he 30 says that he has, I shall reproach him for undervaluing the most valuable things, and overvaluing those that are less valuable. This I shall do to everyone whom I meet, young or old, citizen or stranger, but especially to citizens, since they are more closely related to me. This, you must recognize, the god has commanded me to do. And I think that no greater good has ever befallen you in the state than my service to the god. For I spend my whole life in going about and persuading you all to give your first and greatest care to the improvement of your souls, and not till you have done that to think of your bodies or your wealth. And I tell you that wealth does not bring excellence, but that wealth, and every other good thing which me have, whether in public or in private, comes from excellence. If then I corrupt the youth by this teaching, these things must be harmful. But if any man says that I teach anything else, there is nothing in what he says. And therefore, Athenians, I say, whether you are persuaded by Anytus or not, whether you acquit me or not, I shall not change my way of life; no, not if I have to die for it many times.

XVIII   Do not interrupt me, Athenians, with your shouts. Remember the request which I made to you, and do not interrupt my words. I think that it will profit you to hear them. I am going to say something more to you, at which you may be inclined to protest, but do not do that. Be sure that if you put me to death, I who am what I have told you that I am, you will do .

yourselves more harm than me. Meletus and Anytus can do me no harm: that is impossible, for I am sure it is not allowed that a good man be injured by a worse. He may indeed kill me, or drive me into exile, or deprive me of my civil rights. Perhaps Meletus and others think those things great evils. But I do not think so. I think it is a much greater evil to do what he is doing now, and to try to put a man to death unjustly. And now, Athenians, I am not arguing in my own defense at all, as you might expect me to do, but rather in yours in order you may not make a mistake about the gift of the god to you by condemning me. For if you put me to death, you will not easily find another who, if I may use a ludicrous comparison, clings to the state as a sort of gadfly to a horse that is large and well-bred but rather sluggish because of its size, so that it needs to be aroused. It seems to me that the god has attached me like to the state, for I am constantly alighting upon you at every point to arouse, persuade, and reproach each of you all day long. You will not eas- 31 ily find anyone else, my friends, to fill my place; and if you are persuaded by me, you will spare my life. You are indignant, as drowsy persons are when they are awakened, and, of course, if you are persuaded by Anytus, you could easily kill me with a single blow, and then sleep on undisturbed for the rest of your lives, unless the god in his care for you sends another to arouse you. And you may easily see that it is the god who has given me to your city; for it is not human, the way in which I have neglected all my own interests and allowed my private affairs to be neglected for so many years, while occupying myself unceasingly in your interests, going to each of you privately, like a father or an elder brother, trying to persuade him to care for human excellence. There would have been a reason for it, if I had gained any advantage by this, or if I had been paid for my exhortations; but you see yourselves that my accusers, though they accuse me of everything else without shame, have not had the shamelessness to say that I ever either exacted or demanded payment. To that they have no witness. And I think that I have sufficient witness to the truth of what I say—my poverty.

Perhaps it may seem strange to you that, though XIX I go about giving this advice private and meddling in others' affairs, yet I do not venture to come forward in the assembly and advise the state. You have often heard me speak of my reason for this, and in many places: it is that I have a certain divine guide, which is what Meletus has caricatured in his indictment. I have had it from childhood. It is a kind of voice which, whenever I hear it, always turns me back from something which I was going to do, but never urges me to act. It is this which forbids me to take part in politics. And I think it does well to forbid me. For, Athenians, it is quite certain that, if I had attempted to take part in politics, I should have perished at once and long ago without doing any good either to you or to myself. And do not be indignant with me for telling the truth. There is no man who will preserve his life for long, either in Athens or elsewhere, if he firmly opposes the multitude, and tries to prevent the commission of much injustice and illegality in the state. He who would

32 really fight for justice must do so as a private citizen, not as a political figure, if he is to preserve his life, even for a short time.

xx   I will prove to you that this is so by very strong evidence, not by mere words, but by what you value more—actions. Listen, then, to what has happened to me, that you may know that there is no man who could make me consent to commit an unjust act from the fear of death, but that I would perish at once rather than give way. What I am going to tell you may be commonplace in the law court; nevertheless, it is true. The only office that I ever held in the state, Athenians, was that of councilor. When you wished to try the ten admirals who did not rescue their men after the battle of Arginusae as a group, which was illegal, as you all came to think afterwards, the executive committee was composed of members of the tribe Antiochis, to which I belong.[7] On that occasion I alone of the committee members opposed your illegal action and gave my vote against you. The orators were ready to impeach me and arrest me; and you were clamoring and urging them on with your shouts. But I thought that I ought to face the danger, with law and justice on my side, rather than join with you in your unjust proposal, from fear of imprisonment or death. That was when the state was democratic. When the oligarchy came in, The Thirty sent for me, with four others, to the council-chamber, and ordered us to bring Leon the Salamin-

ian from Salamis, that they might put him to death. They were in the habit of frequently giving similar orders to many others, wishing to implicate as many as possible in their crimes. But then I again proved, not by mere words, but by my actions, that, if I may speak bluntly, I do not care a straw for death; but that I do care very much indeed about not doing anything unjust or impious. That government with all its power did not terrify me into doing anything unjust. When we left the council-chamber, the other four went over to Salamis and brought Leon across to Athens; I went home. And if the rule of The Thirty had not been overthrown soon afterwards, I should very likely have been put to death for what I did then. Many of you will be my witnesses in this matter.[8]

Now do you think that I could have remained alive xxı all these years if I had taken part in public affairs, and had always maintained the cause of justice like a good man, and had held it a paramount duty, as it is, to do so? Certainly not, Athenians, nor could any other man. But throughout my whole life, both in private and in public, whenever I have had to take 33 part in public affairs, you will find I have always been the same and have never yielded unjustly to anyone; no, not to those whom my enemies falsely assert to have been my pupils. But I was never anyone's teacher. I have never withheld myself from anyone, young or old, who was anxious to hear me converse while I was making my investigation; neither do I converse for payment, and refuse to converse without payment. I am ready to ask questions of rich and poor alike, and if any man wishes to answer me, and then listen to what I have to say, he may. And I cannot justly be charged with causing these men to turn out good or bad, for I never either taught or professed to teach any of them any knowledge whatever. And if any man asserts that he ever learned or heard anything from me in private which everyone else did not hear as well as he, be sure that he does not speak the truth.

Why is it, then, that people delight in spending so xxıı much time in my company? You have heard why,

---

[7]The Council was the administrative body in Athens. Actual administrative functions were performed by an executive committee of the Council, and the members of this committee were recruited from each tribe in turn. The case Socrates is alluding to was that of the admirals who were accused of having failed to rescue the crews of ships which sank during the battle of Arginusae. The six admirals who were actually put on trial were condemned as a group and executed.—Ed.

[8]There is evidence that Meletus was one of the four who turned in Leon. Socrates' recalling this earlier lapse from legal procedure is probably also a thrust at Anytus. The Thirty successfully implicated so many Athenians in their crimes that an amnesty was declared, which Anytus strongly favored, in order to enlist wider support for the restored democracy. Thus those who were really implicated could now no longer be prosecuted legally, but Socrates himself being illegally prosecuted (as he now goes on to suggest) because he was guilty of having associated with such "pupils" as Critias, who was a leader of The Thirty.—Ed.

Athenians. I told you the whole truth when I said that they delight in hearing me examine persons who think that they are wise when they are not wise. It is certainly very amusing to listen to. And, as I have said, the god has commanded me to examine men, in oracles and in dreams and in every way in which the divine will was ever declared to man. This is the truth, Athenians, and if it were not the truth, it would be easily refuted. For if it were really the case that I have already corrupted some of the young men, and am now corrupting others, surely some of them, finding as they grew older that I had given them bad advice in their youth, would have come forward today to accuse me and take their revenge. Or if they were unwilling to do so themselves, surely their relatives, their fathers or brothers, or others, would, if I had done them any harm, have remembered it and taken their revenge. Certainly I see many of them in court. Here is Crito, of my own district and of my own age, the father of Critobulus; here is Lysanias of Sphettus, the father of Aeschines; here is also Antiphon of Cephisus, the father of Epigenes. Then here are others whose brothers have spent their time in my company—Nicostratus, the son of Theozotides and brother of Theodotus—and Theodotus is dead, so he at least cannot entreat his brother to be silent; here is Paralus, the son of Demodocus and 34 the brother of Theages; here is Adeimantus, the son of Ariston, whose brother is Plato here; and Aeantodorus, whose brother is Aristodorus. And I can name many others to you, some of whom Meletus ought to have called as witnesses in the course of his own speech; but if he forgot to call them then, let him call them now—I will yield the floor to him—and tell us if he has any such evidence. No, on the contrary, my friends, you will find all these men ready to support me, the corrupter who has injured their relatives, as Meletus and Anytus call me. Those of them who have been already corrupted might perhaps have some reason for supporting me, but what reason can their relatives have who are grown up, and who are uncorrupted, except the reason of truth and justice—that they know very well that Meletus is lying, and that I am speaking the truth?

XXIII   Well, my friends, this, and perhaps more like this, is pretty much all I have to offer in my defense. There may be some one among you who will be indignant when he remembers how, even in a less important trial than this, he begged and entreated the judges, with many tears, to acquit him, and brought forward his children and many of his friends and relatives in court in order to appeal to your feelings; and then finds that I shall do none of these things, though I am in what we would think the supreme danger. Perhaps he will harden himself against me when he notices this; it may make him angry, and he may cast his vote in anger. If it is so with any of you—I do not suppose that it is, but in case it should be so—I think that I should answer him reasonably if I said: "My friend, I have relatives, too, for, in the words of Homer, I am 'not born of an oak or a rock'[9] but of flesh and blood." And so, Athenians, I have relatives, and I have three sons, one of them nearly grown up, and the other two still children. Yet I will not bring any of them forward before you and implore you to acquit me. And why will I do none of these things? It is not from arrogance, Athenians, nor because I lack respect for you—whether or not I can face death bravely is another question—but for my own good name, and for your good name, and for the good name of the whole state. I do not think it right, at my age and with my reputation, to do anything of that kind. Rightly or wrongly, men have made up their minds that in some way Socrates is different from the multitude of men. And it will be 35 shameful if those of you who are thought to excel in wisdom, or in bravery, or in any other excellence, are going to act in this fashion. I have often seen men of reputation behaving in an extraordinary way at their trial, as if they thought it a terrible fate to be killed, and as though they expected to live for ever if you did not put them to death. Such men seem to me to bring shame upon the state, for any stranger would suppose that the best and most eminent Athenians, who are selected by their fellow citizens to hold office, and for other honors, are no better than women. Those of you, Athenians, who have any reputation at all ought not to do these things, and you ought not to allow us to do them. You should show that you will be much more ready to condemn men who make the state ridiculous by these pathetic performances than men who remain quiet.

But apart from the question of reputation, my XXIV friends, I do not think that it is right to entreat the judge to acquit us, or to escape condemnation in that way. It is our duty to teach and persuade him. He does not sit to give away justice as a favor, but to pronounce judgment; and he has sworn, not to favor any man whom he would like to favor, but to

9Homer, *Odyssey*, xix, 163.

judge according to law. And, therefore, we ought not to encourage you in the habit of breaking your oaths; and you ought not to allow yourselves to fall into this habit, for then neither you nor we would be acting piously. Therefore, Athenians, do not require me to do these things, for I believe them to be neither good nor just nor pious; especially, do not ask me to do them today when Meletus is prosecuting me for impiety. For were I to be successful and persuade you by my entreaties to break your oaths, I should be clearly teaching you to believe that there are no gods, and I should be simply accusing myself by my defense of not believing in them. But, Athenians, that is very far from the truth. I do believe in the gods as no one of my accusers believes in them; and to you and to the god I commit my cause to be decided as is best for you and for me.

(He is found guilty by 281 votes to 220.)

xxv I am not indignant at the verdict which you have
36 given, Athenians, for many reasons. I expected that you would find me guilty; and I am not so much surprised at that as at the numbers of the votes. I certainly never thought that the majority against me would have been so narrow. But now it seems that if only thirty votes had changed sides, I should have escaped. So I think that I have escaped Meletus, as it is; and not only have I escaped him, for it is perfectly clear that if Anytus and Lycon had not come forward to accuse me, too, he would not have obtained the fifth part of the votes, and would have had to pay a fine of a thousand drachmae.

xxvi   So he proposes death as the penalty. Be it so. And what alternative penalty shall I propose to you, Athenians?[10] What I deserve, of course, must I not? What then do I deserve to pay or to suffer for having determined not to spend my life in ease? I neglected the things which most men value, such as wealth, and family interests, and military commands, and public oratory, and all the civic appointments, and social clubs, and political factions, that there are in Athens; for I thought that I was really too honest a man to preserve my life if I engaged in these affairs. So I did not go where I should have done no good either to you or to myself. I went, instead, to each one of you privately to do him, as I say, the great-

est of benefits, and tried to persuade him not to think of his affairs until he had thought of himself and tried to make himself as good and wise as possible, nor to think of the affairs of Athens until he had thought of Athens herself; and to care for other things in the same manner. Then what do I deserve for such a life? Something good, Athenians, if I am really to propose what I deserve; and something good which it would be suitable for me to receive. Then what is a suitable reward to be given to a poor benefactor who requires leisure to exhort you? There is no reward, Athenians, so suitable for him as receiving free meals in the prytaneum. It is a much more suitable reward for him than for any of you who has won a victory at the Olympic games with his horse or his chariots. Such a man only makes you seem happy, but I make you really happy; he is not in want, and I am. So if I am to propose the penalty which I really deserve, I propose this—free meals in the prytaneum.   37

Perhaps you think me stubborn and arrogant in xxviii what I am saying now, as in what I said about the entreaties and tears. It is not so, Athenians. It is rather that I am convinced that I never wronged any man voluntarily, though I cannot persuade you of that, since we have conversed together only a little time. If there were a law at Athens, as there is elsewhere, not to finish a trial of life and death in a single day, I think that I could have persuaded you; but now it is not easy in so short a time to clear myself of great prejudices. But when I am persuaded that I have never wronged any man, I shall certainly not wrong myself, or admit that I deserve to suffer any evil, or propose any evil for myself as a penalty. Why should I? Lest I should suffer the penalty which Meletus proposes when I say that I do not know whether it is a good or an evil? Shall I choose instead of it something which I know to be an evil, and propose that as a penalty? Shall I propose imprisonment? And why should I pass the rest of my days in prison, the slave of successive officials? Or shall I propose a fine, with imprisonment until it is paid? I have told you why I will not do that. I should have to remain in prison, for I have no money to pay a fine with. Shall I then propose exile? Perhaps you would agree to that. Life would indeed be very dear to me if I were unreasonable enough to expect that strangers would cheerfully tolerate my discussions and arguments when you who are my fellow citizens cannot endure them, and have found them so irksome and odious to you that you are seeking now

[10]For certain crimes no penalty was fixed by Athenian law. Having reached a verdict of guilty, the court had still to decide between the alternative penalties proposed by the prosecution and the defense.—Ed.

to be relieved of them. No, indeed, Athenians, that is not likely. A fine life I should lead for an old man if I were to withdraw from Athens and pass the rest of my days in wandering from city to city, and continually being expelled. For I know very well that the young men will listen to me wherever I go, as they do here. If I drive them away, they will persuade their elders to expel me; if I do not drive them away, their fathers and other relatives will expel me for their sakes.

XXVIII   Perhaps someone will say, "Why cannot you withdraw from Athens, Socrates, and hold your peace?" It is the most difficult thing in the world to make you understand why I cannot do that. If I say that I cannot hold my peace because that would be to disobey the god, you will think that I am not in earnest and will not believe me. And if I tell you that no 38 greater good can happen to a man than to discuss human excellence every day and the other matters about which you have heard me arguing and examining myself and others, and that an unexamined life is not worth living, then you will believe me still less. But that is so, my friends, though it is not easy to persuade you. And, what is more, I am not accustomed to think that I deserve anything evil. If I had been rich, I would have proposed as large a fine as I could pay: that would have done me no harm. But I am not rich enough to pay a fine unless you are willing to fix it at a sum within my means. Perhaps I could pay you a mina, so I propose that. Plato here, Athenians, and Crito, and Critobulus, and Apollodorus bid me propose thirty minae, and they guarantee its payment. So I propose thirty minae. Their security will be sufficient to you for the money.

(He is condemned to death.)

XXIX   You have not gained very much time, Athenians, and at the price of the slurs of those who wish to revile the state. And they will say that you put Socrates, a wise man, to death. For they will certainly call me wise, whether I am wise or not, when they want to reproach you. If you had waited for a little while, your wishes would have been fulfilled in the course of nature; for you see that I am an old man, far advanced in years, and near to death. I am saying this not to all of you, only to those who have voted for my death. And to them I have something else to say. Perhaps, my friends, you think that I have been convicted because I was wanting in the

arguments by which I could have persuaded you to acquit me, if I had thought it right to do or to say anything to escape punishment. It is not so. I have been convicted because I was wanting, not in arguments, but in impudence and shamelessness—because I would not plead before you as you would have liked to hear me plead, or appeal to you with weeping and wailing, or say and do many other things which I maintain are unworthy of me, but which you have been accustomed to from other men. But when I was defending myself, I thought that I ought not to do anything unworthy of a free man because of the danger which I ran, and I have not changed my mind now. I would very much rather defend myself as I did, and die, than as you would have had me do, and live. Both in a lawsuit and in war, there are some things which neither I nor any 39 other man may do in order to escape from death. In battle, a man often sees that he may at least escape from death by throwing down his arms and falling on his knees before the pursuer to beg for his life. And there are many other ways of avoiding death in every danger if a man is willing to say and to do anything. But, my friends, I think that it is a much harder thing to escape from wickedness than from death, for wickedness is swifter than death. And now I, who am old and slow, have been overtaken by the slower pursuer: and my accusers, who are clever and swift, have been overtaken by the swifter pursuer—wickedness. And now I shall go away, sentenced by you to death; they will go away, sentenced by truth to wickedness and injustice. And I abide by this award as well as they. Perhaps it was right for these things to be so. I think that they are fairly balanced.

And now I wish to prophesy to you, Athenians, xxx who have condemned me. For I am going to die, and that is the time when men have most prophetic power. And I prophesy to you who have sentenced me to death that a far more severe punishment than you have inflicted on me will surely overtake you as soon as I am dead. You have done this thing, thinking that you will be relieved from having to give an account of your lives. But I say that the result will be very different. There will be more men who will call you to account, whom I have held back, though you did not recognize it. And they will be harsher toward you than I have been, for they will be younger, and you will be more indignant with them. For if you think that you will restrain men from reproaching you for not living as you should, by putting them to death, you are very much mistaken. That way of escape is neither possible nor honorable. It is much more honorable and much easier not to suppress others, but to make yourselves as good as you can. This is my parting prophecy to you who have condemned me.

XXXI   With you who have acquitted me I should like to discuss this thing that has happened, while the authorities are busy, and before I go to the place where I have to die. So, remain with me until I go: there is no reason why we should not talk with each other while it is possible. I wish to explain to you, as my friends, the meaning of what has happened to me. An amazing thing has happened to me, judges—for I am right in calling you judges.[11] The prophetic guide has been constantly with me all through my life till now, opposing me even in trivial matters if I were not going to act rightly. And now you yourselves see what has happened to me—a thing which might be thought, and which is sometimes actually reckoned, the supreme evil. But the divine guide did not oppose me when I was leaving my house in the morning, nor when I was coming up here to the court, nor at any point in my speech when I was going to say anything; though at other times it has often stopped me in the very act of speaking. But now, in this matter, it has never once opposed me, either in my words or my actions. I will tell you what I believe to be the reason. This thing that has come upon me must be a good; and those of us who think that death is an evil must needs be mistaken. I have a clear proof that that is so; for my accustomed guide would certainly have opposed me if I had not been going to meet with something good.

XXXII   And if we reflect in another way, we shall see that we may well hope that death is a good. For the state of death is one of two things: either the dead man wholly ceases to be and loses all consciousness or, as we are told, it is a change and a migration of the soul to another place. And if death is the absence of all consciousness, and like the sleep of one whose slumbers are unbroken by any dreams, it will be a wonderful gain. For if a man had to select that night in which he slept so soundly that he did not even dream, and had to compare with it all the other nights and days of his life, and then had to say how many days and nights in his life he had spent better and more pleasantly than this night, I think that a private

person, nay, even the Great King of Persia himself, would find them easy to count, compared with the others. If that is the nature of death, I for one count it a gain. For then it appears that all time is nothing more than a single night. But if death is a journey to another place, and what we are told is true—that all who have died are there—what good could be greater than this, my judges? Would a journey not be worth taking, at the end of which, in the other world, we should be delivered from the pretended [41] judges here and should find the true judges who are said to sit in judgment below, such as Minos and Rhadamanthus and Aeacus and Triptolemus, and the other demigods who were just in their own lives? Or what would you not give to converse with Orpheus and Musaeus and Hesiod and Homer? I am willing to die many times if this be true. And for my own part I should find it wonderful to meet there Palamedes, and Ajax the son of Telamon, and the other men of old who have died through an unjust judgment, and to compare my experiences with theirs. That I think would be no small pleasure. And, above all, I could spend my time in examining those who are there, as I examine men here, and in finding out which of them is wise, and which of them thinks himself wise when he is not wise. What would we not give, my judges, to be able to examine the leader of the great expedition against Troy, or Odysseus, or Sisyphus, or countless other men and women whom we could name? It would be an inexpressible happiness to converse with them and to live with them and to examine them. Assuredly there they do not put men to death for doing that. For besides the other ways in which they are happier than we are, they are immortal, at least if what we are told is true.

And you too, judges, must face death hopefully, XXXIII and believe this one truth, that no evil can happen to a good man, either in life or after death. His affairs are not neglected by the gods; and what has happened to me today has not happened by chance. I am persuaded that it was better for me to die now, and to be released from trouble; and that was the reason why the guide never turned me back. And so I am not at all angry with my accusers or with those who have condemned me to die. Yet it was not with this in mind that they accused me and condemned me, but meaning to do me an injury. So far I may blame them.

Yet I have one request to make of them. When my sons grow up, punish them, my friends, and ha-

---

[11]The form of address hitherto has always been "Athenians," or "my friends." The "judges" in an Athenian court were simply the members of the jury.—Ed.

rass them in the same way that I have harassed you, if they seem to you to care for riches or for any other thing more than excellence; and if they think that they are something when they are really nothing, reproach them, as I have reproached you, for not caring for what they should, and for thinking that they are something when really they are nothing. And if you will do this, I myself and my sons will have re- 42 ceived justice from you.

But now the time has come, and we must go away—I to die, and you to live. Which is better is known to the god alone.

Crito

43 SOCRATES. WHY have you come at this hour, Crito? it must be quite early.

CRITO. Yes certainly.

Soc. What is the exact time?

CR. The dawn is breaking.

Soc. I wonder the keeper of the prison would let you in.

CR. He knows me because I often come, Socrates; moreover. I have done him a kindness.

Soc. And are you only just come?

CR. No, I came some time ago.

b Soc. Then why did you sit and say nothing, instead of awakening me at once?

CR. Why, indeed, Socrates, I myself would rather not have all this sleeplessness and sorrow. But I have been wondering at your peaceful slumbers, and that was the reason why I did not awaken you, because I wanted you to be out of pain. I have always thought you happy in the calmness of your temperament; but never did I see the like of the easy, cheerful way in which you bear this calamity.

Soc. Why, Crito, when a man has reached my age he ought not to be repining at the prospect of death.

c CR. And yet other old men find themselves in similar misfortunes, and age does not prevent them from repining.

Soc. That may be. But you have not told me why you come at this early hour.

CR. I come to bring you a message which is sad and painful; not, as I believe, to yourself but to all of us who are your friends, and saddest of all to me.

Soc. What! I suppose that the ship has come from d Delos, on the arrival of which I am to die?

CR. No, the ship has not actually arrived, but she will probably be here to-day, as persons who have come from Sunium tell me that they have left her there; and therefore to-morrow, Socrates, will be the last day of your life.

Soc. Very well, Crito; if such is the will of God, I am willing; but my belief is that there will be a delay of a day.   44

CR. Why do you say this?

Soc. I will tell you. I am to die on the day after the arrival of the ship?

CR. Yes; that is what the authorities say.

Soc. But I do not think that the ship will be here until to-morrow; this I gather from a vision which I had last night, or rather only just now, when you fortunately allowed me to sleep.

CR. And what was the nature of the vision?

Soc. There came to me the likeness of a woman, fair and comely, clothed in white raiment, who called to me and said: O Socrates—

"The third day hence, to Phthia shalt thou go."   b

CR. What a singular dream, Socrates!

Soc. There can be no doubt about the meaning Crito, I think.

CR. Yes: the meaning is only too clear. But, O! my beloved Socrates, let me entreat you once more to take my advice and escape. For if you die I shall not only lose a friend who can never be replaced, but there is another evil: people who do not know you and me will believe that I might have saved you c if I had been willing to give money, but that I did not care. Now, can there be a worse disgrace than this—that I should be thought to value money more than the life of a friend? For the many will not be persuaded that I wanted you to escape, and that you refused.

Soc. But why, my dear Crito, should we care about the opinion of the many? Good men, and they are the only persons who are worth considering, will d think of these things truly as they happened.

CR. But do you see. Socrates, that the opinion of the many must be regarded, as is evident in your own case, because they can do the very greatest evil to anyone who has lost their good opinion?

Soc. I only wish, Crito, that they could; for then they could also do the greatest good, and that would be well. But the truth is, that they can do neither good nor evil: they cannot make a man wise or make him foolish; and whatever they do is the result of chance.

e CR. Well, I will not dispute about that; but please to tell me, Socrates, whether you are not acting out of regard to me and your other friends: are you not afraid that if you escape hence we may get into trouble with the informers for having stolen you away, and lose either the whole or a great part of our prop-
45 erty; or that even a worse evil may happen to us? Now, if this is your fear, be at ease; for in order to save you, we ought surely to run this or even a greater risk; be persuaded, then, and do as I say.

Soc. Yes, Crito, that is one fear which you mention, but by no means the only one.

CR. Fear not. There are persons who at no great cost are willing to save you and bring you out of prison; and as for the informers, you may observe that they are far from being exorbitant in their de-
b mands; a little money will satisfy them. My means, which, as I am sure, are ample, are at your service, and if you have a scruple about spending all mine, here are strangers who will give you the use of theirs; and one of them, Simmias the Theban, has brought a sum of money for this very purpose; and Cebes and many others are willing to spend their money too. I say, therefore, do not on that account hesitant about making your escape, and do not say, as you c did in the court, that you will have a difficulty in knowing what to do with yourself if you escape. For men will love you in other places to which you may go, and not in Athens only; there are friends of mine in Thessaly, if you like to go to them, who will value and protect you, and no Thessalian will give you any trouble. Nor can I think that you are justified,

Socrates, in betraying your own life when you might be saved; this is playing into the hands of your enemies and destroyers; and moreover I should say that d you were betraying your children; for you might bring them up and educate them; instead of which you go away and leave them, and they will have to take their chance; and if they do not meet with the usual fate of orphans, there will be small thanks to you. No man should bring children into the world who is unwilling to persevere to the end in their nurture and education. But you are choosing the easier part, as I think, not the better and manlier, which would rather have become one who professes virtue in all his actions, like yourself. And, indeed, I am e ashamed not only of you, but of us who are your friends, when I reflect that this entire business of yours will be attributed to our want of courage. The trial need never have come on, or might have been brought to another issue; and the end of all, which 46 is the crowning absurdity, will seem to have been permitted by us, through cowardice and baseness, who might have saved you, as you might have saved yourself, if we had been good for anything (for there was no difficulty in escaping); and we did not see how disgraceful, Socrates, and also miserable all this will be to us as well as to you. Make your mind up then, or rather have your mind already made up, for the time of deliberation is over, and there is only one thing to be done, which must be done, if at all, this very night, and which any delay will render all but impossible; I beseech you therefore, Socrates, to be b persuaded by me, and to do as I say.

Soc. Dear Crito, your zeal is invaluable, if a right one; but if wrong, the greater the zeal the greater the evil; and therefore we ought to consider whether these things shall be done or not. For I am and always have been one of those natures who must be guided by reason, whatever the reason may be which upon reflection appears to me to be the best; and now that this fortune has come upon me, I cannot put away the reasons which I have before given: the principles which I have hitherto honored and revered I still honor, and unless we can find other and better principles on the instant, I am certain not to agree c with you; no, not even if the power of the multitude could inflict many more imprisonments, confiscations, deaths, frightening us like children with hobglobin terrors. But what will be the fairest way of considering the question? Shall I return to your old argument about the opinions of men, some of which are to be regarded, and others, as we were saying, are not to be regarded? Now were we right in maintaining this before I was condemned? And has the argument which was once good now proved to be talk for the sake of talking; in fact an amusement only, and altogether vanity? That is what I want to consider with your help, Crito: whether, under my present circumstances, the argument appears to be in any way different or not; and is to be allowed by me or disallowed. That argument, which, as I believe, is maintained by many who assume to be authorities, was to the effect, as I was saying, that the opinions of some men are to be regarded, and of other men not to be regarded. Now you, Crito, are a disinterested person who is not going to die tomorrow—at least, there is no human probability of this, and you are therefore not liable to be deceived by the circumstances in which you are placed. Tell me, then, whether I am right in saying that some opinions, and the opinions of some men only, are to be valued, and other opinions, and the opinions of other men, are not to be valued. I ask you whether I was right in maintaining this?

CR. Certainly.

Soc. The good are to be regarded, and not the bad?

CR. Yes.

Soc. And the opinions of the wise are good, and the opinions of the unwise are evil?

CR. Certainly.

Soc. And what was said about another matter? Was the disciple in gymnastics supposed to attend to the praise and blame and opinion of every man, or of one man only—his physician or trainer, whoever that was?

CR. Of one man only.

Soc. And he ought to fear the censure and welcome the praise of that one only, and not of the many?

CR. That is clear.

Soc. And he ought to live and train, and eat and drink in the way which seems good to his single master who has understanding, rather than according to the opinion of all other men put together?

CR. True.

Soc. And if he disobeys and disregards the opinion and approval of the one, and regards the opinion of the many who have no understanding, will he not suffer evil?

CR. Certainly he will.

Soc. And what will the evil be, whither tending and what affecting, in the disobedient person?

CR. Clearly, affecting the body; that is what is destroyed by the evil.

Soc. Very good; and is not this true, Crito, of other things which we need not separately enumerate? In the matter of just and unjust, fair and foul, good and evil, which are the subjects of our present consultation, ought we to follow the opinion of the many and to fear them; or the opinion of the one man who has understanding, and whom we ought to fear and reverence more than all the rest of the world: and whom deserting we shall destroy and injure that principle in us which may be assumed to be improved by justice and deteriorated by injustice; is there not such a principle?

CR. Certainly there is, Socrates.

Soc. Take a parallel instance; if, acting under the advice of men who have no understanding, we destroy that which is improvable by health and deteriorated by disease—when that has been destroyed, I say, would life be worth having? And that is—the body? Do you accept this?

CR. Yes.

Soc. Could we live, having an evil and corrupted body?

CR. Certainly not.

Soc. And will life be worth having, if that higher part of man be depraved, which is improved by justice and deteriorated by injustice? Do we suppose that principle, whatever it may be in man, which has to do with justice and injustice, to be inferior to the body?

CR. Certainly not.

Soc. More honored, then?

CR. Far more honored.

Soc. Then, my friend, we must not regard what the many say of us: but what he, the one man who has understanding of just and unjust, will say, and what the truth will say. And therefore you begin in error when you suggest that we should regard the opinion of the many about just and unjust, good and evil, honorable and dishonorable. Well, someone will say, "But the many can kill us."

CR. Yes, Socrates; that will clearly be the answer.

Soc. That is true; but still I find with surprise that the old argument is, as I conceive, unshaken as ever. And I should like to know Whether I may say the same of another proposition—that not life, but a good life, is to be chiefly valued?

CR. Yes, that also remains.

Soc. And a good life is equivalent to a just and honorable one—that holds also?

CR. Yes, that holds.

c SOC. From these premises I proceed to argue the question whether I ought or ought not to try to escape without the consent of the Athenians: and if I am clearly right in escaping, then I will make the attempt; but if not, I will abstain. The other considerations which you mention, of money and loss of character, and the duty of educating children, are, I fear, only the doctrines of the multitude, who would be as ready to call people to life, if they were able, as they are to put them to death—and with as little reason. But now, since the argument has thus far prevailed the only question which remains to be con-

d sidered is, whether we shall do rightly either in escaping or in suffering others to aid in our escape and paying them in money and thanks, or whether we shall not do rightly; and if the latter, then death or any other calamity which may ensure on my remaining here must not be allowed to enter into the calculation.

CR. I think that you are right, Socrates; how then shall we proceed?

SOC. Let us consider the matter together, and do you either refute me if you can, and I will be con-

e vinced; or else cease, my dear friend, from repeating to me that I ought to escape against the wishes of the Athenians: for I am extremely desirous to be persuaded by you, but not against my own better

49 judgment. And now please to consider my first position, and do your best to answer me.

CR. I will do my best.

SOC. Are we to say that we are never intentionally to do wrong, or that in one way we ought and in another way we ought not to do wrong, or is doing wrong always evil and dishonorable, as I was just now saying, and as has been already acknowledged by us? Are all our former admissions which were made within a few days to be thrown away?

b And have we, at our age, been earnestly discoursing with one another all our life long only to discover that we are no better than children? Or are we to rest assured, in spite of the opinion of the many, and in spite of consequences whether better or worse, of the truth of what was then said, that injustice is always an evil and dishonor to him who acts unjustly? Shall we affirm that?

CR. Yes.

SOC. Then we must do no wrong?

CR. Certainly not.

SOC. Nor when injured injure in return, as the

c many imagine; for we must injure no one at all?

CR. Clearly not.

SOC. Again, Crito, may we do evil?

CR. Surely not, Socrates.

SOC. And what of doing evil in return for evil, which is the morality of the many—is that just or not?

CR. Not just.

SOC. For doing evil to another is the same as injuring him?

CR. Very true.

SOC. Then we ought not to retaliate or render evil for evil to anyone, whatever evil we may have suffered from him. But I would have you consider, d Crito, whether you really mean what you are saying. For this opinion has never been held, and never will be held, by any considerable number of persons; and those who are agreed and those who are not agreed upon this point have no common ground, and can only despise one another, when they see how widely they differ. Tell me, then, whether you agree with and assent to my first principle, that neither injury nor retaliation nor warding off evil by evil is e ever right. And shall that be the premise of our agreement? Or do you decline and dissent from this? For this has been of old and is still my opinion; but, if you are of another opinion, let me hear what you have to say. If, however, you remain of the same mind as formerly, I will proceed to the next step.

CR. You may proceed, for I have not changed my mind.

SOC. Then I will proceed to the next step, which may be put in the form of a question: Ought a man to do what he admits to be right, or ought he to betray the right?

CR. He ought to do what he thinks right.

SOC. But if this is true, what is the application? In leaving the prison against the will of the Atheni- 50 ans, do I wrong any? or rather do I not wrong those whom I ought least to wrong? Do I not desert the principles which were acknowledged by us to be just? What do you say?

CR. I cannot tell, Socrates, for I do not know.

SOC. Then consider the matter in this way: Imagine that I am about to play truant (you may call the proceeding by any name which you like), and the laws and the government come and interrogate me: "Tell us, Socrates," they say; "what are you about? b are you going by an act of yours to overturn us— the laws and the whole State, as far as in you lies? Do you imagine that a State can subsist and not be overthrown, in which the decisions of law have no power, but are set aside and overthrown by individuals?" What will be our answer, Crito, to these and the like words? Anyone, and especially a clever rhetorician, will have a good deal to urge about the evil of setting aside the law which requires a senc tence to be carried out; and we might reply, "Yes; but the State has injured us and given an unjust sentence." Suppose I say that?

CR. Very good, Socrates.

SOC. "And was that our agreement with you?" the law would say, "or were you to abide by the sentence of the State?" And if I were to express astonishment at their saying this, the law would probably d add: "Answer, Socrates, instead of opening your eyes: you are in the habit of asking and answering questions. Tell us what complaint you have to make against us which justifies you in attempting to destroy us and the State? In the first place did we not bring you into existence? Your father married your mother by our aid and begat you. Say whether you have any objection to urge against those of us who regulate marriage?" None, I should reply. "Or against those of us who regulate the system of nurture and education of children in which you were trained? Were not the laws, who have the charge of this, right in commanding your father to train you e in music and gymnastic?" Right, I should reply. "Well, then, since you were brought into the world and nurtured and educated by us, can you deny in the first place that you are our child and slave, as your fathers were before you? And if this is true you are not on equal terms with us; nor can you think that you have a right to do to us what we are doing 51 to you. Would you have any right to strike or revile or do any other evil to a father or to your master, if you had one, when you have been struck or reviled by him, or received some other evil at his hands?— you would not say this? And because we think right to destroy you, do you think that you have any right to destroy us in return, and your country as far as in you lies? And will you, O professor of true virtue, say that you are justified in this? Has a philosopher like you failed to discover that our country is more to be valued and higher and holier far than mother b or father or any ancestor, and more to be regarded in the eyes of the gods and of men of understanding? also to be soothed, and gently and reverently entreated when angry, even more than a father, and if not persuaded, obeyed? And when we are punished by her, whether with imprisonment or stripes, the punishment is to be endured in silence; and if

she leads us to wounds or death in battle, thither we follow as is right; neither may anyone yield or retreat or leave his rank, but whether in battle or in a c court of law, or in any other place, he must do what his city and his country order him; or he must change their view of what is just: and if he may do no violence to his father or mother, much less may he do violence to his country." What answer shall we make to this, Crito? Do the laws speak truly, or do they not?

CR. I think that they do.

SOC. Then the laws will say: "Consider, Socrates, if this is true, that in your present attempt you are going to do us wrong. For, after having brought you d into the world, and nurtured and educated you, and given you and every other citizen a share in every good that we had to give, we further proclaim and give the right to every Athenian, that if he does not like us when he has come of age and has seen the ways of the city, and made our acquaintance, he may go where he pleases and take his goods with him; and none of us laws will forbid him or interfere with him. Any of you who does not like us and the city, and who wants to go to a colony or to any other city, may go where he likes, and take his goods with him. But he who has experience of the manner in which e we order justice and administer the State, and still remains, has entered into an implied contract that he will do as we command him. And he who disobeys us is, as we maintain, thrice wrong: first, because in disobeying us he is disobeying his parents; secondly, because we are the authors of his education; thirdly, because he has made an agreement with us that he will duly obey our commands; and he neither obeys them nor convinces us that our commands are 52 wrong; and we do not rudely impose them, but given him the alternative of obeying or convincing us; that is what we offer and he does neither. These are the sort of accusations to which, as we were saying, you, Socrates, will be exposed if you accomplish your intentions; you, above all other Athenians." Suppose I ask, why is this? they will justly retort upon me that I above all other men have acknowledged the agreement. "There is clear proof," they will say, b "Socrates, that we and the city were not displeasing to you. Of all Athenians you have been the most constant resident in the city, which, as you never leave, you may be supposed to love. For you never went out of the city either to see the games, except once when you went to the Isthmus, or to any other place unless when you were on military service; nor did you travel as other men do. Nor had you any cu- c riosity to know other States or their laws: your affections did not go beyond us and our State; we were your especial favorites, and you acquiesced in our government of you; and this is the State in which you begat your children, which is a proof of your satisfaction. Moreover, you might, if you had liked, have fixed the penalty at banishment in the course of the trial—the State which refuses to let you go now would have let you go then. But you pretended that you preferred death to exile, and that you were not grieved at death. And now you have forgotten these fine sentiments, and pay no respect to us, the d laws, of whom you are the destroyer; and are doing what only a miserable slave would do, running away and turning your back upon the compacts and agreements which you made as a citizen. And first of all answer this very question: Are we right in saying that you agreed to be governed according to us in deed, and not in word only? Is that true or not?" How shall we answer that, Crito? Must we not agree?

CR. There is no help, Socrates.

SOC. Then will they not say: "You, Socrates, are e breaking the covenants and agreements which you made with us at your leisure, not in any haste or under any compulsion or deception, but having had seventy years to think of them, during which time you were at liberty to leave the city, if we were not to your mind, or if our covenants appeared to you to be unfair. You had your choice, and might have 53 gone either to Sparta or Crete, which you often praise for their good government, or to some other Hellenic or foreign State. Whereas you, above all other Athenians, seemed to be so fond of the State, or, in other words, of us her laws (for who would like a State that has no laws?), that you never stirred out of her: the halt, the blind, the maimed, were not more stationary in her than you were. And now you run away and forsake your agreements. Not so, Socrates, if you will take our advice; do not make yourself ridiculous by escaping out of the city.

"For just consider, if you transgress and err in this sort of way, what good will you do, either to your- b self or to your friends? That your friends will be driven into exile and deprived of citizenship, or will lose their property, is tolerably certain; and you yourself, if you fly to one of the neighboring cities, c as, for example, Thebes or Megara, both of which are well-governed cities, will come to them as an enemy, Socrates, and their government will be

against you, and all patriotic citizens will cast an evil eye upon you as a subverter of the laws, and you will confirm in the minds of the judges the justice of their own condemnation of you. For he who is a corrupter of the laws is more than likely to be corrupter of the young and foolish portion of mankind. Will you then flee from well-ordered cities and virtuous men? and is existence worth having on these terms? Or will you go to them without shame, and d talk to them, Socrates? And what will you say to them? What you say here about virtue and justice and institutions and laws being the best things among men? Would that be decent of you? Surely not. But if you go away from well-governed States to Crito's friends in Thessaly, where there is great disorder and license, they will be charmed to have the tale of your escape from prison, set off with lu- e dicrous particulars of the manner in which you were wrapped in a goatskin or some other disguise, and metamorphosed as the fashion of runaways is—that is very likely; but will there be no one to remind you that in your old age you violated the most sacred laws from a miserable desire of a little more life? Perhaps not, if you keep them in a good temper; but if they are out of temper you will hear many degrading things; you will live, but how?—as the flatterer of all men, and the servant of all men; and doing what?—eating and drinking in Thessaly, having gone abroad in order that you may get a dinner. And where will be your fine sentiments about justice and 54 virtue then? Say that you wish to live for the sake of your children, that you may bring them up and educate them—will you take them into Thessaly and deprive them of Athenian citizenship? Is that the benefit which you would confer upon them? Or are you under the impression that they will be better cared for and educated here if you are still alive, although absent from them; for that your friends will take care of them? Do you fancy that if you are an b inhabitant of Thessaly they will take care of them, and if you are an inhabitant of the other world they will not take care of them? Nay; but if they who call themselves friends are truly friends, they surely will.

"Listen, then, Socrates, to us who have brought you up. Think not of life and children first, and of justice afterwards, but of justice first, that you may be justified before the princes of the world below. For neither will you nor any that belong to you be happier or holier or juster in this life, or happier in another, if you do as Crito bids. Now you depart in c innocence, a sufferer and not a doer of evil; a victim, not of the laws, but of men. But if you go forth, returning evil for evil, and injury for injury, breaking the covenants and agreements which you have made with us, and wronging those whom you ought least to wrong, that is to say, yourself, your friends, your country, and us, we shall be angry with you while you live, and our brethren, the laws in the world below, will receive you as an enemy; for they will know that you have done your best to destroy d us. Listen, then, to us and not to Crito."

This is the voice which I seem to hear murmuring in my ears, like the sound of the flute in the ears of the mystic; that voice, I say, is humming in my ears, and prevents me from hearing any other. And I know that anything more which you will say will be in vain. Yet speak, if you have anything to say.

CR. I have nothing to say, Socrates.

Soc. Then let me follow the intimations of the e will of God.

Phaedo

Phaedo, a disciple of Socrates, relates to his friend Echecrates Socrates' last conversation before he drank the hemlock. Cebes and Simmias, two of Socrates' disciples, inquire on the nature of the soul and whether it is immortal. Socrates attempts to prove that the soul is indeed immortal. We enter the dialogue as Cebes asks about the moral permissibility of suicide.

'Well then, Socrates, on just what ground do they say it's forbidden to kill oneself? Because—to answer the question you were just asking—I certainly did hear from Philolaus, when he was living with us, and earlier from several others, that one ought not to do that; but I've never heard anything definite about it from anyone.'

62   'Well you must take hear,' he said; 'as maybe you will hear. Perhaps, though, it will seem a matter for wonder to you if this alone of all things is unqualified, and it never happens as other things do sometimes and for some people, that it is better for a man to be dead than alive; and for those for whom it is better to be dead, perhaps it seems a matter for wonder to you if for these men it is not holy to do good to themselves, but they must await another benefactor.'

Cebes chuckled at this. 'Hark at that, now!' he said, speaking in his own dialect.

b   'Well yes,' said Socrates, 'it would seem unreasonable, put that way; but perhaps there is, in fact, some reason for it. The reason given in mysteries on the subject, that we men are in some sort of prison, and that one ought not to release oneself from it or

run away, seems to me a lofty idea and not easy to penetrate; but still, Cebes, this much seems to me well said: it is gods who care for us, and for the gods we men are among their belongings. Don't you think so?'

'I do,' said Cebes.

'Well, if one of your belongings were to kill it- c self, without your signifying that you wanted it to die, wouldn't you be vexed with it, and punish it, if you had any punishment at hand?'

'Certainly.'

'So perhaps, in that case, it isn't unreasonable that one should not kill oneself until God sends some necessity, such as the one now before us.'

'Yes, that does seem fair,' said Cebes. 'But then what you were saying just now—that philosophers should be willing to die lightly—that seems odd, if d what we were just saying, that it is God who cares for us, and that we are his belongings, is well founded. Because it's unreasonable that the wisest of men should not be resentful at quitting this service, where they're directed by the best directors there are—the gods; since a man of that sort, surely, doesn't believe he'll care for himself any better on

Reprinted from Plato's *Phaedo*, translated by David Gallop (1975) by permission of Oxford University Press.

becoming free. A stupid man would perhaps believe
e that: he would think he should escape from his master, and wouldn't reflect that a good master is not
one to escape from, but to stay with as long as possible, and so his escape would be irrational; but a
man of intelligence would surely always want to be
with one better than himself. Yet in that case,
Socrates, the very opposite of what was said just
now seems likely: it's the wise who should be
resentful at dying, whereas the foolish should welcome it.'

When Socrates heard this he seemed to me pleased
at Cebes' persistence, and looking at us he said:
63 'There goes Cebes, always hunting down arguments,
and not at all willing to accept at once what anyone
may say.'

'Well yes,' said Simmias; 'but this time, Socrates,
I think myself there's something in what Cebes says:
why, indeed, should truly wise men want to escape
from masters who are better than themselves, and
be separated from them lightly? So I think it's at you
that Cebes is aiming his argument, because you take
so lightly your leaving both ourselves and the gods,
who are good rulers by your own admission.'

b   'What you both say is fair,' he said; 'as I take you
to mean that I should defend myself against these
charges as if in a court of law.'

'Yes, exactly,' said Simmias.

'Very well then,' he said; 'let me try to defend
myself more convincingly before you than I did before the jury. Because if I didn't believe, Simmias
and Cebes, that I shall enter the presence, first, of
other gods both wise and good, and next of dead
men better than those in this world, then I should be
wrong not to be resentful at death; but as it is, be
assured that I expect to join the company of good
c men—although that point I shouldn't affirm with absolute conviction; but that I shall enter the presence
of gods who are very good masters, be assured that
if there's anything I should affirm on such matters,
it is that. So that's why I am not so resentful, but
rather am hopeful that there is something in store
for those who've died—in fact, as we've long been
told, something far better for the good than for the
wicked.'

'Well then, Socrates,' said Simmias, 'do you mean
to go off keeping this thought to yourself, or would
d you share it with us too? We have a common claim
on this benefit as well, I think; and at the same time
your defence will be made, if you persuade us of
what you say.'

'All right, I'll try,' he said, 'But first let's find out
what it is that Crito here has been wanting to say,
for some time past, I think.'

'Why Socrates,' said Crito, 'it's simply that the
man who's going to give you the poison has been
telling me for some time that you must be warned
to talk as little as possible: he says people get heated
through talking too much, and one must bring nothing of that sort in contact with the poison; people e
doing that sort of thing are sometimes obliged, otherwise, to drink twice or even three times.'

'Never mind him,' said Socrates. 'Just let him prepare his stuff so as to give two doses, or even three
if need be.'

'Yes, I pretty well knew it,' said Crito; 'but he's
been giving me trouble for some while.'

'Let him be,' he said. 'Now then, with you for my
jury I want to give my defence, and show with what
good reason, as it seems to me, a man who has truly
spent his life in philosophy feels confident when
about to die, and is hopeful that, when he has died, 64
he will win very great benefits in the other world.
So I'll try, Simmias and Cebes, to explain how this
could be.

'Other people may well be unaware that all who
actually engage in philosophy aright are practising
nothing other than dying and being dead. Now if this
is true, it would be odd indeed for them to be eager
in their whole life for nothing but this, and yet to be
resentful when it comes, the very thing they'd long
been eager for and practised.'

Simmias laughed at this and said: 'Goodness,
Socrates, you've made me laugh, even though I
wasn't much inclined to laugh just now. I imagine b
that most people, on hearing that, would think it
very well said of philosophers—and our own countrymen would quite agree—that they are, indeed,
verging on death, and that they, at any rate, are well
aware that this is what philosophers deserve to undergo.'

'Yes, and what they say would be true, Simmias,
except for their claim to be aware of it themselves;
because they aren't aware in what sense genuine
philosophers are verging on death and deserving of
it, and what kind of death they deserve. Anyway, c
let's discuss it among ourselves, disregarding them:
do we suppose that death is something?'

'Certainly,' rejoined Simmias.

'And that it is nothing but the separation of the
soul from the body? And that being dead is this: the

body's having come to be apart, separated from the soul, alone by itself, and the soul's being apart, alone by itself, separated from the body? Death can't be anything else but that, can it?'

'No, it's just that.'

'Now look, my friend, and see if maybe you agree with me on these points; because through them I d think we'll improve our knowledge of what we're examining. Do you think it befits a philosophical man to be keen about the so-called pleasures of, for example, food and drink?'

'Not in the least, Socrates,' said Simmias.

'And what about those of sex?'

'Not at all.'

'And what about the other services to the body? Do you think such a man regards them as of any value? For instance, the possession of smart clothes and shoes, and the other bodily adornments—do you think he values them highly, or does he disdain them, e except in so far as he's absolutely compelled to share in them?'

'I think the genuine philosopher disdains them.'

'Do you think in general, then, that such a man's concern is not for the body, but so far as he can stand aside from it, is directed towards the soul?'

'I do.'

'Then is it clear that, first, in such matters as these the philosopher differs from other men in releasing 65 his soul, as far as possible, from its communion with the body?'

'It appears so.'

'And presumably, Simmias, it does seem to most men that someone who finds nothing of that sort pleasant, and takes no part in those things, doesn't deserve to live; rather, one who cares nothing for the pleasures that come by way of the body runs pretty close to being dead.'

'Yes, what you say is quite true.'

'And now, what about the actual gaining of wisdom? Is the body a hindrance or not, if one enlists b it as a partner in the quest? This is the sort of thing I mean: do sight and hearing afford men any truth, or aren't even the poets always harping on such themes, telling us that we neither hear nor see anything accurately? And yet if these of all the bodily senses are neither accurate nor clear, the others will hardly be so; because they are, surely, all inferior to these. Don't you think so?'

'Certainly.'

'So when does the soul attain the truth? Because plainly, whenever it sets about examining anything in company with the body, it is completely taken in by it.'

'That's true.'

'So isn't it in reasoning, if anywhere at all, that c any of the things that *are* become manifest to it?

'Yes.'

'And it reasons best, presumably, whenever none of these things bothers it, neither hearing nor sight nor pain, nor any pleasure either, but whenever it comes to be alone by itself as far as possible, disregarding the body, and whenever, having the least possible communion and contact with it, it strives for that which is.'

'That is so.'

'So there again the soul of the philosopher utterly disdains the body and flees from it, seeking rather d to come to be alone by itself?'

'It seems do.'

'Well now, what about things of this sort, Simmias? Do we say that there is something *just*, or nothing?'

'Yes, we most certainly do!'

'And again, something *beautiful*, and *good*?'

'Of course.'

'Now did you ever yet see any such things with your eyes?'

'Certainly not.'

'Well did you grasp them with any other bodily sense-perception? And I'm talking about them all— about largeness, health, and strength, for example— and, in short, about the Being of all other such things, what each one actually is; is it through the e body that their truest element is viewed, or isn't it rather thus: whoever of us is prepared to think most fully and minutely of each object of his inquiry, in itself, will come closest to the knowledge of each?'

'Yes, certainly.'

'Then would that be achieved most purely by the man who approached each object with his intellect alone as far as possible, neither adducing sight in his thinking, nor dragging in any other sense to accompany his reasoning; rather, using his intellect 66 alone by itself and unsullied, he would undertake the hunt for each of the things that are, each alone by itself and unsullied; he would be separated as far as possible from his eyes and ears, and virtually from his whole body, on the ground that it confuses the soul, and doesn't allow it to gain truth and wisdom when in partnership with it: isn't it this man, Simmias, who will attain that which is, if anyone will?'

'What you say is abundantly true, Socrates,' said Simmias.

'For all these reasons, then, some such view as b this must present itself to genuine philosophers, so that they say such things to one another as these: "There now, it looks as if some sort of track is leading us, together with our reason, astray in our inquiry: as long as we possess the body, and our soul is contaminated by such an evil, we'll surely never adequately gain what we desire—and that, we say, is truth. Because the body affords us countless distractions, owing to the nurture it must have; and c again, if any illnesses befall it, they hamper our pursuit of that which is. Besides, it fills us up with lusts and desires, with fears and fantasies of every kind, and with any amount of trash, so that really and truly we are, as the saying goes, never able to think of anything at all because of it. Thus, it's nothing but the body and its desires that brings wars and factions and fighting; because it's over the gaining of wealth that all wars take place, and we're compelled d to gain wealth because of the body, enslaved as we are to its service; so for all these reasons it leaves us no leisure for philosophy. And the worst of it all is that if we do get any leisure from it, and turn to some inquiry, once again it intrudes everywhere in our researches, setting up a clamour and disturbance, and striking terror, so that the truth can't be discerned because of it. Well now, it really has been shown us that if we're ever going to know anything purely, we must be rid of it, and must view the ob- e jects themselves with the soul by itself; it's then, apparently, that the thing we desire and whose lovers we claim to be, wisdom, will be ours—when we have died, as the argument indicates, though not while we live. Because, if we can know nothing purely in the body's company, then one of two things must be true: either knowledge is nowhere to be gained, or else it is for the dead; since then, but no 67 sooner, will the soul be alone by itself apart from the body. And therefore while we live, it would seem that we shall be closest to knowledge in this way— if we consort with the body as little as possible, and do not commune with it, except in so far as we must, and do not infect ourselves with its nature, but remain pure from it, until God himself shall release us; and being thus pure, through separation from the body's folly, we shall probably be in like company, and shall know through our own selves all that is b unsullied—and that, I dare say, is what the truth is; because never will it be permissible for impure to touch pure." Such are the things, I think, Simmias, that all who are rightly called lovers of knowledge must say to one another, and must believe. Don't you agree?'

'Emphatically, Socrates?'

'Well then, if that's true, my friend,' said Socrates, 'there's plenty of hope for one who arrives where I'm going, that there, if anywhere, he will adequately possess the object that's been our great concern in life gone by; and thus the journey now appointed for me may also be made with good hope by any other c man who regards his intellect as prepared, by having been, in a manner, purified.'

'Yes indeed,' said Simmias.

'Then doesn't purification turn out to be just what's been mentioned for some while in our discussion—the parting of the soul from the body as far as possible, and the habituating of it to assemble and gather itself together, away from every part of the body, alone by itself, and to live, so far as it can, both in the present and in the hereafter, released from d the body, as from fetters?'

'Yes indeed.'

'And is it just this that is named "death"—a release and parting of soul from body?'

'Indeed it is.'

'And it's especially those who practise philosophy aright, or rather they alone, who are always eager to release it, as we say, and the occupation of philosophers is just this, isn't it—a release and parting of soul from body?'

'It seems do.'

'Then wouldn't it be absurd, as I said at the start, for a man to prepare himself in his life to live as e close as he can to being dead, and then to be resentful when this comes to him?'

'It would be absurd, of course.'

'Truly then, Simmias, those who practise philosophy aright are cultivating dying, and for them least of all men does being dead hold any terror. Look at it like this: if they've set themselves at odds with the body at every point, and desire to possess their soul alone by itself, wouldn't it be quite illogical if they were afraid and resentful when this came about—if, that is, they didn't go gladly to the place 68 where, on arrival, they may hope to attain what they longed for throughout life, namely wisdom—and to be rid of the company of that with which they'd set themselves at odds? Or again, many have been willing to enter Hades of their own accord, in quest of human loves, of wives and sons who have died, led by this hope, that there they would see and be united with those they desired; will anyone, then, who truly longs for wisdom, and who firmly holds the same b hope, that nowhere but in Hades will he attain it in any way worth mentioning, be resentful at dying; and will he not go there gladly? One must suppose so, my friend, if he's truly a lover of wisdom; since this will be his firm belief, that nowhere else but there will he attain wisdom purely. Yet if that is so, wouldn't it, as I said just now, be quite illogical if such a man were afraid of death?'

'Yes, quite illogical!'

'Then if you see a man resentful that he is going to die, isn't this proof enough for you that he's no c lover of wisdom after all, but what we may call a lover of the body? And this same man turns out, in some sense, to be a lover of riches and of prestige, either one of these or both.'

'It's just as you say.'

'Well now, Simmias, isn't it also true that what is named "bravery" belongs especially to people of the disposition we have described?'

'Most certainly.'

'And then temperance too, even what most people name "temperance"—not being excited over one's desires, but being scornful of them and well-ordered—belongs, doesn't it, only to those who ut- d terly scorn the body and live in love of wisdom?'

'It must.'

'Yes, because if you care to consider the bravery and temperance of other men, you'll find it strange.'

'How so, Socrates?'

'You know, don't you, that all other men count death among great evils?'

'Very much so.'

'Is it, then, through being afraid of greater evils that the brave among them abide death, whenever they do so?'

'It is.'

'Then, it's through fearing and fear that all men except philosophers are brave; and yet it's surely illogical that anyone should be brave through fear and e cowardice.'

'It certainly is.'

'And what about those of them who are well-ordered? Aren't they in this same state, temperate through a kind of intemperance? True, we say that's impossible; but still that state of simple-minded temperance does turn out in their case to be like this: it's because they're afraid of being deprived of further pleasures, and desire them, that they abstain

from some because they're overcome by others. True, they call it "intemperance" to be ruled by plea- 69 sures, but still that's what happens to them: they overcome some pleasures because they're overcome by others. And this is the sort of thing that was just mentioned: after a fashion, they achieve temperance because of intemperance.'

'Yes, so it seems.'

'Yes, Simmias, my good friend; since this may not be the right exchange with a view to goodness, the exchanging of pleasures for pleasures, pains for pains, and fear for fear, greater for lesser ones, like coins; it may be, rather, that this alone is the right coin, for which one should exchange all these b things—wisdom; and the buying and selling of all things for that, or rather with that, may be real bravery, temperance, justice, and, in short, true goodness in company with wisdom, whether pleasures and fears and all else of that sort be added or taken away; but as for their being parted from wisdom and exchanged for one another, goodness of that sort may be a kind of illusory facade, and fit for slaves indeed, and may have nothing healthy or true about it; whereas, truth to tell, temperance, justice, and bravery may in fact be a kind of purification of all such c things, and wisdom itself a kind of purifying rite. So it really looks as if those who established our initiations are no mean people, but have in fact long been saying in riddles that whoever arrives in Hades unadmitted to the rites, and uninitiated, shall lie in the slough, while he who arrives there purified and initiated shall dwell with gods. For truly there are, so say those concerned with the initiations, "many who bear the wand, but few who are devotees". Now these latter, in my view, are none other than those who d have practised philosophy aright. And it's to be among them that I myself have striven, in every way I could, neglecting nothing during my life within my power. Whether I have striven aright and we have achieved anything, we shall, I think, know for certain, God willing, in a little while, on arrival yonder.

'There's my defence, then, Simmias and Cebes, to show how reasonable it is for me not to take it hard or be resentful at leaving you and my masters e here, since I believe that there also, no less than here, I shall find good masters and companions; so if I'm any more convincing in my defence to you than to the Athenian jury, it would be well.'

When Socrates had said this, Cebes rejoined: 'The other things you say, Socrates, I find excellent; but

what you say about the soul is the subject of much
70 disbelief: men fear that when it's been separated
from the body, it may no longer exist anywhere, but
that on the very day a man dies, it may be destroyed
and perish, as soon as it's separated from the body;
and that as it goes out, it may be dispersed like breath
or smoke, go flying off, and exist no longer anywhere at all. True, if it did exist somewhere, gathered together alone by itself, and separated from
those evils you were recounting just now, there'd be
plenty of hope, Socrates, and a fine hope it would
be, that what you say is true; but on just this point,
b perhaps, one needs no little reassuring and convincing, that when the man has died, his soul exists, and
that it possesses some power and wisdom.'

'That's true, Cebes,' said Socrates; 'but then what
are we to do? Would you like us to speculate on
these very questions, and see whether this is likely
to be the case or not?'

'For my part anyway,' said Cebes, 'I'd gladly hear
whatever opinion you have about them.'

'Well,' said Socrates, 'I really don't think anyone
listening now, even if he were a comic poet, would
c say that I'm talking idly, and arguing about things
that don't concern me. If you agree, then, we should
look into the matter.

'Let's consider it, perhaps, in this way: do the
souls of men exist in Hades when they have died,
or do they not? Now there's an ancient doctrine,
which we've recalled, that they do exist in that
world, entering it from this one, and that they re-en-
ter this world and are born again from the dead; yet
if this is so, if living people are born again from
those who have died, surely our souls would have
d to exist in that world? Because they could hardly be
born again, if they didn't exist; so it would be sufficient evidence for the truth of these claims, if it really became plain that living people are born from
the dead and from nowhere else; but if that isn't so,
some other argument would be needed.'

'Certainly,' said Cebes.

'Well now, consider the matter, if you want to understand more readily, in connection not only with
mankind, but with all animals and plants; and, in
general, for all things subject to coming-to-be, let's
e see whether everything comes to be in this way: opposites come to be only from their opposites—in the
case of all things that actually have an opposite—
as, for example, the beautiful is opposite, of course,
to the ugly, just to unjust, and so on in countless
other cases. So let's consider this: is it necessary that

whatever has an opposite comes to be only from its
opposite? For example, when a thing comes to be
larger, it must, surely, come to be larger from being
smaller before?'

'Yes.'

'And again, if it comes to be smaller, it will come
to be smaller later from being larger before?'   71

'That's so.'

'And that which is weaker comes to be, presumably, from a stronger, and that which is faster from
a slower?'

'Certainly.'

'And again, if a thing comes to be worse, it's from
a better, and if more just, from a more unjust?'

'Of course.'

'Are we satisfied, then, that all things come to be
in this way, opposite things from opposites?'

'Certainly.'

'Now again, do these things have a further feature of this sort: between the members of every pair
of opposites, since they are two, aren't there two
processes of coming-to-be, from one to the other, b
and back again from the latter to the former? Thus,
between a larger thing and a smaller, isn't there increase and decrease, so that in the one case we speak
of "increasing" and in the other of "decreasing"?'

'Yes.'

'And similarly with separating and combining,
cooling and heating, and all such; even if in some
cases we don't use the names, still in actual fact
mustn't the same principle everywhere hold good:
they come to be from each other, and there's a
process of coming-to-be of each into the other?'

'Certainly.'

'Well then, is there an opposite to living, as sleep- c
ing is opposite to being awake?'

'Certainly.'

'What is it?'

'Being dead.'

'Then these come to be from each other, if they
are opposites; and between the pair of them, since
they are two, the processes of coming-to-be are
two?'

'Of course.'

'Now then,' said Socrates, 'I'll tell you one of the
couples I was just mentioning, the couple itself and
its processes; and you tell me the other. My couple d
is sleeping and being awake: being awake comes to
be from sleeping, and sleeping from being awake,
and their processes are going to sleep and waking
up. Is that sufficient for you or not?'

'Certainly.'

'Now it's for you to tell me in the same way about life and death. You say, don't you, that being dead is opposite to living?'

'I do.'

'And that they come to be from each other?'

'Yes.'

'Then what is it that comes to be from that which is living?'

'That which is dead.'

'And what comes to be from that which is dead?'

'I must admit that it's that which is living.'

'Then it's from those that are dead, Cebes, that living things and living people are born?'

e 'Apparently.'

'Then our souls do exist in Hades.'

'So it seems.'

'Now *one* of the relevant processes here is obvious, isn't it? For dying is obvious enough, surely?'

'It certainly is.'

'What shall we do then? Shan't we assign the opposite process to balance it? Will nature be lame in this respect? Or must we supply some process opposite to dying?'

'We surely must.'

'What will this be?'

'Coming to life again.'

'Then if there *is* such a thing as coming to life
72 again, wouldn't this, coming to life again, be a process from dead to living people.'

'Certainly.'

'In that way too, then, we're agreed that living people are born from the dead no less than dead people from the living; and we thought that, if this were the case, it would be sufficient evidence that the souls of the dead must exist somewhere, whence they are born again.'

'I think, Socrates, that that must follow from our admissions.'

'Then look at it this way, Cebes, and you'll see, I think, that our admissions were not mistaken. If
b there were not perpetual reciprocity in coming to be, between one set of things and another, revolving in a circle, as it were—if, instead, coming-to-be were a linear process from one thing into its opposite only, without any bending back in the other direction or reversal, do you realize that all things would ultimately have the same form: the same fate would overtake them, and they would cease from coming to be?'

'What do you mean?'

'It's not at all hard to understand what I mean. If, for example, there were such a thing as going to sleep, but from sleeping there were no reverse process of waking up, you realize that everything would ultimately make Endymion seem a mere trifle: he'd be nowhere, because the same fate as his, c sleeping, would have overtaken everything else. Again, if everything were combined, but not separated, then Anaxagoras' notion of "all things together" would soon be realized. And similarly, my dear Cebes, if all things that partake in life were to die, but when they'd died, the dead remained in that form, and didn't come back to life, wouldn't it be quite inevitable that everything would ultimately be dead, and nothing would live? Because if the living d things came to be from the other things, but the living things were to die, what could possibly prevent everything from being completely spent in being dead?'

'Nothing whatever, in my view, Socrates,' said Cebes; 'what you say seems to be perfectly true.'

'Yes, it certainly is true, Cebes, as I see it; and we're not deceived in making just those admissions: there really is such a thing as coming to life again, living people *are* born from the dead, and the souls of the dead exist.'   e

'Yes, and besides, Socrates,' Cebes replied, 'there's also that theory you're always putting forward, that our learning is actually nothing but recollection; according to that too, if it's true, what we are now reminded of we must have learned at some former time. But that would be impossible, unless our souls existed somewhere before being born in 73 this human form; so in this way too, it appears that the soul is something immortal.'

'Yes, what are the proofs of those points, Cebes?' put in Simmias. 'Remind me, as I don't recall them very well at the moment.'

'One excellent argument,' said Cebes, 'is that when people are questioned, and if the questions are well put, they state the truth about everything for themselves—and yet unless knowledge and a correct account were present within them, they'd be unable to do this; thus, if one takes them to diagrams or anything else of that sort, one has there the b plainest evidence that this is so.'

'But if that doesn't convince you, Simmias,' said Socrates, 'then see whether maybe you agree if you look at it this way. Apparently you doubt whether what is called "learning" is recollection?'

'I don't *doubt* it,' said Simmias; 'but I do need to undergo just what the argument is about, to be "reminded". Actually, from the way Cebes set about stating it, I do almost recall it and am nearly convinced; but I'd like, none the less, to hear now how you set about stating it yourself.'

c   'I'll put it this way. We agree, I take it, that if anyone is to be reminded of a thing, he must have known that thing at some time previously.'

'Certainly.'

'Then do we also agree on this point: that whenever knowledge comes to be present in this sort of way, it is recollection? I mean in some such way as this: if someone, on seeing a thing, or hearing it, or getting any other sense-perception of it, not only recognizes that thing, but also thinks of something else, which is the object not of the same knowledge but of another, don't we then rightly say that he's been d "reminded" of the object of which he has got the thought?'

'What do you mean?'

'Take the following examples: knowledge of a man, surely, is other than that of a lyre?'

'Of course.'

'Well now, you know what happens to lovers, whenever they see a lyre or cloak or anything else their loves are accustomed to use: they recognize the lyre, and they get in their mind, don't they, the form of the boy whose lyre it is? And that is recollection. Likewise, someone seeing Simmias is often reminded of Cebes, and there'd surely be countless other such cases.'

'Countless indeed!' said Simmias.

'Then is something of that sort a kind of recol-
e lection? More especially, though, whenever it happens to someone in connection with things he's since forgotten, through lapse of time or inattention?'

'Certainly.'

'Again now, is it possible, on seeing a horse depicted or a lyre depicted, to be reminded of a man; and on seeing Simmias depicted, to be reminded of Cebes?'

'Certainly.'

'And also, on seeing Simmias depicted, to be reminded of Simmias himself?'

74   'Yes, that's possible.'

'In all these cases, then, doesn't it turn out that there is recollection from similar things, but also from dissimilar things?'

'It does.'

'But whenever one is reminded of something from similar things, mustn't one experience something further: mustn't one think whether or not the thing is lacking at all, in its similarity, in relation to what one is reminded of?'

'One must.'

'Then consider whether this is the case. We say, don't we, that there is something *equal*—I don't mean a log to a log, or a stone to a stone, or anything else of that sort, but some further thing beyond all those, the equal itself: are we to say that there *is* something or nothing?'

'We most certainly are to say that there *is*,' said b Simmias; 'unquestionably!'

'And do we know *what it is*?'

'Certainly.'

'Where did we get the knowledge of it? Wasn't it from the things we were just mentioning: on seeing logs or stones or other equal things, wasn't it from these that we thought of that object, it being different from them? Or doesn't it seem different to you? Look at it this way: don't equal stones and logs, the very same ones, sometimes seem equal to one, but not to another?'

'Yes, certainly.'

'But now, did the equals themselves ever seem to c you unequal, or equality inequality?'

'Never yet, Socrates.'

'Then those equals and the equal itself, are not the same.'

'By no means, Socrates, in my view.'

'But still, it is from *those* equals, different as they are from *that* equal, that you have thought of and got the knowledge of it?'

'That's perfectly true.'

'It being either similar to them or dissimilar?'

'Certainly.'

'Anyway, it makes no difference; so long as on seeing one thing, one does, from this sight, think of another, whether it be similar or dissimilar, this must d be recollection.'

'Certainly.'

'Well now, with regard to the instances in the logs, and, in general, the equals we mentioned just now, are we affected in some way as this: do they seem to us to be equal in the same way as *what it is* itself? Do they fall short of it at all in being like the equal, or not?'

'Very far short of it.'

'Then whenever anyone, on seeing a thing, thinks to himself, "this thing that I now see seeks to be like another of the things that are, but falls short, and e cannot be like that object: it is inferior", do we agree *that the man who thinks this must previously have known the object he says it resembles but falls short of?'*

'He must.'

'Now then, have we ourselves been affected in just this way, or not, with regard to the equals and the equal itself?'

'Indeed we have.'

'Then we must previously have known the equal, before that time when we first, on seeing the equals, 75 thought that all of them were striving to be like the equal but fell short of it.'

'That is so.'

'Yet we also agree on this: we haven't derived the thought of it, nor could we do so, from anywhere but seeing or touching or some other of the senses— I'm counting all these as the same.'

'Yes, they are the same, Socrates, for what the argument seeks to show.'

'But of course it is *from* one's sense-perceptions b that one must think that all the things in the sense-perceptions are striving for *what equal is*, yet are inferior to it; or how shall we put it?'

'Like that.'

'Then it must, surely, have been before we began to see and hear and use the other senses that we got knowledge of the equal itself, of *what it is*, if we were going to refer the equals from our sense-perceptions to it, supposing that all things are doing their best to be like it, but are inferior to it.'

'That must follow from what's been said before, Socrates.'

'Now we were seeing and hearing, and were possessed of our other senses, weren't we, just as soon as we were born?'

'Certainly.'

c   'But we must, we're saying, have got our knowledge of the equal *before* these?'

'Yes.'

'Then it seems that we must have got it before we were born.'

'It seems so.'

'Now if, having got it before birth, we were born in possession of it, did we know, both before birth and as soon as we were born, not only the equal, the larger and the smaller, but everything of that sort? Because our present argument concerns the beautiful itself, and the good itself, and just and holy, no d less than the equal; in fact, as I say, it concerns everything on which we set this seal, "*what it is*",

in the questions we ask and in the answers we give. And so we must have got pieces of knowledge of all those things before birth.'

'That is so.'

'Moreover, if having got them, we did not on each occasion forget them, we must always be born knowing, and must continue to know throughout life: because this is knowing—to possess knowledge one has got of something, and not to have lost it; or isn't loss of knowledge what we mean by "forgetting", Simmias?'

'Certainly it is, Socrates.'   e

'But on the other hand, I suppose that if, having got them before birth, we lost them on being born, and later on, using the senses about the things in question, we regain those pieces of knowledge that we possessed at some former time, in that case wouldn't what we call "learning" be the regaining of knowledge belonging to us? And in saying that this was being reminded, shouldn't we be speaking correctly?'

'Certainly.'

'Yes, because it did seem possible, on sensing an 76 object, whether by seeing or hearing or getting some other sense-perception of it, to think from this of some other thing one had forgotten—either a thing to which the object, though dissimilar to it, was related, or else something to which it was similar; so, as I say, one of two things is true: *either* all of us were born knowing those objects, and we know them throughout life; *or* those we speak of as "learning" are simply being reminded later on, and learning would be recollection.'

'That's quite true, Socrates.'

'Then which do you choose, Simmias? That we are born knowing, or that we are later reminded of b the things we'd gained knowledge of before?'

'At the moment, Socrates, I can't make a choice.'

'Well, can you make one on the following point, and what do you think about it? If a man knows things, can he give an account of what he knows or not?'

'Of course he can, Socrates.'

'And do you think everyone can give an account of those objects we were discussing just now?'

'I only wish they could,' said Simmias; 'but I'm afraid that, on the contrary, this time tomorrow there may no longer be any man who can do so properly.'

'You don't then, Simmias, think that everyone c knows those objects?'

'By no means.'

'Are they, then, reminded of what they once learned?'

'They must be.'

'When did our souls get the knowledge of those objects? Not, at any rate, since we were born as human beings.'

'Indeed not.'

'Earlier, then.'

'Yes.'

'Then our souls did exist earlier, Simmias, before entering human form, apart from bodies; and they possessed wisdom.'

'Unless maybe, Socrates, we get those pieces of knowledge at the very moment of birth; that time still remains.'

d 'Very well, my friend; but then at what other time, may I ask, do we lose them? We aren't born with them, as we agreed just now. Do we then lose them at the very time at which we get them? Or have you any other time to suggest?'

'None at all, Socrates. I didn't realize I was talking nonsense.'

'Then is our position as follows, Simmias? If the objects we're always harping on exist, a beautiful, and a good and all such Being, and if we refer all the things from our sense-perceptions to that Being,
e finding again what was formerly ours, and if we compare these things with that, then just as surely as those objects exist, so also must our soul exist before we are born. On the other hand, if they don't exist, this argument will have gone for nothing. Is this the position? Is it equally necessary that those objects exist, and that our souls existed before birth, and if the former don't exist, then neither did the latter?'

'It's abundantly clear to me, Socrates,' said Simmias, 'that there's the same necessity in either case, and the argument takes opportune refuge in the view that our soul exists before birth, just as surely as the
77 Being of which you're now speaking. Because I myself find nothing so plain to me as that all such objects, beautiful and good and all the others you were speaking of just now, *are* in the fullest possible way; so in my view it's been adequately proved.'

'And what about Cebes?' said Socrates. 'We must convince Cebes too.'

'It's adequate for him, I think,' said Simmias; 'though he's the most obstinate of people when it comes to doubting arguments. But I think he's been sufficiently convinced that our soul existed before we were born. Whether it will still exist, however,

after we've died, doesn't seem, even to me, to have b been shown, Socrates; but the point Cebes made just now still stands—the popular fear that when a man dies, his soul may be dispersed at that time, and that that may be the end of its existence. Because what's to prevent it from coming to be and being put together from some other source, and from existing before it enters a human body, yet when it has entered one, and again been separated from it, from then meeting its end, and being itself destroyed?'

'You're right, Simmias,' said Cebes. 'It seems that c half, as it were, of what is needed has been shown—that our soul existed before we were born; it must also be shown that it will exist after we've died, no less than before we were born, if the proof is going to be complete.'

'That's been proved already, Simmias and Cebes,' said Socrates, 'if you will combine this argument with the one we agreed on earlier, to the effect that all that is living comes from that which is dead. Be- d cause if the soul does have previous existence, and if when it enters upon living and being born, it must come from no other source than death and being dead, surely it must also exist after it has died, given that it has to be born again? So your point has been proved already. But even so, I think you and Simmias would like to thrash out this argument still further; you seem afraid, like children, that as the soul goes out from the body, the wind may literally blow it apart and disperse it, especially when someone e happens not to die in calm weather but in a high wind.'

Cebes laughed at this, and said: 'Try to reassure us, Socrates, as if we were afraid; or rather, not as if we were afraid ourselves—but maybe there's a child inside us, who has fears of that sort. Try to persuade him, then, to stop being afraid of death, as if it were a bogey-man.'

'Well, you must sing spells to him every day,' said Socrates, 'till you've charmed it out of him.'

'And where', he said, 'shall we find a charmer for 78 such fears, Socrates, now that you're leaving us?'

'Greece is a large country, Cebes, which has good men in it, I suppose; and there are many foreign races too. You must ransack all of them in search of such a charmer, sparing neither money nor trouble, because there's no object on which you could more opportunely spend your money. And you yourselves must search too, along with one another; you may not easily find anyone more capable of doing this than yourselves.'

b 'That shall certainly be done,' said Cebes; 'but let's go back to the point where we left off, if you've no objection.'

'Of course not; why should I?'

'Good.'

'Well then,' said Socrates, 'mustn't we ask ourselves something like this: What kind of thing is liable to undergo this fate—namely, dispersal—and for what kind of thing should we fear lest it undergo it? And what kind of thing is not liable to it? And next, mustn't we further ask to which of these two kinds soul belongs, and then feel either confidence or fear for our own soul accordingly?'

'That's true.'

c 'Then is it true that what has been put together and is naturally composite is liable to undergo this, to break up at the point at which it was put together; whereas if there be anything incomposite, it alone is liable, if anything is, to escape this?'

'That's what I think,' said Cebes.

'Well now, aren't the things that are constant and unvarying most likely to be the incomposite, whereas things that vary and are never constant are likely to be composite?'

'I think so.'

'Then let's go back to those entities to which we turned in our earlier argument. Is the Being itself, whose being we give an account of in ask-
d ing and answering questions, unvarying and constant, or does it vary? Does the equal itself, the beautiful itself, *what each thing is* itself, that which *is*, ever admit of any change whatever? Or does *what each of them is*, being uniform alone by itself, remain unvarying and constant, and never admit of any kind of alteration in any way or respect whatever?'

'It must be unvarying and constant, Socrates,' said Cebes.

'But what about the many beautiful things, such as men or horses or cloaks or anything else at all of
e that kind? Or equals, or all things that bear the same name as those objects? Are they constant, or are they just the opposite of those others, and practically never constant at all, either in relation to themselves or to one another?'

'That is their condition,' said Cebes; 'they are never unvarying.'

79 'Now these things you could actually touch and see and sense with the other senses, couldn't you, whereas those that are constant you could lay hold

of only by reasoning of the intellect; aren't such things, rather, invisible and not seen?'

'What you say is perfectly true.'

'Then would you like us to posit two kinds of beings, the one kind seen, the other invisible?'

'Let's posit them.'

'And the invisible is always constant, whereas the seen is never constant?'

'Let's posit that too.'

'Well, but we ourselves are part body and part b soul, aren't we?'

'We are.'

'Then to which kind do we say that the body will be more similar and more akin?'

'That's clear to anyone: obviously to the seen.'

'And what about the soul? Is it seen or invisible?'

'It's not seen by men, at any rate, Socrates.'

'But we meant, surely, things seen and not seen with reference to human nature; or do you think we meant any other?'

'We meant human nature.'

'What do we say about soul, then? Is it seen or unseen?'

'It's not seen.'

'Then it's invisible?'

'Yes.'

'Then soul is more similar than body to the invisible, whereas body is more similar to that which is seen.'

'That must be so, Socrates.' c

'Now weren't we saying a while ago that whenever the soul uses the body as a means to study anything, either by seeing or hearing or any other sense—because to use the body as a means is to study a thing through sense-perception—then it is dragged by the body towards objects that are never constant; and it wanders about itself, and is confused and dizzy, as if drunk, in virtue of contact with things of a similar kind?'

'Certainly.'

'Whereas whenever it studies alone by itself, it d departs yonder towards that which is pure and always existent and immortal and unvarying, and in virtue of its kinship with it, enters always into its company, whenever it has come to be alone by itself, and whenever it may do so; then it has ceased from its wandering and, when it is about those objects, it is always constant and unvarying, because of its contact with things of a similar kind; and this condition of it is called "wisdom", is it not?'

'That's very well said and perfectly true, Socrates.'

'Once again, then, in the light of our earlier and
e present arguments, to which kind do you think that
soul is more similar and more akin?'

'Everyone, I think, Socrates, even the slowest
learner, following this line of inquiry, would agree
that soul is totally and altogether more similar to
what is unvarying than to what is not.'

'And what about the body?'

'That is more like the latter.'

'Now look at it this way too: when soul and body
80 are present in the same thing, nature ordains that the
one shall serve and be ruled, whereas the other shall
rule and be master; here again,which do you think
is similar to the divine and which to the mortal?
Don't you think the divine is naturally adapted for
ruling and domination, whereas the mortal is adapted
for being ruled and for service?'

'I do.'

'Which kind, then, does the soul resemble?'

'Obviously, Socrates, the soul resembles the divine, and the body the mortal.'

'Consider, then, Cebes, if these are our conclusions from all that's been said: soul is most similar
to what is divine, immortal, intelligible, uniform, in-
b dissoluble, unvarying, and constant in relation to itself; whereas body, in its turn, is most similar to
what is human, mortal, multiform, non-intelligible,
dissoluble, and never constant in relation to itself.
Have we anything to say against those statements,
my dear Cebes, to show that they're false?'

'We haven't.'

'Well then, that being so, isn't body liable to be
quickly dissolved, whereas soul must be completely
indissoluble, or something close to it?'

c   'Of course.'

'Now you're aware that when a man has died, the
part of him that's seen, his body, which is situated
in the seen world, the corpse as we call it, although
liable to be dissolved and fall apart and to disinte-
grate, undergoes none of these things at once, but
remains as it is for a fairly long time—in fact for a
very considerable time, even if someone dies with
his body in beautiful condition, and in the flower of
youth; why, the body that is shrunken and embalmed, like those who've been embalmed in Egypt,
d remains almost entire for an immensely long time;
and even should the body decay, some parts of it,
bones and sinews and all such things, are still practically immortal; isn't that so?'

'Yes.'

'Can it be, then, that the soul, the invisible part,

which goes to another place of that kind, noble, pure
and invisible, to "Hades" in the true sense of the
word, into the presence of the good and wise god—
where, God willing, my own soul too must shortly
enter—can it be that this, which we've found to be
a thing of such a kind and nature, should on separation from the body at once be blown apart and perish, as most men say? Far from it, my dear Cebes e
and Simmias; rather, the truth is far more like this:
suppose it is separated in purity, while trailing nothing of the body with it, since it had no avoidable
commerce with it during life, but shunned it; suppose too that it has been gathered together alone into
itself, since it always cultivated this—nothing else
but the right practice of philosophy, in fact, the cultivation of dying without complaint—wouldn't this 81
be the cultivation of death?'

'It certainly would.'

'If it is in that state, then, does it not depart to the
invisible, which is similar to it, the divine and immortal and wise; and on arrival there, isn't its lot to
be happy, released from its wandering and folly, its
fears and wild lusts, and other ills of the human condition, and as is said of the initiated, does it not pass
the rest of time in very truth with gods? Are we to
say this, Cebes, or something else?'

'This, most certainly!', said Cebes.

'Whereas, I imagine, if it is separated from the
body when it has been polluted and made impure,
because it has always been with the body, has served b
and loved it, and been so bewitched by it, by its passions and pleasures, that it thinks nothing else real
save what is corporeal—what can be touched and
seen, drunk and eaten, or used for sexual enjoyment—yet it has been accustomed to hate and shun
and tremble before what is obscure to the eyes and
invisible, but intelligible and grasped by philosophy; c
do you think a soul in that condition will separate
unsullied, and alone by itself?'

'By no means.'

'Rather, I imagine, it will have been interspersed
with a corporeal element, ingrained in it by the
body's company and intercourse, through constant
association and much training?'

'Certainly.'

'And one must suppose, my friend, that this element is ponderous, that it is heavy and earthy and
is seen; and thus encumbered, such a soul is weighed
down, and dragged back into the region of the seen,
through fear of the invisible and of Hades; and it d
roams among tombs and graves, so it is said, around

which some shadowy phantoms of souls have actually been seen, such wraiths as souls of that kind afford, souls that have been released in no pure condition, but while partaking in the seen; and that is just why they are seen.'

'That's likely, Socrates.'

'It is indeed, Cebes; and they're likely to be the souls not of the good but of the wicked, that are compelled to wander about such places, paying the penalty for their former nurture, evil as it was. And they wander about until, owing to the desire of the corporeal element attendant upon them, they are once more imprisoned in a body; and they're likely e to be imprisoned in whatever types of character they may have cultivated in their lifetime.'

'What types can you mean, Socrates?'

'Those who have cultivated gluttony, for example, and lechery, and drunkenness, and have taken 82 no pains to avoid them, are likely to enter the forms of donkeys and animals of that sort. Don't you think so?'

'What you say is very likely.'

'Yes, and those who've preferred injustice, tyranny, and robbery will enter the forms of wolves and hawks and kites. Where else can we say that such souls will go?'

'Into such creatures, certainly,' said Cebes.

'And isn't the direction taken by the others as well obvious in each case, according to the affinities of their training?'

'Quite obvious, of course.'

'And aren't the happiest among these and the ones who enter the best place, those who have practised b popular and social goodness, "temperance" and "justice" so-called, developed from habit and training, but devoid of philosophy and intelligence?'

'In what way are these happiest?'

'Because they're likely to go back into a race of tame and social creatures similar to their kind, bees perhaps, or wasps or ants; and to return to the human race again, and be born from those kinds as decent men.'

'That's likely.'

'But the company of gods may not rightly be joined by one who has not practised philosophy and c departed in absolute purity, by any but the lover of knowledge. It's for these reasons, Simmias and Cebes, my friends, that true philosophers abstain from all bodily desires, and stand firm without surrendering to them; it's not for any fear of poverty or loss of estate, as with most men who are lovers of riches; nor again do they abstain through dread of dishonour or ill-repute attaching to wickedness, like lovers of power and prestige.'

'No, that would ill become them, Socrates,' said Cebes.

'Most certainly it would! And that, Cebes, is just d why those who have any care for their own souls, and don't live fashioning the body, disregard all those people; they do not walk in the same paths as those who, in their view, don't know where they are going; but they themselves believe that their actions must not oppose philosophy, or the release and purifying rite it affords, and they are turned to follow it, in the direction in which it guides them.'

'How so, Socrates?'

'I'll tell you. Lovers of knowledge recognize that when philosophy takes their soul in hand, it has been literally bound and glued to the body, and is forced e to view the things that are as if through a prison, rather than alone by itself; and that it is wallowing in utter ignorance. Now philosophy discerns the cunning of the prison, sees how it is effected through desire, so that the captive himself may co-operate most of all in his imprisonment. As I say, then, lovers of knowledge recognize that their soul is in 83 that state when philosophy takes it in hand, gently reassures it and tries to release it, by showing that inquiry through the eyes is full of deceit, and deceitful too is inquiry through the ears and other senses; and by persuading it to withdraw from these, so far as it need not use them, and by urging it to collect and gather itself together, and to trust none other but itself, whenever, alone by itself, it thinks b of any of the things that are, alone by *itself*; and not to regard as real what it observes by other means, and what varies in various things; that kind of thing is sensible and seen, whereas the object of its own vision is intelligible and invisible. It is, then, just because it believes it should not oppose this release that the soul of the true philosopher abstains from pleasures and desires and pains, so far as it can, reckoning that when one feels intense pleasure or fear, pain or desire, one incurs harm from them not merely to the extent that might be supposed—by being ill, c for example, or spending money to satisfy one's desires—but one incurs the greatest and most extreme of all evils, and does not take it into account.'

'And what is that, Socrates?' said Cebes.

'It's that the soul of every man, when intensely pleased or pained at something, is forced at the same time to suppose that whatever most affects it in this way is most clear and most real, when it is not so; and such objects especially are things seen, aren't they?'

'Certainly.'

'Well, isn't it in this experience that soul is most d thoroughly bound fast by body?'

'How so?'

'Because each pleasure and pain fastens it to the body with a sort of rivet, pins it there, and makes it corporeal, so that it takes for real whatever the body declares to be so. Since by sharing opinions and pleasures with the body, it is, I believe, forced to become of like character and nurture to it, and to be incapable of entering Hades in purity; but it must al-e ways exit contaminated by the body, and so quickly fall back into another body, and grow in it as if sown there, and so have no part in communing with the divine and pure and uniform.'

'What you say is perfectly true, Socrates,' said Cebes.

'It's for these reasons, then, Cebes, that those who deserve to be called "lovers of knowledge" are orderly and brave; it's not for the reasons that count with most people, or do you think it is?'

84 'No, indeed I don't.'

'Indeed not; but the soul of a philosophic man would reason as we've said: it would not think that while philosophy should release it, yet on being released, it should of itself surrender to pleasures and pains, to bind it to the body once again, and should perform the endless task of a Penelope working in reverse at a kind of web. Rather, securing rest from these feelings, by following reasoning and being ever within it, and by beholding what is true and di-b vine and not the object of opinion, and being nurtured by it, it believes that it must live thus for as long as it lives, and that when it has died, it will enter that which is akin and of like nature to itself, and be rid of human ills. With that kind of nurture, surely, Simmias and Cebes, there's no danger of its fearing that on separation from the body it may be rent apart, blown away by winds, go flying off, and exist no longer anywhere at all.'

When Socrates had said this, there was silence for c a long time. To judge from his appearance, Socrates himself was absorbed in the foregoing argument, and so were most of us; but Cebes and Simmias went on talking to each other in a low voice. When he noticed them, Socrates asked: 'What is it? Can it be that you find something lacking in what's been said?

It certainly still leaves room for many misgivings and objections, if, that is, one's going to examine it adequately. If it's something else you're considering, never mind; but if you have some difficulty about these matters, don't hesitate to speak for yourselves and explain it, if you think what was said d could be improved in any way; or again, enlist me too, if you think you'll get out of your difficulty any better with my help.'

Simmias replied: 'All right, Socrates, I'll tell you the truth. For some time each of us has had difficulties, and has been prompting and telling the other to question you, from eagerness to hear, but hesitating to make trouble, in case you should find it unwelcome in your present misfortune.'

When Socrates heard this, he chuckled and said: 'Dear me, Simmias! I'd certainly find it hard to convince other people that I don't regard my present lot e as a misfortune, when I can't convince even you two, but you're afraid that I'm more ill-humoured now than in my earlier life; you must, it seems, think I have a poorer power of prophecy than the swans, who when they realize they must die, then sing more fully and sweetly than they've ever sung before, for 85 joy that they are departing into the presence of the god whose servants they are. Though indeed mankind, because of their own fear of death, malign the swans, and say that they sing their farewell song in distress, lamenting their death; they don't reflect that no bird sings when it is hungry or cold or suffering any other distress, not even the nightingale herself, nor the swallow, nor the hoopoe, birds that are reputed to sing lamentations from distress. But, as I see it, neither they nor the swans sing in dis-b tress, but rather, I believe, because, belonging as they do to Apollo, they are prophetic birds with foreknowledge of the blessings of Hades, and therefore sing and rejoice more greatly on that day than ever before. Now I hold that I myself am a fellow-servant of the swans, consecrated to the same god, that I possess prophetic power from my master no less than theirs, and that I'm departing this life with as good a cheer as they do. . . .

'Now there are many large streams of every kind; but among their number there happen to be four in particular, the largest of which, flowing outermost and round in a circle, is the one called Oceanus; across from this and flowing in the opposite direction is Acheron, which flows through other desert regions, and in particular, flowing underground, reaches the Acherusian Lake, where the souls of 113 most of those who have died arrive, and where, after they have stayed for certain appointed periods, some longer, some shorter, they are sent forth again into the generation of living things. The third river issues between these two, and near the point of issue it pours into a huge region all ablaze with fire, and forms a lake larger than our own sea, boiling with water and mud; from there it proceeds in a b circle, turbid and muddy, and coiling about within the earth it reaches the borders of the Acherusian Lake, amongst other places, but does not mingle with its water; then, after repeated coiling underground, it discharges lower down in Tartarus; this is the river they name Pyriphlegethon, and it is from this that the lava-streams blast fragments up at various points upon the earth. Across from this again issues the fourth river, first into a region terrible and wild, it is said, coloured bluish-grey all over, which they name the Stygian region, and the river c as it discharges forms a lake, the Styx; when it has poured in there, and gained terrible powers in the water, it dips beneath the earth, coils round and proceeds in the opposite direction to Pyriphlegethon, which it encounters in the Acherusian lake from the opposite side; nor does the water of this river mingle with any other, but it too goes round in a circle and discharges into Tartarus opposite to Pyriphlegethon; and its name, according to the poets, is Cocytus.

'Such, then, is their nature. Now when those who d have died arrive at the region to which the spirit conveys each one, they first submit to judgement, both those who have lived honourable and holy lives and those who have not. Those who are found to have lived indifferently journey to Acheron, embark upon certain vessels provided for them, and on these they reach the lake; there they dwell, undergoing purgation by paying the penalty for their wrong-doings, and are absolved, if any has committed any wrong, and they secure reward for their good deeds, each according to his desert; but all e who are found to be incurable because of the magnitude of their offences, through having committed many grave acts of sacrilege, or many wrongful and illegal acts of killing, or any other deeds that may be of that sort, are hurled by the appropriate destiny into Tartarus, whence they nevermore emerge. Those, again, who are found guilty of curable yet 114 grave offences, such as an act of violence in anger against a father or a mother, and have lived the rest of their lives in penitence, or who have committed homicide in some other such fashion, must fall into Tartarus; and when they have fallen and stayed there for a year, the surge casts them forth, the homicides by way of Cocytus, and those who have assaulted father or mother by way of Pyriphlegethon; then, as they are carried along and draw level with the Acherusian lake, they cry out and call, some to those they killed, others to those they injured; calling upon them, they beg and beseech them to allow them to come forth into the b lake and to receive them; and if they persuade them, they come forth and cease from their woes; but if not, they are carried back into Tartarus, and from there again into the rivers, and they do not cease from these sufferings till they persuade those they have wronged; for this is the penalty imposed upon them by their judges. But as for those who are found to have lived exceptionally holy lives, it is they who are freed and delivered from these regions within the earth, as from prisons, and who attain to the pure dwelling above, and make their dwelling above c ground. And among their number, those who have been adequately purified by philosophy live bodiless for the whole of time to come, and attain to dwelling places fairer even than these, which it is not easy to reveal, nor is the time sufficient at present. But it is for the sake of just the things we have related, Simmias, that one must do everything possible to have part in goodness and wisdom during life; for fair is the prize and great the hope.

'Now to insist that these things are just as I've re- d lated them would not be fitting for a man of intelligence; but that either this or something like it is true about our souls and their dwellings, given that the soul evidently is immortal, this, I think, is fitting and worth risking, for one who believes that it is so— for a noble risk it is—so one should repeat such things to oneself like a spell; which is just why I've e so prolonged the tale. For these reasons, then, any man should have confidence for his own soul, who during his life has rejected the pleasures of the body and its adornments as alien, thinking they do more harm than good, but has devoted himself to the pleasures of learning, and has decked his soul with no alien adornment, but with its own, with temperance and justice, bravery, liberality, and truth, thus await- 115 ing the journey he will make to Hades, whenever destiny shall summon him. Now as for you, Simmias and Cebes and the rest, you will make your several journals at some future time, but for myself, "e'en now", as a tragic hero might say, "destiny doth summon me"; and it's just about time I made for the bath: it really seems better to take a bath before drinking the poison, and not to give the women the trouble of washing a dead body.'

b   When he'd spoken, Crito said: 'Very well, Socrates: what instructions have you for these others or for me, about your children or about anything else? What could we do, that would be of most service to you?'

'What I'm always telling you, Crito,' said he, 'and nothing very new: if you take care of yourselves, your actions will be of service to me and mine, and to yourselves too, whatever they may be, even if you make no promises now; but if you take no care for yourselves, and are unwilling to pursue your lives along the tracks, as it were, marked by our present and earlier discussions, then even if you make many c firm promises at this time, you'll do no good at all.'

'Then we'll strive to do as you say,' he said; 'but in what fashion are we to bury you?'

'However you wish,' said he; 'provided you catch me, that is, and I don't get away from you.' And with this he laughed quietly, looked towards us and said: 'Friends, I can't persuade Crito that I am Socrates here, the one who is now conversing and arranging each of the things being discussed; but he imagines I'm that dead body he'll see in a little d while, so he goes and asks how he's to bury me! But as for the great case I've been arguing all this time, that when I drink the poison, I shall no longer remain with you, but shall go off and depart for some happy state of the blessed, this, I think, I'm putting to him in vain, while comforting you and myself alike. So please stand surety for me with Crito, the opposite surety to that which he stood for me with the judges: his guarantee was that I *would* stay behind, whereas you must guarantee that, when I die, I shall *not* stay behind, but shall go off and depart; e then Crito will bear it more easily, and when he sees the burning or interment of my body, he won't be distressed for me, as if I were suffering dreadful things, and won't say at the funeral that it is Socrates they are laying out or bearing to the grave or interring. Because you can be sure, my dear Crito, that misuse of words is not only troublesome in itself, but actually has a bad effect on the soul. Rather, you should have confidence, and say you are burying my body; and bury it however you please, and think 116 most proper.'

After saying this, he rose and went into a room to take a bath, and Crito followed him but told us to wait. So we waited, talking among ourselves about what had been said and reviewing it, and then again dwelling on how great a misfortune had befallen us, literally thinking of it as if we were deprived of a father and would lead the rest of our life as orphans. After he'd bathed and his children had been brought to him—he had two little sons and one big one—and b those women of his household had come, he talked with them in Crito's presence, and gave certain directions as to his wishes; he then told the women and children to leave, and himself returned to us.

By now it was close to sunset, as he'd spent a long time inside. So he came and sat down, fresh from his bath, and there wasn't much talk after that. Then the prison official came in, stepped up to him and said: 'Socrates, I shan't reproach you as I reproach c others for being angry with me and cursing, whenever by order of the rulers I direct them to drink the poison. In your time here I've known you for the most generous and gentlest and best of men who have ever come to this place; and now especially, I feel sure it isn't with me that you're angry, but with others, because you know who are responsible. Well now, you know the message I've come to bring: good-bye, then, and try to bear the inevitable as eas- d ily as you can.' And with this he turned away in tears, and went off.

Socrates looked up at him and said: 'Good-bye to you too, and we'll do as you say.' And to us he added: 'What a civil man he is! Throughout my time here he's been to see me, and sometimes talked with me, and been the best of fellows; and now how generous of him to weep for me! But come on, Crito, let's obey him: let someone bring in the poison, if it has been prepared; if not, let the man prepare it.'

Crito said: 'But Socrates, I think the sun is still e on the mountains and hasn't yet gone down. And besides, I know of others who've taken the draught long after the order had been given them, and after dining well and drinking plenty, and even in some cases enjoying themselves with those they fancied. Be in no hurry, then: there's still time left.'

Socrates said: 'It's reasonable for those you speak of to do those things—because they think they gain by doing them; for myself, it's reasonable not to do them; because I think I'll gain nothing by taking the draught a little later: I'll only earn my own ridicule by clinging to life, and being sparing when there's 117 nothing more left. Go on now; do as I ask, and nothing else.'

Hearing this, Crito nodded to the boy who was standing nearby. The boy went out, and after spending a long time away he returned, bringing the man who was going to administer the poison, and was carrying it ready-pounded in a cup. When he saw the man, Socrates said: 'Well, my friend, you're an expert in these things: what must one do?'

'Simply drink it' he said, 'and walk about till a heaviness comes over your legs; then lie down, and b it will act of itself.' And with this he held out the cup to Socrates.

He took it perfectly calmly, Echecrates, without a tremor, or any change of colour or countenance; but looking up at the man, and fixing him with his customary stare, he said: 'What do you say to pouring someone a libation from this drink? Is it allowed or not?'

'We only prepare as much as we judge the proper dose, Socrates,' he said.

c 'I understand,' he said; 'but at least one may pray to the gods, and so one should, that the removal from this world to the next will be a happy one; that is my own prayer: so may it be.' With these words he pressed the cup to his lips, and drank it off with good humour and without the least distaste.

Till then most of us had been fairly well able to restrain our tears; but when we saw he was drinking, that he'd actually drunk it, we could do so no longer. In my own case, the tears came pouring out in spite of myself, so that I covered my face and wept for myself—not for him, no, but for my own misfortune in being deprived of such a man for a d companion. Even before me, Crito had moved away, when he was unable to restrain his tears. And Apollodorus, who even earlier had been continuously in tears, now burst forth into such a storm of weeping

and grieving, the he made everyone present break down except Socrates himself.

But Socrates said: 'What a way to behave, my strange friends! Why, it was mainly for this reason that I sent the women away, so that they shouldn't make this sort of trouble; in fact, I've heard one e should die in silence. Come now, calm yourselves and have strength.'

When we heard this, we were ashamed and checked our tears. He walked about, and when he said that his legs felt heavy he lay down on his back—as the man told him—and then the man, this one who'd given him the poison, felt him, and after an interval examined his feet and legs; he then pinched his foot hard and asked if he could feel it, and Socrates said not. After that he felt his shins 118 once more; and moving upwards in this way, he showed us that he was becoming cold and numb. He went on feeling him, and said that when the coldness reached his heart, he would be gone.

By this time the coldness was somewhere in the region of his abdomen, when he uncovered his face—it had been covered over—and spoke; and this was in fact his last utterance: 'Crito,' he said, 'we owe a cock to Asclepius: please pay the debt, and don't neglect it.'

'It shall be done,' said Crito; 'have you anything else to say?'

To this question he made no answer, but after a short interval he stirred, and when the man uncovered him his eyes were fixed; when he saw this, Crito closed his mouth and his eyes.

And that, Echecrates, was the end of our companion, a man who, among those of his time we knew, was—so we should say—the best, the wisest too, and the most just.

Meno

Persons of the Dialogue
Meno   A Slave of Meno
Socrates   Anytus

70 MENO: Can you tell me, Socrates, whether virtue is acquired by teaching or by practice; or if neither

by teaching nor by practice, then whether it comes to man by nature, or in what other way?

SOCRATES: There was a time, Meno, when the Thessalians were famous among the other Hellenes for their riches and their riding; but now, if I am not mistaken, they are famous also for their wisdom, es- b pecially at Larisa, which is the native city of your *first definition*

friend Aristippus. And this is Gorgias' doing; for when he came there, he imbued with the love of wisdom the flower of the Aleuadae, among them your
c admirer Aristippus, and the other chiefs of the Thessalians. And he has taught you the habit of answering questions in the grand and bold style, which is natural to those who know, and may be expected from one who is himself ready and willing to be questioned on any subject by any Hellene, and answers all comers. How different is our lot! my dear
71 Meno. Here at Athens there is a dearth of the commodity, and all wisdom seems to have emigrated *[no wisdom]* from us to you. I am certain that if you were to ask any Athenian whether virtue was natural or acquired, he would laugh in your face, and say: 'Stranger, you have far too good an opinion of me, if you think that I can answer your question. For I literally do not know what virtue is, and much less whether it is acquired by teaching or not.'

b   And I myself, Meno, living as I do in this region of poverty am as poor as the rest of the world; and I confess with shame that I know literally nothing about virtue; and when I do not know the 'quid' *[what, property]* of anything how can I know the 'quale'? How, if I knew nothing at all of Meno, could I tell if he was handsome, or the opposite; rich and noble, or the reverse of rich and noble? Do you think that I could?

MEN.: No, indeed. But are you in earnest, Socrates, in saying that you do not know what virtue
c is? And am I to carry back this report of you to Thessaly?

SOC.: *[socratic irony]* Not only that, my dear boy, but you may say further that I have never come across anyone else who did, in my judgement.
d   MEN.: Then you have never met Gorgias when he was at Athens?

SOC.: Yes, I have.

MEN.: And did you not think that he knew?

SOC.: I have not a good memory, Meno, and therefore I cannot now tell what I thought of him at the time. I dare say that he does know, and that you know what he said: please, therefore, to remind me of what he said; or, if you would rather, tell me your own view; for I suspect that you and he think much alike.

MEN.: Very true.

SOC.: Then as he is not here, never mind him, and do you tell me. I adjure you, Meno, be generous, and tell me what you say that virtue is; for I shall esteem myself truly fortunate if I find that I have been mistaken, and that you and Gorgias do really

have this knowledge, when I have been just saying that I have never met anybody who had.

MEN.: There will be no difficulty, Socrates, in answering your question. Let us take first the virtue of e a man—he should know how to administer the state, and in the administration of it should benefit his friends and harm his enemies; and he must also be careful not to suffer harm himself. A woman's virtue, if you wish to know about that, may also be easily described: her duty is to order her household and keep properly what is indoors, and obey her husband. Every age, every condition of life, young or old, male or female, bond or free, has a different 72 virtue: there are virtues numberless, and consequently there is no difficulty about definitions; for there is a virtue relative to the actions and ages of each of us in all that we do. And I take it the same may be said of vice, Socrates.

SOC.: How fortunate I am, Meno! When I ask you for one virtue, you present me with a swarm of them, which are in your keeping. Suppose that I carried on the figure of the swarm, and asked of you, What is b the nature of the bee? and you answered that there are many different kinds of bees, and I replied: But are there many different kinds of bees because they differ quâ bees; or, not differing quâ bees, are they distinguished from one another by something else, some quality such as beauty, or size, or some other such attribute? How would you answer me?

MEN.: I should answer that bees do not differ from one another, quâ bees.

SOC.: And if I went on to say: That is what I desire to know, Meno; tell me what is the quality in which they do differ, but are all alike;—you would c presumably be able to answer?

MEN.: I should.

SOC.: And so of the virtues, however many and different they may be, they have all a common form which makes them virtues; and on this he who would answer the question, 'What is virtue?' would do well to have his eye fixed: Do you understand?

MEN.: I am beginning to understand; but I do not as yet take hold of the question as I could wish.   d

SOC.: When you say, Meno, that there is one virtue of a man, another of a woman, and so on, does this apply only to virtue, or would you say the same of health, and size, and strength? Or is the nature of health always the same, whether in man or woman?

MEN.: I should say that health is the same, both in man and woman.   e

SOC.: And is not this true of size and strength? If

a woman is strong, she will be strong by reason of the same form and of the same strength subsisting in her which there is in the man. I mean to say that strength, as strength, whether of man or woman, is the same. Is there any difference?

MEN.: I think not.

73 SOC.: And will not virtue, as virtue, be the same, whether in a child or in an old man, in a woman or in a man?

MEN.: I cannot help feeling, Socrates, that this case is different from the others.

SOC.: But why? Were you not saying that the virtue of a man was to order a state, and the virtue of a woman was to order a household?

MEN.: I did say so.

SOC.: And can either household or state or anything be well ordered without temperance and without justice?

b MEN.: Certainly not.

SOC.: Then they who order a state or a house temperately and justly order them with temperance and justice?

MEN.: Certainly.

SOC.: Then both men and women, if they are to be good men and women, must have the same virtues of temperance and justice?

c MEN.: Clearly.

SOC.: And could either a young man or an elder one ever become good, while they were intemperate and unjust?

MEN.: Certainly not.

SOC.: They must be temperate and just?

MEN.: Yes.

SOC.: Then all human beings are good in the same way, and become good by possession of the same virtues?

d MEN.: Such is the inference.

SOC.: And they surely would not have been good in the same way, unless their virtue had been the same?

MEN.: They would not.

SOC.: Then now that the sameness of all virtue has been proven, try and remember what Gorgias, and you with him, say that virtue is.   *2nd*

MEN.: I know not what to say, but that virtue is the power of governing mankind—if you really want to have one definition of them all.

SOC.: That is indeed what I want. Now consider this point; can virtue as you define it be the virtue of a child or a slave, Meno? Can the child govern his father, or the slave his master; and would he who governed be any longer a slave?

MEN.: I think not, Socrates.

SOC.: No, indeed; there would be small reason in that. Yet once more, fair friend; according to you, virtue is 'the power of governing'; but shall we not add 'justly and not unjustly'?

MEN.: Yes, Socrates; I agree there; for justice is virtue.

SOC.: Would you say 'virtue', Meno or 'a virtue'? c

MEN.: What do you mean?

SOC.: I mean as I might say about anything; that roundness, for example, is 'a figure' and not simply 'figure', and I should adopt this mode of speaking, because there are other figures.

MEN.: Quite right; and that is just what I say about virtue—that there are other virtues as well as justice.

SOC.: What are they? tell me the names of them, 74 as I would tell you the names of the other figures if you asked me.

MEN.: Courage and temperance and wisdom and a noble way of life are virtues, it seems to me; and there are many others.

SOC.: Yes, Meno; and again we are in the same case: in searching after one virtue we have found many, though not in the same way as before; but we have been unable to find the common virtue which runs through them all.

MEN.: Why, Socrates, even now I am not able to help you in your inquiry and get at one common no- b tion of virtue as in the other cases.

SOC.: No wonder; but I will try to get us nearer if I can. You perhaps understand that this reasoning applies universally: suppose that someone asked you the question which I asked before: Meno, what is figure? if you answered 'roundness', he would reply to you, in my way of speaking, by asking whether roundness is 'figure' or 'a figure'; and you would, of course, answer 'a figure'.

MEN.: Certainly.

SOC.: And for this reason—that there are other figures?   c

MEN.: Yes.

SOC.: And if he proceeded to ask, What other figures are there? you would have told him.

MEN.: I should.

SOC.: And if he similarly asked what colour is, and you answered whiteness, and the questioner rejoined, Would you say that whiteness is colour or a colour? you would reply, A colour, because there are other colours as well.

MEN.: I should.

d SOC.: And if he had said, Tell me what they are?—you would have told him of other colours which are colours just as much as whiteness.

MEN.: Yes.

SOC.: And suppose that he were to pursue the matter in my way, he would say: Ever and anon we are landed in particulars, but that is not what I want; tell me then, since you call them by a common name, and say that they are all figures even when opposed to one another, what is that common nature which you designate as figure—which contains round no less than straight, and, you say, belongs to one no more than to the other—that would be your mode of speaking?

e MEN.: Yes.

SOC.: And in speaking thus, do you mean to say that the round is no more round than straight, or the straight no more straight than round?

MEN.: Of course not.

SOC.: You only assert that the round figure is figure no more than the straight, nor the straight than the round?

MEN.: Very true.

SOC.: To what then do we give the name of figure? Try and answer. Suppose that when a person asked you this question either about figure or colour,
75 you were to reply, My good sir, I do not understand what you want, or know what you mean; he would look rather astonished and say: Do you not understand that I am looking for that which is identical in all the particulars? And then he might put the question in another form: Meno, he might say, what is there identical in the round, the straight, and everything else that you call a figure? Could you not answer that question, Meno? I wish that you would try; the attempt will be good practice for the answer about virtue.

b MEN.: I would rather that you should answer, Socrates.

SOC.: Shall I indulge you?

MEN.: By all means.

SOC.: And then you will tell me about virtue?

MEN.: I will.

SOC.: Then I must do my best, for there is a prize to be won.

MEN.: Certainly.

SOC.: Well, I will try and explain to you what figure is. What do you say to this answer?—Figure is the only thing which accompanies colour. Will you be satisfied with it, as I am sure that I should be if
c you would let me have a similar definition of virtue?

. MEN.: But, Socrates, it is such an artless answer.

SOC.: Why artless?

MEN.: Because, according to you, figure is that which always accompanies colour. Very well; but if a person were to say that he does not know what colour is, any more than what figure is—what sort of answer would you have given him?

SOC.: In my opinion, the truth. And if he were a philosopher of the eristic and contentious sort, I should say to him: You have my answer, and if I am wrong, your business is to take up the argument and d refute me. But if we were friends, and were talking as you and I are now, I ought of course to reply in a milder strain and more in the dialectician's vein; that is to say, I should not only speak the truth, but I should make use of premises which the person interrogated would be willing to admit. And this is the way in which I shall endeavour to approach you. e You will acknowledge, will you not, that there is such a thing as an end, or termination, or extremity?—all which words I use in the same sense, although I am aware that Prodicus might disagree on this point: but still you, I imagine, would speak of a thing as ended or terminated—that is all which I am saying—nothing subtle.

MEN.: Yes, I should; and I believe that I understand your meaning.

SOC.: And you would speak of a surface and also 76 of a solid, as for example in geometry.

MEN.: Yes.

SOC.: Well then, you are now in a condition to understand my definition of figure. I define figure to be always that in which the solid finds its limit; or, more concisely, the limit of solid.

MEN.: And now, Socrates, what is colour?

SOC.: You are outrageous, Meno, in thus plaguing a poor old man to give you an answer, when you will not take the trouble of remembering what is Gorgias' definition of virtue.   b

MEN.: When you have told me what I ask, I will tell you, Socrates.

SOC.: A man who was blindfolded has only to hear you talking, and he would know that you are a beautiful creature and still have lovers.

MEN.: Why do you think so?

SOC.: Why, because you always speak in imperatives, like proud beauties who reign with absolute c power so long as they are in their prime; and also, I suspect, you have found out that I have a weakness for beauty, and therefore to humour you I must answer.

MEN.: Please do.

SOC.: Would you like me to answer you after the manner of Gorgias, in which you may find it easiest to follow me?

MEN.: I should like nothing better.

SOC.: Do not he and you and Empedocles say that there are certain effluences from existing things?

MEN.: Certainly.

SOC.: And passages into which and through d which the effluences pass.

MEN.: Exactly.

SOC.: And some of the effluences fit into the passages, and some of them are too small or too large?

MEN.: True.

SOC.: And there is such a thing as sight?

MEN.: Yes.

SOC.: And now, as Pindar says, 'read my meaning':—colour is an effluence of figures, commensurate with sight, and palpable to sense.

e   MEN.: That, Socrates, appears to me to be an admirable answer.

SOC.: Why, yes, because it happens to be one which you have been in the habit of hearing: and your wit will have discovered, I suspect, that you may explain in the same way the nature of sound and smell, and of many other similar phenomena.

MEN.: Quite true.

SOC.: The answer, Meno, was in the solemn language of tragedy, and therefore was more acceptable to you than the other answer about figure.

MEN.: Yes.

SOC.: And yet, O son of Alexidemus, I cannot help thinking that the other was the better; and I believe that you would be of the same opinion, if you would only stay and be initiated, and were not compelled, as you said yesterday, to go away before the mysteries.

MEN.: But I will stay, Socrates, if you will give me many such answers.

SOC.: Well then, for my own sake as well as for 77 yours, I will do my very best; but I am afraid that I shall not be able to give you very many as good. And now, in your turn, you are to fulfil your promise, and tell me what virtue is in the universal; and do not make a singular into a plural, as the facetious always say of those who break a thing, but leave virtue whole and sound when you tell me its nature. I have b given you the pattern.

MEN.: Well then, Socrates, virtue, as I take it, is when he, who desires things which are lovely, is able to provide them for himself; so the poet says, and I say too that 'virtue is the desire of things that are lovely, with power to attain them'.

SOC.: And does he who desires the things that are lovely also desire the good?

MEN.: Certainly.

SOC.: Then are there some who desire the evil c and others who desire the good? Do not all men, my dear sir, desire good?

MEN.: I think not.

SOC.: There are some who desire evil?

MEN.: Yes.

SOC.: Do you mean that they think the evils which they desire, to be good; or do they know that they are evil and yet desire them?

MEN.: Both, I think.

SOC.: And do you really imagine, Meno, that a man knows evils and desires them notwithstanding?

MEN.: Certainly I do.

SOC.: Desire is of possession?

MEN.: Yes, of possession.   d

SOC.: And does he think that evils do good to him who possesses them, or does he know that their presence does harm?

MEN.: There are some who think that the evils do them good, and others who know that they do harm.

SOC.: And, in your opinion, do those who think that they do them good know that they are evils?

MEN.: I would not go so far as that.   e

SOC.: Is it not obvious that those who are ignorant of their nature do not desire them, but desire what they suppose to be goods although they are really evils; and therefore if in their ignorance they suppose the evils to be goods they really desire goods?

MEN.: In that case, no doubt.

SOC.: Again, those who, as you say, desire evils, and think that evils are hurtful to the possessor of them, presumably know that they will be hurt by them?

MEN.: They must know it.

SOC.: And must they not suppose that those who 78 are hurt are miserable in proportion to the hurt which is inflicted upon them?

MEN.: How can it be otherwise?

SOC.: But are not the miserable ill fated?

MEN.: Yes, indeed.

SOC.: And does anyone desire to be miserable and ill fated?

MEN.: I should say not, Socrates.

SOC.: But if there is no one who desires to be miserable, there is no one, Meno, who desires evil; for what is misery but the desire and possession of evil?

MEN.: That appears to be the truth, Socrates, and b I admit that nobody desires evil.

SOC.: And yet, were you not saying just now that virtue is the desire and power of attaining good?— [Yes, I did say so.]—But of this definition one part, the desire, is common to all, and one man is no better than another in that respect?—[Clearly.]—It is obvious then that if one man is indeed better than another, he must be better in the power of attaining good?

MEN.: Exactly.

c   SOC.: Then, according to your definition, virtue would appear to be the power of attaining good?

MEN.: I entirely approve, Socrates, of the manner in which you now view this matter.

SOC.: Then let us see whether what you now say is true from another point of view; for very likely you may be right:—You affirm virtue to be the power of attaining goods?

MEN.: Yes.

SOC.: And the goods which you mean are such as health and wealth?

MEN.: And the possession of gold and silver, and having office and honour in the state.

SOC.: Those are what you would call goods?

MEN.: Yes, I should include all those.

SOC.: Then, according to Meno, who is the hered- d itary friend of the great king, virtue is the power of getting silver and gold; and would you add that they must be gained piously, justly, or do you deem this to be of no consequence? And is any mode of acquisition, even if unjust, equally to be deemed virtue?

MEN.: Not virtue, Socrates.

SOC.: But vice?

MEN.: Yes.

SOC.: Then justice or temperance or piety, or e some other part of virtue, as would appear, must accompany the acquisition, and without them the mere acquisition of goods will not be virtue.

MEN.: Why, how can there be virtue without these?

SOC.: On the other hand, the failure to acquire gold and silver in an unjust way for oneself or another, or in other words the want of them, may be equally virtue?

MEN.: True.

SOC.: Then the acquisition of such goods is no 79 more virtue than the non-acquisition and want of them, but it seems that whatever is accompanied by justice or honesty is virtue, and whatever is devoid of any such quality is vice.

MEN.: It cannot be otherwise, in my judgement.

SOC.: And were we not saying just now that justice, temperance, and the like, were each of them a part of virtue?

MEN.: Yes.

SOC.: And so, Meno, this is the way in which you mock me.

MEN.: Why do you say that, Socrates?

SOC.: Why, because a short while ago I asked you not to break up virtue and offer it to me in little pieces, and I gave you patterns according to which you were to frame your answer; and you have forgotten already, and tell me that virtue is the power of attaining goods with justice; and justice you ac- b knowledge to be a part of virtue.

MEN.: Yes.

SOC.: Then it follows from your own admissions, that virtue consists in doing with one part of virtue whatever a man does do; for justice and the like are said by you to be parts of virtue, each and all of them. Let me explain further. Did not I ask you to tell me the nature of virtue as a whole? And you are very far from telling me this, but declare every action to be virtue which is done with c a part of virtue; as though you had told me the nature of virtue as a whole, so that I should recognize it even when you fritter it away into little pieces. And, therefore, my dear Meno, I fear that I must begin again and repeat the same question: What is virtue? for otherwise I can only say that every action done with a part of virtue is virtue; what else is the meaning of saying that every action done with justice is virtue? Ought I not to ask the question over again; for can anyone who does not know the nature of virtue know the nature of a part of virtue?

MEN.: No; I do not say that he can.

SOC.: Do you remember how, in the example of figure, we rejected any answer given in terms which d were as yet unexplained or unadmitted?

MEN.: Yes, Socrates; and we were quite right in doing so.

SOC.: But then, my friend, do not suppose that while the nature of virtue as a whole is still undetermined, you can explain it to anyone by reference to some part of virtue; or indeed explain anything at all in that fashion. We should only have to ask over again the old question, What is this virtue of yours? e Am I not right?

MEN.: I believe that you are.

SOC.: Then begin again, and answer me, What,

according to you and your friend Gorgias, is the definition of virtue?

MEN.: O Socrates, I used to be told, before I knew 80 you, that you were always doubting yourself and making others doubt; and now you are casting your spells over me, and I am simply getting betwitched and enchanted, and am at my wits' end. And if I may venture to make a jest upon you, you seem to me both in your appearance and in your power over others to be very like the flat torpedo fish, who torpifies those who come near him and touch him, as you have now torpified me, I think. For my soul and my tongue are really torpid, and I do not know how b to answer you; and though I have been delivered of an infinite variety of speeches about virtue before now, and to many persons—and very good speeches they were, as I thought—at this moment I cannot even say what virtue is. And I think that you are very wise in not voyaging and going away from home, for if you did in other places as you do in Athens, you would be cast into prison as a magician.

SOC.: You are a rogue, Meno, and had all but caught me.

MEN.: What do you mean, Socrates?

c   SOC.: I can tell why you made a simile about me.

MEN.: Why?

SOC.: In order that I might make another simile about you. For I know that all beautiful youths like to have similes made about them—as well they may, since beautiful images, I take it, are naturally evoked by beauty—but I shall not return the compliment. As to my being a torpedo, if the torpedo is itself torpid as well as the cause of torpidity in others, then indeed I am a torpedo, but not otherwise; for I perd plex others, not because I am clear, but because I am utterly perplexed myself. And now I know not what virtue is, and you seem to be in the same case, although you did once perhaps know before you touched me. However, I have no objection to join with you in the inquiry.

MEN.: And how will you investigate, Socrates, that of which you know nothing at all? Where can you find a starting-point in the region of the unknown? And even if you happen to come full upon what you want, how will you ever know that this is the thing which you did not know?

SOC.: I know, Meno, what you mean; but just see e what a tiresome dispute you are introducing. You argue that a man cannot inquire either about that which he knows, or about that which he does not know; for if he knows, he has no need to inquire;

and if not, he cannot; for he does not know the very subject about which he is to inquire.

MEN.: Well, Socrates, and is not the argument 81 sound?

SOC.: I think not.

MEN.: Why not?

SOC.: I will tell you why: I have heard from certain men and women skilled in things divine that— [Here Socrates pauses to change the tone of the dialogue.]

MEN.: What did they say?

SOC.: They spoke of a glorious truth, as I conceive.

MEN.: What is it? and who are they?

SOC.: Some of them are priests and priestesses, who have striven to learn how to give a reasonable account of the things with which they concern b themselves: there are poets also, like Pindar, and the many others who are inspired. And they say— mark, now, and see whether their words are true— they say that the soul of man is immortal, and at one time has an end, which is termed dying, and at another time is born again, but is never destroyed. And the moral is, that a man ought to live always in perfect holiness. 'For in the ninth year Persephone sends the souls of those from whom she has c received the penalty of ancient crime back again from beneath into the light of the sun above, and these are they who become noble kings and mighty men and great in wisdom and are for ever called saintly heroes.'

The soul, then, as being immortal and having been born again many times, and having seen all things that exist, whether in this world or in the world below, has knowledge of them all; and it is no wonder that she should be able to call to remembrance all that she ever knew about virtue, and about everything; for as all nature is akin, and the soul has learned all things, there is no difficulty in d a man eliciting out of a single recollection all the rest—the process generally called 'learning'—if he is strenuous and does not faint; for all inquiry and all learning is but recollection.

And therefore we ought not to listen to this eristic argument about the impossibility of inquiry: for it will make us idle, and it is sweet to the sluggard; but the other doctrine will make us active and in- e quisitive. In that confiding, I will gladly inquire with you into the nature of virtue.

MEN.: Yes, Socrates; but what do you mean by saying that we do not learn, and that what we call learning is only a process of recollection? Can you teach me how this is?

Soc.: I told you, Meno, just now that you were a rogue, and now you ask whether I can teach you, when I am saying that there is no teaching, but only recollection; and thus you imagine that you will expose me in a contradiction.

Men.: Indeed, Socrates, I protest that I had no such intention. I only asked the question from habit; but if you can prove to me that what you say is true, I wish that you would.

Soc.: It will be no easy matter, but I am willing to do my best for you. Suppose that you call one of your numerous attendants, whichever you like, that I may demonstrate on him.

Men.: Certainly. Come hither, boy.

Soc.: He is Greek, and speaks Greek, does he not?

Men.: Yes, indeed; he was born in the house.

Soc.: Attend now, and observe whether he learns of me or only remembers.

Men.: I will.

Soc.: Tell me, boy, do you know that a figure like this is a square?

Boy: I do.

Soc.: And you know that a square figure has these four lines equal?

Boy: Certainly.

Soc.: And these lines which I have drawn through the middle of the square are also equal?

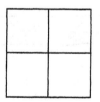

Boy: Yes.

Soc.: A square may be of any size?

Boy: Certainly.

Soc.: And if one side of the figure be of two feet, and the other side be of two feet, how much will the whole be? Let me explain: if in one direction the space was of two feet, and in the other direction of one foot, the whole would be of two feet taken once?

Boy: Yes.

Soc.: But since this side is also of two feet, there are twice two feet?

Boy: There are.

Soc.: Then the square is of twice two feet?

Boy: Yes.

Soc.: And how many are twice two feet? count and tell me.

Boy: Four, Socrates.

Soc.: And might there not be another square twice as large as this, and having like this the lines equal?

Boy: Yes.

Soc.: And of how many feet will that be?

Boy: Of eight feet.

Soc.: And now try and tell me the length of the line which forms the side of that double square: this is two feet—what will that be?

Boy: Clearly, Socrates, it will be double.

Soc.: Do you observe, Meno, that I am not teaching the boy anything, but only asking him questions; and now he fancies that he knows how long a line is necessary in order to produce a figure of eight square feet; does he not?

Men.: Yes.

Soc.: And does he really know?

Men.: Certainly not.

Soc.: He only guesses that because the square is double, the line is double.

Men.: True.

Soc.: Observe him while he recalls the steps in regular order. (To the Boy.) Tell me, boy, do you assert that a double space comes from a double line? Remember that I am not speaking of an oblong, but of a figure equal every way, and twice the size of this—that is to say of eight feet; and I want to know whether you still say that a double square comes from a double line?

Boy: Yes.

Soc.: But does not this line become doubled if we add another such line here?

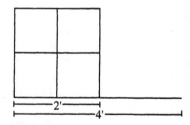

Boy: Certainly.

Soc.: And four such lines will make a space containing eight feet?

BOY: Yes.

SOC.: Let us describe such a figure: Would you not say that this is the figure of eight feet?

BOY: Yes.

SOC.: And are there not these four divisions in the figure, each of which is equal to the figure of four feet?

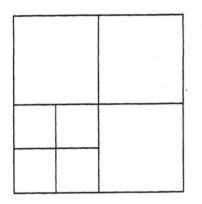

BOY: True.

SOC.: And is not that four times four?

BOY: Certainly.

SOC.: And four times is not double?

BOY: No, indeed.

SOC.: But how much?

BOY: Four times as much.

SOC.: Therefore the double line, boy, has given a space, not twice, but four times as much.

BOY: True.

c   SOC.: Four times four are sixteen—are they not?

BOY: Yes.

SOC.: What line would give you a space of eight feet, as this gives one of sixteen feet;—do you see?

BOY: Yes.

SOC.: And the space of four feet is made from this half line?

BOY: Yes.

SOC.: Good; and is not a space of eight feet twice the size of this, and half the size of the other?

BOY: Certainly.

SOC.: Such a space, then, will be made out of a line greater than this one, and less than that one?

BOY: Yes; I think so.

d   SOC.: Very good; I like to hear you say what you think. And now tell me, is not this a line of two feet and that of four?

BOY: Yes.

SOC.: Then the line which forms the side of eight feet ought to be more than this line of two feet, and less than the other of four feet?

BOY: It ought.

SOC.: Try and see if you can tell me how much it will be.

BOY: Three feet.

SOC.: Then if we add a half to this line of two, that will be the line of three. Here are two and there is one; and on the other side, here are two also and there is one: and that makes the figure of which you speak?

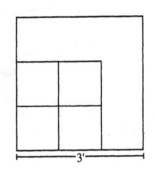

BOY: Yes.

SOC.: But if there are three feet this way and three feet that way, the whole space will be three times three feet?

BOY: That is evident.

SOC.: And how much are three times three feet?

BOY: Nine.

SOC.: And how much is the double of four?

BOY: Eight.

SOC.: Then the figure of eight is not made out of a line of three?

BOY: No.

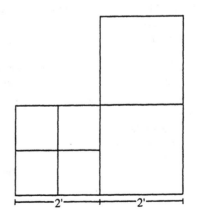

84   Soc.: But from what line?—tell me exactly; and if you would rather not reckon, try and show me the line.

Boy: Indeed, Socrates, I do not know.

Soc.: Do you see, Meno, what advances he has made in his power of recollection? He did not know at first, and he does not know now, what is the side of a figure of eight feet: but then he thought that he knew, and answered confidently as if he knew, and had no difficulty; now he has a difficulty, and neither knows nor fancies that he knows.

b   Men.: True.

Soc.: Is he not better off in knowing his ignorance?

Men.: I think that he is.

Soc.: If we have made him doubt, and given him the 'torpedo's shock,' have we done him any harm?

Men.: I think not.

Soc.: We have certainly, as would seem, assisted him in some degree to the discovery of the truth; and now he will wish to remedy his ignorance, but then he would have been ready to tell all the world
c   again and again that the double space should have a double side.

Men.: True.

Soc.: But do you suppose that he would ever have enquired into or learned what he fancied that he knew, though he was really ignorant of it, until he had fallen into perplexity under the idea that he did not know, and had desired to know?

Men.: I think not, Socrates.

Soc.: Then he was the better for the torpedo's touch?

Men.: I think so.

[Although the slave boy has never been educated, he possesses innate knowledge of geometry. Socrates claims that all he is doing is helping the slave bring to consciousness that which he already knows. That is, education is recollection of innate ideas.]

Soc.: Mark now the farther development. I shall only ask him, and not teach him, and he shall share the enquiry with me: and do you watch and see if you find me telling or explaining anything to him, instead of eliciting his opinion. Tell me, boy, is not
d   this a square of four feet which I have drawn?

Boy: Yes.

Soc.: And now I add another square equal to the former one?

Boy: Yes.

Soc.: And a third, which is equal to either of them?

Boy: Yes.

Soc.: Suppose that we fill up the vacant corner?

Boy: Very good.

Soc.: Here, then, there are four equal spaces?

Boy: Yes.

Soc.: And how many times larger is this space e than this other?

Boy: Four times.

Soc.: But it ought to have been twice only, as you will remember.

Boy: True.

Soc.: And does not this line, reaching from corner to corner, bisect each of these spaces? [BDEF] 85

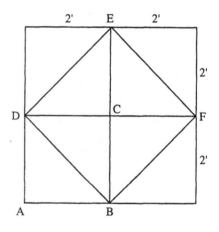

Boy: Yes.

Soc.: And are there not here four equal lines which contain this space? [BD, DE, EF, and FB]

Boy: There are.

Soc.: Look and see how much this space is.

Boy: I do not understand.

Soc.: Has not each interior line cut off half of the four spaces? [BD, DE, EF, and FB]

Boy: Yes.

Soc.: And how many spaces are there in this section? [BDEF]

Boy: Four.

Soc.: And how many in this? [ABCD]   b

Boy: Two.

Soc.: And four is how many times two?

Boy: Twice.

Soc.: And this space is of how many feet? [BDEF]

Boy: Of eight feet.

Soc.: And from what line do you get this figure?

Boy: From this. [BDEF]

Soc.: That is, from the line which extends from corner to corner of the figure of four feet?

Boy: Yes.

Soc.: And that is the line which the learned call the diagonal. And if this is the proper name, then you, Meno's slave, are prepared to affirm that the double space is the square of the diagonal?

Boy: Certainly, Socrates.

Soc.: What do you say of him, Meno? Were not all these answers given out of his own head?

Men.: Yes, they were all his own.

c Soc.: And yet, as we were just now saying, he did not know?

Men.: True.

Soc.: But still he had in him those notions of his—had he not?

Men.: Yes.

Soc.: Then he who does not know may still have true notions of that which he does not know?

Men.: He has.

Soc.: And at present these notions have just been stirred up in him, as in a dream; but if he were fre-
d quently asked the same questions, in different forms, he would know as well as any one at last?

Men.: I dare say.

Soc.: Without any one teaching him he will recover his knowledge for himself, if he is only asked questions?

Men.: Yes.

Soc.: And this spontaneous recovery of knowledge in him is recollection?

Men.: True.

Soc.: And this knowledge which he now has must he not either have acquired or always possessed?

Men.: Yes.

Soc.: But if he always possessed this knowledge he would always have known; or if he has acquired

the knowledge he could not have acquired it in this life, unless he has been taught geometry; for he may be made to do the same with all geometry and ever other branch of knowledge. Now, has any one ever e taught him all this? You must know about him, if, as you say, he was born and bred in your house.

Men.: And I am certain that no one ever did teach him.

Soc.: And yet he has the knowledge?

Men.: The fact, Socrates, is undeniable.

Soc.: But if he did not acquire the knowledge in this life, then he must have had and learned it at 86 some other time?

Men.: Clearly.

Soc.: Which must have been the time when he was not a man?

Men.: Yes.

Soc.: And if there are always to be true thoughts in him, both while he is and while he is not a man, which only need to be awakened into knowledge by putting questions to him, his soul must remain always possessed of this knowledge; for he must always either be or not be a man.

Men.: Obviously.

Soc.: And if the truth of all things always exists b in the soul, then the soul is immortal. Wherefore be of good cheer, and try to discover by recollection what you do not now know, or rather what you do not remember.

Men.: I feel, somehow, that I like what you are saying.

Soc.: And I too like what I am saying. Some things I have said of which I am not altogether confident. But that we shall be better and braver and less helpless if we think that we ought to inquire, than we should have been if we thought that there was no knowing and no duty to seek to know what we do not know;—that is a belief for which I am ready to fight, in word and deed, to the utmost of c my power.

Republic

The first chapter consists of a typical early Platonic dialogue: it was possibly originally written separately from the rest of the book. No firm conclusions are reached about the ostensible purpose of the enquiry—to discover the nature of morality—but the arguments are lively and interesting, and raise themes which will recur later in the book. Once the scene has been set, Socrates whittles away at the unthinking acceptance of conventional views on morality (represented by Cephalus and Polemarchus), before dealing more vigorously with the robust assault on convention (and on Socrates himself) delivered by the sophist Thrasymachus. Socrates accepts neither conventional nor unconventional views unless they survive his logical scrutiny; the ground is prepared for Plato's stress throughout *Republic* on the importance of reason for morality.

CHAPTER I
CONVENTION UNDER ATTACK

Socrates

327a Yesterday I went down to the Piraeus with Glaucon the son of Ariston to worship the goddess and also because I wanted to see how they would conduct the festival on this, its first performance. I was certainly impressed with the splendour of the procession made by the local people, but I have to say that the Thracians rose to the occasion just as well in their pro-
b cession. Once our worshipping and watching were over, we were starting to make our way back to town, when Polemarchus the son of Cephalus spotted us from a distance setting off home, and he told his slave to run over to us and tell us to wait for him. The boy came up behind me, caught hold of my coat, and said, 'Polemarchus wants you to wait.'

I turned around and asked where his master was. 'There,' he said, 'coming up behind you. Please wait.'

'All right, we will,' said Glaucon.

c Polemarchus soon caught up with us, and so did Glaucon's brother Adeimantus, Niceratus the son of Nicias, and some others; they had all apparently been at the procession.

'Socrates,' Polemarchus said, 'it looks to me as though the two of you are setting off back to town.'

'That's right,' I replied.

'Well,' he said, 'do you see how many of us there are?'

'Of course.'

'You'd better choose, then,' he said, 'between overpowering us and staying here.'

'Well, there *is* one further possibility,' I pointed out. 'We might convince you to let us leave.'

'Can you convince people who don't listen?' he asked.

'Impossible,' Glaucon replied.

'Then I think you should know that we won't be listening to you.'

'Anyway,' Adeimantus added, 'don't you realize 328a that there's going to be a horseback torch-race this evening for the goddess?'

'Horseback?' I said. 'That's unusual. Do you mean there'll be a horse-race in which they'll carry torches and pass them on to one another?'

'Precisely,' Polemarchus said. 'And they're also putting on an all-night celebration, which should be worth seeing. We're going to go out to watch it after dinner, and lots of young men will be there too, whom we shall be talking to. So you must do as we suggest and stay.'   b

'It looks as though we'd better stay,' said Glaucon.

'Well, if you think so,' I said, 'then that's what we should do.'

So we went to Polemarchus' house, and there we found his brothers Lysias and Euthydemus, and also Thrasymachus of Chalcedon, Charmantides of Paeania, and Cleitophon the son of Aristonymus. Polemarchus' father Cephalus was in the house too; I

Reprinted from Plato's *Republic*, translated by Robin Waterfield (1993) by permission of Oxford University Press.

c thought he looked very old, but then I hadn't seen him for quite a while. He was sitting on a chair with a cushion, and wearing a chaplet, since he had just been making a ritual offering in the courtyard. Some other chairs had been placed in a circle there, so we sat down beside him.

As soon as Cephalus saw me, he said hello and then went on, 'Socrates, unfortunately for us, you're not in the habit of coming down to the Piraeus. You should, you know. I mean, if I still had the strength to make the journey up to town easily, you wouldn't have to come here, because I'd be visiting you. But as things are, you should come here more of-
d ten. In my case, you see, declining interest in physical pleasures is exactly matched by increasing desire for and enjoyment of conversation. So please do as I ask: by all means spend time with these young men who are your companions, but treat us too as your friends—as your very close friends—and come here to visit us.'

'I certainly will, Cephalus,' I replied. 'I do in fact enjoy talking with very old people, because I think
e we ought to learn from them. They've gone on ahead of us, as it were, on a road which we too will probably have to travel, and we ought to find out from them what the road is like—whether it is rough and hard, or easy and smooth. And I'd be especially glad to ask you your opinion about it, since you've reached the time of life the poets describe as being "on the threshold of old age". Is it a difficult period of one's life, would you say, or what?'

329a   'Of course I'll tell you my opinion, Socrates,' he said. 'You see, it's not uncommon for some of us old men of approximately the same age to get together (and so vindicate the ancient proverb!). These gatherings are invariably used for grumbling, by those who miss the pleasures of youth. They remind themselves of their love lives, drinking, feasting, and the like, and consequently complain of having been robbed of things that are important and claim that in those days they used to live well, whereas nowadays they aren't even alive. Others bleat about how their
b families treat old age like dirt; in fact, this is the main reason they go on and on about all the evils for which old age is responsible. But to my mind, Socrates, they are holding an innocent responsible. If old age were to blame, then I too would have had the same experiences as them—at least as far as old age is concerned—and so would everyone else who has reached this age. But in the past I, at any rate, have met others like myself who do not feel this

way. In particular, I was once with Sophocles the poet when someone asked him, "How do you feel c about sex, Sophocles? Are you still capable of having sex with a woman?" He replied, "Be quiet, man! To my great delight, I have broken free of that, like a slave who has got away from a rabid and savage master." I thought at the time that this was a good response, and I haven't changed my mind. I mean, there's no doubt that in old age you get a great deal of peace and freedom from things like sex. When the desires lose their intensity and ease up, then what happens is absolutely as Sophocles described—freedom from a great many demented masters. How- d ever, the one thing responsible for this, and for one's relationship with relatives as well, is not a person's old age, Socrates, but his character. If someone is self-disciplined and good-tempered, old age isn't too much of a burden; otherwise, it's not just a question of old age, Socrates—such a person will find life difficult when he's young as well.'

I was filled with admiration for him and his words, and because I wanted him to continue, I tried to pro- e voke him by saying, 'Cephalus, I think that most people would react to what you're saying with scepticism; they'd think that you're finding old age easy to bear not because of your character, but because of your great wealth. The rich have many consolations, they say.'

'You're right,' he said, 'they are sceptical. And they do have a point, though not as important a point as they imagine. The story about Themistocles is relevant here—how when the man from Seriphus was rudely saying that his fame was due not to his own merits but to his city, he replied, "It's true that I 330a wouldn't have become famous if I were a Seriphian, but it's also true that you wouldn't if you were an Athenian." The same principle applies to people who aren't rich and are finding old age hard to bear. It's true that a good man wouldn't find old age particularly easy to bear if he were poor, but it's also true that a bad man would never be content with himself even if he were wealthy.'

'Did you inherit most of your wealth, Cephalus,' I asked, 'or did you make it yourself?'

'What's that you say, Socrates?' he asked. 'Make b it myself? As a businessman, I come between my grandfather and my father. My grandfather (after whom I'm named) inherited assets approximately equal to what I have now, and increased them considerably; my father Lysanias, however, decreased them to less than they are now. It'll make me happy if I leave these sons of mine not less, but a little more than I inherited.'

'I'll tell you why I asked,' I said. 'It was because I got the impression that you don't particularly care for money, and this is usually the mark of someone who hasn't made it himself, whereas people who have made it themselves are twice as attached to it as anyone else. Poets are attached to their own compositions, fathers to their sons; in the same way, businessmen are concerned about money not only because it's useful (which is why everyone else is interested in it), but also because it is the product of their own labours. This makes them irritating to be with, since money is the only thing they're prepared to think highly of.'

'You're right,' he said.

'Yes,' I said. 'But there's another question I wanted to ask you. What do you think is the greatest benefit you've gained from being rich?'

'Something which many people might find implausible,' he answered. 'You see, Socrates, when thoughts of death start to impinge on a person's mind, he entertains fears and worries about things which never occurred to him before. In the past he used to laugh at the stories that are told about what goes on in Hades—about how someone who has done wrong here is bound to be punished there— but now they trouble his mind, in case they might be true. This might be due to the weakness of old age or it might be because, now that he's closer to the next world, he sees it more clearly; the result is that he becomes filled with anxiety and fear, and starts to make calculations and to see if he has wronged anyone in any way. Anyone who discovers that during his life he has committed a lot of crimes wakes up constantly in terror from his dreams, as children do, and also lives in dread; on the other hand, anyone who is aware of no wrong in himself faces the future with confidence and optimism which, as Pindar says as well, "comforts him in old age". To my mind, Socrates, he expresses it beautifully when he says that anyone who has spent his life behaving morally and justly has "Sweet hope as a companion, joyfully fostering his heart, comforting him in old age—hope which steers, more than anything else does, men's fickle intention." This is incredibly well put. And this is the context in which I value the possession of money so highly—at least for a decent, orderly person. I mean, the possession of money has a major role to play if one is to avoid cheating or lying against one's bet-

ter judgment, and also avoid the fear of leaving this life still owing some ritual offerings to a god or some money to someone. It serves a lot of other purposes too, but all things considered I'd say that for an intelligent person, Socrates, wealth is particularly useful in this far from insignificant context.'

'A thoroughly commendable sentiment, Cephalus,' I said. 'But what about this thing you mentioned, doing right? Shall we say that it is, without any qualification, truthfulness and giving back anything one has borrowed from someone? Or might the performance of precisely these actions sometimes be right, but sometimes wrong? This is the kind of thing I mean. I'm sure everyone would agree that if you'd borrowed weapons from a friend who was perfectly sane, but he went insane and then asked for the weapons back, you shouldn't give them back, and if you were to given them back you wouldn't be doing right, and neither would someone who was ready to tell the whole truth to a person like that.'

'You're right,' he agreed.

'It follows that this isn't the definition of morality, to tell the truth and to give back whatever one has borrowed.'

'Yes, it is, Socrates,' Polemarchus interjected. 'At least, it is if we're to believe Simonides.'

'Well now,' said Cephalus, 'I shall pass the discussion on to you two, since it's time for me to attend to the ceremony.'

'And shall I be your heir?' asked Polemarchus.

'Of course,' he said with a chuckle, and promptly left for the ceremony.

In a manner strongly reminiscent of Plato's earlier dialogues, Socrates draws inferences about morality by assuming that it is an area of expertise, and that what holds good for other areas of expertise will hold good for morality as well. Polemarchus could have denied that morality has a single field of operation, as crafts do: morality might have some broader function in human relationships, or its purpose might be something general, like promoting happiness. Lacking this insight, Polemarchus is tied into paradoxical knots. In a startling anticipation of Christian ethics (prefigured in the dialogues Crito and Gorgias), Socrates finally concludes that it is never right to harm anyone under any circumstances.

'Well then,' I told him, 'now that you've inherited the discussion, tell us what it is that Simonides says which you think is an accurate statement about morality.'

'That it is right to give anyone back what you owe them,' he said. 'In my opinion, this is a fine remark.'

'Well,' I said, 'it isn't easy to disagree with Simonides: he's a clever man—superhumanly so. But while *you* may understand what he means by this, Polemarchus, I don't. I mean, he obviously doesn't mean what we were talking about a moment ago, the returning of something one has been lent to someone insane who's asking for it back. And yet something lent is owed, wouldn't you say?'

'Yes,'

'And if the person asking for it back is insane, it's inconceivable that it should be given back, isn't it?'

'True,' he replied.

'Then apparently it wasn't this, but something else, that Simonides meant by the assertion that it is right to give back what is owed.'

'Yes, of course it was something else,' he said. 'His view is that friends owe friends good deeds, not bad ones.'

'I see,' I said. 'So if someone gives money back to someone who lent it to him, and this repayment and returning turns out to be harmful, and both the giver and the receiver are friends, then this is not a case of giving back what is owed: is this Simonides' meaning, according to you?'

'Yes, exactly.'

'Now, should we give back what is owed to our enemies?'

'Oh, yes,' he said. 'What is owed to them—yes, absolutely. And what an enemy owes an enemy, I think, is also what is appropriate—something bad.'

'There was apparently a certain obscurity, then, in Simonides' definition of morality,' I remarked. 'How typical of a poet! Although, as it turns out, he meant that it is right to give back to people what is appropriate for them, he called it what is owed to them.'

'I'm surprised you thought any different,' he said.

'But listen,' I said, 'suppose he were asked, "So, Simonides, take the art that we know as medicine. What is it? What does it give that is owed and appropriate, and to what does it give it?" What do you suppose his reply to us would be?'

'Obviously,' he answered, 'he'd reply that it is the art of giving drugs, food, and drink to bodies.'

'What about cookery? What art do we say it is? What does it give that is owed and appropriate, and to what does it give it?'

'It gives taste to cooked food.'

'All right. So which art—the art of giving what to what—might we call morality?'

'In order to be consistent with what was said earlier, Socrates,' he replied, 'it has to be the art of giving benefit and harm to friends and enemies respectively.'

'So Simonides claims that morality is doing good to one's friends and harm to one's enemies, does he?'

'I think so.'

'Now, where sickness and health are concerned, who is best able to do good to his friends and harm to his enemies when they aren't well?'

'A doctor.'

'And where the risks of a sea voyage are concerned, when friends are on board a ship?'

'A ship's captain.'

'And what about a moral person? In which walk of life or for what activity is he best able to benefit his friends and harm his enemies?'

'In fighting against enemies and in support of friends, I'd say.'

'All right. Now, my dear Polemarchus, a doctor is no use unless people are ill.'

'True.'

'And a captain is no use unless people are on a sea voyage.'

'Quite so.'

'Is a moral person, then, no use to anyone who is not at war?'

'No, I don't agree with that.'

'So morality is useful during times of peace too?'

'Yes.'

'And so is farming. Yes?'

'Yes.'

'To provide us with crops?'

'Yes.'

'And shoemaking too?'

'Yes.'

'To provide us with shoes, I imagine you'd say?'

'Exactly.'

'All right, then. What can we use morality for? What does it provide us with? What would you say morality is good for in times of peace?'

'For business contracts, Socrates.'

'By business contracts do you mean when people enter into association with one another, or what?'

'Yes, when people enter into association with one another.'

'So when there's a move to make in backgamb mon, is it a moral person, or an expert backgammon player, who is a good and useful associate?'

'An expert backgammon player.'

'And when it's a question of the positioning of bricks and stones, is a moral person a better and more useful associate than a builder?'

'Not at all.'

'Well, what kind of association is it that people enter into for which a moral person is a better associate than a builder or a musician? I mean, analogously to how a musician is better than a moral person when it comes to an association over melodies.'

'An association involving money, in my opinion.'

'Yes, Polemarchus, but what about when money is put to use? When you jointly need to buy or sell a horse, for instance, then I suppose an expert in c horses is a better associate, don't you think?'

'I suppose so.'

'And if you need to buy or sell a ship, then it's a shipwright or a sailor?'

'You could be right.'

'For what joint usage of money, then, is a moral person more useful than anyone else?'

'When we want to put it on deposit and have it in safe keeping, Socrates.'

'You mean when you don't want to put it to use, but just to have it in store?'

'Yes.'

d 'So morality is useful in relation to money at precisely the time when money is not in use?'

'So it seems.'

'Furthermore, when a pruning-knife needs to be kept safe, then morality is useful (whether you're on your own or have an associate); but when it needs using, then it's viticulture that is useful. Yes?'

'I suppose so.'

'And would you also say that when a shield or a lyre needs to be protected and kept unused, then morality is useful, whereas when they need using, then military or musical expertise is useful?'

'Of course.'

'In every instance, then, morality is useless when anything is being used, and useful when anything is not being used.'

'So it seems.'

'Morality can't be a very important thing, then, can it, my friend, if it is useful for useless objects. And there's another point for us to consider. In a fight—a boxing-match or any other kind of fight—isn't it the person who is expert at hitting who is also expert at protecting himself?'

'Yes.'

'And isn't it the person who knows how to give protection from a disease who is also the expert at secretly inducing the disease?'

'I would say so.'

'Moreover, it's one and the same person who's 334a good at protecting an army and at stealing the enemy's plans and outwitting the rest of his projects, isn't it?'

'Yes,'

'So anything one is good at protecting, one is also good at stealing.'

'So it seems.'

'If a moral person is good at protecting money, therefore, he's also good at stealing it.'

'That's what the argument suggests, anyway,' he said.

'Morality has been exposed, then,' I said. 'A moral person is a kind of thief, apparently. You probably got this notion from Homer. He speaks b warmly of Autolycus, Odysseus' grandfather on his mother's side, and also says that he surpassed everyone "at theft and perjury". So the view that morality is a kind of stealing is yours, Homer's, and Simonides'—with the qualification that it must be done to benefit friends and harm enemies. Was this what you meant?'

'It most certainly was not,' he said, 'but I'm no longer sure what I meant. I do still think this, however—that morality lies in helping one's friends and harming one's enemies.'

'When you say "friends", do you mean those who c appear to a person to be good, or those who genuinely are good (even if they don't appear to be)? And likewise for enemies.'

'It seems plausible to suggest', he said, 'that one treats as friends those one regards as good, and as enemies those one regards as bad.'

'Isn't it common to make mistakes about this, and think that people are good when they aren't, and vice versa?'

'Yes.'

'When this happens, then, doesn't one regard good people as enemies and bad people as friends?'

'Yes.'

'But all the same, in these circumstances it's right for one to help bad people and harm good people, d is it?'

'Apparently.'

'But good people are moral and not the kind to do wrong.'

'True.'

'On your line of reasoning, then, it's right to harm people who do no wrong.'

'Not at all, Socrates,' he said. 'My reasoning must be flawed, I suppose.'

'It's right to harm wrongdoers, then,' I said, 'and to help those who do right?'

'That sounds better.'

'But since there are lots of people who are com-
e pletely mistaken, Polemarchus, then it will commonly turn out to be right for people to harm friends (whom they regard as bad) and to help enemies (whom they regard as good). And in affirming this, we'll be contradicting what we said Simonides meant.'

'Yes,' he said, 'that is a consequence of what we're saying. Let's change tack, however: we're probably making a wrong assumption about friends and enemies.'

'What assumption, Polemarchus?'

'That someone who appears good is a friend.'

'What shall we change that to instead?' I asked.

'That someone who doesn't just appear good, but actually *is* good, is a friend; and that someone who
335a seems good, but actually isn't, is an apparent friend, not a genuine one. And the same goes for enemies.'

'So on this line of reasoning, it's a good man who is a friend, and a bad man who is an enemy.'

'Yes.'

'You're telling us, then, that our original description of morality, when we said that it was right to do good *to a friend* and harm to an enemy, was incomplete. Now you want us to add that it is right to do good to a friend, provided he is good, and to harm an enemy, provided he is bad. Is that right?'

b 'Yes,' he said, 'I think that's a good way to put it.'

'Can a moral person harm *anyone*?' I asked.

'Yes, he can,' he replied. 'He has to harm bad men, people who are his enemies.'

'When horses are harmed, do they improve or deteriorate?'

'Deteriorate.'

'In respect of a state of goodness for dogs or of a state of goodness for horses?'

'In respect of a state of goodness for horses.'

'So the same goes for dogs too: when they are harmed, they deteriorate in respect of what it is to be a good dog, not in respect of what it is to be a good horse. Is that right?'

'No doubt about it.'

'And where people are concerned, my friend, c shouldn't we say that when they're harmed they deteriorate in respect of what it is to be a good human?'

'Yes.'

'And isn't a moral person a good human?'

'There's no doubt about that either.'

'It necessarily follows, Polemarchus, that people who are harmed become less moral.'

'So it seems.'

'Now, can musicians use music to make people unmusical?'

'Impossible.'

'Can skilled horsemen use their skill to make people bad horsemen?'

'No.'

'So can moral people use morality to make people immoral? Or in general can good people use their d goodness to make people bad?'

'No, that's impossible.'

'I imagine this is because cooling things down, for instance, is not the function of warmth but of its opposite.'

'Yes.'

'And moistening things is not the function of dryness but of its opposite.'

'Yes.'

'So harming people is not the function of a good person, but of his opposite.'

'I suppose so.'

'And is a moral person a good person?'

'Of course.'

'It is not the job of a moral person, then, Polemarchus, to harm a friend or anyone else; it is the job of his opposite, as immoral person.'

'I think you're absolutely correct, Socrates,' he said.

'So the claim that it's right and moral to give back e to people what they are owed—if this is taken to mean that a moral person owes harm to his enemies and help to his friends—turns out to be a claim no clever person would make. I mean, it's false: we've found that it is never right to harm anyone.'

'I agree,' he said.

'You and I will join forces, then,' I said, 'to combat anyone who asserts that it is the view of Simonides or Bias or Pittacus or anyone else who is so sublimely clever.'

'Yes,' he said, 'I'm ready to play my part in the battle.'

'Do you know whose view I think it is,' I said, 336a

'that it's right to help one's friends and harm one's enemies?'

'Whose?' he asked.

'I think it was Periander or Perdiccas or Xerxes or Ismenias of Thebes or someone else like that—a rich man who fancied himself to be vastly powerful.'

'You're quite right,' he said.

'All right,' I said. 'Now that we've found that being moral and doing right don't consist in this, can we come up with an alternative definition?'

> Thrasymachus now bursts into the picture. Plato's portrait of Thrasymachus is patently unfavourable, but his position is at least forcefully argued and defended. Socrates first shows that his position— that morality is a convention to enable the stronger party to get the weaker party to act to the stronger party's advantage—cannot be universally true. Thrasymachus intends his view to be a cynical comment on the dog-eat-dog nature of the real world, but is now forced to admit that his views only really apply to ideal, infallible rulers. With a weak inference based on the art of medicine, Socrates concludes that no arts, including morality, are self-serving, but that they all look out for their subjects' interests.

b   Now, Thrasymachus had often made as if to interrupt us in mid-sentence and pounce on the argument, but he'd always been restrained by his neighbours, who had wanted to hear the discussion out. But when we did come to a break, and I'd asked this question, he could no longer remain silent: like a wild animal, he crouched and hurled himself at us as if to tear us apart.

Polemarchus and I were terrified and panic-stricken, but Thrasymachus bellowed out for all to c hear, 'What a lot of drivel, Socrates! Why are you deferentially bowing and scraping to each other like simpletons? If you really want to know what morality is, then don't just ask questions and look for applause by refuting any and every answer you get, because you've realized that it's easier to ask questions than it is to answer them. No, state an opinion yourself: say what you think morality is. And make d sure you state your view clearly and precisely, without saying that it is duty or benefit or profit or gain or advantage; I won't let you get away with any rubbish like that.'

I was scared stiff at his words, and I looked at him in fear. I think that if I hadn't seen him before he saw me, I'd have been unable to speak. But in fact I had got in the first look, when he originally began to get furious at the discussion, and so I was able to respond to him. 'Thrasymachus,' I said, trembling e with fear, 'please don't be cross with us. If Polemarchus and I are going wrong anywhere in the course of investigating the ideas, I assure you that we don't mean to. You can imagine that, if we were looking for money, we wouldn't under any circumstances choose to defer to each other in the course of the search and ruin our chances of finding it. It is morality we are looking for, however, and this is more valuable than pots of money; so you shouldn't think that we'd be so stupid as to give in to each other and not do our level best to discover it. Believe me, Thrasymachus, we're doing all we can. If we lack competence—which I suppose is the case— then pity is a far more reasonable feeling for you experts to have for us than impatience.'   337a

He erupted into highly sarcastic laughter at my words and said, 'God, there goes Socrates again, pretending to be an ignoramus! I knew this would happen; I even told the others here some time ago that you wouldn't be prepared to express opinions, and would feign ignorance and do anything rather than answer a question put to you.'

'That's because you're clever, Thrasymachus,' I said. 'You were well aware of the fact that if you were to ask someone what twelve is, and were to add as a rider to the question, "And just make sure you avoid saying that twelve is two times six, or b three times four, or six times two, or four times three. I won't let you get away with any nonsense like that"—well, I'm sure it was obvious to you that no one would answer a question phrased like that. But suppose this person said, "What do you mean, Thrasymachus? You don't want me to give any of the answers you've mentioned? But what if twelve really is one of those things, Thrasymachus? Shall I still avoid that answer—that is, not tell the truth? Or what would you have me do?" How would you respond to this?'   c

'Well,' he said, 'it's not as if the two cases were similar.'

'Why not?' I replied. 'Anyway, even if they aren't, and it's only that the person you've asked thinks they are, do you think that makes any difference? Won't he still state his opinion, whether or not we rule it out?'

'That's what you're going to do as well, is it?' he asked. 'Respond with one of the answers I ruled out?'

'I wouldn't be surprised if I decided to do that, once I'd looked into the matter,' I said.

d   'What if I were to demonstrate that there's another answer you can give about morality,' he asked, 'which isn't any of those answers and is better than any of them? What penalty would you expect?'

'The penalty which is appropriate for ignorance, of course,' I said, 'which is learning from an expert. That's the penalty I expect.'

'Don't be naïve,' he said. 'You can't just learn: you must pay for it too.'

'If I ever have the money, I will,' I said.

'He has it,' said Glaucon. 'We'll all help Socrates out financially, so as far as the money is concerned, Thrasymachus, go ahead and speak.'

e   'Oh yes, sure!' he said. 'So that Socrates can get his way and not make any claims himself, while he attacks and criticizes someone else's claims.'

'That's because I have no choice, Thrasymachus,' I explained. 'How can anyone express a view when he's not only ignorant, but also admits his ignorance? Moreover, when he's been forbidden to mention any opinion he might happen to hold by a man of considerable calibre? No, it's you who ought to
338a speak, really, since you do claim to have knowledge and to be able to express it. So please do what I'm asking: if you state your view, you'll be doing me a favour, and also generously teaching Glaucon here and all the others too.'

My words prompted Glaucon and the others to urge him to do what I was asking, and although it was clear that Thrasymachus wanted to be heard (since he thought he had an impressive position to state, which would win him acclaim), yet he continued to dissemble and to argue that it should be me who stated my position. Eventually, however,
b   he gave in, and then added, 'Now you can see what Socrates is good at—he refuses to do any teaching himself, but he goes around learning from other people and doesn't even give them thanks in return.'

'You're quite right to say that I learn from other people, Thrasymachus,' I said, 'but quite wrong to say that I don't repay them with gratitude. I pay what I can—and compliments are all I can give, since I don't have money. If I think someone has a good idea, I'm quick to applaud it—as you'll find out very soon when you tell us your opinion, since I'm sure it will be a good one.'

c   'All right, then, listen to this,' he said. 'My claim is that morality is nothing other than the advantage of the stronger party . . . Well, why aren't you applauding? No, you won't let yourself do that.'

'First I need to understand your meaning,' I told him. 'I don't yet. You say that right is the advantage of the stronger party, but what on earth do you mean by this, Thrasymachus? Surely you're not claiming, in effect, that if Poulydamas the pancratiast is stronger than us and it's to his advantage, for the sake of his physique, to eat beef, then this food is advantageous, and therefore right, for us too, who d are weaker than him?'

'Foul tactics, Socrates,' he said, 'to interpret what I say in the way which allows you unscrupulously to distort it most.'

'No, you've got me wrong, Thrasymachus,' I said, 'I just want you to explain yourself better.'

'Don't you know, then,' he said, 'that some countries are dictatorships, some are democracies, and some are aristocracies?'

'Of course I do.'

'And that what has power in any given country is the government?'

'Yes.'

'Now, each government passes laws with a view e to its own advantage: a democracy makes democratic laws, a dictatorship makes dictatorial laws, and so on and so forth. In so doing, each government makes it clear that what is right and moral for its subjects is what is to its own advantage; and each government punishes anyone who deviates from what is advantageous to itself as if he were a criminal and a wrongdoer. So, Socrates, that is what I claim morality is: it is the same in every country, and it is what is to the advantage of the current gov- 339a ernment. Now, of course, it's the current government which has power, and the consequence of this, as anyone who thinks about the matter correctly can work out, is that morality is everywhere the same— the advantage of the stronger party.'

'Now I see what you mean,' I said. 'And I'll try to see whether or not your claim is true. Your position too, Thrasymachus, is that morality is advantage—despite the fact that you ruled this answer out for me—except that you immediately add "of the stronger party".'

'Hardly a trivial addition,' he said.   b

'Whether or not it is important isn't yet clear. What is clear is that we must try to find out whether your claim is true. The point is that I agree that morality is some kind of advantage, but you are qualifying this and claiming that it is the advantage of the stronger party; since I haven't made up my mind about this qualified version, we must look into the matter.'

'Go ahead,' he said.

'All right,' I said. 'Here's a question for you: you're also claiming, I assume, that obedience to the government is right?'

'Yes, I am.'

c 'And is the government in every country infallible, or are they also capable of error?'

'They are certainly capable of error,' he said.

'So when they turn to legislation, they sometimes get it right, and sometimes wrong?'

'Yes, I suppose so.'

'When they get it right, the laws they make will be to their advantage, but when they get it wrong, the laws will be to their disadvantage. Is that what you're saying?'

'Yes.'

'And you're also saying that their subjects must act in accordance with any law that is passed, and that this constitutes doing right?'

'Of course.'

d 'Then it follows from your line of argument that it is no more right to act to the advantage of the stronger party than it is to do the opposite, to act to their disadvantage.'

'What are you saying?' he asked.

'Exactly the same as you, I think; but let's have a closer look. We're agreed that sometimes, when a government orders its subjects to do things, it is utterly mistaken about its own best interest, but that it's right for the subjects to act in accordance with any order issued by the government. Isn't that what we agreed?'

'Yes, I suppose so.'

e 'Then you must also suppose', I continued, 'that you have agreed that it is right to do things which are not to the advantage of the government and the stronger party. When the rulers mistakenly issue orders which are bad for themselves, and since you claim that it is right for people to act in conformity with all the government's orders, then, my dear Thrasymachus, doesn't it necessarily follow that it is right to do the opposite of what your position affirmed? I mean, the weaker party is being ordered to do what is disadvantageous to the stronger party, obviously.'

340a 'Yes, Socrates,' said Polemarchus, 'that's perfectly clear.'

'Of course,' Cleitophon interrupted, 'if you're going to act as a witness for Socrates.'

'There's no need for a witness,' Polemarchus replied. 'Thrasymachus himself admits that rulers sometimes issue orders which are bad for themselves, and that it's right for people to carry out these orders.'

'That's because Thrasymachus maintained that it was right to carry out the rulers' instructions, Polemarchus.'

'Yes, Cleitophon, and he also maintained that right is the advantage of the stronger party. And once b he'd affirmed both of these propositions, he also agreed that sometimes the stronger party tells the weaker party, which is subject to it, to do things which are disadvantageous to it. And from these premisses it follows that morality is no more what is advantageous to the stronger party than it is what is disadvantageous to the stronger party.'

'But,' Cleitophon said, 'what he meant by the advantage of the stronger party was what the stronger party *thinks* is to its advantage. This is what he was maintaining the weaker party ought to do, and this is what he was maintaining morality is.'

'But that's not what he said,' Polemarchus remarked.

'Never mind, Polemarchus,' I said. 'If this is what c Thrasymachus is saying now, then let's accept it as his view. But do please tell me, Thrasymachus: *did* you mean to define morality as to what appears to the stronger party to be to its advantage, whether or not it really is to its advantage? Is that how we are to understand your meaning?'

'Absolutely not!' he protested. 'Do you suppose I would describe someone who makes mistakes as the stronger party when he is making a mistake?'

'Yes,' I replied, 'I did think you were saying this, when you agreed that rulers are not infallible, but also make mistakes.'

'That's because you're a bully in discussions, Socrates,' he said. 'I mean, to take the first exam- d ple that comes to mind, do you describe someone who makes mistakes about his patients as a doctor in virtue of the fact that he makes mistakes? Or do you describe someone who makes mistakes in his calculations as a mathematician, at precisely the time when he is making a mistake, and in virtue of the mistake that he is making? It's true that the expression is in our language: we say that a doctor or a mathematician or a teacher makes mistakes; but in fact, in my opinion, to the extent that each of them e is what we call him, he never makes mistakes. And the consequence of this is that, strictly speaking—

and you're the stickler for verbal precision—no professional makes mistakes: a mistake is due to a failure of knowledge, and for as long as that lasts he is not a professional. Professional, expert, ruler—no ruler makes a mistake at precisely the time when he is ruling, despite the universal usage of expressions like "The doctor made a mistake" or "The ruler made a mistake". So, when I stated my position to you recently, you should appreciate that I too was speaking like that; but the most precise formulation is in 341a fact that a ruler, to the extent that he is a ruler, does not make mistakes; and in not making mistakes he passes laws which are in his best interest; and any subject of his should act in conformity with these laws. Consequently, as I said in the first place, my position is that morality is acting to the advantage of the stronger party.'

'Well, Thrasymachus,' I said, 'so you think I'm a bully, do you?'

'Yes, I do,' he said.

'And that's because you think my questions were premeditated attempts to wrong you?'

'I'm certain of it,' he said. 'And you won't gain b any advantage from it, firstly because I'm aware of your unscrupulous tactics, and secondly because as long as I am aware of them, you won't be able to use the argument to batter me down.'

'My dear Thrasymachus,' I protested, 'the idea would never even occur to me! But we must make sure that this situation doesn't arise again, so please would you make something perfectly clear? Is it, according to you, the ruler and the stronger person in the loose sense, or in what you were just calling the precise sense, whose interest, since he is the stronger party, it is right for the weaker party to act in?'

'I'm talking about the ruler in the most precise sense possible,' he replied. 'You can do anything you like, as far as I'm concerned, so try your unscrupulous and bullying tactics on that, if you can! But you don't stand a chance.'

c   'Do you think I'm crazy enough to try to shave a lion and bully Thrasymachus?' I asked.

'Well, you tried just now,' he said, 'even though you're a nonentity at that too.'

'That's enough of that sort of remark,' I said. 'But let's take this doctor you were talking about a short while ago—the one who's a doctor in the strict sense of the term. Is he a businessman, or someone who attends to sick people? Think about the genuine doctor, please.'

'He attends to sick people,' he replied.

'What about a ship's captain? Is the true captain in charge of sailors or a sailor?'

'In charge of sailors.'

'In other words, we shouldn't take any account of d the fact that he is on board a ship and describe him as a sailor. I mean, it isn't because he's on a ship that he's called a captain, but because of his expertise and because he has authority over the sailors.'

'True,' he said.

'Now, does each of the various parties in these situations have a particular advantage to gain?'

'Yes.'

'And isn't it the case,' I went on, 'that the *raison d'être* of a branch of expertise is to consider the welfare and interest of each party and then procure it?'

'Yes, that is what expertise is for,' he answered.

'Is there anything which is in the interest of any branch of expertise except being as perfect as possible?'

'I don't understand the question.'   e

'For instance,' I said, 'suppose you were to ask me whether it's enough for the body just to be the body, or whether it needs anything else. I'd reply, "There's no doubt at all that it needs something else. That's why the art of medicine has been invented, because the body is flawed and it isn't enough for it to be like that. The branch of expertise has been developed precisely for the purpose of procuring the body's welfare." Would this reply of mine be correct, do you think, or not?' I asked.

'Yes, it would,' he said.

'Well now, is medicine itself flawed? Are all 342a branches of expertise imperfect? For instance, eyes need sight and ears need hearing, and that's why they need a branch of expertise to consider their welfare in precisely these respects and to procure it. Is expertise itself somehow inherently flawed as well, so that each branch of expertise needs a further branch to consider its welfare, and this supervisory branch needs yet another one, and so on *ad infinitum*? Or does every art consider its own interest and welfare? Or is the whole question of it, or another b art, being needed to consider its welfare in view of its flaws irrelevant, in the sense that no branch of expertise is flawed or faulty in the slightest, and it's inappropriate for any branch of expertise to investigate the welfare of anything other than its own area of expertise? In other words, any branch of expertise is flawless and perfect, provided it's a genuine branch of expertise—that is, as long as it wholly is what it is, nothing more and nothing less. Please consider this issue with the same strict use of language we were using before, and tell me: am I right or not?'

'I think you're right,' he said.

c   'It follows, then,' I said, 'that medicine does not consider the welfare of medicine, but the welfare of the body.'

'Yes,' he said.

'And horsemanship considers the welfare of horses, not of horsemanship. In short, no branch of expertise considers its own advantage, since it isn't deficient in any respect: it considers the welfare of its area of expertise.'

'So it seems,' he said.

'But surely, Thrasymachus, the branches of expertise have authority and power over their particular areas of expertise.'

He gave his assent to this with extreme reluctance.

'So no branch of knowledge considers or enjoins the advantage of the stronger party, but the advantage of the weaker party, which is subject to it.'

d Eventually, he agreed to this too, although he tried to argue against it. Once he'd agreed, however, I said, 'Surely, then, no doctor, in his capacity as doctor, considers or enjoins what is advantageous to the doctor, but what is advantageous to the patient? I mean, we've agreed that a doctor, in the strict sense of the term, is in charge of bodies, not a businessman. Isn't that what we agreed?'

He concurred.

'And a ship's captain too is, strictly speaking, in charge of sailors, not a sailor?'

e He agreed.

'So since captains are like this and wield authority in this way, they won't consider and enjoin the interest of the captain, but what is advantageous to the sailor, the subject.'

He reluctantly agreed.

'Therefore, Thrasymachus,' I said, 'no one in any other kind of authority either, in his capacity as ruler, considers or enjoins his own advantage, but the advantage of his subject, the person for whom he practises his expertise. Everything he says and everything he does is said and done with this aim in mind and with regard to what is advantageous to and appropriate for this person.'

Socrates has tried to reduce Thrasymachus' position to the relatively trivial claims that rulers rule in their own interest, and that morality is obeying rulers. Thrasymachus therefore changes his formulation, but not his tack. The important thing about morality being to someone else's advantage, he says, is that it shows that morality is a bad thing, and weak, and unprofitable to its possessor. Socrates' inability (or possibly artificial refusal) to distinguish higher-order arts from lower-order ones results in the strange position that profit-making is a separate art, so that (again) no art— or at least no art other than profit-making—seeks the profit or advantage of the artisan.

Once we'd reached this point in the discussion, it 343a was perfectly clear to everyone that the definition of morality had been turned upside down. Thrasymachus didn't respond to my last remarks, but instead said, 'Tell me, Socrates, do you have a nurse?'

'What?' I asked. 'Shouldn't you come up with some response rather than this question?'

'The point is,' he said, 'that she takes no notice of your runny nose and lets it dribble on when it needs wiping, when you can't even tell her the difference between sheep and shepherd.'

'I haven't the faintest idea what you're getting at,' I said.

'What I'm getting at is your notion that shepherds b or cowherds consider what is good for their sheep or their cows, and fatten them up and look after them, with any aim in mind other than what is good for their masters and for themselves; and also at your supposition that the attitude which people with political authority—who are the real rulers—have towards their subjects differs in the slightest from how one might feel about sheep, and that what they consider day and night is anything other than their own advantage and how to gain it. You're so far off un- c derstanding right and wrong, and morality and immorality, that you don't even realize that morality and right are actually good for someone else—they are the advantage of the stronger party, the ruler— and bad for the underling at the receiving end of the orders. Nor do you realize that the opposite is true for immorality: the wrongdoer lords it over those moral simpletons—that's what they are, really— while his subjects do what is to his advantage, since he is stronger, and make him happy by doing his bidding, but don't further their own happiness in the slightest.

'You fool, Socrates, don't you see? In any and d every situation, a moral person is worse off than an immoral one. Suppose, for instance, that they're doing some business together, which involves one of them entering into association with the other: by the time the association is dissolved, you'll never find the moral person up on the immoral one—he'll be

worse off. Or again, in civic matters, if there's a tax on property, then a moral person pays more tax than an immoral one even when they're both equally well off; and if there's a hand-out, then the one gets noth-
e ing, while the other makes a lot. And when each of them holds political office, even if a moral person loses out financially in no other way, his personal affairs deteriorate through neglect, while his moral-ity stops him making any profit from public funds, and moreover his family and friends fall out with him over his refusal to help them out in unfair ways; in all these respects, however, an immoral person's experience is the opposite.

'I'm talking about the person I described a short
344a while ago, the one with the power to secure huge advantages for himself. This is the person you should consider, if you want to assess the extent to which immorality rather than morality is personally advantageous—and this is something you'll appre-ciate most easily if you look at immorality in its most perfect form and see how it enhances a wrongdoer's life beyond measure, but ruins the lives of his vic-tims, who haven't the stomach for crime, to the same degree. It's dictatorship I mean, because whether it takes stealth or overt violence, a dictator steals what doesn't belong to him—consecrated and unconse-crated objects, private possessions, and public prop-erty—and does so not on a small scale, but com-
b prehensively. Anyone who is caught committing the merest fraction of these crimes is not only punished, but thoroughly stigmatized as well: small-scale criminals who commit these kinds of crimes are called temple-robbers, kidnappers, burglars, thieves, and robbers. On the other hand, when someone ap-propriates the assets of the citizen body and then goes on to rob them of their very freedom and en-slave them, then denigration gives way to congrat-
c ulation, and it isn't only his fellow citizens who call him happy, but anyone else who hears about his con-summate wrongdoing does so as well. The point is that immorality has a bad name because people are afraid of being at the receiving end of it, not of do-ing it.

'So you see, Socrates, immorality—if practised on a large enough scale—has more power, licence, and authority than morality. And as I said at the begin-ning, morality is really the advantage of the stronger party, while immorality is profitable and advanta-geous to oneself.'

d   After flooding our ears, like an attendant in the baths, with this torrential gush of words, Thrasy-machus was thinking of leaving. No one there would let him go, however: they forced him to stay and justify what he'd been saying. I myself was partic-ularly insistent. 'My dear Thrasymachus,' I said, 'you surely aren't thinking of leaving? You can't just pelt us with words, so to speak, and then leave before adequately demonstrating—or before finding out yourself—whether or not they're true. Or do you think that what you're attempting to define is a triv-ial matter, and not how anyone can live his life in e the most rewarding manner?'

'Am I disagreeing with you?' Thrasymachus protested.

'You do give that impression,' I replied, 'unless it's just us you don't care about in the slightest, and you don't spare a thought for whether our ignorance of what you're claiming to know will make us live better or worse lives. No, Thrasymachus, please do 345a your best to enlighten us too: it won't turn out badly for you to do so many of us a favour. I'll tell you my position: I'm not convinced. I do not think that immorality is more profitable than morality, not even if it is given free rein and never prevented from getting its own way; and even if I grant you your immoral person, Thrasymachus, with the power to do wrong either by wealth or by brute force, for my part I'm still not convinced that it is more profitable than morality. It's possible that someone else here feels the same, and that I'm not alone; so, Thrasy- b machus, you must come up with a good enough ar-gument to convince us that rating morality higher than immorality is a mistake.'

'How do you expect me to do that?' he asked. 'If what I've just been saying doesn't convince you, what else can I do? Do you want me to spoonfeed the argument into your mind?'

'No, I certainly don't want you to do that,' I said. 'Above all, I'd like you to be consistent; or if you do change your mind, I'd like you to do so openly, without trying to deceive us. What's happening, you see, Thrasymachus—I mean, we haven't completed our investigation of what you were saying before— c is that although you started by trying to define the true doctor, you didn't maintain the same level of precision when you subsequently turned to the true shepherd. You don't think that the reason a shep-herd, in his capacity as shepherd, herds sheep is what is best for the sheep; you think he's like a dinner-guest when a meal is due, and is interested only in indulging himself—or alternatively that he behaves like a businessman rather than a shepherd, and is in-d terested only in making money. But of course the sole concern of shepherding is to procure the best for what is in its charge, since its own best state has been sufficiently procured, as we know, as long as it wholly and entirely is shepherding. The same reasoning, *I* thought, was what compelled us not long ago to conclude that all authority (whether political or non-political), *qua* authority, considers what is e best for nothing except its subjects, its wards. But do you think that people with political authority—the "real" rulers—exercise authority willingly?'

'I most definitely do not *think* so,' he replied. 'I'm absolutely certain of it!'

'But, Thrasymachus,' I said, 'don't you realize that no other form of authority is willingly exercised by its holder? People demand wages, on the grounds that the power isn't going to benefit *them*, but those who are in their charge. I mean, tell me this: when 346a we want to distinguish one branch of expertise from another, don't we do so by distinguishing what it is capable of doing? And please, Thrasymachus, make sure that your reply expresses what you really believe; otherwise, we won't make any progress.'

'Yes, that's how we distinguish it,' he said.

'And doesn't every branch of expertise have its own particular benefit to bestow as well, rather than one which it shares with other branches of expertise? For instance, medicine confers health, naval captaincy confers safety at sea, and so on.'

'Yes.'

b 'And isn't an income conferred by expertise at earning money? I mean, this is what it is capable of doing. You surely don't identify medicine and captaincy, do you? We must do as you suggested and make precise distinctions, so if a ship's captain recovers from illness because seafaring is good for him, does this lead you to call what he does medicine?'

'Of course not,' he said.

'Nor, I imagine, if someone recovers from illness while earning money, do you describe moneymaking skill as medical skill.'

'Of course not.'

'Well, suppose someone earns money while restoring health? Does this make you describe medicine as moneymaking?'

c 'No.'

'We've agreed that every branch of expertise has its own particular benefit to bestow, haven't we?'

'Yes, I grant you that,' he said.

'So if there's any benefit which the practitioners of every branch of expertise share, then obviously this benefit must come from something which is the same for all of them, and which they all equally make use of, over and above making use of their own particular expertise.'

'I suppose so,' he said.

'And it's our view that practitioners of branches of expertise benefit by earning money because they make use of the skill of moneymaking in addition to their own particular skill.'

He reluctantly agreed.

'It follows that no one benefits, in the sense of d earning money, as a result of practising his own branch of expertise. Instead, given that our enquiry has to be conducted with precision, we should say that medicine creates health, while moneymaking creates an income, and that building creates a house, while moneymaking may accompany building and create an income, and so on for the other branches of expertise: each of them has its own job to do and benefits what is in its charge. But leaving wages aside, is there any benefit which a practitioner gains from his expertise?'

'Apparently not,' he said.

'And what about when he works for free? Does e he in fact fail to confer any benefit at that time?'

'No, I think he does.'

'So, Thrasymachus, it's now clear that no branch of expertise or form of authority procures benefit for itself; as we were saying some time ago, it procures and enjoins benefit for its subject. It considers the advantage of its subject, the weaker party, not that of the stronger party. That, my dear Thrasymachus, is why I was proposing just now that no one willingly chooses authority and the task of righting other people's wrongs; they ask to be paid for it, because 347a anyone who works properly with his expertise consistently fails to work for his own welfare, and also fails to legislate for his own welfare when he gives instructions as a professional. It isn't *his* welfare, but that of his subject, which is his concern. This presumably explains why it is necessary to pay people with money or prestige before they are prepared to hold authority, or to punish them if they refuse.'

'What do you mean, Socrates?' asked Glaucon. 'I recognize your two modes of payment, but I don't know what punishment you are referring to and how it replaces payment.'

'Then you don't know what kind of payment is needed to induce truly excellent people to be pre- b pared to rule,' I said. 'Don't you realize that to say that someone is interested in prestige or money is thought—and rightly thought—to be insulting?'

'Yes, I know that,' he said.

'Well,' I explained, 'that's why neither money nor prestige tempts good people to accept power. You see, if they overtly require money for being in charge, they'll be called hired hands, and if they covertly make money for themselves out of the possession of power, they'll be called thieves; and they don't want either of these alternatives. On the other hand, they won't do it for prestige either, since they aren't ambitious. So one has to pressurize them and c threaten them with punishment, otherwise they'll never assume power; and this is probably the origin of the conventional view that it's shameful to *want* to take power on, rather than waiting until one has no choice. The ultimate punishment for being unwilling to assume authority oneself is to be governed by a worse person, and it is fear of this happening, I think, which prompts good men to assume power occasionally. On these occasions, they don't embark d upon government with the expectation of gaining some advantage or benefit from it: their attitude is that they have no choice in the matter, in the sense that they haven't been able to find people better than themselves, or even their equals, to whom they might entrust the task. The chances are that were a community of good men to exist, the competition to avoid power would be just as fierce as the competition for power is under current circumstances. In such a community, it would be glaringly obvious that any genuine ruler really is incapable of considering his own welfare, rather than that of his subject, and the consequence would be that anyone with any sense would prefer receiving benefit to all the problems that go with conferring it. So anyway, I utterly disagree with Thrasymachus' assertion that e morality is the advantage of the stronger party; but we've examined that topic enough for the time being.'

Thrasymachus has also claimed that immorality is more rewarding than morality. Socrates now attacks this claim, which is also the target of much of the rest of Republic. In an argument which is rather too clever for its own good, Socrates first argues that an immoral person's behaviour resembles that of bad, stupid people in other areas of expertise, rather than that of good, intelligent people. The argument exploits an ambiguity in superiority, which can mean 'doing better than' or 'having more than'; and, by means of the analogy between morality and skill, it assumes that an immoral person is a failure where a moral person succeeds. In fact, however, moral and immoral people have different goals.

'Thrasymachus' current claim, however, is that a life of crime is better than a life of integrity, and this seems to me to be a far more important assertion. Do you have a preference, Glaucon?' I asked. 'Which view do you think is closer to the truth?'

'I think a moral life is more rewarding.'

'Did you hear Thrasymachus' recent long list of 348a the advantages of an immoral life?' I asked.

'I did,' he answered, 'but I'm not convinced.'

'Shall we try to convince him, then, if we possibly can, of the falsehood of his claim?'

'Yes, of course, let's,' he said.

'Well,' I said, 'if we counter his claim by drawing up an alternative list of all the advantages of morality, and then he responds to that, and we respond to his response, we'll find ourselves in the position of having to add up advantages and measure the lengths of our respective lists, and before we b know it we'll need jurors to adjudicate for us. On the other hand, if we conduct the investigation as we did just now, by trying to win each other's consent, then we'll be our own jurors *and* claimants.'

'Quite so,' he said.

'Which plan do you like, then?' I asked.

'The latter,' he said.

'All right, then, Thrasymachus,' I said, 'let's go back to the beginning. Could you please confirm for us that your claim is that perfect immorality is more profitable than perfect morality?'

'Yes, that's my claim,' he said, 'and I've ex- c plained why too.'

'And here's another question about them: do you think that one of them is a good state and the other is a bad one?'

'Of course.'

'That is, morality is a good state, and immorality a bad one?'

'Don't be so naïve, Socrates,' he said. 'Would I say that when I'm claiming that it's immorality which is profitable, not morality?'

'What *is* your position, then?'

'The opposite of what you said,' he replied.

'That morality is bad?'

'No, it's sheer simplicity.'

'So you're saying that immorality is duplicity, are d you?'

'No, it's sound judgement,' he said.

'Do you really think that criminals are clever, good people, Thrasymachus?'

e 'Yes, if their criminality is able to manifest in a perfect form and they are capable of dominating countries and nations. I suppose you think I was talking about pickpockets. Actually,' he added, 'activities like that are rewarding too, if you can get away with them, but they're insignificant—unlike the ones I've just mentioned.'

'Yes, I see what you mean,' I said. 'But I'm surprised you count immorality as a form of goodness and cleverness, and morality as the opposite.'

'Nevertheless, that's exactly what I do.'

'You've come up with a rather intractable idea this time,' I commented. 'It's not easy to know how to respond to it. If you were proposing that immorality is profitable, but also conceding (as others do) that it's contemptible and bad, then our conversation could proceed against a background of convention. However, since you've made the enterprising suggestion that it's to be classified along with goodness and cleverness, you're obviously going to 349a say that it is a fine, effective quality, and will attribute to it all the other properties which we tend to ascribe to morality.'

'Your prophecy couldn't be more accurate,' he said.

'All the same,' I said, 'I musn't be put off. I must continue with the discussion and carry on with the investigation, as long as I feel that you're speaking your mind. I mean, I get the impression, Thrasymachus, that now you aren't toying with us in the slightest, but are expressing your beliefs about the way things truly are.'

'What does it matter to you whether or not it's what I believe?' he said. 'Why don't you just tackle what I'm saying?'

'It doesn't matter to me at all,' I said. 'But here's another question I'd like you to try to answer, over b and above what you've already said. Do you think a moral person would wish to set himself up as superior to another moral person?'

'Of course he wouldn't,' he replied. 'Otherwise he wouldn't be the civilized simpleton he is.'

'Well, would he want to set himself up as superior to moral behaviour?'

'Again, no,' he replied.

'Would he, or would he not, want and intend to set himself up as superior to an immoral person?'

'He would intend to,' he replied, 'but he wouldn't be able to.'

'I'm not asking whether he'd be able to do it,' I said. 'My question is: isn't it the case that a moral person does not intend or wish to set himself up as superior to another moral person, but only to an im- c moral person?'

'That's correct,' he said.

'What about an immoral person? Does he want to set himself up as superior to a moral person and to moral behaviour?'

'Of course,' he replied. 'He wants to gain the upper hand in everything.'

'So will an immoral person also try to set himself up as superior to another immoral person and to immoral behaviour? In short, will he struggle to gain the upper hand over everyone else in everything?'

'Yes.'

'Let's put it this way,' I said. 'A moral person doesn't set himself up as superior to people who are like him, but only to people who are unlike him; an immoral person, on the other hand, sets himself up as superior to people who are like him as well as to people who are unlike him.'

'You couldn't have put it better,' he said. d

'Now, an immoral person is clever and good, and a moral person is neither clever nor good. Isn't that right?'

'Yes, you've put that well too,' he said.

'So is it the case that an immoral person also *resembles* a clever, good person, while a moral person does not?' I asked.

'Naturally,' he replied. 'Since that's the type of person he is, then of course he resembles others of the same type; and of course a moral person does not resemble them.'

'Fine. So each of them is of the same type as people he resembles?'

'That goes without saying,' he said.

'All right, Thrasymachus. Do you acknowledge that some people are musical and some aren't?' e

'I do.'

'Which ones are clever and which aren't?'

'The musical ones are clever, of course, and the unmusical ones aren't.'

'And if someone is clever at something, isn't he also good at it, and bad at it if he isn't clever at it?'

'Yes.'

'And doesn't the same apply to medicine?'

'Yes.'

'Do you think, then, Thrasymachus, that when a

musical person is tuning a lyre—tightening and slackening the strings—he would want to set himself up as superior to, and gain the upper hand over, another musical person?'

'No, I don't think so.'

'As superior to an unmusical person, then?'

'Inevitably,' he said.

350a 'And what about a doctor? Do you think that in dietary matters he would have the slightest desire to set himself up as superior to another doctor or to medical practice?'

'Of course not.'

'But as superior to non-medical people and practice?'

'Yes.'

'Consider any instance of knowledge or ignorance. Do you think that the actions or words of anyone who is knowledgeable in anything are motivated by a desire to surpass the actions or words of another person with the same knowledge? Don't you think that his actions and words would be identical to those of someone like him in the same circumstances?'

'Yes, I suppose that's bound to be the case,' he said.

'What about an ignoramus? Wouldn't he try to set
b himself up as superior to knowledgeable people and to ignorant people equally?'

'I suppose so.'

'A knowledgeable person is clever, isn't he?'

'Yes.'

'And a clever person is good?'

'Yes.'

'So it's if someone is good and clever that he won't want to set himself up as superior to people who are like him, but only to people who are unlike him and have nothing in common with him.'

'So it seems.'

'If someone is bad and ignorant, however, he'll want to set himself up as superior to people who are like him as well as to people who are unlike him.'

'I suppose so.'

'Well, Thrasymachus,' I said, 'we found that it was an immoral person who sets himself up as superior to people who are like him as well as to people who are unlike him, didn't we? Isn't that what you said?'

'I did,' he replied.

c 'And a moral person won't set himself up as superior to people who are like him, but only to people who are unlike him?'

'Yes.'

'It follows,' I said, 'that it is a moral person who resembles a clever, good person, and an immoral person who resembles a bad, ignorant person.'

'It looks that way.'

'And we agreed that each of them is of the same type as people he is like.'

'Yes, we did.'

'We've proved, then, that it is a moral person who is good and clever, whereas an immoral person is ignorant and bad.'

Socrates launches an attack on the effectiveness of immoral behaviour. Criminals fall out with one another, and therefore cannot act in concert; an immoral individual, such as Thrasymachus' dictator, falls out with himself. Thrasymachus meekly accepts this idea (which prefigures the psychology and the definition of morality which will occur later in Republic) because he accepts that immorality is essentially destructive of concord.

Now, although Thrasymachus did concede all these points, it wasn't as easy as I'm making it sound by describing it: he was hauled along with great re- d luctance, sweating profusely (since it was the hot season). And I also saw then something I'd never seen before—a red-faced Thrasymachus.

So anyway, we agreed that morality was a good state and was knowledge, and that immorality was a bad state and was ignorance. Next I said, 'All right. We may have settled that issue, but we also have before us the claim that immorality is effective. Do you remember, Thrasymachus?'

'Yes, I remember,' he replied. 'But I'm not satisfied with the statements you've just been making. I could address them, but I'm sure that if I did, you'd claim that I was holding forth like an orator. So either let me say what I want and for as long as I want, e or go on with your questions, if you insist on doing that, and I'll go on saying "All right" and nodding and shaking my head as if I were listening to old women telling stories.'

'But you must never go against what you actually believe,' I said.

'Why shouldn't I?' he said. 'It makes you happy. You won't let me speak—do you want more from me than that?'

'No, not at all,' I replied. 'If you'll do what you said, that's fine, and I'll ask the questions.'

'Go ahead, then.'

'Well, here's the question I was getting at just now; I think it's the logical next one for our investigation. When morality is compared with immorality, what do we learn about morality? I mean, the suggestion was made that immorality is more powerful and more effective than morality; but the fact that we've now established that morality is a good state and is knowledge will make it easy to prove, I think, that it's also more effective than immorality, given that immorality is ignorance, as everyone knows by now. However, I don't want our investigation to be couched in such abstract terms, Thrasymachus, but rather as follows: would you agree that it is wrong for a community to undertake the domination of other communities, to deprive other communities of their freedom, and to keep a number of other communities subservient to itself?'

'Of course it is,' he said. 'And the better the community—the more perfectly immoral—the more it will act in exactly that way.'

'I appreciate that this is your position,' I said, 'but what I'm doing is exploring an aspect of it and asking whether a community which is stronger than another community will retain its power if it doesn't have morality, or whether it can do so only if it has morality.'

'If your recent assertion was correct,' he replied, 'that morality is knowledge, then it will take morality; but if I'm right, it takes immorality.'

'Thrasymachus,' I said, 'I'm really pleased that you're not just nodding and shaking your head, but are giving these excellent answers.'

'I'm doing it to make you happy,' he said.

'Thank you. You'll carry on making me happy if you answer this question of mine. Do you think that a community or an army or pirates or thieves or any other band which forms for the purpose of wrongdoing would be capable of doing anything if the members of the band wrong one another?'

'Of course not,' he said.

'But if they don't wrong one another, then they stand a better chance of success?'

'Yes.'

'Because immorality makes for mutual conflict, hatred, and antagonism, while moral behaviour makes for concord and friendship. Is that right?'

'I'll grant you that: I don't want to quarrel with you,' he said.

'Thank you, Thrasymachus. Now here's another question for you. If it's a function of immorality to generate hatred in its train, then whenever it arises among people—people from any walk of life—won't it make them hate one another and clash with one another and be incapable of doing things together?'

'Yes.'

'What about when it arises between two people? Won't it make them quarrel with and feel hatred and hostility towards not only each other but also moral people?'

'It will.'

'And, Thrasymachus, if immorality arises within a single person, it won't lose its power, surely, will it? Won't it retain it in an undiminished form?'

'I dare say it does,' he said.

'Evidently, then, its power is twofold. First, its occurrence makes things incapable of co-ordinated action, because of their internal conflict and dissension; second, as well as generating internal hostility, it generates hostility between them and anything which is completely different from them—that is, anything which is moral. And this is the case whether it arises in a community, a family, an army, or anything else. Isn't this right?'

'Yes.'

'And when it arises within a single individual, it will, I suppose, produce exactly the same results— the results it is inherently bound to have. First, it will make him incapable of action, because of internal dissension and discord; second, as well as generating internal hostility, it will generate hostility between him and moral people. Right?'

'Yes.'

'Now, my friend, aren't the gods moral beings?'

'I dare say.'

'Therefore, an immoral person will be an enemy of the gods, Thrasymachus, and a moral person will be in their favour.'

'That's right, indulge yourself,' he said. 'And don't worry: I won't contradict what you're saying. I mean, I don't want to fall out with our friends here.'

'All right, then,' I went on. 'You'll treat me to all the food I still need to be satisfied, if you continue to answer my questions as you have been just now. I mean, we've found that moral people are more expert at getting things done, are better at it, and are more capable of it, and that immoral people are not capable of acting together at all. Moreover, if we ever claim that immoral people have been effective and have performed some concerted action together, then we are not telling the whole truth, because if they were absolutely immoral, they'd have been at one another's throats; there was obviously a degree of morality in them, which enabled them to refrain from wronging one another as well as their victims and which allowed them to do what they did. Immorality had only half perverted them when they embarked upon their misdeeds, since people who are rotten through and through and are perfectly immoral are perfectly incapable of doing anything either. I now see that all this is correct, and that your original position was quite wrong.'

At last Socrates turns to a direct refutation of Thrasymachus' claim that immorality is rewarding. Everything has a particular job to do, and the good state of anything is what enables it to do its job well. Therefore, if morality is a good state, it enables one to do a good job at life—to live well, and be happy and fulfilled. The argument is, as with most of the arguments in this chapter, as weak or as strong as the pervasive analogy between morality and skill or being good at something.

'However, we must also look into the postponed issue of whether moral people have a better and a more fulfilled life than immoral people. I must say that at the moment it does look to me as though they do, on the basis of what we've been saying. All the same, we must look more closely at the matter, since what is at stake is far from insignificant: it is how one should live one's life.'

'Go ahead with your investigation, then,' he said.

'All right,' I said. 'Tell me, please: do you think that a horse has a function?'

e 'Yes.'

'And would you say that a horse's function, or anything else's function, is what can be done only with that thing, or can be done best only with that thing?'

'I don't understand,' he said.

'Look at it this way: can you see with anything except eyes?'

'Of course not.'

'And can you hear with anything except ears?'

'No.'

'Would it be right, then, for us to say that these are their functions?'

'Yes.'

353a 'Now, you could cut a vine-twig with a short-sword or a cobbler's knife or plenty of other things, couldn't you?'

'Of course.'

'But I should think that the best tool for the job

would be a pruning-knife, the kind made especially for this purpose.'

'True.'

'Shall we say that this is its function, then?'

'Yes.'

'No doubt you can now see the point of the question I asked a moment ago, whether the function of anything is what it alone can do, or what it can do better than anything else.'

'Yes, I can,' he said. 'And I agree that this is anything's function.'   t

'All right,' I said. 'Now, don't you think that anything which has been endowed with a function also has a state of being good? Let's go back to the same examples. We're saying that eyes have a function?'

'Yes.'

'And do eyes also have a state of being good?'

'Yes, that too.'

'And do ears have a function?'

'Yes.'

'And a state of being good as well?'

'Yes, that too.'

'And does the same go for everything else?'

'Yes.'

'Now then, could eyes do a good job if they weren't in their own special good state, but were in- c stead in a bad state?'

'Of course not,' he replied. 'I suppose you mean if they were blind instead of capable of seeing.'

'I mean whatever their good state is,' I said. 'You've answered a question I haven't yet asked. At the moment I'm asking only whether it is thanks to its own special state of goodness that anything with a job to do performs its function well, and thanks to badness that it does its job badly.'

'Well, that's true,' he said.

'And in the absence of their goodness, will ears do their job badly?'

'Yes.'

'And so on, on the same principle, for everything d else?'

'I think so.'

'All right, now here's the next point to think about. Does the mind have a function—something you couldn't do with anything else? Consider, for instance, management, the exercise of authority, planning, and so on: would it be right for us to ascribe them to anything except the mind or to say that they were the particular province of anything except the mind?'

'No.'

'And what about one's way of life? Won't we say that this is a function of the mind?'

'Absolutely,' he said.

'And do we also think that the mind has a good state?'

'Yes.'

e   'Will the mind, then, Thrasymachus, ever perform its functions well in the absence of its own special goodness? Or is that impossible?'

'Yes, it's impossible.'

'Therefore, management and authority will inevitably be handled badly by a bad mind, whereas a good mind will do all these things well.'

'Inevitably.'

'Now, we agreed that morality is a good mental state, and that immorality is a bad state.'

'We did.'

'So a moral mind and a moral person will live a good life, and an immoral person will live a bad life.'

'Apparently,' he said, 'on your line of reasoning.'

'Now, anyone who lives a good life is happy and fulfilled, and anyone who doesn't is the opposite.'

'Of course.'

354a   'Therefore, a moral person is happy, whereas an immoral person is unhappy.'

'I dare say,' he said.

'Now, no one is well off because they're unhappy, but because they're happy.'

'Of course.'

'Therefore, my dear Thrasymachus, immorality is never more rewarding than morality.'

'There's your treat, Socrates,' he said, 'for this festival of Bendis.'

'And the meal was provided by you, Thrasymachus,' I said, 'since you were kind to me and
b stopped being cross. I've not had a proper meal, however—but that's my fault, not yours. I think I've behaved like those gluttons who can't wait to taste every dish that's served up, before they've given themselves a proper chance to enjoy the previous one. I gave up before we discovered what we set out to discover—the nature of morality—and I embarked instead on an investigation into whether it was a bad state and ignorance, or whether it was knowledge and a good state; then later, when the idea cropped up that immorality was more profitable than morality, I couldn't resist turning to that next. Consequently, the effect of our discussion on me has been ignorance. I mean, if I don't know what morality actually is, it's going to be difficult for me to know whether or not it is good, and

whether its possession makes someone unhappy or happy.'

CHAPTER 2
THE CHALLENGE TO SOCRATES

Glaucon and Adeimantus (Plato's brothers) now become Socrates' interlocutors for the rest of the book. Socrates has claimed (352d–354a) that morality enables us to prosper; they demand a full justification of this claim. Instead of the more usual views that morality is (a) not good, but a lesser evil (Glaucon), and (b) valued only for its external rewards (Adeimantus), they challenge Socrates to prove that morality is intrinsically good and rewarding, and that it contributes towards a moral person's happiness.

At this point, I thought I'd be exempt from further 357a talking, but apparently that was only the preamble. You see, it's not in Glaucon's nature to cut and run from anything, and on this occasion he refused to accept Thrasymachus' capitulation, but said, 'Socrates, do you want us *really* to be convinced that in all circumstances morality is better than im- b morality or merely to pretend to be?'

'If it were up to me,' I replied, 'I'd prefer your conviction to be genuine.'

'Well,' he remarked, 'your behaviour is at odds with your wishes, then. I mean, here's a question for you. Don't you describe as good something which is welcomed for its own sake, rather than because its consequences are desired? Enjoyment, for instance, and all those pleasures which are harmless and whose future consequences are only enjoyable?'

'Yes,' I agreed, ' "good" seems to me the right description for that situation.'

'And what about things which are welcome not c just for their own sakes, but also for their consequences? Intelligence, sight, and health, for instance, are evidently welcomed for both reasons.'

'Yes,' I said.

'And isn't there, in your experience,' he asked, 'a third category of good things—the category in which we find exercise, medical treatment, and any moneymaking job like being a doctor? All these things are regarded as nuisances, but beneficial, and are not welcomed for their own sakes, but for their financial rewards and other consequences.'   d

'Yes,' I agreed, 'there is this third category as well. What of it?'

'To which category do you think morality belongs?' he asked.

358a 'In my opinion,' I replied, 'it belongs in the best category—the category which anyone who expects to be happy should welcome both for its own sake and for its consequences.'

'That's not the usual view,' he said, 'which consigns morality to the nuisance category of things which have to be done for the sake of financial reward and for the prospect of making a good impression, but which, taken in isolation, are so trying that one should avoid them.'

'I'm aware of this view,' I said, 'and it's the reason why Thrasymachus has been running morality down all this time, and praising immorality. But I'm slow on the uptake, apparently.'

b 'All right, then,' he said, 'listen to what I have to say too, and see if you agree with me. The point is that Thrasymachus gave up too soon, in my opinion: you charmed him into docility as if he were a snake. The arguments that have been offered about both morality and immorality leave *me* unsatisfied, however, in the sense that I still want to hear a definition of them both, and to be told what the effect is of the occurrence of each of them in the mind—each of them in isolation, without taking into consideration financial reward or any other consequence they might have.

'So if it's all right with you, what I'll do is revive c Thrasymachus' position. First, I'll explain the usual view of the nature and origin of morality; second, I'll claim that it is only ever practised reluctantly, as something necessary, but not good; third, I'll claim that this behaviour is reasonable, because people are right to think that an immoral person's life is much better than a moral person's life.

'Now, I don't agree with any of this, Socrates, but I don't know what to think. My ears are ringing from listening to Thrasymachus and countless others, but I've never yet heard the kind of support for d morality, as being preferable to immorality, that I'd like to hear, which is a hymn to the virtues it possesses in and of itself. If I can get this from anyone, it'll be you, I think. That is why I'll speak at some length in praise of the immoral life; by doing so, I'll be showing you the kind of rejoinder I want you to develop when you criticize immorality and commend morality. What do you think of this plan?'

'I thoroughly approve,' I replied. 'I mean, I can't think of another topic which any thinking person

would more gladly see cropping up again and again in his conversations.'

'That's wonderful,' he said. 'Well, I promised I'd e talk first about the nature and origin of morality, so here goes. The idea is that although it's a fact of nature that doing wrong is good and having wrong done to one is bad, nevertheless the disadvantages of having it done to one outweigh the benefits of doing it. Consequently, once people have experienced both committing wrong and being at the receiving end of it, they see that the disadvantages are unavoidable and the benefits are unattainable; so they 359a decide that the most profitable course is for them to enter into a contract with one another, guaranteeing that no wrong will be committed or received. They then set about making laws and decrees, and from then on they use the terms "legal" and "right" to describe anything which is enjoined by their code. So that's the origin and nature of morality, on this view: it is a compromise between the ideal of doing wrong without having to pay for it, and the worst situation, which is having wrong done to one while lacking the means of exacting compensation. Since morality is a compromise, it is endorsed because, while it may not be good, it does gain value by preventing people from doing wrong. The point is that any real b man with the ability to do wrong would never enter into a contract to avoid both wronging and being wronged: he wouldn't be so crazy. Anyway, Socrates, that is what this view has to say about the nature and origin of morality and so on.

'As for the fact that morality is only ever practised reluctantly, by people who lack the ability to do wrong—this would become particularly obvious if we performed the following thought-experiment. Suppose we grant both types of people—moral and c immoral—the scope to do whatever they want, and we then keep an eye on them to see where their wishes lead them. We'll catch our moral person red-handed: his desire for superiority will point him in the same direction as the immoral person, towards a destination which every creature naturally regards as good and aims for, except that people are compelled by convention to deviate from this path and respect equality.

'They'd have the scope I'm talking about especially if they acquired the kind of power which, we hear, an ancestor of Gyges of Lydia once acquired. He was a shepherd in the service of the Lydian ruler d of the time, when a heavy rainstorm occurred and an earthquake cracked open the land to a certain ex-

tent, and a chasm appeared in the region where he was pasturing his flocks. He was fascinated by the sight, and went down into the chasm and saw there, as the story goes, among other artefacts, a bronze horse, which was hollow and had windows set in it; he stooped and looked in through the windows and saw a corpse inside, which seemed to be that of a
c giant. The corpse was naked, but had a golden ring on one finger; he took the ring off the finger and left. Now, the shepherds used to meet once a month to keep the king informed about his flocks, and our protagonist came to the meeting wearing the ring. He was sitting down among the others, and happened to twist the ring's bezel in the direction of his body, towards the inner part of his hand. When he did this, he became invisible to his neighbours, and
360a to his astonishment they talked about him as if he'd left. While he was fiddling about with the ring again, he turned the bezel outwards, and became visible. He thought about this and experimented to see if it was the ring which had this power; in this way he eventually found that turning the bezel inwards made him invisible and turning it outwards made him visible. As soon as he realized this, he arranged to be one of the delegates to the king; once he was
b inside the palace, he seduced the king's wife and with her help assaulted and killed the king, and so took possession of the throne.

'Suppose there were two such rings, then—one worn by our moral person, the other by the immoral person. There is no one, on this view, who is iron-willed enough to maintain his morality and find the strength of purpose to keep his hands off what doesn't belong to him, when he is able to take whatever he wants from the market-stalls without fear of
c being discovered, to enter houses and sleep with whomever he chooses, to kill and to release from prison anyone he wants, and generally to act like a god among men. His behaviour would be identical to that of the other person: both of them would be heading in the same direction.

'Now this is substantial evidence, it would be claimed, that morality is never freely chosen. People do wrong whenever they think they can, so they act morally only if they're forced to, because they regard morality as something which isn't good for one personally. The point is that everyone thinks the
d rewards of immorality far outweigh those of morality—and they're right, according to the proponent of this view. The sight of someone with that kind of scope refusing all those opportunities for wrongdo-

ing and never laying a finger on things that didn't belong to him would lead people to think that he was in an extremely bad way, and was a first-class fool as well—even though their fear of being wronged might make them attempt to mislead others by singing his praises to them in public.

'That's all I have to say on this. As for actually assessing the lives of the people we're talking about, e we'll be able to do that correctly if we make the gap between a moral person and an immoral person as wide as possible. That's the only way to make a proper assessment. And we should set them apart from each other by leaving their respective immorality and morality absolutely intact, so that we make each of them a consummate professional. In other words, our immoral person must be a true expert. A top-notch ship's captain, for instance, or doctor, recognizes the limits of his branch of expertise and undertakes what is possible while ignoring what 361a is impossible; moreover, if he makes a mistake, he has the competence to correct it. Equally, our immoral person must get away with any crimes he undertakes in the proper fashion, if he is to be outstandingly immoral; getting caught must be taken to be a sign of incompetence, since the acme of immorality is to give an impression of morality while actually being immoral. So we must attribute consummate immorality to our consummate criminal, and if we are to leave it intact, we should have him equipped with a colossal reputation for morality even though he is a colossal criminal. He should be b capable of correcting any mistakes he makes. He must have the ability to argue plausibly, in case any of his crimes are ever found out, and to use force wherever necessary, by making use of his courage and strength and by drawing on his fund of friends and his financial resources.

'Now that we've come up with this sketch of an immoral person, we must conceive of a moral person to stand beside him—someone who is straightforward and principled, and who, as Aeschylus says, wants genuine goodness rather than merely an aura of goodness. So we must deprive him of any such c aura, since if others think him moral, this reputation will gain him privileges and rewards, and it will become unclear whether it is morality or the rewards and privileges which might be motivating him to be what he is. We should strip him of everything except morality, then, and our portrait should be of someone in the opposite situation to the one we imagined before. I mean, even though he does no

wrong at all, he must have a colossal reputation for immorality, so that his morality can be tested by seeing whether or not he is impervious to a bad reputation and its consequences; he must unswervingly
d follow his path until he dies—a saint with a lifelong reputation as a sinner. When they can both go no further in morality and immorality respectively, we can decide which of them is the happier.'

'My dear Glaucon,' I said, 'I'm very impressed at how industriously you're ridding each of them of defects and getting them ready for assessment. It's as if you were working on statues.'

'I'm doing the best I can,' he replied. 'And now that we've established what the two of them are like, I'm sure we won't find it difficult to specify what sort of life is in store for either of them. That's what
e I must do, then—and if my words are rather coarse, Socrates, please remember that the argument is not mine, but stems from those who prefer immorality to morality.

'Here's what they'll say: for a moral person in the situation I've described, the future holds flogging, torture on the rack, imprisonment in chains, having his eyes burnt out, and every ordeal in the book, up
362a to and including being impaled on a stake. Then at last he'll realize that one's goal should be not actual morality, but the appearance of morality. In fact, that phrase of Aeschylus' has far more relevance for an immoral person, in the sense that, as they will claim, it is really an immoral person who wants genuine immorality rather than merely an aura of immorality, because his occupation takes account of the way things are and his life is not concerned with appearances. He is the one who "reaps the harvest of
b wise plans which grow in his mind's deep furrow"— and what he plans is first to use his reputation for morality to gain control over his country, and then to marry a woman from any family he wants, to have his children marry whomever he wants, to deal and do business with whomever he wants, and, over and above all this, to secure his own benefit by ensuring that his lack of distaste for crime makes him a financial profit. If he's challenged privately or publicly, he wins the day and comes off better than his
c enemies; because he gains the upper hand, he gets rich; he therefore does good to his friends and harm to his enemies, and the religious rites he performs and the offerings he makes to the gods are not just adequate but magnificent; his service to the gods and to the men he favours is far better than a moral person's; and consequently it is more appropriate for

the gods to smile on him rather than on a moral person, and more likely that they will. And this, Socrates, is why both gods and men provide a better life for an immoral person than for a moral person, according to this view.'

After Glaucon's speech, I was intending to make
d some reply to what he'd been saying, but his brother Adeimantus asked, 'Surely you don't consider that an adequate treatment of the issue, do you, Socrates?'

'Why shouldn't I?' I said.

'It's precisely the most important point which has been omitted,' he said.

'Well,' I said, 'as the saying goes, a man and his brother should stick together. So if Glaucon here has left anything out, you should back him up. As far as I'm concerned, however, even what he's already said is enough to floor me and make me a totally ineffective ally of morality.'

'Rubbish,' he said. 'But don't let that stop you lis-
e tening to what I have to say as well. In order to clarify Glaucon's meaning, we also have to go into the arguments for the opposite of his point—the arguments in favour of morality and against immorality. As you know, fathers point out to their sons the importance of morality and impress it upon them (as every guardian impresses it upon his ward) by singing the praises not of morality itself but of the
363a good reputation it brings. The inducement they offer is that power, good marriage, and all the things Glaucon mentioned a moment ago come to someone who is thought to be moral as a result of this reputation: if a moral persons gets them, it is because he is well thought of.

'They have more to say about the consequences of reputation. They adduce being well thought of by the gods, and then they have benefits galore to talk of, all the ones the gods are said to award to just people. There are, for instance, the statements of noble Hesiod and of Homer. Hesiod says that the gods make "oaks bear acorns on their outsides and bees in their centres" for moral people; and he says that
b "their wooly sheep are weighed down by their fleeces", and that they gain many other advantages. Homer makes very similar claims: "As of some righteous king," he says, "who pleases the gods by upholding justice, and the dark earth bears wheat and barley, the trees hang heavy with fruit, the sheep steadily give birth, and the sea-waters yield fish."
c
'Musaeus and his son claim that the gods give moral people even more exciting advantages. Once

they've transported them, in their account, to Hades and got them reclining on couches for the party they've laid on for just people, they next have them spending eternity wearing chaplets on their heads and drinking, on the assumption that the best possi-
d ble reward for goodness is perpetual intoxication. Others have the gods' rewards for morality lasting even longer: they say that the legacy left behind by a person who is just and keeps his promises is that his children's children are better people.

'These, and others like them, are the glowing terms in which they speak of morality. As for un-just and immoral people, they bury them in Hades in a kind of mud and force them to carry water in sieves, and they make sure that while they remain alive they are thought badly of; and they claim that
e all the punishments which Glaucon specified for people who, despite being moral, are thought to be immoral are destined for immoral people. They have no novel punishments to add to this list, however.

'Anyway, that's how morality is commended and immorality condemned. But there's also another point for you to take into consideration, Socrates. It's the sort of thing ordinary people say to one an-
364a other about morality and immorality, but it occurs in the poets as well. They all unanimously go on and on about how self-discipline and morality may be commendable, but are also difficult and trouble-some, whereas self-indulgence and immorality are enjoyable and easily gained, and it's only in peo-ple's minds and in convention that they are con-temptible. They also say that, on the whole, im-morality is more rewarding than morality; and whereas they're perfectly ready to admire bad men, if they're affluent and powerful in other respects as well, and to award them political office and personal prestige, they have disrespect and look down on peo-ple who are in any way powerless or are poor, even
b while admitting their moral superiority to the oth-ers.

'The most astonishing thing of all, however, is what gets said about the gods and goodness—that the gods often assign misfortune and a terrible life to good people, and the opposite to the other type of person. Beggar-priests and soothsayers knock on the doors of wealthy households and try to persuade the owners that (as long as there's some enjoyable feasting involved) the gods have granted them the power to use rituals and spells to expiate any sin
c committed by a person or by any of his ancestors, and that if anyone has an enemy he'd like to hurt,

then it'll cost hardly anything to injure him—and it makes no difference whether the target is a moral or an immoral person—by means of certain incanta-tions and formulae, since they can persuade the gods, they say, to do their bidding.

'The poets are called on to support all these claims. Some people concede that vice involves nothing arduous, on the grounds that "There's no difficulty in choosing vice in abundance: the road is d smooth and it's hardly any distance to where it lives. But the gods have put sweat in the way of good-ness", and a long, rough, steep road. Others cite Homer in support of the idea that humans can in-fluence the gods, pointing out that he too said, "Even the gods themselves can be moved by entreaty: men appeal to them by means of rites and softly spoken prayers, libations and sacrifices, and influence them, when a crime has been committed and a wrong has e been done." They come up with a noisy mob of books written by Musaeus and Orpheus (who are de-scended from the Moon and the Muses, they say), which are source-books for their rituals; and they convince whole countries as well as individuals that there are in fact ways to be free and cleansed of sin. While we remain on earth, this involves rituals and enjoyable diversions, which also work for us after 365a we have died and which they call initiations. These initiations, they say, free us from all the terrors of the other world, but ghastly things await anyone who didn't take part in the rituals.

'This, my dear Socrates,' he went on, 'is the kind of thing that gets said—and at this kind of length—about how highly gods and men regard virtue and vice. Can we tell what the effect of being exposed to all this is on a young mind which is naturally gifted and is capable of working out, as a result of flitting (so to speak) from one idea to another and dipping into them all, what type of person he has to be and what road he has to take to have as good a life as possible? He would probably follow Pindar b and ask himself, " 'Is it honesty or crooked deceit that enables me to scale the higher wall' and so live my life surrounded by secure defences? What I hear is people telling me that, unless I also gain a repu-tation for morality, my actually being moral will do me no good, but will be a source of private troubles and public punishments. On the other hand, an im-moral person who has managed to get a reputation for morality is said to have a wonderful life. There-fore, since the experts tell me that 'Appearance over- c powers reality' and is responsible for happiness, I must wholeheartedly devote myself to appearance. I must surround myself with an illusion of goodness. This must be my front, what people see of me, but behind me I must have on a leash that cunning, subtle fox of which Archilochus, the greatest of all experts, speaks. Someone might object, 'But it's not easy to cloak one's badness for ever.' That's because no important project is easy, we shall reply; nevertheless, everything we hear marks this as the road d to take if we are to be happy. To help us with our disguise, we shall form clubs and pressure-groups, and we can acquire skill at political and forensic speaking from teachers of the art of persuasion. Consequently, by a combination of persuasion and brute force, we shall dominate others without being punished for it."

' "But you can't hide from the gods, or overpower them." "Well, suppose there are no gods, or suppose they aren't bothered in the slightest about human affairs: then why should we in our turn bother about hiding from them? On the other hand, if the gods do exist, and do care for us, then our only sources of e knowledge and information about them are tradition and the poets who have described their lineage. And these are precisely the people who are telling us that the gods can be persuaded and influenced by 'rites and softly spoken prayers' and offerings. Their credibility in one respect stands or falls with their credibility in the other respect. So if we listen to them, our course is to do wrong and then make offerings to the gods from the proceeds of our crimes. The point is that if we behave morally, then the most that 366a we'll avoid is being punished by the gods, but we'll also pass up the opportunity for making a profit from our immorality; if we are immoral, however, we'll not only get rich, we'll win the gods over with our entreaties and get off scot-free, for all the crimes we commit and wrong we do."

' "But we'll pay in Hades for the crimes we've committed here on earth—or if we don't ourselves, then our children's children will." He'll think about it and then reply, "No, my friend, we won't. Initiations are very effective and the gods whose domain is exoneration have a great deal of power: that is the message we are given by very important countries b and by the offspring of the gods, who have become poets and the gods' interpreters, and who reveal that this is so."

'Is there any argument left, then, which might persuade us not to choose out-and-out immorality, but to prefer morality? I mean, if we combine immorality with a fraudulent, but specious, façade, then we can do as we please in this world and in the next, in the presence of both gods and men. This is what both ordinary people and outstanding people are telling us. So after all these arguments, Socrates, is c there any strategy to enable someone with potential—whether it is due to mental attributes or wealth or physique or lineage—to be prepared to rate morality highly, rather than laugh when he hears it being praised?

'I tell you, if there's anyone who can not only refute the arguments I've been stating, but is also secure in his knowledge that morality is best, then what he feels for immoral people is not anger but a large measure of forgiveness. He knows that people abstain from wrong either because, by divine dispensation, they instinctively find it distasteful, or because of some realization they've come to, and that otherwise no one chooses to be moral, although peo- d ple find fault with immorality when cowardice or old age or some other form of weakness prevents them from doing wrong. This is obviously the case: the first of these people to gain power is the first to behave immorally—and as immorally as he possibly can.

'One thing is responsible for all this, and it is the same thing which constituted the starting-point of this whole discussion. Both Glaucon and I, Socrates, are saying to you, "My friend, we can start with those original heroes whose writings are e extant and end with our contemporaries, but we find that not a single one of you self-styled supporters of morality has ever found fault with immorality or commended morality except in terms of the reputation, status, and rewards which follow from them. What each of them does on its own, however, and what the effect is of its occurrence in someone's mind, where it is hidden from the eyes of both gods and men, has never been adequately explained either in poetry or in everyday conversation; nor has it ever been proven that the worst possible thing that can occur in the mind is immorality, and that morality is the best. If this is how all of you had approached the matter from the 367a outset, and if you had started trying to convince us when we were young, then we wouldn't now be defending ourselves against one another's wrongdoing, but everyone would be his own best defender, since he'd be afraid that if he did wrong he'd be opening his doors to the worst of all possible residents."

'That, Socrates, is what Thrasymachus—though he's not the only one, of course—might say on the subject of morality and immorality, and he'd probably have even more to add. Now, *I* think he's crudely misrepresenting their functions, but the reason I've taken his argument as far as I can is, to be perfectly candid, because I want to hear you mak-
b ing the opposite claims. It's not enough just to demonstrate that morality is better than immorality. Why does one of them, in and of itself, make anyone who possesses it bad, while the other one, in and of itself, makes him good? And, as Glaucon suggested, don't bring reputation into it. You see, if you leave them with reputations which genuinely reflect their natures, and don't attribute to each of them reputations which fail to do justice to them, then we'll accuse you of praising a reputation for morality rather than morality itself, and of criticizing a reputation for immorality rather than immorality itself;
c and we'll claim that what you're recommending is being immoral and getting away with it, and that you actually agree with Thrasymachus that morality is good for someone else—that it is the advantage of the stronger party—while it is immorality that is to one's own advantage and profit, but is disadvantageous to the weaker party.

'So, since it is your expressed opinion that morality is one of those paramount good things which are worth having not just for their consequences, but also and especially for themselves (like sight, hearing, intelligence—health, of course—and any other good things which are not
d just thought to be worth while, but are inherently so), then this is the aspect of morality which you should pay tribute to. You should show how morality is worth while in and of itself for anyone who possesses it and how immorality harms him, and leave others to praise rewards and reputations. I mean, I can accept the fact that others praise morality and criticize immorality in these terms, by eulogizing or abusing their reputations and rewards, but I won't put up with that from you (unless you
e insist), because this and this alone is what you've spent your whole life investigating. So it's not enough just to demonstrate that morality is better than immorality: show us why one of them, in and of itself, makes anyone who possesses it good, whether or not it is hidden from the eyes of gods and men, while the other one, in and of itself, and whether or not it is hidden from the eyes of gods and men, makes him bad.'

CHAPTER 3
FUNDAMENTALS OF INNER POLITICS

In order to meet the challenge issued in the last chapter, Plato begins to imagine the constitution of a community which will correspond to human psychology and make it easier to understand morality. The first community consists of workers alone living a life of rude and primitive health, each with a single talent and therefore a single job, responding cooperatively to one another's selfish needs. In political terms, economics underpins society; in psychological terms, our desires or needs are fundamental.

Now, I've always admired Glaucon's and Adeimantus' temperaments, but I was particularly delighted with them on this occasion, once I'd heard what they had to say. 'Like father, like sons,' I re- 368a marked. 'The first line of the elegiac poem which Glaucon's lover composed when you distinguished yourselves at the battle of Megara wasn't wrong in addressing you as "sons of Ariston, godlike offspring of an eminent sire". I think this is quite right: "godlike" is certainly the word for your state, if you can speak like that in support of immorality, and yet remain unconvinced that it is better than morality. I *do* think that you really are unconvinced; my evidence is what I know of your characters from other b occasions. If I'd had to judge from your words alone, I would have doubted it. But it's precisely because I don't doubt it that I'm in a quandary. On the one hand, I can't come to the assistance of morality, since I am incompetent—as is proven by the fact that although I thought the points I'd made to Thrasymachus had shown that morality was better than immorality, you weren't satisfied. On the other hand, I can't not come to morality's assistance, since I'm afraid that it might actually be sacrilegious to stand idly by while morality is being denigrated and not try to assist as long as one has breath in one's body and a voice to protest with. Anyway, the best c thing is for me to offer it whatever help I can.'

Glaucon and the others begged me to do everything I could to help; they implored me not to abandon the discussion, but to make a thorough enquiry into the nature of both morality and immorality, and to search out the truth about their expediency. I told them what occurred to me: 'We're undertaking an investigation which, in my opinion, requires care and sharp eyesight. Now, we're not experts,' I d pointed out, 'so I suggest we conduct the investigation as follows. Suppose we were rather short-sighted and had been told to read small writing from a long way off, and then one of us noticed the same letters written elsewhere in a larger size and on a larger surface: I'm sure we'd regard this as a godsend and would read them there before examining the smaller ones, to see if they were really identical.'

'Of course we would,' said Adeimantus. 'But how is this analogous to our investigation into morality,
e Socrates, in your view?'

'I'll tell you,' I replied. 'Wouldn't we say that morality can be a property of whole communities as well as of individuals?'

'Yes,' he said.

'And a community is larger than a single person?'

'Yes,' he said.

'It's not impossible, then, that morality might exist on a larger scale in the larger entity and be easier to discern. So, if you have no objection, why
369a don't we start by trying to see what morality is like in communities? And then we can examine individuals too, to see if the larger entity is reflected in the features of the smaller entity.'

'I think that's an excellent idea,' he said.

'Well,' I said, 'the theoretical observation of a community in the process of formation would enable us to see its morality and immorality forming too, wouldn't it?'

'I should think so,' he said.

'And once the process is complete, we could expect to see more easily what we're looking for?'
b 'Yes, much more easily.'

'Are we agreed, then, on the necessity of trying to see this plan through? I'm asking because I think it'll take a lot of work. So are you sure?'

'Yes, we are,' said Adeimantus. 'Please do what you're proposing.'

'Well,' I said, 'a community starts to be formed, I suppose, when individual human beings find that they aren't self-sufficient, but that each of them has plenty of requirements which he can't fulfil on his own. Do you have an alternative suggestion as to why communities are founded?'

'No,' he said.
c 'So people become involved with various other people to fulfil various needs, and we have lots of needs, so we gather lots of people together and get them to live in a single district as our associates and assistants. And then we call this living together a community. Is that right?'

'Yes.'

'And people trade goods with one another, because they think they'll be better off if each gives or receives something in exchange, don't they?'

'Yes.'

'All right, then,' I said. 'Let's construct our theoretical community from scratch. Apparently, its cause is our neediness.'

'Of course.'

'And the most basic and most important of our d needs is that we are provided with enough food for existence and for life.'

'Absolutely.'

'The second most important is our need for somewhere to live, and the third is our need for clothing and so on.'

'True.'

'All right,' I said. 'How will our community cope with all this provisioning? Mustn't one member of it be a farmer, another a builder, and another a weaver? Is that all the people we need to look after our bodily needs? Shall we add a shoemaker to it as well?'

'Yes.'

'And there we'd have our community. Reduced to its bare essentials, it would consist of four or five people.'

'So it seems.'   e

'Well now, should each of them make what he produces publicly available for everyone? For instance, although the farmer is only one person, should he supply all four people with food? Should he spend four times as long and work four times as hard on supplying food and share it out, or should he ignore everyone else and spend a quarter of his time producing only a quarter of this amount of food for himself, and divide the other three-quarters be- 370a tween getting a house and clothes and shoes for himself, and not have all the bother of associating with other people, but look after his own affairs on his own?'

Adeimantus said, 'It looks as though the first alternative is simpler, Socrates.'

'That's not surprising, of course,' I said. 'I mean, it occurred to me while you were speaking that, in the first place, different people are inherently suitable for different activities, since people are not particularly similar to one another, but have a wide va- b riety of natures. Don't you agree?'

'I do.'

'And is success a more likely consequence of an

individual working at several jobs or specializing in only one?'

'Of his specializing in only one,' he said.

'Now, here's another obvious point, I'm sure—that missing the critical opportunity has a deleterious effect.'

'Yes, obviously.'

c 'The reason being that the work isn't prepared to wait for the worker to make time for it. No, it's crucial for the worker to fall in with the work and not try to fit it into his spare time.'

'Yes, that's crucial.'

'So it follows that productivity is increased, the quality of the products is improved, and the process is simplified when an individual sets aside his other pursuits, does the one thing for which he is naturally suited, and does it at the opportune moment.'

'Absolutely.'

'We need more than four citizens, then, Adeimantus, to supply the needs we mentioned. I mean, if the farmer's going to have a good plough, he will d apparently not be making it himself, and the same goes for his hoe and all the rest of his farming implements. Moreover, the builder won't be making his own tools either, and he too needs plenty of them; nor, by the same token, will the weaver and the shoemaker. True?'

'True.'

'So plenty of other craftsmen—joiners, metalworkers, and so on—will join our little settlement and swell its population.'

'Yes.'

'It still won't be very big, though, even when we've added shepherds and other herdsmen—who are also needed, otherwise the farmers won't have oxen to plough with, and there'll be no draught-e animals for them and the builders to use for pulling things, and no leather or wool for the weavers and shoemakers.'

'No,' he said, 'but it won't be small either with all that lot.'

'Now, it's practically impossible to build the actual community in a place where it will have no need of imports,' I pointed out.

'Yes, that's too much to expect.'

'Then they'll need more people, to bring in what it needs from elsewhere.'

'Yes.'

'But if their man goes empty-handed, in the sense of taking nothing with him which satisfies the re-371a quirements of the people from whom they're trying

to get what they need, then he'll depart empty-handed, won't he?'

'I should say so.'

'Then their home production must not only be enough to satisfy their own requirements, but must also be of a type and a quantity which satisfies the requirements of the people they need.'

'Yes, it must.'

'So our community had better increase the number of its farmers and other craftsmen.'

'Yes.'

'And also the number of its workers, I suppose, who import and export all the different kinds of goods—which is to say, merchants. Don't you agree?'

'Yes.'

'We'll need merchants too, then.'

'Certainly.'

'And if they deal with overseas countries, then a great many other people will be needed—experts in all sea-related work.'

b 'Yes, we'll certainly need a lot of them.'

'Now, within the actual community, how will people trade their produce with one another? I mean, that was why we established an association and founded a community in the first place.'

'They'll trade by buying and selling, obviously,' he said.

'Then a consequence of this is that we'll have a market-place and coinage as a system of trading.'

'Yes.'

'So if a farmer or one of the other producers brings c some of his produce to the market-place, but doesn't arrive at the same time as the people who want to trade with him, won't he be sitting in the market-place neglecting his own work?'

'No,' he replied, 'because there are people who notice the situation and take it on themselves to supply this service; in properly organized communities, they tend to be those who are physically the weakest and who are therefore unsuited for any other kind of work. Their job is to stay there in the market-place and to give people who want to sell something money in exchange for their goods, and then to give d goods in exchange for money to people who want to buy something.'

'So this need', I said, 'gives rise to stallholders in our community. I mean, aren't people who stay put in a market-place and do the job of buying and selling called "stallholders", as distinct from those who travel from community to community, who are called "merchants"?'

'Yes, that's right.'

e 'I think there's another category of worker too, consisting of people who don't really deserve to join our community for their mental abilities, but who are physically strong enough to undertake hard labour. They sell the use of their strength, "pay" is the name of the reward they get for this, and that is why they're called "paid hands", I suppose, don't you?'

'Yes.'

'With paid hands as well, then, our community has reached its limit, I should think.'

'I agree.'

'Well, Adeimantus, our community has certainly grown. Is it now just right?'

'I suppose so.'

'Does it contain morality and immorality, then? If so, where and thanks to which of the people we've considered?'

372a 'I've no idea, Socrates,' he said, 'unless it has something to do with how these people treat one another.'

'You might be right,' I said. 'We must look into your idea: it deserves to be taken seriously. Let's start by considering how people who've been provided for like this will live. Surely they'll spend their time producing food, wine, clothes, and shoes, won't they? Once they've built their houses, they'll turn to production, which they'll invariably work at in the summer naked and with bare feet, and in the winter with adequate protective clothing and footwear.
b Their food will be barley-meal and wheat-meal, which will sometimes be cooked and sometimes pulped, and the resulting honest fare of barley-cakes and wheat-cakes will be served up on reeds or on clean leaves, as they and their children, wearing chaplets and singing hymns to the gods, recline on carpets of bryony and myrtle and eat their fill, while drinking wine. They'll enjoy having sex, except that
c concern about poverty or war will stop them procreating beyond their means.'

At this point Glaucon interrupted and said, 'This diet you're giving them dispenses with savouries, apparently.'

'You're right,' I said. 'I was forgetting that they'll also have savouries—salt, obviously, and olives and cheese—and they'll boil up the kinds of roots and vegetables which country stews are made of. We'll serve them with desserts too, I suppose, of figs, chick-peas, and beans; and they'll roast myrtle-berries and acorns in the fire as they sip their drinks.

And so, it seems, their life will pass in peace and d good health, and at their death in old age they will pass on a similar way of life to their offspring.'

'Socrates,' he remarked, 'isn't this exactly the fodder you'd lay on if you were devising a community for pigs?'

'What would you suggest, then, Glaucon?' I asked.

'Nothing abnormal,' he replied. 'I think they should recline on couches, if they're to be comfortable, and eat from tables, and have the kinds of e savouries and desserts which are in current usage.'

Realistically, there is more to human life than the first community can provide—more to the human psyche than mere needs. The community is expanded to include non-necessary needs, until it threatens the integrity of others with which it comes into contact, and is itself threatened in the same way. It therefore needs guardians, to protect its integrity. The job of protection requires passion and love of knowledge.

'All right,' I said. 'I see. We're not just investigating the origins of a community, apparently, but of an indulgent community. Well, that may not be wrong: if we extend our enquiry like that, we might perhaps see how morality and immorality take root in communities. Now, I think that the true community—the one in a healthy condition, as it were—is the one we've described; but if you want us to inspect an inflamed community as well, so be it. There's no reason not to. I mean, some people apparently won't be satisfied with the provisions and 373a the lifestyle we've described, but will have all sorts of furniture like couches and tables, and a wide selection of savouries, perfumes, incense, prostitutes, and pastries. Moreover, the essential requirements can no longer be restricted to the houses and clothing and shoes we originally mentioned; no, we have to invent painting and ornamentation, and get hold of gold and ivory and so on. Don't you agree?'

'Yes,' he said. b

'So we have to increase the size of our community once again. That healthy community will no longer do; it must become bloated and distended with occupations which leave the essential requirements of a community behind—for instance, with all kinds of hunters and imitators. Among the latter will be hordes of people concerned with shapes and colours, and further hordes concerned with music (poets and their dependants—rhapsodes, actors,

dancers, producers), and manufacturers of all kinds of contraptions and all sorts of things, especially
c women's cosmetics. Furthermore, we'll need a larger number of workers—don't you think?—such as children's attendants, nurses, nannies, hairdressers, barbers, and savoury-cooks and meat-cooks too. And that's not the end of it: we'll need pig-farmers as well—a job which didn't exist in our previous community, since there was no need of it, but which will be needed in the present one—and huge numbers of cows and sheep, if they are to be eaten, won't we?'

'Of course.'

d   'And with this lifestyle won't we be in far greater need of doctors than we were before?'

'Yes.'

'And, of course, although the inhabitants of our former community could live off the produce of the land, the land will be too small now, don't you think?'

'I agree.'

'So we'll have to take a chunk of our neighbours' land, if we're going to have enough for our herds and our crops, won't we? And suppose they too have stopped limiting themselves to necessities and have gone in for the uncontrolled acquisition of innumerable possessions: then they'll have to take a chunk of our land too, won't they?'

e   'That's more or less inevitable, Socrates,' he replied.

'And the next step will be war, Glaucon, don't you think?'

'I agree,' he said.

'Now, let's not commit ourselves yet to a view on whether the effects of war are good or bad,' I said. 'All we're saying at the moment is that we've now discovered the origin of war. It is caused by those factors whose occurrence is the major cause of a community's troubles, whether it's the community as a whole which is afflicted or any individual member of it.'

'Yes.'

'We need another sizeable increase in our com-
374a munity, then, Glaucon—an army-sized increase. We need an army to go out and defend all the community's property and all the people we were talking about a moment ago against invaders.'

'But can't the inhabitants do this themselves?' he asked.

'No,' I replied. 'At any rate, they can't if the proposition we all—including you—agreed to when

we were forming our community was correct. The proposition was, if you remember, that it is impossible for one person to work properly at more than one area of expertise.'

'You're right.'

'Well,' I said, 'don't you think that warfare re- b quires expertise?'

'I certainly do,' he answered.

'So should we take more trouble over our shoemakers than we do over our soldiers?'

'Not at all.'

'Well now, we prohibited a shoemaker from simultaneously undertaking farming or weaving or building, but had him concentrating exclusively on shoemaking, to ensure quality achievements in shoemaking; and we similarly allotted every single person just one job—the one for which he was naturally suited, and which he was to work at all his life, setting aside his other pursuits, so as not to miss the opportunities which are critical for quality achievement. c Isn't it crucial, however, that the achievements of warfare are of a high standard? Or is soldiering so easy that someone can be expert at it while carrying on with his farming or shoemaking or whatever his profession might be, despite the fact that no one could even become a competent backgammon-player or dice-player if he took it up only in his spare time and didn't concentrate on it for years, starting when he was a young man? Does someone just have to pick up a shield (or whatever military implement or in- d strument it may be) and he instantaneously becomes a competent fighter in a heavy infantry engagement (or in whatever form of armed conflict it may be)? This would be unique, since no other implement makes a person a craftsman or an athlete if he just holds it, and no other implement is the slightest good to anyone unless he's acquired the knowledge of how to use it and has devoted sufficient attention to it.'

'Yes,' he said, 'if tools could do that, they'd be highly prized.'

'Now,' I said, 'the amount of time allotted just to it, and also the degree of professionalism and training, should reflect the supreme importance of the e guardians' work.'

'I certainly think so,' he said.

'And a natural talent for the job would help too, wouldn't it?'

'Of course.'

'Our job, then, if we're up to it, would seem to be to select which people and what types of person have a natural gift for protecting our community.'

'Yes, it is.'

'We've certainly taken on an awesome task, then,' I said. 'Still, we mustn't be intimidated; we must do the best we can.'

375a 'I agree.'

'Well,' I went on, 'do you think there's any difference, as far as suitability for guarding is concerned, between the nature of the best type of dog and that of a well-born young man?'

'What are you getting at?'

'That both of them have to be acutely perceptive, quick on their feet (so as to chase after anything they do perceive) and strong as well, in the case they have to fight someone they've cornered.'

'Yes,' he said, 'they need all these qualities.'

'And a good fighter must be brave, of course.'

'That goes without saying.'

'Now, you'll never find courage without passion, in a horse or a dog or any other creature, will you? I mean, you must have noticed how indomitable and invincible passion is. It always takes passion in a b mind to make it capable of facing any situation without fear and without yielding, doesn't it?'

'Yes.'

'It's obvious what physical attributes a guardian must have, then.'

'Yes.'

'And the importance of a passionate temperament is also clear.'

'Again, yes.'

'Well, aren't people of this type bound to behave like brutes to one another and to the rest of their fellow citizens, Glaucon?' I asked.

'Yes, it certainly won't be easy to stop them,' he replied.

'However, they should really behave with civic lized gentleness towards their friends and neighbours and with ferocity towards their enemies. Otherwise, it won't be a question of waiting for others to come and destroy them: they'll do the job first themselves!'

'True,' he said.

'What shall we do, then?' I asked. 'Where are we going to find a character that is simultaneously gentle and high-spirited, when gentleness and passion are opposites?'

'Yes, they do seem to be mutually exclusive.'

'And yet if a guardian is deprived of either of them he can't be a good guardian. We seem to be faced d with an impasse; it turns out that a good guardian is an impossibility.'

'I suppose so.'

I was stuck. I surveyed the course of the discussion and then said, 'We deserve to be stuck, Glaucon. We haven't kept to the analogy we proposed.'

'What do you mean?'

'We've overlooked the fact that the supposedly impossible type of character, which contains these opposite qualities, does exist.'

'Where?'

'In animals. You could find the combination primarily—though not exclusively—in the animal we used as an analogy for our guardian. I mean, as I'm e sure you know, there's no creature more gentle towards people it knows and recognizes, and no creature more savage towards strangers, then the best type of dog; and this is due to its innate character.'

'Yes, I'm aware of that.'

'So it is a possibility, then,' I said. 'We're not looking for something unnatural in looking for a guardian of this type.'

'No, I suppose not.'

'Now, don't you think there's another quality which a would-be guardian needs as well? Don't you think that in addition to being naturally passionate he should also have a philosopher's love of knowledge?'

'Why?' he asked. 'I don't see why.' 376a

'Take dogs again,' I said. 'It's noticeable that they have a remarkable feature.'

'What?'

'They get fierce with strangers even before the slightest harm has been done them, and they welcome familiar people even if they've never been benefited by them. Has this never struck you as surprising?'

'I hadn't really thought about it until now,' he said. 'But yes, they do clearly do that.'

'But don't you think that this feature shows how naturally smart they are and how genuinely they love b knowledge?'

'How?'

'Because', I explained, 'their sole criterion for the friendliness or hostility of what they see is whether or not they have learnt to recognize it. Now, anything that relies on familiarity and unfamiliarity to define what is congenial and what is alien must prize learning, mustn't it?'

'Yes,' he said, 'inevitably.'

'Well,' I went on, 'isn't loving learning the same thing as loving knowledge?'

'Yes, it is,' he said.

'So why don't we stick our necks out and suggest that the same goes for a human being too—that if ᴄ he's going to be gentle with his friends and acquaintances, he must be an innate lover of knowledge and learning?'

'All right,' he said.

'Anyone who is going to be a truly good guardian of our community, then, will have a philosopher's love of knowledge, and will be passionate, quick on his feet, and strong.'

'Absolutely,' he said.

CHAPTER 4
PRIMARY EDUCATION FOR THE GUARDIANS

The would-be guardians have natural aptitude, but how should their characters be moulded? (Academic-education is reserved for the few, and for when they are older.) Plato begins with the stories they hear from childhood onwards. These inculcate values, so they must hear only morally sound stories, which will help them gain the appropriate social attitudes, such as respect for their parents, the desire for political unity, and, above all, correct beliefs about God, who is good, straight-forward, and unchanging. Any stories which could inculcate the wrong attitudes in any of these respect is to be censored.

'So those are his attributes. But how are we going to bring these people up? What education shall we give them? If we look into these issues, does it further the overall purpose of our enquiry, which is 376d to see how morality and immorality arise in society? We have to be careful not to leave out any relevant argument or to swamp the discussion with too many topics.'

It was Glaucon's brother who said, 'I expect the consideration of these issues will substantially further it.'

'In that case, my dear Adeimantus' I said, 'we must certainly not give up, even if the investigation turns out to be rather lengthy.'

'No, we mustn't.'

'All right, then, let's devise a theoretical education for these people, as if we were making up a story and weren't worried about time.'

ᴇ 'Yes, that's a good idea.'

'How shall we educate them, then? Or is it hard to improve on the educational system which has

evolved over a long period of time? This, as you known, consists of exercise for the body and cultural studies for the mind.'

'Yes.'

'And shall we begin the cultural programme before the physical one?'

'Of course.'

'Cultural studies include literature, don't you think?' I asked.

'I do.'

'Aren't there two kinds of literature, true and false?'

'Yes.'

'Should we include both kinds in our educational 377a system, and start with the untrue kind?'

'I don't understand what you're getting at,' he said.

'Don't you realize,' I asked, 'that we start by telling children stories which are, by and large, untrue, though they contain elements of truth? And stories precede physical exercise in our education of children.'

'True.'

'Which is why I suggested that cultural studies should be taken up before physical exercise.'

'It was a good suggestion,' he said.

'Now, do you appreciate that the most important stage of any enterprise is the beginning, especially when something young and sensitive is involved? You see, that's when most of its formation takes ʙ place, and it absorbs every impression that anyone wants to stamp upon it.'

'You're absolutely right.'

'Shall we, then, casually allow our children to listen to any old stories, made up by just anyone, and to take into their minds views which, on the whole, contradict those we'll want them to have as adults?'

'No, we won't allow that at all.'

'So our first job, apparently, is to oversee the work of the story-writers, and to accept any good story they write, but reject the others. We'll let nurses and mothers tell their children the acceptable ones, and ᴄ we'll have them devote themselves far more to using these stories to form their children's minds than they do to using their hands to form their bodies. However, we'll have to disallow most of the stories they currently tell.'

'Which stories?' he asked.

'If we examine the grander kind of story,' I said, 'that will give us insights into the more lightweight kind as well, because the same principle must be in- ᴅ volved and both kinds are bound to have the same effect, don't you think?'

'That sounds fine to me,' he replied, 'but I don't even understand which stories you're describing as grander.'

'The ones which Hesiod, Homer, and their fellow poets tell us. In the past, it's always been the poets who've composed untrue stories to tell people, and it's no different nowadays.'

'Which stories?' he asked. 'And what's their defect, in your view?'

'There is no defect which one ought to condemn more quickly and more thoroughly,' I replied, 'especially if the lies have no redeeming feature.'

'Yes, but what *is* the defect?'

e 'Using the written word to give a distorted image of the nature of the gods and heroes, just as a painter might produce a portrait which completely fails to capture the likeness of the original.'

'Yes,' he said, 'it's quite right to find fault with that sort of thing. But how do they do that? What kinds of things do they say?'

'First and most important, since the subject is so important,' I said, 'there is no redeeming feature to 378a the lies which Hesiod repeats, about Uranus' deeds and Cronus' revenge on Uranus. Then there are Cronus' deeds and what his son did to him. Now, I think that even if these stories are true, they oughtn't to be told so casually to young people and people who lack discrimination; it's better to keep silent, and if one absolutely has to speak, to make them esoteric secrets told to as few people as possible, who are to have sacrificed no mere piglet, but something so large and rare that the smallest conceivable number of people get to hear them.'

'Yes,' he said, 'these stories are definitely dangerous.'

b 'And we must censor them in our community, Adeimantus,' I said. 'No young person is to hear stories which suggest that were he to commit the vilest of crimes, and were he to do his utmost to punish his father's crimes, he wouldn't be doing anything out of the ordinary, but would simply be behaving like the first and the greatest gods.'

'No, I absolutely agree,' he said. 'I share your view that these stories are unsuitable and shouldn't be repeated.'

'And that's not all,' I said. 'The stories which have gods fighting and scheming and battling against one c another are utterly unsuitable too, because they're just as untrue. If the prospective guardians of our community are to loathe casual quarrels with one another, we must take good care that battles between gods and giants and all the other various tales of gods and heroes coming to blows with their relatives and friends don't occur in the stories they hear and the pictures they see. No, if we're somehow to convince them that fellow citizens never fall out with one another, that this is wrong, then that is the kind of story d they must hear, from childhood onwards, from the community's elders of both sexes; and the poets they'll hear when they're older must be forced to tell equivalent stories in their poetry. But we'd better not admit into our community the story of Hera being tied up by her son, or the episode when Hephaestus is hurled away by his father for trying to save his mother from a beating, or any of the battles between the gods which Homer has in his poetry, whether or not their intention is allegorical. The point is that a young person can't tell when something is allegorical and when it isn't, and any idea admitted by a person of that age tends to become almost ineradicable and permanent. e All things considered, then, that is why a very great deal of importance should be placed upon ensuring that the first stories they hear are best adapted for their moral improvement.'

'Yes, that makes sense,' he said. 'But suppose we were once again to be asked, in this context as well, what stories we meant, how would we respond?'

'Adeimantus,' I said, 'you and I are not making up stories at the moment; we're founding a community. Founders ought to know the broad outlines 379a within which their poets are to compose stories, so that they can exclude any compositions which do not conform to those outlines; but they shouldn't themselves make stories up.'

'You're right,' he said. 'But that's precisely the point: what are these guidelines for talking about the gods?'

'They'd be something like this,' I said. 'Whatever the type of poetry—epic, lyric, or tragic—God must of course always be portrayed as he really is.'

'Yes, he must.'

'Well, isn't God good, in fact, and shouldn't he b be described as such?'

'Of course.'

'And nothing good is harmful, is it?'

'I don't think so.'

'Now, can anything harmless cause damage?'

'No, of course not.'

'Can anything incapable of causing damage do anything bad?'

'Again, no.'

'And something which never does bad couldn't be responsible for bad, could it?'

'Of course not.'

'Well now, is goodness beneficial?'

'Yes.'

'And it's responsible for doing good, then?'

'Yes.'

'So goodness is not responsible for everything: it's responsible for things that are in a good state, but bad things cannot be attributed to it.'

c 'Exactly,' he said.

'The same goes for Good too, then,' I said. 'Since he is good, he cannot be responsible for everything, as is commonly said. He is responsible only for a small part of human life, and many things cannot be attributed to him—I mean, there's far more bad than good in the world. He and he alone must be held responsible for the good things, but responsibility for bad things must be looked for elsewhere and not attributed to God.'

'I think you're absolutely right,' he said.

'So,' I said, 'we shouldn't connive at Homer or d any other poet making the stupid mistake of saying about the gods, "Two jars sit on Zeus' threshold: one is full of good destinies, but the other is full of wretched destinies", and that if Zeus mixes the two up together and doles them out to someone, that person "sometimes meets with bad, sometimes with good", whereas if he doesn't mix them up, but allots the pernicious ones to someone in an unadulterated form, that person "is driven over the glorious earth by the evil of poverty". Nor will we e connive at them claiming that "Zeus is the dispenser of both good and evil".

'Moreover, we'll disapprove of the attribution of Pandarus' perjury and truce-breaking to the agency of Athena and Zeus, and of the gods' quarrel and its resolution to Themis and Zeus; and we'll not allow the younger generation to hear the idea which Aeschylus expresses as "When God wants to visit utter ruin on a household, he implants the cause in 380a men." No, if plays are composed (such as the one these lines are from) about Niobe's afflictions, or about the trials and tribulations of the descendants of Pelops, or about the Trojan War, the playwrights must either be prohibited from saying that God was responsible for these events, or if they do attribute them to God, they have to come up with an explanation which approximates to the one we're looking b for at the moment, and say that what God did was right and good, in the sense that the people in question were being punished and therefore benefited; but poets should be prohibited from saying that these people were in a *bad* way as a result of being punished and that this was God's doing. The claim that the sinners were badly off because they were in need of punishment, and that in punishing them God was benefiting them, is permissible; but the claim that God, who is good, is responsible for any instance of badness is to be resisted as forcefully as possible by anyone who wants a well-regulated community, until it is never spoken and never heard by anyone, of whatever age, whether the tale is told in verse or in c prose. And the reasons are that the voicing of these views is sacrilege, they do us no good, and they are inconsistent with one another.'

'I approve of this law,' he said. 'I'll be right behind you when you cast your vote for it.'

'So now we have the first of the laws and guidelines which pertain to the gods,' I said. 'Any spoken words or composed works will have to conform to the principle that God is not responsible for everything, but only for good.'

'Well, I'm certainly happy with it,' he said.

'All right, then. What about a second principle, as follows? Do you think that God is a sorcerer and can d by exercising his will vary his appearance from time to time, sometimes by actually changing and transforming his appearance into a large number of forms, and at other times by deluding us into thinking that's what he's done? Or do you think he's uniform and extremely unlikely to abandon his own appearance?'

'I'm not in a position to say just at the moment,' he replied.

'Look at it this way. Isn't it inevitable that if anything sheds its form, the change is due either to it- e self or to something else?'

'Yes.'

'Now, really good things are extremely unlikely to be altered or moved by an external agent, aren't they? For instance, a human body is altered by food, drink, and exercise, and plants are altered by the heat of the sun and by wind and phenomena like that; but the more healthy and strong a thing is, the less likely 381a it is to be altered.'

'Of course.'

'And the more courageous and intelligent a mind is, the less likely it is that an external agent would disturb it and alter it?'

'Yes.'

'Moreover, the same principle applies universally even to manufactured items, such as utensils, houses, and clothes: things which are well made and are in good condition are less likely to be altered by time and other phenomena.'

'True.'

b 'So anything which is in a good state—whether that is due to nature or human skill or both—can hardly be changed at all by an external agent.'

'That sounds right.'

'But God and the divine realm are of course in all respects as perfect as anything can be.'

'Of course.'

'From this point of view, then, God is extremely unlikely to have at his disposal a large number of forms.'

'Yes, extremely unlikely indeed.'

'Would he, however, change and alter himself internally, by his own resources?'

'If he changes in the first place,' he said, 'then obviously this must be how.'

'Well, does he enhance and improve himself, or does he worsen and debase himself?'

c 'If he changes,' he said, 'then it must be for the worse, since it's unthinkable that God's goodness and excellence are anything less than perfect.'

'You're absolutely right,' I said. 'And, Adeimantus, in this context, do you think that anyone—human or divine—deliberately makes himself deteriorate in any respect?'

'That's impossible,' he said.

'It is equally impossible, then,' I said, 'for God to want to change himself. Since, as we have found, the divine nature is as perfect and as good as anything could be, then any god retains his own form in a uniform, direct fashion for ever.'

'I think that's absolutely inevitable,' he said.

'It follows, Adeimantus,' I said, 'that none of our d poets is to say, "The gods travel around human habitations disguised as all sorts of visitors from other lands." Nor are they to tell lies about Proteus and Thetis, or present Hera in a tragedy or any other kind of poem in an altered form, as a mendicant holy woman begging alms "for the life-giving children of the Argive river Inachus", or repeat the mass of other similar lies that have been told. Furthermore, we e should neutralize the poets' influence on mothers, which makes them scare their children with terrible stories about how some gods tend to prowl around during the hours of darkness in a wide variety of unfamiliar human guises, so that we stop the mothers

blaspheming against the gods, and at the same time stop them making their children too timid.'

'Yes, we should,' he said.

'But even if it isn't in the gods' nature actually to change,' I said, 'do they magically delude us into seeing them appear in all kinds of guises?'

'It's not inconceivable,' he said.

'Well, would God willingly mask the truth behind 382a appearance and deceive us by his words or actions?' I asked.

'I don't know,' he answered.

'Don't you know that a true falsehood (if you'll allow me the phrase) is loathed by everyone, divine or human?' I asked.

'What do you mean?' he asked.

'I mean', I said, 'that no one chooses and wants to be deceived in the most important part of himself and about the most important things. The presence of falsehood there is his worst fear.'

'I still don't understand,' he said.

'That's because you think I'm trying to make a b high-powered point,' I said. 'But all I'm saying is that no one is at all happy at being lied to and deceived in his mind about the facts; no one likes being ignorant, and the existence and presence of falsehood there are extremely unwelcome to everyone; they particularly hate it there.'

'They certainly do,' he said.

'Well, I might have been perfectly correct when I described this state a moment ago as true falsehood—the state of misapprehension caused by falsehood in the mind. I mean, a spoken lie is a kind of copy and subsequent reflection of the mental con- c dition, and no pure lie, don't you think?'

'Yes.'

'Now, a genuine lie is hated by men as well as gods.'

'I think so.'

'What about a spoken lie? Aren't there occasions and situations when telling lies is helpful and doesn't therefore warrant hatred? What about when we're dealing with enemies, or with people we count as friends, but who are trying to do something bad because they've gone mad or have somehow taken leave of their senses? Isn't telling lies helpful under these circumstances as a preventative medicine? Moreover, consider those stories we were discussing d not long ago: we cannot know the truth about events in the past, so we make something up which approximates as closely as possible to the truth, and that helps us, doesn't it?'

'Yes,' he said, 'you're quite right.'

'Which of these reasons, then, makes telling lies helpful to God? Would he make up something which resembles the truth because he doesn't know the past?'

'That's a ridiculous suggestion,' he said.

'So there's nothing of the lying poet in God.'

'I don't think so.'

'Would he lie out of fear for his enemies?'

e   'Hardly.'

'Because his friends have taken leave of their senses or gone mad?'

'Anyone witless or insane is no friend of God,' he said.

'So God has no reason to lie.'

'No.'

'So it is not in the nature of deities or gods to deceive.'

'Absolutely not,' he said.

'Whether acting or speaking, then, God is entirely uniform and truthful. He doesn't actually change himself, and he doesn't delude others either, during their sleeping or their waking hours, in how he appears or in what he says or in the signs he sends.'

383a   'Listening to you speak,' he said, 'I find myself agreeing with you.'

'So do you agree,' I said, 'that this is the second principle to which religious discussions and literature must conform—that the gods are not shapeshifting wizards and do not mislead us by lying in what they say or do?'

'I agree.'

'Although there is much to commend in Homer, then, we won't approve of the passage when Zeus sends the dream to Agamemnon. Likewise, we won't approve of the bit of Aeschylus where Thetis says that at her wedding Apollo "celebrated in song how happy my children would make me—how they

b wouldn't know sickness and would live for many long years—and went on and on about how lucky I was and how the gods smiled on me, until he made my heart glad. And since Phoebus is a god and abounds in prophetic skill, I expected his words to be true. But for all his singing, for all his sharing of our feast, for all these claims of his, it is he who has now killed my son." We'll come down hard on anyone who says anything like this about the gods: we'll

c refuse him a chorus and ban teachers from using his works to educate our children. Otherwise, our guardians won't grow up to be religious people, or to be as godlike themselves as is humanly possible.'

'I'm in complete agreement with these principles,' he said, 'and would want them enshrined as laws.'

Poets—especially Homer—also carelessly promote cowardice, servility, lying, over-indulgence in emotion and sensual desire, avarice, and disrespect. To the extent that story-telling, which was the domain of the poets, is an important psychological influence (and it formed a major part of a child's education in Plato's Athens), we must prevent poets from promoting these values, and permit only the opposite values to be inculcated in the community.

'All right, then,' I said. "If people are going to re- 386a vere the gods, respect their parents, and not belittle friendship with one another, then apparently those are the kinds of stories they should and shouldn't hear about the gods, from childhood onwards.'

'I'm sure we're right about this,' he said.

'What about if they are to be brave? Won't they also need stories which are designed to make them fear death as little as possible? I mean, don't you b think that courage and fearing death are mutually exclusive?'

'Yes, I certainly do,' he answered.

'What about the idea that Hades doesn't just exist, but is terrifying? Do you think this goes with facing death fearlessly and with preferring death in battle to defeat and slavery?'

'Of course not.'

'So here's another aspect of story-telling for us to oversee, apparently. We must ask those who take on the job of telling stories not to denigrate Hades in the simple fashion they have been, but to speak well of it, because otherwise they'll not only be lying, but also not speaking in a way that is conducive to courage in battle.'   c

'Yes, we must,' he said.

'Then we'll start with the following lines,' I said, 'and delete everything which resembles them: "I'd rather be a slave labouring for someone else—someone without property, who can hardly make a living—than rule over all the spirits of the dead"; and "The vile, dank halls, which even the gods hate, d might appear to men and gods"; and "Amazing! The soul, the likeness of a person, really does exist in Hades' halls, but it is completely witless"; and "He alone had consciousness, while the rest were darting shadows"; and "His soul flew from his body and went to Hades bewailing its fate, forfeiting courage and the glory of young manhood"; and "Like a wisp 387a of smoke, his soul went down to the underworld with a shrill cry"; and "As when bats flit about squeaking in the depths of an awful cave, when one of them loses its perch on the crowded rock, and they cling to one another, so the flock of souls went with shrill b cries." We'll implore Homer and the rest of the poets not to get cross if we strike these and all similar lines from their works. We'll explain that it's not because the lines are not good poetry and don't give pleasure to most people; on the contrary, the better poetry they are, the more they are to be kept from the ears of children and men who are to be autonomous and to be more afraid of losing this freedom than of death.'

'Absolutely.'

'Now, we'd better get rid of all the frightening and terrifying names which crop up here. I mean names like Cocytus and Styx, ghost and wraith, and c so on—all the names which are designed to make everyone who hears them shudder. In another context, they may have a useful purpose to serve; but our worry is that this shivering might make our guardians too feverish and enervated.'

'It's a legitimate worry,' he remarked.

'Should we ban them, then?'

'Yes.'

'It's names which have the opposite effect that should be used in both prose and poetry, isn't it?'

'Clearly.'

'Shall we also remove the passages where emi- d nent men weep and wail in mourning, then?'

'We have to,' he said. 'It follows from what we've already done.'

'Let's see whether or not we're right to remove them,' I said. 'We can agree that one good man will not regard death as a terrible thing for another good man—a friend of his—to suffer.'

'Yes, we can.'

'So a good man won't mourn as if the other person had suffered something terrible.'

'No.'

'Moreover, we can also agree that a good man is preeminently capable of providing himself with a good life entirely from his own resources, and is ab- e solutely the last person to need anyone or anything else.'

'True.'

'So he'd be the last person to be overwhelmed by the loss of a son or a brother or some money and so on and so forth.'

'Yes, definitely.'

'He'll also be the last person to mourn, then, when some such disaster overtakes him: no one will endure it with more equanimity than him.'

'Very true.'

'We'd be right, then, not to have famous men mourning. We can allow women to do that (as long as they aren't admirable women) and any bad men there might be, so that the people we claim to be training for guardianship of our land find all that sort 388a of behaviour distasteful.'

'That's right,' he said.

'So we have a further request to make of Homer and the rest of the poets. We'll ask them not to portray Achilles, who was the son of a goddess, "at one point lying on his side, then later on his back, and then on his front; and then getting to his feet and sailing, crazed with grief, over the sands of the bit- b ter sea", or as "pouring handfuls of filthy ashes over his head", or generally as weeping and wailing to the extent and in the fashion that the poet portrays him. And we'll ask them not to have Priam, a close relative of the gods by birth, "begging, and rolling in the dung as he calls out to each man by name". We'll be even more forceful, however, in our request that they don't portray the *gods* lamenting and saying things like, "Oh, poor me! How wretched I c am to have borne the noblest of children!"; or at the very least they ought to stop short of giving such an inaccurate portrait of the greatest of the gods that they have him saying, "Alas! The man I now see being chased around Troy is dear to me, and my heart grieves", and "Alas that Sarpedon, the dearest of men to me, is destined to fall at the hands of Patro- d clus the son of Menoetius."

'The point is, my dear Adeimantus, that if the young men of our community hear this kind of thing and take it seriously, rather than regarding it as despicable and absurd, they're hardly going to regard such behaviour as despicable in human beings like themselves and feel remorse when they also find themselves saying or doing these or similar things. Instead, they won't find it at all degrading to be constantly chanting laments and dirges for trivial incidents, and they won't resist doing so.'

'You're quite right,' he said.

'And what we've just been arguing, in effect— e and at the moment no one's come up with a better argument, so we should stick to this one—is that we must prevent this happening.'

'Yes, we must.'

'Now, they'd better not be prone to laughter either. I mean, the stronger the laughter, the stronger the consequent emotional reaction too—that's almost inevitable.'

'I agree,' he said.

'We should, therefore, refuse admittance to any poetry which portrays eminent humans as being 389a overcome by laughter, and do so even more vigorously if it shows gods in that state.'

'Yes, indeed,' he said.

'So we'll also reject the lines of Homer where he says about the gods, "Unquenchable laughter arose among the blessed gods as they watched Hephaestus bustling about the house." According to your argument, we should disallow this type of passage.'

'Yes, if you want to attribute the argument to me,' b he said. 'At any rate, we should disallow it.'

'Next, they must rate honesty highly. You see, if we were right in what we were saying a short while ago, and the gods really have no use for falsehood, although it can serve as a type of medicine for us humans, then clearly lying should be entrusted to doctors, and laymen should have nothing to do with it.'

'Clearly,' he said.

'If it's anyone's job, then, it's the job of the rulers of our community: they can lie for the good of the community, when either an external or an internal threat makes it necessary. No one else, however, should have anything to do with lying. If an ordinary person lies to these rulers of ours, we'll count c that as equivalent in misguidedness, if not worse, to a patient lying to his doctor about his physical condition, or an athlete in training lying to his trainer about his physical condition, or someone misleading a ship's captain, with respect to his ship or crew, by telling him lies about his own state or that of one of his fellow crewmen.'

'You're absolutely right,' he said.

'So if anyone else is caught lying in our com- d munity—"any artisan, whether diviner or healer of ills or carpenter"—he is to be punished on the grounds that he's introducing a practice which is just as liable to wreck and ruin a community as a ship.'

'Yes, it would,' he said, 'if what people did was influenced by what he had said.'

'Now, won't the young men of our community need self-discipline?'

'Of course.'

'And aren't the most important aspects of self-dis- e cipline, at least for the general rank and file, obedi-

ence to those in authority and establishing one's own authority over the pleasures of drink, sex, and food?'

'I think so.'

'So I'm sure we'll approve of the kind of thing Homer has Diomedes say—"Sit down, shut up, and listen to me"—and related passages, like "Exuding an aura of courage, the Greeks advanced in silence, respecting their leaders", and so on and so forth.'

'Yes, we will.'

'Well, what about lines like "You're groggy with wine, you have the eyes of a dog and the heart of a deer" and the next few lines? Are they all right? And 390a what about all the other impertinent things people have said to their rulers in works of prose or poetry?'

'We won't approve of them.'

'That, I suppose, is because they don't encourage self-discipline in their audience, though they may well be enjoyable from another point of view. What do you think?'

'I agree,' he said.

'What about having your cleverest character saying that in his opinion the best thing in the world is when "The nearby tables are laden with bread and meat, and the steward draws wine from the mixing- b bowl, brings it, and pours it into the cups"? Do you think this is the right material for a young man to hear if he is to be self-controlled? Or "There is no death worse than death by starvation, no more wretched fate to face"? And then there's the passage where, while everyone else—mortal and immortal— is asleep, Zeus stays awake to do some planning, but in no time at all it is driven completely out of his mind by his sexual desire, and he is so overwhelmed c by the sight of Hera that he doesn't even want to go to their room, but wants to have sex with her there and then, on the ground, and he says that he's feeling more desire for her even than the first time they slept together, "without our parents knowing". And the story of how Hephaestus ensnared Ares and Aphrodite for similar reasons is equally inappropriate material for them to hear.'

'I couldn't agree with you more,' he said. 'It's quite unsuitable.'

'On the other hand,' I said, 'it's worth their paying attention to the portrayal on stage or in writing d of occasions when famous men express, by their words or actions, resistance to all kinds of temptations. For instance, there are the lines, "He struck his breast and spoke sternly to his heart: 'Patience, heart—you've put up with worse in the past.' "

'Absolutely,' he said.

'Then again, we shouldn't let them be mercenary or avaricious.'

e   'Of course not.'

'So they shouldn't repeat the verse "Gifts win over even gods and magnificent kings". And we won't compliment Achilles' attendant Phoenix on his restraint in advising Achilles to accept the gifts he was being offered and help the Greeks in their fight, but not to refrain from his "wrath" unless he was bribed. It will also go against our wishes and our convic-
391a tions for Achilles himself to be mercenary enough to accept Agamemnon's gifts and to refuse to release a corpse until he'd been given a ransom.'

'Yes, it would be wrong to approve of that kind of behaviour,' he said.

'Now, the fact that it's Homer makes me hesitate,' I said, 'but I'm not sure it's not actually sacrilegious for us to say things like this about Achilles and accept them when others say them. The same goes also for when Achilles says to Apollo, "There's no god more baneful than you—you with your aloofness. You misled me, and I'd pay you back if I could." We shouldn't believe that he refused to obey the river-god either, and was ready to fight him, and that he said of his hair, which was dedicated to another
b river, the Spercheius, "I hereby give my hair to the hero Patroclus: may he take it with him", when Patroclus was dead—we shouldn't believe that he did this. And we'll deny the truth of the stories that he dragged Hector around Patroclus' tomb and slaughtered prisoners on his funeral pyre. And we won't allow our citizens to believe that Achilles—the child
c of a goddess and of Peleus (who was himself a model of self-discipline and a grandson of Zeus) and tutored by the sage Cheiron—was so full of turmoil that he suffered from the two conflicting diseases of mean-spirited avarice and disdain for gods and men.'

'You're right,' he said.

'Moreover,' I went on, 'we won't believe or tolerate the story about those horrific kidnap projects by Theseus and Peirithous, who were respectively
d the sons of Poseidon and Zeus; and in general, we find it unthinkable that anyone with a god as a parent, or any hero, would be unscrupulous enough to do the terrible, sacrilegious things people falsely attribute to them. No, we should force the poets to deny either that the heroes did these things or that their parents were gods, but not to say both; and they should also be forcibly prevented from trying to persuade the young men of our community that the gods are the source of evil and that the heroes are no better than ordinary people. We demonstrated earlier the impossibility of bad things originating with the e gods; so, as we said then, these stories are not only sacrilegious, but also false.'

'Of course.'

'And they have a pernicious effect on their audience as well, in the sense that no one will find his own badness reprehensible once he's been persuaded that these things are and always have been done by "immediate descendants of the gods, close relatives of Zeus, people whose altar to Zeus, their father-protector, is high on Mount Ida, above the clouds" and "in whom the blood of deities is still fresh". That's why we must put an end to stories of this nature: if we don't, they will engender in the 392a young men of our community a casual attitude towards badness.'

'I quite agree,' he said.

'Now,' I said, 'if we want to distinguish what in literature should be allowed and what should be censored, there's one further type of writing we should still look at, isn't there? I mean, we've discussed how gods must be portrayed—and deities, heroes, and the dead.'

'Yes.'

'So wouldn't we be left with writing which has human beings as its subject?'

'Yes, obviously.'

'In fact, though, we can't evaluate this kind of writing at the moment.'

'Why not?'

'Because what we'd claim, I imagine, is that poets and prose-writers misrepresent people in extremely important ways, when—as they often do— b they portray immoral people as happy and moral people as unhappy, and write about the rewards of undiscovered immorality and how morality is good for someone else, but disadvantageous to oneself. I suppose we'd proscribe assertions of that kind, and tell them that their poems and stories are to make the opposite points, don't you think?'

'I'm certain we would,' he said.

'Well, if you concede this, then won't I claim that you've conceded the original purpose of the enquiry?'

'Yes, I take your point,' he said.

'So we'll postpone our conclusion that these are the types of stories that should be told about people until we've got to the bottom of morality and found out how, given its nature, it rewards its pos- c sessor whether or not he gives an impression of morality.'

'You're quite right,' he said.

Turning from content to form, Plato classifies poetry according to how much 'representation' or 'impersonation' it uses—how much the poet speaks for himself as opposed to having characters speak in their persons. This is a form of dishonesty, but more importantly, it allows people to take on characteristics which may be alien to what they themselves actually are, and undesirable. This habituation would warp their true natures, whereas the principle of 'one man, one job' requires adherence to one's own nature.

'Let's take our discussion of stories no further, then. But the next thing we should look at, in my opinion, is style. Then we'll have considered not only the content, but also the form the stories should have, and our enquiry will be complete.'

'I don't understand what you're getting at here,' said Adeimantus.

'But it's important that you do,' I responded. d 'Maybe this will clarify matters for you: isn't everything told by story-tellers or poets actually a narrative of events in the past, present, or future?'

'Of course,' he said.

'And don't they achieve their effect by making use either of pure narrative, or of representational narrative, or of both?'

'I'm still finding this very obscure,' he said.

'What a ridiculous teacher I seem to be!' I said. 'I don't make things plain at all. I'll stop trying to behave like a professional speaker, and instead of talking in general terms, I'll take a particular exame ple and use that to try to explain my meaning. So here's a question for you. You know the very beginning of the *Iliad*, where Homer has Chryses ask Agamemnon to release his daughter, and Agamemnon gets annoyed, and Chryses doesn't get his way 393a and so calls on his god to curse the Greeks?'

'Yes.'

'Well, as you know, Homer starts by speaking in his own voice and doesn't try to lead us astray by pretending that anyone else is the speaker; this goes on up to the lines "He implored all the Greeks, but especially their leaders, the two sons of Atreus." Next, however, he speaks in Chryses' voice and tries b his very hardest to make us believe that it isn't Homer who is speaking, but the old priest. And the same method of composition is employed through-

out nearly all his narrative of events in Troy and Ithaca and in the *Odyssey* in general.'

'Quite so,' he said.

'Now, the term "narrative" covers all the speeches as well as the passages in between the speeches, doesn't it?'

'Of course.'

'And when he assumes someone else's voice to c make a speech, don't you think that on those occasions he does his very best to adapt his own style to whoever he tells us is about to do the talking?'

'Yes, certainly.'

'Now, to adapt oneself—one's voice or one's appearance—to someone else is to represent that person, isn't it?'

'Of course.'

'So this turns out to be a case of Homer and the rest of the poets composing representational narrative.'

'Yes.'

'And if Homer were to remain undisguised throughout, then all his poetry and all his narrative d would be free of representation. But I don't want you saying that you don't understand again, so I'll tell you how this might happen. If Homer had described Chryses as coming with his daughter's ransom to appeal to the Greeks, but especially their kings, and had then gone on to continue speaking in his own voice rather than taking on the role of Chryses, then it would be pure narrative, not representation. It would go something like this, in my prose version—I'm no poet. "The priest came and prayed that the gods would allow the Greeks to take Troy e and come through unscathed, and also prayed that the Greeks would accept the ransom and, out of reverence for Apollo, release his daughter. Although everyone else gave their assent and approval to what he said, Agamemnon became incensed and ordered him to leave immediately and not to return, or else he would find that his staff and its Apolline garlands were insufficient protection; he said that his daughter would grow old in Argos with him sooner than be released, and he told him to leave and not to make him angry, if he wanted to get home safe. The old 394a man was frightened by what Agamemnon had said, and left without a word, but once he was away from the encampment he prayed over and over to Apollo. He invoked the god's titles, reminded him of all favours he had done him, and asked to be recompensed for any shrine he had built or ritual sacrifice he had performed which had pleased the god. He prayed that, in recognition of these favours, the Greeks would be made to pay for his tears with Apollos' darts." That, my friend,' I concluded, 'is b how we get pure narrative, which is free of representation.'

'I see,' he said.

'Well,' I went on, 'do you also appreciate that we get the opposite when all the passages which the poet composed in between the speeches are excised and only the dialogue is left?'

'Yes,' he said, 'I understand this as well: this is what happens in tragedies for instance.'

'You've grasped my meaning perfectly,' I said. 'I think I'm now getting across to you what I couldn't explain before. There are several varieties of poetry c and story-telling. Some—tragedy and comedy, as you say—is entirely representational; some is in the poet's own voice—you'd find this particularly in dithyrambic poetry; finally, the kind which employs both methods is what we find in epic poetry, but also in many other types of poetry too. Do you see what I mean?'

'Yes,' he said, 'and I understand what you were trying to tell me earlier.'

'Now cast your mind back to what we were saying even before that—that we had discussed the required content of stories, but still had their form to consider.'

'I remember.'

'What I was getting at, then, was just this: we have d to decide whether to allow our poets to compose representational narratives, or to compose narratives which are partly representational and partly not (and if so, we have to decide what kinds of subjects should be treated in either of these ways), or to insist that they avoid representation altogether.'

'The underlying point of your enquiry seems to me', he said, 'to be whether or not we'll allow tragedy and comedy into our community.'

'It could be,' I said, 'but it may be far broader. I certainly don't know yet; we must let our destination be decided by the winds of the discussion.'

'Well said,' he commented.

e 'What I want you to consider carefully, Adeimantus, is whether or not our guardians should be good at representation. Or do you think the answer follows from what we've already established—that whereas an individual can do one job well, he cannot do lots of jobs well, and if he were to try to do so, he would fail to achieve distinction in any occupation, despite undertaking a lot of them?'

'Of course it does.'

'So the same principle applies to representation too: it's impossible for a single individual to play lots of roles as successfully as he plays a single role.'

'That's right.'

'It would be unreasonable, then, to expect a sin- 395a gle individual to work at one of the commendable pursuits and at the same time play lots of parts and be good at representation. I mean, as you know, it isn't possible for the same people simultaneously to be successful in two representational spheres at once, even when those spheres are arguably closely related. Witness, for example, the composition of comedy and the composition of tragedy. Didn't you just describe them as representational?'

'I did—and you're right: people are incapable of doing both at once.'

'And they can't be competent rhapsodes and competent actors at the same time either.'

'True.'

'In fact, the same people can't be competent comic actors and also competent tragic actors. These b are all representational, wouldn't you say?'

'Yes.'

'And the totality of human nature seems to me, Adeimantus, to have been broken down into even smaller slivers than this, until an individual is incapable of successfully playing more than one representational role, or of doing more than one of the actual things which the roles represent.'

'You're absolutely right,' he said.

'Our original position was that our guardians ought to be released from all other sorts of work: they are to be precision craftsmen of the community's autonomy, and must not engage in any work c which does not tend towards this goal. If we're not to undermine this position, then, our guardians have to concentrate exclusively on this work and on this role. Any representational roles they do take on must, from childhood onwards, be appropriate ones. They should represent people who are courageous, self-disciplined, just, and generous and should play only those kinds of parts; but they should neither do nor be good at representing anything mean-spirited or otherwise contemptible, in case the harvest they reap from representation is reality. I mean, haven't you noticed how if repeated representation contin- d ues much past childhood, it becomes habitual and ingrained and has an effect on a person's body, voice, and mind?'

'I certainly have,' he replied.

'So,' I said, 'we won't allow people we claim to care for, and who we're saying have to be good men, to represent (despite being men) a woman, young or old, as she hurls insults at her husband, or pits herself against the gods and arrogantly imagines herself to be happy, or is gripped by catastrophe, grief, and sorrow; and it goes without saying that the same goes for representing a woman who's ill or is suffering pangs of love or labour.'

'I couldn't agree more,' he said.

'And the same prohibition applies to representing slaves of either sex going about their servile duties.'

'I agree.'

'And also, I suppose, to representing bad men who are cowards and whose conduct is the opposite of what we mentioned a short while ago—who abuse and mock and revile one another when they're drunk, or even when they're sober, or who in general, by their words and their actions, sin against themselves and others. Moreover, I'm sure they shouldn't get into the habit of adapting their behaviour to the words and actions of mad people; they must be able to recognize madness and badness in men and women, but they mustn't do or represent any of these things.'

'You're absolutely right,' he said.

'And should they represent artisans like metal-workers,' I asked, 'or oarsmen on a trireme or the petty officers in charge of them, or the like?'

'There'll be no chance of that,' he said, 'since there won't even be the opportunity for any of these concerns to occupy their attention.'

'And will they represent horses neighing, bulls bellowing, rivers splashing, the sea crashing, thunderclaps, and so on and so forth?'

'No,' he said. 'We've already forbidden them to behave abnormally or like madmen.'

'So what you're saying, if I'm getting it right,' I said, 'is that there are two kinds of style, two kinds of narrative. There's one kind which a truly good person would use, when called upon to deliver a narrative; and then there's another, quite different kind, which would be the staple narrative method of someone who by nature and upbringing was the opposite of truly good.'

'What are they?' he asked.

'My impression', I said, 'is that when a moderate man comes in the course of a narrative to something said or done by a good man, he'll happily assume the role of that good man and read it out. He won't find representation of this kind ignominious. He'll

concentrate on representing a good man who is acting reliably and in full possession of his senses, but he'll be less enthusiastic about and will tend to avoid representing a good man who has become unreliable as a result of illness, love, drink, or in general some catastrophe. However, when he comes across a degrading character, he won't be prepared to assimilate himself seriously to this inferior person, except on the few occasions when this character does something good. He'd be ashamed to do so, not only because he's untrained in representing this type of person, but also because he finds it distasteful to mould and conform himself to an inferior stamp, which his mind finds contemptible, except for fun.'

'Yes, that's likely,' he said.

'So the sort of narrative he'll use will be the kind we described a short while ago when we were discussing the Homeric epics: he'll employ the style which incorporates both representation and narrative, but the proportion of representation in the text will be small. So you think I'm right, or am I talking nonsense?'

'What you're talking is certainly not nonsense,' he replied. 'You're describing the principle that kind of person is bound to follow when speaking.'

'All right, then,' I said. "Now, what about the other kind of person? The less good he is, the less he'll be inclined to omit any of the narrative and regard anything as degrading. We'll end up with someone who's prepared to represent anything and everything, and to do so seriously and publicly. He'll even represent sounds and noises and cries like those of the things we mentioned just now—thunder, wind and hail, axles and pulleys, trumpets, reed-pipes, wind-pipes, and every single musical instrument, and also dogs, sheep, and birds. His style will be the one which relies entirely on vocal or bodily representation (though it may contain a small amount of narrative), won't it?'

'Yes, it's bound to be,' he said. 'You're right again.'

'Well, that's what I meant when I said that there were two kinds of style,' I said.

'And there are,' he said.

'Now, one of them involves little variation. Suppose a suitable musical mode and rhythm is assigned to a speaker's style: it turns out that anyone who uses this style correctly is not far off speaking in one and the same mode (given that the variation is only slight), and also with a rhythm that is similarly almost constant. Do you agree?'

'Yes, that's exactly how it is,' he said.

d   'What about the other speaker's style? Won't it be the opposite? For it to be used properly, won't it need every mode and every rhythm there is, since it involves every conceivable kind of variation?'

'Yes, that's an excellent description of it.'

'Now, doesn't every poet—everyone who expresses himself in any way at all, in fact—conform to one of these two styles or to one which he concocts by mixing the two together?'

'Necessarily,' he said.

'What shall we do, then?' I asked. 'Shall we allow all these styles into our community, or one of the two unmixed styles, or the mixed one?'

'I'd vote for the unmixed style which represents the good man,' he said.

'But the mixed style does at least give pleasure, Adeimantus; and the one which gives by far the most pleasure to children and their attendants, and the general run of people, is the one which is the opposite of your choice.'

'Yes, that's because it *is* very enjoyable.'

'But perhaps you'd say that it isn't compatible with our community's political system,' I went on, e 'because each of our people has a single job to do, and therefore none of them is two-sided or many-sided.'

'That's right: it's incompatible.'

'And this was the principle which meant that ours is the only kind of community where we'll find a shoemaker who is a shoemaker and not a ship's captain as well, and a farmer who is a farmer and not a judge as well, and a soldier who is a soldier and not a businessman as well, and so on, wasn't it?'

'True,' he said.

398a   'So it follows that were a man who was clever enough to be able to assume all kinds of forms and to represent everything in the world to come in person to our community and want to show off his compositions, we'd treat him as an object of reverence and awe, and as a source of pleasure, and we'd prostate ourselves before him; but we'd tell him that not only is there no one like him in our community, it is also not permitted for anyone like him to live among us, and we'd send him elsewhere, once we had anointed his head with myrrh and given him a chaplet of wool. Left to ourselves, however, with benefit as our goal, we would em-b ploy harsher, less entertaining poets and story-tellers, to speak in the style of a good man and to keep in their stories to the principles we originally

established as lawful, when our task was the education of our militia.'

'Yes,' he said, 'that's certainly what we'd do, if it were up to us.'

'So now, Adeimantus,' I said, 'I should think we've exhausted the aspect of cultural studies which relates to stories and fables. I mean, we've discussed both the content and the form which the stores should have.'

'I agree,' he said.

A great deal of Greek poetry was chanted or sung, so Plato has to deal with music too. Only certain modes and rhythms are to be allowed: they are the ones which do not titillate or indulge one's emotions.

'Next, we still have to discuss the procedure for c singing and music,' I said.

'Evidently.'

'Well, what we have to say about them—about which types are permitted—if we are to be consistent with what has already been said, must by now be universally obvious, surely?'

Glaucon laughed and said, 'It looks as though I don't belong to this universe, then, Socrates. It's not sufficiently clear to me at the moment what we ought to say, though I have a vague idea.'

'Well,' I said, 'I'm sure that here, in the first place, is a notion you have a perfectly adequate grasp of: that a song is a blend of three ingredients—words, d music, and rhythm.'

'Yes,' he said, 'I understand that.'

'Now, surely the verbal component doesn't differ at all from words which are not part of a song, in the *sense that the words* still have to conform to those same principles we mentioned a moment ago and to the same style, don't they?'

'True,' he said.

'And the music and the rhythm must be in keeping with the words.'

'Of course.'

'Well, we said that laments and dirges need never be voiced.'

'That's right.'

'So which are the plaintive musical modes? You e must tell me—you're the musician.'

'The Mixed Lydian', he replied, 'and the Taut Lydian, and any others like them.'

'We should exclude them, then,' I said. 'They don't help even women achieve the required goodness, let alone men.'

'Right.'

'Now, it's utterly inappropriate for our guardians to be drunk and soft and idle.'

'Of course.'

'Well, which modes are soft and suitable for drinking-parties?'

'There's an Ionian mode which is called "loose",' he answered, 'and another Lydian one as well.'

399a   'Can you find any use for them, Glaucon, when you're dealing with military men?'

'None at all,' he replied. 'It looks as though you're left with the Dorian and Phrygian modes.'

'I'm no expert on the modes,' I said, 'but please leave me with a mode which properly captures the tones and variations of pitch of a brave man's voice during battle or any other enterprise he'd rather not b be involved in—the voice of a man who, even when he fails and faces injury or death or some other catastrophe, still resists fortune in a disciplined and resolute manner. And leave me another mode which captures his voice when he's engaged in peaceful enterprises, where there's no lack of will and he can choose what to do; or when he's trying to win someone over to his point of view and is appealing to him, whether this involves praying to a god or explaining to a human being where he has gone wrong; or alternatively when he patient submits to others' appeals or explanations or arguments, and when he has subsequently completed an action to his satisfaction, and doesn't get big-headed, but acts with self-discipline and restraint throughout and accepts whatever outc come there may be. Leave me these two modes, then—the voluntary and the involuntary ones—which perfectly capture the tones of self-disciplined and courageous men in failure and success.'

'But you're asking to be left with exactly the modes I just mentioned,' he said.

'We'll not need in our songs and music a wide range of notes and the full range of modes, then,' I remarked.

'No, I suppose not,' he said.

'Then we won't keep artisans to make psalteries and harps and any other instruments which are ded signed to produce a wide range of notes and modes.'

'I suppose we won't.'

'Well, will you allow into our community people who make reed-pipes or people who play them? I mean, doesn't this produce a wider range of notes than any other instrument? Don't all instruments which can play the full range of modes in fact take after the reed-pipe in this respect?'

'Obviously they do,' he said.

'So you're left with the lyre and the cithara', I said, 'as instruments which serve some purpose in an urban setting; and then in the countryside the herdsmen can have wind-pipes.'

'That's what the argument suggests, anyway,' he said.

'It's not as if we were doing anything startlingly original', I pointed out, 'in preferring Apollo and e Apollo's kind of instrument to Marsyas and his kind of instrument.'

'How interesting!' he said. 'I suppose we aren't.'

'You know what strikes me?' I said. 'Without realizing it, we've been re-purging the community of the indulgence we mentioned a while back.'

'That just shows how disciplined we are!' he said.

'All right, then, let's finish the purging. We should discuss rhythm next, after music, and make sure we avoid chasing after complexity of rhythm and a wide variety of tempos. We should try to discern the rhythms of a life which is well regulated and courageous. When we've done so, we'll force the metre and the tune to conform to the words which express such a life, rather than forcing the words to conform 400a to the metre and the tune. And it's up to you to tell us what those rhythms are, just as you did with musical modes.'

'Good heavens, no!' he said. 'I can't do that. Because of my studies, I could tell you that there are three elements of tempo, just as in the case of sound there are four basic constituents of all the musical modes. But I can't tell you which rhythmic elements b represent which lifestyle.'

'Well,' I said, 'we'll have to bring in Damon too, and consult him about which tempos suit meanness and promiscuity or derangement, and other forms of badness, and which rhythms should be reserved for the opposite qualities. I remember having heard a difficult talk of his in which he described one compound rhythm as martial, finger-like, and heroic, and he somehow divided it into ordered parts and made it equal in its rise and its fall; and, as I recall, he described an iamb as involving a short period and a long period, and he c described a trochee too; and he assigned to all of these their long and short quantities. And I think he condemned and commended the cadences of some of these rhythms just as much as he did the rhythms themselves; or perhaps it was the combination of cadence and rhythm he was talking about—I can't say. As I said, let's put this on one

side for Damon, since it would take us ages to resolve the issue. What do you think?'

'I couldn't agree more,' he said.

The arguments of the previous sections are now
generalized and expanded. Not only poetry, but
every artefact and every natural entity can display
grace or inelegance, and so be poor food for the
guardians. Moreover, not only do inelegant things
harm a person's character, but they are also products in the first place of a bad character. This could
create a downward spiral of increasing badness in
a community, whereas a spiral of increasing appreciation of goodness and beauty is possible
through proper education. And this appreciation
in turn binds the members of a community together in shared authentic (non-sexual) love.

'But at least you're sure that grace and inelegance
depend on good and bad rhythm, aren't you?'

'Of course.'

d 'Furthermore, good and bad rhythm depend, respectively, on assimilation to a good speaking style
or its opposite, and the same goes for harmony and
disharmony. This follows from what we were just
saying—that rhythm and the harmony of music
should conform to language, not vice versa.'

'Yes, they should,' he said.

'As for speaking style and language,' I said, 'they
depend on a person's character, don't they?'

'Of course.'

'And everything else depends on speaking style?'

'Yes.'

'It follows, then, that good use of language, harmony, grace, and rhythm all depend on goodness of
e character. I'm not talking about the state which is
actually stupidity, but which we gloss as goodness
of character; I'm talking about when the mind really has equipped the character with moral goodness
and excellence.'

'Absolutely,' he said.

'And shouldn't the young people of our community take every opportunity to cultivate these qualities, if they are to do their jobs?'

'Yes, they should.'

'Now, painting and related arts, and weaving, em-
401a broidery, architecture, and the manufacture of utensils, in general, and also the physical structures of
creatures and plants, are all pervaded by these qualities, in the sense that they may display grace or inelegance. And inelegance, lack of rhythm, and
disharmony are allied to abuse of language and a

corrupt character, whereas their opposites are allied
to and reflect a disciplined and good character.'

'Absolutely,' he said.

'Is it only the poets we should oversee, then, and b
compel to choose between imbuing their compositions with the image of goodness of character or not
practising their art in our community? Don't we also
have to oversee artisans in general and stop them
imbuing their portraits of animals, their edifices, and
whatever else they may produce, with corruption,
lack of self-restraint, meanness of spirit, and inelegance, and punish failure to comply with a ban on
working in our community? Otherwise, during their
upbringing our guardians will be surrounded by the
pernicious pasturage of images of badness, which c
will be so common that they'll often be nibbling and
feeding on them, day in and day out, a little at a
time, until without realizing it they'll amass badness
in their minds. No, we must look for craftsmen who
have the innate gift of tracking down goodness and
grace, so that the young people of our community
can live in a salubrious region where everything is
beneficial and where their eyes and ears meet no influences except those of fine works of art, whose effect is like a breeze which brings health from
favourable regions, and which imperceptibly guides d
them, from childhood onwards, until they are assimilated to, familiar with, and in harmony with the
beauty of reason.'

'Yes, that would be an outstandingly fine upbringing for them,' he said.

'Now, Glaucon,' I said, 'isn't the prime importance of cultural education due to the fact that
rhythm and harmony sink more deeply into the mind
than anything else and affect it more powerfully than
anything else and bring grace in their train? For
someone who is given a correct education, their
product is grace; but in the opposite situation it is
inelegance. And isn't its importance also due to the e
fact that a proper cultural education would enable a
person to be very quick at noticing defects and flaws
in the construction or nature of things? In other
words, he'd find offensive the things he ought to
find offensive. Fine things would be appreciated and
enjoyed by him, and he'd accept them into his mind
as nourishment and would therefore become truly
good; even when young, however, and still inca- 402a
pable of rationally understanding why, he would
rightly condemn and loathe contemptible things.
And then the rational mind would be greeted like an
old friend when it did arrive, because anyone with

this upbringing would be more closely affiliated with rationality than anyone else.'

'Yes,' he said, 'to my mind those are the kinds of reasons for cultural education.'

'It's analogous to the process of becoming literate, then,' I said. 'We weren't literate until we realized that, despite being few in number, the letters are fundamental wherever they occur, and until we appreciated their importance whether the word b which contained them was great or small, and stopped thinking that we didn't need to take note of them, but tried hard to recognize them everywhere, on the grounds that literacy would elude us until we were capable of doing so.'

'True.'

'And we won't be able to tell which letters are which when they're reflected in water or a mirror either, until we can recognize the letters themselves, will we? It takes the same expertise and training, doesn't it?'

'Absolutely.'

'Then this is incredibly similar to what I've been c saying. We won't be cultured either (and this doesn't apply only to us, but to the people we're claiming to educate for guardianship) until we recognize the types—self-discipline, courage, generosity, broadness of vision, and all the qualities which are allied and opposed to them—wherever they occur, and notice instances of their presence, whether it is the qualities themselves or their reflections that we are noticing, and don't underestimate them whether the situation in which they're occurring is great or small, but bear in mind that it takes the same expertise and training. Right?'

'Definitely,' he said.

'Now,' I went on, 'imagine a situation where d someone combines beautiful mental characteristics with physical features which conform to the same principle and so are consistent and concordant with the beauty of his mind. Could there be a more beautiful sight for anyone capable of seeing it?'

'Hardly.'

'And the more beautiful a thing is, the more lovable it is?'

'Naturally.'

'Therefore, the more people are of this type, the more a cultured person will love them. If they're dis-e cordant, however, he will not love them.'

'No, he won't,' he said, 'if they have a mental defect; but if their flaw is physical, he'll put up with it and not refuse his affection.'

'I appreciate what you're saying,' I said. 'I know you are or were in love with someone like that, and I concede the point. But answer me this: can self-discipline and excessive pleasure go together?'

'Of course not,' he said. 'Pleasure deranges people just as effectively as distress.'

'Can excessive pleasure partner any of the other virtues?'

'No.'

'What about promiscuity and dissoluteness?' 403a

'Yes, they're its chief partners.'

'Can you think of any pleasure which is greater and more intense than sexual pleasure?'

'No, I can't,' he said, 'and I can't think of any pleasure which is more manic either.'

'And authentic love is a disciplined and cultured love of someone who is restrained as well as good-looking. Yes?'

'Definitely,' he said.

'Authentic love should have no involvement, then, with anything manic or anything which bears the trace of dissoluteness, should it?'

'No, it shouldn't.'

'Doesn't it follow, then, that lovers and their b boyfriends who love and are loved authentically should have no involvement with this pleasure and should have nothing to do with it?'

'That's right, Socrates,' he said. 'They most certainly should not.'

'So you'll apparently be making a regulation in the community we're founding to the effect that although a lover can (if he can persuade his boyfriend to let him) kiss and spend time with and touch his boyfriend, as he would his son—which is to say, for honourable reasons—still his relationship with anyone he cares for will basically be such that he never gives the impression that there is more to it than that. Otherwise, he'll be liable to condemnation for lack- c ing culture and moral sensibility.'

'Exactly,' he said.

'Now, do you join me in thinking that we've completed our discussion of cultural studies?' I asked. 'At any rate, we've reached a good place to finish: I mean, it's good for cultural studies to lead ultimately to love of beauty.'

'I agree,' he said.

The sketch of physical training which follows stresses moderation of diet. Neglect of moderation in diet is the cause of a great deal of ill health, as the neglect of discipline in emotion is the cause of crime (and the legal profession). Hypochondria is an indulgence born of idleness, and interferes with life. Incurably ill people should accept death gracefully (just as incurable criminals should be executed), because they cannot exercise their talents.

'Well, after their cultural education, our young men should receive physical training.'

'Of course.'

'And this too should be a precise course of training which starts in childhood and continues throughout a person's life. See what you think too, but my thinking is that this is the way things are: I am not of the opinion that if the body is in a good condition, then this state of physical excellence makes the mind good too. I think it's the other way round: a good mind, by being in a state of excellence, allows a body to maximize its potential for physical goodness. What about you? What do you think?'

'I agree with you,' he replied.

'So if the education we've provided for the mind is adequate, then wouldn't it be best for us to leave the mind to attend to the details of the physical training, and steer clear of a lengthy discussion by just outlining the principles?'

'Yes, certainly.'

'Now, we've already said that they should avoid getting drunk. I mean, a guardian is, of course, the last person who should get so drunk that he doesn't know where on earth he is.'

'Yes,' he said, 'because then our guardians would need guardians, and that would be ridiculous.'

'What about their food? These men are competitors in the greatest contest of all, aren't they?'

'Yes.'

'So would the condition of one of today's athletes be suitable for them?'

'Maybe.'

'But it's a sluggish condition, and makes health precarious. Can't you see how these athletes spend their lives sleeping and only need to deviate a tiny bit from their prescribed regimen to come down with serious and severe illnesses?'

'Yes, I can.'

'Then our warriors need a less crude form of training,' I said. 'It's essential for them to be as vigilant as watchdogs, with the best possible eyesight and hearing, and for their health to be not so precariously balanced that it is affected by changes in their drinking-water and their diet generally, and in the

heat or cold of the weather, because these changes are commonly encountered during warfare.'

'I agree.'

'Doesn't it follow that the best physical training for them would be comparable in simplicity to the cultural education we described a short while ago?'

'In what sense?'

'I mean a simple and moderate form of physical training, and one designed particularly for warfare.'

'How?'

'Even Homer's a good source for the sort of thing I mean,' I said. 'As you know, when he portrays the heroes eating, he doesn't feed them, while they're campaigning, either on fish (despite the fact that they are in the Hellespont by the sea) or on boiled meat, but only on roasted meat. This is the diet which would be particularly convenient for soldiers, in the sense that they can cook on an open fire almost anywhere, whereas it's less easy for them to carry cooking-pots around wherever they go.'

'Quite so.'

'Nor, I think, does Homer ever mention savoury sauces. In fact, the necessity of avoiding this kind of food if you want to be physically fit is common knowledge among athletes, isn't it?'

'Yes, it is,' he said, 'and they're right to avoid it.'

'If you think they're right to do this, my friend, I suppose you disapprove of Syracusan rations and the wide variety of savouries that can be found in Sicily.'

'Yes, I think I do.'

'Then you also take exception to anyone having a Corinthian lady friend, if he intends to get fit.'

'Absolutely.'

'And to him enjoying the apparent delights of Attic pastries?'

'No doubt about it.'

'And the reason for your disapproval, I imagine, is because we'd be right to draw an analogy between everything that constitutes this kind of diet and lifestyle, and the composition of songs and ballads which use the full range of modes and rhythms.'

'Of course that would be a fair analogy.'

'Now, although in the case of music variety tends to engender lack of discipline, in the present case it engenders illness. Simplicity in music, however, engenders self-control, and simplicity in physical training gives rise to bodily health. Right?'

'Perfectly true,' he said.

'When dissoluteness and disease proliferate in a community, then lawcourts and doctors' surgeries open up all over the place, and the professions of lawyer and doctor have high opinions of themselves, when even large numbers of free men regard them as extremely important.'

'That's inevitable.'

'Could you produce more telling evidence of when a community's educational system is bad and contemptible than when top-notch doctors and lawyers are needed not only by low-ranking people and labourers, but also by those who pride themselves on their privileged upbringing? I mean, don't you think it's despicable, and highly indicative of

b lack of culture, to feel compelled to rely on a moral code which has been imported from others, as if they were one's masters and judges, and to lack one's own moral sense?'

'Nothing could be more contemptible,' he replied.

'Really?' I asked. 'Don't you think that it's more contemptible to waste most of one's life in the law-courts as a prosecutor or defendant, and moreover to be so lacking in moral sensibility that one confidently preens oneself on this fact, and regards one-

c self as a skilful criminal, accomplished in every manoeuvre, in dodges and subterfuges for slipping through every loophole which enables one to avoid being punished, and to do all this for the sake of matters which are trivial and of no importance, because one is ignorant of how much finer and better it is to arrange one's life so that one has no need of a drowsy juror?'

'Yes, you're right,' he said. 'This ranks even higher on the scale of contemptibility.'

'What about needing the art of medicine', I continued, 'for anything except serious injuries and when infected by certain of the seasonal epidemics? What about when it's needed instead because peo-

d ple are, thanks to inactivity and the diet we described, as full of fluids and gases as a marsh, and leave the ingenious Asclepiadae no choice but to come up with names like flatulence and catarrh for their disorders? Doesn't this strike you as contemptible?'

'Yes,' he said, 'these words certainly are really unfamiliar and odd when used as the names of diseases.'

'And I don't think they were used like that in Asclepius' time,' I said. 'The reason I think this is be-

e cause when Eurypylus was wounded at Troy and was treated with Pramnian wine which had lots of pearl barley and grated cheese stirred in it (which is

406a supposed to be an inflammatory brew), Asclepius'

sons didn't tick the woman off for giving it him to drink, and didn't criticize Patroclus' treatment of him either.'

'Well, it *was* an odd drink for someone in his condition,' he remarked.

'Not if you bear in mind the fact that doctors didn't use this modern medical technical of pampering illness until Herodicus' time,' I said. 'Herodicus was a physical-education instructor who became chronically ill and combined the arts of physical exercise and medicine into a means of tormenting first and foremost himself, and then subse- b quently a lot of other people.'

'How?' he asked.

'By prolonging his death,' I answered. 'Although he danced attendance on his illness, it was terminal, and there was no way he could cure himself, of course. He was so busy doctoring himself that for the rest of his life he had no time for anything else and suffered torments every time he deviated in the slightest from his usual regimen; thanks to his cleverness he reached old age, but had one foot constantly in the grave.'

'His expertise earned him a fine reward, then!' he said.

'A suitable one for someone who didn't realize that Asclepius' omission of this type of medical method in the art he invented and handed down to c his successors was not due to his being ignorant and unaware of it,' I said. 'It was because he knew that every citizen of a well-regulated community is assigned a single job which he has to do, and that no one has the time to spend his life ill and doctoring himself. Ridiculously enough, it is noticeable today that while the working class conform to this principle, people who are rich and supposedly happy do not.'

'What do you mean?' he asked.

'If a joiner gets ill,' I explained, 'what he expects d from his doctor is an emetic drug to drink to vomit up the illness, or an aperient for his bowels, or to resort to cautery or surgery to get rid of the affliction. If he's prescribed a long course of treatment, and told to wrap his head in dressings and so on, then his immediate response is to say that he has no time to be ill, and that this way of life, which involves concentrating on his illness and neglecting the work he's been set, holds no rewards for him. Then he takes his leave of this type of doctor, returns to his usual regimen, regains his health, and e lives performing his proper function; alternatively, if his body isn't up to surviving, he gets rid of his troubles by dying.'

'That's the right way for an artisan to approach medical science, I think,' he said.

407a 'Isn't that because he has a job to do,' I asked, 'and because if he doesn't do it, his life is unrewarding?'

'Obviously,' he said.

'But a rich person, by definition, has no job assigned to him such that if he were forced to abstain from it his life would become intolerable.'

'He isn't said to, anyway.'

'If you say that, then you haven't heard what Phocylides said about how as soon as one's livelihood is secure, one should practise goodness.'

'I think one should do so even earlier,' he said.

'Let's not quarrel with him about this,' I said. 'Let's be our own teachers, and find out whether a rich person ought to practise what Phocylides says and whether life becomes intolerable for a rich per-
b son if he doesn't practise it. Let's see whether despite the fact that pampering an illness prevents a person applying himself to joinery and all the other branches of expertise, it is no impediment to anyone carrying out Phocylides' injunction.'

'Of course it is,' he exclaimed. 'It's hard to think of any impediment greater than this excessive attention to the body, this attempt to improve on physical exercise. It's a nuisance in the context of estate-management, of military service, and of sedentary political office too.'

'Its worst aspect, however, is that it makes it difficult to study anything and to think and concentrate, since one is constantly worried about headaches and
c dizziness, and blaming philosophy for their occurrence. So if you're practising this philosophical type of goodness, then excessive attention to the body is a thorough hindrance, since it constantly makes you imagine that you're ill and you're always agonizing about your body.'

'Yes, that's likely,' he said.

'Well, shall we say that Asclepius realized this as well? He invented the art of medicine for people who are physically healthy, thanks to both their constil-
d tutions and their lifestyles, but who contract some isolated illness. This is the type of person and condition he had in mind. He used drugs and surgery to get rid of their illnesses, and then he told them to continue with their usual lifestyles, because he didn't want to damage the functioning of the community. However, he didn't try to use diet gradually to

drain and fill bodies which were diseased to the core, and so be responsible for the person having a long and horrible life and in all probability producing children with the same afflictions. He didn't see any point in treating anyone who was incapable of liv-
c ing a normal life, because such a person does neither himself nor his community any good.'

'Asclepius was a public-spirited person, according to you,' he remarked.

'Obviously he was,' I said. 'And look at his sons 408a too: it was because this was his nature that at Troy they proved themselves to be good fighters and practised the kind of medicine I'm describing. Don't you remember how when Pandarus wounded Menelaus, "they sucked the blood" from the wound "and applied soothing medicines", but didn't tell him (any more than they did Eurypylus) what to eat and drink after this treatment? They were acting on the assumption that the medicines were enough to cure men who had, before being wounded, been healthy and had led orderly lives, even if they happened to b be drinking potions at that precise moment. But they didn't think that the people themselves or anyone else would gain by someone who was constitutionally sickly and who lacked self-discipline remaining alive; they didn't want to waste their art on these people or treat them, even if they were richer than Midas.'

'Asclepius' sons were very clever, according to you,' he said.

'Just as clever as they should be,' I responded. 'And yet the tragedians and Pindar don't see things the way we do, and they claim that Asclepius, despite being the son of Apollo, was bribed to treat a rich man who was already at death's door, and that this is why he was struck by lightning. However, c we'll stick to the principles we formulated earlier and therefore not let them convince us of the truth of both assertions: either he was the son of a god, in which case (we'll claim) he wasn't attracted by dirty money; or he was attracted by dirty money, in which case he wasn't the son of a god.'

'Yes, you're quite right,' he said. 'But here's a question for you, Socrates: surely we need to have good doctors in our community, don't we? And, I suppose, the more healthy and sick people they've dealt with, the more likely they are to be good. The d same goes for legal experts too: it's those who've been involved with people of all sorts and characters who are most likely to be good.'

'I am certainly saying that we need good ones,' I

replied. 'But do you know which ones I regard as good?'

'You'll have to tell me,' he said.

'I'll try,' I said. 'Your question combined dissimilar cases, however.'

'In what way?' he asked.

'Well, take doctors first. In order for doctors to attain perfect skill, they must not only have learnt their trade. In addition, from childhood onwards, they should have come into contact with as many bodies as they possibly could, in the worst condition they could find; moreover, they themselves
e should have contracted every single disease there is, and should be constitutionally rather unhealthy. I mean, it's not their bodies they use to treat other people's bodies, of course; if that were the case, it would be out of the question for their bodies to be bad or to get into a bad state. No, it's their minds they use to treat bodies, and it's impossible for a mind which is or has become bad to treat anything well.'

'Right,' he said.

409a   'On the other hand, Glaucon, a legal expert does use his mind to wield authority over other people's minds. And it's out of the question for a legal expert to be brought up, from childhood onwards, in the company of minds which are in a bad condition, and for his mind to have thoroughly explored the whole arena of immorality until it has become immoral itself and can quickly use itself as a criterion by which to assess the immorality of others' actions (by the analogy of a doctor using his body to assess others' illnesses). Instead, his mind must, while young, have no experience of bad characters, and must not be contaminated by them, if it's to become truly good at assessing the morality of actions in a reliable manner. This also explains why good people are, in their youth, thought by immoral people
b to be gullible simpletons: they don't contain within themselves standards of behaviour which are compatible with anything which is bad.'

'Yes, that's always happening to them,' he said.

'That's why a young man doesn't make a good legal expert,' I said, 'and why advanced age is a prerequisite. A good legal expert must have been slow to learn the nature of immorality, because he's been observing something which is not an inherent quality in his own mind, but an alien quality in other people's minds. He must have trained himself over many years to discern its badness by making use of
c information, not his own experience.'

'At any rate,' he said, 'I suppose the best kind of legal expert is like that.'

'So is a good one,' I said, 'and that was what you were asking about. I mean, it's a good mind that makes someone good. As for that clever paranoiac, who has done wrong himself many times and thinks of himself as smart and unscrupulous: in the company of people similar to himself, his caution—induced by his looking at the standards of behaviour he contains within himself—does make him appear clever. On the other hand, when he associates with good people and older people, then his excessive d mistrust and his inability to recognize reliability—induced by the fact that he has no standard by which to recognize it—make him appear stupid. Since he more commonly encounters bad people than good people, however, he thinks himself clever rather than stupid, and this opinion is endorsed by others.'

'That's perfectly true,' he said.

'Our search for a good, skilful legal expert had better not end with him, then,' I said, 'but with the type of person we described before, because whereas a bad person can never recognize either goodness or badness, a good person will, with time and education, come to understand both goodness and bad- e ness—and therefore it is he, not a bad person, who acquires skill, in my opinion.'

'And I agree with you,' he said.

'So at the same time as legislating for this type of legal practice in our community, you'll also legislate for the kind of medical practice we described. These two practices will treat the bodies and minds of those of your citizens who are naturally well en- 410a dowed in these respects; as for the rest, those with a poor physical constitution will be allowed to die, and those with irredeemably rotten minds will be put to death. Right?'

'Yes, we've shown that this is the best course', he said, 'for those at the receiving end of the treatment as well as for the community.'

'And so your young men', I said, 'will obviously be careful about getting themselves into a position where they need legal expertise; they'll rely on that simple cultural training which, as we said, engenders self-discipline.'

'Naturally,' he said.

'And won't anyone culturally trained in this way b who follows the same trail find, if he wants to, the form of physical exercise he's after, with the result that he'll not need doctors at all, except in emergencies?'

'I think so.'

Harking back to the two poles of a guardian's nature (375c–376c), Plato concludes that the primary education whose principles have been outlined in this chapter will produce people in whom the poles of aggressiveness and gentleness have been adequately trained, when neither side is emphasized to the neglect of the other, and they offset each other.

'Now, the goal he aims for even with this physical exercise and effort is the passionate aspect of his nature. This is what he wants to wake up. This, not developing physical strength, will be the goal of his efforts, as distinct from all other athletes, who diet and train for the sake of physical fitness.'

'Definitely,' he said.

'Doesn't it follow, then, Glaucon,' I asked, 'that c it's wrong to think that the people who are making cultural studies and physical exercise the constituents of our educational system are doing so for the purpose of using the one to look after the body and the other to look after the mind?'

'Why is it wrong?' he asked.

'It rather looks as though the mind is the main objective in both cases,' I said.

'I don't understand.'

'Haven't you noticed the psychological effect of people spending their whole lives on physical exercise, but excluding culture,' I asked, 'or the effect of doing the opposite?'

'In what respect to you mean?' he asked.

d 'I mean in respect of the brutality and intractability of the one lot, and the softness and docility of the others,' I replied.

'Yes,' he said, 'I've noticed that people who engage exclusively in physical exercise end up being excessively brutal, while people who engage exclusively in cultural studies end up shamefully soft.'

'Now, brutality is a product of the passionate part of one's nature. With the correct training, this passionate part is brave; but if it is over-stretched, it becomes intractable and unmanageable, as you can imagine.'

'I agree,' he said.

e 'And docility is an attribute of a philosophical temperament. Over-relaxation results in excessive softness, but if a philosophical temperament is properly trained it becomes docile and orderly, doesn't it?'

'Yes.'

'And we said that our guardians had to possess both characteristics.'

'Yes, they must.'

'So these two features have to fit harmoniously together, don't they?'

'Of course.'

'If they do, the result is a mind which is self- 411a controlled and courageous, isn't it?'

'Yes.'

'And if they don't, the result is a mind which is timid and insensitive?'

'Yes.'

'So when a person allows the music of culture to charm him and makes his ears a channel for his mind to be flooded with the modes we described not long ago as enchanting and soft, and the ones we described as plaintive, and spends his whole life humming and entranced by song, then at first he softens his passionate side, like iron in a forge, and makes it useful, instead of useless and intractable; but if he b goes on and on, and never lets up, but is beguiled, then the result is that he dissolves and melts his passionate side, until it becomes completely fluid and he has, so to speak, cut the sinews out of his mind and made himself a "feeble fighter".'

'Quite,' he said.

'If right from the start he was endowed with a mind which lacked passion,' I went on, 'then it doesn't take long for this to happen; but if he had a passionate mind, then he weakens the passion and destabilizes it, so that even trivial matters make it quickly blaze up and die down again. People like this have exchanged passion for peevishness and ir- c ritability, and are seething with discontent.'

'Absolutely.'

'And what about when someone puts a lot of effort into physical exercise and eats very well, but has nothing to do with culture and philosophy? At first, because he's physically fit, he gets all proud and passionate, and braver than he was before, doesn't he?'

'Yes, exactly.'

'But what if he restricts himself entirely to these activities and has absolutely no contact with the Muse of culture? The intellectual side of his mind is completely starved of intellectual studies and in- d vestigations, and never joins in a discussion or any other cultural activity. Won't it become weak and deaf and blind, because it never receives any stimulation or nourishment and its senses are never purified?'

'Yes.'

'Then this type of person ends up, I suppose, devoid of culture and with a hatred of rationality. He stops relying on the persuasive force of rational argument and instead, like a wild beast, uses brute violence to attain all his ends. He lives his life in blundering ignorance, lacking elegance or refinement.'

'You're absolutely right,' he said.

'So in my opinion what we find is that, since we have a dual nature, God gave us two corresponding areas of expertise—culture and physical exercise—for our passionate and our philosophical aspects. He didn't give them for the mind and the body, except 412a incidentally; the purpose was for those two aspects of our nature to fit harmoniously together by being stretched and relaxed as much as is appropriate.'

'Yes, that seems to be so,' he said.

'Therefore, it isn't the person who attunes the strings of a lyre to one another, it's the person who makes the best blend of physical exercise and culture, and who applies them to the mind in the right proportions, whom we should really describe as a virtuoso and as having the most harmony in his life.'

'That's hard to deny, Socrates,' he said.

'So, Glaucon, we'll always need someone of this type to oversee our community, if its political system is to remain intact, won't we?'

b   'Yes, that'll be the most important of our requirements.'

CHAPTER 5
THE GUARDIANS' LIFE AND DUTIES

This chapter covers various topics, which are loosely strung together, in a sketchy form, because Plato is in pursuit of morality, and other features of the community are of less interest to him in this context. Still, important points are made. First, the guardians are divided into guardians proper, who are to rule, and auxiliaries, who are the militia. Selection of full guardians will take years (see also Chapter 10) of checking that they always have the community's best interests at heart. We now have three classes—guardians, auxiliaries, and workers—whom we may call the castes of gold, silver, and copper or iron. The members of the castes have to believe that this is the way God wants them to be, but there is a little room for change.

'So much for our educational principles. I mean, we don't have to describe in detail the guardians'

dances, hunts, sporting competitions, and horse-races: it's fairly obvious that these activities must conform to the same principles, and their elucidation shouldn't cause any problems now.'

'No, I suppose they shouldn't,' he said.

'All right,' I said. 'What do we have to decide about next? Shouldn't we decide which members of this particular class will be the rulers and which will be the subjects?'

'Of course.'   412c

'It's obvious that the older ones should be the rulers and the younger ones the subjects, isn't it?'

'Yes.'

'And only the best of the older ones?'

'Yes, that's obvious too.'

'Now, the best farmers are the most accomplished farmers, aren't they?'

'Yes.'

'And in the present case, since we're after the best guardians, they must be those who are particularly good at safeguarding the community, mustn't they?'

'Yes.'

'They not only have to have the intelligence and the competence for the job, but they also have to care for the community, wouldn't you say?'

'Yes.'   d

'Now, you care most for things that happen to be dear to you.'

'Inevitably.'

'And something is particularly dear to you if you regard your interests and its interests as identical, and if you think that your success and failure follow from its success and failure.'

'Yes,' he said.

'It follows that we should select from among the guardians men who particularly strike us, on investigation, as being the type to devote their whole lives to wholeheartedly doing what they regard as advantageous to the community, and to completely refusing to do anything they regard as disadvantageous to it.'

'Yes, they would make suitable rulers,' he said.

'I think we'll have to watch them at every stage of their lives, then, to make sure that they're good at safeguarding this idea and aren't magically or forcibly induced to shed and forget the notion that it's essential to do what's best for the community.'

'What do you mean by this shedding?' he asked.

'I'll explain,' I said. 'It seems to me that the departure of an idea from a person's mind can be either intentional or unintentional. It's intentional if

the idea is false and the person learns better, and un-
413a intentional whenever the idea is true.'

'I understand intentional loss,' he said, 'but I still don't understand unintentional loss.'

'But don't you think that the loss of good things is unintentional, while the loss of bad things is intentional?' I asked. 'And don't you think that being deceived about the truth is a bad thing, while having a grasp of the truth is good? And don't you think that having a grasp of the truth is having a belief that matches the way things are?'

'Yes, you're right,' he said. 'I agree that the loss of a true belief is unintentional.'

b 'So when this happens, it's the result of robbery, magic, or brute force, wouldn't you say?'

'I don't understand again,' he said.

'I suppose I am talking pompously,' I said. 'When I talk of a person being robbed of a belief, I mean that he's persuaded by an argument to change his mind, or time causes him to forget it: in either case, he doesn't notice the departure of the belief. I should think you understand now, don't you?'

'Yes,'

'And when I talk of a person being forced out of a belief, I mean that pain or suffering makes him change his mind.'

'Yes, I understand that too,' he said, 'and you're right.'

c 'And I'm sure you'd agree that anyone who changes his mind because he's been beguiled by pleasure or terrified by threats has had magic used on him.'

'Yes,' he said, 'any deception is a form of magic, I suppose.'

'As I was starting to say a moment ago, then, we must try to discover which of our guardians are particularly good at safeguarding within themselves the belief that they should only ever pursue courses of action which they think are in the community's best interests. We must watch them from childhood onwards, and set them tasks which maximize the possibility of their forgetting a belief like this and being misled; those who bear the belief in mind and prove hard to mislead are the ones we should select, d while excluding the others. Do you agree?'

'Yes.'

'And we should also set them tough and painful assignments and ordeals, and watch for exactly the same things.'

'Right,' he said.

'Now, we'll have to invent a selection procedure

for our third category, magic, as well,' I said, 'and observe how they perform. People test a foal's nervousness by introducing it to noise and commotion, and in the same way we must bring our guardians, while they're young, face to face with fear and then shift them into facing pleasure. People use fire to test gold, but our test must be far more thorough, e and must show us how well they resist magic and whether they remain graceful whatever the situation, keep themselves and their cultural education intact, and display rhythm and harmony throughout; if they're capable of doing this, their value to themselves and to the community will be very high. Anyone who emerges without impurities from every single test—as a child, as a young man, and as an adult—should be made a ruler and guardian 414a of our community, and should be honoured in life and in death, in the sense of being awarded the most privileged of funerals and tombs. Anyone who gets corrupted, however, should be excluded. So, Glaucon,' I concluded, 'I think that this is how we should select and appoint our rulers and guardians. These are just guidelines, though: I haven't gone into details.'

'I agree,' he said. 'It must be something like this.'

'And we really and truly could hardly go wrong b if we reserved the term "guardian" in its fullest sense for these people, who ensure that neither the desire nor the capacity for harming the community arises, whether from external enemies or from internal friends. As for the young men we've been calling guardians up to now, we should strictly call them auxiliaries and assistants of the guardians and their decision-making, don't you think?'

'Yes, I do,' he said.

'Now,' I said, 'can we devise one of those lies— the kind which crop up as the occasion demands, which we were talking about not long ago—so that with a single noble lie we can indoctrinate the rulers c themselves, preferably, but at least the rest of the community?'

'What sort of lie?' he asked.

'Nothing too outlandish,' I replied, 'just a tall story about something which happened all over the place in times past (at least, that's what the poets claim and have persuaded us to believe), but which hasn't happened in our lifetimes and I'm not sure it could, and people would need a great deal of convincing about it.'

'You seem reluctant to tell us the story,' he remarked.

'And you'll see that my reluctance was well founded', I said, 'when I do tell you about it.'

'Don't worry,' he said. 'Just talk.'

d   'What I'm saying is . . . I'm not sure where to find the gall or the words to tell the story . . . I'll be trying above all to convince the rulers themselves and the military, and secondarily the rest of the community, that all the nurture and education we provided happened to them in a kind of dream-world; in actual fact, they were at that time being formed and nurtured deep inside the earth, and their weaponry and their equipment in general were also e being made there. When they were finished products, the earth, their mother, sent them up above ground; and now in their policy-making they must regard the country they find themselves in as their mother and their nurse, they must defend her against invasion, and they should think of the rest of the inhabitants of the community as their earth-born brothers.'

'I'm not surprised you were ashamed to tell us the lie before,' he remarked.

415a   'I had good reason,' I said. 'All the same, do please listen to the rest of the story as well. "Although all of you citizens are brothers," we'll continue the tale by telling them, "nevertheless, during the kneading phase, God included gold in the mixture when he was forming those of you who have what it takes to be rulers (which is why the rulers have the greatest privileges), silver when he was forming the auxiliaries, and iron and copper when he was forming the farmers and other workers. Now, despite the fact that in general your offspring will be similar in kind to yourselves, nevertheless, because you're all related, sometimes a silver child b might be born to a gold parent, a gold one to a silver parent, and so on: any of them might be produced by any of the others. Therefore, of all his instructions to the rulers, there is none that God stresses more than this: there is no aspect of their work as guardians which they shall be so good at or dedicated to as watching over the admixture of elements in the minds of the children of the community. If one of their own children is born with a nature tinged with copper or iron, they shall at all costs avoid feeling sorry for it: they shall assign it the sta- c tus appropriate to its nature and banish it to the workers or the farmers. On the other hand, if a child born to a worker or a farmer has a nature tinged with gold or silver, they shall honour it and elevate it to the rank of either guardian or auxiliary, because of an

oracle which states that the community will be destroyed when it has a copper or iron guardian." Can you think of any tactics to make them believe this story?'

'No, not for this particular lot, anyway,' he said, 'but I can for the immediately succeeding genera- d tions and all the generations to follow.'

'I've got a pretty good idea of what you're getting at,' I said.

'It would help them care even more for the community and for one another. But the future of all this will be decided by popular consensus, not by us.'

Within the community, the guardians and auxiliaries are to live an alert, military life (which resembles that of the Spartans), without owing property, which would corrupt them (by turning them into members of the lower class) and cause the downfall of the community. It is true that they will not be happy in the common, materialistic sense of the term, but arguably they will have the greatest happiness (see Chapter 12). In any case, the happiness of the whole is more important than that of any of its parts.

'What we can do, however, is arm these earthborn men and mobilize them under the leadership of their rulers. They must go and look for the best location within the community for their barracks, a lo- e cation from where they can control any disobedience to the laws on the part of the internal inhabitants, and repel the assault of an external enemy who falls on the community like a wolf on a flock of sheep. When they've occupied the site, they must sacrifice to the appropriate gods and construct shelters, don't you think?'

'Yes,' he said.

'And these shelters should provide adequate protection whatever the weather?'

'Of course,' he said. 'I mean, these are their living-quarters you're talking about, I think.'

'Yes,' I said, 'but military quarters, not places of business.'

'*Now* what distinction are you getting at?' he 416a asked.

'I'll try to explain,' I answered. 'Consider, for example, the dogs which shepherds train to act as their auxiliaries, to help them look after their flocks: there could be nothing more dreadful or despicable than for these dogs, thanks to their nature or thanks to the shepherds' training, to be capable of being influenced by indiscipline or hunger or some other bad habit to try to harm the sheep and behave like wolves rather than sheepdogs.'

'It goes without saying that this would be dreadful,' he said.

b 'So we must do everything possible to guard against the possibility of our auxiliaries treating the inhabitants of our community like that and using their greater power to behave like brutal despots rather than well-intentioned allies.'

'Yes, we must,' he said.

'Wouldn't a really excellent education have equipped them to take the maximum amount of care?'

'But they did receive an excellent education,' he said.

'That's not something we should stake our lives on, my dear Glaucon,' I said. 'But we should stand c firmly by our present position, that whatever constitutes a proper education, it is the chief factor in the guardians' treating themselves and their wards in a civilized fashion.'

'That's right,' he said.

'Now, doesn't it make sense to say that this education isn't all they need? That in addition their living-quarters and their property in general should be designed not to interfere with their carrying out their work as guardians as well as possible or to encour- d age them to commit crimes against their fellow citizens?'

'Yes, it does.'

'I wonder if they'd turn out as we want if their lifestyle and living-quarters were somewhat as follows,' I said. 'See what you think. In the first place, none of them is to have any private property, except what is absolutely indispensable. In the second place, none of them is to have living-quarters and storerooms which are not able to be entered by anyone who wants to. Their provisions (which should be suitable in quantity for self-controlled and coura- e geous warriors) are to be their stipend, paid by their fellow citizens for their guarding, the amount being fixed so that, at the end of a year, there is no excess or shortfall. There will be shared mess-halls for them to go to, and their lives will be communal, as if they were on campaign. We'll tell them that the permanent presence in their minds of divine gold and silver, which they were granted by the gods, means that they have no need of earthly gold and silver as well; and we'll add that it is sacrilegious for them to adulterate and contaminate that heavenly possession by owning the earthly variety, because in the past this earthly variety, which is accepted as cur- 417a rency by the masses, has provoked many acts of desecration, whereas theirs is untainted. So, unlike any of their fellow citizens, they are not permitted to have any contract or involvement with gold and silver: they are not to come under the same roof as gold and silver, or wear them on their bodies, or drink from gold and silver cups. These precepts will guarantee not only their own integrity, but also the integrity of the community which is in their safe keeping. If they do come to own land and homes and money, they will be estate-managers and farmers instead of guardians; they will become despots, and enemies rather than allies of the inhabitants of b the community; they will spend their lives hating and being hated, plotting and being plotted against; they will have internal enemies to fear more, and more intensely, than their external enemies. With private property, they will be racing ever closer to the ruin of themselves and the whole community. All this confirms the importance of our stated arrangements for the guardians' living-quarters and so on,' I concluded, 'so shall we enshrine them in law, or not?'

'We certainly must,' said Glaucon.

Adeimantus came in with an objection: 'Tell me, 419a Socrates,' he said. 'How are you going to reply to the accusation that you're not making these men at all happy, and moreover you're making it their own fault? In a real sense, the community belongs to them, but they don't derive any benefit from the community. Others own estates, build beautiful mansions and stock them with suitable furniture, perform their own special religious rites, entertain, and of course own the items you were just talking about, gold and silver, and everything else without which happiness is, on the usual view, impossible. Instead of all this, a critic might say, their role in our community really is just like that of auxiliary troops—mercenaries—with nothing to do except maintain a garrison.'   420a

'Yes,' I agreed. 'And they don't even get paid like other auxiliary troops: they get no more than their provisions. Consequently, they can't even take a trip for personal reasons out of town if they want to, or give presents to mistresses, or spend money on anything else they might want to, as so-called happy people can. You're leaving all this out of your accusation, and plenty of other things too.'

'All right,' he said. 'Please assume that the accusation includes them.'

b 'So you're asking how we'll defend ourselves, are you?'

'Yes.'

'I don't think we need to change direction at all to come across a suitable defence,' I said. 'We'll reply that although it wouldn't surprise us in the slightest if in fact there were no people happier than these men, all the same we're not constructing our community with the intention of making one group within it especially happy, but to maximize the happiness of the community as a whole. We thought we'd be most likely to find morality in a community like ours and also immorality in a community with the worst possible management, and that once c we'd examined them we'd reach the decision which is the original purpose of our investigation. What we're doing at the moment, we think, is forming a community which is happy as a whole, without hiving off a few of its members and making them the happy ones; and before long we'll be looking at a community in the opposite condition.

'Suppose we were painting a statue and someone came up and criticized us for not using the most beautiful paint for the creature's most beautiful features, because the eyes are the most beautiful part and they hadn't been painted purple but black. It would be perfectly reasonable, in our opinion, for d us to reply to this critic by saying, "My dear chap, you can't expect us to paint beautiful eyes in a way which stops them looking like eyes, or to do that to the other parts of the body either. Don't you think that if we treat every single part in an appropriate fashion, we're making the creature as a whole beautiful? Likewise, in the present case, please don't force us to graft the sort of happiness on to the guardians which will make them anything but e guardians. You see, we know we could dress our farmers in soft clothes and golden jewellery and tell them to work the land only when they have a mind to, and we know we could have our potters lie basking in their kiln-fire's warmth on a formal arrangement of couches, drinking and feasting with their wheel beside them as a table, and doing pottery only as much as they feel like, and we know we could make everyone else happy in this sort of way, and so have a community which was happy overall; but please don't advise us to do so, because if we follow your recommendation, then our farmers won't 421a be farmers and our potters won't be potters and no one else will retain that aspect of himself which is a constituent of a community. Now, this isn't so im-

portant where the rest of the community is concerned. I mean, if cobblers go to the bad and degenerate and pretend to be other than what they are, it's not catastrophic for a community; but if the people who guard a community and its laws ignore their essence and start to pose, then obviously they're utterly destroying the community, despite the fact that its good management and happiness are crucially in their hands and their hands alone."

'Now, if we're creating genuine guardians, who can hardly harm their community, and the origina- b tor of that other idea is talking about a certain kind of farmer and people who are, as it were, happy to fill their stomachs on holiday, but aren't members of a community, then he's not talking about a community, but something else. What we have to consider is whether our intention in putting the guardians in place is to maximize their happiness, or whether we ought to make the happiness of the community as a whole our goal and should, by fair means and foul, convince these auxiliaries and guardians that their task is to ensure that they, and c everyone else as well, are the best at their own jobs. Then, when the community as a whole is flourishing and rests on a fine foundation, we can take it for granted that every group within it will find happiness according to its nature.'

'I'm sure you're right,' he said.

The continued integrity, unity, and stability of the community require the guardians to prevent the workers neglecting their work by becoming too rich or too poor, and to keep the population from becoming too great. Since they lack the material resources for prolonged warfare, diplomacy and the threat of their military prowess will be the preferred means of resolving conflicts with other states. To save discussing every possible topic, Plato stresses the overall importance of education: good men, with an understanding of principle, will not need endless rules to guide their lives. Once you have a good system of education and a good political system, beware of change and innovation.

'Well, I wonder if a closely related idea of mine will also strike you as sensible,' I said.

'What is it?'

'That there are other factors which corrupt the rest d of the workers and make them bad at their jobs.'

'What factors?'

'Affluence and poverty,' I replied.

'What do you mean?'

'This is what I mean. If a potter gets rich, do you think he'll still be willing to devote himself to his profession?'

'Not at all,' he answered.

'He'll become less hard-working and less conscientious than before, won't he?'

'Considerably less.'

'Then he'll be a worse potter?'

'Again, considerably worse,' he said.

'But if he's so poor that he lacks the means to provide himself with tools and other essentials for his job, then he's going to be turning out inferior products and he'll not be able to provide his sons (or e whoever else is apprenticed to him) with adequate training.'

'Of course.'

'Both affluence and poverty, then, are causes of degeneration in the products and the practitioners of a craft.'

'So it seems.'

'So we've come up with more things which the guardians must at all costs prevent from sneaking into the community without their noticing it.'

'What things?'

422a 'Affluence and poverty,' I said. 'The first brings indulgence, indolence, and innovation; the second entails miserliness and bad workmanship, as well as also bringing innovation.'

'Quite so,' he said. 'But, Socrates, here's a question for you. How will our community be capable of waging war if its coffers are empty, especially if it has to face an enemy who is large and wealthy?'

'Obviously it would be easier to have two such opponents ranged against us than one, relatively b speaking,' I said.

'What are you getting at?' he asked.

'Chiefly this,' I said. 'If they do have to fight, won't it be a case of warriors versus plutocrats?'

'Yes,' he said.

'Well, Adeimantus,' I went on, 'don't you think that a single boxer who has received the best possible training can easily take on two non-boxers who are rich and fat?'

'Maybe not at the same time,' he answered.

'Not even if it were possible for him to draw back and then turn around and strike whichever opponent is bearing down on him first?' I asked. 'And what c about if he could do this over and over again in the sunshine and stifling heat? Under these circumstances, couldn't he overcome even more opponents of the kind we're postulating?'

'Without a doubt,' he said. 'It wouldn't be at all surprising.'

'Well, don't you think that rich people are better and more experienced boxers than they are soldiers?'

'I do,' he replied.

'Our warriors will, then, in all likelihood, have no difficulty in taking on two or three times the number of rich opponents.'

'I'll concede the point,' he said. 'I think you're right.'

'All right, then. Suppose they send a herald to one d of the two communities with the following true message: "We have no use for gold and silver; it is taboo for us, though not for you. Side with us in the war, and you can have the other side's assets." Do you think that anyone who received this message would choose the option of fighting tough, lean dogs rather than siding with the dogs against fat, tender sheep?'

'No, I don't. But if all the assets of all the other communities are gathered up by a single community, then don't you think this situation might entail e some danger for our asset-free community?'

'It's naïve of you to think that any community other than the one we're constructing deserves the name,' I said.

'What should I call them?' he asked.

'They should have a more capacious title,' I replied, 'since each of them is not so much a community as a great many communities, as in the game. Minimally, they contain two warring communities—one consisting of the rich and one of the poor. 423a Then each of these two contains quite a number of further communities. It would be quite wrong to treat this plurality as a unity. However, if you treat them as a plurality and offer one section's assets and power and personnel to another section, then you'll always have a lot of allies and few enemies. And as long as your community's administration retains its discipline and is arranged in accordance with our recent regulations, it will have no equal. I don't mean that it will merely have the reputation of having no equal, but that it really won't, even if its militia numbers no more than a thousand. You'll be hard put to find a community of this size in Greece or abroad which is actually single, though there are plenty of communities which are far larger in size and which b might be thought to be single. Do you agree, or not?'

'I most certainly do,' he said.

'Now, this could also provide our rulers with the best criterion for deciding on the appropriate size for the community,' I said, 'and how much territory they should reserve for a community of this size, without expanding any further.'

'What criterion?' he asked.

'To allow growth as long as growth doesn't jeopardize its unity,' I said, 'but no further. This is the criterion I'm thinking of.'

c 'It's a good one,' he commented.

'So here's another instruction we'll be giving the guardians,' I said. 'They are to do everything possible to guard against the community either being small or merely appearing large, and to ensure that it is just the right size and is a unity.'

'I suppose you think that's a simple instruction for them to carry out,' he said.

'And here's an even simpler one,' I said, 'which we mentioned earlier as well. We were talking of the necessity of banishing to the other ranks any inferior child who is born to the guardians, and of having any outstanding child who is born to the other ranks join the guardians. And the point of this idea was that every single member of the community, from the other ranks as well as any of the guardians, has to dedicate himself to the single job for which he is naturally suited, because this specialization of function will ensure that every person is not a plurality but a unity, and thus that the community as a whole develops as a unity, not a plurality.'

'Oh yes, that's simpler—hardly worth mentioning!' he said.

'As a matter of fact, my dear Adeimantus,' I said, 'the instructions we're giving them are not as numerous or as difficult as they might seem: they're all simple, provided they follow the saying and e "stick to the one thing that's important"—or rather, not important so much as decisive.'

'What is this thing?' he asked.

'Their education and upbringing,' I replied. 'If they receive a good education which makes them moderate, then they'll easily discover everything we're talking about for themselves—and everything we've missed out so far as well, such as what they are to do with their wives, and what to do about marriage and childbirth, and how all these matters have to be dealt with in accordance with the proverbial 424a saying that friends share everything they can.'

'Yes, that would be best,' he said.

'Now, provided our community's constitution is given a good initial start,' I said, 'then it'll get into a spiral of growth. I mean, a good educational system, if maintained, engenders people of good character; and then people of good character, if they in their turn receive the benefits of an education of this kind, become even better than their predecessors in every respect, but especially—as is the case with other crea- b tures too—in that they produce better children.'

'Yes, that seems reasonable,' he said.

'To put it succinctly, then, the government of the community must adhere to this educational system, and make sure that its integrity is not subtly compromised; they should constantly be on their guard against innovations which transgress our regulations about either physical exercise or cultural studies. They should look out for these to the best of their ability, and should worry if they hear the claim that "the most popular song is the one which happens to be on singers' lips at the moment", in case the poet might c commonly be taken to be talking not about new songs, but a new type of singing, and might be commended for doing so. This kind of thing should be frowned on, however, and it surely is not what the poet meant. The point is that caution must be taken in adopting an unfamiliar type of music: it is an extremely risky venture, since any change in the musical modes affects the most important laws of a community. This is what Damon claims, and I believe him.'

'You can count me as another convert to this view,' said Adeimantus.

'So now we know where the guardians should build their lookout post,' I said. 'It's in the field of d music and culture.'

'Yes,' he said. 'At any rate, indiscipline can easily creep in here without being noticed.'

'Yes,' I agreed. 'because it's not taken seriously and is assumed to have no harmful effects.'

'That's because it doesn't,' he said, 'except that it gradually establishes itself and then silently seeps into people's mannerisms and habits, which become the basis from which it erupts, now enlarged, into their business dealings with one another, which in turn become the basis from which it assaults the laws and the constitution with gross indecency, Socrates, e until it eventually throws everything into chaos in both the private and the public spheres.'

'Really?' I asked.

'I think so,' he said.

'Our original position was correct, then: the children of our community must engage in more lawful amusements right from the start, because when pastimes become lawless and children follow suit, it is impossible for them to grow into law-abiding, exemplary adults. Yes?'

425a 'Of course,' he said.

'Therefore, when children play in a proper manner right from the start, and their cultural education introduces them to the orderliness of law, there is the opposite result: lawfulness accompanies them in everything they do, guides their growth, and corrects any aspect of the community which was formerly aberrant.'

'You're right,' he said.

'And they therefore rediscover those apparently trivial rules which their predecessors had completely lost.'

'What rules?'

b 'For example, that one should be silent in the presence of people older than oneself. Younger people should also give up their seats for their elders, stand up when they enter the room, and look after their parents. Then there are the rules about hairstyle, clothing, footwear, and in general the way one presents oneself, and so on and so forth. Do you agree?'

'Yes.'

'But in my opinion only an idiot would legislate on these matters. I don't think these rules come into being, and I don't think they would remain in force either, through being formulated and written down.'

'How could they?'

'Anyway, Adeimantus,' I said, 'education is the c factor which determines a person's subsequent direction in life. I mean, doesn't like always attract like?'

'Of course.'

'And I suppose we'd say that the final result is a single, dynamic whole, whether or not it's good.'

'Naturally,' he said.

'And that's why I for one wouldn't try to legislate further than we already have done in this area,' I said.

'It makes sense not to,' he remarked.

'Now then,' I said, 'what on earth shall we do about the world of the agora? I mean the commercial deals people make with one another and, of d course, contracts with labourers, lawsuits for slander and assault, indictments, empanelling juries, the collecting or paying of any money due for renting space in the agora or the port, and any business which concerns the general regulation of the agora or the city or the ports or whatever. Shall we take it on ourselves to make any rules and regulations about these matters?'

'It isn't right to tell truly good men what to do,' e he said. 'They won't have any difficulty, in the ma-

jority of cases, in finding out which matters need legal measures.'

'No, my friend, they won't,' I said, 'as long as, by God's will, the laws we've already discussed are preserved intact.'

'Otherwise,' he said, 'they'll spend their whole lives making rule after rule, and then trying to improve them, in the hope that they'll hit on a successful formula.'

'You mean they'll live like people who are ill, but lack the discipline to give up a way of life that is bad for them,' I said.

'That's it.'

'And what a nice time *they* have! All their treat- 426a ments get them nowhere (except that they increase the variety and seriousness of their ailments) and they're constantly expecting every medicine they are recommended to make them better.'

'Yes, that's typical of this kind of invalid,' he said.

'And here's another nice feature of theirs,' I said. 'The thing they can abide least of all is someone telling the truth—that until they stop getting drunk, stuffing themselves, whoring, and doing no work, no medicine or cautery or surgery, and no spell or b amulet or anything like that either, is going to do them the slightest good.'

'That's not at all nice,' he said. 'There's nothing nice about getting angry at good advice.'

'You don't think highly of this type of person, it seems,' I commented.

'No, I certainly don't.'

'And you also won't think highly of a whole community, then, if it carries on in the equivalent way we mentioned a moment ago. I mean, wouldn't you describe as identical the actions of all those badly governed states which forewarn their citizens not to interfere with the general political system and c threaten with death anyone who does so, while anyone who treats them, despite the condition of their government, in a way which pleases them a great deal, and who gets into their good books by flattering them and anticipating their wishes and by being good at satisfying these wishes, is accounted and acclaimed by them a man of virtue and high skill?'

'Yes, I think they're doing exactly the same,' he said, 'and I've got nothing good to say about them at all.'

'And what about people who are prepared, and even determined, to look after such communities? d Don't you admire their courage—and their casual attitude?'

'Yes, I do,' he replied, 'except when they're deluded into imagining that they're true statesmen simply because the masses think highly of them.'

'What do you mean?' I asked. 'Don't you feel compassion for them? I mean, do you suppose there's any way in which a man who is incapable of measuring can avoid thinking he's four cubits tall
e when others (who are just as ignorant) are frequently telling him he is?'

'No, he can't,' he said.

'Don't be so hard on them, then: they're the nicest of people. They make the kinds of laws we mentioned a short while ago and then try to improve them, and constantly expect the next breach of contract to be the last one, and likewise for the other crimes we mentioned just now, because they are unaware that in fact they're slashing away at a kind of Hydra.'

427a   'Yes, that's exactly what they're doing,' he said.

'So I wouldn't have thought that in either a badly governed or a well-governed community a genuine legislator need occupy himself with laws and administration of this kind. In the one community they can't help and don't accomplish anything; in the other some of them will be obvious and others will follow automatically from habits the citizens will already have acquired.'

b   'Is there any legislation for us still to see to, then?' he asked.

'Not for us,' I replied, 'but Delphic Apollo still has to make the most important, valuable, and fundamental laws.'

'Which ones?' he asked.

'How to site temples, how to conduct sacrifices, and how in general to worship the gods, deities, and heroes. Then there's the burial of the dead and all the services we have to perform to propitiate those who have gone to the other world. You see, we aren't experts in this area, and in founding our city we won't—
c perts in this area, and in founding our city we won't—if we have any sense—trust anyone else's advice or consult any arbiter except our ancestral one. Apollo is, of course, the traditional arbiter in this area for the whole human race, and he performs his function as arbiter from his seat at the earth's navel.'

'That's a good idea,' he said. 'We must do as you suggest.'

CHAPTER 6
INNER AND OUTER MORALITY

Plato now locates the four presumed elements of goodness in the community he has imagined. The thought and resourcefulness of the guardians, as they take care of the community as a whole, are its wisdom; the lawful bravery of the auxiliaries is its courage; the lower orders tolerating the control of the rulers is its self-discipline; the members of the three classes doing what they are best equipped to do, without usurping the functions of others, is its morality, because (as Plato supposes morality must) it allows the other elements of goodness to exist.

'So there you are, Adeimantus,' I said. 'Your community seems to have been founded. The next thing for you to do is to get hold of a bright enough light 427d and explore the community—you should invite your brother and Polemarchus and the rest of us to join you—to see if we can locate morality and immorality within it, discover how they differ from each other, and find out which of them is a prerequisite for happiness, whether or not its possession is hidden from the eyes of gods and men.'

'Rubbish,' said Glaucon. 'You promised you'd do the investigating, on the grounds that it was sacrilegious for you not to do everything you could to assist morality.'   e

'You're right,' I said. 'Thanks for the reminder. But you should still help me while I do so.'

'We will,' he said.

'I think I know how we'd better conduct the search,' I said. 'I assume that if the community has been founded properly, it has everything it takes to be good.'

'Necessarily,' he replied.

'Obviously, then, it has wisdom, courage, self-discipline, and morality.'

'Obviously.'

'And clearly, as we go about our search, we'll discover some of these elements and there'll be some we have yet to discover.'

'Of course.'   428a

'Now, imagine any set of four things, and imagine we're exploring something for one of the four. Either we'd recognize it straight away and that would do the job, or we would recognize the one we're looking for by first recognizing the other three, in the sense that whatever is left is bound to be the one we're looking for.'

'Right,' he said.

'Well, we're faced with a set of four things here, so the principles of exploration are the same. Yes?'

'Obviously.'

'Now, the first thing which I think is visible here is wisdom. And there's a peculiarity in its case.'   b

'What?' he asked.

'Well, I do think that the community we've described really is wise. I mean, it's resourceful, isn't it?'

'Yes.'

'And this thing, resourcefulness, is obviously a kind of knowledge. I mean, it's not ignorance which makes people resourceful; it's knowledge.'

'Obviously.'

'Now, there are many branches of knowledge in our community, of all different kinds.'

'Naturally.'

'So is it the knowledge its carpenters have which makes the community deserve to be described as wise and resourceful?'

c   'No, that only entitles us to call it good at carpentry,' he replied.

'It shouldn't be called wise, then, because of its knowledge of carpentry and because it is resourceful at ensuring the excellence of its furniture.'

'Certainly not.'

'Because it knows how to make mental implements, then, or anything like that?'

'Definitely not that either,' he said.

'And the fact that it knows how to grow crops only entitles us to describe it as good at agriculture.'

'That's what I think.'

'All right,' I said. 'Is there a branch of knowledge which some of the inhabitants of the community we've just founded have, which enables it to think d resourcefully about the whole community, not just some element of it, and about enhancing the whole community's domestic and foreign policies?'

'There certainly is.'

'What is it?' I asked. 'And which of the citizens have it?'

'It is guardianship,' he replied, 'and the people who have it are those rulers—the ones we not long ago called guardians in the strict sense of the word.'

'And what description does this branch of knowledge earn the community, in your opinion?'

'Resourceful and genuinely wise,' he answered.

'Now, do you think that in our community met-e alworkers will outnumber these true guardians, or the other way round?' I asked.

'There'll be far more metalworkers,' he said.

'And wouldn't these guardians be outnumbered by any of the other acknowledged categories of experts?' I asked.

'Yes, by a long way.'

'So when a community is founded on natural principles, the wisdom it has as a whole is due to the smallest grouping and section within it and to the knowledge possessed by this group, which is the authoritative and ruling section of the community. And we also find that this category, which is naturally the least numerous, is the one which inherently pos- 429a sesses the only branch of knowledge which deserves to be called wisdom.'

'You're absolutely right,' he said.

'So we've somehow stumbled across one of the four qualities we were looking for and found whereabouts in the community it is located.'

'*I* think it's clear enough, anyway,' he said.

'Now, it's not too hard to spot courage and to see which section of the community possesses it and enables the community to be described as courageous.'

'Why?'

'The only feature of a community which might justify describing it as either cowardly or coura- b geous', I answered, 'is its defensive and military arm.'

'Yes, that's the only one,' he agreed.

'The point is', I went on, 'that whether the rest of its inhabitants are cowardly or brave wouldn't affect the nature of the community either way, I imagine.'

'No, it wouldn't.'

'Again, then, it is a section of a community that earns it the right to be called courageous. This section possesses the ability to retain under all circumstances the notion that the things and kinds of things c to be feared are precisely those things and kinds of things which during their education the legislator pronounced fearful. Isn't this what you call courage?'

'I haven't understood your point,' he said. 'Please could you repeat it.'

'I'm saying that courage is a sort of retention,' I explained.

'What do you mean, retention?'

'I mean the retention of the notion, which has been inculcated by law through the agency of education, about what things and what kinds of things are to be feared. And by its retention "under all circumstances" I meant keeping it intact and not losing it d whether one is under the influence of pain or pleasure, desire or aversion. I can tell you what strikes me as analogous, if you like.'

'Yes, please.'

'Well,' I said, 'you know how when dyers want to dye wool purple, they first select something which is naturally white, rather than any other colour; then they subject it to a lengthy preparatory treatment designed to ensure that the colour will take as well as possible; and when it's in the required condition, e they dye it. Anything dyed in this way holds its colour, and the colour can't be washed out, whether or not one uses solvent. But you know what happens to anything which isn't dyed in this way, when something of another colour is dyed, or when something white is dyed without having been treated first.'

'Yes,' he said. 'The dye washes out and they look ridiculous.'

'So I want you to imagine', I said, 'that we too were doing our best to achieve something similar, when we selected our militia and put them through 430a their cultural and physical education. You should assume that the educational programme was designed for one purpose only: to indoctrinate them so thoroughly that the laws take in them like a dye, so that their notions about what is to be feared and about everything else hold fast (which requires a suitable character as well as a suitable upbringing), with the dye being incapable of being washed out by those solvents which are so frighteningly good at scouring—pleasure, which is a more efficient cleanser b than any soda and lye, and pain and aversion and desire, which outclass any solvent. So this ability to retain under all circumstances a true and lawful notion about what is and is not to be feared is what I'm calling courage. That's how I'll use the term, unless you have an alternative suggestion.'

'No, I don't,' he said. 'I mean, I think your idea is that any true notion about these matters which is formed in an animal or a slave without the benefit of education is not really lawful, and I suppose you'd find some other name for it, not courage.'

c   'You're quite right,' I said.

'I accept your definition of courage, then.'

'Accept it by all means,' I said, 'but as a definition of the kind of courage a community has; then your acceptance will be all right. We'll go into the subject more thoroughly later, if you want; you see, at the moment our quarry is morality, not courage, which I think we've explored enough.'

'That's fine by me,' he said.

'Well, we've still got two qualities to detect in the community,' I said, 'self-discipline and the purpose d of the whole enquiry, morality.'

'Quite so.'

'Can we somehow locate morality and not bother any more about self-discipline?'

'I don't know if we can,' he said, 'and anyway I wouldn't like morality to be discovered first if that entails dropping the search for self-discipline. I'd be

grateful if you'd look for self-discipline before morality.'

'Then it's my duty to do so, of course,' I said.

'Go on, then,' he said.

'All right,' I said. 'From my point of view, we're faced here with a closer similarity to some kind of harmony and attunement than we were before.'

'Why?'

'To be self-disciplined', I replied, 'is somehow to order and control the pleasures and desires. Hence the opaque expression "self-mastery"; and there are other expressions which hint at its nature. Yes?'

'Absolutely,' he said.

'Isn't the phrase "self-mastery" absurd? I mean, anyone who is his own master is also his own slave, of course, and vice versa, since it's the same person 431a who is the subject in all these expressions.'

'Of course.'

'What this expression means, I think,' I continued, 'is that there are better and worse elements in a person's mind, and when the part which is naturally better is in control of the worse part, then we use this phrase "self-mastery" (which is, after all, complimentary). But when, as a result of bad upbringing or bad company, the smaller better part is defeated by the superior numbers of the worse part, then we use critical and deprecatory language and b describe someone in this state as lacking self-mastery and discipline.'

'That sounds plausible,' he said.

'Have a look at our new community, then,' I said, 'and you'll find that the first of these alternatives is attributable to it. I mean, you must admit the justice of describing it as having self-mastery, since anything whose better part rules its worse part should be described as having self-discipline and self-mastery.'

'Yes, I can see the truth of what you're saying,' he said.

'Now, children, women, slaves, and (among so-called free men) the rabble who constitute the ma- c jority of the population are the ones who evidently experience the greatest quantity and variety of forms of desire, pleasure, and pain.'

'Yes.'

'Whereas simple and moderate forms, which are guided by the rational mind with its intelligence and true beliefs, are encountered only in those few people who have been endowed with excellence by their nature and their education.'

'True,' he said.

'And is it clear to you that this is a property of your community, where the desires of the common majority are controlled by the desires and the intelligence of the minority of better men?'

'It is,' he said.

'So if any community deserves to be described as having mastered pleasure and desire, and as having self-mastery, it is this one.'

'Without the slighest doubt,' he said.

'So it also deserves to be called self-disciplined, doesn't it?'

'Yes, indeed,' he said.

'Moreover, it is in this community, more than in any other conceivable community, that the rulers and their subjects agree on who the rulers should be, don't you think?'

'Definitely,' he said.

'In a situation like this, then, is it the rulers or the subjects of the community who, in your opinion, possess self-discipline?'

'Both,' he replied.

'Is it clear to you, then,' I asked, 'that our recent conjecture that self-discipline resembles a kind of attunement wasn't bad?'

'Why?'

'Because unlike courage and wisdom, both of which imbued the community with their respective qualities while being properties of only a part of the community, self-discipline literally spans the whole octaval spread of the community, and makes the weakest, the strongest, and the ones in between all sing in unison, whatever criterion you choose in order to assess their relative strengths—intelligence, physical strength, numerical quantity, wealth, and so on. And the upshot is that we couldn't go wrong if we claimed that self-discipline was this unanimity, a harmony between the naturally worse and naturally better elements of society as to which of them should rule both in a community and in every individual.'

'I certainly agree,' he said.

'All right,' I said. 'We've detected three of the qualities in our community, as far as we can tell. But there's one final way in which a community achieves goodness. What precisely is morality? I mean, morality is this missing type of goodness, clearly.'

'Clearly.'

'We must now imitate hunters surrounding a thicket, Glaucon, and make sure that morality doesn't somehow elude us and disappear into obscurity. I mean, we know it's somewhere round here. Keep your eyes peeled and try to spot it. If you see it before I do, let me know where it is.'

'I wish I could,' he said. 'But in fact it would be more realistic of you to regard me as someone who follows in your footsteps and can see things only when they're pointed out to him.'

'Follow me, then,' I said, 'and pray for success.'

'I will,' he said. 'You have only to lead on.'

'Now, we're in a rather rugged and overcast spot, it seems,' I said. 'At any rate, it's gloomy and hunting won't be easy. Still, we must carry on.'

'Yes, we must,' he said.

I caught a glimpse of something and shouted, "Hurray! Glaucon, I believe we're on its trail! I don't think it will get clean away from us.'

'That's good news,' he said.

'What a stupid state to find ourselves in!' I exclaimed.

'What do you mean?'

'It looks as though it's been curled up at our feet all the time, right from the beginning, my friend, and we didn't see it, but just made absolute fools of ourselves. You know how people sometimes go in search of something they're holding in their hands all the time? That's what we've been like. We've been looking off into the distance somewhere, instead of at our quarry, and that was why we didn't notice it, I suppose.'

'What do you mean?'

'I'll tell you,' I said. 'I think it's been the subject of our discussion all along and we just didn't appreciate that we were in a sense talking about it.'

'What a long preamble,' he said, 'when I'm so keen to hear what you're getting at!'

'All right,' I said. 'See if you think there's anything in what I say. From the outset, when we first started to found the community, there's a principle we established as a universal requirement—and this, or some version of it, is in my opinion morality. The principle we established, and then repeated time and again, as you'll remember, is that every individual has to do just one of the jobs relevant to the community, the one for which his nature has best equipped him.'

'Yes, that's what we said.'

'Furthermore, the idea that morality is doing one's own job and not intruding elsewhere is commonly voiced, and we ourselves have often said it.'

'Yes, we have.'

'So, Glaucon,' I said, 'it seems likely that this is in a sense what morality is—doing one's own job. Do you know what makes me think so?'

'No,' he answered. 'Please tell me.'

'We've examined self-discipline, courage, and wisdom,' I said, 'and it occurs to me that this principle is what is left in the community, because it is the principle which makes it possible for all those other qualities to arise in the community, and its continued presence allows them to flourish in safety c once they have arisen. And we did in fact say that if we found the other three, then whatever was left would be morality.'

'Yes, that's necessarily so,' he said.

'But if we had to decide which of these qualities it was whose presence is chiefly responsible for the goodness of the community,' I said, 'it would be hard to decide whether it's the unanimity between d rulers and subjects, or the militia's retention of the lawful notion about what is and is not to be feared, or the wise guardianship which is an attribute of the rulers, or the fact that it is an attribute of every child, woman, slave, free person, artisan, ruler, and subject that each individual does his own job without intruding elsewhere, that is chiefly responsible for making it good.'

'Yes, of course that would be a difficult decision,' he said.

'When it comes to contributing to a community's goodness, then, there's apparently a close contest between the ability of everyone in a community to do their own jobs and its wisdom, self-discipline, and courage.'

'There certainly is,' he said.

'And wouldn't you say that anything which rivals these qualities in contributing towards a commu- e nity's goodness must be morality?'

'Absolutely.'

'See if you also agree when you look at it from this point of view. Won't you be requiring the rulers to adjudicate when lawsuits occur in the community?'

'Of course.'

'And won't their most important aim in doing so be to ensure that people don't get hold of other people's property and aren't deprived of their own?'

'Yes.'

'Because this is right?'

'Yes.'

'So from this point of view too we are agreed that morality is keeping one's own property and keeping 434a to one's own occupation.'

'True.'

'See if you agree with me on this as well: if a joiner tried to do a shoemaker's job, or a shoemaker a carpenter's, or if they swapped tools or status, or even if the same person tried to do both jobs, with all the tools and so on of both jobs switched around, do you think that much harm would come to the community?'

'Not really,' he said.

'On the other hand, when someone whom nature has equipped to be an artisan or to work for money in some capacity or other gets so puffed up by his b wealth or popularity or strength or some such factor that he tries to enter the military class, or when a member of the militia tries to enter the class of policy-makers and guardians when he's not qualified to do so, and they swap tools and status, or when a single person tries to do all these jobs simultaneously, then I'm sure you'll agree that these inter- c changes and intrusions are disastrous for the community.'

'Absolutely.'

'There's nothing more disastrous for the community, then, than the intrusion of any of the three classes into either of the other two, and the interchange of roles among them, and there could be no more correct context for using the term "criminal".'

'Indubitably.'

'And when someone commits the worst crimes against his own community, wouldn't you describe this as immorality?'

'Of course.'

'Then this is what immorality is. Here's an alternative way of putting it. Isn't it the case (to put it the other way round) that when each of the three classes—the one that works for a living, the auxiliaries, and the guardians—performs its proper function and does its own job in the community, then this is morality and makes the community a moral one?'

'Yes, I think that's exactly right,' he said.   d

The existence of conflict within a person's mind proves that there are different 'parts' to the mind. On examination, we can claim that there are three parts. Plato's description of them is rather hard to pin down, and the discussion in this section should be supplemented by reference to 580d–588a, 602c–605c, and Chapter II as a whole. He distinguishes a part which includes our desires or wants or instinctive appetites; our intellect, which uses both pure and applied thinking; and our passionate, assertive, proud, brave side, which (in non-Platonic terms) enhances or defends our 'sense of

I'. This is Plato's famous theory of the tripartite mind, which recurs in *Phaedrus* and *Timaeus*. Since all three parts have aims and objectives and distinctive pleasures, the most profitable way to think of them is to describe them as forms of desire: instinctive desire; the desire for one's overall good; and the desire for good results based on one's self-image.

'Let's not be too inflexible about it yet,' I warned. 'If we also conclude that this type of thing constitutes morality in the case of individual human beings as well, then we'll have no reservations. I mean, how could we under those circumstances? However, if we find that it doesn't apply to humans as well, then we'll have to take the enquiry into new areas. So let's now wind up that aspect of the enquiry which is based on the idea we had that it would be easier to detect the nature of morality in an individual human being if we first tried to observe it in something larger and to watch its operation there. We decided that the larger thing was a community, e and so we founded as good a community as we could, because we were well aware that it would have to be a good community for morality to exist in it. What we have to do now is apply the results we found in the case of the community to an individual. If there's a match, that will be fine; but if we find something different in the case of an individual, then we'll return to the community to test the new result. With luck, the friction of comparing the two cases will enable morality to flare up from these 435a fire-sticks, so to speak, and once it's become visible we'll make it more of a force in our own lives.'

'That's a viable notion,' he said. 'We should do as you suggest.'

'Well,' I said, 'if a single property is predicated of two things of different sizes, then in so far as it's the same predicate, is it in fact dissimilar or similar in the two instances?'

'Similar,' he said.

b 'So in respect of the actual type of thing morality is, a moral person will be no different from a moral community, but will resemble it.'

'Yes,' he said.

'Now, we decided that a community was moral when each of the three natural classes that exist within it did its own job, and also that certain other states and conditions of the same three classes made it self-disciplined and courageous and wise.'

'True.'

'It follows, my friend, that we should expect an individual to have the same three classes in himself, c and that the same conditions make him liable to the same predicates as the community receives.'

'That's absolutely inevitable,' he said.

'Glaucon,' I said, 'now we're faced with another simple enquiry, to see whether or not the mind contains these three features.'

'It hardly seems to me to be a simple one,' he remarked. 'But then it's probably a true saying, Socrates, that anything fine is difficult.'

'I think that's right,' I said. 'In fact, I have to tell you, Glaucon, that in my opinion we'll never com- d pletely understand this issue by relying on the kinds of methods we've employed so far in our discussion: a longer and fuller approach is needed. Still, we can hope to come up with something which is in keeping with what we've already said in the earlier stages of our enquiry.'

'Shouldn't we be content with that?' he asked. 'I for one would be satisfied with that for the time being.'

'And it'll do perfectly well for me too,' I said.

'No flagging, then,' he said. 'On with the enquiry.'

'Well, here's something we're bound to agree on, e aren't we?' I asked. 'That we do contain the same kinds of features and characteristics as the community. I mean, where else could it have got them from? When the general population of a community consists of people who are reputedly passionate—Thracians and Scythians, for example, and almost any northerner—it would be absurd to think that passion arises in this community from any other source. And the same goes for love of knowledge, for which our 436a country has a strong reputation; and being mercenary might be claimed to be a particular characteristic of Phoenicians and Egyptians.'

'Certainly.'

'This is a matter of fact, then,' I said, 'and it wasn't hard to discover.'

'No.'

'But here's a hard one: is there just a single thing which we use for doing everything, or are there three and we use different things for different tasks? Do we learn with one of our aspects, get worked up with another, and with a third desire the pleasures of eating, sex, and so on, or do we use the whole of our mind for every task we actually get going on? These b questions won't be easy to answer satisfactorily.'

'I agree,' he said.

'Well, let's approach an answer by trying to see whether these aspects are the same as one another or are different.'

'How?'

'It's clear that the same one thing cannot simultaneously either act or be acted on in opposite ways in the same respect and in the same context. And consequently, if we find this happening in the case of these aspects of ourselves, we'll know that there c are more than one of them.'

'All right.'

'What about this, then?'

'What?'

'Is it possible for the same thing to be simultaneously at rest and in motion in the same respect?' I asked.

'Of course not.'

'Let's take a closer look before agreeing, otherwise we'll start arguing later. My assumption is that if someone claims that a person who is standing still, but moving his hands and head, is the same person simultaneously being still and moving, we won't approve of this way of putting it, as opposed to say- d ing that one part of him is still, and another part of him is moving. Yes?'

'Yes.'

'So even if the advocate of the claim were to get even more subtle and ingeniously maintain that when a top is spinning round with its peg fixed in place, then this is definitely a case of something simultaneously being still and moving as a whole, or that the same goes for anything else which spins round on one spot, we wouldn't accept this assertion. We'll say that in this situation these objects are e not still and moving in the same respects. We'll point out that they include an axis and a circumference, and that they may be still in respect of their axes (in the sense that they're not tipping over at all), but they have circular motion in respect of their circumferences; and we'll add that when one of these objects tips its upright to the right or left or front or back while simultaneously spinning round, then it has no stillness in any respect.'

'Yes, that's right,' he said.

'No assertion of this kind will put us off, then, or make us in the slightest inclined to believe that the same thing could ever simultaneously be acted on 437a or exist or act in opposite ways in the same respect and in the same context.'

'I won't be put off, anyway,' he said.

'That's as may be,' I said. 'But let's not feel com-pelled to have all the bother of going through every single one of these arguments and proving them false. Let's assume that we're right and carry on, with the understanding that if we ever turn out to have been mistaken, all the conclusions we draw on the basis of this assumption will be invalidated.'

'Yes, that's what we'd better do,' he said.

'Wouldn't you count assent and dissent,' I asked, b 'seeking and avoidance, and liking and disliking, as all pairs of opposites? It'll make no difference whether you think of them as ways of acting or of being acted on.'

'Yes, they're opposites,' he answered.

'What about thirst and hunger and the desires generally,' I went on, 'and what about wishing and wanting? Wouldn't you say that all these things belong somewhere among the sets we've just men- c tioned? For example, won't you describe the mind of anyone who is in a state of desire as seeking to fulfil his desires, or as liking whatever the desired object is? Or gain, to the extent that it wants to get hold of something, don't you think it is internally assenting to this thing, as if in response to a question, and is longing for it to happen?'

'Yes, I do.'

'And what about the states of antipathy, reluctance, or unwillingness? Won't we put these states in the opposite category, which includes dislike and aversion?'

'Of course.'

'Under these circumstances, then, won't we say d that there is a category which consists of the desires, and that the most conspicuous desires are the ones called thirst and hunger?'

'Yes,' he said.

'And the one is desire for drink, the other desire for food?'

'Yes.'

'Now, is thirst, in itself, the mental desire for anything more than the object we mentioned? For example, is thirst thirst for a hot drink or a cold one, a lot of drink or a little, or in short for any particular kind of drink at all? Doesn't it take heat in addition to thirst to give it the extra feature of being e desire for something cold, and cold to make it desire for something hot? Doesn't it take a thirst which has been aggravated into becoming strong to produce the desire for a lot of drink, and doesn't it take a weak thirst to produce the desire for a little drink? The actual state of being thirsty, however, cannot possibly be desire for anything other than its natural object, which is just drink; and the same goes for hunger and food.'

'Yes,' he said. 'Each desire is for its natural object only, and the desire for an object of this or that type is a result of some addition.'

438a 'It should be quite impossible, then,' I said, 'for anyone to catch us unawares and rattle us with the claim that no one desires drink, but a good drink, and no one desires food, but good food. Everyone desires good, they say, so if thirst is a desire, it must be desire for a good drink or whatever; and so on for the other desires.'

'There might seem to be some plausibility to the claim,' he remarked.

'But there are only two categories of things whose nature is to be relative,' I said. 'The first category consists, in my opinion, of things which have par- b ticular qualities and whose correlates have particular qualities; the second category consists of things which are just what they are and whose correlates are just what they are.'

'I don't understand,' he said.

'Don't you realize', I said, 'that anything which is greater is greater than something?'

'Yes.'

'Than something smaller?'

'Yes.'

'Whereas anything which is a lot greater is relative to something which is a lot smaller. Agreed?'

'Yes.'

'And anything which was once greater (or will be) is relative to something which was once smaller (or will be), isn't it?'

'Of course,' he said.

c 'And the same goes for more in relation to less, and double in relation to half (and all similar numerical relations); also for heavier in relation to lighter, quicker in relation to slower, and moreover hot in relation to cold, and so on and so forth, don't you think?'

'Yes.'

'And what about the branches of knowledge? Isn't it the same story? Knowledge in itself is knowledge of information in itself (or whatever you choose to call the object of knowledge), but a particular branch of knowledge, knowledge qualified, is d knowledge of a particular qualified kind of thing. Here's an example: when the knowledge of making houses was developed, didn't it differ from the rest of the branches of knowledge and consequently gain its own name, building?'

'Of course.'

'And didn't it do so by virtue of the fact that it is a particular kind of knowledge, a kind which none of the other branches of knowledge is?'

'Yes.'

'And wasn't it when its object came into being as a particular kind of thing that it too came into being as a particular kind of knowledge? And doesn't the same go for all the other branches of expertise and knowledge?'

'Yes, it does.'

'I wonder if you've grasped my meaning now,' I said. 'You should think of this as the point I was trying to make before, when I said that there are two categories of things whose nature it is to be relative: some are only themselves and are related to objects which are only themselves; others have particular e qualities and are related to objects with particular qualities. I don't mean to imply that their quality is the same as the quality of their objects—that knowledge of health and illness is itself healthy and ill, and knowledge of evil and good is itself evil and good. I mean that when knowledge occurs whose object is not the unqualified object of knowledge, but an object with a particular quality (say, health and illness), then the consequence is that the knowledge itself also acquires a particular quality, and this is why it is no longer called just plain knowledge: the qualification is added, and it is called medical knowledge.'

'I do understand,' he said, 'and I agree as well.'

'As for thirst, then,' I said, 'don't you think it finds 439a its essential place among relative things? And what it essentially is, of course, is thirst . . .'

'. . . for drink,' he said. 'Yes, I agree.'

'So for drink of a particular kind there is also thirst of a particular kind; but thirst in itself is not thirst for a lot of drink or a little drink, or a beneficial drink or a harmful drink, or in short for drink of any particular kind. Thirst in itself is essentially just thirst for drink in itself.'

'Absolutely.'

'When someone is thirsty, then, the only thing—in so far as he is thirsty—that his mind wants is to drink. This is what it longs for and strives for.'

'Clearly.'   b

'So imagine an occasion when something is making it resist the pull of its thirst: isn't this bound to be a different part of it from the thirsty part, which is impelling it towards drink as if it were an animal? I mean, we've already agreed that the same one thing cannot thanks to the same part of itself simultaneously have opposite effects in the same context.'

'No, it can't.'

'As an analogy, it isn't in my opinion right to say that an archer's hands are simultaneously pushing the bow away and pulling it closer. Strictly, one hand is pushing it away and the other is pulling it close.'

c   'I quite agree,' he said.

'Now, do we know of cases where thirsty people are unwilling to drink?'

'Certainly,' he said. 'It's a common occurrence.'

'What could be the explanation for these cases?' I asked. 'Don't we have to say that their mind contains a part which is telling them to drink, and a part which is telling them not to drink, and that this is different part and overcomes the part which is telling them to drink?'

'I think so,' he said.

'And those occasions when thirst and so on are countermanded occur thanks to rationality, whereas d the pulls and impulses occur thanks to afflictions and diseased states, don't they?'

'I suppose so.'

'So it wouldn't be irrational of us to expect that these are two separate parts,' I said, 'one of which we can describe as rational, and the other as irrational and desirous. The first is responsible for the mind's capacity to think rationally, and the second—which is an ally of certain satisfactions and pleasures—for its capacity to feel lust, hunger, and thirst, and in general to be stirred by desire.'

e   'No, it wouldn't be irrational,' he said. 'This would be a perfectly reasonable view for us to hold.'

'Let's have these, then,' I said, 'as two distinct aspects of our minds. What about the passionate part, however, which is responsible for the mind's capacity for passion? Is it a third part, or might it be interchangeable with one of the other two?'

'I suppose it might be the same as the desirous part,' he said.

'But there's a story I once heard which seems to me to be reliable,' I said, 'about how Leontius the son of Aglaeon was coming up from the Piraeus, outside the North Wall but close to it, when he saw some corpses with the public executioner standing near by. On the one hand, he experienced the desire to see them, but at the same time he felt disgust and averted his gaze. For a while, he strug-
440a gled and kept his hands over his eyes, but finally he was overcome by the desire; he opened his eyes wide, ran up to the corpses, and said, "There you

are, you wretches! What a lovely sight! I hope you feel satisfied!" '

'Yes, I've heard the story too,' he said.

'Now, what it suggests', I said, 'is that it's possible for anger to be at odds with the desires, as if they were different things.'

'Yes, it does,' he agreed.

'And that's far from being an isolated case, isn't it?' I asked. 'It's not at all uncommon to find a person's desires compelling him to go against his reason, and to see him cursing himself and venting his b passion on the source of the compulsion within him. It's as if there were two warring factions, with passion fighting on the side of reason. But I'm sure you wouldn't claim that you had ever, in yourself or in anyone else, met a case of passion siding with the desires against the rational mind, when the rational mind prohibits resistance.'

'No, I certainly haven't,' he said.

'And what about when you feel you're in the wrong?' I asked. 'If someone who in your opinion c has a right to do so retaliates by inflicting on you hunger and cold and so on, then isn't it the case that, in proportion to your goodness of character, you are incapable of getting angry at this treatment and your passion, as I say, has no inclination to get worked up against him?'

'True,' he said.

'But suppose you feel you're being wronged. Under these circumstances, your passion boils and rages, and fights for what you regard as right. Then hunger, cold, and other sufferings make you stand firm and conquer them, and only success or death can stop it fighting the good fight, unless it is re- d called by your rational mind and calmed down, as a dog is by a shepherd.'

'That's a very good simile,' he said. 'And in fact the part we've got the auxiliaries to pay in our community is just like that of dogs, with their masters being the rulers, who are, as it were, the shepherds of the community.'

'Yes, you've got it,' I said. 'That's exactly what I mean. But there's something else here too, and I wonder if you've noticed it as well.'

'What is it?'   e

'That we're getting the opposite impression of the passionate part from what we did before. Previously, we were thinking that it was an aspect of the desirous part, but now that seems to be way off the mark, and we're saying that when there's mental conflict, it is far more likely to fight alongside reason.'

'Absolutely,' he said.

'Is it different from the rational part, then, or is it a version of it, in which case there are two, not three, mental categories—the rational and the desirous? Or will the analogy with the community hold good? 441a Three classes constituted the community—the one which works for a living, the auxiliaries, and the policy-makers—so is there in the mind as well a third part, the passionate part, which is an auxiliary of the rational part, unless it is corrupted by bad upbringing?'

'It must be a third party,' he said.

'Yes,' I said, '*if* we find that it's as distinct from the rational part as it is from the desirous part.'

'But that's easy,' he said. 'Just look at children. It's evident that from the moment of their birth they have a copious supply of passion, but I'm not con-b vinced that some of them ever acquire reason, and it takes quite a time for most of them to do so.'

'Yes, you've certainly put that well,' I said. 'And animals provide further evidence of the truth of what you're saying. Moreover, we can adduce the passage from Homer we quoted earlier: "He struck his breast and spoke sternly to his heart." Clearly, Homer here has one distinct part rebuking another c distinct part—the part which has thought rationally about what is better and worse rebuking the part whose passion is irrationally becoming aroused.'

'You're absolutely right,' he said.

'It's not been easy,' I said, 'but we've made it to the other shore: we've reached the reasonable conclusion that the constituent categories of a community and of any individual's mind are identical in nature and number.'

'Yes, they are.'

Since the three mental parts are precisely analogous to the three social classes of Plato's community, Plato now analyses individual wisdom, courage, self-discipline, and morality in ways which precisely parallel his analysis of their civic manifestations. Morality, then, is an inner state and has little to do with external appearances. It is harmony between the parts of a person's mind under the leadership of his or her intellect; immorality is anarchy and civil war between the parts. The remaining question, whether morality or immorality is rewarding, is raised, but then deferred to Chapter 11.

'Isn't it bound to follow that the manner and cause of a community's and an individual's wisdom are identical?'

'Naturally.'

'And that the manner and cause of a community's d and an individual's courage are identical, and that the same goes for every other factor which contributes in both cases towards goodness?'

'Inevitably.'

'So no doubt, Glaucon, we'll also be claiming that human morality is the same in kind as a community's morality.'

'Yes, that's absolutely inevitable too.'

'We can't have forgotten, however, that a community's morality consists in each of its three constituent classes doing its own job.'

'No, I'm sure we haven't,' he said.

'So we should impress upon our minds the idea that the same goes for human beings as well. Where each of the constituent parts of an individual does its own job, the individual will be moral and will do e *his* own job.'

'Yes, we certainly should do that,' he said.

'Since the rational part is wise and looks out for the whole of the mind, isn't it right for it to rule, and for the passionate part to be its subordinate and its ally?'

'Yes.'

'Now—to repeat—isn't it the combination of culture and exercise which will make them attuned to each other? The two combined provide fine discussions and studies to stretch and educate the rational part, and music and rhythm to relax, calm, and 442a soothe the passionate part.'

'Absolutely.'

'And once these two parts have received this education and have been trained and conditioned in their true work, then they are to be put in charge of the desirous part, which is the major constituent of an individual's mind and is naturally insatiably greedy for things. So they have to watch over it and make sure that it doesn't get so saturated with physical pleasures (as they are called) that in its bloated and strengthened state it stops doing its own job, and tries to dominate and rule over things which it is not b equipped by its hereditary status to rule over, and so plunges the whole of everyone's life into chaos.'

'Yes, indeed,' he said.

'Moreover, these two are perfect for guarding the entire mind and the body against external enemies, aren't they?' I asked. 'The rational part will do the planning, and the passionate part the fighting. The passionate part will obey the ruling part and employ its courage to carry out the plans.'

'True.'

'I imagine, then, that it is the passionate part of a
c person which we are taking into consideration when
we describe him as courageous: we're saying that
neither pain nor pleasure stops his passionate part
retaining the pronouncements of reason about what
is and is not to be feared.'

'That's right,' he agreed.

'And the part we take into consideration when we
call him wise is that little part—his internal ruler,
which made these pronouncements—which knows
what is advantageous for each of the three parts and
for their joint unity.'

'Yes.'

'And don't we call him self-disciplined when
there's concord and attunement between these same
parts—that is, when the ruler and its two subjects
d unanimously agree on the necessity of the rational
part being the ruler and when they don't rebel
against it?'

'Yes, that's exactly what self-discipline is, in both
a community and an individual,' he said.

'And we're not changing our minds about the
manner and cause of morality.'

'Absolutely not.'

'Well,' I said, 'have we blunted the edge of our
notion of morality in any way? Do we have any
grounds for thinking that our conclusions about its
nature in a community don't apply in this context?'

'I don't think so,' he replied.

'If there's still any doubt in our minds,' I said,
e 'we can eradicate it completely by checking our conclusion against everyday cases.'

'What cases?'

'Take this community of ours and a person who
resembles it by virtue of both his nature and his upbringing, and suppose, for instance, we had to state
whether, in our opinion, a person of this type would
steal money which had been deposited with him. Is
it conceivable to you that anyone would think our
443a man capable of this, rather than any other type of
person?'

'No one could think that,' he said.

'And he could have nothing to do with temple-
robbery, theft, and betrayal either of his personal
friends or, on a public scale, of his country, could
he?'

'No, he couldn't.'

'Moreover, nothing could induce him to break an
oath or any other kind of agreement.'

'No, nothing.'

'And he's the last person you'd expect to find
committing adultery, neglecting his parents, and failing to worship the gods.'

'Yes, of course,' he said.

'And isn't the reason for all of this the fact that
each of his constituent parts does its own job as ruler b
or subject?'

'Yes, that's the only reason.'

'Do you need to look any further for morality,
then? Don't you think it can only be the capacity
we've come up with, which enables both people and
communities to be like this?'

'I for one certainly don't need to look any further,' he said.

'Our dream has finally come true, then. We said
we had a vague impression that we had probably—
with the help of some god—stumbled across the origin and some kind of outline of morality right at the c
start of our foundation of the community.'

'Absolutely.'

'It turns out, then, Glaucon—and this is why it
was so useful—that the idea that a person who has
been equipped by nature to be a shoemaker or a
joiner or whatever should make shoes or do joinery
or whatever was a dreamt image of morality.'

'So it seems.'

'And we've found that in real life morality is the
same kind of property, apparently, though not in the
field of external activities. Its sphere is a person's inner activity: it is really a matter of oneself and the
parts of oneself. Once he has stopped his mental con- d
stituents doing any job which is not their own or intruding on one another's work; once he has set his
own house in order, which is what he really should
be concerned with; once he is his own ruler, and is
well regulated, and has internal concord; once he has
treated the three factors as if they were literally the
three defining notes of an octave—low, high, and
middle—and has created a harmony out of them and
however many notes there may be in between; once
he has bound all the factors together and made him- e
self a perfect unity instead of a plurality, self-disciplined and internally attuned: then and only then does
he act—if he acts—to acquire property or look after
his body or play a role in government or do some
private business. In the course of this activity, it is
conduct which preserves and promotes this inner
condition of his that he regards as moral and describes as fine, and it is the knowledge which oversees this conduct that he regards as wisdom; however, it is any conduct which disperses this condition

444a that he regards as immoral, and the thinking which oversees this conduct that he regards as stupidity.'

'You're absolutely right, Socrates,' he said.

'All right,' I said. 'I imagine that we'd regard as no more than the truth the claim that we had found out what it is to be a moral person and a moral community, and had discovered what morality actually is when it occurs in them.'

'Yes, we certainly would,' he said.

'Shall we make the claim, then?'

'Yes.'

'So be it,' I said. 'Next, I suppose, we should consider immorality.'

'Obviously.'

b 'Isn't it bound to involve these three factors being in conflict, intruding into one another's work, and exchanging roles, and one part rebelling against the mind as a whole in an improper attempt to usurp rulership—improper because its natural function is to be dominated unless it belongs to the ruling class? Our position, I'm sure, will be that it is disruption and disorder of the three parts along these lines that constitutes not only immorality, but also indiscipline, cowardice, and stupidity—in a word, badness of any kind.'

'Precisely,' he said.

c 'Now that morality and immorality are in plain view, doesn't that mean that wrongdoing and immoral conduct, and right conduct too, are as well?' I asked.

'Why?'

'Because their role in the mind happens to be identical to that of healthy or unhealthy factors in the body,' I said.

'In what sense?'

'Healthy factors engender health, and unhealthy ones illness.'

'Yes.'

'Well, doesn't moral behaviour engender morald ity, while immoral behaviour engenders immorality?'

'Inevitably.'

'But you create health by making the components of a body control and be controlled as nature intended, and you create disease by subverting this natural order.'

'Yes.'

'Doesn't it follow,' I said, 'that you create morality by making the components of a mind control and be controlled as nature intended, and immorality by subverting this natural order?'

'Absolutely,' he said.

'Goodness, then, is apparently a state of mental health, bloom, and vitality; badness is a state of mental sickness, deformity, and infirmity.'

e

'That's right.'

'Isn't it the case, therefore, that goodness is a consequence of good conduct, badness of bad conduct?'

'Necessarily.'

'Now we come to what is, I suppose, the final topic. We have to consider whether moral conduct, fine behaviour, and being moral (whether or not the 445a person is known to be moral) are rewarding, or whether it is wrongdoing and being immoral (provided that the immoral person doesn't have to pay for his crimes and doesn't become a better person as a result of being punished).'

'It seems to me that it would be absurd to consider that topic now, Socrates,' he said. 'Life isn't thought to be worth living when the natural constitution of the body is ruined, even if one has all the food and drink and wealth and power in the world. So how could it be worth living when the natural constitution of the very life-force within us is disrupted and ruined? How could life be worth living b if a person's chosen course of action is to avoid the path which will lead him away from badness and immorality and towards the possession of morality and goodness, given the evident accuracy of our descriptions of both of these states?'

'Yes, it is absurd,' I agreed. 'All the same, since we've reached a point which affords the clearest possible view of the truth of these matters, we shouldn't give up now.'

'I couldn't agree more,' he said. 'Giving up should be the last thing on our minds.'

'Come and join me here, then,' I said, 'and you'll c see, I think, all the types of badness there are—at least, the ones that are worth seeing.'

'I'm coming,' he said. 'You have only to tell me.'

'Well,' I said, 'the impression I get from the vantage-point we've reached at this point of our discussion is that while there's only one kind of goodness, there are countless types of badness, of which four are worth mentioning.'

'What do you mean?' he asked.

'There are probably as many types of character,' I said, 'as there are identifiable forms of political system.'

'And how many is that?'

'There are five types of political system,' I replied, d 'and five types of character.'

'Please tell me what they are,' he said.

'All right,' I said. 'One of the forms of political system would be the one we've described. There are two possible ways of referring to it, however: if a single outstanding individual arises within the ruling class, it's called a kingship; but if there is a plurality of rulers, it's called an aristocracy.'

'True,' he said.

'This is the first of the types of political system I had in mind,' I said. 'The point is that whether there is a single ruler in the community, or whether there e are more than one, they won't disturb any of the community's important laws, since they'll have been brought up and educated in the manner we've explained.'

'No, it's implausible to think that they will,' he said.

CHAPTER 7
WOMEN, CHILDREN, AND WELFARE

The discussion of morality is now interrupted until Chapter II. However, the intervening chapters are of great importance, and deepen our understanding of some issues already raised. For many readers, these chapters constitute the heart of the book; the metaphysics of Chapters 8–9 is particularly famous, and recurs in several other dialogues. But first we meet Plato's most radical social proposals.

449a 'So that's the kind of community and political system—and the kind of person—I'm calling good and right. Given the rightness of this community, I'm describing all the others as bad and flawed: not only are their political systems wrong, but they also influence individuals' characters incorrectly. And I see them as falling into four categories.'

'What four categories?' he asked.

I was on the point of listing them and explaining how, in my opinion, each in turn evolved out of the b preceding one, when Polemarchus (who was sitting just beyond Adeimantus) reached out and got hold of Adeimantus' cloak high up, by his shoulder. He drew Adeimantus towards himself, leaned forward and whispered something with his mouth to his ear, so that all we heard of his words was: 'Shall we let it drop or what?'

'Of course not,' Adeimantus replied—this was out loud.

'What aren't you going to let drop?' I asked.

'You,' he said.

'What have I done?' I asked.   c

'We think you're being lazy,' he said. 'We think you're doing us out of a whole aspect of the discussion, and a not unimportant aspect at that, so that you don't have to spell out the details. You seem to think you can get away with casually saying, as if it were obvious to everyone, that where wives and children are concerned "friends share".'

'But that's right, isn't it, Adeimantus?' I asked.

'Yes,' he replied. 'But it still needs explaining, just as you've explained everything else. What makes this sharing right? I mean, there are all sorts of ways it could happen, so don't leave us guessing d as to which one you have in mind. For a long time now we've been patiently expecting you to make some mention of their approach to procreation and how they'll bring up their children, and to discuss the whole issue of the sharing of wives and children, which is a subject you raised, because in our opinion, as far as society is concerned, a great deal—no, everything—hinges on whether or not it happens in the right way. That is why, when you were starting to criticize another type of political system before you'd adequately discussed this issue, we made the decision you overheard—not to let you go on until 450a you'd discussed this whole topic as well.'

'You should know that I share his view,' said Glaucon. 'This decision gets my vote too.'

'In fact, you'd better count us as unanimous about this decision, Socrates,' said Thrasymachus.

'If only you knew what you'd done, laying into me like this,' I said. 'You're touching off a huge discussion about the constitution of our community; it'll be like starting again from the beginning. And I was so pleased that I'd finished describing it, and so happy that the description I'd given had been found acceptable and allowed to stand! You've no idea how massive a swarm of arguments you're stir- b ring up now with your appeals. It's because I noticed its size that I did nothing about it, to avoid all the bother it would cause us.'

'Do you think it's gold fever that's brought these people here?' demanded Thrasymachus. 'Don't you suppose they've come to hear arguments?'

'Yes,' I replied, 'but not endless ones.'

'Anyone with any sense lets only death put an end to this kind of discussion,' Glaucon said. 'Please don't spare us a thought: just persevere and explain your views on the matters we're asking c about. How will our guardians share children and wives? What upbringing will they provide for young children between birth and schooling, which is regarded as the most difficult period? Please try to explain it to us.'

'It's not an easy matter to go into, Glaucon,' I said. 'There are plenty of reasons for misgivings— even more than in the matters we've already discussed. I mean, one might doubt the viability of the proposal, and even granting its viability, there'll be room for doubting whether it's the best course of action. That, my dear friend, is why I'm rather hesi-d tant about addressing the topic: I'm scared of my ideas being thought to be wishful thinking.'

'Don't worry,' he said. 'You won't be faced with an audience of dunces or sceptics or grumblers.'

'Was that remark supposed to raise my morale, Glaucon?' I asked.

'Yes,' he answered.

'Well, it's having exactly the opposite effect,' I said. 'If I was sure I knew what I was talking about, then your attempt at encouragement would go down well. I mean, there's no danger or uncertainty when someone who knows the truth speaks among intel-e ligent friends about crucial matters which are close to their hearts, but when someone who is vacillating and who still hasn't formed any definite conclusions does the talking, as I am, it's a cause for 451a alarm and caution. My worry is not that I might make a fool of myself: that would be a childish worry. But I'm frightened of dragging my friends down with me when I stumble and fall short of the truth in matters where uncertainty is the lasting thing one wants. I humbly beg Nemesis, Glaucon, to pardon what I'm about to say. You see, I'm sure that deceiving people about customs which are truly good and moral is more of a sin than accidentally killing someone. That is why it's preferable to take this risk when one is in the company of enemies rather than friends— b and that's why I really appreciated your encouragement!'

Glaucon smiled and said, 'Socrates, if anything nasty happens to us as a result of what you say, we'll acquit you of murder, so to speak, and find you free of all taint of deceit. So you can talk with confidence.'

'Well, it's true that in homicide cases there's a law guaranteeing that anyone who has been acquitted is free of the taint of pollution,' I said, 'so I suppose the same rule applies here too.'

'Then there's nothing to stop you getting on with the discussion,' he said.

Socrates unveils his plans for the equality of female guardians with male guardians. In the first place, their primary education (see Chapter 4) is to be identical. Anyone who finds this idea ludicrous is confusing relevant and irrelevant properties of human nature; the ideas are both feasible and good for the community. Men may be better at most things, but that does not mean they have exclusive rights to those functions. Concern for the welfare of the community should have priority over convention in this context, especially since the convention may be wrong.

'We'd better backtrack, then,' I said. 'The proper time for the discussion may have been earlier, but we'll have to have it now. It'll probably be all right c this way, though—to proceed with the women's business now that the men's business is completed and done, especially since that's what you're asking me to do. It is my opinion that there is only one correct way for people with the character and education we've described to have and deal with their children and wives, and that is if they continue in the direction we gave them at the outset. What we tried to do, as you know, was make the men in theory like guardians of a flock.'

'Yes.'

'So let's keep to the same path and have the d women born and brought up in a closely similar way, and see whether or not it turns out right for us.'

'How?' he asked.

'Well, should female guard-dogs share with the males the guarding and hunting and whatever other duties the males might have, do you think? Or should they stay indoors, incapacitated by their bearing and rearing of whelps, while the males work and do all the overseeing of the flocks?'

'They should share in everything,' he said. 'The e only qualification is that we're dealing with a physically weaker sex: the males are stronger.'

'Can you employ any two creatures for the same purposes if you haven't given them the same upbringing and education?' I asked.

'No.'

'Therefore, if we're going to use the women for the same purposes as the men, we have to educate them in the same way.'

'Yes.'

'Now, the men were set cultural studies and phys- 452a ical exercise.'

'Yes.'

'So these two subjects had better be set the women

too. Then there's the military training: we ought to put them through exactly what we put the men through.'

'That's a reasonable deduction from what you're saying,' he said.

'I suppose a lot of our suggestions would seem ludicrous and outlandish if they became practical realities,' I said.

'No doubt,' he said.

'Which of them do you think would be the most ludicrous?' I asked. 'Isn't it obviously the idea of having women exercising naked in the gymnasia along with the men—and not only young women, b but older ones as well? I mean, there are old men who come to the gymnasia and are still fond of exercise despite their wrinkled flesh and ugly appearance.'

'Good heavens, yes!' he said. 'That would certainly be thought ludicrous, as things stand to day.'

'Well,' I said, 'we've chosen the course of our argument, so we shouldn't let sarcastic jibes worry us. People would crack lots of jokes of all kinds if they were faced in practice with changes of this nature in physical and cultural education, let alone in how arc mour was worn and horses were ridden.'

'You're right,' he said.

'We've started out on this argument, however, so we must take the legislative rough with the smooth. We'll ask those wits not to do what they usually do, but to be serious for a change, and we'll remind them that until quite recently the Greeks used to regard it as shocking and ludicrous for *men* to be seen naked—in fact, in most foreign countries this is still the case. The Cretans were the first to exercise naked (followed by the Spartans), and when they started to do so, it was an opportunity for the wags of the day d to make fun of it all, don't you think?'

'Yes.'

'But when experience proved the superiority of nakedness to clothing in all these kinds of contexts, then superficial mockery waned in the light of what reasoned argument revealed to be best. It was shown to be inane to think anything ludicrous except badness, to try to raise a laugh by regarding as absurd the spectacle of anything except foolishness and e badness, and also to seriously hold any standard of beauty except goodness.'

'Absolutely.' he said.

'The first thing we have to reach agreement on, then, is whether or not these proposals are viable, isn't it? And shouldn't we allow that there is room

for doubting—whether the doubt is expressed humourously or seriously—whether women do have 453a the natural ability to co-operate with men in all their jobs, or in none, or in some but not others (in which case there's the further question of which category warfare belongs to)? Don't you think that this would be the best way for us to make a start and would probably lead to the best conclusion?'

'By far the best,' he said.

'Shall we voice their doubts between ourselves, then, on their behalf,' I asked, 'so that the opposite point of view is not left to fend for itself?'

'Why not?' he replied.   b

'So let's have them say, "You don't need external sceptics, Socrates and Glaucon. You yourselves asserted, right at the start of the founding of your community, that everyone had to do the one job for which his nature had equipped him." '

'Yes, I should say so. Of course we did.'

' "And doesn't a woman's nature differ a great deal from a man's?" '

'Of course it does.'

' "So the members of each sex should properly be assigned different work—work which suits their particular nature—shouldn't they?" '   c

'Of course.'

' "So your current proposal is bound to be incorrect, and you're contradicting yourselves with the claim that men and women should do the same jobs, despite the enormous differences between their natures." Can you defend our proposals against this accusation, Glaucon?'

'Hardly,' he replied, 'not without some preparation. What I'd do is ask *you* to come up with the response for us—so that's what I am doing.'

'I foresaw this accusation a long time ago, Glaucon,' I said, 'and plenty of other similar criticisms too. That's why I was afraid and didn't really want to get involved with regulations about what to do d with wives and how to bring up children.'

'No, it certainly doesn't seem to be an easy task,' he remarked.

'No, it isn't,' I said. 'But it's like this: it makes no difference whether you fall into a little pool or into the middle of the largest ocean—you're still swimming.'

'Yes.'

'So we'd better try swimming to safety out of this sea of argument, hoping for some improbable rescue like a dolphin picking us up.'

'I suppose so,' he said.   e

'Let's see if we can find a way out, then,' I continued. 'We maintain that different natures should do different work, and that men and women do have different natures; and now we're claiming that these different natures should do the same work. Is that what we're accused of?'

'Exactly.'

454a 'You know, Glaucon, skill at disputation is a splendid thing,' I said.

'Why?'

'Because a lot of people, I think,' I replied, 'find themselves unconsciously seduced by it: they think they're practising dialectic, not eristic. The reason for this is their inability to conduct the enquiry by dividing the subject-matter into its various aspects. Instead their goal is the contradiction of statements at the purely verbal level, and they converse with one another eristically, not dialectically.'

'Yes,' he said, 'that's a common phenomenon. But does it have any relevance to our current situation?'

b 'Nothing could be more relevant,' I answered. 'At any rate, we're in danger of unconsciously resorting to disputation.'

'How?'

'We're pursuing the idea that different natures should get different occupations with considerable vigour and eristic force at the verbal level, but we haven't spent any time at all enquiring precisely what type of inherent difference and identity we meant when we assigned different occupations to different natures and identical occupations to identical natures, and whether context makes any difference to what we said.'

'No, we haven't looked into that,' he said.

c 'By the same token,' I said, 'we might as well ask ourselves, apparently, whether bald men and men with hair have the same nature of completely different natures. And suppose we agreed that they have completely different natures, then we might have bald shoemakers, and make hair disqualify people from being shoemakers, or vice versa.'

'Which would be absurd,' he said.

'And the reason it would be absurd,' I said, 'is because earlier we weren't talking about identity or difference of nature in any absolute sense. We had in mind only that type of difference or similarity d which is relevant to identity of occupation, didn't we? We meant, for example, that a man with a medical mind and a woman with a medical mind have the same nature. Don't you agree?'

'I do.'

'Whereas a male doctor and a male joiner have different natures?'

'Absolutely.'

'So if either the male or the female gender turns out to be better than the other gender at some profession or occupation, then we'll claim that this is an occupation which ought to be assigned to that gender. But if the only difference turns out to be that females bear offspring, while males mount females, then we'll say that this doesn't yet bring us any e closer at all to proving that men and women are different in the context we're talking about, and we'll continue to think that our guardians and their women should have the same occupations.'

'Right,' he said.

'This is exactly what we'll require our opponent to explain to us next, then—for which of the pro- 455a fessions or occupations which bear on the organization of a community are there inherent differences between men and women?'

'Yes, that would be a fair question.'

'And he might well copy what you said a few moments ago, and reply that it's hard to come up with an adequate response on the spur of the moment, but that research would make it easy.'

'Yes, he might.'

'Shall we ask our disputatious friend to accompany us, then, to see if we can prove to him that there is no occupation which bears on the administration of a community which belongs especially to b women or to men?'

'Yes.'

' "All right, then," we'll say to him, "here's a question for you. When you distinguish people as naturally competent or incompetent in a particular context, don't you mean that some people find it easy to learn that subject, while others find it hard? And that some people start to do their own broadly speaking original work in the subject after only a little study, while others can't even retain what they've learnt after even a lot of study and care? And that some people's bodies are sufficiently subservient to their minds, while others' are obstructive? Aren't these the features—there are more too—which enable you to define some people as naturally compe- c tent, and others as naturally incompetent?" '

'Indisputably,' he said.

' "Well, do you know of any subject on earth in which men do not outclass women in all these respects?" Anyway, do we need to extend the conversation by discussing sewing, looking after pancakes, and boiling vegetables, which women are supposed to be good at, and where defeat makes them the most ridiculous creatures in the world?'

'You're right,' he said. 'The one gender is far superior to the other in just about every sphere. It may be that many women are better than many men at many things, but by and large it is as you say.'

'Therefore, my friend, there's no administrative job in a community which belongs to a woman *qua* woman, or to a man *qua* man,' I said. 'Innate qualities have been distributed equally between the two sexes, and women can join in every occupation just e as much as men, although they are the weaker sex in all respects.'

'Yes.'

'So shall we assign the men all the work and leave the women nothing?'

'Definitely not.'

'The point being that some women may be good at medicine or music, even if others aren't. That's what we'll say, I suppose.'

'Of course.'

456a   'And isn't it the case that some women may be good at sports or warfare, while others aren't?'

'I should say so.'

'And philosophically inclined or disciplined too? And some may be passionate, while others aren't?'

'Again, yes.'

'Some women may make good guardians, then, while others won't, since these were the innate qualities we selected as the marks of men who would make good guardians, weren't they?'

'They were.'

'Both women and men, then, have the same natural ability for guarding a community, and it's just that women are innately weaker than men.'

'I suppose so.'

b   'These are the women, then, who should be selected to live with the male guardians and to join them in guardianship. They are endowed with the natural ability to do so, and they are from the same stock as the male guardians.'

'Quite.'

'And the same occupations should be assigned to people with the same natures, shouldn't they?'

'Yes.'

'So we've come full circle back to where we were before. We're agreed that it isn't unnatural for the wives of our guardians to be set cultural studies and physical exercise.'

'Absolutely.'

'Our regulations were viable, then, and weren't just wishful thinking, since they're compatible with c nature. In fact, it is current practice, which contravenes this, which is apparently more likely to be unnatural.'

'So it seems.'

'Now, we were trying to discover whether our proposals were viable and for the best, weren't we?'

'Yes.'

'And we've concluded that they're viable, haven't we?'

'Yes.'

'So next we need to reach agreement on whether they're for the best, don't we?'

'Obviously.'

'Well, in order to make women good at guarding, we won't be providing them with a different education from the one that works for men, will we? After all, it's the same nature the educational system takes on in both cases.'   d

'Yes, it is.'

'Now, I wonder what you think about this idea.'

'Which one?'

'The notion that some men are better than others. Perhaps you think they're all the same?'

'Definitely not.'

'In the community we're founding, then, do you think the guardians or the shoemakers will prove to be the better people, when the guardians have been educated in the way we've described and the shoemakers have been educated in their craft?'

'I'm not going to treat that as a serious question,' he said.

'I see,' I said. 'And what about the rest of the citizen body? Will the guardians be the best?'   e

'By far the best.'

'And won't the women we're talking about be better than all the rest of the women?'

'Again, by a long way,' he said.

'Is anything better for a community than for it to engender women and men who are exceptionally good?'

'No.'

'And this is the effect of cultural studies and physical education when they're employed as we have described, isn't it?'   457a

'Of course.'

'In addition to being viable, then, the regulation we were making for our community was for the best as well.'

'Yes.'

'So the wives of the guardians ought to strip off; they'll be protected by goodness rather than clothes. They'll take part in warfare and whatever else guarding the community involves, and this will be their one and only occupation. However, they will receive lighter duties than the men, because of the weakness of their sex. Any man who treats the fact that women b are exercising naked with goodness as their goal as a reason for laughter is "plucking laughter unripe"; we now appreciate that he has no awareness of what he's laughing at or what he's doing, since it's impossible, and will remain impossible, to improve on the idea that anything beneficial is commendable, and anything harmful is deplorable.'

'Absolutely.'

The guardians will have no family life—or rather, they will regard one another as all belonging to a vastly extended family. There will be no formal marriages between them, and their children will be brought up communally. In the context of maximizing the community's benefit, it is both morally and eugenically sensible to control sexual pairing (in the senses of who mates with whom, and when), and to dispose of unsound children.

'So may we now claim to have escaped this first wave, as it were? We've discussed what legislation to enact where women are concerned and managed c to avoid being completely swamped while decreeing that our male and female guardians have to share all their occupations. In fact, the argument was internally consistent in its claim that the proposals were both viable and beneficial.'

'It's a pretty sizeable wave you're escaping,' he remarked.

'You'll be saying it's pretty insignificant when you see the next one,' I said.

'I won't see it unless you tell me about it,' he said.

'It's legislation which follows from what we've just enacted and from all the laws we made earlier too, I think,' I said.

'But what is it?'

'That there's to be no such thing as private mard riage between these women and these men: all the women are to be shared among all the men. And that the children are also to be shared, with no parent knowing which child is his, or child knowing his parent.'

'This is a far bigger wave than the first one,' he said, 'and its viability and value are far more likely to be doubted.'

'I don't see how its advantages can be called into question,' I said. 'If the sharing of wives and children is feasible, it's bound to be extremely valuable. I should think that most of the doubt will be concentrated upon whether or not it's viable.'

'No, there are plenty of reasons to be sceptical e about both aspects,' he said.

'You mean I can't separate the two arguments?' I said. 'I was hoping I'd escape from one of them, by securing your agreement to the idea's advantages, and that I'd only be left with discussing its viability.'

'But you were caught escaping,' he said, 'and you have to justify both aspects.'

'I must pay the penalty,' I said, 'but I ask for a little bit of leniency: please let me indulge in some lazy thinking, as someone out for a solitary stroll 458a might well do. You know how someone like that doesn't bother with the prior question of how to fulfil his desires. He doesn't want to exhaust himself wondering whether or not their fulfilment is viable, so he just imagines that they've been fulfilled and then sorts everything else out and happily details the kinds of things he's going to do when they are realized—and so makes a mind that was already lazy even lazier. Now, I'm feeling enervated myself at the moment, and I'd like to delay investigating the b proposals' viability until later. On the assumption that they are viable, I'll now—with your permission—look into how the rulers will sort them out in practice and prove that nothing could be more advantageous to the community and to the guardians than their enactment. This is what we'll try to investigate together first, if you approve of my suggestion, and then we'll tackle the other issue later.'

'That's all right by me,' he said. 'Go ahead.'

'Well, in my opinion,' I said, 'if the rulers and their auxiliaries live up to their names, then the auxiliaries will be prepared to carry out instructions, and c the rulers will be prepared to given them instructions. These instructions will sometimes be in direct conformity with law, but sometimes—where we've left the possibility—they'll simply reflect our legal principles.'

'That sounds reasonable,' he said.

'Now, you are their legislator,' I said, 'and once the women have been through the same selection procedure as the men, you'll send the ones who match the men's innate qualities as closely as possible to join them. Since they share living-quarters and mess-halls and since none of them has any pri- d vate property of this kind, they will coexist and commingle during their exercises and their educational programme in general, and consequently their instincts are bound to lure them into having sex with one another. Don't you think that's bound to happen?'

'I don't think it's logically necessary,' he replied, 'but the imperative is coming from the sex drive, and I suppose most people find the proddings of the sex drive far more influential and compelling than those of logic!'

'They certainly do,' I said. 'The next point, Glaucon, is that in a community which is to be happy, undisciplined sex (or undisciplined anything else, e for that matter) is a profanity, and the rulers won't allow it.'

'That's because it's wrong,' he said.

'So obviously our next task is to ensure that marriages are as far removed from profanity as possible—which will happen if they contribute as much as possible towards the community's welfare.'

'Absolutely.'

459a   'So we need to ask how to maximize this contribution of theirs. Now, Glaucon, I've seen lots of hunting dogs and fine birds in your house, so I wonder whether you've noticed a particular aspect of their mating and procreation.'

'What?' he asked.

'The main point is this. Isn't it true that although they're all pedigree creatures, some of them prove to be exceptionally good?'

'Yes.'

'So do you breed from all of them indiscriminately, or do you take care to choose the outstanding ones as much as possible?'

'I choose the outstanding ones.'

'And of these, do you choose the youngest ones or the oldest ones or, wherever feasible, the ones in their prime?'

'The ones in their prime.'

b   'And wouldn't you expect the result of failure to follow this breeding programme to be the deterioration of your strain of birds and dogs?'

'Yes,' he said.

'Does a different principle apply to horses and other creatures, do you think?' I asked.

'It would be odd if it did,' he said.

'My dear Glaucon!' I exclaimed. 'We're going to need really exceptional rulers if the same principle applies to humans too.'

'Well, it does,' he said. 'What do you make of it?' c

'That they'll be compelled to rely a great deal on medicines,' I said. 'As you know, we regard treating people whose bodies don't require medicine, but who are prepared to follow a diet, as within the competence of a less accomplished doctor; when medicines are called for, however, a more courageous doctor is evidently required.'

'This is true,' but what are you driving at?'

'That the rulers will probably have to rely a lot on falsehood and deceit,' I said, 'to help their subjects. You'll remember our claim that lies and so on are useful as a type of medicine.'   d

'Yes, and there's nothing wrong with using them like that,' he said.

'Well, it occurs to me that this usage is particularly important in the domain of mating and procreation.'

'Why?'

'It follows from our conclusions so far that sex should preferably take place between men and women who are outstandingly good, and should occur as little as possible between men and women of a vastly inferior stamp. It also follows that the offspring of the first group should be brought up, while the offspring of the second group shouldn't. This is how to maximize the potential of our flock. And the fact that all this is happening should be concealed e from everyone except the rulers themselves, if the herd of guardians is to be as free as possible from conflict.'

'You're quite right,' he said.

'So what we, as legislators, have to do is institute certain holidays and religious ceremonies, during which we'll bring the brides and the grooms together; and we'll have our poets compose suitable wedding-odes for them. We'll leave the quantity of 460a marriages up to the rulers: they'll want to keep the number of men in the community more or less constant, bearing in mind wars and epidemics and so on, so as to do their best to avoid increasing or decreasing the community's size.'

'Right,' he said.

'We'd better set up a subtle lottery, then, so that those inferior men we spoke of blame chance and not the rulers every mating-time.'

'Definitely,' he said.

'And the main privilege and reward that any b young men who are good at fighting or at some other activity ought to receive is the right to sleep with the women more frequently, so that as many as possible of the children are fathered by this kind of person, and there is at the same time a plausible reason for this happening.'

'Right.'

'Now, the officials whose job it is to take charge of any children who are born—and they could be men, women, or some of each, since positions of authority are open to both men and women equally, of course . . .'

'Yes.'

c 'Well, I suppose they'll take the children of good parents to the crèche and hand them over to nurses (who live in a separate section of the community); and they'll find some suitable way of hiding away in some secret and secluded spot the children of worse parents and any handicapped children of good parents.'

'Otherwise our breed of guardians will become tainted,' he said.

'And they'll take care of the children's feeding by bringing the mothers to the crèche when their breasts d are full of milk, although they'll devise all sorts of stratagems to make sure that no mother recognizes her own child. If the mothers' supply of milk is inadequate, they'll bring in other women to supplement it. They'll take care that the mothers don't breast-feed for too long, and they'll assign sleepless nights and all the hard work to wet-nurses and nannies.'

'You're making child-bearing very easy for the wives of the guardians,' he remarked.

'Which is only right and proper,' I said. 'But let's get on with the next item of our proposals. We said that the children's parents should be in their prime, didn't we?'

'True.'

e 'Do you agree that a woman is in her prime for twenty years or so, and a man for thirty years or so?'

'Which twenty or thirty years?' he asked.

'A woman can serve the community by producing children between the ages of twenty and forty, a man by fathering children from when he passes his peak as a runner until the age of fifty-five.'

461a 'Yes, in both cases this is the period when they're in their physical and intellectual prime,' he said.

'Therefore, if the production of children for the community is encroached on by anyone too old or too young, we'll say that he has sinned against both gods and men by fathering a child who (if the matter goes unnoticed and the child is born) will not have been affected by the rites and prayers which

the priestesses and priests and the whole community pray at each wedding-festival—for every generation of children to improve on their parents' goodness and value—but will instead have been born under b the influence of darkness and dire lack of self-control.'

'Right,' he said.

'And even if a man's age doesn't exclude him from procreation,' I said, 'the same regulation will apply if he has sex with a woman of the right age when a ruler has not paired them. We'll declare the child he's trying to foist on the community a bastard, without standing or sanction.'

'Quite right,' he said.

'When the men and women get past the age for procreation, I imagine we'll release them and allow them the freedom to have sex with anyone they want—except that a man is forbidden to have sex with a daughter and her female offspring, and a c mother and her female precursors, and a woman is forbidden to have sex with a son, a father, and their male descendants and precursors. But before we release them, we'll impress upon them the importance of trying their best to abort absolutely every pregnancy that occurs, and of ensuring that any baby born despite their efforts is not brought up.'

'Yes, that's a sensible proposal,' he said. 'But how are they to tell who are whose fathers and daughters and so on?'   d

'They won't be able to,' I said. 'However, a man will call any child born in the tenth month, and in the seventh month of course, after he participated in one of the wedding-ceremonies a son (if the child is male) or daughter (if female); they'll call him father and their children will be his grandchildren, who'll regard his generation as grandfathers and grandmothers, and who'll count anyone born in the period when their mothers and fathers were producing children as their sisters and brothers. The result will e be what we were just saying: they'll avoid sex with one another. However, the law will allow brothers and sisters to sleep together, if the lottery turns out that way and the Delphic oracle has no objection.'

'You're quite right,' he said.

These proposals will prevent conflict and ensure the unity of the community by abolishing from the guardians not only possessions, but the feeling of possessiveness. They will extend the mutual respect and fellow-feeling, typically found within a family, to the whole community.

'So this is how your community's guardians will share women and children, Glaucon. We next need to have the argument confirm that this is basically in keeping with the constitution and that it is by far the best course of action. Isn't that the thing to do?'

'Definitely,' he said.

462a 'Shouldn't we initiate the enquiry by asking ourselves which factor, in our opinion, makes the most important positive contribution towards the organization of a community—and this is the factor a legislator has to aim for when he's making his laws—and which factor does the most harm? Then we should try to see whether these new proposals of ours match the traces of the good factor and not of the harmful one.'

'Absolutely.'

'Could we describe anything as worse for a com-
b munity, do you think than something which tears it apart and destroys its unity? And could we describe anything as better for a community than something which binds it together and unifies it?'

'No, we couldn't.'

'And isn't it the sharing of feelings of pleasure and distress which binds a community together—when (in so far as it is feasible) the whole citizen body feels more or less the same pleasure or distress at the same gains and losses?'

'Absolutely,' he said.

'And isn't it, on the other hand, the non-sharing of these feelings which causes disintegration—when something happens to the community or some of its members and the attendant feelings range from de-
c pression to delight?'

'Naturally.'

'And doesn't this privatization of feelings happen when the members of a community are out of tune with one another when they use expressions like "mine" and "not mine", and likewise when they identify something as foreign?'

'Absolutely.'

'So the best-run community is the one in which as many people as possible use these expressions, "mine" and "not mine", to refer to the same things in the same respects. Yes?'

'Definitely.'

'And the one which approximates as much as possible to a single human being? I mean, when someone's finger is hurt, the whole federation, which encompasses body and mind in its span and forms a single organized system under its ruling part, is
d aware of the pain and feels it, as a whole, along with

the injured part, and that's why we say that the person has hurt his finger. And the same principle applies to any other part of a person, whether it's experiencing the discomfort of pain or the relief of pleasure.'

'Yes, I agree,' he said. 'And, to answer your question, yes—the more closely a community's organization approximates to this situation, the better run that community is.'

'So in this kind of community, any experience—whether good or bad—of any of its members will in all likelihood be regarded as its own experience, and the community as a whole will share the affected e member's feelings of pleasure or pain.'

'Yes, that's bound to be the case in a well-regulated community,' he said.

'Now would be a good time', I said, 'for us to return to our community, and see whether it is the pre-eminent example of a community with the qualities we've just formulated, or whether some other community surpasses it.'

'Yes, we ought to do that,' he said.

'All right. Now, our community—like every 463a community—contains both rulers and commoners, doesn't it?'

'Yes.'

'Who all refer to one another as fellow citizens?'

'Of course.'

'But in other communities the commoners call the rulers something else besides "fellow citizens", don't they?'

'Yes, in most communities they call them "masters", and in democracies they call them just that—"rulers".'

'What about in our community? How will the general populace think of the rulers, apart from thinking of them as fellow citizens?'   b

'As their protectors and defenders,' he said.

'And how will *they* regard the general populace?'

'As their paymasters and quartermasters.'

'In other communities how do rulers regard the general populace?'

'As slaves,' he said.

'And one another?'

'As fellow rulers,' he said.

'How do our rulers regard one another?'

'As fellow guardians.'

'Would you say that in other communities a ruler might regard some of his fellow rulers as friends and others as strangers?'

'Yes, that commonly happens.'

'And he regards and describes his friends as be-
c longing to his circle, and the strangers as nothing to
do with him?'

'Yes.'

'What about the guardians in your community?
Could any of them regard or refer to a fellow
guardian as a stranger?'

'Certainly not,' he said. 'He'll be regarding everyone he meets as a brother or a sister, a father or a
mother, a son or a daughter, a grandchild or a grand-
parent.'

'Excellently put,' I said. 'But here's another question for you. As legislator, will you be obliging them
only to label one another relatives, or also to make
d all their behaviour conform to these labels? Take
their fathers, for instance: will they have to show
their fathers all the usual respect and care and obedience due to parents, or else have both gods and
men think the worse of them for their unjust and immoral behaviour? Will these be the traditions which
every single citizen of your community will din into
the ears of the children from their earliest years
about the people they are told to regard as fathers
and about all their other relatives, or will you have
different traditions?'

e 'No, I'll have the ones you've mentioned,' he said.
'It would be ridiculous for them only to mouth these
family labels without it affecting their behaviour.'

'So there's no community in which it's more
likely that, when one of its members does well or
badly, people will be in tune with one another in using the expression we mentioned, and will say, "The
success is mine" or "The failure is mine." '

'That's absolutely true,' he said.

464a 'Well, didn't we say that when people hold this
belief and use this expression they start to share feelings of pleasure and distress?'

'We did, and we were right.'

'Isn't it above all the members of our community,
then, who will genuinely share and refer to the same
thing as "mine"? And because they share in this way,
they'll share feelings of pleasure and distress more
than anyone else, won't they?'

'Much more.'

'And, apart from the general constitution of the
community, it's the fact that the guardians share
their women and children that is responsible for this,
isn't it?'

'Yes, that's by far the most important factor,' he
said.

'Now, our conclusion was that there is nothing

better for a community than this sharing of feelings. b
We compared a well-run community to a body, and
pointed out what a body does in relation to the pleasure and pain of its parts.'

'Yes, and the conclusions was right,' he said.

'So we've demonstrated that the community's
greatest benefit is due to the fact that its defenders
share their women and children.'

'We certainly have,' he said.

'Moreover, this conclusion goes with what we
were saying earlier. I mean, we did say that genuine
guardians shouldn't own houses or land or anything,
but should be given their food by others, as payment c
for their guarding, and should all eat together.'

'Right,' he said.

'Isn't it the case, as I say, that both our earlier proposals and the current ones increase the likelihood
of their being genuine guardians, and prevent them
tearing the community apart by using the expression
"mine" to refer not to the same thing, but to various
things? Different people call different things "mine"
when they each have their own houses into which d
they pull anything they can keep out of the hands of
others, and when they each have their own wife and
children; and this situation introduces into the community the personal pleasures and pains of private
individuals. Aren't they more likely to be genuine
guardians if they all regard the same things as within
their circle of interest, tend in the same direction,
and feel pleasure and pain, as much as possible, under the same circumstances?'

'Absolutely,' he said.

'And won't trials and lawsuits against one another
be almost non-existent, since they'll own nothing
except their bodies and share everything else? And
consequently they'll be free of all the conflict that e
arises when people have money or children and relatives.'

'That's more or less inevitable,' he said.

'Lawsuits for assault or bodily harm won't be part
of their moral code either, because we'll make it a
moral obligation for people in any given age-group
to defend themselves against their peers, which will
force them to take care of their bodies.'

'Right,' he said.

'There's something else that makes this regula- 465a
tion right too,' I said. 'If an angry person satisfies
his rage like this, he's less likely to escalate the matter into a major conflict.'

'Yes.'

'Now, we'll have given older people authority

over younger ones and made them responsible for disciplining them.'

'Obviously.'

'And it's unlikely that younger people will ever try to assault or strike their elders (unless ordered to do so by the rulers), or show them disrespect in any other way. There are two guardians whose presence is enough to stop them—fear and respect. Respect b will stop them laying hands on their parents, and they'll be afraid of all the help any victim would get from people who regard themselves as his sons or brothers or fathers.'

'Yes, that's what would happen,' he said.

'So thanks to our legislation they'll live together in perfect peace, don't you think?'

'Definitely.'

'And because of their freedom from in-fighting, there is no danger of a rift ever forming between them and the rest of the community or within the rest of the community.'

'No, there isn't.'

'For fear of sounding a discordant note, I hardly like even to mention the trivial mischiefs they'll avoid. There's how poor people have to flatter the c rich; there are all the problems and worries they suffer while they're having their children educated and because in order to support a household they're forced to raise money by borrowing, by refusing to pay back debts, by doing whatever it takes to make an income—only to hand the accumulated money over to their wives and servants to spend on housekeeping. There are a number of different burdens one finds in this context, but they're too obvious and demeaning to be worth mentioning.'

d   'Yes, even a blind man could see them,' he said.

'So they'll avoid all these troubles, and they'll live more happily than any Olympic victor.'

'Why?'

'The happiness which people attribute to Olympic victors is due to a tiny fraction of what our guardians have. The guardians' victory is more splendid, and their upkeep by the general populace is more thorough-going. The fruit of their victory is the preservation of the whole community, their prize the maintenance of themselves and their children with food and all of life's essentials. During their lifetimes they are honoured by their community, and e when they die they are buried in high style.'

'These are excellent prizes,' he said.

'Do you remember', I asked, 'that earlier someone or other criticized us for failing to make the

guardians happy because although they could take possession of the property of everyone in the community, they actually had nothing? We said we'd 466a look into the matter later, if it was convenient, and that for the time being we were making our guardians guardians and making our community as happy as we could, and that it wasn't our intention to single out one particular group within the community and devise happiness just for them.'

'I remember,' he said.

'Well, since we now think that our auxiliaries live a far better and more rewarding life than any Olympic victor, we're hardly going to place it at the b same level as the life of a shoemaker or any of our other urban or rural workers, are we?'

'I don't think so,' he answered.

'Nevertheless, the comment I made at the time is also fair in this context. If a guardian aims for the kind of happiness which is incompatible with his being a guardian—if the moderate, secure, and outstanding lifestyle we've described is not enough for him and, under the influence of some idiotic and immature conception of happiness, he sets about exploiting his power to appropriate all the community's assets for himself, he'll start to appreciate how c wise Hesiod was when he said that in a sense "half is more than a whole".'

'I'd recommend him to keep to the guardian's life,' he said.

'Do you agree, then,' I said, 'that the best course is for the men and women to receive the same education, share children, and co-operate in the guarding of the rest of their fellow citizens, as we've described? And do you agree that whether it involves staying within the community or going out to war, the women should help in the guarding and hunting, d as female dogs do? They should share in everything as much as they can, and this will not only be the best course of action for them, but is also not incompatible with their nature, as compared with masculinity, and is the kind of partnership which nature intended for the two sexes?'

'Yes, I agree,' he said.

Having decided that these arrangements are for the best, Plato again (see 458b) postpones the issue of their feasibility (until 471cff.) and turns to warfare instead. Male and female auxiliaries will fight side by side, and young apprentice guardians will observe and participate as much as possible. The prescriptions for punishing cowardice and rewarding bravery, and of how to regard enemies, are all governed by the concern to preserve unity within the community and between natural friends.

'Well, we still have to decide', I said, 'whether in fact, and under what circumstances, this sharing is viable among humans, as it is among other species.'

'I was just about to take you up on that very point,' he said, 'but you got in first.'

e   'Because it's obvious what they'll do about warfare, I suppose,' I said.

'What?' he asked.

'Men and women will campaign together, and they'll also take any sturdy children with them to war, so that they see the work they'll have to do when they become adults, just as the children of 467a other kinds of workmen do. But the children won't just watch: they'll also act as apprentices and servants in all aspects of war, and look after their fathers and mothers. I mean, you must have noticed what happens in the case of other occupations—how the children of potters, say, spend a long time as apprentices and observers before getting involved in any actual pottery.'

'Yes, I know.'

'And should potters take more care than the guardians over educating their children by familiarizing them and letting them observe their duties?'

'That would be ridiculous,' he said.

'Moreover, every creature fights better, anyway, b when its offspring are around.'

'True. But Socrates, aren't they running quite a risk? If they fail, which is always a possibility in war, then they'll be responsible for their children being killed as well as themselves, and for the rest of the community finding it impossible to recover.'

'You're right,' I said. 'But the main point is: do you think they should be provided with a risk-free life?'

'Certainly not.'

'Well, if they have to face danger, shouldn't it be when the result of success will be an improvement in their conditions?'

'Obviously.'

c   'And do you think it hardly matters—not enough to compensate for the danger—whether or not the children who are to become soldiers when they're adults observe warfare and all it entails?'

'No, it does make a difference, in the sense you're talking about.'

'It'll be best, then, if our primary objective is having the children observe warfare, but we also find ways to keep them safe. Right?'

'Yes.'

'Well, the chief point', I said, 'is that their fathers will know all that can humanly be known about warfare, and will therefore be able to distinguish risky d military ventures from safe ones.'

'That's likely,' he said.

'So they'll take them to the one kind and steer clear of the others.'

'Right.'

'And they'll not be putting second-rate supervisors in charge of them, but people who thanks to their experience and their age are qualified to act as guides and attendants.'

'Yes, that's the right thing to do.'

'Still, we're agreed that the unexpected often occurs.'

'Yes.'

'And that is why we'd better equip our children with wings from an early age, my friend, so that they can escape by flying away, if they have to.'

'I don't understand,' he said.   e

'We have to put them on horseback', I explained, 'from the earliest possible age, and they can go and watch campaigns only when they've been taught to ride. The horses they go on won't be excitable or aggressive, but will be the fastest and most manageable ones available. That's the best way for them to take stock of their work, and they'll have no difficulty in following the older people who are their guides to safety if necessary.'

'I think you're right,' he said.

'What about warfare?' I asked. 'What attitudes do 468a you want your soldiers to have towards themselves and towards the enemy? Do you think my ideas are correct or not?'

'Tell me them,' he said.

'Shouldn't anyone who deserts or discards his weapons or does anything cowardly like that be made an artisan or a farmer?' I asked.

'Yes.'

'And anyone who is taken alive by the enemy should be presented to his captors, and they can treat this catch of theirs in any way they choose.'

'Absolutely.'   b

'What about someone who distinguishes himself for outstanding bravery? Shouldn't he first, before returning home from the campaign, be crowned with chaplets by each of his comrades-in-arms—the young men and the children—one by one? Is that a good idea, do you think, or not?'

'I think so.'

'And should they take him by the hand?'

'Yes, that too.'

'But I don't think you'll go so far as to agree with my next idea,' I said.

'What is it?'

'That he should kiss and be kissed by each of his comrades.'

'That's very important indeed,' he said. 'In fact, I'll add a rider to your regulation: for the duration c of that campaign, no one he wants to kiss is allowed to refuse. This will make anyone who happens to be in love with a male or female comrade try harder to win the prize for bravery.'

'That's an excellent idea,' I said, 'because we've already said that a good man will be allowed to participate in a greater number of marriage ceremonies than others and that it will invariably be a good man rather than anyone else who is selected for them, so that as many children as possible are fathered by men of this type.'

'Yes, I remember,' he said.

'Moreover, Homer too approved of rewarding young men for their goodness. He said that for dis- d tinguishing himself in a battle Ajax "was awarded the whole length of the chine"—this being an appropriate reward for vigour and valour because it's simultaneously a source of strength as well as a reward.'

'You're quite right,' he said.

'We'll let Homer be our guide in this matter, then,' I said. 'I mean, we too will use religious rites and so on as occasions for rewarding anyone who has displayed virtue not only with odes and the privileges we've been talking about, but also "with the seat of honour, with the best cuts of meat, and with goblets full of wine", so that we simultaneously give our virtuous men and women an opportunity for e training as well as a reward.'

'That's an exceptionally good idea,' he said.

'All right. Now, what about those who die during the course of a campaign? In the first place, we must count anyone who dies a glorious death as a member of the golden caste, mustn't we?'

'Definitely.'

'And we'll believe Hesiod when he says that after people of this kind die "they become pure deities 469a attached to the earth, who in their goodness guard mortal men and keep them from harm". Right?'

'Yes, we will.'

'So won't we consult Apollo to find out how to lay to rest men of superhuman stature and what special things to do, and then bury them in the way he prescribes?'

'Of course.'

'And thereafter we'll regard their tombs as the tombs of deities, and we'll tend to them and wor- b ship there, won't we? And don't you think we should institute the same custom whenever anyone who during his lifetime was acknowledged to be exceptionally good dies of old age or whatever?'

'Yes, that's the right thing to do,' he said.

'Now, what attitude will our soldiers have towards their enemies?'

'In what sense?'

'Take enslavement first. Do you think it's right for communities of Greeks to enslave other Greeks? Shouldn't they do their best to prevent any other community from enslaving Greeks and make it the norm to spare anyone of Greek stock, for fear of c themselves being enslaved by non-Greeks?'

'It's absolutely crucial that they spare Greeks,' he said.

'Not only should they not own Greek slaves themselves, then, but they should also advise other Greeks to follow their example.'

'Yes,' he said. 'That should encourage them to concentrate on non-Greeks and leave one another alone.'

'And what about the victors despoiling the dead? Taking their weapons is all right, but otherwise is it a good practice? I mean, doesn't it provide an excuse for cowards not to advance against an enemy d who is still fighting, because they can make out that they're doing their duty by poking around among the corpses? This sort of looting has often in the past been the ruin of armies.'

'I quite agree.'

'Plundering corpses seems mean and mercenary, don't you think? And treating the body of a dead person as an enemy, when the hostile element has flown off and only the instrument it once used for fighting remains, seems to indicate a womanly, petty mind. I mean, do you think there's any difference between this behaviour and that of dogs who, if they're hit with stones, get annoyed at the stones, e but don't go anywhere near the person who threw them?'

'That's an absolutely perfect analogy,' he replied.

'So we'd better avoid the practice of plundering

corpses and also preventing our opponents from recovering the bodies of their dead, don't you think?'

'Yes, we certainly should,' he said.

'And we won't be taking arms and armour to our temples as trophies either, especially if they came 470a from Greeks, if we're the slightest bit interested in being on good terms with other Greeks. We're more likely to be afraid of the possible pollution involved in robbing our kin of their weapons and taking them to a sacred site, except when the practice is divinely sanctioned.'

'You're quite right,' he said.

'What about devastating the land and burning the homes of Greeks? How will your troops behave towards their enemies?'

'I'd be glad to hear what you have to say about this,' he said.

'Well, I think they'll avoid both practices,' I said, b 'and only steal the annual harvest. Shall I tell you why?'

'Yes, please.'

'I think that the fact that there are these two separate terms, war and conflict, is indicative of the existence of two things with separate distinguishing features. One of the two is an internal affair, within a single domain; the other is an external affair, crossing borders. "Conflict" refers to the hostility of an internal element, "war" to that of an external element.'

'No one could fault what you're saying in the slightest,' he said.

c 'I wonder if you'll find the next point just as sound. I maintain that Greeks are bonded to one another by internal ties of blood and kinship, but interact with non-Greeks as people who are foreign and live outside their domain.'

'That's right,' he said.

"When Greeks and non-Greeks fight, then, we"ll describe this as warfare, and claim that they are natural enemies and that the term "war" should refer to this type of hostility. But when Greeks get involved in this kind of thing with other Greeks, we"ll claim that they are natural friends, and that in a situation like this Greece is diseased and in conflict, and we"ll d maintain that term "conflict" should refer to this type of hostility."'

'I for one agree with your view,' he said.

'Now that we've agreed what conflict is,' I said, 'imagine it happening, imagine a community divided against itself, and you'll see that, if each side devastates the other side's land and burns their homes, conflict comes across as an abomination and neither side can be regarded as patriotic, since if they were, they would stop short of ravaging their nurse and their mother. However, it seems reasonable for the winners to take the losers' crops, and it smacks e of aiming for reconciliation rather than perpetual warfare.'

'Yes, there's far more compassion in this aim,' he said.

'Well, this community you're founding is going to be Greek, isn't it?' I asked.

'Of course,' he answered.

'And its members will be good, compassionate people, won't they?'

'Certainly.'

'Won't they feel warmth for their fellow Greeks? Won't they regard Greece as their own land and join all other Greeks in their common religious rites?'

'They certainly will.'

'Then they'll regard any dissension between 471a themselves and Greeks as conflict, since Greeks are their own people, and they won't even use the term "war" in this context, will they?'

'No.'

'So in times of dissension they'll be looking for reconciliation, won't they?'

'Yes.'

'So they won't be motivated by hatred, but by wanting to bring their opponents to their senses. As disciplinarians, then, rather than enemies, they won't punish their opponents with enslavement or death.'

'That's right,' he said.

'And as Greeks, they won't ravage Greece either, or burn homes, or conclude that the whole population of a given community—men, women, and children—is hostile to them, but only those few hostile people who were responsible for the dissension. All these reasons will make them unwilling to ravage b their opponents' land or demolish their houses, since the majority of the population will be their friends; instead, they will see the dispute through until the point is reached when those who are innocent have suffered enough and they force the guilty few to pay for what they've done.'

'I agree that this is the attitude the members of our community ought to have towards their opponents,' he said. 'And they'll reserve for non-Greeks the treatment Greeks currently give one another.'

'Shall we include this rule among our regulations for the guardians then—that they are not to devastate land or burn houses?'   c

'Yes,' he said, 'and let's add that it and our earlier regulations are all good.'

CHAPTER 8
PHILOSOPHER KINGS

Plato faces the third wave—the question of the imaginary community's feasibility—and comes up with what is perhaps the most famous (or notorious) proposal a philosopher has ever made: that the only solution to political and personal troubles is for true philosophers to become kings, or for current rulers to become true philosophers. As Plato recognizes, this assertion throws up an urgent need to define what it is to be a true philosopher. A philosopher loves knowledge, but what exactly is knowledge? And then the basic question which will be explored throughout Chapter 8–10, and which connects them to the rest of the book, is the relation between morality and knowledge.

'I get the impression, though, Socrates, that this is the kind of topic where, if no one interrupts you, you'll forget that it is all a digression from a previous topic—that is, whether this political system is viable, and if so, how. I accept that all these practices, if realized, would be good for any community they were practised in, and I can supplement your 471d account: they are highly likely to fight well against enemy forces, in so far as they are highly unlikely to abandon one another, since they regard one another as brothers, fathers, sons, and call one another by these names; if women joined them on a campaign (whether their task was to fight alongside the men or to support them in the rear), they'd have the effect of terrifying the enemy and could come up as reinforcements in an emergency, and I'm sure this would make our militia completely invincible; and I can see all the domestic benefits they'd bring which e you haven't mentioned. You can take for granted my agreement that the realization of the constitution would result in all these advantages and innumerable others as well; so you don't have to talk about the actual constitution any more. Let's just try now to convince ourselves that it is viable and to find out how it is viable, and let's not bother with anything else.'

472a   'I wasn't expecting you to ambush my argument like this,' I said. 'Can't you sympathize with my procrastination? Perhaps you don't realize that it was

hard enough for me to escape from the first two waves, and now you're invoking the largest and most problematic of the set of three waves. When you see it and hear it, then you'll sympathize with me and see that it was perfectly realistic of me to have misgivings and qualms about proposing such a paradoxical idea for investigation.'

'The more you say this kind of thing,' he said, 'the less likely we are to let you off discussing how b this political system might be realized. Please don't waste any more time: just get on with it.'

'Well, the first thing we have to do,' I said, 'is remember that it's our search for the nature of morality and immorality that has brought us here.'

'All right,' he said. 'So what?'

'Nothing really. It's just that if we do discover what morality is, will we expect a moral man to be indistinguishable from it, and to be a perfect image of morality? Or will we be satisfied if he resembles c it as closely as possible and participates in it more thoroughly than anyone else?'

'Yes, we'll be happy with that,' he said.

'Therefore,' I said, 'it's because we need a paradigm that we're trying to find out what morality is, and are asking whether a perfectly moral man could exist and, if so, what he would be like (and likewise for immorality and an immoral man). We want to be able to look at these men, to see how they stand as regards happiness and misery, and to face the inevitable conclusion about ourselves, that the more we resemble these exemplars, the more our condi- d tion will resemble their condition. In other words, the purpose of our enquiry is not to try to prove that perfect morality or immorality could ever actually exist.'

'True,' he said.

'Do you doubt an artist's competence if he paints a paradigmatically good-looking human being, and portrays everything perfectly well in the painting, but can't prove that a person like that could actually exist?'

'I certainly do not,' he protested.

'Well, aren't we saying that we're trying to construct a theoretical paradigm of a good community?'

'Yes.'   e

'Then do you doubt our competence as theoreticians in this context if we can't prove that a community with our theoretical constitution could actually exist?'

'Of course not,' he said.

'So that's how matters really stand,' I said. 'However, if for your sake I also have to apply myself to proving how and under what circumstances it might get as close as possible to viability, then although this is a different kind of argument, I must ask you to make the same concession as before.'

'What concession?'

473a 'Is it possible for anything actual to match a theory? Isn't any actual thing bound to have less contact with truth than a theory, however, much people deny it? Do you agree or not?'

'I do,' he said.

'So please don't force me to point to an actual case in the material world which conforms in all respects to our theoretical construct. If we can discover how a community's administration could come very close to our theory, then let's say that b we've fulfilled your demands and discovered how it's all viable. I mean, won't you be satisfied if we get that close? I would.'

'I would too,' he said.

'Next, then, I suppose we should try to discover and show what the flaw is in current political systems which stops communities being governed as well as we've described, and what the smallest change in which could enable a community to achieve this type of constitution. By the smallest change, I mean preferably a single change, but if that's impossible, then two changes, or at any rate as few as possible and the least drastic ones possible.'

c 'Absolutely,' he said.

'Well,' I said, 'I think there is a single change which can be shown to bring about the transformation. It's not a small change, however, or easy to achieve, but it is feasible.'

'What is it?' he asked.

'I'm now about to confront the difficulty which, in our image, is the largest wave,' I said. 'Still, it must be voiced, even if it's going to swamp us, exactly like a wave, with scornful and contemptuous laughter. Are you ready for me to speak?'

'Go ahead,' he said.

'Unless communities have philosophers as kings,' I said, 'or the people who are currently called kings d and rulers practise philosophy with enough integrity—in other words, unless political power and philosophy coincide, and all the people with their diversity of talents who currently head in different directions towards either government or philosophy have those doors shut firmly in their faces—there can be no end to political troubles, my dear Glau-

con, or even to human troubles in general, I'd say, e and our theoretical constitution will be stillborn and will never see the light of day. Now you can appreciate what made me hesitate to speak before: I saw how very paradoxical it would sound, since it is difficult to realize that there is no other way for an individual or a community to achieve happiness.'

'What a thing to say, Socrates!' Glaucon said in response. 'This is quite an idea! Now that it's out in the open, you'd better expect hordes of people—and not second-rate people either—to fling off their clothes (so to speak), pick up the nearest weapon, 474a and rush naked at you with enough energy to achieve heroic feats. And if you don't come up with an argument to keep them at bay while you make your escape, then your punishment will be to discover what scorn really is.'

'And it'll all be your fault, won't it?' I said.

'I've no regrets,' he replied. 'But that doesn't mean I'll desert you: I'll defend you to the best of my ability. Goodwill and encouragement are my arsenal, and my answers probably suit you more than someone else's might. You can count on this assis- b tance, so please try to win the sceptics round to your point of view.'

'You're providing such major support that I must make the effort,' I said. 'Now, in my opinion, we'll never escape from the people you mentioned unless we offer them a definition of a philosopher so that it is clear what we mean by our rash claim that philosophers should have political power. When there's no doubt about what it is to be a philosopher, then a defence becomes possible, if we can show that some people are made to practise philosophy c and to be political leaders, while others shouldn't engage in philosophy and should follow a leader.'

'The definition would be timely,' he remarked.

'All right. I wonder if this route leads to any kind of adequate clarification. Why don't you join me, and we'll see?'

'Lead on,' he said.

'I'm sure you're aware, without me having to remind you,' I said, 'that if the claim that someone loves something is to be accurate, he must undeniably love that thing as a whole, not just some aspects of it.'

'You've got to remind me, apparently,' he said, 'because I don't quite understand.'   d

'I'd have expected someone else to say that, Glaucon, not you,' I said. 'It's unlike an expert in love to forget that an amorous lover finds some pretext for being smitten and unhinged by every single alluring boy. They all seem to deserve his attention and devotion. I mean, isn't this how you and others like you behave towards good-looking young men? Don't you compliment a snub nose by calling it "pert", describe a hooked nose as "regal", and call one which falls between these two extremes "perfectly proportioned"? Don't you call swarthy young men "virile" and pallid ones "children of the gods"? And who do you think invented the term "honey-coloured"? It could only have been some lover glossing over and making light of a sallow complexion, because its possessor was in the alluring period of adolescence. In short, you come up with every conceivable excuse and all kinds of terms to ensure that you can give your approval to every alluring lad.'

'If you insist on trying out your ideas of how lovers behave on me,' he said, 'you can have my assent, because I don't want to jeopardize the argument.'

'And haven't you seen people who are fond of drinking behave in exactly the same way?' I went on. 'They make all kinds of excuses for their devotion to wine of every kind.'

'Yes.'

'And I'm sure you've noticed that if ambitious people can't get the command of a whole army, they take a company; and if they can't win the respect of important and high-powered people, they're happy to be respected by lesser people. It's status in general which they desire.'

'Absolutely.'

'So tell me where you stand on this question. If in our opinion someone desires something, are we to say that he desires that type of thing as a whole, or only some aspects of it?'

'The whole of it,' he replied.

'So the same goes for a philosopher too: we're to say that what he desires is the whole of knowledge, not just some aspects of it. True?'

'True.'

'If someone fusses about his lessons, then, especially when he's still young and without rational understanding of what is and isn't good for him, we can't describe him as a lover of knowledge, a philosopher, just as we can't describe someone who is fussing about his food as hungry, as desiring food, and don't call him a gourmand, but a poor eater.'

'Yes, it would be wrong to call him anything else.'

'On the other hand, if someone is glad to sample every subject and eagerly sets about his lessons with an insatiable appetite, then we'd be perfectly justified in calling him a philosopher, don't you think?'

In a very important argument, Plato describes a philosopher as one who perceives things 'in themselves'. A philosopher is awake rather than asleep; he has knowledge, while everyone else has mere belief or opinion, which is fallible and has less access to reality, because it can see no further than the sensible world, which is deceptive and deficient. Knowledge is correlated with the truth of things, which is a property of what each thing is itself, and which never changes; belief is correlated with the less real aspect of things, in which they are no more beautiful (say) than ugly.

'Then a motley crowd of people will be philosophers,' Glaucon said. 'For instance, sightseers all do what they do because they enjoy learning, I suppose; and it would be very odd to count theatre-goers as philosophers, when they'd never go of their own accord to hear a lecture or spend time over anything like that, but they rush around the festivals of Dionysus to hear every theatrical troupe, as if they were getting paid for the use of their ears, and never miss a single festival, whether it's being held in town or out of town. Are we to describe all these people and the disciples of other amusements as philosophers? And what about students of trivial branches of expertise?'

'No,' I replied, 'they're not philosophers, but they resemble philosophers.'

'Who are the true philosophers you have in mind?' he asked.

'Sightseers of the truth,' I answered.

'That must be right, but what exactly does it mean?' he asked.

'It wouldn't be easy to explain to anyone else,' I said. 'But you'll grant me this, surely.'

'What?'

'Since beautiful is the opposite of ugly, they are two things.'

'Of course.'

'In so far as they are two, each of them is single?'

'Yes.'

'And the same principle applies to moral and immoral, good and bad, and everything of any type: in itself, each of them is single, but each of them has a plurality of manifestations because they appear all over the place, as they become associated with actions and bodies and one another.'

'You're right,' he said.

'Well,' I continued, 'this is what enables me to distinguish the sightseers (to borrow your term) and the ones who want to acquire some expertise or other and the men of action from the people in question, b the ones who are philosophers in the true sense of the term.'

'What do you mean?' he asked.

'Theatre-goers and sightseers are devoted to beautiful sounds and colours and shapes, and to works of art which consist of these elements, but their minds are constitutionally incapable of seeing and devoting themselves to beauty itself.'

'Yes, that's certainly right,' he said.

'However, people with the ability to approach beauty itself and see beauty as it actually is are bound to be few and far between, aren't they?'

c 'Definitely.'

'So does someone whose horizon is limited to beautiful things, with no conception of beauty itself, and who is incapable of following guidance as to how to gain knowledge of beauty itself, strike you as living in a dream-world or in the real world? Look at it this way. Isn't dreaming precisely the state, whether one is asleep or awake, of taking something to be the real thing, when it is actually only a likeness?'

'Yes, that's what I'd say dreaming is,' he said.

'And what about someone who does the oppo-d site—who does think that there is such a thing as beauty itself, and has the ability to see it as well as the things which partake in it, and never gets them muddled up? Do you think he's living in the real world or in a dream-world?'

'Definitely in the real world,' he said.

'So wouldn't we be right to describe the difference between their mental states by saying that while this person has knowledge, the other one has beliefs?'

'Yes.'

'Now, suppose this other person—the one we're saying has beliefs, not knowledge—were to get cross with us and query the truth of our assertions. Will e we be able to calm him down and gently convince him of our point of view, while keeping him in the dark about the poor state of his health?'

'We really ought to,' he said.

'All right, but what shall we say to him, do you think? Perhaps this is what we should ask him. We'll tell him that we don't resent any knowledge he might have—indeed, we'd be delighted to see that he does know something—and then we'll say, "But can you

tell us, please, whether someone with knowledge knows something or nothing?" You'd better answer my questions for him.'

'My answer will be that he knows something,' he said.

'Something real or something unreal?'

'Real. How could something unreal be known?'

'We could look at the matter from more angles, 477a but we're happy enough with the idea that something completely real is completely accessible to knowledge, and something utterly unreal is entirely inaccessible to knowledge. Yes?'

'Perfectly happy.'

'All right. But if something is in a state of both reality and unreality, then it falls between that which is perfectly real and that which is utterly unreal, doesn't it?'

'Yes.'

'So since the field of knowledge is reality, and since it must be incomprehension whose field is un-reality, then we need to find out if there is in fact something which falls between incomprehension b and knowledge, whose field is this intermediate, don't we?'

'Yes.'

'Now, we acknowledge the existence of belief, don't we?'

'Of course.'

'Is it a different faculty from knowledge, or is it the same?'

'Different.'

'Every faculty has its own distinctive abilities, so belief and knowledge must have different domains'

'Yes.'

'Now, since the natural field of knowledge is reality—its function is to know reality as reality . . . Actually, I think there's something else we need to get clear about first.'

'What?'

'Shall we count as a distinct class of things the c faculties which give human beings and all other creatures their abilities? By "faculties" I mean things like sight and hearing. Do you understand the type of thing I have in mind?'

'Yes, I do,' he said.

'Let me tell you something that strikes me about them. I can't distinguish one faculty from another the way I commonly distinguish other things, by looking at their colours or shapes or anything like that, because faculties don't have any of those sorts of qualities for me to look at. The only aspect of a d faculty I can look at is its field, its effect. This is what enables me to identify each of them as a particular faculty. Where I find a single domain and a single effect, I say there is a single faculty; and I distinguish faculties which have different fields and different effects. What about you? What do you do?'

'The same as you,' he said.

'Let's go back to where we were before, then, Glaucon,' I said. 'Do you think that knowledge is a faculty, or does it belong in your opinion to some other class?'

'I think it belongs to that class,' he said, 'and is the most powerful of all the faculties.'

e 'And shall we classify belief as a faculty, or what?'

'As a faculty,' he said. 'Belief is precisely that which enables us to entertain beliefs.'

'Not long ago, however, you agreed that knowledge and belief were different.'

'Of course,' he said. 'One is infallible and the other is fallible, so anyone with any sense would keep them separate.'

478a 'Good,' I said. 'There can be no doubt of our position: knowledge and belief are different.'

'Yes.'

'Since they're different faculties, then, they have different natural fields, don't they?'

'Necessarily.'

'The field of knowledge is reality, isn't it? Its function is to know the reality of anything real?'

'Yes.'

'And the function of belief, we're saying, is to entertain beliefs?'

'Yes.'

'Does it entertain beliefs about the same thing which knowledge knows? Will what is accessible to knowledge and what is accessible to belief be identical? Or is that out of the question?'

'It's ruled out by what we've already agreed,' he said. 'If different faculties naturally have different fields, and if both knowledge and belief are facul-

b ties, and different faculties too, as we said, then it follows that it is impossible for what is accessible to knowledge and what is accessible to belief to be identical.'

'So if it is reality that is accessible to knowledge, then it is something else, not reality, that is accessible to belief, isn't it?'

'Yes.'

'Does it entertain beliefs about what is unreal? Or is it also impossible for that to happen? Think about

this: isn't it the case that someone who is entertaining a belief is bringing his believing mind to bear on something? I mean, is it possible to have a belief, and to be believing nothing?'

'That's impossible.'

'In fact, someone who has a belief has some single thing in mind, doesn't he?'

'Yes.'

'But the most accurate way to refer to something unreal would be to say that it is nothing, not that it is a single thing, wouldn't it?'   c

'Yes.'

'Didn't we find ourselves forced to relate incomprehension to unreality and knowledge to reality?'

'That's right,' he said.

'So the field of belief is neither reality nor unreality?'

'No.'

'Belief can't be incomprehension or knowledge, then?'

'So it seems.'

'Well, does it lie beyond their limits? Does it shed more light than knowledge or spread more obscurity than incomprehension?'

'It does neither.'

'Alternatively, does belief strike you as more opaque than knowledge and more lucid than incomprehension?'

'Considerably more,' he said.

'It lies within their limits?'   d

'Yes.'

'Then belief must fall between them.'

'Absolutely.'

'Now, didn't we say earlier that something which is simultaneously real and unreal (were such a thing to be shown to exist) would fall between the perfectly real and the wholly unreal, and wouldn't be the field of either knowledge or incomprehension, but of an intermediate (again, if such a thing were shown to exist) between incomprehension and knowledge?'

'Right.'

'And now we've found that what we call belief is such an intermediate, haven't we?'

'We have.'

'So the only thing left for us to discover, appar- e ently, is whether there's anything which partakes of both reality and unreality, and cannot be said to be perfectly real or perfectly unreal. If we were to come across such a thing, we'd be fully justified in describing it as the field of belief, on the principle that extremes belong together, and so do intermediates. Do you agree?'

'Yes.'

479a 'Let's return, on this basis, to the give and take of conversation with that fine fellow who doesn't acknowledge the existence of beauty itself or think that beauty itself has any permanent and unvarying character, but takes the plurality of beautiful things as his norm—that sightseer who can't under any circumstances abide the notion that beauty, morality, and so on are each a single entity. What we'll say to him is, "My friend, is there one beautiful thing, in this welter of beautiful things, which won't turn out to be ugly? Is there one moral deed which won't turn out to be immoral? Is there one just act which won't turn out to be unjust?" '

b 'No, there isn't,' he said. 'It's inevitable for these things to turn out to be both beautiful and ugly, in a sense, and the same goes for all the other qualities you mentioned in your question.'

'And there are doubles galore—but they turn out to be halves just as much as doubles, don't they?'

'Yes.'

'And do things which are large, small, light, and heavy deserve these attributes any more than they deserve the opposite attributes?'

'No, each of them is bound to have both qualities,' he said.

'So isn't it the case, then, that any member of a plurality no more *is* whatever it is said to be than it *is not* whatever it is said to be?'

c 'This is like those *double entendres* one hears at parties,' he said, 'or the riddle children tell about the eunuch and his hitting a bat—they make a riddle by asking what he hit it with and what it was on—in the sense that the members of the plurality are also ambiguous: it is impossible to form a stable conception of any of them as either being what it is, or not being what it is, or being both, or being neither.'

'How are you going to cope with them, then?' I asked. 'Can you find a better place to locate them than between real being and unreality? I mean, they can't turn out to be more opaque and unreal than un-
d reality, or more lucid and real than reality.'

'True,' he said.

'So there we are. We've discovered that the welter of things which the masses conventionally regard as beautiful and so on mill around somewhere between unreality and perfect reality.'

'Yes, we have.'

'But we have a prior agreement that were such a thing to turn up, we'd have to call it the field of belief, not of knowledge, since the realm which occupies some uncertain intermediate point must be accessible to the intermediate faculty.'

'Yes, we do.'

'What shall we say about those spectators, then, e who can see a plurality of beautiful things, but not beauty itself, and who are incapable of following if someone else tries to lead them to it, and who can see many moral actions, but not morality itself, and so on? That they only ever entertain beliefs, and do not *know* any of the things they believe?'

'That's what we have to say,' he said.

'As for those who can see each of these things in itself, in its permanent and unvarying nature, we'll say they have knowledge and are not merely entertaining beliefs, won't we?'

'Again, we have to.'

'And won't our position be that they're devoted to and love the domain of knowledge, as opposed to 480a the others, who are devoted to and love the domain of belief? I mean, surely we haven't forgotten our claim that these others love and are spectators of beautiful sounds and colours and so on, but can't abide the idea that there is such a thing as beauty itself?'

'No, we haven't forgotten.'

'They won't think us nasty if we refer to them as "lovers of belief" rather than as philosophers, who love knowledge, will they? Are they going to get very cross with us if we say that now?'

'Not if they listen to me,' he replied. 'It's not right to get angry at the truth.'

'But the term "believers" is inappropriate for those who are devoted to everything that is real: they should be called philosophers, shouldn't they?'

'Absolutely.'

A philosopher's inherent virtues are displayed. Though they stem from his or her love of knowledge, they coincide with commonly recognized virtues, and are far from incompatible with rulership.

'It's taken a long and thorough discussion, Glau- 484a con,' I said, 'and it's not been easy, but we've now demonstrated the difference between philosophers and non-philosophers.'

'A short discussion probably wouldn't have been enough,' he replied.

'I suppose you're right,' I said. 'Anyway, I think the conclusion would have been clearer if that had

been the only subject we'd had to discuss, and there weren't plenty of topics left for us to cover if we're to see the difference between a moral and an im-
b moral life.'

'What's the next issue for us to look into?' he asked.

'The next one's the one that follows, of course,' I replied. 'Given that philosophers are those who are capable of apprehending that which is permanent and unvarying, while those who can't, those who wander erratically in the midst of plurality and variety, are not lovers of knowledge, which set of people ought to be rulers of a community?'

'What would be a sensible answer for us to give?' he asked.

'That the position of guardianship should be given to whichever set we find capable of guarding the laws and customs of a community,' I said.

'Right,' he said.

'I assume it's clear whether someone who's going to guard something should be blind or have good eyesight?' I said.

'Of course it is,' he answered.

'Well, imagine someone who really lacks the ability to recognize any and every real thing and has no paradigm to shed light for his mind's eye. He has nothing absolutely authentic to contemplate, as painters do, and use as a reference-point whenever
d he needs to, and gain a completely accurate picture of, before establishing human norms of right, morality, and goodness (if establishing is what is required), and before guarding and protecting the norms that have already been established. Do you think there's any difference between his condition and blindness?'

'No, there's hardly any difference at all,' he said.

'Is this the type of person you'd prefer us to appoint as guardians? Or shall we appoint those who can recognize every reality, and who not only have just as much practical experience as the others, but are also at least as good as them in every other respect?'

'If they really are at least equal in every other sphere,' he said, 'and since they are pre-eminent in the sphere you've mentioned, which is just about the most important one there is, then it would be ridiculous to choose anyone else.'

485a   'So what we'd better explain is how a single person can combine both sets of qualities, hadn't we?'

'Yes.'

'Well, right at the beginning of this argument we said that the first thing we had to grasp was what it is to be a philosopher. I'm sure that if we reached a satisfactory agreement on that point, we'd also agree that despite being a single person, he can combine both sets of qualities, and that philosophers are the only ones who should rule over communities.'

'Why?'

'Let's start by agreeing that it's natural for philosophers to love every field of study which re- b veals to them something of that reality which is eternal and is not subject to the vicissitudes of generation and destruction.'

'All right.'

'Moreover,' I said, 'we can agree that they're in love with reality as a whole, and that therefore their behaviour is just like that of ambitious people and lovers, as we explained before, in that they won't willingly give up even minor or worthless parts of it.'

'You're right,' he said.

'The next thing for you to think about is whether there's a further feature they must have, if they're c going to live up to our description of them.'

'What feature?'

'Honesty—the inability consciously to tolerate falsehood, rather than loathing it, and loving truth.'

'It makes sense that they should,' he said.

'It doesn't only make sense, my friend: a lover is absolutely bound to love everything which is related and belongs to his beloved.'

'Right,' he said.

'Well, can you conceive of anything more closely related to knowledge than truth?'

'Of course not,' he replied.

'Is it possible, then, for love of knowledge and love of falsehood to be found in the same nature?'   d

'Definitely not.'

'Then a genuine lover of knowledge will from his earliest years find nothing more attractive than truth of every kind.'

'Indisputably.'

'And we know that anyone whose predilection tends strongly in a single direction has correspondingly less desire for other things, like a stream whose flow has been diverted into another channel.'

'Of course.'

'So when a person's desires are channelled towards learning and so on, that person is concerned with the pleasure the mind feels of its own accord, and has nothing to do with the pleasures which reach

the mind through the agency of the body, if the per-
e son is a genuine philosopher, not a fake one.'

'Inevitably.'

'He'll be self-disciplined, then, and not mercenary, since he's constitutionally incapable of taking
seriously the things which money can buy—at considerable cost—and which cause others to take
money seriously.'

'Yes.'

486a   'And here's another point you'd better take into
consideration, to help you distinguish a philosophical from a non-philosophical character.'

'What?'

'You must watch out for the presence of small-
mindedness. Nothing stops a mind constantly striving for an overview of the totality of things human
and divine more effectively than involvement in
petty details.'

'Very true,' he said.

'When a mind has broadness of vision and contemplates all time and all existence, do you think it
can place much importance on human life?'

'Impossible,' he said.

b   'So it won't find death terrifying either, will it?'

'Not at all.'

'Then a cowardly and small-minded person is excluded from true philosophy, it seems.'

'I agree.'

'Well now, take a person who's restrained and un-
interested in money, and who isn't small-minded or
specious or cowardly. Could he possibly drive hard
bargains or act immorally?'

'No.'

'So when you're trying to see whether or not
someone has a philosophical mind, you'll watch out
for whether, from his earliest years, he shows himself to be moral and well mannered, or antisocial
and uncouth.'

'Yes.'

c   'And there's something else you won't forget to
look out for as well, I imagine.'

'What?'

'Whether he's quick or slow at learning. I mean,
you wouldn't expect someone to be particularly fond
of something it hurt him to do and where slight gains
were hard to win, would you?'

'I'd never do that.'

'What about if he's incapable of retaining anything he's learnt? Is there any way he can have room
for knowledge, when he's full of forgetfulness?'

'Of course not.'

'In the end, don't you think, after all his thank-
less toil, he's bound to loathe both himself and intellectual activity?'

'Yes.'

'So we'd better count forgetfulness as a factor d
which precludes a mind from being good enough at
philosophy. We'd better make a good memory a prerequisite.'

'Absolutely.'

'Now, isn't it the case that lack of culture and
grace in someone can only lead him to lack a sense
of proportion?'

'Of course.'

'And do you think that truth is closely related to
proportion or to its opposite?'

'To proportion.'

'So we need to look for a mind which, in addition to the qualities we've already mentioned, has
an inherent sense of proportion and elegance, and
which makes a person instinctively inclined towards
anything's essential character.'

'Of course we do.'

'All right. Surely you don't think that any of the e
interconnected qualities we've mentioned are at all
inessential for a competent and complete mental
grasp of reality?'

'No, they're absolutely essential,' he said.   487a

'Can you find any flaw, then, in an occupation
like this, which in order to be competently practised
requires the following inherent qualities in a person:
a good memory, quickness at learning, broadness of
vision, elegance, and love of and affiliation to truth,
morality, courage, and self-discipline?'

'Not even Momus could criticize this occupation,'
he replied.

'Now, aren't people who, thanks to their education
and their age, have these qualities in full the only ones
to whom you would entrust your community?'

To the objection that the popular impression of
philosophers is that they are either useless or bad,
Socrates replies that the 'useless' ones are so described because people simply fail to understand
their value, and the 'bad' ones are either those who
have been corrupted by the general populace (and
the sophists who pander to the general populace),
until they use their natural talents for base ends,
or those who try to take up philosophy despite
their lack of talent. Both are cases where the 'one
man, one job' principle is transgressed; in neither
case should we really describe these people as
philosophers.

Adeimantus spoke up. 'Socrates,' he said, 'no b one's going to take you up on this point; but that may be due to the fact that there's a particular experience which people who hear you speak on any occasion always have. They get the impression that, because they lack expertise at the give and take of discussion, they're led a little bit astray by each question, and then when all the little bits are put together at the end of the discussion, they find that they were way off the mark and that they've contradicted their original position. They're like unskilled backgammon players, who end up being shut out by skilled ones and incapable of making a move: c they too end up being shut out and incapable of making an argumentative move in this alternative version of backgammon, which uses words rather than counters, since they feel that this is not necessarily a certain route to the truth. From my point of view, what I'm saying is relevant to our current situation. You see, someone might object that his inability to find the words to challenge you doesn't alter the evident fact that the majority of the people who take d up philosophy and spend more than just their youth on it—who don't get involved in it just for educational purposes and then drop it—turn out to be pretty weird (not to say rotten to the core), and that the effect of this pursuit you're praising even on those of its practitioners who are supposed to be particularly good is that they become incapable of performing any service to their communities.'

I responded by asking, 'Do you think this view is right?'

'I don't know,' he replied. 'But I'd be happy to hear what you have to say on the matter.'

'What you'd hear from me is that I think they're telling the truth.'

e 'Then how can it be right', he said, 'to say that there'll be no end to political troubles until philosophers have power in their communities, when we agree that philosophers are not use to them?'

'It'll take an analogy to answer your question,' I said.

'And you never use analogies, of course,' he said.

'What?' I exclaimed. 'It's hard enough to prove my point without you making fun of me as well as forc- 488a ing me to try. Anyway, here's my analogy: now you'll be in a better position to see how inadequate it is. I mean, what society does to the best practitioners of philosophy is so complex that there's no other single phenomenon like it: in order to defend them from criticism, one has to compile an analogy out of lots of different elements, like the goat-stags and other compound creatures painters come up with.

'Imagine the following situation on a fleet of ships, or on a single ship. The owner has the edge over everyone else on board by virtue of his size and b strength, but he's rather deaf and short-sighted, and his knowledge of naval matters is just as limited. The sailors are wrangling with one another because each of them thinks that he ought to be the captain, despite the fact that he's never learnt how, and can't name his teacher or specify the period of his apprenticeship. In any case, they are ready to butcher anyone who says it is. They're for ever crowding closely around the owner, pleading for with him and c stopping at nothing to get him to entrust the rudder to them. Sometimes, if their pleas are unsuccessful, but others get the job, they kill those others or throw them off the ship, subdue their worthy owner by drugging him drunk or something, take control of the ship, help themselves to its cargo, and have the kind of drunken and indulgent voyage you'd expect from people like that. And that's not all: they think highly of anyone who contributes towards their gaining power by showing skill at winning over or subduing the owner, and describe him as an accomplished seaman, a true captain, a naval expert; but d they criticize anyone different as useless. They completely fail to understand that any genuine sea-captain has to study the yearly cycle, the seasons, the heavens, the stars and winds, and everything relevant to the job, if he's to be properly equipped to hold a position of authority in a ship. In fact, they think it's impossible to study and acquire expertise at how to steer a ship (leaving aside the question of e whether or not people want you to) and at the same time be a good captain. When this is what's happening on board ships, don't you think that the crew of ships in this state would think of any true captain as nothing but a windbag with his head in the clouds, 489a of no use to them at all?'

'They definitely would,' Adeimantus replied.

'I'm sure you don't need an analysis of the analogy to see that it's a metaphor for the attitude of society towards true philosophers,' I said. 'I'm sure you take my point.'

'I certainly do,' he said.

'You'd better use it, then, in the first instance, to clarify things for that person who expressed surprise at the disrespect shown to philosophers by society, and try to show him how much more astonishing it would be if they were respected.'   b

'All right, I will,' he said.

'And that you're right to say that the best practitioners of philosophy are incapable of performing any public service. But you'd better tell him to blame their uselessness on the others' failure to make use of them, rather than on the fact that they are accomplished philosophers. I mean, it's unnatural for the captain to ask the sailors to accept his authority and it's unnatural for wise men to dance attendance on rich men; this story is misleading. The truth of the matter is that it makes no difference whether you're rich or poor: if you feel ill, you're bound to c dance attendance on a doctor, and if you need to accept authority, you must dance attendance on someone in authority who is capable of providing it. If he is really to serve any useful purpose, it's not up to him to ask those under him to accept his authority. And you won't be mistaken if you compare present-day political leaders to the sailors in our recent tale, and the ones they call useless airheads to the genuine captain.'

'You're absolutely right,' he said.

'Under these conditions and circumstances, it's not easy for the best of occupations to gain a good reputation, when reputations are in the hands of peo- d ple whose occupations are incompatible with it. But by far the worst and most influential condemnation of philosophy comes about as a result of the people who claim to practise it—the ones the critic of philosophy was talking about, in your report, when he described the majority of the people who take up philosophy as rotten to the core (although the best of them are merely useless). And I agreed that you were telling the truth, didn't I?'

'Yes.'

'Well, we've described the reasons for the uselessness of the good practitioners, haven't we?'

'We certainly have.'

'Shall we next describe why the corruption of most philosophers is inevitable, and try to explain e why this shouldn't be blamed on philosophy either, if we can?'

'Yes.'

'Let's start our discussion by reminding ourselves of the fundamental points in our description of the kind of character a truly good person will inevitably have. If you remember, above all he was led by truth: 490a if he didn't pursue truth absolutely and wholeheartedly, he was bound to be a specious impostor, with nothing whatsoever to do with true philosophy.'

'That's what we said.'

'Well, that in itself is diametrically opposed to current opinion about philosophers, isn't it?'

'It certainly is,' he said.

'Now, our response will be to point out that a genuine lover of knowledge innately aspires to reality, and doesn't settle on all the various things which are b assumed to be real, but keeps on, with love remaining keen and steady, until the nature of each thing as it really is in itself has been grasped by the appropriate part of his mind—which is to say, the part which is akin to reality. Once he has drawn near this authentic reality and united with it, and thus fathered intellect and truth, then he has knowledge; then he lives a life which is true to himself; then he is nourished; and then, but not before, he finds release from his love-pangs. Would this be a reasonable response for us to make?'

'Nothing could be more reasonable,' he said.

'And will he be the sort of person to love falsehood or will exactly the opposite be the case, and he'll loathe it?' c

'He'll loathe it,' he said.

'I'm sure we'd insist that no array of evils could follow the leadership of truth.'

'Of course we would.'

'But rather, a character imbued with health and morality, and the self-discipline that accompanies them.'

'Right,' he said.

'Anyway, there's no need for us to have the whole array of the philosopher's characteristics line up all over again. I'm sure you remember how we found that philosophers naturally have courage, broadness of vision, quickness at learning, and a good memory. You interrupted by saying that although our argument was absolutely incontrovertible, it was still possible for someone to leave arguments out of it d and look at the actual people we were talking about, and to conclude that while some philosophers are evidently merely useless, the majority of them are bad through and through. We're trying to uncover the reasons for their bad name, and so we're now up against the question why the majority are bad. That's why we brought the true philosopher's characteristics back in again and felt compelled to provide a clear statement of them.'

'True,' he said. e

'What we have to do', I said, 'is see how this philosophical nature is corrupted and why it is often completely ruined, while immunity from corruption is rare—and these escapees are the people who get called useless, rather than bad. After that, 491a we'll turn to pseudo-philosophical natures and the kinds of people who take up the occupation which is proper to a philosophical nature, and we'll try to discern what it is in the make-up of their minds which drives them towards an occupation which is too good and too sublime for them, so that they commit a wide variety of offences and make everyone, all over the world, think of philosophy in the way you've mentioned.'

'What sources of corruption do you have in mind?' he asked.

'I'll do my best to explain,' I replied. 'I suppose it's indisputable that a fully philosophical nature— of the kind we've described, with the whole array b of qualities we lined up not long ago—is a rare human phenomenon: there aren't going to be very many of them. Don't you agree?'

'Definitely.'

'Well, look how heavily these few people are outnumbered by powerful sources of corruption.'

'What are they, though?'

'The most astounding thing of all is that there isn't one of their commendable characteristics which doesn't ruin a mind which possess it and cause a rift between it and philosophy. I'm talking about courage, self-discipline, and all the qualities we went through.'

'It's not easy to make sense of this idea,' he said.

c 'And that's not all,' I said. 'Every single one of the acknowledged good things of life is a factor in its corruption and the rift—good looks, affluence, physical fitness, influential family relationships in one's community, and so on and so forth. I've cut the list short, because you can see what I'm saying.'

'I can,' he said. 'And I wouldn't mind hearing a more detailed explanation.'

'If you grasp the general principle of the matter,' I said, 'everything will fall into place and what I've already said will start to make sense.'

'What are you getting at?' he asked.

d 'We know', I said, 'that if any plant or creature, at the stage when it is a seed or a new growth, fails to get the right nourishment or weather or location, then the number of its deficiencies, in respect to properties it should have, is proportionate to its vigour. I mean, bad is the opposite of good, rather than of not-good.'

'Of course.'

'So I suppose it's plausible to think that a very good thing will end up in a worse state than a sec-ond-rate thing if the conditions of its nurture are less suited to its nature.'

'Yes.'

'Well, by the same token, Adeimantus,' I asked, e 'won't we claim that if the most gifted minds are subjected to a bad education, they become exceptionally bad? I mean, do you imagine that horrendous crimes and sheer depravity stem from a second-rate nature, rather than from a vigorous one which has been ruined by its upbringing? Could significant benefit or significant harm conceivably proceed from innate weakness?'

'No, you're right,' he said.

'Now, in my opinion, if it receives a suitable ed- 492a ucation, the philosophical nature we proposed is bound to grow and arrive at perfect goodness. However, if its germination and growth take place in an unsuitable educational environment, then without divine intervention its destination will inevitably be completely the opposite. Or do you follow the masses and believe that there are members of the younger generation who are corrupted by professional teachers, and that there are professional teachers who, despite being private citizens, can be a source of corruption to any degree worth mentioning? Don't you think, rather, that it is the very people who make this claim who are the most influential teachers, and who provide the most thorough education and form men and women of all ages into b any shape they want?'

'When do they do this?' he asked.

'When a lot of them huddle together on seats in the assembly or lawcourt or theatre,' I said, 'or when they convene for military purposes, or when there's any other general public gathering, and the boos and applause of their criticism or praise (excessive in both cases) of whatever is being said or done make a terrible din, and it's not only them—the rocks and their surroundings double the noise of their approval c and disapproval by echoing it. In a situation like this, how do you think a young man's heart, as they say, will be affected? How can the education he received outside of this public arena stand up to it, do you suppose, without being overwhelmed by criticism or praise of this kind and swept away at the mercy of the current? Won't he end up just like them, with the same moral standards and the same habits as them?'

'He's bound to, Socrates,' he said.   d

'And we haven't yet mentioned the most irresistible pressure they bring to bear,' I said.

'What is it?' he asked.

'It's the concrete pressure these consummate professional educators apply when they turn to action, if their words have failed to indoctrinate someone. I mean, surely you're aware that they punish disobedience with forfeiture of rights, and with fines and death?'

'Yes, I'm certainly well aware of that,' he said.

'Can you think of any teacher or any kind of privately received instruction with the strength to hold out against these pressures?'

e 'I think it's impossible,' he said.

'Yes, and it's extremely stupid even to try to be that kind of teacher,' I said. 'You see, it's quite impossible, as the present and the past show, for any educational programme to alter anyone's character, as far as goodness is concerned, contrary to the conditioning he receives in the public arena—by "anyone" I mean any human, of course, Adeimantus: as the proverb recommends, we'd better make an ex-

493a ception of divinity. I mean, I can tell you that you'd be quite right to see God at work when anything does retain its integrity and fulfil its potential within current political systems.'

'That's what I think too,' he said.

'And I wonder whether you agree with me on a further point as well,' I said.

'What?'

'Even though they call it knowledge, every one of those private fee-charging individuals—the ones who are called sophists and are regarded as rivals by these educators we've been talking about—teaches nothing but the attitudes the masses form by consensus. Imagine that the keeper of a huge, strong beast notices what makes it angry, what it desires,

b how it has to be approached and handled, the circumstances and conditions under which it becomes particularly fierce or calm, what provokes its typical cries, and what tones of voice make it gentle or wild. Once he's spent enough time in the creature's company to acquire all this information, he calls it knowledge, forms it into a systematic branch of expertise, and starts to teach it, despite total ignorance, in fact, about which of the creature's attitudes and desires is commendable or deplorable, good or bad,

c moral or immoral. His usage of all these terms simply conforms to the great beast's attitudes, and he describes things as good or bad according to its likes and dislikes, and can't justify his usage of the terms any further, but describes as right and good things which are merely indispensable, since he hasn't re-

alized and can't explain to anyone else how vast a gulf there is between necessity and goodness. Wouldn't you really and truly find someone like this implausible as a teacher?'

'Yes, I would,' he said.

'Well, do you think there's anything to choose between him and someone who's noticed what makes the motley masses collectively angry and happy and d thinks he has knowledge—whether it's in the field of painting or music or government? I mean, whenever someone's relationship with the masses consists of displaying his composition (or whatever product it may be) or his political service to them, and giving them power over him—or rather, more power than they need have—then the proverbial necessity of Diomedes forces him to compose things of which they approve. Sometimes one of the sophists might argue that what the masses like coincides with what is genuinely good and fine, but this argument always comes across as utterly absurd, don't you think?'

'It always has and it always will, in my opinion,' c he said.

'So, against this background, please remember what we were saying before. Is it possible for the masses to accept or conceive of the existence of beauty itself, rather than the plurality of beautiful things? Or anything in itself, rather than the plurality of instances of each thing?'

'Not at all,' he said. 494a

'It's impossible, then, for the masses to love knowledge,' I said.

'Yes, it is.'

'They're bound to run philosophers down, then, as well.'

'That's inevitable.'

'And so are those individuals whose relationship with the masses consists of wanting to please them.'

'Obviously.'

'In this context, can you see how any innate philosopher will preserve the integrity of his nature, and consequently stay with the occupation and see it through to the end? Look at it in the context of what we were saying earlier. We agreed that a b philosopher has quickness at learning, a good memory, courage, and broadness of vision.'

'Yes.'

'From his earliest years, then, he'll outclass other children at everything, especially if he's as gifted physically as he is mentally, won't he?'

'Of course,' he answered.

'So when he grows up, his friends and fellow citizens will want to make use of him for their own affairs.'

'Naturally.'

c 'They'll be a constant presence, then, with their requests and courtesies, as they flatter him and try to get him on their side in anticipation of the influence that will one day be his.'

'Yes, that's what invariably happens,' he said.

'What do you imagine he'll do in this situation,' I asked, 'especially if he happens to come from a wealthy and noble family within a powerful state, and is also good-looking and well built? Don't you think he'll be filled with unrealizable hopes, and will expect to be capable one day of managing the affairs not only of Greece, but of the
d non-Greek world as well? In these circumstances, won't he get ideas above his station and puff himself up with affection and baseless, senseless price?'

'He certainly will,' he said.

'Now, suppose someone gently approaches him while he's in this frame of mind and tells him the truth—that he's taken leave of his senses and should try to dispel this inanity, but that he won't gain intelligence unless he works like a slave for it—do you think it's going to be easy for the message to penetrate all these pernicious influences and get through to him?'

'No, far from it,' he said.

'And,' I went on, 'supposing his innate gifts and
e his affinity with the rationality of what's being said do enable him to pay attention at all, and he is swayed and attracted towards philosophy, what reaction would you expect from those others, when they think they're losing his services and his friendship? Won't they do and say absolutely anything to stop him being won over? And as for the person who's trying to win him over, won't they come up with all kinds of private schemes and public court-cases to stop him succeeding?'

495a 'Inevitably,' he said.

'What chance does this young man have of becoming a philosopher?'

'No chance, really.'

'So, as you can see,' I went on, 'we were right to say that it is, in fact, the actual ingredients of a philosophical nature which are in a sense responsible (given a pernicious educational environment) for someone being deflected from his occupation, and that the acknowledged good things of life—affluence and similar resources—are also responsible. Do you agree?'

'Yes,' he said. 'We were quite right.'

'There we are, then, Adeimantus,' I said. 'Those are the powerful factors which ruin and corrupt any- b one who is, by nature, best suited for the best occupation—and such people are rare anyway, as we said. Moreover, these are the men who have the potential to do the greatest harm to communities and to individuals, and the greatest good too, if that's the course they happen to take. An insignificant person, however, never has any effect of any significance on any individual or society.'

'You're quite right,' he said.

'So that's how the most appropriate people are deflected and desert philosophy, without consummating the relationship. They end up living a life which c is inappropriate for them and which isn't true to their natures, and they leave philosophy, like an orphan with no relatives, to the mercy of others who aren't good enough for her, and who defile her and gain her the kind of tarnished reputation you say her detractors ascribe to her—for going about with people who are either worthless or obnoxious.'

'Yes, that's the usual view,' he said.

'And it's not unreasonable,' I said. 'You see, when the abandonment of this territory is noticed by others—inferior members of the human race—and when they also see how rich it is in renown and sta- d tus, they behave like escaped convicts who take sanctuary in temples: they break away from their professions, with no regrets, and encroach on philosophy. In fact, they're the ones who do have some facility at their own paltry professions, because in spite of this treatment, philosophy still remains more prestigious than other occupations; and this prestige attracts a lot of people—immature people, who have been physically deformed by their jobs and work, and are mentally just as warped and stunted by their e servile business. Don't you think that's inevitable?'

'It certainly is.'

'Do you think the impression they give', I went on, 'is any different from that of a small, bald metal-worker who's come into some money? He's just got himself out of debtor's prison, he's had a bath and is wearing brand-new clothes and a bridegroom's outfit, and he's about to marry his master's daughter because she's hard up and has no one to look after her.'

'No, they're exactly the same, really,' he said. 496a

'What sort of offspring are they likely to father,

then? Second-rate half-breeds, don't you think?'

'Inevitably.'

'Now, when people who are unworthy of education force their presumptuous attentions on her, what sorts of ideas and thoughts do they produce, would you say? Isn't it perfectly appropriate to call them sophisms, and to claim that they are all illegitimate and lacking in true intelligence?'

'Absolutely,' he said.

'That leaves us with only a tiny number of people, Adeimantus,' I said, 'who have the right to consort with philosophy. A person of high character and sound education might fortuitously have been exiled, and so have remained true to his nature and faithful to philosophy by being out of the reach of corrupting influences; or occasionally a great mind is born in some backwater of a community and finds the politics petty and beneath him. And I suppose a few, because of their natural gifts, do have the right to find some other occupation demeaning and to turn from it to philosophy. Then there is also the bridle of our friend Theages, which can act as a curb: Theages was in all other respects well equipped to be deflected from philosophy, but he had to pamper his physical ailment and so he was curbed and prevented from taking up politics. It's not worth mentioning my own case—the communications I receive from my deity—because there's either very little or no precedent for the phenomenon.

'When the few members of this band have glimpsed the joy and happiness to be found in mastering philosophy and have also gained a clear enough impression of the madness of the masses; when they've realized that more or less every political action is pernicious and that if someone tries to assist morality there will be no one to back him up and see that he comes out unscathed, but it would be like an encounter between a human being and wild beasts; since he isn't prepared to join others in their immorality and isn't capable, all alone, of standing up to all those ferocious beasts, but would die before doing his community or his friends any good, and so would be useless to himself and to everyone else—once he has grasped all this with his rational mind, he lies low and does only what he's meant to do. It's as if he's taken shelter under a wall during a storm, with the wind whipping up the dust and rain pelting down; lawlessness infects everyone else he sees, so he is content if he can find a way to live his life here on earth without becoming tainted by immoral or un-

just deeds, and to depart from life confidently, and without anger and bitterness.'

'If he could do that,' he said, 'he'd really have done something with his life.'

Despite the gloomy realism of the previous section, Plato now argues that his imaginary community could, in principle, exist. It would take a correct educational programme, which did not trivialize philosophy but made it the acme of one's life; it would take a correct assessment of the value of philosophy; and it would take radical political changes. However, it is still clear that Plato regards the possibility of all this actually happening as extremely remote; he is more interested in the principle than the practical reality.

'But he could do much more with his life', I replied, 'if he just lived in a suitable political system, which enabled him to develop more and to preserve the integrity of public business as well as his own affairs. Anyway, I think we've said enough about why philosophy has a bad name, and why it doesn't deserve it, unless you've got something to add.'

'No, I've nothing to add on this issue,' he said. 'But which contemporary political system do you think is suitable for philosophy?'

'Not a single one,' I replied. 'That's exactly what I'm critical of—that no current political system is good enough for a philosophical nature to grow in without getting modified and altered. It's like a seed which has been brought from its native land and planted in foreign soil: its vitality tends to become drained, and the species become absorbed into the dominant local variety. In the same way, this type of person can't retain his native qualities, but is deflected and assumes properties that don't really belong to him. If he comes across a political system with the same degree of excellence as his character, then the divinity of the philosophical character will become apparent, as distinct from the humanity of all other natures and occupations. Now, your next question is obviously going to be what this political system is.'

'You've got me wrong there,' he said. 'I wasn't going to ask that, but whether the community we're founding and describing is the one you mean, or whether there's another candidate.'

'On the whole, it's our community,' I said. 'But there's an earlier point that needs repeating, that the community would have to contain an element which understands the rationale of the political system and d keeps to the same principles which you as legislator followed when you made the laws.'

'Yes, that did come up,' he agreed.

'I didn't make it sufficiently clear, however,' I said, 'because I was worried about the objections you were raising which have shown how long and complicated an argument it takes to prove the point. And what we're still faced with is hardly the easiest part of the account.'

'What is it?'

'How a community can engage in philosophy and survive. I mean, great enterprises are always hazardous, and anything fine really is, as the saying puts it, difficult.'

e 'All the same,' he said, 'the account won't be complete until this point has been cleared up. So we'd better explore it.'

'The only thing that could stop us doing so is lack of ability,' I said. 'It won't be lack of will, and you'll be an eyewitness to my determination. Look at it now, in fact—and how I'm prepared to stick my neck out and say that our community should turn the current approach to philosophy upside down.'

'What do you mean?'

'At the moment,' I said, 'those who actually do engage in it are young men, scarcely out of childhood. In the interval before they take up estate-man-498a agement and moneymaking, they dabble in the most difficult aspect of philosophy—the bit which has to do with rational argument—and then they drop it. And they are supposed to be the most advanced philosophers! After that, they count it as no mean achievement actually to accept an invitation to listen to a philosophical debate, since they think that philosophy should be merely an incidental occupation. And in old age they are—with a few excep-b tions—snuffed out more thoroughly than Heraclitus' sun, since they are never rekindled later.'

'Whereas they should do what?' he asked.

'Exactly the opposite. While they're young, they should be educated and should study philosophy in a way which suits their age. Their bodies are growing and developing during this period, and they should concentrate on getting them into a state where they minister to philosophy. In due course of time, when their minds are beginning to mature, they should put more effort into mental exercise; and when their physical strength starts to wane and they are too old to play a public part in the community c or to serve in the militia, they should be allowed to roam free and graze at will, and to concentrate on

philosophy, with everything else being incidental. This is the correct programme for people who are going to live a happy life and guarantee for themselves circumstances in the next world, after their death, which match the life they lived here.'

'You certainly give the impression of being wholehearted about this, Socrates,' he said. 'But I think most of the people who hear you express these views will be even more wholehearted about challenging them, since they won't be convinced in the slightest. And Thrasymachus will take the lead in this, I imagine.'

'Please don't cause trouble between me and Thrasymachus,' I said, 'when we've only just be- d come friends—not that we were enemies before. I'll spare no effort until I've either won him and everyone else over to my point of view—or at least done something to prepare them in case they ever meet these arguments again in future incarnations!'

'You're thinking in the short term, then!' he remarked.

'It's nothing compared with eternity,' I responded. 'But I'm not at all surprised that most people find what I'm saying incredible: after all, it's never been within their experience. They're used to carefully e assimilated phrases, rather than hearing words tumbling out without preparation as they are now. And they've never come across even a single case of a man who is, in both his actions and his words, as perfectly identified and assimilated with goodness as is possible, and who is in a position of authority in an equally good community. Do you think they 499a have?'

'Definitely not.'

'Then again, Adeimantus, they've not been adequately exposed to discussions which aren't dishonourable and mean, but are designed for a thorough and intense quest for the truth, for the sake of knowledge, and which are hardly on nodding terms with those subtleties and eristic tricks whose sole purpose, whether they occur during lawsuits or private conversations, is to increase the speaker's reputation and his chances of winning the argument.'

'No, they haven't,' he said.

'These are the reasons and considerations', I said, 'which led me earlier, despite my anxieties—since b the truth left me no option—to claim that no community or political system, and by the same token on person either, could ever attain perfection until some accident forced those few philosophers (the ones who are currently called useless, rather than the ones who are called rotten) to take charge of a community whether or not they wanted to, and made the citizens obey them, or alternatively until, thanks to c divine providence, either current kings and rulers or their sons were gripped by authentic love for authentic philosophy. In my opinion, it's unreasonable to claim that either or both of these alternatives are impossible; if this were so, then we'd deserve to be ridiculed for our empty assertions, our wishful thinking. Don't you agree?'

'Yes.'

'So whether the outstanding practitioners of philosophy were compelled to take charge of a community at some point in the infinity of past time, or whether they are now being compelled to do so in some foreign land which lies far beyond the limits d of our awareness, or whether they will be compelled to do so in the future, we are prepared to insist that the political system we've described either did or does or will exist, whenever it is that the Muse of philosophy gains control of a community. The point is that the compulsion is feasible, and we aren't talking about unrealizable theories—though we're the first to admit that it wouldn't be easy.'

'I agree,' he said.

'Most people don't, however, wouldn't you say?' I asked.

'I suppose so,' he said.

'Adeimantus,' I said, 'you really shouldn't condemn the masses like that. They'll change their e minds if you don't approach them argumentatively. You mustn't rub them up the wrong way while trying to remove their low opinion of intellectualism. You must show them who you mean by philosophers, and explain (as we did just now) what it takes to be a philosopher and what the pursuit involves, 500a so that they realize that you're not talking about the people they think of as philosophers. I mean, do you think that, even if they see things this way, they won't change their minds and adopt a different position? Do you think that someone open-minded and even-tempered can get angry unless he's in the presence of anger, or can be resentful unless he's in the presence of resentment? I won't even let you reply before telling you my opinion: this kind of intransigence is a rare phenomenon, and the majority of people don't have it.'

'I agree,' he said, 'without hesitation.'

b 'Do you also agree that responsibility for the usual disparagement of philosophy is to be laid at the door of those gate-crashers who barge in where they have

no right to be, call one another names, behave offensively, and constantly gossip about people, which is a highly unphilosophical activity?'

'Definitely,' he replied.

'The point is, of course, Adeimantus, that someone whose mind really is fixed on reality has no time to cast his gaze downwards on to the affairs of men c and to enter into their disputes (and so be infected with resentment and malice). His eyes are occupied with the sight of things which are organized, permanent, and unchanging, where wronging and being wronged don't exist, where all is orderly and rational; and he makes this realm the model for his behaviour, and assimilates himself to it as much as is feasible. I mean, don't you think that one's behaviour is bound to resemble anyone or anything whose company one enjoys?'

'Inevitably,' he said.

'So because a philosopher's links are with a realm which is divine and orderly, he becomes as d divine and orderly as is humanly possible. Even so, he still meets with plenty of criticism from all quarters.'

'Absolutely.'

'Now, if a philosopher were compelled not to restrict his modelling to himself, but to work both publicly and in his private life to stamp men's characters with what he sees in that realm, do you think he'd make a poor artisan of self-discipline, morality, and in general of what it is to be, in ordinary terms, a good person?'

'Not at all,' he answered.

'And if people realize that what we're saying about him is the truth, will they still get angry at e philosophers? Will they still doubt our claim that there is no way in which a community is going to be happy unless its plan is drawn up by artists who refer to a divine model?'

'No, they won't get angry if they realize that,' he said. 'But how will these artists go about their 501a work?'

'They must treat a community and people's characters like a painting-board,' I said, 'and their first job is to wipe it clean. This isn't a particularly easy thing to do, but you'll appreciate that the main way they differ from everyone else is in refusing to deal with an individual or a community, and not being prepared to sketch out a legal code, until they've either been given a clean slate or have made it so themselves.'

'Yes, and they're right,' he said.

'Next they'll make an outline of the constitution, don't you think?'

'Of course.'

b 'I imagine the next stage would involve their constantly looking this way and that as they work—looking on the one hand towards that which is inherently moral, right, self-disciplined, and so on, and on the other hand towards what they're creating in the human realm. By selecting behaviour-patterns and blending them, they'll produce a composite human likeness, taking as their reference-point that quality which Homer too called "godly" and "godlike" in its human manifestation.'

'Right,' he said.

'And I suppose they'd rub bits out and paint them in again, until they've done all they can to create hu-
c man characters which stand the best chance of meeting the gods' approval.'

'It should be a very beautiful painting, anyway,' he remarked.

'Well,' I asked, 'are we making any progress towards persuading those energetic opponents of ours, the ones you mentioned, that this is the kind of painter of constitutions we were recommending to them before? They got angry with him then, because we were putting political power in his hands, but are they rather more mollified now that they've heard our account?'

'They'll be much less upset,' he said, 'if they've got any sense.'

'I mean, how could they have any reservations?
d Could they doubt that philosophers are lovers of reality and truth?'

'Hardly,' he said.

'But could they doubt the affiliation of the philosophical nature we described to excellence?'

'No, they couldn't doubt that either.'

'Well, could they argue against the idea that, under the right circumstances, this sort of person is more likely than anyone to become perfectly good and a consummate philosopher? Will our critic maintain that the other lot—the ones we ruled out—are more likely?'

e 'Of course not.'

'Will they stop getting cross at us, then, for saying that until philosophers gain political power, there'll be no end to troubles for communities or their citizens, and our fictional political system will never become a full-fledged reality?'

'They might be less upset,' he said.

'How about if we say that they are completely mollified and utterly convinced,' I suggested, 'rather than that they might be less upset? That should 502a shame them into agreeing with us, if they can't do so for any other reason.'

'All right,' he said.

'Even if we can assume, then, that we've convinced them of this point,' I said, 'will they still argue that there's no chance of the children of kings or rulers being born with the philosophical characteristics?'

'They couldn't do that,' he said.

'Could they claim that these philosophical children of kings and rulers are absolutely bound to be corrupted? I mean, even we are admitting that it's difficult for them to preserve their integrity, but is b it plausible to argue that, out of all of them, not even a single one could ever, in the entire passage of time, remain unspoilt?'

'Of course not.'

'If even one remains uncorrupted', I said, 'in a community which is prepared to obey him, then that is enough: everything which is now open to doubt would become a full-fledged reality.'

'Yes, one would do,' he agreed.

'Because if he, as ruler, establishes the laws and practices we've described,' I went on, 'then it's surely not inconceivable that the citizens of the community will be prepared to carry them out.'

'Of course it isn't.'

'But is it unimaginable and inconceivable that others might agree with our point of view?'

'I don't think so,' he said.   c

'And our earlier discussion of the question whether our proposals are for the best (if they are feasible) was, in my opinion, adequate.'

'Yes, it was.'

'So what we've found by now is this, apparently: if our proposed legislation were actually to happen, it would be impossible to improve on it; and its realization may be difficult, but is not impossible.'

'Yes, that's what we've found,' he said.

CHAPTER 9
THE SUPREMACY OF GOOD

Plato now recommends the 'longer route'—a more thorough approach to morality than that of Chapter 6. Morality will never be understood—nor will it become a reality in the guardians' lives—without knowledge of goodness. After briefly dismissing the equation of goodness with either pleasure or knowledge, Plato stresses the importance of goodness: no one does anything which he does not think is good for him; goodness is a universal goal. Therefore, the analysis of morality which has been accepted up till now must be deepened by understanding its relation to goodness. However, Plato does not actually undertake this longer route himself, and goes on to offer only elusive images and allegories about goodness and its importance.

'Well, it was quite a struggle, but we've completed that topic. Next we'd better go on to the remaining issues. What will it take—what studies and 502d practices—for these preservers of our political system to be a possibility? And at what ages should they undertake the various subjects to be studied?'

'Yes, we ought to discuss these issues,' he agreed.

'So I gained nothing', I said, 'whether earlier I cleverly delayed the awkward matter of their marital arrangements, and the topics of procreation and what rulers to appoint. I was aware that the whole truth about what rulers to appoint would arouse resentment and anger. It didn't make any difference, though, because now I'm up against the necessity of discussing these matters anyway. There's noth-
c ing more to say about women and children, but I've got to start all over again, more or less, in exploring the question of the rulers. I'm sure you re-
503a member our claim that they have to demonstrate love of their community while being tested in both pleasant and painful circumstances, and make it clear that they won't shed this patriotism whatever ordeals or fears they meet with, or whatever changing situations they endure. Anyone who is incapable of retaining it is to be excluded, whereas anyone who emerges from every test without impurities (like gold tested in fire) is to be made a ruler and given privileges and rewards in life and in death. We spoke along these lines, but the discussion was starting to deviate and hide itself, be-
b cause it was afraid of broaching the matter we're now facing.'

'Yes, I remember,' he said. 'You're quite right.'

'I was too scared to make the reckless assertions that have now been expressed,' I said, 'but now the presumptuous statement that if we are to have absolutely authentic guardians, then we must appoint philosophers, is out in the open.'

'Yes, it is,' he said.

'Do you realize how few they'll be, in all likelihood? Consider the nature which, in our account, they have to have and how rare it is for its various

parts to coalesce into a single entity: it usually ends up in bits and pieces.'

'What do you mean?' he asked.   c

'People who are quick at learning, have good memories, and are astute and smart and so on, tend—as you know—not to combine both energy and broadness of mental vision with the ability to live an orderly, peaceful, and stable life. Instead, their quickness carries them this way and that, and stability plays no part at all in their lives.'

'You're right,' he said.

'On the other hand, a sound and stable character, which makes people more dependable and slow to d respond to frightening situations in battle, also makes them approach their studies in the same way. They're as slow to respond and to learn as if they'd been drugged, and they're constantly dozing off and yawning when they're asked to do anything intellectually arduous.'

'True,' he said.

'But our claim is that a good and sufficient helping of both sets of qualities is a prerequisite for anyone to be allowed to take part in an authentic educational programme or to be awarded political office and power.'

'Right,' he said.

'So it'll be a rare phenomenon, don't you think?'

'Of course it will.'

'It's not just a matter of testing someone in the ways we've already mentioned, then—by means of e ordeals and fear and pleasure. There's a further point we omitted before, but are including now: we must give him plenty of intellectual exercise as well, so that we can see whether he is capable of enduring fundamental intellectual work, or whether he'll cut and run as cowards do in other spheres.'

'Yes, we certainly ought to try to find that out,' 504a he said. 'But what do you mean by fundamental intellectual work?'

'I'm sure you remember when, as a result of distinguishing three aspects within the mind, we defined morality, self-discipline, courage, and wisdom,' I said.

'If I didn't,' he said, 'then we might as well stop right now.'

'Do you also remember how we prefaced our discussion of those qualities?'

'How?'

'We said that it would take a different route, a b longer one, to reach the best possible vantage-point and that they would be plainly visible to anyone who went that way, but that it was possible to come up with arguments which were in keeping with the kinds of discussions we'd already been having. You said that would do, and we proceeded at the time on that basis. I think the argument was defective, in terms of precision, but it's up to you to say whether you were happy with it.'

'Yes, I was happy enough with it,' he said, 'and so was everyone else.'

'But in these sorts of matters, my friend,' I said, c 'anything which misses the truth by even a tiny amount is nowhere near "enough". Anything less than perfect is not up to the mark at all, though people occasionally think it's adequate and that they don't need to look any further.'

'Yes, a great many people feel this,' he said, 'because they're lazy.'

'But it's a completely inappropriate feeling for a guardian of a community and its laws to have,' I said.

'I suppose so,' he said.

'Then a guardian had better take the longer route, Adeimantus,' I said, 'and put just as much effort into d his intellectual work as his physical exercise. Otherwise, as we said a moment ago, he'll never see that fundamental field of study through to the end—and it's not just fundamental, but particularly appropriate for him.'

'Are you implying that morality and the other qualities we discussed are not the most important things there are—that there's something even more fundamental than them?' he asked.

'It's not only more fundamental,' I said, 'but it's exactly the kind of thing which requires viewing as a completely finished product, without skimping and looking merely at an outline, as we did just now. I e mean, wouldn't it be absurd to devote extremes of energy and effort to getting as precise and clear a picture as possible of insignificant matters, and then not to think that the most important matters deserve the utmost precision too?'

'An excellent sentiment,' he said. 'But surely you don't expect to get away without being asked what this fundamental field of study of yours is, and what it is concerned with?'

'No, I don't,' I answered. 'Go ahead and ask your questions. In actual fact, you've not infrequently been told what it is, but it's either slipped your mind for the moment, or you're intending to make trou-505a ble for me by attacking my position. I incline towards the latter alternative, since you've often been

told that the most important thing to try to understand is the character of goodness, because this is where anything which is moral (or whatever) gets its value and advantages from. It can hardly have escaped your notice that this is my position, and you must know what I'm going to add: that our knowledge of goodness is inadequate. And you appreciate, I'm sure, that there's absolutely no point in having expert knowledge of everything else, but lacking knowledge of goodness, just as there isn't in having anything else either, unless goodness comes with it. b I mean, do you think there's any advantage in owning everything in the world except good things, or in understanding everything else except goodness, and therefore failing to understand anything worthwhile and good?'

'I certainly don't,' he said.

'Now, it can't have escaped your notice either that the usual view of goodness is that it's pleasure, while there's also a more ingenious view around, that it's knowledge.'

'Of course it hasn't.'

'As you also know, however, my friend, the people who hold the latter view are incapable of explaining exactly *what* knowledge constitutes goodness, but are forced ultimately to say that it is knowledge of goodness.'

'And so to make complete fools of themselves,' he remarked.

'Of course they do,' I said. 'First they tell us off c for not knowing what goodness is, then they talk to us as if we did know what it is. I mean, to say it's knowledge of goodness is to assume that we understand what they're saying when they use the term "goodness".'

'You're absolutely right,' he said.

'What about the definition of goodness as pleasure? Aren't its proponents just as thoroughly misguided as the others? I mean, they too are forced to make a concession, in this case that there are bad pleasures, aren't they?'

'Certainly.'

'So their position ends up being that it is possible for a single thing to be both good and bad, doesn't it?'

'Naturally.'   d

'It's clear, therefore, that there's plenty of scope for serious disagreement where goodness is concerned. Yes?'

'Of course.'

'Well, isn't it also clear that whereas (whether it's

a matter of doing something, or owning something, or having a certain reputation) people usually prefer the appearance of morality and right, even if there's no reality involved, yet no one is content with any possession that is only apparently good? It's the reality of goodness they want; no one thinks at all highly of mere appearance in this sphere.'

'Yes, that's perfectly clear,' he said.

'So here we have something which everyone, whatever their temperament, is after, and which is the goal of all their activities. They have an inkling e of its existence, but they're confused about it and can't adequately grasp its nature or be as certain and as confident about it as they can about other things, and consequently they fail to derive any benefit even from those other activities. When something of this kind and this importance is involved, can we allow 506a the best members of our community, the ones to whom we're going to entrust everything, to be equally in the dark?'

'Certainly not,' he protested.

'Anyway,' I said, 'I imagine that anyone who is ignorant about the goodness of moral and right conduct would make a second-rate guardian of morality and right, and I suspect that no one will fully understand them until he knows about their relation to goodness.'

'Your suspicion is right,' he said.

'So the constitution and organization of our community will be perfect only if they are overseen by the kind of guardian who has this knowledge, won't they?'

'Necessarily,' he said. 'But Socrates, do *you* identify goodness with knowledge or pleasure, or with something else?'

'Just listen to him!' I exclaimed. 'It's been perfectly obvious all along that other people's views on the matter weren't going to be enough for you.'

'That's because I don't think it's right, Socrates,' he said, 'for someone who's devoted so much time c to the matter to be in a position to state others' beliefs, but not his own.'

'But do you think it's right', I responded, 'for someone to talk as if he knew what he doesn't know?'

'Of course not,' he said. 'Not as if he knew, but as if he'd formed opinions—he should be prepared to say what he thinks.'

'But aren't ideas which aren't based on knowledge always defective, in your experience?' I asked. 'The best of them are blind. I mean, don't people who have a correct belief, but no knowledge, strike you as exactly like blind people who happen to be taking the right road?'

'Yes,' he said.

'Well, do you want to see things which are defective, blind, and deformed,' I asked, 'when you d could be getting lucid, correct views from elsewhere?'

Socrates professes himself incapable of defining goodness and proposes a simile instead. This is the Simile of the Sun, the first of the three great, and justly famous, interconnected images which Plato uses to convey some of his core views. The Sun consists of an extended analogy between the visible and intelligible realms: just as the sun is the source of light and growth, and is responsible for sight and seeing, and is the acme of the visible realm, so goodness is the source of truth and reality, and is responsible for knowledge and knowing, and is the acme of the intelligible realm. Belief, on the other hand, is like partial sight.

'Socrates,' said Glaucon, 'please don't back away from the finishing-line, so to speak. We'd be happy with the kind of description of goodness that you gave of morality, self-discipline, and so on.'

'So would I, Glaucon,' I said, 'very happy. But I'm afraid it'll be more than I can manage, and that my malformed efforts will make me ridiculous. What I suggest, my friends, is that we forget about trying to define goodness itself for the time being. e You see, I don't at the moment think that our current impulse is enough to take us to where I'd like to see us go. However, I am prepared to talk about something which seems to me to be the child of goodness and to bear a very strong resemblance to it. Would you like me to do that? If not, we can just forget it.'

'Please do,' he said. 'You can settle your account 507a by discussing the father another time.'

'I hope I can make the repayment,' I said, 'and you can recover the debt, rather than just the interest, as you are now. Anyway, as interest on your account, here's an account of the child of goodness. But please be careful that I don't cheat you—not that I intend to—by giving you a counterfeit description of the child.'

'We'll watch out for that as best we can,' he replied. 'Just go ahead, please.'

'First I want to make sure that we're not at cross purposes,' I said, 'and to remind you of something that came up earlier, though you've often heard it on other occasions as well.'

b   'What?' he asked.

'As we talk,' I said, 'we mention and differentiate between a lot of beautiful things and a lot of good things and so on.'

'Yes, we do.'

'And we also talk about beauty itself, goodness itself and so on. All the things we refer to as a plurality on those occasions we also conversely count as belonging to a single class by virtue of the fact that they have a single particular character, and we say that the x itself is "what really is".'

'True.'

'And we say that the first lot is visible rather than intelligible, whereas characters are intelligible rather than visible.'

'Absolutely.'

c   'With what aspect of ourselves do we see the things we see?'

'With our sight,' he replied.

'And we use hearing for the things we hear, and so on for all the other senses and the things we perceive. Yes?'

'Of course.'

'Well, have you ever stopped to consider', I asked, 'how generous the creator of the senses was when he created the domain of seeing and being seen?'

'No, not really,' he said.

'Look at it this way. Are hearing and sound deficient? Do they need an extra something to make the one hear and the other be heard—some third thing d without which hearing won't hear and sound won't be heard?'

'No,' he answered.

'And in my opinion', I went on, 'the same goes for many other domains, if not all: they don't need anything like this. Or can you point to one that does?'

'I can't,' he said.

'But do you realize that sight and the visible realm are deficient?'

'How?'

'Even if a person's eyes are capable of sight, and he's trying to use it, and what he's trying to look at is coloured, the sight will see nothing and the colours e will remain unseen, surely, unless there is also present an extra third thing which is made specifically for this purpose.'

'What is this thing you're getting at?' he asked.

'It's what we call light,' I said.

'You're right,' he said.

'So if light has value, then because it links the sense of sight and the ability to be seen, it is far and 508a away the most valuable link there is.'

'Well, it certainly does have value,' he said.

'Which of the heavenly gods would you say is responsible for this? Whose light makes it possible for our sight to see and for the things we see to be seen?'

'My reply will be no different from what yours or anyone else's would be,' he said. 'I mean, you're obviously expecting the answer, "the sun".'

'Now, there are certain conclusions to be drawn from comparing sight to this god.'

'What?'

'Sight and the sun aren't to be identified: neither the sense itself nor its location—which we call the eye—is the same as the sun.'   b

'True.'

'Nevertheless, there's no sense-organ which more closely resembles the sun, in my opinion, than the eye.'

'The resemblance is striking.'

'Moreover, the eye's ability to see has been bestowed upon it and channelled into it, as it were, by the sun.'

'Yes.'

'So the sun is not to be identified with sight, but is responsible for sight and is itself within the visible realm. Right?'

'Yes,' he said.

'The sun is the child of goodness I was talking about, then,' I said. 'It is a counterpart to its father, goodness. As goodness stands in the intelligible c realm to intelligence and the things we know, so in the visible realm the sun stands to sight and the things we see.'

'I don't understand,' he said. 'I need more detail, please.'

'As you know,' I explained, 'when our eyes are directed towards things whose colours are no longer bathed in daylight, but in artificial light instead, then they're less effective and seem to be virtually blind, as if they didn't even have the potential for seeing clearly.'

'Certainly,' he said.

'But when they're directed towards things which d are lit up by the sun, then they see clearly and obviously do have that potential.'

'Of course.'

'Well, here's how you can think about the mind as well. When its object is something which is lit up by truth and reality, then it has—and obviously has—intelligent awareness and knowledge. However, when its object is permeated with darkness (that is, when its object is something which is subject to generation and decay), then it has beliefs and is less effective, because its beliefs chop and change, and under these circumstances it comes across as devoid of intelligence.'

'Yes, it does.'

c 'Well, what I'm saying is that it's goodness which gives the things we know their truth and makes it possible for people to have knowledge. It is responsible for knowledge and truth, and you should think of it as being within the intelligible realm, but you shouldn't identify it with knowledge and truth, otherwise you'll be wrong: for all their value, it is

509a even more valuable. In the other realm, it is right to regard light and sight as resembling the sun, but not to identify either of them with the sun; so in this realm it is right to regard knowledge and truth as resembling goodness, but not to identify either of them with goodness, which should be rated even more highly.'

'You're talking about something of inestimable value,' he said, 'if it's not only the source of knowledge and truth, but is also more valuable than them. I mean, you certainly don't seem to be identifying it with pleasure!'

'How could you even think it?' I exclaimed. 'But we can take our analogy even further.'

b 'How?'

'I think you'll agree that the ability to be seen is not the only gift the sun gives to the things we see. It is also the source of their generation, growth, and nourishment, although it isn't actually the process of generation.'

'Of course it isn't.'

'And it isn't only the known-ness of the things we know which is conferred upon them by goodness, but also their reality and their being, although goodness isn't actually the state of being, but surpasses being in majesty and might.'

c 'It's way beyond human comprehension, all right,' was Glaucon's quite amusing comment.

'It's your fault for forcing me to express my views on the subject,' I replied.

'Yes, and please don't stop,' he said. 'If you've left anything out of your explanation of the simile of the sun, then the least you could do is continue with it.'

'There are plenty of omissions, in fact,' I said.

'Don't leave any gaps,' he said, 'however small.'

'I think I'll have to leave a lot out,' I said, 'but I'll try to make it as complete as I can at the moment.'

'All right,' he said.

The image of the Line, in which now follows, is expressly (509c) supposed to supplement the Sun.

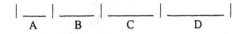

As *A* stands to *B* in terms of clarity and opacity, so *C* stands to *D* as well. *A* consists of likenesses, which are identified by conjecture; *B* consists of the solid things of the material world, which are identified confidently; *C* and *D* consist of the types, which are knowable, but the two sections are distinguished because of a difference in methodology. As *B* stands to *A* in terms of truth, so *C* and *D* together stand to *A* and *B* together. *A* and *B* together constitute the visible realm, which is the realm of belief; *C* and *D* together constitute the intelligible realm, which is the realm of knowledge.

'So bear in mind the two things we've been talk- d ing about,' I said, 'one of which rules over the intelligible realm and its inhabitants, while the other rules over the visible realm—I won't say over the heavens in case you think I'm playing clever word-games. Anyway, do you understand this distinction between visible things and intelligible things?'

'Yes.'

'Well, picture them as a line cut into two unequal sections and, following the same proportion, subdivide both the section of the visible realm and that of the intelligible realm. Now you can compare the sections in terms of clarity and unclarity. The first section in the visible realm consists of likenesses, by which I mean a number of things: shadows, re- e flections (on the surface of water or on anything else 510a which is inherently compact, smooth, and bright), and so on. Do you see what I'm getting at?'

'I do.'

'And you should count the other section of the visible realm as consisting of the things whose likenesses are found in the first section: all the flora and fauna there are in the world, and every kind of artefact too.'

'All right.'

'I wonder whether you'd agree,' I said, 'that truth and lack of truth have been the criteria for distinguishing these sections, and that the image stands to the original as the realm of beliefs stands to the realm of knowledge?'

b   'Yes,' he said, 'I certainly agree.'

'Now have a look at how to subdivide the section which belongs to the intelligible realm.'

'How?'

'Like this. If the mind wants to explore the first subdivision, it can do so only by using those former originals as likenesses and by taking things for granted on its journey, which leads it to an end-point, rather than to a starting-point. If it wants to explore the second subdivision, however, it takes things for granted in order to travel to a starting-point where nothing needs to be taken for granted, and it has no involvement with likenesses, as before, but makes its approach by means of types alone, in and of themselves.'

'I don't quite understand what you're saying,' he said.

c   'You will if I repeat it,' I said, 'because this preamble will make it easier to understand. I'm sure you're aware that practitioners of geometry, arithmetic, and so on take for granted things like numerical oddness and evenness, the geometrical figures, the three kinds of angle, and any other things of that sort which are relevant to a given subject. They act as if they know about these things, treat them as basic, and don't feel any further need to explain them either to themselves or to anyone else,
d on the grounds that there is nothing unclear about them. They make them the starting-points for their subsequent investigations, which end after a coherent chain of reasoning at the point they'd set out to reach in their research.'

'Yes, I'm certainly well aware of this,' he said.

'So you must also be aware that in the course of their discussions they make use of visible forms, despite the fact that they're not interested in visible forms as such, but in the things of which the visible forms are likenesses: that is, their discussions are concerned with what it is to be a square, and with what it is to be a diagonal (and so on), rather than
e with the diagonal (and so on) which occurs in their diagrams. They treat their models and diagrams as likenesses, when these things have likenesses themselves, in fact (that is, shadows and reflections on
511a water); but they're actually trying to see squares and so on in themselves, which only thought can see.'

'You're right,' he said.

'So it was objects of this type that I was describ-

ing as belonging to the intelligible realm, with the rider that the mind can explore them only by taking things for granted, and that its goal is not a starting-point, because it is incapable of changing direction and rising above the things it is taking for granted. And I went on to say that it used as likenesses those very things which are themselves the originals of a lower order of likenesses, and that relative to the likenesses, the originals command respect and admiration for their distinctness.'

'I see,' he said. 'You're talking about the objects b of geometry and related occupations.'

'Now, can you see what I mean by the second subdivision of the intelligible realm? It is what reason grasps by itself, thanks to its ability to practise dialectic. When it takes things for granted, it doesn't treat them as starting-points, but as basic in the strict sense—as platforms and rungs, for example. These serve it until it reaches a point where nothing needs to be taken for granted, and which is the starting-point for everything. Once it has grasped this starting-point, it turns around and by a process of depending on the things which depend from the starting-point, it descends to an end-point. It makes absolutely no use of anything perceptible by the senses: it aims for types by means of types alone, in c and of themselves, and it ends its journey with types.'

'I don't quite understand,' he said. 'I mean, you're talking about crucial matters here, I think. I do understand, however, that you want to mark off that part of the real and intelligible realm which is before the eyes of anyone who knows how to practise dialectic as more clear than the other part, which is before the eyes of practitioners of the various branches of expertise, as we call them. The latter make the things they take for granted their starting-points, and although they inevitably use thought, not the senses, to observe what they observe, yet because of their failure to ascend to a starting-point— because their enquiries rely on taking things for d granted—you're saying that they don't understand these things, even though they are intelligible, when related to a starting-point. I take you to be describing what geometers and so on do as thinking rather than knowing, on the grounds that thinking is the intermediate state between believing and knowing.'

'There's nothing wrong with your understanding,' I said. 'And you should appreciate that there are four states of mind, one for each of the four sections. There's knowledge for the highest section and ₑ thought for the second one; and you'd better assign confidence to the third one and conjecture to the final one. You can make an orderly progression out of them, and you should regard them as possessing as much clarity as their objects possess truth.'

'I see,' he said. 'That's fine with me: I'll order them in the way you suggest.'

The final image, the Allegory of the Cave, is the longest and most famous of the three. It is introduced rather abruptly, but is meant to fit in with the preceding two images (517b–c, 532a–d). Further details of the fit are a matter of dispute, although the broad outlines are clear enough. Like all the great images of the world's greatest literature, Plato's Cave manages simultaneously to appear transparent and yet unexpectedly rich and surprising. Those readers who believe that philosophy is a dry academic pursuit will be surprised at its presentation here as a pursuit which frees us from a terrible slavery; but for Plato and his peers philosophy is a way of life, not just a course of study.

514a   'Next,' I said, 'here's a situation which you can use as an analogy for the human condition—for our education or lack of it. Imagine people living in a cavernous cell down under the ground; at the far end of the cave, a long way off, there's an entrance open to the outside world. They've been there since childhood, with their legs and necks tied up in a way
ᵇ which keeps them in one place and allows them to look only straight ahead, but not to turn their heads. There's firelight burning a long way further up the cave behind them, and up the slope between the fire and the prisoners there's a road, beside which you should imagine a low wall has been built—like the partition which conjurors place between themselves and their audience and above which they show their tricks.'

'All right,' he said.

'Imagine also that there are people on the other side of this wall who are carrying all sorts of artefacts. These artefacts, human statuettes, and animal
ᶜ models carved in stone and wood and all kinds of materials stick out over the wall; and as you'd ex-
515a pect, some of the people talk as they carry these objects along, while others are silent.'

'This is a strange picture you're painting,' he said, 'with strange prisoners.'

'They're no different from us,' I said. 'I mean, in the first place, do you think they'd see anything of themselves and one another except the shadows cast by the fire on to the cave wall directly opposite them?'

'Of course not,' he said. 'They're forced to spend their lives without moving their heads.'   ᵇ

'And what about the objects which were being carried along? Won't they only see their shadows as well?'

'Naturally.'

'Now, suppose they were able to talk to one another: don't you think they'd assume that their words applied to what they saw passing by in front of them?'

'They couldn't think otherwise.'

'And what if sound echoed off the prison wall opposite them? When any of the passers-by spoke, don't you think they'd be bound to assume that the sound came from a passing shadow?'

'I'm absolutely certain of it,' he said.

'All in all, then,' I said, 'the shadows of artefacts ᶜ would constitute the only reality people in this situation would recognize.'

'That's absolutely inevitable,' he agreed.

'What do you think would happen, then,' I asked, 'if they were set free from their bonds and cured of their inanity? What would it be like if they found that happening to them? Imagine that one of them has been set free and is suddenly made to stand up, to turn his head and walk, and to look towards the firelight. It hurts him to do all this and he's too dazzled to be capable of making out the objects whose shadows he'd formerly been looking at. And suppose someone tells him that what he's been seeing ᵈ all this time has no substance, and that he's now closer to reality and is seeing more accurately, because of the greater reality of the things in front of his eyes—what do you imagine his reaction would be? And what do you think he'd say if he were shown any of the passing objects and had to respond to being asked what it was? Don't you think he'd be bewildered and would think that there was more reality in what he'd been seeing before than in what he was being shown now?'

'Far more,' he said.

'And if he were forced to look at the actual fire- ₑ light, don't you think it would hurt his eyes? Don't you think he'd turn away and run back to the things he could make out, and would take the truth of the matter to be that these things are clearer than what he was being shown?'

'Yes,' he agreed.

'And imagine him being dragged forcibly away from there up the rough, steep slope,' I went on, 'without being released until he's pulled out into the 516a sunlight. Wouldn't this treatment cause him pain and distress? And once he's reached the sunlight, he wouldn't be able to see a single one of the things which are currently taken to be real, would he, because his eyes would be overwhelmed by the sun's beams?'

'No, he wouldn't,' he answered, 'not straight away.'

'He wouldn't be able to see things up on the surface of the earth, I suppose, until he'd got used to his situation. At first, it would be shadows that he could most easily make out, then he'd move on to the reflections of people and so on in water, and later he'd be able to see the actual things themselves. Next, he'd feast his eyes on the heavenly bodies and the heavens themselves, which would be easier at b night: he'd look at the light of the stars and the moon, rather than at the sun and sunlight during the daytime.'

'Of course.'

'And at last, I imagine, he'd be able to discern and feast his eyes on the sun—not the displaced image of the sun in water or elsewhere, but the sun on its own, in its proper place.'

'Yes, he'd inevitably come to that,' he said.'

'After that, he'd start to think about the sun and he'd deduce that it is the source of the seasons and the yearly cycle, that the whole of the visible realm c is its domain, and that in a sense everything which he and his peers used to see is its responsibility.'

'Yes, that would obviously be the next point he'd come to,' he agreed.

'Now, if he recalled the cell where he'd originally lived and what passed for knowledge there and his former fellow prisoners, don't you think he'd feel happy about his own altered circumstances, and sorry for them?'

'Definitely.'

'Suppose that the prisoners used to assign prestige and credit to one another, in the sense that they rewarded speed at recognizing the shadows as they passed, and the ability to remember which ones normally come earlier and later and at the same time as d which other ones, and expertise at using this as a basis for guessing which ones would arrive next. Do you think our former prisoner would covet these honours and would envy the people who had status and power there, or would he much prefer, as Homer describes it, "being a slave labouring for someone else—someone without property", and would put up with anything at all, in fact, rather than share their beliefs and their life?'

'Yes, I think he'd go through anything rather than e live that way,' he said.

'Here's something else I'd like your opinion about,' I said. 'If he went back underground and sat down again in the same spot, wouldn't the sudden transition from the sunlight mean that his eyes would be overwhelmed by darkness?'

'Certainly,' he replied.

'Now, the process of adjustment would be quite long this time, and suppose that before his eyes had settled down and while he wasn't seeing well, he had once again to compete against those same old 517a prisoners at identifying those shadows. Wouldn't he make a fool of himself? Wouldn't they say that he'd come back from his upward journey with his eyes ruined, and that it wasn't even worth trying to go up there? And wouldn't they—if they could—grab hold of anyone who tried to set them free and take them up there and kill him?'

'They certainly would,' he said.

'Well, my dear Glaucon,' I said, 'you should apply this allegory, as a whole, to what we were talk- b ing about before. The region which is accessible to sight should be equated with the prison cell, and the firelight there with the light of the sun. And if you think of the upward journey and the sight of things up on the surface of the earth as the mind's ascent to the intelligible realm, you won't be wrong—at least I don't think you'd be wrong, and it's my impression that you want to hear. Only God knows if it's actually true, however. Anyway, it's my opinion that the last thing to be seen—and it isn't easy c to see either—in the realm of knowledge is goodness; and the sight of the character of goodness leads one to deduce that it is responsible for everything that is right and fine, whatever the circumstances, and that in the visible realm it is the progenitor of light and of the source of light, and in the intelligible realm it is the source and provider of truth and knowledge. And I also think that the sight of it is a prerequisite for intelligent conduct either of one's own private affairs or of public business.'

'I couldn't agree more,' he said.

'All right, then,' I said. 'I wonder if you also agree with me in not finding it strange that people who've travelled there don't want to engage in human business: there's nowhere else their minds would ever

rather be than in the upper region—which is hardly
d surprising, if our allegory has got this aspect right
as well.'

'No, it's not surprising,' he agreed.

'Well, what about this?' I asked. 'Imagine someone returning to the human world and all its misery
after contemplating the divine realm. Do you think
it's surprising if he seems awkward and ridiculous
while he's still not seeing well, before he's had time
to adjust to the darkness of his situation, and he's
forced into a contest (in a lawcourt or wherever)
about the shadows of morality or the statuettes which
e cast the shadows, and into a competition whose
terms are the conceptions of morality held by people who have never seen morality itself?'

'No, that's not surprising in the slightest,' he said.

518a 'In fact anyone with any sense,' I said, 'would
remember that the eyes can become confused in
two different ways, as a result of two different sets
of circumstances: it can happen in the transition
from light to darkness, and also in the transition
from darkness to light. If he took the same facts
into consideration when he also noticed someone's
mind in such a state of confusion that it was incapable of making anything out, his reaction would-
n't be unthinking ridicule. Instead, he'd try to find
out whether this person's mind was returning from
a mode of existence which involves greater lucidity and had been blinded by the unfamiliar darkness, or whether it was moving from relative ignorance to relative lucidity and had been
overwhelmed and dazzled by the increased brightness. Once he'd distinguished between the two conditions and modes of existence, he'd congratulate
b anyone he found in the second state, and feel sorry
for anyone in the first state. If he did choose to
laugh at someone in the second state, his amusement would be less absurd than when laughter is
directed at someone returning from the light
above.'

'Yes,' he said, 'you're making a lot of sense.'

Since the Cave was expressly introduced as being
relevant to education, its immediate educational
implications are now drawn out. We all have the
capacity for knowledge (in the Platonic sense, not
just information), and education should develop
that potential. But since it requires knowledge of
goodness to manage a community well, then those
who gain such knowledge have to 'return to the
cave': paradoxically, those who least want power
are the ones who should have it.

'Now, if this is true,' I said, 'we must bear in mind
that education is not capable of doing what some
people promise. They claim to introduce knowledge
into a mind which doesn't have it, as if they were c
introducing sight into eyes which are blind.'

'Yes, they do,' he said.

'An implication of what we're saying at the moment, however,' I pointed out, 'is that the capacity
for knowledge is present in everyone's mind. If you
can imagine an eye that can turn from darkness to
brightness only if the body as a whole turns, then
our organ of understanding is like that. Its orientation has to be accompanied by turning the mind as
a whole away from the world of becoming, until it
becomes capable of bearing the sight of real being
and reality at its most bright, which we're saying is d
goodness. Yes?'

'Yes.'

'That's what education should be,' I said, 'the art
of orientation. Educators should devise the simplest
and most effective methods of turning minds around.
It shouldn't be the art of implanting sight in the organ, but should proceed on the understanding that
the organ already has the capacity, but is improperly aligned and isn't facing the right way.'

'I suppose you're right,' he said.

'So although the mental states which are described
as good generally seem to resemble good physical
states, in the sense that habituation and training do e
in fact implant them where they didn't use to be, yet
understanding (as it turns out) is undoubtedly a property of something which is more divine: it never
loses its power, and it is useful and beneficial, or
useless and harmful, depending on its orientation. 519a
For example, surely you've noticed how the petty
minds of those who are acknowledged to be bad, but
clever, are sharp-eyed and perceptive enough to gain
insights into matters they direct their attention towards. It's not as if they weren't sharp-sighted, but
their minds are forced to serve evil, and consequently the keener their vision is, the greater the evil
they accomplish.'

'Yes, I've noticed this,' he said.

'However,' I went on, 'if this aspect of that kind
of person is hammered at from an early age, until
the inevitable consequences of incarnation have
been knocked off it—the leaden weights, so to b
speak, which are grafted on to it as a result of eating and similar pleasures and indulgences and which
turn the sight of the mind downwards—if it sheds
these weights and is reoriented towards the truth,

then (and we're talking about the same organ and the same people) it would see the truth just as clearly as it sees the objects it faces at the moment.'

'Yes, that makes sense,' he said.

'Well, doesn't this make sense as well?' I asked. 'Or rather, isn't it an inevitable consequence of what we've been saying that uneducated people, who have no experience of truth, would make incompetent ad-

c ministrators of a community, and that the same goes for people who are allowed to spend their whole lives educating themselves? The first group would be no good because their lives lack direction: they've got no single point of reference to guide them in all their affairs, whether private or public. The second group would be no good because their hearts would-n't be in the business: they think they've been transported to the Isles of the Blessed even while they're still alive.'

'True,' he said.

'Our job as founders, then,' I said, 'is to make sure that the best people come to that fundamental field of study (as we called it earlier): we must have them make the ascent we've been talking about and see goodness. And afterwards, once they've been up

d there and had a good look, we mustn't let them get away with what they do at the moment.'

'Which is what?'

'Staying there,' I replied, 'and refusing to come back down again to those prisoners, to share their work and their rewards, no matter whether those rewards are trivial or significant.'

'But in that case,' he protested, 'we'll be wrong-ing them: we'll be making the quality of their lives worse and denying them the better life they could be living, won't we?'

e   'You're again forgetting, my friend,' I said, 'that the point of legislation is not to make one section of a community better off than the rest, but to engineer this for the community as a whole. Legislators should persuade or compel the members of a com-munity to mesh together, should make every indi-vidual share with his fellows the benefit which he

520a is capable of contributing to the common welfare, and should ensure that the community does contain people with this capacity; and the purpose of all this is not for legislators to leave people to choose their own directions, but for them to use people to bind the community together.'

'Yes, you're right,' he said. 'I was forgetting.'

'I think you'll also find, Glaucon,' I said, 'that we won't be wronging any philosophers who arise in

our community. Our remarks, as we force them to b take care of their fellow citizens and be their guardians, will be perfectly fair. We'll tell them that it's reasonable for philosophers who happen to oc-cur in other communities not to share the work of those communities, since their occurrence was spon-taneous, rather than planned by the political system of any of the communities in question, and it's fair for anything which arises spontaneously and does-n't owe its nurture to anyone or anything to have no interest in repaying anyone for having provided its nourishment. "We've bred *you*, however," we'll say, "to act, as it were, as the hive's leaders and kings, for your own good as well as that of the rest of the community. You've received a better and more thor-ough education than those other philosophers, and you're more capable of playing a part in both c spheres. So each of you must, when your time comes, descend to where the rest of the community lives, and get used to looking at things in the dark. The point is that once you become acclimatized, you'll see infinitely better than the others there; your experience of genuine right, morality, and goodness will enable you to identify every one of the images and recognize what it is an image of. And then the administration of our community—ours as well as yours—will be in the hands of people who are awake, as distinct from the norm nowadays of com-munities being governed by people who shadow-box and fall out with one another in their dreams over who should rule, as if that were a highly desirable thing to do. No, the truth of the matter is this: the d less keen the would-be rulers of a community are to rule, the better and less divided the administration of that community is bound to be, but where the rulers feel the opposite, the administration is bound to be the opposite." '

'Yes,' he said.

'And do you think our wards will greet these views of ours with scepticism and will refuse to join in the work of government when their time comes, when they can still spend most of their time living with one another in the untainted realm?'

'No, they couldn't,' he answered. 'They're fair- e ·minded people, and the instructions we're giving them are fair. However, they'll undoubtedly ap-proach rulership as an inescapable duty—an attitude which is the opposite of the one held by the people who have power in communities at the moment.'

'You're right, Glaucon,' I said. 'You'll only have a well-governed community if you can come up with 512a a way of life for your prospective rulers that is preferable to ruling! The point is that this is the only kind of community where the rulers will be genuinely well off (not in material terms, but they'll possess the wealth which is a prerequisite of happiness—a life of virtue and intelligence), whereas if government falls into the hands of people who are impoverished and starved of any good things of their own, and who expect to wrest some good for themselves from political office, a well-governed community is an impossibility. I mean, when rulership becomes something to fight for, a domestic and internal war like this destroys not only the perpetrators, but also the rest of the community.'

'You're absolutely right,' he said.

b 'Apart from the philosophical life,' I said, 'is there any way of life, in your opinion, which looks down on political office?'

'No, definitely not,' he answered.

'In fact, political power should be in the hands of people who aren't enamoured of it. Otherwise their rivals in love will fight them for it.'

'Of course.'

'There's no one you'd rather force to undertake the guarding of your community, then, than those who are experts in the factors which contribute towards the good government of a community, who don't look to politics for their rewards, and whose life is better than the political life. Agreed?'

'Yes,' he said.

CHAPTER 10
EDUCATING PHILOSOPHER KINGS

Granted that the rulers need to understand goodness, what kind of education will take them there? This was a delicate subject for Plato. Higher education—intellectual rather than character-building—had been in the hands of the sophists, who also claimed to teach goodness, but whose chameleonic values Plato mistrusted. He first draws a distinction, based on the metaphysics of Chapter 8, between pure and applied subjects. The philosophers will need both, but in the present context Plato stresses the ability of some subjects to lead the mind away from mundane reality and towards the realm at whose apex goodness stands.

'So would you like us to consider next how to produce people of this type in our community, and how to lead them up to the light—like the people we hear about who rise from Hades to dwell among the gods?'

'Yes, of course I'd like us to do that,' he replied.

'Now, what we're dealing with here, it would seem, is not the spinning of a potsherd, but the reorientation of a mind from a kind of twilight to true daylight—and this reorientation is an ascent to reality, or in other words true philosophy.'

'Quite so.'

'We ought to try to see which intellectual pursuits d can have this effect, then, oughtn't we?'

'Of course.'

'What intellectual pursuit, then, Glaucon, might attract a mind away from the realm of becoming and towards reality? Oh, something just occurred to me while I was speaking: we said that in their youth these people had to be warriors, didn't we?'

'Yes, we did.'

'Therefore, the area of study we're after must have an additional feature.'

'What?'

'It must be of value to men of war.'

'Yes, it certainly must,' he said, 'if possible.'

'Now, the education we've arranged for them so far consists of physical exercise and cultural stud- e ies.'

'Yes,' he said.

'And physical exercise is concerned with the world of coming into being and passing away, since its domain is physical growth and decay.'

'I suppose so.'

'So it isn't the area of study we're after.'

'No.'   522a

'What about the cultural education we described earlier?'

'But that merely complemented the physical exercise,' he said. 'I'm sure you remember that it trains the guardians by habituation: it doesn't produce knowledge, but harmony in the sphere of music, elegance in the sphere of rhythm, and other allied habits in the field of literature, whether the literature in question is fictional or closer to non-fiction. There's nothing in it which can lead a student towards the kind of goal you're after at the moment.' b

'Your memory is very accurate,' I said. 'Thanks for reminding me: it's true that there's nothing like that in it. But then, what sort of intellectual pursuit *are* we after? I mean, all the professions seemed servile, somehow.'

'Of course they did. But if we exclude cultural studies, physical exercise, and the professional occupations, what else is there that anyone could study?'

'Well,' I said, 'if they're all we can take, then let's take something which applies to them all.'

'What?'

c 'For example, there's that everyday thing—one of the first things everyone has to learn—which all the modes of expertise, thinking, and knowledge make use of.'

'What are you getting at?' he asked.

'It's nothing special,' I said. 'It's the ability to distinguish one, two, and three—in short, I'm talking about number and counting. I mean, isn't it the case that every branch of expertise and knowledge is bound to have some involvement with numbers and with counting?'

'Definitely,' he said.

'Even military expertise?' I asked.

'Yes, certainly. It has to,' he said.

d 'At any rate, tragedy after tragedy has Palamedes showing up Agamemnon's utterly ridiculous deficiencies as a military commander,' I said. 'Haven't you noticed how Palamedes claims that, once he'd invented counting, he deployed the troops at Troy and added up the ships and so on? The implication is that previously none of them had been counted, and Agamemnon's inability to count presumably means that he didn't even know how many feet he had. What sort of military commander do you think he was?'

'A peculiar one, I'd say, if there's any truth in this,' he replied:

e 'So our position will be—won't it?—that it's essential for a man of war to learn how to calculate and count,' I asked.

'He absolutely has to,' he said, 'if he's going to know anything at all about deploying troops, or rather, if he's even going to be a human being.'

'Now, there's an idea I have about this subject, and I wonder whether you share it,' I said.

'What is it?'

523a 'It rather looks as though it's one of the subjects we're after, which stimulate a student's intellect. But it also seems likely that no one makes correct use of its consummate ability to attract one towards reality.'

'What do you mean?' he asked.

'I'll try to clarify my point of view,' I said. 'In my mind, I distinguish between things which are and things which are not attractive in the way we're talking about. I'll try to get you to appreciate the dis-

tinction as well, and then you can tell me whether or not you agree, so that we can be better placed to see how accurate my hunch is.'

'Yes, do explain,' he said.

'All right,' I said. 'I'm sure you'll see what I mean if I say that at the level of the senses, some things don't encourage the intellect to explore further, be- b cause the situation can be adequately assessed by the relevant sense, while other things can't help provoking an enquiring attitude, because sense-perception fails to produce a sound result.'

'You're obviously talking about distant impressions and illusory paintings,' he said.

'No, you haven't quite got my point,' I said.

'What are you talking about, then?'

'In order to count as thought-provoking, in my opinion,' I explained, 'they have to produce contradictory sense-impressions at the same time; other- c wise, they aren't thought-provoking. The impression sense-perception has to give of an object is that it is no more X than the opposite of X, however, close or far away it is when you encounter it. An example will help you understand what I'm getting at. Here are three fingers, we'd say, the little finger, the second one and the middle one.'

'Yes,' he said.

'And please assume that I'm talking about seeing them from close range. Now, here's what I want you to think about.'

'What?'

'Well, each of them equally gives the impression of being a finger. There's no difference between them in this respect, and it doesn't matter whether d the finger that's being looked at is in the middle or on either end, pale or dark, thick or thin, and so on and so forth. It's almost inconceivable that anyone's mind would feel impelled in any of these circumstances to think and try to come up with an answer to the question what a finger is, since sight has given the mind no grounds for supposing that the finger is at the same time the opposite of a finger.'

'That's right,' he agreed.

'So it makes sense to say that this situation doesn't provoke or arouse thought,' I said.   e

'Agreed.'

'What about the bigness or smallness of the fingers, however? Is what sight sees adequate in this case? Does it make no difference to it whether or not the finger it's looking at is in the middle or on either end? And doesn't the same go for touch and the fingers' thickness and thinness or hardness and softness? And the other senses also give inadequate impressions in this kind of situation, don't they? I mean, here's how each sense works: the main point 524a is that the sense into whose domain hardness falls is inevitably also the sense into whose domain softness falls; and the message it passes on to the mind is that, in its perception, the same thing is both hard and soft. True?'

'True,' he said.

'So isn't what happens in *these* situations that the mind inevitably feels puzzled about what this sense means by hardness, since it's saying that the same thing is soft as well? And when the sense that perceives weight reports that something heavy is light and that something light is heavy, isn't the mind bound to wonder what lightness and heaviness are?'

b 'Yes,' he said, 'because the messages it's receiving are strange and demand clarification.'

'It makes sense to suppose, then,' I went on, 'that these are the circumstances in which the chief thing the mind does is summon up calculation and thought to help it examine whether in any given case it's being informed about one object or two objects.'

'Of course.'

'And if there turn out to be two objects, then each of them is single and they're different from each other, aren't they?'

'Yes.'

'If each of them is single, then, and it takes two of them to make two, then it'll think about them as two separate objects. I mean, if they were insepara- c ble, it wouldn't be thinking about two objects: it would be thinking about one object.'

'Right.'

'However, in our current example sight sees both big and small as a kind of mixture, not as separate from each other. Yes?'

'Yes.'

'And in order to clarify the situation, the intellect is forced in its turn to look at big and small as distinct entities, not mixed together, which is the opposite of what sight does.'

'True.'

'And this, in outline, is why it occurs to us to ask what in fact bigness and smallness really are, isn't it?'

'Absolutely.'

'And that's how we come to distinguish what we call the intelligible realm from the visible realm.'

'You're quite right,' he said.

d 'So that's what I was getting at just now, when I was saying that some things are thought-provoking, and some things aren't. I define as thought-provoking the things which impinge upon our sense-perception along with their opposites, whereas I describe things which don't do that as incapable of arousing thought.'

'I understand now,' he said, 'and I agree.'

The curriculum is laid out. Trainee philosopher kings must study arithmetic, plane geometry, solid geometry, astronomy, and musicology. In each case, these subjects are interpreted until they reveal an aspect which will help to 'extricate' would-be philosophers from the 'world of becoming'; they also serve to sharpen the mind generally. Mathematics is chosen because it was, in Plato's day, the subject which had been developed furthest towards being laid out along systematic lines (leading within fifty or so years to Euclid's Elements), and Plato wants dialectic to achieve that kind of coherence.

'All right, then. Which of these two categories do you think number—which is to say, oneness—belongs to?'

'I don't know,' he answered.

'Well, you can work it out from what we've already said,' I replied. 'If oneness is adequately seen (or grasped by any other sense) for what it is, then it doesn't have any power to attract towards real- e ity—as a finger doesn't, we were saying. However, if it's never seen without its opposite simultaneously being seen, so that the impression it gives is no more of oneness than of the opposite, then evaluation becomes imperative and the mind has no choice but to be puzzled: it sets its thought-processes in motion, and casts about for an answer to the question what oneness itself actually is. And if this is what happens, then oneness is one of those subjects which guide and turn people towards the contemplation of 525a reality.'

'But that's exactly what seeing oneness does, in fact,' he said. 'We see the same thing simultaneously as one and as infinitely many.'

'And if oneness is like that,' I said, 'then number as a whole is as well.'

'Naturally.'

'Now, calculation and arithmetic are entirely concerned with number.'

'Certainly.'

'And they clearly guide one towards truth.'

'Yes, they're exceptionally good at that.'

b 'Then arithmetic is one of the subjects we're after, apparently. A man of war can't do without it, because he deploys troops, and a philosopher can't do without it, because he has to extricate himself from the world of becoming and make reality his field of operation, or else he'll never be able to reason and calculate.'

'True,' he said.

'And our guardians are, in fact, both warriors and philosophers.'

'Of course.'

'Therefore, Glaucon, we ought to provide for this subject in our legislation, and to persuade the people who are going to undertake our community's c most important tasks to take up arithmetic. They shouldn't engage in it like dilettantes, but should keep at it until they reach the point where they can see in their mind's eye what numbers really are, and they shouldn't study it as merchants and stallholders do, for commercial reasons, but for the sake of warfare and in order to facilitate the mind's turning away from becoming and towards truth and reality.'

'You're absolutely right,' he said.

'Now that arithmetic has been mentioned,' I said, 'it also occurs to me how neatly it fits in the con- d text we're getting at, and how commonly it could be used by anyone who applies himself to it for intellectual rather than commercial purposes.'

'How?' he asked.

'Because it's particularly good at guiding the mind upwards—which is what we've been talking about—and forcing one to discuss numbers in themselves. It excludes the slightest hint, in a discussion, of numbers which have attendant visible or tangible material objects. I mean, I'm sure you're aware that e the experts in the field pour scorn on any attempt to divide the actual number one and refuse to allow it. If you chop it up, they multiple it; they take steps to preserve one's oneness and to prevent it ever appearing to contain a multiplicity of factors.'

'You're absolutely right,' he said.

526a 'What do you think they'd say, then, Glaucon, if someone were to ask them, in surprise, "What are these numbers you're talking about? What numbers involve a oneness which fulfils your requirements, where every single unit is equal to every other unit, without even the smallest variation, and without being divisible in the slightest?" '

'I think they'd reply that the numbers they're talking about are only accessible to thought, and cannot be grasped in any other way.'

'So can you see, Glaucon,' I said, 'that it really does seem as though this subject is essential, since it apparently forces the mind to rely purely on in- b tellectual processes and to aim for truth in itself?'

'Yes,' he said. 'It certainly does do that.'

'Now, have you ever noticed that people who are naturally good at arithmetic are also naturally quick at just about every subject? And that if you make slow-witted people learn and study arithmetic, then without exception they end up quicker than they used to be, even if they gain nothing else from it?'

'That's true,' he said.

'Moreover, I don't suppose it would be easy for c you to find many subjects which require more effort from the student learning them.'

'No.'

'For all these reasons, then, this is a subject we'd better take seriously; we must have our best people study it.'

'I agree,' he said.

'That's the first subject dealt with, then,' I said. 'But in the second place, let's consider whether the subject which follows on its heels suits our purposes.'

'What subject do you mean?' he asked. 'Geometry?'

'Exactly,' I said.

'It obviously suits our purposes,' he said, 'because it has some military applications. You see, it does d make a difference whether or not a person is good at geometry when he comes to organize an encampment, occupy territory, deploy an army over a narrow or wide extent, and form up troops in any other way in the course of a battle or while on the move.'

'Yes,' I said,' but it hardly takes the whole of geometry and arithmetic to enable someone to cope with that kind of situation. What we have to consider is whether the more advanced aspects of geometry which constitute the bulk of the subject have any relevance in the context of smoothing the way towards seeing the character of goodness. And what e we're saying is that anything is relevant in this context if it forces the mind to turn towards the realm where the most blessed part of reality is to be found, which the mind should do its utmost to see.'

'You're right,' he said.

'So if it impels the mind to see reality, it suits our purposes; but if it impels the mind to see the world of becoming, it does not.'

'Yes, that's what we're saying.'

527a 'Even people who know very little geometry', I said, 'won't dispute the fact that this branch of knowledge is quite different from how it is described by its practitioners.'

'In what sense?' he asked.

'They have a very absurd, if very inevitable, way of talking about geometry. They talk as if they were actually doing something and as if the point of all their theorems was to have some actual effect: they come up with words like "squaring" and "applying" and "adding" and so on, whereas in fact the sole pur-b pose of the subject is knowledge.'

'Absolutely,' he said.

'And there's something else we'd better agree on.'

'What?'

'That this knowledge is of things which exist for ever, rather than of things which come into existence at some time and subsequently pass away.'

'There's no difficulty in agreeing to that,' he said. 'The objects of geometrical knowledge do exist for ever.'

'Therefore, Glaucon, geometry can attract the minds towards truth. It can produce philosophical thought, in the sense that it can reverse the misguided downward tendencies we currently have.'

'It's particularly effective at that,' he agreed.

c 'Then you'd better be particularly effective at telling the inhabitants of your Goodland to do their utmost not to dismiss geometry,' I told him. 'I mean, its by-products are not unimportant either.'

'What are they?' he asked.

'There are the military ones you mentioned,' I replied, 'and also, as we know, people who've studied geometry are much more receptive than those who haven't to do intellectual work in general; it makes absolutely all the difference in the world.'

'Yes, it certainly does,' he said.

'So shall we make this a second subject for the young people of our community to study?'

'Yes,' he said.

d 'And don't you think the third should be astronomy?'

'I do, anyway,' he said. 'I mean, it's not only farmers and sailors who need to be sensitive to the seasons, months, and phases of the year: it's just as important for military commanders as well.'

'You seem to be naïvely worried about what people will think of you,' I remarked. 'You don't want them to think you're recommending studies which have no practical benefit. It is, in fact, really hard for people to have confidence in the fact that studying this kind of subject cleans and re-ignites a particular mental organ which everyone has (while other e occupations ruin it and blind it), and that this organ is a thousand times more worth preserving than any eye, since it is the only organ which can see truth. People who acknowledge this fact will be incredibly happy with your ideas, but all those people who are completely unaware of it will in all likelihood think you're talking rubbish, because, as they can see, this kind of study doesn't produce any worthwhile benefit of any other kind. So you'd better hurry up and decide which group of people you're addressing. Alternatively, you're not really addressing either group: you're mainly framing your arguments for your own 528a sake—which is not to say that you'd resent anyone else profiting from them as well.'

'That's what I'd prefer to do—talk, ask questions, and answer them chiefly for my own sake,' he said.

'Well,' I said, 'I'd like you to backtrack a bit. Just now we chose the wrong thing to follow geometry.'

'What do you mean?' he asked.

'We went straight from surfaces to solidity in circular motion,' I said, 'before we'd taken solidity on its own. The correct procedure is to go from the sec-b ond dimension to the third—which is, of course, the domain of cubes and anything else with volume.'

'True,' he said. 'But I don't think this domain has been explored yet, Socrates.'

'There are two reasons for that,' I replied. 'First, no society respects it, and therefore its complexity makes people diffident about looking into it. Second, exploration isn't feasible unless the research is conducted under supervision, but a supervisor is unlikely to be found, and moreover, even if one were to be found, the current situation is that the people doing the research in the field are so self-assured c that they wouldn't listen to him. However, they would listen if a whole community treated the subject with respect and supervised it, and once research was undertaken with continuity and determination, then facts would be discovered. I mean, even under the current circumstances of its general disrespect and depreciation—at the hands of the researchers as well, since they can't explain what good it is—it still manages to be attractive enough to overcome all this opposition and to develop, and I wouldn't be surprised if discoveries were made.'

'Yes, it certainly is a particularly attractive sub-d ject,' he agreed. 'But please can you explain what you were getting at just now. You referred to geometry as the study of surfaces . . .'

'Yes,' I said.

'. . . and then at first you said that astronomy came next, but later you took this back,' he said.

'I was in a hurry to complete the discussion,' I explained, 'and that was slowing me down. Although investigation of three-dimensionality came next, the research in the field has made the subject so difficult e to take seriously that I missed it out and put astronomy, which is solidity in motion, after geometry.'

'You're right,' he said.

'So let's make astronomy the fourth subject,' I said, 'on the understanding that, if a community were to underwrite the research, the branch of knowledge we're omitting at the moment would be available.'

'Yes, that sounds reasonable,' he said. 'And since you ticked me off just now for my crude endorsement of astronomy, Socrates, I'll now give it the kind of endorsement you're after. I mean, I can't 529a imagine anyone doubting that it forces the mind to look upwards and guides it from this realm to another realm.'

'It seems as though I'm the only one to doubt it, then,' I said. 'You see, I disagree.'

'On what grounds?' he protested.

'Because I think its current usage, in the hands of those who try to interest people in philosophy, is guaranteed to make people look downwards.'

'What do you mean?' he asked.

'I get the impression,' I said, 'that your conception of the study of things up on high is rather generous! It looks as though you'd think that the study b of decorations on a ceiling by bending one's neck back, and the acquisition of information that way, makes use of the intellect rather than the eyes! You may be right, and I'm probably being simple-minded, but it's only a field of study which is concerned with immaterial reality that I can regard as making the mind look upwards, and I wouldn't describe the attempt to study perceptible things by gawping upwards or squinting downwards as learning (since there's no knowledge involved in these cases); neither would I say that in these cases the mind is looking upwards rather than downwards, c even if the studying takes place while lying on one's back on the ground or in the sea.'

'That's a fair comment,' he said. 'You're right to have told me off. But apart from how it's studied at the moment, then, how do you think astronomy should be studied, if studying it is to have some point in the context we're talking about?'

'Like this,' I replied. 'It may be that there's nothing in the visible realm which is more beautiful or less erratic than these decorations in the sky, but even so, since they're within the visible realm, they d should be regarded as considerably inferior to true decorations, in respect of the beauty and precision of the movements which, in the realm of true number and all the true figures, genuine speed and slowness make relative to each other as they transport things which are not accessible to sight, but only to reason and thought. Don't you agree?'

'Definitely,' he said.

'Therefore,' I continued, 'we should use the heavenly decorations merely as illustrations to help us study the other realm, as we would if we were faced with exceptional geometrical figures drawn in fine detail by Daedalus or some other artist or painter. e On seeing figures of this kind, an expert geometer would think that for all the beauty of their execution, it would be absurd seriously to expect an examination of them to reveal the truth about equals 530a or doubles or some other ratio.'

'Of course it would be absurd,' he agreed.

'Don't you think that a genuine astronomer feels the same when he looks at the movements of the heavenly bodies?' I asked. 'He'll certainly think that the artist of the heavens has constructed them and all they contain to be as beautiful as such works could ever possibly be, but what about the ratio between night and day, between them and a month, between a month and a year? And what about the relations of the heavenly bodies in general to these b phenomena or to one another? Don't you think he'd regard it as ludicrous to suppose that these things are constant and unvarying, and never change in the slightest, when they're material and visible, and to devote all one's energy to discovering the truth about these things?'

'I agree,' he said, 'or anyway, I do when I hear your account.'

'So the way we'll do astronomy will be identical to the way we do geometry,' I said, 'since in both cases we'll be making use of matters that require elucidation. And if we don't ignore the heavenly bodies, we'll never be engaged in true astronomy, and we'll never develop rather than atrophy our c mind's innate intelligence.'

'Your instructions will involve astronomers in a great deal more work than they're used to at the moment,' he remarked.

'Yes, and I think we'll be issuing further instructions of the same kind,' I said, 'if our legislation is to do any good. But are there any other suitable fields of study that you can think of?'

'Not just at the moment,' he replied.

'There are, however, several types of movement, d I think,' I said. 'An expert would probably be able to give us a complete list, but even we can easily see two of them.'

'What are they?'

'In addition to the astronomical variety, there's one that complements it too,' I said.

'Which one do you mean?'

'The eyes are made for astronomy,' I said, 'and by the same token the ears are presumably made for the type of movement that constitutes music. If so, these branches of knowledge are allied to each other. This is what the Pythagoreans claim, and we should agree, Glaucon, don't you think?'

'Yes,' he said.

e 'Music is a difficult subject,' I said, 'so we'll consult the Pythagoreans to find out their views, and to see if they've anything to add. But throughout we'll be looking after our own agenda.'

'Which is what?'

'To make sure that our wards don't set about learning any pointless aspects of music—any aspect which doesn't unfailingly fetch up at the place which (as we were just saying in the case of astronomy) ought to be the destination of all these subjects.

531a Don't you realize that people get music wrong too? They laboriously measure the interrelations between audible concords and sounds, which is as useless an activity as anything astronomers get up to.'

'Yes, they really make fools of themselves,' he said. 'They talk about "concentrations" and bring their ears close to the source of the sound—as if they were trying to hear what the people next door were saying! And then some of them claim to be able to detect a further intermediate resonance and maintain that they've found the smallest possible interval, which should be used as the basis of measurement, while others dispute all this and claim that the notes in question are to all intents and purposes identical.

b But both camps rate their ears above their intellect.'

'You're talking', I said, 'about those excellent characters who make life hard for strings and torture them by twisting them on pegs. I don't want to push the image too far and mention how they strike the strings with a plectrum and challenge them, and how the strings refuse to talk and come up with specious pleas. So I'll drop the image and tell you that

I wasn't thinking of those people, but the ones we were saying just now would explain music to us, because they act in the same way that astronomers do. They limit their research to the numbers they can c find within audible concords, but they fail to come up with general matters for elucidation, such as which numbers form concords together and which don't, and why some do and some don't.'

'That's a superhuman task you're talking about,' he remarked.

'But a useful one,' I said, 'if it serves the aim of trying to understand what morality and goodness are. In any other context, however, it's a pointless pursuit.'

'I suppose so,' he said.

'What I'd say', I continued, is that engaging in all the subjects we've been discussing has some rele- d vance to our purposes, and all that effort isn't wasted, if the work takes one to the common ground of affinity between the subjects, and enables one to work out how they are all related to one another; otherwise it's a waste of time.'

'I suspect you're right,' he said. 'But you're talking about an awful lot of hard work, Socrates.'

Following the course in the mathematical sciences, the crowning part of the curriculum is dialectic, which gives one the ability to understand things as they are in themselves, and therefore to understand their relation to goodness. Without dialectic, we are condemned to the semi-conscious level of belief.

'What?' I asked. 'The prelude is hard, you say? Don't you realize that this is all just the prelude to the main theme, which is the important subject? I mean, you surely don't think that being accomplished in these subjects makes one good at dialec- e tic.'

'No, certainly not,' he answered, 'although it does happen sometimes—very occasionally—in my experience.'

'But don't you think the inability to explain anything, and to understand explanations, rules out the possibility of knowing any of the things we're saying are important?' I asked.

'Yes, I agree with you on this too,' he replied.

'And isn't this exactly the theme which dialectic 532a develops, Glaucon?' I asked. 'It may be an intelligible theme, but sight can be said to reflect it, when, as we were saying, it sets about looking at actual creatures, at the heavenly bodies themselves, and finally at the sun itself. Just as, in this case, a person ends up at the supreme point of the visible realm, so the summit of the intelligible realm is reached when, by means of dialectic and without relying on anything perceptible, a person perseveres in using b rational argument to approach the true reality of things until he has grasped with his intellect the reality of goodness itself.'

'Absolutely,' he said.

'And this is the journey a practitioner of dialectic makes, wouldn't you say?'

'Of course.'

'And the prisoners' release from their bonds,' I went on, 'their orientation away from shadows and towards figurines and firelight, their ascent out from under the ground into sunlight, their lingering inability to look in the upper world at creatures and plants and the light of the sun, rather than gazing at c reflections in water and at shadows (shadows, that is, of real things, not the shadows of figurines cast by a light which, relative to the sun, is of the same order as the figurines)—just as, in this case, the most lucid part of the body is taken up to see the most lucid part of the material, visible realm, so the whole business of studying the areas of expertise we've been discussing has the ability to guide the best part of the mind upwards until it sees the best part of red ality.'

'I'm happy with that,' he said, 'despite the fact that acceptance and rejection both seem to me to be problematic, from different points of view. However, we shouldn't let this be just a one-off discussion today, but should often return to the issue. So let's assume that our ideas are correct, and get on with discussing the actual main theme in as much detail as we did the prelude. So please tell us the ins e and outs of the ability to do dialectic, and how many different types of it there are, and what methods it employs, since they'd presumably be the means of approaching that place which, once reached, is travellers' rest and journey's end.'

533a 'You won't be able to follow me there, my dear Glaucon,' I said, 'which is a pity, because there'd be no shortage of determination from me, and what you'd see there wouldn't be an image of what we're talking about: you'd see the truth itself—or that's what I think, anyway. I may be right, and I may be wrong—that's not for us to insist on at the moment; but we can state with confidence that there'd be something of the kind to be seen, don't you think?'

'Of course.'

'And what about the idea that dialectic alone can elucidate these matters, to someone with experience in the subjects we've discussed, and that otherwise it's impossible?'

'Yes, we should state that confidently too,' he said.

'Anyway, what is indisputable in what we're say- b ing', I said, 'is that dialectic is the only field of enquiry which sets out methodically to grasp the reality of any and every thing. All the other areas of expertise, on the other hand, are either concerned with fulfilling people's beliefs and desires, or are directed towards generation and manufacture or looking after things while they're being generated and manufactured. Even any that are left—geometry and so on, which we were saying do grasp reality to some extent—are evidently dreaming about reality. There's no chance of their having a conscious c glimpse of reality as long as they refuse to disturb the things they take for granted and remain incapable of explaining them. For if your starting-point is unknown, and your end-point and intermediate stages are woven together out of unknown material, there may be coherence, but knowledge is completely out of the question.'

'Yes, it is,' he agreed.

'So dialectic is the only field of enquiry', I went on, 'whose quest for certainty causes it to uproot the things it takes for granted in the course of its journey, which takes it towards an actual starting-point. d When the mind's eye is literally buried deep in mud, far from home, dialectic gently extracts it and guides it upwards, and for this reorientation it draws on the assistance of those areas of expertise we discussed. It's true that we've often called them branches of *knowledge* in the past, but that's only a habit and they really need a different word, which implies a higher degree of clarity than belief has, and a higher degree of opacity than knowledge has. Earlier, we used the term "thought". But I don't suppose we'll quarrel about terminology when we're faced with e matters as important as the ones we're looking into at the moment.'

'No, we won't,' he said, 'just so long as whatever term is used expresses the state of mental clarity.'

'So the terms we used earlier will do,' I said. 'We'll call the first section knowledge, the second thought, the third confidence, and the fourth conjecture; and the first pair constitute intellect (which 534a is concerned with real being), the second pair belief (which is concerned with becoming). As being

stands to becoming, so intellect stands to belief; and
as intellect stands to belief, so knowledge stands to
confidence and thought to conjecture. However,
we'd better pass over the proportionate relations between the objects of intellect and belief, Glaucon,
and the twofold division of each of the two realms—
the domain of belief and the domain of intellect—
if we want to avoid getting entangled in an argument which would be many times as long as the ones
our discussion has already thrown up.'

b   'Well, I agree with everything else you've said,
in so far as I can follow it,' he said.

'And don't you think that the ability to understand
what it is to be any given thing, when someone else
explains it, is indicative of a dialectician? And
wouldn't you say that, in so far as anyone who lacks
this ability is incapable of explaining anything to
himself or to anyone else either, then he doesn't
know anything?'

'Of course I would,' he answered.

'The same principle applies to goodness, then, as
well. If someone is incapable of arguing for the separation and distinction of the character of goodness
from everything else, and cannot, so to speak, fight
c all the objections one by one and refute them (responding to them resolutely by referring to the reality of things, rather than to people's beliefs), and
can't see it all through to the end without his position suffering a fall—if you find someone to be in
this state, you'll deny that he has knowledge of
goodness itself or, in general, of anything good at
all. Instead, if he does somehow manage to make
contact with a reflection of goodness, you'll claim
that the contact is due to belief, not knowledge. He
dreams his current life away in a state of semi-con-
sciousness, you'll say, and he'll never wake up here:
d he'll go to Hades, the place of total sleep, first.
Agreed?'

'Yes, definitely,' he said. 'I'll certainly be making all of these claims.'

'Now, suppose your theoretical upbringing and
education of your younger generation were to become a reality. I imagine you'd deny them power
and crucial responsibility in the community if they
were as irrational as surds.'

'Yes, I would,' he said.

'Will you include in your legislation, then, the ruling that a major part of the education they engage
in must be the subject which will enable them to acquire particular expertise at the give and take of discussion?'

'I will,' he replied, 'if you join me.'   e

'Don't you think', I asked, 'that dialectic occupies the highest position and forms, as it were, the
copestone of the curriculum? And that, if so, there's
no subject which ought to occupy a higher position,
and therefore it completes our educational pro- 535a
gramme?'

'Yes, I agree,' he answered.

Plato repeats (from Chapter 8) the qualities potential philosopher kings must have, stressing in
this context their enthusiasm for intellectual pursuits. The main educational stages are allotted to
ages: the primary education of Chapter 4 goes up
to about 17 or 18; there will follow a couple of
years of intense military training; then ten years
spent with the mathematical sciences; then five
years of solid dialectic. Trainees who are found to
be unsuited to each successive stage will be
weeded out. Those who make it through to the end
will now become executives and teachers for fifteen years, until finally they understand goodness
and are allowed to alternate periods of contemplative philosophy with periods of rulership. Now
that we have seen (a) what it is to be a true philosopher, and (b) how to produce true philosophers,
we can see the truth of the proposal that the imaginary community will be feasible (if at all) only
when philosophers are kings.

'All that remains for you to do,' I said, 'is distribute the subjects: to whom, and on what basis,
shall we assign them?'

'Yes, that's obviously what we're left with,' he
said.

'Well, do you remember what kind of people we
chose as rulers, when we made our choice earlier?'

'Of course I do,' he answered.

'Now, on the whole,' I went on, 'the characteristics we should favour ought to remain the same, I
suggest. I mean, we should prefer people with a high
degree of reliability and courage, and also, within
reason, people who are very goodlooking. In addition, however, to being good and solid, we must also b
look for people with a natural talent for these studies.'

'What special qualities do you have in mind?'

'They must be sharp and quick at learning, Glaucon,' I said. 'You see, physical exercise is far less
appalling to the mind than intense intellectual work,
since intellectual work is more exclusively mental.
It belongs to the mind, rather than being shared with
the body.'

'True,' he said.

'And we should also look for people who have c good memories, are tenacious, and enjoy all kinds of work. Otherwise, there's no way that they'll be prepared to complete such a long course of intellectual study over and above all the hard work of the physical programme.'

'That's right,' he said. 'That'll take all the advantages nature can provide.'

'The problem nowadays, anyway,' I said, 'and the reason why philosophy has become devalued, is (to repeat ourselves) that its practitioners are people who aren't good enough for it. It should be practised by men of true pedigree, not by bastards.'

'What do you mean?' he asked.

'The main thing', I explained, 'is that the practi- d tioner must not be hamstrung in his enjoyment of work, with half of him enjoying it and half of him not. That's what you get when someone enjoys exercising and hunting and all kinds of physical work, but doesn't enjoy using his mind or listening to lectures or undertaking research, and instead loathes working in all these contexts. Then there are also people who are hamstrung in their enjoyment of work by having the opposite attitude.'

'You're absolutely right,' he said.

'By the same token,' I continued, 'we'll call a mind handicapped in the context of truth if, while e loathing conscious lying (in that it not only finds it hard to stomach from itself, but also gets highly irritated when others do it), it happily puts up with unconscious lying and doesn't get irritated when its ignorance is exposed, but wallows in ignorance as cheerfully as any pig.'

536a 'Absolutely,' he said.

'And the same goes for self-control, courage, broadness of vision, and all the other aspects of virtue,' I said. 'It's particularly important to distinguish men of true pedigree from bastards in all these contexts. The inability to look at these qualities from every possible angle leads people and communities to use crippled bastards for some purpose or other— as their friends, maybe, or as their rulers.'

'Very true,' he said.

'It's important for us to take precautions against b all traps of this kind,' I said. 'If we bring people who are in perfect physical and mental condition to this lengthy study programme and course of training, and educate them in it, we'll have done nothing wrong even by the strictest standards of moral behaviour, and we'll be preserving the integrity of our com-

munity and political system. However, if we introduce people of any other kind to it, we'll not only achieve the opposite results, but we'll also increase the flood of ridicule which pours down on philosophy.'

'That would be disgraceful,' he said.

'Yes, it would,' I agreed. 'But it looks as though I'm open to ridicule myself at the moment.'

'In what respect?' he asked.

'I forgot that our tone has been light-hearted,' I c answered, 'and I spoke with rather too much intensity. You see, while I was speaking, I looked at philosophy and saw how unjustly it has been dragged in the gutter. That made me cross, and I suppose I used the over-serious tone that I did because I felt a kind of rage.'

'Well, from my point of view as a member of the audience,' he said, 'it didn't strike me as excessive.'

'But from my point of view as the speaker,' I said, 'it did. Anyway, we should bear in mind that although our earlier selection procedure favoured old men, our present one rules them out. I mean, we d shouldn't let Solon convince us that while growing old there is still plenty of scope for learning: in fact, there's more scope for running than for learning! In any given sphere, it's up to young people to work long and hard.'

'That's necessarily true,' he said.

'So it's while they're young that we should set them arithmetic, geometry, and the rest of the studies which are the essential preliminaries before taking up dialectic. But we shouldn't present the work as compulsory.'

'Why not?'

'Because an autonomous person should never e learn a subject in a slavish fashion,' I explained. 'It's true that if physical work is performed under compulsion, the body isn't impaired, but compulsory intellectual work never remains in the mind.'

'True,' he said.

'So the educational environment in which you foster your younger generation, Glaucon,' I said, 'should be light-hearted rather than authoritarian. 537a This will also help you to see what natural abilities every one of them has.'

'That's plausible,' he said.

'And do you remember', I continued, 'our assertion that the children should be taken on horseback to observe warfare and, if they can do so safely, should also be taken up to the front and given a taste of blood, as young dogs are?'

'Yes, I do,' he replied.

'Well, any of them who demonstrates a high degree of proficiency in his exercising, studying, and facing fear should be enrolled in a special unit,' I said.'

b 'At what age, do you mean?' he asked.

'When they've finished with the basics of physical exercise,' I said. 'The point is that it's out of the question for them to do anything else during the period in question, which may last for two or three years, because exertion and exhaustion don't mix with intellectual work. Also, one of the crucial ways we'll be testing them will be by seeing what impression each of them gives during the period when they're concentrating on physical exercise.'

'Of course,' he said.

'After this period', I went on, 'a select group of the twenty-year-olds will receive promotion above the rest, and will be required to consolidate the subjects they were taught unsystematically as children c until they gain an overview of the relationships these subjects have to one another and to reality.'

'Yes,' he said, 'it's only when this has occurred that one's learning has a secure foundation.'

'And it's also the main way of testing whether or not someone is naturally suited for dialectic,' I said, 'since the ability to take an overview is the distinguishing mark of a dialectician.'

'I agree,' he said.

'What you'll have to do, then,' I said, 'is look out for this quality and try to see which of your people d are particularly capable in this respect, and have staying power in their intellectual work, in warfare, and in their other duties. These are the ones who, once they're past the age of thirty, you must select from among the select and promote even further; and you must subject them to dialectical training, to try to see which of them is capable of letting go of vision and of sense-perception in general, and can proceed to the realm of truth and reality itself. But you have to be very careful at this point, Glaucon.'

'Why?' he asked.

e 'Don't you realize how much harm occurs in the way dialectic is practised nowadays?' I said.

'What harm?' he asked.

'People become thoroughly rebellious,' I answered.

'They certainly do,' he said.

'Well', it's not a surprising state for them to get into, is it, do you think?' I asked. 'Can't you forgive them?'

'Why should I?' he asked.

'Here's an analogy,' I said. 'Suppose an illegiti- 538a mate child is brought up in affluent circumstances, in the midst of a large, powerful family with hordes of flatterers; and suppose that, when he grows up, he becomes aware that he isn't the child of his self-styled parents, but can't find out who his real parents are. Can you guess what his attitude would be towards the flatterers and towards his surrogate parents when he didn't know that this wasn't his rightful place, and then when he learnt the truth? Or shall I tell you what I suspect?'

'Please do,' he said.

'I suspect', I said, 'that, before he learnt the truth, he'd be more inclined to respect his father and b mother and the rest of the people he'd presumed to be his relatives than he would the flatterers, and less inclined to turn a blind eye to any need of theirs, and to do or say anything rebellious to them, and to disobey them in any important respect.'

'That's likely,' he said.

'However, once he'd become aware of the true state of affairs, I suspect he'd leave off giving them his respect and concern, and transfer his attention to the flatterers instead. He'd listen to them more than c he did before, model his lifestyle on theirs, openly spend time with them, and not have the slightest interest in that father of his and the rest of his pseudo-family—unless he's inherently a person of high principles.'

'Yes, that's exactly what would happen,' he agreed. 'But how does this analogy apply to people who are exposed to rational arguments?'

'Like this. From childhood, we've held certain views about moral and right conduct. These views formed the environment of our upbringing, we are subject to them as we are to our parents, and we obey them and respect them.'

'True.'

'Now, there are also enjoyable practices which run d counter to this moral code. These practices flatter and tempt our minds, but anyone with even a scrap of restraint doesn't give in, and continues instead to respect and obey those traditional views.'

'True.'

'Well, suppose', I went on, 'that the kind of person we're imagining is faced with a question like "What is right?" He answers that it consists in the conduct enjoined by the originator of his society's code, but the argument proves him wrong, and proves him wrong again and again, until he's bat-

tered into thinking that this code is no more right than wrong. Then the same happens with morality
e and goodness and all the qualities he used particularly to respect. What do you think the consequences of this are on his behaviour? What will happen to his respect and obedience?'

'He'll inevitably become more disrespectful and disobedient than he was before,' he said.

'Now, when he's changed his mind about what to respect and about his former familiar code,' I said, 'and at the same time can't discover the truth, where can he turn? Doesn't it only make sense to think of
539a him being seduced by the tempting lifestyle?'

'Yes,' he said.

'So he'll stop being law-abiding and become rebellious.'

'Inevitably.'

'People who are exposed to rational arguments, then,' I said, 'are quite likely to rebel and, as I suggested a moment ago, we should forgive them, don't you think?'

'Yes, and feel sorry for them,' he added.

'So if you want to avoid having to feel sorry for your thirty-year-olds, then you must handle rational arguments with the utmost circumspection, mustn't you?'

'Yes, definitely,' he said.

b   'And one important precaution you can take is not to let them get wind of rational arguments when they're young, don't you think? I mean, I'm sure you've noticed how when adolescents get their first taste of argumentation, they abuse it and treat it like a game. They can't find any other use for it except disputation; they use knock-down arguments which they borrow from others to demolish people's positions. Like puppies, they love to tug away at anyone they come across and to tear his argument to shreds with theirs.'

'Yes, it's incredible,' he said.

'So before long—once they've demolished a lot
c of arguments and often had their own demolished as well—they find they've radically changed their minds about everything. And the result of this is that people take a dim view of them, and of philosophy in general.'

'You're absolutely right,' he said.

'An older person, however,' I went on, 'is hardly likely to succumb to this insanity: he'd sooner resemble someone who's willing to practise dialectic and look for the truth, than someone who trivializes everything with his game-playing and disputatious-

ness. His own behaviour will be more moderate, and he'll increase, rather than decrease, dialectic's rep- d utation.'

'Right,' he said.

'And hasn't the point of what we've been saying been to get rid of the current practice of letting absolutely anyone, even when entirely unsuitable, come to rational argumentation, and to ensure that it is only orderly and stable people who get involved in it?

'Yes,' he said.

'Suppose, in order to complement the way physical exercise was approached, someone were to study, with constancy and concentration, nothing but rational argumentation for twice as many years as he devoted to physical exercise. Would that do?'

'Do you mean six years or four years?' he asked. e

'Why don't you just make it five?' I suggested. 'You see, the next thing you have to do is make them go back down into that cave and force them to take charge of warfare and whatever other areas young people should be responsible for, so that they gain just as much practical experience as everyone else. Moreover, while they hold these positions of responsibility, you'd better test them to see whether they remain unmoved by all the various temptations 540a they're exposed to, or whether they go astray.

'How long do you suggest for this?' he asked.

'Fifteen years,' I replied. 'Not all of them will reach their fiftieth year unscathed and with absolutely outstanding performances in every task they undertook and branch of knowledge they studied, but you can guide those who do to the climax of their lives. You must make them open up the beam of their minds and look at the all-embracing source of light, which is goodness itself. Once they've seen it, they must use it as a reference-point and spend the rest of their lives ordering the community, its b members, and themselves. They take turns at this: they spend most of their time doing philosophy, but when their turn comes, then for the community's sake they become involved in its affairs and slog away at them as rulers. This is something they do as an obligation, not as a privilege. Because they have this attitude, they're constantly training others to follow suit, and once they've completed this process and have bequeathed guardianship of the community to others in their place, they depart for a new home in the Isles of the Blessed. And the community constructs public memorials and establishes ceremonies in their honour, and treats them (if the c Delphic oracle gives its blessing) as deities, or otherwise as happy and godlike men.'

'You've created an image of the rulers which makes them as thoroughly attractive as a master sculptor makes his statues, Socrates,' he remarked.

'And there are female rulers too, Glaucon,' I said. 'Please don't think that what I've been saying doesn't apply equally to any women in the community with the required natural abilities.'

'That's right,' he said. 'Men and women will share everything equally, as we explained.'

'Well then, do you agree that our community and d political system weren't just wishful thinking?' I said. 'The community may be difficult to realize, but it's feasible; the essential prerequisite, as we've insisted, is that genuine philosophers—one or more of them—wield power. They have to be born in a community, but grow up to regard the political rewards currently available to them as despicable, as mean and worthless. Instead, they have to find nothing e more valuable than integrity and its rewards, and nothing more important and essential than morality, which they serve and foster as they take in hand every detail of their community.'

'How do they go about this?' he asked.

'First, they banish everyone over the age of ten 541a into the countryside,' I answered. 'Then the take charge of the community's children and make sure that they're beyond the reach of existing conventions, which their parents adhere to, and bring them up under their own customs and laws, which are similar to the ones we were describing before. That's the quickest and simplest way for the community and political system we've been discussing to be established, to attain happiness, and to benefit the people among whom they occur.'

'Yes, definitely,' he said. 'And I think you've b given an excellent explanation of how our community would be realized, if it ever were.'

'So is that it, then?' I asked. 'Have we finished discussing this community of ours and its human counterpart? I mean, I suppose it's obvious what kind of person we'll claim he has to be.'

'Yes, it is,' he said. 'And, to answer your question, yes, I think we've finished.'

CHAPTER 11
WARPED MINDS, WARPED SOCIETIES

Plato now returns to the question of morality, apparently interrupted since the end of Chapter 6. He has said

what it is, but he has yet to show that it benefits its possessor. Since the best form of society and type of individual have already been described, he proposes to describe debased versions, and to slant the descriptions so that the question of their relative happiness may become clear. This will involve some rather schematic and simplistic psychology based on the analogy between communities and types of individual, but also some brilliant and much-admired vignettes of these individuals.

'All right, Glaucon. Now, we concluded that the 543a best government of a community depends on sharing women, children, and education in all its aspects, and by the same token on peacetime and wartime functions being performed by women as well as by men, and on their kings being those who have proved outstanding at philosophy and warfare.'

'Yes, we did,' he agreed.

'And we also agreed that, once they're in office, b the rulers are to take the militia and settle them in the kind of quarters we described earlier—that is, where nothing is exclusive to any individual, but everything is shared. Furthermore, apart from their quarters being like this, we also drew some conclusions about their possession of property, as you may remember.'

'I do,' he said. 'We thought that, contrary to current practice, none of them should own any property, but that as warriors and guardians they should be paid by everyone else an annual stipend for their guarding, consisting of the provisions appropriate to c their duties, and that they should look after the community as a whole, as well as themselves.'

'That's right,' I said. 'But now that we've finished with all that, let's try to resume our journey by recalling where we were when we took the side-turning that led us here.'

'That's no problem,' he said. 'You were talking, much as you are now, as if your discussion of our community were complete. You were saying that you'd call good the kind of community you'd described at that point, and its human counterpart— d even though, as it turns out, you were in a position to describe an even better community and an even better person. Anyway, you claimed that, given the 544a rightness of our community, all the rest were flawed, and you said, if my memory serves me well, that of these remaining political systems, four types would be worth mentioning, and that we ought to see where they and their human counterparts go wrong, so that we can decide whether or not the best person is also the happiest person, and the worst the unhappiest, which we can only do once we've seen all these types of human being and reached agreement as to which is best and which is worst. I had just asked which four political systems you had in mind, when b Polemarchus and Adeimantus interrupted. You responded to them, and that's how the discussion reached this point.'

'Your memory is spot on,' I said.

'Why don't you resume your stance, then, as if you were a wrestler? I'll ask the same question, and you can have a go at saying what you were poised to say then.'

'I'll try,' I said.

'In fact, speaking for myself, I really would like to hear which four political systems you had in mind,' he said.

c 'I should be able to tell you that without any difficulty,' I said, 'since the ones I mean are recognized political systems with names. There's that popular favourite, the Cretan and Spartan system; the second one, which is also the second most popular, is the thoroughly rotten system known as oligarchy; then next there's democracy, oligarchy's adversary; and the fourth, the ultimate political disease, which leaves all the rest behind, is noble dictatorship. Can you think of any other type of political system which d counts as a distinct variety? I mean, there are autocracies and monarchies which can be bought, and other political systems (to be found among both Greeks and non-Greeks) which equally fall somewhere among the ones I've mentioned.'

'Yes, there are all sorts of odd systems one hears about,' he remarked.

'Well, do you appreciate that there are bound to be as many types of human being as there are of political system?' I asked. 'Or do you imagine that political systems somehow come into being from oak or from rock, rather than from the characters of the communities' inhabitants? If one type of character outweighs the rest, so to speak, then don't you think e it draws all the other types with it?'

'Yes, that's the only possible way in which political systems arise,' he agreed.

'So if there are five types of society, then any given individual should also have one of five kinds of mental trait.'

'Naturally.'

'Now, we've already described the individual counterpart to aristocracy, and no one could fault our claim that it's a person of goodness and morality.'

'Yes, we have.' 　　　　　　　　　　　　　　545a

'So next we'd better describe the inferior kinds of person—the competitive and ambitious person who corresponds to the Spartan system, then the oligarchic, democratic, and dictatorial types. This will enable us to see which of them is the least moral; we can then contrast him with the most moral type, and that will complete our enquiry into how absolute morality compares with absolute immorality in respect of the happiness or unhappiness they entail for people who possess them. Then we'll be in a position either to follow Thrasymachus and pursue immorality, or to follow the argument which is developing at the moment and pursue morality. Do you b think that's what we'd better do?'

'Yes, most definitely,' he said.

'Well, we started off by looking at characteristics as they manifested in societies, before turning to individuals, on the grounds that this would make it easier for us to see them. So we'd better continue by looking first at the "ambitious" political system—I can't think of another familiar word for it: perhaps we should call it "timocracy" or "timarchy". We'll examine its human counterpart, by comparing him with it; then oligarchy and an oligarchic person; next we'll look at democracy and try to form an impression of c a democratic person; and in the fourth place we'll turn our attention to dictatorial government of a community and then we'll look at a dictatorial temperament. Don't you think this is how we should try to gain the competence to assess the matter before us?'

'Yes, that's a perfectly reasonable way to go about the investigation and the assessment,' he replied.

Time and again, Plato has stressed the stability of his 'aristocratic' community, in such a way as to make its degeneration seem unlikely. But nothing in this world is permanent, and the rulers of the aristocracy will, sooner or later, be less than perfect. 'Timarchy' will take the place of 'aristocracy'. Timarchy is rule by people governed by the passionate part of the mind, who value military ideals and success, but have begun to be corrupted by money. The degeneration will begin when the community ceases to be a unity and ceases to keep to the Principle of Specialization. The behaviour of the corresponding timarchic individual is based on the fact that he is torn between the highest and lowest parts of his mind, and so compromises on the intermediate part.

'All right, then,' I said. 'Let's try to account for the transition from aristocracy to timocracy. I suppose this much is straightforward—that all political d change is due to the actual power-possessing members of society themselves, when conflict arises among them. Even if there are very few of them, instability is out of the question as long as they're of one mind. Yes?'

'Yes.'

'How, then, Glaucon,' I asked, 'will change become a feature of our community? How will conflict arise between and among the auxiliaries and the rulers? Perhaps you'd like us to imitate Homer and pray for the e Muses to tell us "how conflict first occurred", and to have them speak in a pompous and highfalutin fashion, using the kind of semi-serious tone one uses when teasing and making fun of children.'

'What do you mean?'

546a 'Something like this. Hard though it may be for a community with this structure to undergo change, yet everything that is born must die, and so even this kind of structure will not last for ever, but will fall apart. This is how it will happen. Fertility and infertility are not restricted to plants: surface-dwelling creatures also periodically experience both mental and physical fertility and infertility, each time their cycles complete a revolution. Short-lived creatures have short cycles, long-lived ones the opposite. Where the human species is concerned, despite the b cleverness of the people you've trained to be in charge of your community, they'll still fail to catch the times of fertility and barrenness, although they supplement the evidence of their senses with rationality. They'll mistime things and produce children when they shouldn't.

'Now, a divine creature's cycle is defined by a perfect number; but a human creature's number is the smallest one in which increases entailing potential and realized potential gain three intervals and four terms from among the causes of similarity and dissimilarity, and from among the things that increase and decrease, and so make everything mutu- c ally conformable and rational. The base numbers involved—3 in relation to 4, along with 5—produce two harmonies when they are increased three times. One harmony is made up of a factor squared, times a hundred times itself; the other harmony is in a sense made up of equal factors, but in a sense of unequal factors—one factor being 100 of the numbers from the rational diagonals of 5, each diminished by 1 (or 100 of the numbers from the irrational diagonals of 5, each diminished by 2), and the other factor being 100 of the cubes of 3.

'The geometrical number produced is responsible for this area—for the quality of children born—and when your guardians are unaware of this, they pair men and women sexually on the wrong occasions, d and the resulting children will not be naturally gifted or fortunate. It may be that the preceding generation will choose only the best of these children for office, but all the same they won't be as good as they should be, and when they in turn inherit their fathers' positions of authority, despite being guardians they'll begin to neglect us: they'll underrate the importance of cultural studies, and then of physical exercise, and consequently the young people of your community will become rather uncultured. As a result, the next generation of rules to be appointed will not be particularly good at guarding, in the sense that they won't be so good at assessing those castes of Hesiod's and yours—the castes of gold and sil- e ver, of copper and iron. Iron will get all mixed up 547a with silver, copper with gold; discrepancy and discordant incongruity will occur, and they always breed hostility and antagonism, wherever they occur. It has to be admitted that "this is the lineage" of conflict, whatever the circumstances of its occurrence on any given occasion.'

'Yes, we'll endorse their opinion,' he said.

'We have to,' I said. 'They are the Muses, after all.'

'What are they going to say next?' he asked. — b

'Once conflict has been born,' I said, 'the two castes start to pull in different directions. The iron and copper caste incline towards business and want to possess land, houses, gold, and silver. The gold and silver caste, on the other hand, don't feel in need of money: thanks to their innate wealth, they tend to be temperamentally attracted towards goodness and the traditional ways. Because of the tension and antipathy between them, they compromise by agreeing to assign themselves land and houses for private c ownership, and at the same time they subjugate their former friends and wards, whom they used to guard, and make them their dependants and slaves, while they take responsibility for warfare and for guarding themselves against them.'

'Yes, I think that's the cause of the transition,' he agreed.

'And wouldn't this political system fall between aristocracy and oligarchy?' I asked.

'Yes.'

'Anyway, that's how the transition will take place. But once it has taken place, how will the commud nity be governed? Perhaps the answer's obvious: won't it in some respects take after both oligarchy and the system which preceded it (since it falls between them), and in other respects have its own distinctive features?'

'Yes,' he answered.

'Now, there'll be respect for the rulers, and its militia won't get involved in any businesses like farming and manufacture, but will have arranged common mess-halls for themselves and will devote themselves to physical exercise and to training for war. In all these respects, it'll reflect the political system which preceded it, won't it?'

'Yes.'

e 'On the other hand, there'll be reluctance to choose men of knowledge for political office, since the only intellectuals within the community by then will be complex characters, lacking in robust directness. The community will incline towards the greater directness of passionate types, who are by their natures more suited for war than for peace; it will value the ruses and stratagems which war entails, and will spend all 548a its time on warfare. Most of these sorts of features will be peculiar to it, won't they?'

'Yes.'

'Furthermore,' I went on, 'the members of this kind of community will share with people under oligarchies a craving for money. They'll have a fanatical respect for gold and silver—but a furtive respect, because they'll have storerooms and vaults in their homes where they can put them and hide them away, and they'll also have surrounded their homes with walls, for all the world as if their houses were private dens within whose confines they can exb travagantly spend their money on their wives and anyone else they choose.'

'True,' he said.

'But because they value money and aren't open about possessing it, they'll actually be mean about it—although they'll be happy to satisfy their craving by spending other people's money. They'll pluck their pleasures in secret, hiding away from the law like children running and hiding from their father. The background to all this will be the fact that their education will have been forced on them, rather than finding willing ears, and this will be due to their neglect of the authentic Muse—and of her companions, reason and philosophy—and to their placing c more value on physical exercise than on cultural studies.'

'You're talking about a political system which is a thorough mixture of good and bad,' he remarked.

'Yes, it is a mixture,' I agreed, 'but thanks to the predominance of the passionate element, there's only one aspect which particularly stands out—all its competitiveness and ambition.'

'Yes, that's extrèmely noticeable,' he said.

'So much, then,' I said, 'for the origin and nature of this political system. I assume that a verbal sketch of the outline of the system will do, rather than filling in all the details, since even a sketch will enable d us to see where the extremes of human morality and immorality lie, and it would take for ever to go through every possible political system and human characteristic in minute detail.'

'Yes, that's right,' he said.

'What about the person who corresponds to this political system, then? What's his background? And what's he like?'

'I think he'd approximate pretty closely to Glaucon here,' said Adeimantus, 'with his competitiveness.'

'Maybe he would in this respect,' I said, 'but there e are traits he has which do not resemble any of Glaucon's, I think.'

'Which ones?'

'He's bound to be more obstinate,' I said, 'and to have spent less time on cultural studies. He'll approve of culture, however, and he'll enjoy listening to lectures, even though he won't be any good at speaking himself. This kind of person will treat 549a slaves harshly (rather than finding them beneath consideration, which is the attitude of a properly educated person), but he'll be gentle with those he likes. He'll be excessively submissive to authority, and ambitiously eager for authority himself. He'll regard military achievements as qualifying someone for political office, rather than ability at speaking and so on, and he'll be fond of sports and hunting.'

'Yes,' he said, 'because these are the characteristics of the political system we've been describing.'

'Now, as a young man,' I continued, 'a person of this type will disdain money, but the older he gets, b the more he'll welcome it at every opportunity, don't you think? This is because his mercenary side will have come to the fore, and because his attitude towards goodness will be tainted, thanks to his lack of the best guardian.'

'What guardian is that?' asked Adeimantus.

'A mind which combines reason and culture,' I replied. 'It's only when this resides in someone throughout his life that his goodness is kept intact.'

'You're right,' he said.

'So that's what a timocratic person is like in his youth,' I said. 'And he is the counterpart to the kind of community we've been talking about.'

c 'Yes.'

'As for his background,' I went on, 'it's something like this. As a young man, he's the son of a father who is good, but who lives in a badly governed community and therefore steers clear of status and office, and lawsuits and all that kind of involvement in public affairs, and is happy to be discounted and consequently to avoid all the nuisance of involvement.'

'Yes, but how does this produce a timocratic type?' he asked.

'It all starts', I explained, 'when he hears his mother complaining that her husband doesn't have political power, and that this is why she is snubbed by all the other women. Then she sees that he isn't d especially interested in money, and plays no part in the fighting and mud-slinging that occur in private lawsuits or in political situations, and doesn't get worked up about all that kind of thing; she also notices that he's always minding his own business, and doesn't overrate her (not that he underrates her either). All this makes her cross and she tells him that his father isn't a real man, and that he's too nonchalant, and goes on and on with all the usual complaints women routinely come up with in these kinds e of circumstances.'

'Yes, there are plenty of these typical complaints,' said Adeimantus.

'As you know, then,' I continued, 'even the supposedly loyal servants of this sort of man whisper the same kinds of things to his sons, and if the servants notice that a young man's father is failing to prosecute someone who owes him some money or is wronging him in some other way, they encourage the son to make sure that he gets even with all these 550a people when he's an adult, and to be more of a man than his father. Outside of the house, the young man hears and sees more of the same sort: he notices that people who mind their own business are regarded by the rest of the community as stupid and are despised, while those who don't are respected and admired. So, when the young man hears and sees all this, and also listens to what his father has to say, and sees his way of life from close quarters and compares it with the alternative, he is pulled in two di-b rections: his father irrigates and nurtures his rational mind, while everyone else nurtures the desirous

and passionate parts of his mind. Now, he isn't a bad person, but he's been exposed to some bad influences, so he resolves these contrary impulses by reaching a compromise: he transfers authority within himself to the intermediate part of himself—the competitive and passionate part—and so he becomes a supercilious, ambitious man.'

'I think you've described his background perfectly,' he said.

'So there's our second political system and our c second type of person,' I said.

'Yes,' he agreed.

After timarchy, oligarchy. This is not described neutrally as 'the rule of the few', otherwise Plato's aristocracy would be an oligarchy. It is rule by the wealthy few (i.e. plutocracy), who value money over goodness, and do not necessarily have the expertise rulership requires. They are governed by the third, acquisitive part of the mind. Even more than timarchy, oligarchy transgresses the two fundamental principles of the ideal state: it lacks unity, its members are not restricted to a single occupation, and they do not all contribute to the good of the whole. In fact, some of its members may lack any occupation at all. It is a society of 'drones'. There is a strong criminal element, which is barely suppressed. The psychology of the corresponding individual is an exact introjected counterpart to this oligarchic society.

'Next, to paraphrase Aeschylus, shall we "tell who else has been deployed, to stand before which community"—or rather, shall we keep to our plan and speak of the community first?'

'Yes,' he said.

'I think that oligarchy would follow the kind of political system we've described.'

'But what kind of constitution do you mean by oligarchy?' he asked.

'A political system which is based on property value,' I replied, 'so that the rich have political d power, and the poor are excluded from government.'

'I see,' he said.

'Hadn't we better explain the initial transition from timarchy to oligarchy?'

'Yes.

'But even a blind man could see how it happens,' I said.

'How?'

'The downfall of timarchy is brought about by trying to keep that storeroom we spoke of—the one people have for their gold—full up. You see, first people invent ways to spend their money and they subvert the laws for this purpose, in the sense that they and their wives refuse to obey them.'

'That makes sense,' he said.

e 'Next, I suppose, everyone starts to look at everyone else with envy, and that becomes the normal attitude.'

'That's likely.'

'And then,' I said, 'they get more and more involved in making money; and the higher they rate money, the lower they rate goodness. I mean, isn't the difference between wealth and goodness analogous to them each lying in one of the pans of a pair of scales and constantly tending in opposite directions?'

'It certainly is,' he said.

551a 'So if wealth and wealthy people are admired in a community, then goodness and good people are despised there.'

'Obviously.'

'Now, you cultivate what you admire, whatever it may be, and ignore what you despise.'

'Yes.'

'So eventually they stop being competitive and ambitious, and become acquisitive and mercenary instead. They acclaim and admire anyone rich, and make it easy for him to gain political power, but they despise anyone poor.'

'Yes.'

'They then enact the legislation which is the distinctive feature of an oligarchic political system, in which they ordain a certain amount of money—a b larger amount if the oligarchy is more of an oligarchy, a smaller amount if it is less of one—and announce that only those whose property attains the ordained value shall play a part in government. They either use force of arms to get this legislation passed, or they've already used fear to make this kind of constitution a *fait accompli*. Do you agree?'

'Yes.'

'So that's more or less how it comes to be established.'

'Yes,' he said, 'but what kind of system is it? We c said it was flawed—what are these flaws?'

'You should start by thinking about its distinctive feature,' I said. 'I mean, what do you think it would be like if ships' captains were appointed in this way, because of the value of their property, and poverty ruled someone out even if he was a better captain?'

'Then people would have terrible voyages,' he said.

'And does the same go for positions of authority in other spheres?'

'I'd say so.'

'Except political power?' I asked. 'Or does it also apply to political power?'

'It applies there above all,' he said, 'because it's the most difficult and important kind of power there is.'

'That's the first major mistake oligarchy makes, d then, apparently.'

'So it seems.'

'Well, here's another flaw, and I wonder if it's any less serious.'

'What is it?'

'That a community of this kind can't be single: it's inevitably divided into the haves and the have-nots. They may live in the same place, but they're constantly plotting against one another.'

'No, that's certainly just as serious a flaw,' he said.

'Another deplorable feature is that they'd probably be incapable of going to war against an enemy. They could either arm the populace at large, in order to use them in the war—but that would in- e evitably give them more cause for fear than the enemy; or they could avoid using the populace, and then, when it came to actual fighting, they'd be revealed as true oligarch! At the same time their mercenary nature makes them unwilling to levy a war-tax.'

'That's no good.'

'Then there's something we've been expressing disapproval of all along—the fact that in this kind of political system people won't stick to a single oc- 552a cupation, but will be farmers, businessmen, and soldiers at the same time. Do you think that's the right way to go about things?'

'No, I certainly don't.'

'Now, would you agree that this is the first political system to admit the ultimate evil?'

'What are you getting at?'

'It's possible for someone to sell everything (and for someone else to acquire his property) and continue to live in the community without being one of its limbs—without being a businessman or a manufacturer, or in the cavalry or the heavy infantry. He'd be classified instead as impoverished and destitute.'

'Yes,' this is the first system it could happen in,' b he agreed.

'Anyway, that kind of thing isn't ruled out by an oligarchy, otherwise we wouldn't find both excessive affluence and utter poverty at the same time.'

'Right.'

'Now what do you think about this? Did the person we're imagining actually benefit his community in the respects we're considering while he was well off and was spending his money? Or is it true to say that he was only a pseudo-ruler, and that in reality he didn't rule over the community or serve it in any capacity, but merely consumed whatever he could lay his hands on?'

c 'Yes, that's right,' he said. 'He wasn't an authentic ruler: he was nothing but a consumer.'

'Shall we describe him as a drone, then?' I asked. 'His home is equivalent to the cell in a honeycomb where a drone is born, and he becomes the bane of his community as a drone becomes the bane of the hive.'

'I like that idea, Socrates,' he said.

'Now, the first variety of drones, Adeimantus— the ones with wings—have been denied stings by God. The second variety, however—the ones that go on foot—fall into two categories: some of them are stingless, but some have terrifying stings, don't they? The stingless ones end up in their old age as beggars, while everyone who's designated a criminal started life as one of the drones with stings. Yes?'

'True,' he said.

'It obviously follows,' I said, 'that any community where you can find beggars also has thieves, pickpockets, temple-robbers, and perpetrators of similar crimes concealed somewhere about the place.'

'Yes, obviously,' he agreed.

'Well, don't you find beggars in communities which are governed by oligarchies?'

'Yes,' he said, 'just about everyone except for the rulers!'

e 'Isn't the implication of what we're saying that these communities also contain plenty of criminals with stings,' I asked, 'who are deliberately and forcibly repressed by the authorities?'

'Yes, it is,' he said.

'And we're claiming that the presence of these criminals is a direct result of lack of education, bad upbringing, and a bad political system?'

'We are.'

'There you are, then. That's what a community is like when it's governed by an oligarchy, and those are its major flaws—though there may be more.'

'That all sounds about right,' he said.

'So much, then,' I concluded, 'for our description 553a of the kind of political system which uses property value as a criterion for rulership, and which is called "oligarchy". Next, we'd better look at the background and nature of its human counterpart.'

'Yes,'

'The transition from a timocratic person to an oligarchic one invariable happens as follows, wouldn't you say?'

'How?'

'When a child is born to a timocratic man, he initially looks up to his father and follows in his footsteps. Later, however, he sees him suddenly wrecked on some political reef, and watches as his father and b all his property are washed overboard. His father might have been a military commander or held some other important position, and then have ended up in court as a result of sycophants making trouble for him, and been put to death or exiled or deprived of his citizenship and had all his property confiscated.'

'Yes, that's not at all impossible,' he said.

'The effect of seeing and experiencing all this, Adeimantus, and of losing his property, is (I should think) that the son gets afraid and immediately tosses c ambition and his passionate side headlong from the throne they'd been occupying in his mind. Laid low by poverty, he turns to tawdry commercial activities, and gradually accumulates wealth by thrift and hard work. Don't you think that under these circumstances he'd install his desirous and mercenary side on that throne? Don't you think he'd make it his internal equivalent of the Persian king, and deck it out with tiaras and necklaces and scimitars?'

'I do,' he said.

'While his rational and passionate aspects, I imag- d ine, are made to sit on the ground on either side of the king's feet in abject servitude. The only calculations and researches he allows his rational mind to make are concerned with how to start with a little money and increase it, the only admiration and respect he allows his passionate side to feel are for wealth and wealthy people, and he restricts his ambition to the acquisition of money and to any means towards that end.'

'There's no transition so quick or so complete in its effects', he remarked, 'as when a young person becomes mercenary instead of ambitious.'

'So do you think we've found our oligarchic type?' I asked. e

'Well, he does evolve from the type who corresponds to the political system from which oligarchy evolves.'

'Let's see if he has similar characteristics, then.'

554a 'All right.'

'The first point of similarity is the supreme value he places on money, wouldn't you say?'

'Of course.'

'Then there's the fact that he's thrifty and hard-working. He satisfies only those of his desires which are essential, and suppresses all the rest (he thinks they're pointless), so as not to incur any further expenses.'

'Yes.'

'He's rather ascetic,' I said. 'He tries to make a profit out of every situation, and he's a hoarder—an attribute which is commonly admired in people. Aren't these characteristics of the person who cor-
b responds to the political system we've been describing?'

'I'd say so,' he said. 'At any rate, money is the be-all and end-all for that community as well as for him.'

'It's because he never bothered about his education, I suppose,' I said.

'Yes, I think so,' he replied. 'Otherwise, he wouldn't have thought so highly of a blind person and made him the leader of his troupe.'

'Good point,' I said. 'Now, what about this? Don't you think we should say that his lack of education engenders within him drone-like desires—some in the beggarly mode, some in the criminal mode—
c which are forcibly and deliberately repressed, on the whole?'

'I certainly do,' he replied.

'Do you know where you'll find these people behaving like criminals?' I asked.

'Where?' he asked.

'When they're entrusted with the guardianship of orphans, and when similar easy opportunities for wrongdoing come their way.'

'True.'

'This makes it clear that it's only because some remnant of decency makes them forcibly repress their evil desires that they have a reputation for fair
d dealing in other contexts. And they repress these desires not because they're convinced that they should, or because they've used reason to tame them, but because they have no choice and because they're afraid—afraid for the rest of their property. Do you agree?'

'Yes, definitely,' he said.

'But when it's a case of them spending someone else's money, Adeimantus,' I went on, 'then, I swear, the drone-like desires most of them contain will be exposed.'

'Yes,' he said, 'I couldn't agree more.'

'So internal conflict will characterize this kind of person: he isn't single, he's divided into two. His condition is simply that his better desires by and e large control his worse ones.'

'True.'

'That is why, in my opinion, although this sort of person gives a better impression than lots of people do, he still comes nowhere near true goodness, which requires mental unity and harmony.'

'I agree.'

'Moreover, because he's mean about money, he doesn't put himself personally on the line and strive to win some political victory or generally to gain pub- 555a lic recognition for good deeds. He's reluctant to spend money for the sake of prestige or for anything else like that which involves rivalry against others, because he's afraid of waking up desires which would require him to spend money and of summoning up their assistance in a competitive situation. So he fights in true oligarchic fashion, with just a few parts of himself, and he's usually defeated—but rich.'

'That's right,' he said.

'So we have no reason now to doubt the correspondence between a community governed by an oligarchy and a mean, mercenary type of person, do b we?' I asked.

'None at all,' he said.

After oligarchy, democracy. Plato is obviously thinking to some extent of the system familiar to him from the Athens of his day. The brutality of oligarchy leads (usually) to a violent revolution and the establishment of democracy, which is a kind of free-for-all. It does not correspond to rule by any of the three divisions of the mind: it is disarray, the rule of none of the parts of the mind, or of different parts at different times. The community has no unity, and anyone can do any job he likes—even govern without the required expertise. The psychology of the democratic individual is characterized by a similar lack of discipline. Each passing whim is indulged, just as in a democracy leaders come and go.

'Next, I suppose, we'd better try to see how democracy starts, and what its characteristics are once it exists. That will help us identify the corresponding individual, and then we can assess his merits, relative to those of the other types.'

'Yes, that would be in keeping with what we've been doing so far,' he said.

'Don't you think,' I said, 'that the transition from oligarchy to democracy is a result of people being insatiably greedy for what they've come to accept as good—that they ought to get as rich as they possibly can?'

'In what sense?'

c 'The way I see it is that because political power within the community depends on the possession of wealth, the rulers aren't disposed to curb by legal means the undisciplined elements of the younger generation, to prevent them from spending their money and ruining their estates, because this enables them to buy up those estates and to loan money at interest, and so get even richer and gain even more public standing.'

'That's extremely plausible.'

'We need no further evidence, then, for the impossibility of the citizen body of a community simultaneously rating affluence highly and being adequately self-disciplined: they are bound to neglect either one or the other.'

'Yes, that's clear enough,' he said.

'Now, the negligent sanctioning of indiscipline which occurs within oligarchies has been known in the past to reduce men of some calibre to poverty.'

'It certainly has.'

'There they squat in the community, I imagine, equipped with their stings—and with weapons. Some are in debt, some have lost their citizenship, some are enduring both these hardships. In their hatred of the people who have acquired their property, they long for revolution, and plot against them and everyone else as well.'

'True.'

'But their targets, stooped businessmen that they are, appear not to notice. They continue to inject the venom of money into any remaining member of the community who submits to them, they continue to collect compound rates of interest, the offspring of the loan, and they continue to fill the community with drones and beggars.'

556a

'Of course they do,' he said.

'Nor do they show any inclination to extinguish the blaze of this kind of trouble', I went on, 'by banning indiscriminate usage of one's assets or by some alternative legislation which gets rid of behaviour of that sort.'

'What alternative legislation?'

'It's not as effective as the first option, but it does force the members of a community to cultivate goodness. I mean, if there were a rule to the effect that most categories of voluntary contract should be entered upon at the lender's own risk, then the pursuit of money within the community would become less shameless, and fewer evils of the kind we've been talking about would develop.'

'Considerably fewer,' he said.

'As things are, however,' I said, 'it's thanks to the rulers of the community—for all the kinds of reasons we've been describing—that their subjects are in the state they're in. Meanwhile, they make themselves and their families ... well, their children never know what it's like to work, physically or mentally, so they become spoilt and too soft and lazy to resist pleasure and pain, don't they?'

'Of course.'

'And they themselves ignore everything except making money: there's nothing to tell between them and the poor in terms of how little attention they pay to goodness, is there?'

'No, there isn't.'

'So this is the basis on which the rulers and their subjects meet one another, as they walk in the streets or come together under any circumstances—for a show, say, or as fellow sailors or fellow soldiers on a campaign. Even in the teeth of danger, they eye one another; but there's no way that the poor are despised by the rich in this situation. Poor people tend to be lean and sun-tanned, and when they stand in the battle-line next to the rich with their indoor pallor and plentiful extra flesh, they notice their breathlessness and utter ineptitude. Don't you think they'll conclude that it's their own cowardice that has allowed the rich to get rich, and they'll get together in private and tell one another, "They're ours for the taking. There's nothing to them"?'

'I'm sure that's what they do,' he said.

'Now, it takes only a slight external influence to push an unhealthy body towards illness, and sometimes nothing external need be involved at all for the body's elements to start fighting one another. Likewise, a community which is in a similarly unhealthy state needs only a slight pretext—one party might bring in reinforcements from an external oligarchy, or the other from an external democracy—to fall ill and start fighting with itself, and sometimes no external influence at all is needed for conflict to begin. Do you agree?'

557a   'Definitely.'

'So democracy starts, in my opinion, when the poor members of the community are victorious. They kill some of the rich, they expel others, and they give everyone who's left equal social and political rights: in a democratic system governmental posts are usually decided by lot.'

'Yes,' he said, 'that's how democracy is founded, but it might not involve force of arms: fear might have been used to drive their enemies away.'

'All right,' I said, 'but what kind of constitution b is it? What's a democratic political system actually like? I mean, this is how we'll learn about the corresponding democratic individual, obviously.'

'Obviously,' he agreed.

'Well, in the first place, the members of the community are autonomous, aren't they? The community is informed by independence and freedom of speech, and everyone has the right to do as he chooses, doesn't he?'

'That's the claim, anyway,' he answered.

'And given this right, then clearly every individual can make for himself the kind of life which suits him.'

'Clearly.'

c   'I should think, then, that there'd be a wider variety of types of people in this society than in any other.'

'Of course there would.'

'It's probably the most gorgeous political system there is,' I continued. 'Its beauty comes from the fact that it is adorned with every species of human trait, as a cloak might be adorned with every species of flower. And I suppose', I added, 'that plenty of people would find it highly attractive, just as women and children are attracted by the sight of colourful variety.'

'Yes, a great many would,' he said.

d   'It's a good place to look for a constitution, Adeimantus, as well,' I said.

'Why?'

'Because it's so open that it contains every type of political system there is. For anyone wanting to construct a community, as we were a short while ago, a visit to a democratically governed community is essential, to help him choose the kind he likes. It's a sort of general store for political systems: you can visit it, make your choice, and then found your community.'

e   'Yes, I suppose it would be easy to find samples,' he said.

'You're not forced to hold political office in this kind of community,' I said, 'even if you'd be good at it; you're not forced to be a subject either, unless you want to. You don't have to go to war when there's a war on, or to keep the peace when everyone else is, if peace isn't to your liking. Then again, even if you're legally forbidden to play a part in governmental or judicial procedures, you can still do 558a both, if you feel like it. Isn't this an extraordinarily pleasant way to spend one's life, in the short term?'

'Yes, probably,' he said, 'but not in the long term'

'And what about the exquisite calmness of some condemned criminals? I'm sure it's within your experience of this kind of society how people who've been sentenced to death or exile still stay on and go about their daily business in full view of everyone. No one cares or notices as they roam around, as invisible as the dead.'

'Yes, this is not uncommon,' he said.

'One could hardly call this system's attitude to- b wards the principles we took seriously when we were founding our community pendantic—"flexible" and "high-handed" would be more accurate. We said that no one could be good (short of having been born with really exceptional talents), unless even his childhood games had taken place within a good environment and his way of life had been the same. This political system, however, arrogantly spurns all of that, and doesn't care what kinds of provenance people had before coming to government; as long as someone claims to be sympathetic to the general populace, he is honoured within this political sys- c tem.'

'A very vulgar way of going about things,' he commented.

'So these are democracy's features—these and others like them,' I said. 'It looks as though it's an enjoyable, lax, and variegated kind of political system, which treats everyone as equal, whether or not they are.'

'Yes, this is all perfectly familiar,' he said.

'Now, what do you think the corresponding private individual is like?' I asked. 'I suppose we'd better start by considering his background, as we did in the case of the political system.'

'Yes,' he said.

'Here's my idea. Any son born to that mean, oligarchic character would, I imagine, be brought up by his father to behave in the same way.'   d

'Naturally.'

'So he too would forcibly control his desires for

any pleasures which involve spending money rather than making it—that is, for the pleasures which have been classified as unnecessary.'

'Obviously he would,' he agreed.

'Shall we start by defining what we mean by necessary and unnecessary desires, then?' I asked. 'We don't want our conversation to be shrouded in obscurity.'

'Yes, let's,' he replied.

'Wouldn't it be right to describe as necessary any e desires which we're incapable of stopping, and any whose satisfaction is beneficial to us? I mean, both these categories of desire are essential to human nature, wouldn't you say?'

'Definitely.'

559a   'We'd be right to think of them in terms of necessity, then.'

'Yes.'

'What about desires which can be dispensed with (given training from childhood onwards) and whose presence certainly does not good, and may even do harm? Wouldn't we be right to call them unnecessary?'

'Yes, we would.'

'Shall we find an example of each type, so that we can get a rough idea of their nature?'

'We'd better.'

'Don't you think the desire for eating (provided it doesn't go beyond what's required for a healthy b physical condition), the desire simply for bread and savouries, is a necessary one?'

'Yes, I do.'

'In fact, the desire for bread is necessary in both senses: it's beneficial, and it's impossible for a living creature to stop it.'

'Yes.'

'Whereas the desire for savouries is necessary only as an aid towards physical fitness.'

'Yes.'

'What about the desire for more food than this, however, or for a varied diet? It can usually be eliminated by the habit of restraint, learnt young in life, and it's harmful to both the body and the mind (in c the context of intelligence and self-discipline), so we wouldn't be wrong to call it unnecessary, would we?'

'No, that would be perfectly correct.'

'Shall we say that unnecessary desires involve spending money, while necessary desires help one work and therefore make money?'

'Of course.'

'And doesn't the same principle apply to the desire for sex, and desire in general?'

'Yes.'

'So, to put this in the context of a distinction we drew earlier, the type of person we've been calling a drone is overflowing with these pleasures and desires, and is ruled by the unnecessary ones, whereas the mean, oligarchic type is ruled by the necessary d ones. Right?'

'No doubt about it.'

'Let's return, then, to the transition from the oligarchic type to the democratic one,' I said. 'It seems to me that it invariably happens as follows.'

'How?'

'When a young person, whose upbringing has been as uncultured and mean as we were saying a short while ago, tastes the drones' honey and starts to associate with ferocious, dangerous beasts who are capable of arranging for him pleasures of every conceivable kind, form, and description—that, I suggest, is how the transition begins from an internal e oligarchic state to a democratic one.'

'It's almost inevitable,' he said.

'Now, we found that the transition occurs at a political level when one party is helped by like-minded reinforcements from outside. In the same way, doesn't our young man change when one of his aspects is supported from outside by desires of the same persuasion and breed?'

'Absolutely.'

'And if his oligarchic aspect is reinforced in response to this threat, as a result of his being scolded and ticked off by his father or by the rest of his relatives, I should think the upshot would be conflict 560a and counter-conflict, an internal civil war.'

'Of course it would.'

'Sometimes, I imagine, the democratic aspect is routed by the oligarchic aspect, and some of his desires are killed or expelled. This happens when inhibitions are implanted in the young man's mind, and he puts his life in order again.'

'Yes, that sometimes happens,' he said.

'Then later, I suppose, the father's ignorance of how to bring up his child leads to other desires, of the same breed as the exiled ones, growing up and b becoming plentiful and powerful.'

'Yes, that tends to happen,' he said.

'They draw him back to his old associates, and these secret liaisons result in the birth of a horde of them.'

'Of course.'

'In the end, I suppose, they seize the fortress in the young man's mind and find it deserted: it holds no information of value, no sound habits and true ideas—none of the sentinels and guardians which best protect the minds of men who find favour in God's sight.'

c 'Yes, they are by far the best,' he agreed.

'So false and specious ideas and thoughts charge up the hill and occupy the young man's fortress instead of these sentinels.'

'I'm sure you're right,' he said.

'Then he returns to those lotus-eaters and lives with them openly. If his relatives send reinforcements for the mean part of his mind, those specious ideas shut the gates of the royal fortress within him. Not only do they not let these reinforcements in, but they also refuse to accept any mediation by older d people from outside the family. Once they've won the war, they denounce inhibition as simple-mindedness, deprive it of rights, and send it out into exile; they call self-control "cowardice", drag its name in the gutter, and then expel it; they perpetuate the view that moderation shows lack of style and that frugality is stinginess, and then, with the help of a horde of futile desires, they banish them beyond their borders.'

'They certainly do.'

'Once they've taken over the mind of the neo- e phyte, and purged and purified it for the great mysteries, they next waste no time before recalling from exile insubordination, disorder, extravagance, and uninhibitedness. They parade them in glory, with chaplets on their heads and with a full complement of attendants. They sing the praises of these qualities and gloss over their true nature: they call insubordination "erudition", disorder "freedom", extravagance "magnificence", and uninhibitedness 561a "courage". Isn't this', I asked, 'more or less how a young person exchanges conditioning by necessary desires for the permissiveness and laxity of unnecessary, futile pleasures?'

'Yes, you've explained it very well,' he said.

'From then on, I imagine, he spends as much money, effort, and time in his life on unnecessary pleasures as on necessary ones. With luck, how- b ever—and if he doesn't overdo the high life—and if, when he's older and the main disturbance has passed, he allows the exiles back to some extent and doesn't succumb utterly to the invaders, then he finds a way of life which involves a balance of pleasures. He submits to every passing pleasure as its turn comes to hold office, as it were, until it has been satisfied, and then submits to the next one, and so on. He doesn't deprive any pleasure of its rights, but tends all of them equally.'

'Yes.'

'And', I continued, 'he refuses to listen to—to let into his fortress—the truth of the idea that there are differences between pleasures. Some are the result c of fine, good desires, and these are worth cultivating and valuing; but some are the result of bad desires, and these are to be curbed and kept down. He denies this, however, and insists that they are all alike and of equal value.'

'Yes, I quite agree,' he said. 'That's his attitude, and that's what he does.'

'So that's how he lives,' I said. 'He indulges in every passing desire that each day brings. One day he gets drunk at a party, the next day he's sipping water and trying to lose weight; then again, he sometimes takes exercise, sometimes takes things easy d without a care in the world, and sometimes he's apparently a student of philosophy. At frequent intervals, he gets involved in community affairs, and his public speaking and other duties keep him leaping around here, there, and everywhere. If military types arouse his admiration, he inclines towards the military life; if it's businessmen, he's all for business. His lifestyle has no rhyme or reason, but he thinks it enjoyable, free, and enviable and he never dispenses with it.'

'You've given a perfect description of an egali- e tarian,' he said.

'Yes,' I said, 'and I think he's also multi-hued and multi-faceted, as gorgeous and varied a patchwork as that community is. His way of life can be admired by many men and women, because he contains examples of so many political systems, and walks of life.'

'Yes, he does,' he agreed.

'I suggest, then, that we designate this type of in- 562a dividual the counterpart to democracy and assume that we'd be correct to call him the democratic type.'

'I agree,' he said.

After democracy, dictatorship. If democracy is the idle indulgence and satisfaction of every kind of pleasure, the dictatorial type is driven by insatiable, base pleasures alone. He is so extreme that he cannot be equated with one of the three divisions of the mind: he is a criminal, beyond social castes. The three layers of Plato's imaginary community find a vague reflection in the fact that a democratic society consists of wealthy people, demagogues, and the general populace. The demagogues side with the people, so it is basically a case of rich versus poor—and again there is no unity. The poor find themselves a champion, who acquires a taste for power and gradually becomes an autocratic, bloodthirsty dictator, who is surrounded by a bodyguard of ex-slaves and mercenaries, loathed by anyone with any goodness, and whose subjects can only be described as slaves.

'All that's left for us to do, then,' I said, 'is describe the political system and the individual which are the ultimate in excellence—dictatorship and the dictator.'

'Exactly,' he said.

'All right, then. How does dictatorship begin, Adeimantus? I mean, apart from the fact that we can be pretty certain that it evolves out of democracy.'

'Yes, that's clear.'

'I wonder whether dictatorship evolves out of b democracy in more or less the same way that democracy evolves out of oligarchy.'

'How is that?'

'There is something', I said, 'which the members of an oligarchy have come to accept as good, and which is the *raison d'être* of oligarchy. This is wealth, isn't it?'

'Yes.'

'And it is insatiable greed for wealth—being too busy making money to pay attention to anything else—which causes its downfall, we found.'

'True,' he said.

'So what I'm wondering is whether democracy's downfall is also brought about by insatiable greed for what it defines as good.'

'What's that, do you think?'

'Freedom,' I replied. 'I'm sure you've been in a community with a democratic government and heard them claim that there is nothing finer than freedom, c and that this is why democracy is the only suitable environment for a free man.'

'Yes, one hears the claim repeatedly,' he said.

'So, to complete the question I was about to ask a moment ago,' I said, 'is it insatiable greed for freedom and neglect of everything else which causes this political system to change and creates the need for dictatorship?'

'How would it do that?' he asked.

'In its thirst for freedom, a democratically governed community might get leaders who aren't any d good at serving wine. It gets drunk on excessive

quantities of undiluted freedom, and then, I suppose, unless the rulers are very lenient and keep it provided with plenty of freedom, it accuses them of being foul oligarchs and punishes them.'

'Yes,' he agreed, 'that's what it does.'

'Then those who obey authority have abuse heaped on them,' I said, 'and are described as voluntary slaves, nonentities; admiration and respect are given to people who, in both their private life and in public, behave like subjects if they're rulers, and behave like rulers if they're subjects. Isn't it inevitable that a community of this kind will take free- e dom as far as it can go?'

'Of course.'

'Equally inevitably, my friend,' I said, 'lawlessness seeps into everyone's homes; ultimately, even animals are infected.'

'Can you explain this for us?' he asked.

'For instance,' I said, 'the pursuit of freedom makes it increasingly normal for fathers and sons to swap places: fathers are afraid of their sons, and sons no longer feel shame before their parents or stand in awe of them. And it starts to make no difference whether one is a citizen or a resident alien, or even a visitor from abroad: everyone is at the same level.' 563a

'Yes, that happens,' he said.

'Those are the most important cases,' I said, 'but there are others. In these circumstances, for example, teachers are afraid of their pupils and curry favour with them, while pupils despise their teachers and their attendants as well. In short, the younger generation starts to look like the older generation, and they turn any conversation or action into a trial of strength with their elders; meanwhile, the older members of the community adapt themselves to the younger ones, ooze frivolity and charm, and model their behaviour on that of the young, because they b don't want to be thought disagreeable tyrants.'

'Right,' he said.

'The peak of popular freedom for this community is reached', I continued, 'when male and female slaves have as much freedom as the people who bought them. And I almost forgot to mention the extent to which men and women meet as autonomous equals.'

'Why don't we just do what Aeschylus suggests,' c he said, 'when he asks, "Shall we voice what we were poised to say?" '

'All right,' I said. 'This is what I have to say. If you hadn't seen it, you'd never believe how much more freedom pets have in this community com-

pared with any other. The dogs really do start to resemble their mistresses, as the proverb says, but so
do horses and donkeys as well, in the way they learn
to strut about with absolute freedom, bumping into
anyone they meet on the road who doesn't get out
of the way. And everything else is just as saturated
d with freedom.'

'You're telling me my own dream,' he said. 'I often experience just that on my way out of town.'

'Taking all this into consideration,' I said, 'the
long and short of it is that the minds of the citizens
of a democracy become so sensitive that they get
angry and annoyed at the slightest hint of enslavement. Do you know what I mean? And they're so
worried about the possibility of anyone having authority over them that they end up, as I'm sure you're
e aware, taking no notice of the laws either, whether
written or unwritten.'

'Yes, I'm well aware of that,' he said.

'So there, I think,' I said, 'you have the fine, vigorous shoot from which dictatorship grows.'

'No one could deny its vigour,' he said. 'But
what's the next stage?'

'The same sickness that infected oligarchy and
caused its demise', I said, 'erupts in democracy too,
but in a more widespread and virulent form, because
of its openness, and reduces it to slavery. In fact, it's
a general principle that overdoing anything leads to
a huge compensatory shift towards the opposite: seasons, plants, and bodily health are all subjects to this
564a principle, and political systems are particularly good
examples of it.'

'That sounds plausible,' he said.

'In other words, it's plausible to claim that excessive freedom, at both the individual and the political level, can only change into excessive slavery.'

'Exactly.'

'It makes sense, then,' I continued, 'to say that
dictatorship is bound to arise out of democracy—
from what, I take it, is the peak of freedom to the
most severe and savage form of slavery.'

'Yes, it does,' he agreed.

'But what wasn't the point of your question, I
think,' I said. 'You wanted to know what the sick-
b ness is which proliferates in a democracy as well as
in an oligarchy, and reduces it to slavery.'

'That's right,' he said.

'Well,' I said, 'I've already mentioned that breed
of lazy, extravagant people and how they're divided
into leaders or followers, depending on the degree
to which they possess courage. They're the ones we

said were like drones—the leaders with stings, the
followers stingless.'

'Yes, that's right,' he said.

'Well, the presence of these two kinds of drone,'
I said, 'throws any political system into chaos, as
phlegm and bile do in the case of the body. The ability to look a long way ahead and take precautions
against them is a sign of a good doctor and legislator, just as much as it is a sign of a skilful beekeeper. c
Ideally, they should try to prevent their birth; but if
they're already been born, they should try to eradicate them as quickly as possible, cells and all.'

'Yes, you're absolutely right,' he said.

'Now, we'll never be in a position to make the assessment we want without a clear enough view,' I
said. 'Here's a move that'll help.'

'What move?'

'Let's assume that there are three distinct components to a democratically governed community—
as in fact there are. First, its openness allows the
drone element to develop within it, and in this re- d
spect it resembles an oligarchy.'

'True.'

'But this element is far more vigorous in a democracy than an oligarchy.'

'Why?'

'In an oligarchy it isn't given any respect and is
excluded from political office, so it never gets a
chance to flex its muscles and become strong. In almost all democracies, however, it is the leading element: its most vigorous members make speeches
and do things, while the rest settle in a buzzing
swarm around the rostra and prevent anyone presenting alternative points of view, and consequently e
the government of a democratic community is almost entirely in the hands of this element.'

'Yes, indeed,' he said.

'Now, the second element is constantly being
propagated by the inhabitants.'

'What is it?'

'Although everyone is trying to make money, it's
invariably the most disciplined people who do best
financially.'

'That's likely.'

'They're a rich source of honey for the drones, I
should think: it's very easy for them to siphon it off
from there.'

'Well, it's hardly possible to siphon it from the
have-nots,' he remarked.

'And this element, the drones' fodder, is called
the moneyed class.'

'That sounds about right,' he said.

565a 'The third element would be the general populace—the smallholders, who don't spend all their time on politics and don't have a great deal of property. They form the largest section of the population, and when they gather in one spot they are the most authoritative group in a democracy.'

'True,' he said. 'But they tend not to gather very often, unless there's honey to be gained.'

'And they always get it,' I said. 'Those champions of theirs do their very best to rob the rich and distribute the trivial amounts they don't keep for themselves to the general populace.'

b 'Yes, that's how they get their honey,' he said.

'Their victims are forced to defend themselves, I suppose, by making speeches to the people and acting wherever possible.'

'Of course.'

'And then they're accused by the democratic leaders of plotting against the people and of being oligarchs, even if revolution is the last thing on their minds.'

'Of course.'

'Ultimately, when they realize that the populace at large is out to wrong them, not because it really wants to, but because in its ignorance it's been misled by the lies and slanders of their opponents,
c then—and only then—they do in fact willy-nilly become oligarchs. It's not that they really want to, but the drones' stings inject this poison into their systems as well, to grow inside them.'

'That's undeniable.'

'And the result is that the two sides turn to arraignments, lawsuits, and trials about each other's conduct.'

'Yes.'

'And aren't the people always given to setting up a particular individual as their special champion, who under their caring nurture grows to a prodigious size?'

'Yes, they do tend to do that.'

d 'It's clear, then,' I said, 'that this champion is the only possible root from which any dictatorial shoot that appears is bound to have grown.'

'Perfectly clear.'

'So what makes a champion change into a dictator? Isn't it obviously when a champion starts to behave in the same way as what the stories tell us happens to people in the sanctuary of Zeus Lycaeus in Arcadia?'

'What's that?' he asked.

'That anyone who tastes even a single morsel of human entrails mixed in among those of other sacrificial offerings is bound to become a wolf. Haven't e you heard this story?'

'Yes, I have.'

'Doesn't the same thing happen to a champion of the people? Suppose the masses are more or less totally under his thumb and he feels no compunction about shedding the blood of a fellow citizen; suppose he trumps up the usual charges against someone, takes him to court, and murders him, thereby eliminating a human life; suppose on his tongue and in his unholy mouth is the taste of the blood of a kinsman, and he turns to demanding banishment and 566a death, and to hinting at the cancellation of debts and the reassignment of land. Isn't it unalterably inevitable that this man will next either be assassinated by his enemies or change into a wolf instead of a human being—that is, become a dictator?'

'It's absolutely inevitable,' he agreed.

'And he's the one who stirs up conflict against the propertied class.'

'Yes.'

'Now, he might be exiled and return to his home country in spite of his enemies. If so, then he comes back as a complete dictator, doesn't he?'

'Obviously.'

'Alternatively, his enemies might not be able to b arouse enough hostility against him to have him exiled or executed, so they start to try to find a secret way to assassinate him.'

'Yes, that's the usual course of events,' he said.

'And then, at this stage, every dictator comes up with the notorious and typical demand: he asks the people for bodyguards to protect him, the people's defender.'

'Yes,' he agreed.

'And because they're afraid for his safety, and at the same time optimistic about their own future, they give him his bodyguards, I'm sure.'

'That's right.'   c

'This is when anyone wealthy, whose wealth has made him suspected of being opposed to democracy, acts in accordance with the oracle given to Croesus and "flees beside the pebbly Hermus without delay and without worrying about cowardice".'

'Yes, because he won't get a second chance to worry,' he said.

'And if he's caught, he'll be put to death,' I added.

'Inevitably.'

'Now, that champion obviously doesn't "lie

d sprawled in his vastness over a vast area", but topples numerous others and stands firm on the chariot of the state, a complete dictator now, instead of a champion.'

'That's bound to be the case,' he said.

'How happy do you think he is?' I asked. 'And how happy is the community which contains a creature of this sort? Shall we talk about this?'

'Yes, let's,' he said.

'In the early days,' I said, 'in the first period of his supremacy, he greets everyone he meets with a smile. He claims not to be a dictator, makes a lot of promises to his close associates and in his public e speeches, rescinds debts, gives land to the people and to his supporters, and poses as an altogether amiable and gentle person, doesn't he?'

'Inevitably,' he said.

'Meanwhile he is, I imagine, settling his differences with some of his exiled enemies, and killing others. Once that threat is a thing of the past, he turns to provoking warfare, so as to keep the people in need of a leader.'

'Yes, that's likely.'

'And also, wouldn't you say, so as to tax them 567a and make them poor, so that they're forced to concentrate on their daily business and have less time to plot against him?'

'Obviously.'

'And also, I think, to find a plausible way of killing people he suspects of entertaining notions of freedom, and of consequently being likely to resist his authority: he simply makes sure that the enemy get their hands on them. Don't you agree? All of these reasons guarantee that a dictator must constantly be provoking wars, mustn't he?'

'He has to.'

'Now, these actions of his will probably be reb sented by the citizens of his community, won't they?'

'Of course they will.'

'And some—they'll have to be the bravest—of those who helped him on his way and who are in positions of power will speak their minds to him, as well as to one another, and will criticize what's going on, won't they?'

'I should think so.'

'So a dictator has to eliminate the lot of them— or else relinquish power—until there's no one of any value left among either his friends or his enemies.'

'Obviously.'

'He has to keep a sharp eye out, then, for anyone with courage, self-confidence, intelligence, or wealth. He has no choice in the matter: he's bound c to treat them as enemies and to intrigue against them, until he's purged the community of them. That's the nature of his happy state.'

'A fine purge that is,' he remarked.

'Yes,' I said, 'and quite different from a medical purge of the body. Doctors remove the worst and leave the best; he does the opposite.'

'He has to, if he's to retain power, apparently,' he said.

'He's caught in an enviable dilemma, then,' I said, d 'which requires him to choose between sharing his life with people who are, on the whole, second-rate, and who hate him, or not living at all.'

'That's right,' he said.

'Now, the greater the resentment felt by the citizens of his community at his conduct, the larger and more reliable his bodyguard will have to be, won't it?'

'Of course.'

'Well, who can he rely on? Where will he get his soldiers from?'

'Swarms of them will wing their way to him as if by magic,' he said, 'if he offers them the payment they want.'

'You wouldn't be talking about drones, by any chance, would you?' I asked. 'Drones of all differ- e ent shapes and sizes from abroad?'

'You've understood me perfectly,' he said.

'But who can he rely on from his own community? Do you think he'd. . . ?'

'What?'

'. . . steal slaves from his citizens, emancipate them, and include them among his bodyguard?'

'He undoubtedly would,' he replied. 'He could surely rely on them more than anyone else.'

'Dictatorship is certainly an enviable thing, then,' I said. 'Look at the friends he has and the people he 568a can depend on, once he's killed all his previous associates.'

'Yes, well, that is the kind of person he keeps company with,' he said.

'These companions of his, these newly created citizens, form his circle of admiring friends, while decent people avoid him like the plague, don't they?'

'Of course they do.'

'It's not surprising', I said, 'that tragedy in general is thought to be a clever affair and Euripides is taken to be the most outstanding tragic playwright.'

'Why?'

'Because with his penetrating mind he's already
b expressed this idea: "Dictators are clever because of
the clever company they keep," he says. He was obviously referring to the clever people we've been
saying form a dictator's circle.'

'He also eulogizes dictatorship in a number of
ways,' he added, 'by calling it "godlike", for instance. And he's joined in this by all the other poets.'

'And it's precisely because tragic poets are
clever', I said, 'that they'll forgive us (and others
with a similar political system) for refusing to allow
them into our society, on the grounds that they sing
the praises of dictatorship.'

c 'I expect the gifted ones will forgive us, anyway,'
he said.

'They can tour around other communities instead,
where they'll attract huge audiences and use the
beauty, carrying-power, and persuasiveness of the
voices of the actors they hire to convert them to dictatorship or democracy.'

'Yes.'

'And that's not all. They'll be paid and acclaimed
for doing this. They'll get the most from dictatorships, and somewhat less from democracies; and
then the higher up our scale of political systems they
d go, the more the acclaim will die away, as if it were
short of breath and unable to continue.'

'Yes.'

'But we digress,' I said. 'We'd better return to
that army which a dictator possesses, in all its splendour, size, variety, and inconstancy, and discuss how
he'll maintain it.'

'He'll obviously use up any wealth the community's temples have,' he said, 'whenever his victims'
money runs out, so that he won't have to tax the
people too much.'

e 'What about when there's no longer enough in the
temples?'

'He and all the men and women who hobnob with
him will obviously be maintained by his father's
wealth,' he said.

'I see,' I said. 'You're implying that the general
populace, which is the dictator's father, will keep
him and his companions.'

'They'll have little choice in the matter,' he said.

'What do you mean?' I said. 'Suppose the people
get annoyed with him and tell him it's wrong for a
son in his prime to be kept by a father, and that, on
the contrary, the son should be keeping the father;
569a suppose they tell him that the purpose of their giv-

ing him life and power was not for them to be dominated, now that he's grown up, by their own slaves
and for them to support him and their slaves and all
the rest of the riff-raff, but so that he could be their
champion in freeing them from the dominion of the
rich and the so-called gentlemen of their community; suppose they now behave like a father throwing his son out of the home, along with his free-
loading friends, and they order him to leave the
community, and to take his companions with him.
What would happen then, do you think?'

'Then it'll certainly take hardly any time for the
people to find out what sort of creature they've fa- b
thered, cared for, and nurtured to maturity,' he said.
'And they'll soon see that the people they're trying
to expel are the stronger party.'

'What?' I exclaimed. 'Do you mean that the dictator will be unscrupulous enough to lay hands on
his father—to respond to a difference of opinion
with physical violence?'

'Yes,' he said, 'once he's deprived his father of
his weapons.'

'In other words,' I said, 'a dictator is guilty of the
crime of father-beating, and is no comfort to his father in his old age. This, it turns out, is what dictatorship is and would be acknowledged to be. And,
as the saying goes, the people would escape the
smoke of being the slaves of free men only to fall
into the fire of having slaves as their masters. They c
exchange considerable, and even excessive, freedom
for the worst and harshest kind of enslavement—enslavement to slaves.'

'Yes, this is exactly what happens,' he agreed.

'In that case,' I said, 'it would be reasonable for
us to claim that we've done enough to explain how
dictatorship evolves out of democracy, and what it's
like as a fully fledged entity. Yes?'

'Yes, we've certainly done enough,' he said.

'All there is left for us to do', I said, 'is study an 571a
actual dictatorial person, to try to see how he evolves
out of the democratic type, what he's like once he
does exist, and whether his life is happy or unhappy.'

'Yes, that's right,' he said.

'Well, there's still a deficiency to remedy, I think,'
I said.

'What?'

'I don't think we've finished distinguishing the
various kinds of desires or finding out how many
different kinds there are. And as long as this job remains unfinished, our enquiry will be veiled in ob- b
scurity.'

'But it's not too late, is it?' he asked.

'No. The thing about them I want to have out in the open is that some of the unnecessary pleasures and desires strike me as lawless. We probably all contain these pleasures and desires, but they can be kept under control by convention and by the co-operation of reason and the better desires. Some people, in fact, control them so well that they get rid of them altogether or leave only a few of them in a weakened state, but they remain stronger and more c numerous in others.'

'What pleasures and desires are you thinking of?' he asked.

'The ones that wake up while we're asleep,' I replied. 'When all the rest of the mind—the rational, regulated, controlling part—is asleep, then if the wild, unruly part is glutted with food or drink, it springs up and longs to banish sleep and go and satisfy its own instincts. I'm sure you're aware of how in these circumstances nothing is too outrageous: a person acts as if he were totally lacking in moral principle and unhampered by intelligence. In his dreams, he doesn't stop at trying to have sex with his mother and with d anyone or anything else—man, beast, or god; he's ready to slaughter anything; there's nothing he wouldn't eat. In short, he doesn't hold back from anything, however bizarre or disgusting.'

'You're quite right,' he said.

'On the other hand, I imagine, when someone who's self-disciplined and who keeps himself healthy goes to sleep, he's made sure that his rational mind is awake and has eaten its fill of fine ideas and arguments, which he's brought to an agreed conclusion within himself. Since he hasn't either starved or over-indulged his desirous part, it can settle down e to sleep and not bother the best part of him with its feelings of pleasure or pain, and consequently the 572a best part is free to get on with the enquiries it carries out all by itself, when it is secluded and untarnished by anything else, and to try to fulfil its impulse for perceiving something in the past or present or future that it doesn't know. He's also calmed down his passionate part and doesn't go to bed in an emotionally disturbed state because he's been angry with someone. In other words, he's quietened down two aspects of himself, but woken up the third—the one in which intelligence resides—and that's how he takes his rest; and, as you know, in this state he can maximize his contact with the truth and minimize the lawlessness of the visions he sees b in his dreams.'

'I'm sure you're absolutely right,' he said.

'Now, we've wandered rather far from the main course of the argument, but the point I'm trying to get across is this: every one of us—even someone who seems very restrained—contains desires which are terrible, wild, and lawless, and this category of desire becomes manifest during sleep. Do you agree? Do you think I have a point?'

'Yes, I do agree.'

'Well, remember the nature of the democratic man, as we described him: his formative childhood c upbringing was by a skinflint of a father who valued only desires which helped him make money, and despised all the unnecessary ones with their frivolity and frippery, wasn't it?'

'Yes.'

'But then he fell in with a more elegant crowd, consisting of people who indulge in the desires we've just been describing, and his dislike of his father's meanness drove him to all kinds of outrageous behaviour, and to modelling himself on them. However, he was essentially better than these corrupters of his, and since he was being pulled in both directions, he found between the two ways of life a com- d promise in which he drew on each of them to a reasonable extent, in his opinion, and lived a life which wasn't miserly, but at the same time wasn't lawless either. And that's how he made the transition from being oligarchic to being democratic.'

'Yes, that's what we thought earlier, and it still seems valid,' he said.

'Now imagine', I said, 'that our democratic type has grown older and has a son who's been brought up, in his turn, in his father's ways.'

'All right.'

'And imagine that the same thing happens to him as happened to his father: he's attracted by complete lawlessness (although the people who are advertising it to him call it complete freedom), his father e and his family in general reinforce the desires he settled on as a compromise, and others reinforce his lawless side. When these black magicians, these creators of dictators, realize that there's only one way they're going to gain control of the young man, they arrange matters until they implant in him a particular lust, to champion the rest of his desires which are too idle to do more than share out anything that readily comes their way. And don't you think this 573a kind of lust is exactly like a great, winged drone?'

'Yes, that seems to me to be a perfect description of it,' he said.

'Then the rest of the desires buzz in a swarm around their champion, reeking of incense and perfumes, laden with garlands, overflowing with wine, and offering all the indulgent pleasures that go with that kind of social life. Under their caring nurture, he grows to his fullest extent and gains a sting whose poison is unfulfilled longing. This inner champion now takes frenzy for his bodyguard and runs amok. b If he finds that the person contains any apparently good beliefs or desires which still cause him to feel shame, he kills them and banishes them, until he's purged the person of self-discipline and imported frenzy in its place.'

'That's a perfect description of a dictatorial type's evolution,' he said.

'And isn't this also the kind of reason why lust is traditionally called a dictator?' I asked.

'I suppose so,' he said.

'Now, there's something dictatorial about a drunken person's arrogance too, isn't there, c Adeimantus?' I asked.

'Yes, there is.'

'And people who are insane and mentally disturbed try to dominate the gods, let alone other human beings, and expect to be able to do so.'

'Yes,' he agreed.

'So strictly speaking, Adeimantus,' I said, 'the dictatorial type is the result of someone's nature or conditioning—or both—making him a drunken, lustful maniac.'

'Absolutely.'

'So that's how the dictatorial type evolves, apparently. Now, what's his life like?'

d   'At the risk of sounding like a tease,' he said, 'it's you who'll have to tell me.'

'All right,' I said. 'I think he proceeds to give himself over to feasting and revelry, parties and prostitutes, and all the activities which typically indicate that the dictator lust has taken up residence within a person and is in complete control of his mind.'

'Yes, that's bound to happen,' he agreed.

'Every day and every night, terrible desires with prodigious appetites branch out in large numbers from the main stem, don't they?'

'Yes, they do.'

'So his income is soon exhausted.'

'Of course.'

e   'And then he starts borrowing and working his way through is estate.'

'Naturally.'

'And when there's nothing left, his young brood of desires is bound to clamour long and loud. He's driven by the stinging swarm of his desires (and especially by lust, the captain of the bodyguard the others form) to run amok—to see if there's anyone he can steal anything from by deceit or by force. 574a Yes?'

'Definitely,' he said.

'He has no choice: he can either filch from every available source, or be racked with agonizing pains.'

'Agreed.'

'Now, every passing pleasant sensation he feels takes precedence over the ones which are in the past and steals from them, so by the same token he expects to take precedence over his parents, despite being younger than them, and to steal from them, in the sense of appropriating his father's property once he's exhausted his own. Yes?'

'Of course,' he agreed.

'And if his parents refused to hand it over to him, b he'd initially resort to obtaining money from them on false pretences, wouldn't he?'

'Absolutely.'

'And if that didn't work, he'd turn to robbery with violence?'

'I think so,' he said.

'If his elderly parents resisted and fought back, Adeimantus, do you think he'd be circumspect and hesitant about doing anything dictatorial?'

'No, I don't hold out much hope for the parents of someone like this,' he said.

'Would he really beat up his mother, who's cared for him for years, Adeimantus, and whom he could never have lived without, for the sake of his latest dispensable girlfriend, whom he's just fallen in love with? Would he really beat up his aged, indispens- c able father, who may not be much to look at any more, but whose affection has lasted for so many years, for the sake of his latest alluring, but dispensable, boyfriend? Would he honestly let his parents be dominated by them, if he had them all living together in the same house?'

'Yes, he certainly would,' he said.

'What a happy thing it is, then,' I exclaimed, 'to be the parent of a dictator!'

'That's right,' he agreed.

'What happens when there's none of his parents' d property left, but a large number of pleasures have gathered together in a swarm within him? Won't he first turn his hand to a bit of burglary or to mugging travellers late at night, and then try emptying out a temple? At the same time a gang of beliefs which

had until recently been suppressed, but now form lust's bodyguard, come to his assistance to enable him to overpower all the views about good and bad behaviour he'd been brought up to hold and which he'd assumed to comprise morality. This gang consists of attitudes which had formerly—during the period when there was still a democratic government within him, and he was still subject to the laws and
e to his father—broken free only at night, while he was asleep. Once he's under the dictatorship of lust, however, his constant waking state is one that was formerly rare and restricted to dreams: there's no form of murder, however vile, that he isn't willing to commit; there's nothing he won't eat, no deed he isn't ready to perform. Lust lives within him like a
575a dictator, with no regard for law and convention. It uses its absolute power to influence the person in whom it lives, as an autocrat influences his community, to stop at nothing as long as the result is the perpetuation of itself and the pandemonium it generates. Some of this pandemonium is the result of bad company, and has therefore been introduced from outside; the rest is the result of the person's own practice of the same bad habits, and so has been released and set free internally. Don't you think this is how he lives?'

'Yes,' he said.

'Now, if people of this kind form a small propor-
b tion of a community's population, while the rest are self-disciplined,' I said, 'then they leave and serve in the bodyguard of a dictator somewhere else, or as mercenaries in some war or other. But if they occur in a time of peace and stability, they stay in their community and commit lots of trivial crimes.'

'What sort of crimes do you mean?'

'They're thieves, burglars, pickpockets, muggers, temple-robbers, kidnappers; if they have any ability at public speaking, they might be sycophants, and they're the kind of people who commit perjury in court and take bribes.'
c 'Yes, these are trivial crimes, as long as there aren't many people committing them,' he said.

'Anything trivial is only trivial in comparison with something important,' I went on, 'and all these crimes are (as the saying goes) well wide of the mark of dictatorship in the effect they have on how rotten and unhappy a community is. In fact, it's when these people and their followers start to form a significant proportion of a community's population, and realize how many there are of them, that they—assisted by the folly of the people—become

the ones to whom the dictator we discussed owes his origin: he is simply whichever one of them has the greatest and most thriving dictator in his own mind.'
d
'Yes, that's likely,' he agreed. 'Dictatorship would come most naturally to him.'

'There's no problem if they're happy to defer to him, but if the community refuses to submit, then, if he can, it'll be his fatherland's turn for the same punishment he inflicted on his mother and father before. He'll bring new friends in from abroad and, for all her long-standing care, he'll make sure that his motherland (as the Cretans call their country) and fatherland are kept and maintained—in a state of enslavement to these new friends of his. After all, that's how the desire of this sort of person is fulfilled.'

'Yes, it is, absolutely,' he said.
e
'Now, don't people of this sort behave like dictators in their private lives even before they gain political power?' I asked. 'Take their relationships with others, for instance. They either go about with people who flatter them and are ready to carry out their every whim, or they're deferential themselves, if they want something from someone. As long as 576a that's the case, there's nothing they wouldn't do to make him believe they're his friends, but once they've got what they want, they're distant again.'

'Definitely.'

'They never have any friends, then, throughout their lives: they can only be masters or slaves. Dictatorial people can never experience freedom and true friendship.'

'No.'

'We couldn't exactly call them reliable, could we?'

'Of course not.'

'And, assuming that our earlier conclusions about the nature of morality were correct, we'd have to say that there's no one more immoral than them.' b

'Well, our earlier conclusions *are* right,' he said.

'In short, then,' I said, 'the worst type of person is one whose waking life resembles the dreams we discussed.'

'Yes.'

'He's the product of absolute power falling into the hands of an inherently dictatorial person, and the longer he spends as a dictator, the worse he becomes.'

'Glaucon took over the job of talking with me, and said, 'Yes, that's bound to happen.'

CHAPTER 12
HAPPINESS AND UNHAPPINESS

Plato now declares himself to be in a position to adjudicate the relative happiness or unhappiness of the five types of individuals. As usual, he starts by looking at the equivalent communities. Happiness is circumscribed by a number of properties—freedom, lack of need, lack of fear—and it is concluded that a community ruled by a dictator, and a dictatorial person (especially if he becomes an actual dictator), are in the most miserable condition. On the weak basis of the fact that in the previous chapter the five types were presented as a series of degenerations, with the dictator at the bottom, the happiness and unhappiness of the five types are now ranked according to the order of degeneration.

576c   'Now,' I continued, 'won't we find that the worst person is also the unhappiest person? And won't we find—whatever most people think—that it's the most enduring and thorough dictator who has the most enduring and thorough unhappiness?'

'Yes,' he said, 'that's inevitable.'

'Now, isn't it the case', I asked, 'that a dictatorial person is the counterpart of a community which is ruled by a dictator, and a democratic person corresponds to a community with a democratic government, and so on for the rest?'

d   'Of course.'

'So we can compare the state of goodness and the happiness of one type of community with another and apply the results to their corresponding human types, can we?'

'Of course.'

'How does the state of goodness of a community which is ruled by a dictator compare, then, with that of the one we described first, with its kings?'

'They're at opposite ends of the scale,' he answered. 'One is the best type of community, the other is the worst.'

'I don't need to ask which is which,' I said, 'because it's obvious. But now what about their happiness and unhappiness? Would you come up with the same estimate, or a different one? We shouldn't be rushed into a decision by our impressions of just one person, the dictator himself, or by the few people who constitute his immediate circle. We should visit
e the community and see all the sights, immerse ourselves thoroughly in it and look everywhere, and then express an opinion.'

'That's a good suggestion,' he said. 'And everyone would see that a community under a dictator is as unhappy as any community can be, while a community under kingship is the happiest one possible.'

'And suppose I were to make the same suggestion as regards their human equivalents too,' I said. 'Would that be a good suggestion? I'd be expecting 577a someone to come up with his assessment of their happiness and unhappiness only if he has the ability to gain insights into a person by using his mind to take on that person's characteristics. Rather than childishly looking from the outside and being won over by the ostentatious façade a dictator presents to the outside world, he should be capable of insight. Suppose we found someone who's not only this good at assessment, but who has also lived in close proximity with a dictator, and has been an eyewitness to what goes on inside a dictator's house and how he treats the various members of his household, because these are the best circumstances for seeing a dictator stripped of his pompous clothing; and sup- b pose he'd also seen how a dictator reacts to the risks involved in political life. Would I be right to claim that we should all listen to what this person has to say? Should we ask him to draw on all this firsthand experience to tell us how a dictator fares, as regards happiness and unhappiness, compared with our other types?'

'Yes, that would be a very good idea as well,' he said.

'Shall we pretend, then', I said, 'that *we* are expert assessors, and have in the past met dictators? Otherwise, there'll be no one to answer our questions for us.'

'Yes, let's.'

'All right, then,' I said, 'here's how you'd better c proceed with the enquiry. You should bear in mind the equivalence between community and individual and submit them one after another to a detailed examination; then you'll be in a position to describe the attributes either or both of them have.'

'What attributes?' he asked.

'Starting with a community,' I said, 'do you think a community which is ruled by a dictator is free or oppressed?'

'It's impossible to imagine a more complete state of oppression,' he replied.

'But some of its members are evidently free and are doing the oppressing.'

'Yes,' he said, 'but they're the minority. Wretched servitude, with no civil rights, is pretty much the universal condition of the citizen body—certainly of the truly good elements.'

d 'Given the correspondence between individual and community,' I said, 'then isn't his structure necessarily identical? Oppression and servitude must pervade his mind, with the truly good parts of it being oppressed, and an evil, crazed minority doing the oppressing.'

'Necessarily,' he agreed.

'Well, do you think a mind in this condition is free or enslaved?'

'Enslaved, I'd say—definitely.'

'Then again, a community which is enslaved and ruled by a dictator is hardly ever free to do what it wants, is it?'

'I quite agree.'

e 'What about a mind which is ruled by an inner dictator, then? Treating the mind as a single whole, it'll hardly ever be free to do what it wants, will it? It'll constantly be subject to the overpowering whims of its lust, and this will make it highly inconsistent and fickle.'

'Of course.'

'And would a community under a dictator be poor or well off?'

'Poor.'

578a 'So a person with a dictatorial mind is bound to be in a constant state of poverty and need.'

'Yes,' he agreed.

'Now, isn't fear ever-present in communities and individuals of this sort?'

'It certainly is.'

'Is there any other community, do you think, where you'd come across more moaning, complaining, grievances, and hardships?'

'No, definitely not.'

'Would you come across more of them in any other type of individual, do you think? Or has the limit been reached with this dictatorial type and the frenzy caused by his desires and lusts?'

'Of course it has,' he said.

'I imagine all this was the kind of evidence which b led you to conclude that the community is as unhappy as any community can be.'

'Do you disagree?' he asked.

'Not at all,' I replied. 'But what does the same evidence lead you to think about a dictatorial person?'

'That he is far unhappier than any of the other types,' he answered.

'Now you've made a claim I *do* disagree with,' I said.

'Why?' he asked.

'I don't think he's that outstandingly unhappy,' I said.

'Who is, then?'

'I should think you'd agree that here's an even more miserable person than the one we've been discussing.'

'Who?'

'A dictatorial person who can't remain a private c citizen all his life,' I said, 'but has the misfortune to end up, by force of circumstance, as an actual dictator.'

'If I'm to be consistent with our earlier argument,' he said, 'I have to admit that you're right.'

'Yes,' I said, 'but it's important for us not to rely on assumptions in these sorts of cases. We're looking into the most important issue there is—which kind of life is good, and which is bad—so we must conduct a really thorough investigation, and I think I see how to proceed.'

'You're quite right,' he said.

'Well, I wonder what you'll make of my idea that we should start the investigation by bearing in mind the following points.'   d

'Which ones?'

'Every single wealthy citizen in a community owns a lot of slaves. In this respect—that they have a number of people under their control—they resemble dictators; the only difference is that dictators control larger numbers of people.'

'That's right.'

'Well, do you appreciate that these slave-owners aren't in a state of fear? They aren't afraid of their slaves, are they?'

'What reason would they have to be?'

'None,' I answered. 'But do you realize shy?'

'Yes. It's because behind every single citizen is the community as a whole.'

'Exactly,' I said. 'Now, imagine that a man who e owns fifty or more slaves is plucked by some god from his community—wife, children, and all—and deposited in some isolated spot along with all his property, especially his slaves. There are no other free men around to help him. Would he be afraid of his slaves killing him and his family? And if so, how frightened do you think he'd be?'

'He'd be absolutely terrified, I expect,' he replied.

'What he'd have to do, then, despite their being 579a his slaves, is immediately get on the right side of some of them, make them extravagant promises, and given them their freedom, whatever misgivings he may have. In fact, he'd end up being dependent on the goodwill of his servants, wouldn't he?'

'It's either that or be killed,' he said, 'so he doesn't really have a choice.'

'And what do you think would happen if this god also surrounded him with a lot of neighbours in nearby settlements, and these neighbours of his couldn't abide anyone presuming to be anyone else's master, and punished with extreme severity any case they came across of this kind of oppression?'

b 'He'd be in an even worse trap,' he said, 'with all those enemies hemming him in on every side.'

'Well, is there any difference between this and the prison a dictator finds himself in, because of all the fears and lusts his nature, as we've described it, makes him liable to? He may be greedy for new experiences, but he's the only person in the community who can't travel abroad or see all the sights every other free man longs to see. Instead, he lives like a woman, buried indoors most of the time, re-

c senting any of his fellow citizens who go abroad and see something worth while.'

'Absolutely,' he said.

'So these are the kinds of troubles which swell the harvest of evils reaped by the individual who, in your recent assessment, is as unhappy as anyone can be— the dictatorial type, whose bad government is restricted to himself—when he can't remain a private citizen all his life, but is forced by some misfortune to take on the government of others, despite his inability to control even himself. This is like someone ill with spastic paralysis being forced to enter the public arena and spend his life competing as an ath-

d lete against others or fighting in wars.'

'That's a perfect analogy, Socrates,' he said. 'You're quite right.'

'There's nothing but misery in a dictator's life, then, is there, Glaucon?' I asked. 'You thought you'd identified the worst life possible, but there's even more hardship in his, isn't there?'

'Definitely,' he said.

'The truth of the matter, then, even if people deny it, is that a real dictator is actually a real slave—judging by the extent of his obsequiousness and servitude—and a flatterer of the worst kinds of people. His desires are completely insatiable as

e well: any expert observer of the totality of the mind can see that a dictator is actually never fulfilled and is therefore poor. Moreover, fear pervades his whole life, and he's convulsed with constant pains. This is what he's like, if his condition resembles

that of the community he rules over—and it does, doesn't it?'

'Yes, it does,' he agreed.

'And we haven't finished with his attributes yet: 580a there are also all the ones we mentioned earlier, which he's not only bound to have, but bound to have even more thoroughly than before because of being in office. He's resentful, unreliable, immoral, friendless, and unjust; and he gives room and board to every vice. And the result of all this is not just the extreme wretchedness of his own condition; these attributes of his also rub off on people who come near him.'

'That's beyond all reasonable doubt,' he said.

'All right, then,' I continued. 'Now is the time for you to play the part of the judge with overall authority and reveal your verdict. Of the five types— b regal, timocratic, oligarchic, democratic, and dictatorial—which comes first, in your opinion, in the contest of happiness? Which comes second? You'd better grade all five of them.'

'It's an easy decision to make,' he said, 'because the order in which they made their entrance, like troupes of dancers on a stage, corresponds to how I rate them. That's my estimate of where they come on the scale of goodness and badness, and of happiness and unhappiness.'

'Shall we hire a town crier, then,' I asked, 'or shall I be the one to proclaim that the son of Ariston has judged the happiest person to be the best and most c moral person—that is, the person who possesses the highest degree of regal qualities and who rules as king over himself? And that he has also judged the unhappiest person to be the worst and most immoral person—that is, the person who possesses the highest degree of dictatorial qualities and rules as completely as possible as a dictator over himself and his community?'

'*You* make the announcement,' he said.

'And can I add a rider that this is so whether or not their condition is hidden from the eyes of god and men?' I asked.

'You can,' he said.

A second proof of the philosopher's happiness proceeds on the basis of the threefold division of the human mind (Chapter 6) and the corresponding types of individual—philosophical, competitive, avaricious. Each enjoys different things, and each claims that what he or she enjoys is best. However, the philosopher's claim is the most authoritative since he has the experience and intelligence to decide the issue.

'All right, then,' I said. 'That's the first proof, but
d I wonder how the second one strikes you.'

'What is it?'

'I think the correspondence between the three
classes into which the community was divided was
divided and the threefold division of everyone's
mind provides the basis for a further argument,' I
said.

'What argument?'

'It seems to me that each of the three mental categories has its own particular pleasure, so that there
are three kinds of pleasure as well. The same would
also go for desires and motivations.'

'What do you mean?' he said.

'We found that one part is the intellectual part of
a person, another is the passionate part, and the third
has so many manifestations that we couldn't give it
a single label which applied to it and it alone, so we
named it after its most prevalent and powerful aspect: we called it the desirous part, because of the
intensity of our desires for food, drink, sex, and so
on, and we also referred to it as the mercenary part,
because desires of this kind invariably need money
581a for their fulfilment.'

'And we were right,' he said.

'What if we said that what it enjoys, what it cares
for, is profit? This would be the best way for us to
clarify the issue for ourselves: we could keep our
references to this part of the mind concise, and call
it mercenary and avaricious. Would that description
hit the mark?'

'I think so,' he said.

'And isn't our position that the passionate part always has its sights set wholly on power, success,
and fame?'

'Yes.'

b   'So it would be fair for us to call it competitive
and ambitious, wouldn't it?'

'Perfectly fair.'

'And it's patently obvious that our intellectual part
is entirely directed at every moment towards knowing the truth of things, and isn't interested in the
slightest in money and reputation.'

'Certainly.'

'So we'd be right to call it intellectual and philosophical, wouldn't we?'

'Of course.'

'Now, sometimes this intellectual part is the motivating aspect of one's mind; sometimes—as cir-
b cumstances dictate—it's one of the other two. Yes?'

'Yes,' he said.

'Which is why we're also claiming that there are
three basic human types—the philosophical, the
competitive, and the avaricious.'

'Exactly.'

'And it also explains why there are three kinds of
pleasure as well, one for each of the human types,
doesn't it?'

'Yes.'

'Now, I'm sure you're aware', I said, 'that if you
were to approach representatives of these three types
one by one and ask them which of these ways of life
was the most enjoyable, they'd each swear by their
own way of life, wouldn't they? A money-minded d
person wouldn't think that respect or learning, and
their pleasures, were anywhere near as important as
making money, unless there was also a profit to be
made out of them, would he?'

'True,' he said.

'Then again, an ambitious person would regard
enjoyment of money as vulgar,' I continued, 'and
would think that only some concomitant respect
could redeem enjoyment of intellectual activities
from being an impractical waste of time, wouldn't
he?'

'Yes,' he agreed.

'What about a philosopher?' I asked. 'How do you
think he rates other pleasures compared with know- e
ing the truth of things and with constantly employ-
ing his intellect and feeling that kind of pleasure?
Doesn't he think they miss the mark by a long way?
Doesn't he describe them as necessary, in the strict
sense that, apart from intellectual pleasures, he needs
only those which are unavoidable?'

'We can be perfectly certain about that,' he
replied.

'Now, when people are arguing about the various
pleasures which accompany aspects of themselves,'
I said, 'and even about the kind of life one should
lead, and when the only criterion they're using is
where a way of life comes on the scale of pleasure
and distress, rather than on the scales of right and
wrong or good and bad, then how can we know who 582a
has truth on his side?'

'I really couldn't tell you,' he said.

'Well, look at it this way. What does it take to
make a good decision? Doesn't it take experience,
intelligence, and rationality? Aren't these the best
means of reaching a decision?'

'Of course,' he said.

'All right, then. Which of the three men has had
the greatest exposure to all the pleasures we've men-

tioned? Do you think the avaricious type understands the truth of things and has therefore had more b experience of intellectual pleasure than a philosopher has of the pleasure of moneymaking?'

'There's a world of difference,' he replied. 'From his earliest years onward a philosopher has inevitably experienced both the other kinds of pleasure; there's never been any reason, however, for an avaricious person to experience the sweetness of intellectual pleasure and it remains unfamiliar to him—in fact, even if he wanted to get a taste of it, he'd find it difficult.'

'In other words,' I commented, 'a philosopher's experience of both intellectual and moneymaking pleasures puts him in a better position than an avaricious person, anyway.'

c   'A far better position.'

'And how does he compare with an ambitious person? Is he more familiar with the enjoyment of respect than an ambitious person is with the enjoyment of intelligence?'

'But anyone can get respect: it's a result of attaining one's objective,' he said. 'Respect is showered on people for their wealth, their courage, and their intelligence: all three types are familiar with what it's like to enjoy being respected, at any rate. But only a philosopher can have found out by experience what it's like to enjoy contemplating reality.'

d   'As far as experience is concerned, then,' I said, 'it's a philosopher who's in the best position to make a decision.'

'By far the best position,' he agreed.

'And he's the only one who'll be in a position to combine experience and intelligence.'

'Naturally.'

'Moreover, the resources for making a decision are available only to a philosopher, not to an avaricious or an ambitious person.'

'What resources?'

'We did say that decisions require rational argumentation, didn't we?'

'Yes.'

'And rational argumentation is a particularly important resource in this context.'

'Of course.'

'Now, if money and wealth were the best means of making decisions, then the likes and dislikes of e the avaricious type would necessarily be closest to the truth.'

'Yes.'

'And if prestige, success, and courage were best, it would be the likes and dislikes of the ambitious, competitive type. Yes?'

'Obviously.'

'But since it takes experience, intelligence and rationality. . . ?'

'Then it's the philosophical type, with his appreciation of rationality, whose tastes are closest to the truth,' he said.

'Of the three kinds of pleasure, the most enjoy- 583a able, then, is that which belongs to the intellectual part of the mind; one's life becomes most enjoyable when this part of the mind is one's motivating force.'

'Of course,' he said. 'I mean, when a thoughtful person recommends his own way of life, he ought to be taken seriously.'

'Which way of life—which pleasure—comes second, in his assessment?'

'Obviously the pleasure which accompanies the military, ambitious life, since it differs less from his own way of life than the moneymaking one does.'

'Apparently, then, the way of life pursued by the avaricious type comes last, in his estimate. Yes?'

'Of course,' he said.

The third proof of the philosopher's happiness is again concerned with pleasure. In a suggestive fashion, Plato distinguishes between true (genuine) pleasures and false (illusory) pleasures. The vast majority of so-called pleasures are actually only relief from pain—a state intermediate between pleasure and pain. Genuine pleasures are pure, unsullied by pain in this way. They are, above all, the pleasures of the mind, since the things of the rational mind, being more real, offer more real or genuine satisfaction. Since only the philosopher is familiar with these mental pleasures, then only he has true pleasure. Since morality is the rule of the rational mind, then a moral life is far happier and more desirable—involves far more true pleasure—than the immoral life of a dictator. In fact, one could say that a philosopher was 729 times happier than a dictator!

'That makes it two, then, one after another: im- b morality has twice been defeated by morality. In Olympic fashion, here's the third round—for Zeus the Saviour and Zeus of Olympus. I wonder whether you agree that only the philosopher's pleasure is true and pure, while the others are illusory; I seem to remember having heard some clever fellow or other expressing this idea. And in fact that would be the most important and serious fall of the whole competition.'

'It certainly would. But what are you getting at?'

'I'll find out, if you'll help my investigation by answering my questions,' I said.

'Go ahead,' he said.

'All right,' I said. 'Pain is the opposite of pleasure, wouldn't you say?'

'Yes.'

'And is there a state which involves no pleasure or pain?'

'Yes, there certainly is.'

'It's an intermediate state in which the mind isn't active in either of these ways, isn't it? What do you think?'

'I agree,' he said.

'Now, can you remember what people say when they're ill?' I asked.

'What?'

'They claim that health really is the most pleasant thing in the world, but that they didn't appreciate the fact until they got ill.'

'Yes, that's familiar,' he said.

'And you're aware that when people are in great pain they say that the most pleasant thing in the world would be for the pain to end.'

'Yes.'

'And you've come across all sorts of other situations, I should think, in which people are feeling pain and claim that there is nothing more pleasant than the remission and absence of pain. It's not pleasure whose praises they sing in these situations.'

'That's because under these circumstances remission does become pleasant and desirable, I suppose,' he remarked.

'And it follows that when someone stops feeling pleasure, the remission of pleasure will be painful.'

'I suppose so,' he said.

'So the intermediate state, as we called it a moment ago—the state of inactivity—will at different times be both pleasure and pain.'

'So it seems.'

'Is it possible for anything to be both of two things if it is neither of those two things?'

'I don't think so.'

'Now, the mental feelings of pleasure and pain are both activities, aren't they?'

'Yes.'

584a 'And didn't we just find that the state which involves no pain or pleasure is actually a state of *in*activity which falls between the two?'

'Yes, we did.

'How can it be right, then, to regard absence of pain as pleasant, or absence of pleasure as painful?'

'It can't be.'

'There's no reality here, then, just some superficial effect,' I said. 'Inactivity merely appears pleasant and painful on those occasions, because it's being contrasted respectively with pain and with pleasure. These appearances aren't reliable in the slightest: they're a kind of deception.'

'Yes, that *is* what the argument suggests,' he said.

'Well, I'd like to show you pleasures which aren't products of pain,' I said. 'I'm worried about the possibility of your currently regarding all pleasure as the cessation of pain, and all pain as the cessation of pleasure, and thinking that this is how things are.'

'Where shall I look?' he asked. 'What pleasures are you talking about?'

'If you'd care to consider the enjoyment of smells,' I replied, 'you'd see particularly clear examples, though there are plenty of other cases too. The point is that there's no preceding feeling of pain, and yet you can suddenly get an incredibly intense pleasure at a scent, which also leaves no distress behind when it's over.'

'That's true,' he said.

'So we'd better resist the notion that pure pleasant pleasure is escape from pain, and pure pain is escape from pleasure.'

'Yes.'

'All the same,' I went on, 'I dare say that most so-called pleasures—the most intense ones, anyway—which reach the mind through the body are of this kind: in some way or other they involve escape from pain.'

'True.'

'And doesn't the same go for anticipatory pleasure and distress, which happen before the event as a result of expectations?'

'Yes.'

'Do you know what they're like—what the best analogy for them is?' I asked.

'What?' he answered.

'You know how things can be high, low, or in between?' I asked.

'Yes.'

'Well, someone moving from the bottom of anything to the middle is bound to get an impression of upward motion, isn't he? And once he's standing at the halfway point and looking down to where he travelled from, then if he hasn't seen the true heights, he's bound to think he's reached the top, isn't he?'

'Yes, I'd certainly have to agree with that,' he said.

'And if he retraced his steps, he'd think—
e rightly—that he was travelling downwards, wouldn't he?' I asked.

'Of course.'

'And all these experiences of his would be due to his ignorance of the true nature of high, middle, and low, wouldn't they?'

'Obviously.'

'So would you think it odd for people who have never experienced truth, and who therefore have unreliable views about a great many subjects, to be in the same position where pleasure, pain, and the intermediate state are concerned? They not only hold
585a the correct opinion that they are feeling pain, and do in fact feel pain, when they move into a state of pain, but they're also certain about the satisfaction and pleasure they fell when they move away from pain and into the intermediate state. But they're being misled: there's no difference between people who've never experienced pleasure comparing pain with absence of pain, and people who've never experienced white comparing black with grey.'

'No, I don't find this at all odd,' he replied. 'In fact, I'd be far more surprised if it didn't happen.'

'Here's something for you to think about,' I said.
b 'Aren't hunger, thirst, and so on states in which the body is lacking something?'

'Naturally.'

'While stupidity and unintelligence are states in which the mind is lacking something?'

'Yes.'

'So food and intelligence are the sources of satisfaction in these cases?'

'Of course.'

'Is it the case that the more real something is, the more it can be a source of true satisfaction? Or is it the less real it is?'

'Obviously it's the more real it is.'

'Well, is reality present in a purer form in things like bread, drink, savouries, and food in general, do you think, or in things like true belief, knowledge, intelligence, and in short in all the things that con-
c stitute goodness? Here's another issue to help you decide. There are objects which never alter, never perish, and are never deceptive, and which are not only like that in themselves, but are found in an environment which is also like that; on the other hand,

there are objects which are constantly altering and are perishable, and which are not only like that in themselves, but are found in an environment which is also like that. Which class of objects, do you think, contains a higher degree of reality.'

'The class of objects which never alter is far superior in this respect,' he replied.

'And isn't the reality of that which never alters just as knowable as it is real?'

'Yes.'

'And just as true?'

'Again, yes.'

'If it were less true, it would be less real as well, wouldn't it?'

'Necessarily.'

'To sum up, then, the kinds of things which tend d to the body are less true and less real than the kinds of things which tend to the mind. Yes?'

'Yes, certainly.'

'And don't you think the same goes for the body, compared to the mind?'

'I do.'

'Is it the case, then, that an object which is satisfied by more real things, and which is itself more real, is more really satisfied than an object which is satisfied by less real things, and which is itself less real?'

'Of course.'

'Therefore, assuming that being satisfied by things which accord with one's nature is pleasant, an object which is really satisfied more (that is, by more real things) would be enabled more really and truly to feel true pleasure, while an object which e comes by less real things would be less truly and steadily satisfied and would come by a less dependable and less true version of pleasure.'

'That's absolutely inevitable,' he agreed.

'It turns out, then, that people to whom intelli- 586a gence and goodness are unfamiliar, whose only interest is self-indulgence and so on, spend their lives moving aimlessly to and fro between the bottom and the halfway point, which is as far as they reach. But they never travel any further towards the true heights: they've never even looked up there, let alone gone there; they aren't really satisfied by anything real; they don't experience steady, pure pleasure. They're no different from cattle: they spend their lives grazing, with their eyes turned down and heads bowed towards the ground and their tables. Food and sex are their only concerns, and their insatiable greed for more and more drives them to kick

and butt one another to death with their horns and
b hoofs of iron, killing one another because they're
seeking satisfaction in unreal things for a part of
themselves which is also unreal—a leaky vessel
they're trying to fill.'

'Socrates,' Glaucon declared, 'you've given an inspired and perfect description of the life most people lead.'

'Isn't it also inevitable that the pleasures they're
involved with are, in fact, combinations of pleasure
and pain, mere effigies of true pleasure? Like those
illusory paintings, the pleasure and pain are vivid
c only because of the contrast between them, and their
intensity is therefore no more than apparent. They
impregnate people with an insane lust for the pleasure they offer, and these fools fight over them, as
the Trojans in Stesichorus' story, out of ignorance
of the truth, fought over the mere apparition of Helen.'

'Yes, something like that's bound to be the case,'
he said.

'What about the passionate part of the mind?
Won't the situation be more or less the same for anyone who brings its desires to a successful conclusion? He's either ambitious, in which case he's motivated by resentment and seeks satisfaction in
status; or he's competitive, in which case he relies
on force and seeks satisfaction in success; or he's
bad-tempered, in which case he resorts to anger and
d seeks satisfaction in an angry outburst. But none of
these involve reason and intelligence.'

'Again, yes, something like that's bound to be the
case,' he said.

'All right, then,' I said. 'Shall we confidently state
that, where avarice and competitiveness are concerned, any desire which succeeds in attaining its
objective will get the truest pleasure available to it
when it is guided by truth, which is to say when it
follows the leadership of knowledge and reason in
its quest for those pleasures to which intelligence di-
e rects it? And shall we add that the pleasures it gets
will also be the ones which are particularly suitable
for it—that is, if suitability and benefit coincide?'

'Well, they do coincide,' he said.

'It follows that when the whole mind accepts the
leadership of the philosophical part, and there's no
internal conflict, then each part can do its own job
and be moral in everything it does, and in particular can enjoy its own pleasures, and thus reap as
587a much benefit and truth from pleasure as is possible
for it.'

'Exactly.'

'When one of the other two parts is in control,
however, it not only fails to attain its own pleasure,
but it also forces the other parts to go after unsuitable, false pleasures.'

'Right,' he agreed.

'Now, the further removed something is from philosophy and reason, the more it'll have an effect of
this kind.'

'Certainly.'

'And aren't things separated from law and order
to the same extent that they're separated from rea- b
son?'

'Obviously.'

'And didn't we find that it's the lustful, dictatorial desires which are the furthest removed from law
and order?'

'We certainly did.'

'While the regal, restrained desires are closest to
them?'

'Yes.'

'The more of a dictator a person is, then, the
greater the distance between him and pleasure which
is both true and suitable; the more of a king a person is, the shorter the distance.'

'Necessarily.'

'It follows that there is no life less enjoyable than
a dictator's, and no life more enjoyable than a
king's.'

'No doubt about it.'

'Do you know, in fact, how much less enjoyable
a dictator's life is than a king's?' I asked.

'No. Please tell me,' he replied.

'There are three kinds of pleasure, apparently, and
one of them is genuine, while two are spurious. A
dictator, in his flight from law and reason, crosses c
over into the land beyond the spurious pleasures and
settles down with his bodyguard of slavish pleasures.
Perhaps the best way to describe the extent of his
degeneration, which isn't all that easy to describe,
is as follows.'

'How?' he asked.

'The dictator occupies the third place in the series
which starts with the oligarchic type, since the democratic type comes in between them.'

'Yes.'

'So the pleasure he beds down with is also, assuming the truth of our earlier conclusions, a reflection three places away from oligarchic pleasure.
Yes?'

'Yes.'

'Moreover, counting from the regal type (and assuming that aristocracy and kingship belong to the d same category), it's the oligarchic type's turn to come third.'

'Yes.'

'It follows', I said, 'that a dictator's distance from true pleasure is, in numerical terms, triple a triple.'

'I suppose so.

'So it appears', I said, 'that the reflection which constitutes a dictator's pleasure is a plane number based on the quantity of the linear number.'

'Yes, definitely.'

'And the extent of the distance can be expressed as a square and a cube.'

'It can be a mathematician, anyway,' he said.

'So suppose you wanted to put it the other way e round and state how far a king is from a dictator in terms of the truth of pleasure, the completed multiplication would show that his life is 729 times more pleasant than a dictator's. And a dictator is that much more wretched than a king.'

'You've had to spout some complex mathemat- 588a ics,' he remarked, 'to describe the difference, in terms of pleasure and distress, between the two men—the moral one and the immoral one.'

'Yes, but I'm right,' I said, 'and it's a number which suits lives, assuming that days, nights, months, and years are related to lives.'

'Well, they certainly are,' he said.

'Now, if this is how decisive a victory a good, moral person wins over a bad, immoral one on the field of pleasure, just think how infinitely more resounding his victory will be on the field of elegance and propriety of life, and of goodness.'

'Yes, that's absolutely right,' he said.

Plato concludes that he has responded to the challenge of Chapter 2: he has demonstrated that morality is intrinsically rewarding and desirable. He rounds this off with a graphic image of the tripartite mind as consisting of three creatures: a human being (reason), a lion (passion), and a mutable monster (desire). Morality feeds the human being, tames the lion, and subdues the monster; immorality—especially if it goes undiscovered—makes one a monster. Self-discipline (as a result of the educational programme of Chapters 4 and 10) is best, but the externally imposed discipline of law and convention is a good second best. One must use the imaginary community as a paradigm on which to model one's own inner constitution.

'All right,' I said. 'At this point in the argument, let's remind ourselves of the original assertion which b started us off on our journey here. Wasn't it someone saying that immorality was rewarding if you were a consummate criminal who gave an impression of morality? Wasn't that the asssertion?'

'Yes, it was.'

'Well, now that we've decided what effect moral and immoral conduct have,' I said, 'we can engage him in conversation.'

'What shall we say?' he asked.   c

'Let's construct a theoretical model of the mind, to help him see what kind of idea he's come up with.'

'What sort of model?' he asked.

'Something along the lines of those creatures who throng the ancient myths,' I said, 'like the Chimera, Scylla, Cerberus, and so on, whose form is a composite of the features of more than one creature.'

'Yes, that's how they're described,' he said.

'Make a model, then, of a creature with a single— if varied and many-headed—form, arrayed all around with the heads of both wild and tame animals, and possessing the ability to change over to a different set of heads and to generate all these new bits from its own body.'

'That would take some skilful modelling,' he remarked, 'but since words are a more plastic mater- d ial than wax and so on, you may consider the model constructed.'

'A lion and a man are the next two models to make, then. The first of the models, however, is to be by far the largest, and the second the second largest.'

'That's an easier job,' he said. 'It's done.'

'Now join the three of them together until they become one, as it were.'

'All right,' he said.

'And for the final coat, give them the external appearance of a single entity. Make them look like a person, so that anyone incapable of seeing what's inside, who can see only the external husk, will see e a single creature, a human being.'

'It's done,' he said.

'Now, we'd better respond to the idea that this person gains from doing wrong, and loses from doing right, by pointing out to its proponent that this is tantamount to saying that we're rewarded if we indulge and strengthen the many-sided beast and the lion with all its aspects, but starve and weaken the 589a man, until he's subject to the whims of the others, and can't promote familiarity and compatibility between the other two, but lets them bite each other, fight, and try to eat each other.'

'Yes. that's undoubtedly what a supporter of immorality would have to say,' he agreed.

'So the alternative position, that morality is profitable, is equivalent to saying that our words and be-
b haviour should be designed to maximize the control the inner man has within us, and should enable him to secure the help of the leonine quality and then tend to the many-headed beast as a farmer tends to his crops—by nurturing and cultivating its tame aspects, and by stopping the wild ones growing. Then he can ensure that they're all compatible with one another, and with himself, and can look after them all equally, without favouritism.'

'Yes, that's exactly what a supporter of morality has to say,' he agreed.

'Whichever way you look at it, then, a supporter
c of morality is telling the truth, and a supporter of immorality is wrong. Whether your criterion is pleasure, reputation, or benefit, a supporter of morality is right, and a critic of morality is unreliable and doesn't know what he's talking about.'

'I quite agree: he doesn't in the slightest,' he said.

'But he doesn't mean to make a mistake, so let's be gentle with him. Here's a question we can ask him, to try to win him over: "My friend, don't you think that this is also what accounts for conventional standards of what is and is not acceptable? Things are acceptable when they subject the bestial aspects
d of our nature to the human—or it might be more accurate to say the divine—part of ourselves, but they're objectionable when they cause the oppression of our tame side under the savage side." Will he agree, do you think?'

'Well, I'll be recommending him to,' he answered.

'So what follows from this argument? Can there be any profit in the immoral acquisition of money, if this entails the enslavement of the best part of one-
e self to the worst part? The point is, if there's no profit in someone selling his son or daughter into slavery—slavery under savage and evil men—for even a great deal of money, then what happens if he cruelly enslaves the most divine part of himself to the vilest, most godless part? Isn't unhappiness the result? Isn't the deadly business he's being paid for
590a far more terrible than what Eriphyle did when she accepted the necklace as the price for her husband's death?'

'Yes, by a long way,' Glaucon said. 'I mean, I'll answer on behalf of our supporter of immorality.'

'Now, do you think the reason for the traditional condemnation of licentiousness is the same—because it allows that fiend, that huge and many-faceted creature, greater freedom than it should have?'

'Obviously,' he said.

'And aren't obstinacy and bad temper considered bad because they distend and invigorate our leonine, serpentine side to a disproportionate extent?'   b

'Yes.'

'Whereas a spoilt, soft way of life is considered bad because it makes this part of us so slack and loose that it's incapable of facing hardship?'

'Of course.'

'And why are lack of independence and autonomy despised? Isn't it still to do with the passionate part, because we have to subordinate it to the unruly beast and, from our earliest years, get the lion used to being insulted and to becoming a monkey instead of a lion—and all for the sake of money and to satisfy our greed?'

'Yes.'   c

'What about mundane, manual labour? Why do you think it has a bad name? Isn't it precisely because there's an inherent weakness in the truly good part of the person which makes him incapable of controlling his internal beasts, so that all he does is pander to them, and all he can learn is their whims?'

'I suppose that's right,' he said.

'The question is, how can a person in this condition become subject to the kind of rulership which is available to a truly good person? By being the slave, we suggest, of a truly good person, whose divine element rules within him. But we're not sug-
d gesting, as Thrasymachus did about subjects, that his status as a subject should do him harm; we're saying that subjection to the principle of divine intelligence is to everyone's advantage. It's best if this principle is part of a person's own nature, but if it isn't, it can be imposed from outside, to foster as much unanimity and compatibility between us as might be possible when we're all governed by the same principle.'

'You're right,' he said.

'It's also clear', I continued, 'that this is the func- e
tion of law: this is why every member of a community has the law to fall back on. And it explains why we keep children under control and don't allow them their freedom until we've formed a government within them, as we would in a community. What we do is use what is best in ourselves to cultivate the

591a equivalent aspect of a child, and then we let him go free once the equivalent part within him has been established as his guardian and ruler.'

'Yes, that's clear,' he said.

'Is there any conceivable argument, then, Glaucon, which will enable us to claim that immorality or licentiousness is rewarding, when the result of any kind of shameful behaviour may be a richer or otherwise more powerful person, but is certainly a worse person?'

'No, there isn't,' he replied.

'And how can it be profitable for a person's imb morality to go unnoticed and unpunished? The consequence of a criminal getting away with his crimes is that he becomes a worse person. If he's found out and punished, however, then his bestial side is tamed and pacified, his tame side is liberated, and in short his mental state becomes as good as it can be. And, in so far as the mind is a more valuable asset than the body, it's more important for the mind to acquire self-discipline, morality, and intelligence than it is for the body to become fit, attractive, and healthy.'

'You're absolutely right,' he said.

'Then anyone with any sense will put all his enc ergies, throughout his life, into achieving this goal. In the first place, he'll value only those intellectual pursuits which have the effect we've described on the mind, and regard any others as trivial, won't he?'

'Obviously,' he said.

'In the second place,' I went on, 'there's more to his attitude towards the care and condition of his body than simply the fact that he won't give himself over to bestial and irrational pleasure and make that the whole point of his life. He won't, in fact, be interested in physical health and he won't take the pursuit of physical fitness, health, and beauty serid ously unless they also lead to self-discipline. We'll find him, throughout his life, attuning his body in order to make music with his mind.'

'Yes, that's exactly what it takes to be a true virtuoso,' he said.

'And won't the same attunement and harmony guide his acquisition of money? He's hardly going to be swayed by the usual standards of happiness and amass an inexhaustible pile of money, along with its inexhaustible troubles, is he?'

'I don't think so,' he said.

'What he'll do, however,' I said, 'is keep an eye e on his own inner society and watch out for trouble brewing among its members, caused by his having either too much or too little property. He'll stick to

this guiding principle as much as possible, and increase and decrease his assets accordingly.'

'Exactly,' he agreed.

'And the same consideration will also guide his 592a attitude towards honours. He won't hesitate to accept and experience those which will, in his view, make him a better person, but in his private life as well as in public life he'll avoid those which he thinks would cause the downfall of his established constitution.'

'If that's what's important to him,' he said, 'he's unlikely to have anything to do with government.'

'Actually,' I said, 'he certainly will, in his own community. But I agree that he probably won't in the country of his birth, short of divine intervention.'

'I see,' he said. 'You mean that he will in the community we've just been founding and describing, which can't be accommodated anywhere in the world, and therefore rests at the level of ideas.'

'It may be, however,' I replied, 'that it is retained b in heaven as a paradigm for those who desire to see it and, through seeing it, to return from exile. In fact, it doesn't make the slightest bit of difference whether it exists or will exist anywhere: it's still the only community in whose government he could play a part.'

'Yes, I suppose so,' he said.

CHAPTER 13
POETRY AND UNREALITY

Plato now launches his notorious attack on poetry (with painting introduced in a supporting role); the critique is supplementary to that of Chapter 4. The attack begins with the claim that artistic products are two stages removed from reality and truth, and that they represent things as they appear to be, not as they are. It is easy to be a master of representing appearances, since it involves no understanding of any of the things represented, no penetration beyond the surface of things to its function or to whether or not it serves some moral purpose.

'You know,' I said, 'the issue of poetry is the main 595a consideration—among many others—which convinces me that the way we were trying to found our community was along absolutely the right lines.'

'What are you thinking of?' he asked.

'That we flatly refused to admit any representational poetry. I mean, its total unacceptability is even b clearer, in my opinion, now that we've distinguished the different aspects of the mind.'

'How is it clearer?'

'Well, this is just between ourselves: please don't denounce me to the tragic playwrights and all the other representational poets. But it looks as though this whole genre of poetry deforms its audience's minds, unless they have the antidote, which is recognition of what this kind of poetry is actually like.'

'What do you mean? What do you have in mind?' he asked.

'It's fairly clear', I said, 'that all these fine trage-dians trace their lineage back to Homer: they're Homer's students and disciples, ultimately. And this c makes it difficult for me to say what I have to say, because I've had a kind of fascinated admiration for Homer ever since I was young. Still, we should value truth more than we value any person, so, as I say, I'd better speak out.'

'Yes,' he said.

'And you'll listen to what I have to say, or rather respond to any questions I ask?'

'Yes. Go ahead and ask them.'

'Can you tell me what representation basically is? You see, I don't quite understand its point myself.'

'And I suppose I do!' he said.

'It wouldn't surprise me if you did,' I said. 'Just because a person can't see very well, it doesn't mean 596a that he won't often see things before people with better eyesight than him.'

'That's true,' he said. 'All the same, I'd be too shy to explain any views I did have in front of you, so please try to come up with an answer yourself.'

'All right. Shall we get the enquiry going by draw-ing on familiar ideas? Our usual position is, as you know, that any given plurality of things which have a single name constitutes a single specific type. Is that clear to you?'

'Yes.'

'So now let's take any plurality you want. Would it be all right with you if we said that there were, b for instance, lots of beds and tables?'

'Of course.'

'But these items of furniture comprise only two types—the type of bed and the type of table.'

'Yes.'

'Now, we also invariably claim that the manu-facture of either of these items of furniture involves the craftsman looking to the type and then making the beds or tables (or whatever) which we use. The point is that the type itself is not manufactured by any craftsman. How could it be?'

'It couldn't.'

'There's another kind of craftsman, too. I wonder what you think of him.'

'What kind?'

'He makes everything—all the items which every c single manufacturer makes.'

'He must be extraordinarily gifted.'

'Wait: you haven't heard the half of it yet. It's not just a case of his being able to manufacture all the artefacts there are: every plant too, every creature (himself included), the earth, the heavens, gods, and everything in the heavens and in Hades under the earth—all these are made and created by this one man!'

'He really must be extraordinarily clever,' he said. d

'Don't you believe me?' I asked. 'Tell me, do you doubt that this kind of craftsman could exist under any circumstances, or do you admit the possibility that a person could—in one sense, at least—create all these things? I mean, don't you realize that you yourself could, under certain circumstances, create all these things?'

'What circumstances?' he asked.

'I'm not talking about anything complicated or rare,' I said. 'It doesn't take long to create the cir-cumstances. The quickest method, I suppose, is to get hold of a mirror and carry it around with you e everywhere. You'll soon be creating everything I mentioned a moment ago—the sun and the heavenly bodies, the earth, yourself, and all other creatures, plants, and so on.'

'Yes, but I'd be creating appearances, not actual real things,' he said.

'That's a good point,' I said. 'You've arrived just in time to save the argument. I mean, that's pre-sumably the kind of craftsman a painter is. Yes?'

'Of course.'

'His creations aren't real, according to you; but do you agree that all the same there's a sense in which even a painter creates a bed?'

'Yes,' he said, 'he's another one who creates an apparent bed.'

'What about a joiner who specializes in making 597a beds? Weren't we saying a short while ago that what he makes is a particular bed, not the type, which is (on our view) the real bed?'

'Yes, we were.'

'So if there's no reality to his creation, then it isn't real; it's similar to something real, but it isn't actually real. It looks as though it's wrong to attribute full reality to a joiner's or any artisan's product, doesn't it?'

'Yes,' he said, 'any serious student of this kind of argument would agree with you.'

'It shouldn't surprise us, then, if we find that even these products are obscure when compared with the truth.'

b 'No, it shouldn't.

'Now, what about this representer we're trying to understand? Shall we see if these examples help us?' I asked.

'That's fine by me,' he said.

'Well, we've got these three beds. First, there's the real one, and we'd say, I imagine, that it is the product of divine craftsmanship. I mean, who else could have made it?'

'No one, surely.'

'Then there's the one the joiner makes.'

'Yes,' he said.

'And then there's the one the painter makes. Yes?'

'Yes, agreed.'

'These three, then—painter, joiner, God—are responsible for three different kinds of bed.'

'Yes, that's right.'

'Now, God has produced only that one real bed.
c The restriction to only one might have been his own choice, or it might just be impossible for him to make more than one. But God never has, and never could, create two or more such beds.'

'Why not?' he asked.

'Even if he were to make only two such beds,' I said, 'an extra one would emerge, and both the other two would be of that one's type. It, and not the two beds, would be the real bed.'

'Right,' he said.

'God realized this, I'm sure. He didn't want to be
d a kind of joiner, making a particular bed: he wanted to be a genuine creator and make a genuine bed. That's why he created a single real one.'

'I suppose that's right.'

'Shall we call him its progenitor, then, or something like that?'

'Yes, he deserves the name,' he said, 'since he's the maker of this and every other reality.'

'What about a joiner? Shall we call him a manufacturer of beds?'

'Yes.'

'And shall we also call a painter a manufacturer and maker of beds and so on?'

'No, definitely not.'

'What do you think he does with beds, then?'

'I think the most suitable thing to call him would e be a representer of the others' creations,' he said.

'Well, in that case', I said, 'you're using the term "representer" for someone who deals with things which are, in fact, two generations away from reality, aren't you?'

'Yes,' he said.

'The same goes for tragic playwrights, then, since they're representers: they're two generations away from the throne of truth, and so are all other representers.'

'I suppose so.'

'Well, in the context of what we're now saying about representation, I've got a further question about painters. Is it, in any given instance, the ac- 598a tual reality that they try to represent, or is it the craftsmen's products?'

'The craftsmen's products,' he said.

'Here's another distinction you'd better make: do they try to represent them as they are, or as they appear to be?'

'What do you mean?' he asked.

'I'll tell you. Whether you look at a bed from the side or straight on or whatever, it's still just as much a bed as it ever was, isn't it? I mean, it doesn't actually alter it at all: it just *appears* to be different, doesn't it? And the same goes for anything else you can mention. Yes.'

'Yes,' he agreed. 'It seems different, but isn't actually.'

'So I want you to consider carefully which of b these two alternatives painting is designed for in any and every instance. Is it designed to represent the facts of the real world or appearances? Does it represent appearance or truth?'

'Appearance,' he said.

'It follows that representation and truth are a considerable distance apart, and a representer is capable of making every product there is only because his contact with things is slight and is restricted to how they look. Consider what a painter does, for instance: we're saying that he doesn't have a clue about shoemaking or joinery, but he'll still paint pictures of artisans working at these and all other areas c of expertise, and if he's good at painting he might paint a joiner, have people look at it from far away, and deceive them—if they're children or stupid adults—by making it look as though the joiner were real.'

'Naturally.'

'I think the important thing to bear in mind about cases like this, Glaucon, is that when people tell us they've met someone who's mastered every craft, and is the world's leading expert in absolutely every branch of human knowledge, we should reply that
d they're being rather silly. They seem to have met the kind of illusionist who's expert at representation and, thanks to their own inability to evaluate knowledge, ignorance, and representation, to have been so thoroughly taken in as to believe in his omniscience.'

'You're absolutely right,' he said.

'Now, we'd better investigate tragedy next,' I said, 'and its guru, Homer, because one does come across the claim that there's no area of expertise,
e and nothing relevant to human goodness and badness either—and nothing to do with the gods even—that these poets don't understand. It is said that a good poet must understand the issues he writes about, if his writing is to be successful, and that if he didn't understand them, he wouldn't be able to write about them. So we'd better try to decide between the alternatives. Either the people who come across these representational poets are being taken in and are failing to appreciate, when they see their products, that these products are two steps away
599a from reality and that it certainly doesn't take knowledge of the truth to create them (since what they're creating are appearances, not reality); or this view is valid, and in fact good poets are authorities on the subjects most people are convinced they're good at writing about.'

'Yes, this definitely needs looking into,' he said.

'Well, do you think that anyone who was capable of producing both originals and images would devote his energy to making images, and would make out that this is the best things he's done with his life?'
b 'No, I don't.'

'I'm sure that if he really knew about the things he was copying in his representations, he'd put far more effort into producing real objects than he would into representations, and would try to leave behind a lot of fine products for people to remember him by, and would dedicate himself to being the recipient rather than the bestower of praise.'

'I agree,' he said. 'He'd gain a lot more prestige and do himself a great deal more good.'
c 'Well, let's concentrate our interrogation of Homer (or any other poet you like) on a single area. Let's not ask him whether he can tell us of any patients cured

by any poet in ancient or modern times, as Asclepius cured his patients, or of any students any of them left to continue his work, as Asclepius left his sons. And even these questions grant the possibility that a poet might have had some medical knowledge, instead of merely representing medical terminology. No, let's not bother to ask him about any other areas of expertise either. But we do have a right to ask Homer about the most important and glorious areas he undertakes to expound—warfare, tactics, politics, and human education. Let's ask him, politely, "Homer, maybe you d aren't two steps away from knowing the truth about goodness; maybe you aren't involved in the manufacture of images (which is what we called representation). Perhaps you're actually only one step away, and you do have the ability to recognize which practices—in their private or their public lives—improve people and which ones impair them. But in that case, just as Sparta has its Lycurgus and communities of all different sizes have their various reformers, please tell us which community has you to thank for improvements to its government. Which community attributes the benefits of its good legal code to you? Italy and e Sicily name Charondas in this respect, we Athenians name Solon. Which country names you?" Will he have any reply to make?'

'I don't think so,' said Glaucon. 'Even the Homeridae themselves don't make that claim.'

'Well, does history record that there was any war 600a fought in Homer's time whose success depended on his leadership or advice?'

'No.'

'Well, then, are a lot of ingenious inventions attributed to him, as they are to Thales of Miletus and Anacharsis of Scythia? I mean the kinds of inventions which have practical applications in the arts and crafts and elsewhere. He is, after all, supposed to be good at creating things.'

'No, there's not the slightest hint of that sort of thing.'

'All right, so there's no evidence of his having been a public benefactor, but what about in private? In there any evidence that, during his lifetime, he was a mentor to people, and that they used to value him for his teaching and then handed down to their b successors a particular Homeric way of life? This is what happened to Pythagoras: he wasn't only held in extremely high regard for his teaching during his lifetime, but his successors even now call their way of life Pythagorean and somehow seem to stand out from all other people.'

'No, there's no hint of that sort of thing either,' he said. 'I mean, Homer's associate Creophylus' cultural attainments would turn out to be even more derisory than his name suggests they are, Socrates, if the stories about Homer are true. You see, Creophylus is said to have more or less disregarded c Homer during his lifetime.'

'Yes, that *is* what we're told,' I agreed. 'But, Glaucon, if Homer really had been an educational expert whose products were better people—which is to say, if he had knowledge in this sphere and his abilities were not limited to representation—don't you think he'd have been surrounded by hordes of associates, who would have admired him and valued his company highly? Look at Protagoras of Abdera, Prodicus of Ceos, and all the rest of them: they can use their exclusive tuition to make their contemporaries believe that without them in charge of their education they won't be capable of managing their own estates, let alone their communities, and d they're so appreciated for this expertise of theirs that their associates almost carry them around on their heads. So if Homer or Hesiod had been able to help people's moral development, would their contemporaries have allowed them to go from town to town reciting their poems? Wouldn't they have kept a tighter grip on them than on their money, and tried to force them to stay with them in their homes? And if they couldn't persuade them to do that, wouldn't e they have danced attendance on them wherever they went, until they'd gained as much from their teaching as they could?'

'I don't think anyone could disagree with you, Socrates,' he said.

'So shall we classify all poets, from Homer onwards, as representers of images of goodness (and of everything else which occurs in their poetry), and claim that they don't have any contact with the truth? 601a The facts are as we said a short while ago: a painter creates an illusory shoemaker, when not only does he not understand anything about shoemaking, but his audience doesn't either. They just base their conclusions on the colours and shapes they can see.'

'Yes.'

'And I should think we'll say that the same goes for a poet as well: he uses words and phrases to block in some of the colours of each area of expertise, although all he understands is how to represent things in a way which makes other superficial people, who base their conclusions on the words they can hear, think that he's written a really good poem about

shoemaking or military command or whatever else it is that he's set to metre, rhythm, and music. It only b takes these features to cast this powerful a spell: that's what they're for. But when the poets' work is stripped of its musical hues and expressed in plain words, I think you've seen what kind of impression it gives, so you know what I'm talking about.'

'I do,' he said.

'Isn't it', I asked, 'like what noticeably happens when a young man has alluring features, without actually being goodlooking, and then this charm of his deserts him?'

'Exactly,' he said.

'Now, here's another point to consider. An image-maker, a representer, understands only appearance, while reality is beyond him. Isn't that our po- c sition?'

'Yes.'

'Let's not leave the job half done: let's give this idea the consideration it deserves.'

'Go on,' he said.

'What a painter does, we're saying, is paint a picture of a horse's reins and a bit. Yes?'

'Yes.'

'While they're made by a saddler and a smith, aren't they?'

'Yes.'

'Does a painter know what the reins and the bit have to be like? Surely even their makers, the smith and the saddler, don't know this, do they? Only the horseman does, because he's the one who knows how to make use of them.'

'You're quite right.'

'In fact, won't we claim that it's a general principle?'

'What?'

'That whatever the object, there are three areas of expertise: usage, manufacture, and representation.' d

'Yes.'

'Now, is there any other standard by which one assesses the goodness, fineness, and rightness of anything (whether it's a piece of equipment or a creature or an activity) than the use for which it was made, by man or by nature?'

'No.'

'It's absolutely inevitable, then, that no one knows the ins and outs of any object more than the person who makes use of it. He has to be the one to tell the manufacturer how well or badly the object he's using fares in actual usage. A pipe-player, for example, tells a pipe-maker which of his pipes do what e they're supposed to do when actually played, and goes on to instruct him in what kinds of pipes to make, and the pipe-maker does what he's told.'

'Of course.'

'So as far as good and bad pipes are concerned, it's a knowledgeable person who gives the orders, while the other obeys the orders and does the manufacturing. Right?'

'Yes.'

'Justified confidence, then, is what a pipe-maker has about goodness and badness (as a result of spending time with a knowledgeable person and having to listen to him), while knowledge is the 602a province of the person who makes use of the pipes.'

'Yes.'

'Which of these two categories does our representer belong to? Does he acquire knowledge about whether or not what he's painting is good or right from making use of the object, or does he acquire true belief because of having to spend time with a knowledgeable person and being told what to paint?'

'He doesn't fit either case.'

'As far as goodness and badness are concerned, then, a representer doesn't have either knowledge or true beliefs about whatever it is he's representing.'

'Apparently not.'

'How nicely placed a poetic representer is, then, to know what he's writing about!'

'Not really.'

b   'No, because all the same, despite his ignorance of the good and bad aspects of things, he'll go on representing them. But what he'll be representing, apparently, is whatever appeals to a large, if ignorant, audience.'

'Naturally.'

'Here are the points we seem to have reached a reasonable measure of agreement on, then: a representer knows nothing of value about the things he represents; representation is a kind of game, and shouldn't be taken seriously; and those who compose tragedies in iambic and epic verse are, without exception, outstanding examples of representers.'

'Yes.'

Since poetry deals with appearances, it appeals to—and fattens up—the lower part of the mind, not the rational part. It makes us indulge in emotional feelings which hamper reason, even when we would not normally sanction those feelings. Reason uses measurement to combat some illusory appearances, and calculation of benefit to combat unnecessary feelings. In short, poetry does

nothing to establish an ordered, moral inner constitution, and if one is already established, it threatens to subvert it. Until or unless it can be proven that feelings foster philosophy, rather than hinder it, we must be extremely wary of them.

'So the province of representation is indeed two c steps removed from truth, isn't it?' I said.

'Yes.'

'But on which of the many aspects of a person does it exert its influence?'

'What are you getting at?'

'Something like this. One and the same object appears to vary in size depending on whether we're looking at it from close up or far away.'

'Yes.'

'And the same objects look both bent and straight depending on whether we look at them when they're in water or out of it, and both concave and convex because sight gets misled by colouring. Our mind obviously contains the potential for every single kind of confusion like this. It's because illusory d painting aims at this afflicting in our natures that it can only be described as sorcery; and the same goes for conjuring and all trickery of that sort.'

'True.'

'Now, methods have evolved of combating this—measuring, counting, and weighing are the most elegant of them—and consequently of ending the reign within us of apparent size, number, and weight, and replacing them with something which calculates and measures, or even weighs. Right?'

'Of course.'

'And this, of course, is the job of the rational part e of the mind, which is capable of performing calculations.'

'Yes.'

'Now, it's not uncommon for the mind to have made its measurements, and to be reporting that x is larger than y (or smaller than it, or the same size as it), but still to be receiving an impression which contradicts its measurements of these very objects.'

'Yes.'

'Well, didn't we say that it's impossible for a single thing to hold contradictory beliefs at the same time about the same objects?'

'Yes, we did, and we were right.'

'So the part of the mind whose views run counter 603a to the measurements must be different from the part whose views fall in with the measurements.'

'Yes.'

'But it's the best part of the mind which accepts measurements and calculations.'

'Of course.'

'The part which opposes them, therefore, must be a low-grade part of the mind.'

'Necessarily.'

'Well, all that I've been saying has been intended to bring us to the point where we can agree that not only does painting—or rather representation in general—produce a product which is far from truth, but it also forms a close, warm, affectionate relationship with a part of us which is, in its turn, far from in-b telligence. And nothing healthy or authentic can emerge from this relationship.'

'Absolutely,' he said.

'A low-grade mother like representation, then, and an equally low-grade father produce low-grade children.'

'I suppose that's right.'

'Does this apply only to visual representation,' I asked, 'or to aural representation as well—in other words, to poetry?'

'I suppose it applies to poetry as well,' he said.

'Well, we'd better not rely on mere suppositions based on painting,' I said. 'Let's also get close c enough to that part of the mind which poetic representation consorts with to see whether it's of low or high quality.'

'Yes, we should.'

'We'd better start by having certain ideas out in the open. We'd say that representational poetry represents people doing things, willingly or unwillingly, and afterwards thinking that they've been successful or unsuccessful, and throughout feeling distressed or happy. Have I missed anything out?'

'No, nothing.'

'Well, does a person remain internally unanimous d throughout all this? We found that, in the case of sight, there's conflict and people have contradictory views within themselves at the same time about the same objects. Is it like that when one is doing things too? Is there internal conflict and dissent? But it occurs to me that there's really no need for us to decide where we stand on this issue now, because we've already done so, perfectly adequately, in an earlier phase of the discussion, when we concluded that, at any given moment, our minds are teeming with countless thousands of these kinds of contradictions.'

'That's right,' he said.

'Yes,' I said. 'But that earlier discussion of ours was incomplete, and I think it's crucial that we fin-e ish it off now.'

'What have we left out?' he asked.

'If a good man meets with a misfortune such as losing a son or something else he values very highly, we've already said, as you know, that he'll endure this better than anyone else.'

'Yes.'

'But here's something for us to think about. Will he feel no grief, or is that impossible? If it's impossible, is it just that he somehow keeps his pain within moderate bounds?'

'The second alternative is closer to the truth,' he said.

'But now I've got another question for you about him. Do you think he'll be more likely to fight and 604a resist his distress when his peers can see him, or when he's all alone by himself in some secluded spot?'

'He'll endure pain far better when there are people who can see him, of course,' he said.

'When he's all alone, however, I imagine he won't stop himself expressing a lot of things he'd be ashamed of anyone hearing, and doing a lot of things he'd hate anyone to see him do.'

'That's right,' he agreed.

'Isn't it the case that reason and convention recommend resistance, while the actual event pushes b him towards distress?'

'True.'

'When a person is simultaneously pulled in opposite directions in response to a single object, we're bound to conclude that he has two sides.'

'Of course.'

'One of which is prepared to let convention dictate the proper course of action, isn't it?'

'Can you explain how?'

'Convention tells us, as you know, that it's best to remain as unruffled as possible when disaster strikes and not to get upset, on the grounds that it's never clear whether an incident of this nature is good or bad, that nothing positive is gained by taking it badly, that no aspect of human life is worth bothering about a great deal, and that grief blocks our ac- c cess to the very thing we need to have available as quickly as possible in these circumstances.'

'What do you have in mind?' he asked.

'The ability to think about the incident', I replied, 'and, under the guidance of reason, to make the best possible use of one's situation, as one would in a game of dice when faced with how the dice had fallen. When children bump into things, they clutch the hurt spot and spend time crying; instead of behaving like that, we should constantly be training our minds to waste no time before trying to heal anything which is unwell, and help anything which has fallen get up from the floor—to banish mourning by means of medicine.'

'Yes, that's the best way to deal with misfortune,' he said.

'Now, our position is that the best part of our minds is perfectly happy to be guided by reason like this.'

'That goes without saying.'

'Whereas there's another part of our minds which urges us to remember the bad times and to express our grief, and which is insatiably greedy for tears. What can we say about it? That it's incapable of listening to reason, that it can't face hard work, that it goes hand in hand with being frightened of hardship?'

'Yes, that's right.'

'Now, although the petulant part of us is rich in a variety of representable possibilities, the intelligent and calm side of our characters is pretty well constant and unchanging. This makes it not only difficult to represent, but also difficult to understand when it is represented, particularly when the audience is the kind of motley crowd you find crammed into a theatre, because they're simply not acquainted with the experience that's being represented to them.'

'Absolutely.'

'Evidently, then, a representational poet has nothing to do with this part of the mind: his skill isn't made for its pleasure, because otherwise he'd lose his popular appeal. He's concerned with the petulant and varied side of our characters, because it's easy to represent.'

'Obviously.'

'So we're now in a position to see that we'd be perfectly justified in taking hold of him and placing him in the same category as a painter. He resembles a painter because his creations fall short of truth, and a further point of resemblance is that the part of the mind he communicates with is not the best part, but something else. Now we can see how right we'd be to refuse him admission into any community which is going to respect convention, because now we know which part of the mind he wakes up. He destroys the rational part by feeding and fattening up this other part, and this is equivalent to someone de-

stroying the more civilized members of a community by presenting ruffians with political power. There's no difference, we'll claim, between this and what a representational poet does: at a personal level, he establishes a bad system of government in people's minds by gratifying their irrational side, which can't even recognize what size things are—an object which at one moment it calls big, it might call small the next moment—by creating images, and by being far removed from truth.'

'Yes.'

'However, we haven't yet made the most serious allegation against representational poetry. It has a terrifying capacity for deforming even good people. Only a very few escape.'

'Yes, that *is* terrifying. Does it really do that?'

'Here's my evidence: you can make up your own mind. When Homer or another tragedian represents the grief of one of the heroes, they have him deliver a lengthy speech of lamentation or even have him sing a dirge and beat his breast; and when we listen to all this, even the best of us, as I'm sure you're aware, feels pleasure. We surrender ourselves, let ourselves be carried along, and share the hero's pain; and then we enthuse about the skill of any poet who makes us feel particularly strong feelings.'

'Yes, I'm aware of this, of course.'

'However, you also appreciate that when we're afflicted by trouble in our own lives, then we take pride in the opposite—in our ability to endure pain without being upset. We think that this is manly behaviour, and that only women behave in the way we were sanctioning earlier.'

'I realize that,' he said.

'So,' I said, 'instead of being repulsed by the sight of the kind of person we'd regret and deplore being ourselves, we enjoy the spectacle and sanction it. Is this a proper way to behave?'

'No, it certainly isn't,' he said. 'It's pretty unreasonable, I'd say.'

'I agree,' I said, 'and here's even more evidence.'

'What?'

'Consider this. What a poet satisfies and gratifies on these occasions is an aspect of ourselves which we forcibly restrain when tragedy strikes our own lives—an aspect which hungers after tears and the satisfaction of having cried until one can cry no more, since that is what it is in its nature to want to do. When the part of us which is inherently good has been inadequately trained in habits enjoined by reason, it relaxes its guard over this other part, the b part which feels sad. Other people, not ourselves, are feeling these feelings, we tell ourselves, and it's no disgrace for us to sanction such behaviour and feel sorry for someone who, even while claiming to be good, is over-indulging in grief; and, we think, we are at least profiting from the pleasure, and there's no point in throwing away the pleasure by spurning the whole poem or play. You see, few people have the ability to work out that we ourselves are bound to store the harvest we repeat from others: these occasions feed the feeling of sadness until it is too strong for us easily to restrain it when hardship occurs in our own lives.'

c 'You're absolutely right,' he said.

'And doesn't the same go for humour as well? If there are amusing things which you'd be ashamed to do yourself, but which give you a great deal of pleasure when you see them in a comic representation or hear about them in private company—when you don't find them loathsome and repulsive—then isn't this exactly the same kind of behaviour as we uncovered when talking about feeling sad? There's a part of you which wants to make people laugh, but your reason restrains it, because you're afraid of being thought a vulgar clown. Nevertheless, you let it have its way on those other occasions, and you don't realize that the almost inevitable result of giving it energy in this other context is that you become a comedian in your own life.'

'Yes, that's very true,' he said.

d 'And the same goes for sex, anger, and all the desires and feelings of pleasure and distress which, we're saying, accompany everything we do: poetic representation has the same effect in all these cases too. It irrigates and tends to these things when they should be left to wither, and it makes them our rulers when they should be our subjects, because otherwise we won't live better and happier lives, but quite the opposite.'

'I can't deny the truth of what you're saying,' he said.

e 'Therefore, Glaucon,' I went on, 'when you come across people praising Homer and saying that he is the poet who has educated Greece, that he's a good source for people to learn how to manage their affairs and gain culture in their lives, and that one should structure the whole of one's life in accordance with his precepts, you ought to be kind and 607a considerate: after all, they're doing the best they can. You should concede that Homer is a supreme poet and the original tragedian, but you should also rec-

ognize that the only poems we can admit into our community are hymns to the gods and eulogies of virtuous men. If you admit the entertaining Muse of lyric and epic poetry, then instead of law and the shared acceptance of reason as the best guide, the kings of your community will be pleasure and pain.'

'You're quite right,' he agreed.

'So,' I said, 'since we've been giving poetry another hearing, there's our defence: given its nature, b we had good grounds for banishing it earlier from our community. No rational person could have done any different. However, poetry might accuse us of insensitivity and lack of culture, so we'd better also tell her that there's an ancient quarrel between poetry and philosophy. There are countless pieces of evidence for this enmity between them, but here are just a few: there's that "bitch yelping and baying at her master"; there's "featuring prominently in the idle chatter of fools"; there's "control by a crowd of c know-alls"; there are those whose "subtle notions" lead them to realize that they do indeed have "notional incomes". All the same, we ought to point out that if the kinds of poetry and representation which are designed merely to give pleasure can come up with a rational argument for their inclusion in a well-governed community, we'd be delighted—short of compromising the truth as we see it, which wouldn't be right—to bring them back from exile: after all, we know from our own experience all about their spell. I mean, haven't *you* ever fallen under the spell of poetry, Glaucon, especially when the spectacle is d provided by Homer?'

'I certainly have.'

'Under these circumstances, then, if our allegations met a poetic rebuttal in lyric verse or whatever, would we be justified in letting poetry return?'

'Yes.'

'And I suppose we'd also allow people who champion poetry because they like it, even though they can't compose it, to speak on its behalf in prose, and to try to prove that there's more to poetry than mere pleasure—that it also has a beneficial effect on society and on human life in general. And we won't listen in a hostile frame of mind, because we'll be e the winners if poetry turns out to be beneficial as well as enjoyable.'

'Of course we will,' he agreed.

'And if it doesn't, Glaucon, then we'll do what a lover does when he thinks that a love affair he's involved in is no good for him: he reluctantly detaches himself. Similarly, since we've been conditioned by

608a our wonderful societies until we have a deep-seated love for this kind of poetry, we'll be delighted if there proves to be nothing better and closer to the truth than it. As long as it is incapable of rebutting our allegations, however, then while we listen to poetry we'll be chanting these allegations of ours to ourselves as a precautionary incantation against being caught once more by that childish and pervasive love. Our message will be that the commitment appropriate for an important matter with access to the truth shouldn't be given to this kind of poetry. People should, instead, be worried about the possible effects, on one's own inner political system, of listening to it and should tread cautiously; and they b should let our arguments guide their attitude towards poetry.'

'I couldn't agree more,' he said.

'You see, my dear Glaucon,' I said, 'what's in the balance here is absolutely crucial—far more so than people think. It's whether one becomes a good or a bad person, and consequently has the calibre not to be distracted by prestige, wealth, political power, or even poetry from applying oneself to morality and whatever else goodness involves.'

'Looking back over our discussion,' he said, 'I can only agree with you. And I think anyone else would do the same as well.'

CHAPTER 14
REWARDS NOW AND HEREAFTER

Plato has argued that morality is intrinsically rewarding, in that it is the vital component of individual happiness. He now allows himself to claim that it also brings external advantages: the discussion moves from 'being moral' to 'appearing moral'. The brevity and dogmatism of the claim show that Plato thought this to be by far the less interesting and important part of the response to the challenge formulated in Chapter 2. First, however, to pave the way for the aspect of the claim which depends on the doctrine of reincarnation, we get an unusual (and rather dense) argument for the mind's immortality: everything has a specific affliction which is the only thing that can destroy it; the mind's specific affliction—immorality—cannot destroy it; therefore the mind is indestructible and immortal.

608c   'But, you know,' I said, 'we haven't discussed the most substantial rewards and wages which goodness entails.'

'You mean there's more?' he said. 'They must be stupendous, if they're bigger than the ones we've already talked about.'

'How can anything grow big in a short span of time?' I asked. 'I mean, a complete lifetime, from childhood to old age, is tiny compared with the whole of time.'

'It's nothing at all,' he agreed.

'Well then, don't you think that anything immortal should concern itself with the whole of time, d rather than with such a short extent?'

'Yes, I do,' he said. 'But what are you getting at?'

'Don't you realize that our mind is immortal and never dies?' I asked.

He looked straight at me in surprise and said, 'No, I certainly don't. Are *you* in a position to claim that it is?'

'Certainly,' I said. 'So are you, I'd say. I mean, it's a relatively straightforward subject.'

'Not to me, it isn't,' he replied. 'But I'd be glad to hear what you have to say on this "relatively straightforward subject"!'

'All right,' I said.

'Go on, then,' he said.

'You acknowledge the existence of good and bad, don't you?' I asked.

'Yes.'

'I wonder if your conception of them is the same e as mine.'

'What is that?'

'Badness always manifests in destruction and corruption, while goodness always manifests in preservation and benefit.'

'I agree,' he said.

'Now, would you say that there are things which are good and bad for a given object? For example, ophthalmia is bad for eyes, illness for the body as a 609a whole, blight for corn, rot for wood, rust for bronze and iron I say, nearly every object has some specific thing to afflict it, which is bad for it.'

'I agree,' he said.

'Isn't it the case that whenever one of these objects is afflicted by its affliction, it deteriorates, and ultimately decomposes and perishes?'

'Of course.'

'Therefore, any given object is destroyed by its specific affliction and defect; apart from this, there's nothing else that can destroy it, because goodness is never destructive, and neither is anything which is b intermediate between good and bad.'

'Of course,' he said.

'Suppose that we come across something, then, which is certainly subject to the degenerative action of its defect, but which cannot be decomposed and destroyed by it. Won't we immediately realize that we're faced with something which, by its very nature, is indestructible?'

'I should think we would,' he replied.

'Now, is there anything which makes a mind bad?' I asked.

'Yes, definitely,' he said. 'All the things which have cropped up in the course of our discussion—c immorality, lack of self-control, cowardice, and ignorance.'

'Well, do any of these defects cause it to decompose and perish? Be careful now: we don't want to fall into the trap of thinking that when an immoral person is stupid enough to have his crimes found out, this is an instance of his being destroyed by his mental defect—in this case, by his immorality. No, here's how to proceed. You know how illness, which is a body's defect, wastes and ruins a body, until it is actually annihilated; and you know how all the objects we mentioned a moment ago are brought to a state of annihilation when they're taken over and d afflicted by their specific defect, with its destructive power. Yes?'

'Yes.'

'All right, let's apply the same line of argument to the mind. When immorality (or some other kind of defect) occupies a person's mind, does its presence and occupancy cause his mind to deteriorate and decay, and does it eventually bring his mind to death and cause it to separate from the body?'

'No, it doesn't do that,' he said.

'On the other hand,' I said, 'it doesn't make sense to think that anything could be destroyed by some other object's defect, rather than by its own.'

'No, it doesn't.'

'You see, Glaucon,' I continued, 'I want you to e appreciate that a body does not, in our view, have to be destroyed by some defect or other in its food—staleness or mouldiness or whatever. No, we'll explain any instance of bad food making a body deteriorate by saying that the *cause* of the body's destruction was its specific defect, illness, and that the food was the *reason* it became ill. But since a body and food are quite different from each other, we'd better resist the temptation to say that a body 610a is destroyed by bad food—that is, by something else's defect—unless it engenders the body's specific defect.'

'You're quite right,' he said.

'By the same token,' I went on, 'if a bad physical state can't cause a bad mental state, we'd better not claim that a person's mind is destroyed (unless its own special defect is present) by a defect from elsewhere: that would be an instance of one thing being destroyed by something else's defect.'

'Yes, that makes sense,' he agreed.

'We've got a choice, then. We can either prove this idea of ours wrong, or (in the absence of such proof) we have to say that no fever, no illness of any b kind, and no injury either—not even chopping the whole body up into the tiniest possible pieces—has the slightest destructive effect on the mind. In order for us to accept that it does, someone would have to demonstrate that these physical afflictions cause an increase in immorality and injustice in the mind. But we should refuse to accept the assertion that the mind or anything else is destroyed if its own specific defect doesn't occur, and it's just a case of one c thing providing an environment for something else's defect to occur.'

'But no one will ever prove that death makes a dead person's mind more immoral,' he said.

'Someone might venture to tackle our argument head on, however,' I said, 'and might try to avoid having to concede the mind's immortality by claiming that a dying person degenerates and becomes less moral. In that case, I suppose, if our opponent was right, we'd have to deny our current claim that the *cause* of death for immoral people is other people administering justice, while immorality is the *reason* they do so. Instead, we'd have to claim that immorality is as fatal as a disease for anyone who possesses it; that people who contract it die of it, be- d cause it is in its nature to kill; and that the speed at which it kills them depends on the extent of their immorality!'

'Yes, and if immorality is fatal to its possessor,' he added, 'then it obviously gives him no cause for alarm, since it'll put an end to all his troubles. No, I'm sure we're more likely to find that, on the contrary, immorality kills other people, if it can, not its e possessor. In fact, an immoral person even gains quite a lot of vitality from it, and restless vigour as well. In other words, the impression it gives is that it's found a billet a long way from being fatal.'

'You're right,' I said. 'Now, since we've found that the mind can't be exterminated by its specific defect and destroyed by its specific affliction, it's hardly likely that a defect which is designed for the destruction of something else is going to destroy the mind—or anything else, for that matter, except whatever it's designed for.'

'Yes, that's hardly likely,' he agreed.

'It cannot be destroyed, then, by any defect specific to itself, or any defect specific to anything else. 611a It plainly follows that it must exist for ever. And if it exists for ever, then it is immortal.'

'Yes, inevitably,' he agreed.

'So much for that, then,' I said. 'Now, if this is so, you'll appreciate that there must always be the same minds in existence. None of them can be destroyed, so their number cannot decrease; and it can't increase either, because any additional immortal entity of any kind would have to come, as I'm sure you realize, from a mortal entity, and therefore everything would eventually become immortal.'

'You're right.'

'But that's too implausible an idea for us to believe,' I said. 'And we'll also find it hard to believe b that, in essence, the mind is the kind of thing to be pervaded by internal diversity, inconsistency, and dissension.'

'What do you mean?' he asked.

'That something is unlikely to be immortal if it's a compound, formed imperfectly from diverse parts,' I replied. 'But that's what we found the mind to be not long ago.'

'Yes, that would make immortality improbable.'

'Well, the immorality of the mind would seem to have been conclusively proved by the argument we've just been through, and by our other arguments as well. What we have to do, however, is try to see what the mind is really and truly like, when it's not deformed by its association with the body and with other evils (which is how we've been looking at it so far). We should try to see what it's like when it's c untainted, and we'll have to rely on reason to get a clear enough view of that. You'll find that its beauty is greatly enhanced, and you'll gain far more insight into cases of morality and immorality, and all the qualities we've been discussion. Our current ideas about the mind are true, in so far as they correspond to what we can see of it at the moment; but the condition in which we're observing it is like that of Glaucus the sea-deity. If people were to see Glaucus, it would be hard for them to discern his origi- d nal state any more, because some of the original parts of his body have been knocked off, some have been worn away and generally deformed by the waves, and other things—shells, seaweed, and stones—have grown on him, so that his appearance is quite different from what it used to be, and he looks altogether more like a monster. Similarly, when we look at the mind too, its condition, as we see it, is the result of countless malign influences. What we have to do, Glaucon, is look in a different direction.'

'Where?' he asked.

'We should take note of the fact that it is attracted e towards wisdom, and consider what it is related to and the affiliations it desires, given that it is of the same order as the divine, immortal, and eternal realm. And we should consider what would happen to the mind if the *whole* of it allowed this realm to dictate its direction, and if this impulse carried it out of its current underwater location, and all the stones and shells were broken off—all the accretions of 612a earth and rock (since earth is its food) which currently grow uncontrollably in large numbers all over it because it indulges in the pleasures which men say bring happiness. Then we'd be able to see what it's really like—whether it is manifold or uniform, or what its true nature and condition is. Anyway, I think we've given a reasonable account of what happens to it and the forms it assumes in human life.'

'Definitely,' he said.

A recurrent problem in Greek popular ethics was why immoral people's external affairs often appeared to prosper, while those of moral people suffered. Plato's response here is to insist that a moral person must be in the gods' favour and therefore, even if he does not prosper at first, he will eventually, while an immoral person will sooner or later suffer catastrophe.

'Now,' I said, 'haven't we succeeded in refuting all the charges that were mentioned? In particular, haven't we avoided praising the respects in which b morality is rewarding and enhances a person's reputation, which is what you all said Hesiod and Homer did, and discovered that, when morality and the mind are both taken just in themselves, there's nothing better for the mind than morality, and that a person ought to behave morally whether or not he owns Gyges' ring, and whether or not he owns Hades' helmet as well a magical ring?'

'You're quite right,' he said.

'Surely, then, Glaucon,' I said, 'no one will mind if, as an appendix, we now go on to assign rewards to morality and virtue in general, and describe all the various ways in which men and gods remunerate morality during a person's lifetime and after his death?'

'Of course they won't,' he said.

'Now, you incurred a debt in the course of our discussion. Are you going to pay me back?'

'What debt?'

'I allowed you a moral man with a reputation for immorality, and an immoral man with a reputation for morality, You were asking for this concession to be made, for the sake of argument, because even though it might in fact be impossible for the true state of affairs not to be known by gods and men, you thought it would still help us compare and assess morality and immorality on their own terms. Do
d you remember?'

'Of course I do,' he said.

'Well, our assessment *has* been made,' I said, 'and so I am now, on behalf of morality, asking you for a favour in return: I want us to agree, along with everyone else, that morality does have the reputation it enjoys among gods and men. We've found that actually being moral entails benefits, and that those in whom morality is genuinely present are not gaining a false impression of morality, so if you grant me this favour, morality can also collect the prize for its reputation and gain the benefits it bestows on its possessors.'

'It's a fair request,' he said.

e   'Well, the first idea I want to redeem from you', I said, 'is that the gods don't notice what these two characters are like. All right?'

'Yes, we'll repay that debt,' he said.

'Now, if they're both known to the gods, then the one must be in the gods' favour and the other must be their enemy, as we agreed at the beginning too.'

'True.'

'Now, I'm sure we'll agree that everything the gods have to give will happen, in as beneficial a way
613a as possible, to the person who's in their favour (unless he's already owed some unavoidable harm as a result of a former misdemeanour).'

'Yes.'

'If a moral person appears to be in a bad way, then, we're bound to assume that his poverty or illness or whatever will eventually be good for him, whether this happens during his lifetime or after it. The point is that the gods never neglect anyone who is prepared to devote himself to becoming moral and, by practising virtue, to assimilate himself to
b God as much as is humanly possible.'

'Yes, it doesn't seem likely that he'd be neglected by God, when he resembles him,' he remarked.

'Now, we have to suppose that an immoral person is in the opposite situation, don't we?'

'Definitely.'

'Anyway, these are the kinds of prizes that a moral person would get from the gods.'

'That's what I think, at any rate,' he said.

'What about from men?' I asked. 'In all honesty, isn't it true that clever criminals are exactly like those runners who do well on the way up the track, and then flag on the way back? They spring away at the beginning, but end up being jeered off the track, and have to beat a hasty retreat with their ears c on their shoulders and without winning any chaplets. Genuine runners, however, complete the course and earn themselves rewards as well as chaplets. Isn't that the usual outcome in the case of moral people? Aren't they acclaimed, and rewarded as well, at the end of every activity and transaction they're involved in, and at the end of their lives?'

'Yes, they certainly are.'

'You're not in a position to object if I make the same claims about moral people that *you* made about immoral people, then, are you? I'm going to claim d that moral people can, in later life, have political power in their own communities if they want, can marry women from any families they want, can have their children marry whomever they want, and so on. Everything you said about immoral people I am now claiming applies to moral people. On the other hand, my position as regards immoral people is that, even if they get away with it when they're young, at the end of the race they're found out. Their old age is made miserable by the jeering insults of strangers and countrymen alike; they're flogged and they undergo the punishments you rightly described e as coarse . . . and then they'll be tortured on the rack, and they'll have their eyes burnt out . . . well, you'd better imagine that I've given you the whole list of the torments they suffer. Anyway, as I say, please see if you have any objections to all this.'

'No, I don't,' he said. 'What you're saying is perfectly fair.'

Finally, morality also brings rewards after death. By means of a myth which interweaves traditional and mystical eschatology, and Greek and Near Eastern notions, Plato depicts the horrors of the punishments which await an immoral person in Hades. A moral person avoids these, and can also remain conscious and rational enough to choose his next incarnation with care. Plato also offers a stupendous rationalistic vision of the universe. The myth as a whole emphasizes the orderliness of things, under necessity, and underscores the importance of having order in one's mind, which is morality. There can be no possible grounds for doubting that Plato believed in all the ingredients of the myth: he uses this literary form because he accepts that they are not susceptible of reasoned proof.

614a 'So in addition to the benefits which stem from morality in itself,' I said, 'those are the kinds of prizes and rewards and trophies which a moral person comes by during his lifetime from gods and men.'

'They're wonderful,' he said, 'and well founded.'

'Actually they're nothing,' I said. 'They are few and insubstantial compared with what our two characters will meet after their death. I'd better explain: we owe it to both of them to do so, and if I don't, the debt won't be repaid in full.'

'Please do,' he said. 'There's hardly anything I'd
b rather hear a description of.'

'Well, I'm not going to tell you the kind of saga Alcinous had to endure,' I said. 'Endurance will be my theme, however—that of brave Er the son of Armenius, who was a Pamphylian by birth. Once upon a time, he was killed in battle, and by the time the corpses were collected, ten days later, they had all putrefied except his, which was still in good shape. He was taken home and, twelve days after his death, just as his funeral was about to start and he was lying on the pyre, he came back to life. Then he told people what he'd seen in the other world.

'He said that his soul left his body and went on a journey, with lots of other souls as his companions.
c They came to an awesome place, where they found two openings next to each other in the earth, and two others directly opposite them up in the sky. There were judges sitting between the openings who made their assessment and then told the moral ones to take the right-hand route which went up and through the sky, and gave them tokens to wear on their fronts to show what behaviour they'd been assessed for, but told the immoral ones to take the left-hand, downward route. These people also had tokens, but on their backs, to show all their past deeds.
d When Er approached, however, the judges said that he had to report back to mankind about what goes on there, and they told him to listen and observe everything that happened in the place.

'From where he was, he could see souls leaving, once they'd been judged, by one or the other of the two openings in the sky and in the earth, and he noticed how the other two openings were used too: one was for certain souls, caked in grime and dust, to arise out of the earth, while the other was for other, clean souls to come down out of the sky. They ar- e rived periodically, and he gained the impression that it had taken a long journey for them to get there; they were grateful to turn aside into the meadow and find a place to settle down. The scene resembled a festival. Old acquaintances greeted one another; those who'd come out of the earth asked those from the heavens what had happened to them there, and were asked the same question in return. The tales of the one group were accompanied by groans and 615a tears, as they recalled all the awful things they'd experienced and seen in the course of their underworld journey (which takes a thousand years), while the souls from heaven had only wonderful experiences and incredibly beautiful sights to recount.

'It would take ages to tell you a substantial proportion of their tales, Glaucon, but here's a brief outline of what Er said. Each individual had been punished—for every single crime he'd ever committed, and for every person he'd ever wronged—ten times, which is to say once every hundred years (assum- b ing that the span of human life is a hundred years), to ensure that the penalty he paid was ten times worse than the crime. Take people who had caused a great many deaths, by betraying a country or an army, and people who had enslaved others or been responsible for inflicting misery in some other way: for every single person they had hurt, they received back ten times the amount of pain. Conversely, the same principle applied to the rewards people received for their good deeds, their morality and justice. Things are different, however, for those who die at birth or shortly afterwards, but what he told c me about them isn't worth mentioning. However, he did tell a story about the even greater rewards and penalties for observance and non-observance of the proper behaviour towards gods and one's parents, and for murder with one's own hand.

'He said that he overheard someone asking someone else where Ardiaeus the Great was. (A thousand years earlier, this Ardiaeus had been the dictator of a certain city-state in Pamphylia, and is said to have committed a great many abominable crimes, including killing his aged father and his elder brother.) The person who'd been asked the question replied, d "He's not here, and he never will be. One of the terrible sights we saw was when we were near the exit. At last, after all we'd been through, we were about to come up from underground, when we suddenly caught sight of Ardiaeus. There were others with him, the vast majority of whom had been dictators, while the rest had committed awful nonpolitical e crimes. They were under the impression that they were on the point of leaving, but the exit refused to take them. Whenever anyone whose wickedness couldn't be redeemed tried to go up, or anyone who hadn't been punished enough, it made bellowing sounds. Fierce, fiery-looking men were standing there," he went on, "and they could make sense of the sounds. These men simply grabbed hold of some of the criminals and took them away, but they placed fetters on Ardiaeus' wrists, ankles, and neck, and 616a others got the same treatment; then they threw their prisoners to the ground and flayed them, and finally dragged them away along the roadside, tearing them to pieces on the thorny shrubs. They told any passers-by that they were taking them away to hurl them into Tartarus, and explained why as well."

'He added that of all the various terrors they experienced there, the worst was the fear they each felt that, as they started their ascent, they'd encounter the bellowing sound, and that there was nothing more gratifying than hearing no sound and making the ascent.

'So much for Er's description of the penalties and punishments, and the equivalent rewards. They spent b seven days in the meadow, and on the eighth day they had to leave and go elsewhere. On the fourth day after that they reached a place from where they could see a straight shaft of light stretching from on high through the heavens and the earth; the light was like a pillar, and it was just like a rainbow in colour, except that it was brighter and clearer. It took another day's travelling to reach the light, and when they got there they were at the mid-point of the light c and they could see, stretching away out of the heavens, the extremities of the bonds of the heavens (for this light binds the heavens together, and as the girth that underpins a trireme holds a trireme together, so this light holds the whole rotation together), while stretching down from the extremities was the spindle of Necessity, which causes the circular motion of all the separate rotations.

'The spindle's stem and hook are made of adamant, while its whorl consists of various substances, including adamant. In appearance, the whorl

basically looks like whorls here on earth, but, given d Er's description, one is bound to picture it as if there was first a large hollow whorl, with its insides completely scooped out, and with a second, smaller one lying snugly inside it (like those jars which fit into one another), and then, on the same arrangement, a third whorl, a fourth one, and finally four others. For he said that there were eight concentric whorls in all, and that their circular rims, looked at from above, e formed a solid surface, as if there were just a single whorl attached to the stem, which was driven right through the middle of the eighth whorl.

'The circle which constituted the rim of the first whorl, the one on the outside, was the broadest; next broadest was the rim of the sixth whorl; third was the rim of the fourth whorl; fourth was the rim of the eighth whorl; fifth was the rim of the seventh whorl; sixth was the rim of the fifth whorl; seventh was the rim of the third whorl; and eighth was the rim of the second whorl. The rim of the largest whorl was spangled; the rim of the seventh whorl was brightest; the rim of the eighth whorl gained its 617a colour by reflecting the light of the seventh one; the rims of the second and fifth whorls were more yellow than the rest, and were almost identical in hue; the third was the whitest; the fourth was reddish; the sixth was white, but not as white as the third.

'Now, although the rotation of the spindle as a whole was uniform, nevertheless within the motion of the whole the seven inner circles moved, at regular speeds, in orbits which ran counter to the direction of the whole. The seven inner circles varied in speed: the eighth was the fastest; then second fastest were, all at once, the seventh, sixth, and fifth; b the third fastest seemed to them (Er said) to be the fourth, which was in retrograde motion; the fourth fastest was the third, and the fifth fastest was the second. The spindle was turning in the lap of Lady Necessity. Each of the spindle's circles acted as the vehicle for a Siren. Each Siren, as she stood on one of the circles, sounded a single note, and all eight notes together made a single harmonious sound.

'Three other women were also sitting on thrones c which were evenly spaced around the spindle. They were the Fates, the daughters of necessity, robed in white, with garlands on their heads; they were Lachesis, Clotho, and Atropos, accompanying the Sirens' song, with Lachesis singing of the past, Clotho of the present, and Atropos of the future. Clotho periodically laid her right hand on the outer circle of the spindle and helped to turn it; Atropos did the same

with her left hand to the inner circles; and Lachesis
d alternately helped the outer circle and the inner circles on their way with one hand after the other.

'As soon as the souls arrived, they had to approach
Lachesis. An intermediary arranged them in rows
and then, once he'd taken from Lachesis' lap lottery
tokens and sample lives, stepped up on to a high ros-
trum and said, "Hear the words of Lady Lachesis,
daughter of Necessity. You souls condemned to im-
permanence, the cycle of birth followed by death is
beginning again for you. No deity will be assigned
to you: you will pick your own deities. The order of
e gaining tokens decides the order of choosing lives,
which will be irrevocably yours. Goodness makes
its own rules: each of you will be good to the extent that you value it. Responsibility lies with the
chooser, not with God."

'After this announcement, he threw the tokens into
the crowd, and everybody (except Er, who wasn't
allowed to) picked up the token that fell beside him.
Each soul's position in the lottery was clear once
he'd picked up his token. Next, the intermediary
618a placed on the ground in front of them the sample
lives, of which there were far more than there were
souls in the crowd; every single kind of human and
animal life was included among the samples. For instance, there were dictatorships (some lifelong, others collapsing before their time and ending in
poverty, exile, and begging), and also male and fe-
b male versions of lives of fame for one's physique,
good looks, and general strength and athleticism, or
for one's lineage and the excellence of one's ancestors; and there were lives which lacked these distinctions as well. Temperament wasn't included,
however, since that inevitably varies according to
the life chosen; but otherwise there was every possible combination of qualities with one another and
with factors like wealth, poverty, sickness, and
health, in extreme or moderate amounts.

'Now, it looks as though this is an absolutely critical point for a person, my dear Glaucon. And that
c is why every single one of us has to give his undi-
vided attention—to the detriment of all other areas
of study—to trying to track down and discover
whether there is anyone he can discover and unearth
anywhere who can give him the competence and
knowledge to distinguish a good life from a bad one,
and to choose the better life from among all the possibilities that surround him at any given moment. He
has to weigh up all the things we've been talking
about, so as to know what bearing they have, in com-

bination and in isolation, on living a good life. What
are the good or bad results of mixing good looks
with poverty or with wealth, in conjunction with d
such-and-such a mental condition? What are the effects of the various combinations of innate and acquired characteristics such as high and low birth, involvement and lack of involvement in politics,
physical strength and frailty, cleverness and stupidity, and so on? He has to be able to take into consideration the nature of the mind and so make a rational choice, from among all the alternatives,
between a better and a worse life. He has to be in a
position to think of a life which leads his mind towards a state of increasing immorality as worse, and
consider one which leads in the opposite direction
as better. There's no other factor he'll regard as im- e
portant: we've already seen that this is the cardinal
decision anyone has to make, whether he does so
during his lifetime or after he's died. By the time he
reaches Hades, then, this belief must be absolutely 619a
unassailable in him, so that there too he can resist
the lure of afflictions such as wealth, and won't be
trapped into dictatorship or any other activity which
would cause him to commit a number of foul crimes,
and to suffer even worse torments himself. Instead,
he must know how to choose a life which occupies
the middle ground, and how to avoid either extreme,
as much as possible, in this world and throughout
the next. For this is how a person guarantees happi- b
ness for himself.

'Anyway, according to the report the messenger
from the other world delivered on the occasion I'm
talking about, the intermediary continued: "Even the
last to come forward will find an acceptable life, not
a pernicious one, if he chooses wisely and exerts
himself during his lifetime. The first to choose
should take care, and the last need not despair."

'Er said that no sooner had the intermediary fallen
silent than the person whose turn was first stepped
up and chose the most powerful dictatorship available. His stupidity and greed made him choose this
life without inspecting it thoroughly and in sufficient
detail, so he didn't notice that it included the fate of
eating his own children and committing other hor- c
rible crimes. When he took the time to examine his
choice, he beat his breast and wept, but he didn't
comply with the intermediary's earlier words, because he didn't hold himself responsible for his afflictions; instead he blamed fortune, the gods, and
anything rather than himself. He was one of those
who had come out of the heavens, since he'd spent

his previous life in a well-regulated community, and
d so had been good to a certain extent, even though it
was habituation rather than philosophy that had
made him so. In fact, those who had come from the
heavens fell into this trap more or less as often as
the others, since they hadn't learnt how to cope with
difficult situations, whereas the majority of those
who had come out of the earth didn't rush into their
decisions, because they knew about suffering from
their own experiences as well as from observing others. That was one of the main reasons—another being the unpredictability of the lottery—that most of
the souls met with a reversal, from good to bad or
vice versa. The point is this: if during his lifetime
e in this world a person practises philosophy with integrity, and if it so happens, as a result of the lottery, that he's not one of the last to choose, then the
report brought back from that other world makes it
plausible to expect not only that he'd be happy here,
but also that he'd travel from here to there and back
again on the smooth roads of the heavens, rather than
on rough underground trails.

'It was well worth seeing, Er said, how particular
620a souls chose their lives; the sight was by turns sad,
amusing, and astonishing. Their choice was invariably dictated by conditioning gained in their former
incarnation. For instance, he said he saw the soul
which had once belonged to Orpheus choose the life
of a swan; because women had killed him, he hated
everything female, and wanted to avoid a female incarnation. He saw Thamyras choose a nightingale's
b life, while a swan and other songbirds opted for
change and chose to live as human beings. The soul
which was twentieth in line picked the life of a lion;
it was Ajax the son of Telamon, and he didn't want
a human incarnation because he was unable to forget the decision that had been made about the armour. The next soul was that of Agamemnon: again,
his sufferings had embittered him against humanity,
and he chose instead to be reborn as an eagle. About
halfway through, it was the turn of Atalanta's soul,
and she caught sight of a male athlete's life: when
she noticed how well rewarded it was, she couldn't
walk on by, and she took it. After Atalanta, Er saw
c the soul of Epeius the son of Panopeus becoming a
craftswoman; and later, towards the end, he saw the
soul of Thersites the funny man taking on a monkey's form. As the luck of the lottery had it,
Odysseus' soul was the very last to come forward
and choose. The memory of all the hardship he had
previously endured had caused his ambition to sub-

side, so he walked around for a long time, looking
for a life as a non-political private citizen. At last he d
found one lying somewhere, disregarded by everyone else. When he saw it, he happily took it, saying
that he'd have done exactly the same even if he'd
been the first to choose. And the same kind of thorough exchange and shuffling of roles occurred in the
case of animals too, as they became men or other
animals—wild ones if they'd been immoral, tame
ones otherwise.'

'When the souls had all finished choosing their
lives, they approached Lachesis in the order the lottery had assigned them. She gave each of them the
personal deity they'd selected, to accompany them
throughout their lives, as their guardians and to ful- e
fil the choices they had made. Each deity first led
its soul to Clotho, to pass under her hand and under
the revolving orbit of the spindle, and so to ratify
the destiny the soul had chosen in the lottery. Then,
once a connection had been made with her, the deity led the soul to Atropos and her spinning, to make
the web woven by Clotho fixed and unalterable. Afterwards, the soul set a fixed course for Lady Necessity's throne and passed under it; once it was on 621a
the other side, and when everyone else had joined it
there, they all travelled through terrible, stifling heat
(since no trees or plants grew in that place) to the
Plain of Oblivion. Since the day was now drawing
to a close, they camped there by the River of Neglect, whose waters no vessel can contain.

'Now, they were all required to drink a certain
amount of water, but some were too stupid to look
after themselves properly and drank more than the
required amount. As each person drank, he forgot
everything. They lay down to sleep, and in the mid- b
dle of the night there was thunder and an earthquake.
All of a sudden, they were lifted up from where they
were, and they darted like shooting stars away in
various directions for rebirth. As for Er, although he
hadn't been allowed to drink any of the water he had
no idea what direction he took, or how he got back
to his body, but he suddenly opened his eyes and
found that it was early in the morning and that he
was lying on the funeral pyre.

'There you are, then, Glaucon. The story has made
it safely through to the end, without perishing on the
way. And it might save us too, if we take it to heart,
and so successfully cross the River of Oblivion without defiling our souls. Anyway, my recommenda- c
tion would be for us to regard the soul as immortal
and as capable of surviving a great deal of suffer-

Chapter 3
ARISTOTLE

Aristotle (384–322 B.C.), son of a physician, student in Plato's Academy for twenty years, teacher of Alexander the Great, rivals Plato as the most important philosopher in the Western tradition. He started the second great university, the Lyceum, nicknamed "Peripatetic" because he and the students frequently walked in the courtyard while conversing. Reputed to have written 400 books, he was an encyclopedic scholar and writer. The Father of Logic, a great biologist and physicist, writer of the second great work on ethics (accepting the *Republic* as the first), and great works on political philosophy, he made significant contributions to every area of philosophy. He stammered. He wrote his treatise *Ethics* (included below) to his son Nicomachus. After Alexander's death, finding himself unpopular in Athens, charged with the crime of impiety, he fled the city, "lest the Athenians sin twice against philosophy" (the fist time was in executing Socrates).

COMPARISON OF ARISTOTLE'S THOUGHT WITH PLATO'S

Both Plato and Aristotle sought knowledge as a good in its own right. Both were *teleologists* in that they believed in a universal goal for all things, the Good or the *final cause*. In this they differ from modern science (nature knows no purposes), especially Darwinian evolution where chance or random selection and survival of the fittest replace rational order. Aristotle believed in teleology because of the regularity in generation, astronomy, and physical behavior. Nature has unconscious purposes.

Whereas Plato was mystical, an idealist, loved abstract ideas, and scorned the physical, empirical, and sensual, Aristotle was more commonsensical, loved facts, physics, biology, and scientific observation. Plato offers us grand allegories and myths to convey a comprehensive world view, whereas Aristotle sought to remove myth and symbol from philosophy, substituting rational explanation and logical precision.

Aristotle's main disagreement with Plato is over the theory of the Forms. He criticizes it from various points of view—as a logician he offers a different analysis of predication; as an ontologist and epistemologist he argues that it is the concrete particular, not the universal or form, that is substance in the primary sense, and that provides the starting point in our investigation of form. Third, as a physicist he points out that the separate and transcendent forms are useless in accounting for change and coming into existence. Plato's Forms belong to the world of unchanging being, but the study of change involves the investigator of forms in the changing objects of the world of becoming. Aristotle shifted the focus from the study of pure, immutable being to physics, the study of Nature (and natural change).

Aristotle sets forth three basic ingredients for the explanation of change:

a. The Substrata (Substance)—that which persists through change.

b. The Privation or absence of form.

c. The Form which appears in the process of change, always a part of the concrete thing.

Change consists in a substratum (matter) acquiring a form which it didn't previously possess. Non-being is associated with privation, and the substratum, since it is always in existence, is in itself free of non-being. But since form follows privation, there is a sense in which we do have a creation out of non-being. Before matter and form merge in an individual, they are only potential; in becoming a particular they are acutalized. The result is *Substance* ("primary substance"), a particular individual. Hence Aristotle brings Plato's Forms down from heaven to concrete reality. Universals do not have any existence of their own as individuals but only subsist in things (we can refer to them only apart from things as abstractions, i.e., an ideal triangle or horse).

Aristotle complains that Plato's Forms neither cause movement nor change. Change and motion are especially related to physics. It is in this regard that Aristotle offers an alternative account to what has gone before (*Physics* I, II).

Aristotle's Metaphysics

Aristotle inherited from earlier philosophers of Nature the view that change takes place between opposites of one kind or another. This provides the basis of his own general theory of form or privation. Change takes place between a pair of opposites, such as hot and cold, one of which represents the form and the other the privation. But a third factor is necessary, i.e., that which is subject to or undergoes the change (*hypokeimenon*, substratum or matter). For example, boiling a kettle of water—there is an underlying matter that begins in the form of water and is changed to air (matter is *qualityless* and never present—a sort of nonbeing). Here we have two causes: (1) Form—change either from the form to the privation or vice versa and (2) Matter (substratum). Aristotle adds two more types: (3) Efficient or Moving Cause, and (4) Final or End Cause (*telos*), ending with four types of causes:

1. Matter or Material Cause—the substratum out of which the change occurs, the underlying subject which persists through change (e.g., the bronze or wood out of which a statue is made—the Greek word for matter is *hule* = wood).

2. Formal Cause—the essence of the thing, that from or to which a thing changes [shape] (e.g., the statue is a figure of Athene of Apollo).

3. Efficient Cause—the moving or proximate cause (the sculptor who makes the statue).

4. The Final or End Cause (*telos*)—the goal or purpose (the sculptor has in mind) toward which the change is moving (e.g., the statue is to represent Athene or Apollo as a symbol for worship and admiration).

The formal cause is Socrates' essence (his reason, being a bipedal animala, etc.); the material cause is his mother; the efficient cause is his father, whose semen does not contribute the matter of the embryo (which is the mother's) but serves to activate the matter; the final cause in his end, a fully functioning reality as a mature philosopher.

Some of the implications of the theory are:

1. No conscious purpose exists in Nature (*Physics* 119b). Nature does not deliberate but there are nevertheless *unconscious* purposes or ends in nature.

2. Nature fulfills its ends only as a general rule, not as an absolute rule without exceptions (there are mistakes). As Aristotle says, Natural processes take place "always or for the most part."

3. Nevertheless, final causes exist in nature in spite of the fact that nature does not deliberate because of the regularity of natural change. First the movements of the heavenly bodies provide a model of regularity and uniformity; then there is uniformity in the repro-

duction of natural species, in that each kind produces its own kind, a man generating man, mice generating mice, oak trees generating oak trees; and regularity is also to be found in the natural movements of the four elements, earth always falling and fire rising when nothing impedes their motion. Therefore it would seem reasonable to conclude via induction that Nature is not random or haphazard but exhibits order and regularity and if these, then Ends, though not conscious ones.

4. Aristotle's craftsman is reminiscent of Plato's demiurge (*Timaeus*) with the difference that Aristotle goes a lot farther in trying to demythologize and naturalize explicitly this process—more a metaphor for Aristotle. It's not clear how literal Plato believes his explanation to be, but Aristotle clearly views his metaphors as such, Nature has its ends not from without but from within (inner *telos*).

Another way to look at change is in terms of *potentiality* and *actuality*. For example, take a tree: the seed of the tree is *potentially* the mature tree (acorn, the oak). Similarly the fetus is potentially the adult human; a piece of wood, potentially the table; a piece of marble, potentially the statue of Apollo.

In each instance it is the relatively formless matter, the shapless wood or marble that may be said to possess potentiality. Qualityless matter, the abstraction, is pure potentiality. But relatively formless matter possesses potentialities in different senses and to different degrees. (e.g., a fetus is potentially a man to a higher degree than earth, fire, air, and water are potentially a man).

Aristotle's point in tying potentiality and actuality together is to show that even the relatively formless matter is potentially what the end product is actually. Form is not something transcendent and separate, as Plato claimed, but something that is gradually acquired and brought to actuality during the process of change. That is, Aristotle did not hold that something came out of nothing [*ex nihilo nihil fit*, nothing comes from nothing], but all coming into existence is relative: something comes from something else which is potentially what it later is actually. In each case the substratum acquires a new form. Hence in a sense a seed is and is not a tree—potentially it is but actually it is not.

Finally, we say a word about Aristotle's *Ethics* and *Politics*, which are included as our two final readings in this chapter. After a general discussion of the nature of ethics, Aristotle turns to the nature of virtue. Virtues are simply those characteristics that enable individuals to live well in communities. In order to achieve a state of well-being (*eudaimonia*, usually translated happiness), proper social institutions are necessary. Thus the moral person cannot really exist apart from a flourishing political setting that enables the individual to develop the requisite virtues for the good life. Ethics is thus a species of politics.

Next, Aristotle distinguishes moral virtues from intellectual ones. Whereas the intellectual virtues may be taught directly, the moral ons must be lived in order to be learned. By living well we acquire the right habits. These habits are in fact the virtues, which are to be sought as the best guarantee to the happy life. But, again, happiness requires that one be lucky enough to live in a flourishing state. The morally virtuous life consists in living in moderation, according to the "golden mean."

Politics rivals the *Republic* as the greatest political treatise of ancient philosophy. It consists of a series of essays which discuss the definitions and structure of the state, as well as criticize Plato's Utopianism and forms of democracy. Aristotle argues for aristocracy (rule by the excellent) as the best form of government.

In our first reading, *Categories*, Aristotle offers a theory of predication, that is an explanation of how the terms of language apply to things in the world (the Greek word *kategoriai* from which we derive the word 'categories' comes from the verb meaning 'to predicate'). Aristotle argues that underlying all reality is substance, fundamental and independent reality. Everything else depends for its existence on substance.

FOR FURTHER READING

Ackrill, J. L. *Aristotle the Philosopher*. (Oxford University Press, 1981).

Allan, D. J. *The Philosophy of Aristotle*. (Oxford University Press, 1970).

Barnes, Jonathan. *The Complete Works of Aristotle*, 2 vols. (Princeton University Press, 1984).

Barnes, Jonathan. *Aristotle*. (Oxford University Press, 1982).

Guthrie, W. K. C. *A History of Greek Philosophy*, vol VI. (Cambridge University Press, 1981).

Irwin, Terrance. *Aristotle's First Principles*. (Oxford University Press, 1988).

Rorty, A. O., ed. *Essays on Aristotle's Ethics*. (University of California Press, 1980).

Ross, W. D. *Aristotle*. (1923 reprinted by Meridian Books, 1959).

Taylor, A. E. *Aristotle*. (Dover, 1955).

Categories

1ᵃ **1.** When things have only a name in common and the definition of being which corresponds to the name is different, they are called *homonymous*. Thus, for example, both a man and a picture are animals. These have only a name in common and the definition of being which corresponds to the name is different; for if one is to say what being an animal is for each of them, one will give two distinct ₅ definitions.

When things have the name in common and the definition of being which corresponds to the name is the same, they are called *synonymous*. Thus, for example, both a man and an ox are animals. Each of these is called, by a common name, an animal, and the definition of being is also the same; for if ₁₀ one is to give the definition of each—what being an animal is for each of them—one will give the same definition.

When things get their name from something, with a difference of ending, they are called *paronymous*. Thus, for example, the grammarian gets his name ₁₅ from grammar, the brave get theirs from bravery.

2. Of things that are said, some involve combination while others are said without combination. Examples of those involving combination are: man runs, man wins; and of those without combination: man, ox, runs, wins.

Of things there are: (*a*) some are *said of* a subject ₂₀ but are not *in* any subject. For example, man is said of a subject, the individual man, but is not in any subject. (*b*) Some are in a subject but are not said of any subject. (By 'in a subject' I mean what is in something, not as a part, and cannot exist separately from what it is in.) For example, the individual ₂₅ knowledge-of-grammer is in a subject, the soul, but is not said of any subject; and the individual white is in a subject, the body (for all colour is in a body), but is not said of any subject. (*c*) Some are both said of a subject and in a subject. For example, knowledge is in a subject, the soul, and is also said of a 1ᵇ subject, knowledge-of-grammar. (*d*) Some are neither in a subject nor said of a subject, for example, the individual man or the individual horse—for nothing of this sort is either in a subject or said of ₅ a subject. Things that are individual and numerically one are, without exception, not said of any subject, but there is nothing to prevent some of them from being in a subject—the individual knowledge-of-grammar is one of the things in a subject.

3. Whenever one thing is predicated of another ₁₀ as of a subject, all things said of what is predicated will be said of the subject also. For example, man is predicated of the individual man, and animal of man; so animal will be predicated of the individual

Reprinted from Aristotle's *Categories*, translated by J. L. Ackrill (1963) by permission of Oxford University Press.

15 man also—for the individual man is both a man and an animal.

The differentiae of genera which are different and not subordinate one to the other are themselves different in kind. For example, animal and knowledge: footed, winged, aquatic, two-footed, are differentiae
20 of animal, but none of these is a differentia of knowledge; one sort of knowledge does not differ from another by being two-footed. However, there is nothing to prevent genera subordinate one to the other from having the same differentiae. For the higher are predicated of the genera below them, so that all differentiae of the predicated genus will be differentiae of the subject also.

25 **4.** Of things said without any combination, each signifies either substance or quantity or qualification or a relative or where or when or being-in-a-position or having or doing or being-affected. To give a rough idea, examples of substance are man, horse; of quantity: four-foot, five-foot; of qualification: white, grammatical; of a relative: double, half,
2ª1 larger; of where: in the Lyceum, in the market-place; of when: yesterday, last-year; of being-in-a-position: is-lying, is-sitting; of having: has-shoes-on, has-armour-on; of doing: cutting, burning; of being-affected: being-cut, being-burned.

5 None of the above is said just by itself in any affirmation, but by the combination of these with one another an affirmation is produced. For every affirmation, it seems, is either true or false; but of things said without any combination none is either true or
10 false (e.g. man, white, runs, wins).

5. A *substance*—that which is called a substance most strictly, primarily, and most of all—is that which is neither said of a subject nor in a subject,
15 e.g. the individual man or the individual horse. The species in which the things primarily called substances are, are called *secondary substances*, as also are the genera of these species. For example, the individual man belongs in a species, man, and animal is a genus of the species; so these—both man and animal—are called secondary substances.

It is clear from what has been said that if something is said of a subject both its name and its definition are necessarily predicated of the subject. For
20 example, man is said of a subject, the individual man, and the name is of course predicated (since you will be predicating man of the individual man), and also the definition of man will be predicated of the individual man (since the individual man is also a
25 man). Thus both the name and the definition will be

predicated of the subject. But as for things which are in a subject, in most cases neither the name nor the definition is predicated of the subject. In some cases there is nothing to prevent the name from being predicated of the subject, but it is impossible for 30 the definition to be predicated. For example, white, which is in a subject (the body), is predicated of the subject; for a body is called white. But the definition of white will never be predicated of the body.

All the other things are either said of the primary 35 substances as subjects or in them as subjects. This is clear from an examination of cases. For example, animal is predicated of man and therefore also of the individual man; for were it predicated of none of the individual men it would not be predicated of man at all. Again, colour is in body and therefore also in an 2ᵇ1 individual body; for were it not in some individual body it would not be in body at all. Thus all the other things are either said of the primary substances as subjects or in them as subjects. So if the primary 5 substances did not exist it would be impossible for any of the other things to exist.

Of the secondary substances the species is more a substance than the genus, since it is nearer to the primary substance. For if one is to say of the primary substance what it is, it will be more informative and apt to give the species than the genus. For 10 example, it would be more informative to say of the individual man that he is a man than that he is an animal (since the one is more distinctive of the individual man while the other is more general); and more informative to say of the individual tree that it is a tree than that it is a plant. Further, it is because the primary substances are subjects for all the 15 other things and all the other things are predicated of them or are in them, that they are called substances most of all. But as the primary substances stand to the other things, so the species stands to the genus: the species is a subject for the genus (for the genera are predicated of the species but the species are not predicated reciprocally of the genera). Hence for this reason too the species is more a substance 20 than the genus.

But of the species themselves—those which are not genera—one is no more a substance than another: it is no more apt to say of the individual man that he is a man than to say of the individual horse that it is a horse. And similarly of the primary sub- 25 stances one is no more a substance than another: the individual man is no more a substance than the individual ox.

It is reasonable that, after the primary substances, their species and genera should be the only other things called secondary substances. For only they, of things predicated, reveal the primary substance. For if one is to say of the individual man what he is, it will be in place to give the species or the genus (though more informative to give man than animal); but to give any of the other things would be out of place—for example, to say white or runs or anything like that. So it is reasonable that these should be the only other things called substances. Further, it is because the primary substances are subjects for everything else that they are called substances most strictly. But as the primary substances stand to everything else, so the species and genera of the primary substances stand to all the rest: all the rest are predicated of these. For if you will call the individual man grammatical, then you will call both a man and an animal grammatical; and similarly in other cases.

It is a characteristic common to every substance not to be in a subject. For a primary substance is neither said of a subject nor in a subject. And as for secondary substances, it is obvious at once that they are not in a subject. For man is said of the individual man as subject but is not in a subject: man is not *in* the individual man. Similarly, animal also is said of the individual man as subject, but animal is not *in* the individual man. Further, while there is nothing to prevent the name of what is in a subject from being sometimes predicated of the subject, it is impossible for the definition to be predicated. But the definition of the secondary substances, as well as the name, is predicated of the subject: you will predicate the definition of man of the individual man, and also that of animal. No substance, therefore, is in a subject.

This is not, however, peculiar to substance, since the differentia also is not in a subject. For footed and two-footed are said of man as subject but are not in a subject; neither two-footed nor footed is *in* man. Moreover, the definition of the differentia is predicated of that of which the differentia is said. For example, if footed is said of man the definition of footed will also be predicated of man; for man is footed.

We need not be disturbed by any fear that we may be forced to say that the parts of a substance, being in a subject (the whole substance), are not substances. For when we spoke of things *in a subject* we did not mean things belonging in something as *parts*.

It is a characteristic of substances and differentiae that all things called from them are so called synonymously. For all the predicates from them are predicated either of the individuals or of the species. (For from a primary substance there is no predicate, since it is said of no subject; and as for secondary substances, the species is predicated of the individual, the genus both of the species and of the individual. Similarly, differentiae too are predicated both of the species and of the individuals.) And the primary substances admit the definition of the species and of the genera, and the species admits that of the genus; for everything said of what is predicated will be said of the subject also. Similarly, both the species and the individuals admit the definition of the differentiae. But synonymous things were precisely those with both the name in common and the same definition. Hence all the things called from substances and differentiae are so called synonymously.

Every substance seems to signify a certain 'this'. As regards the primary substances, it is indisputably true that each of them signifies a certain 'this'; for the thing revealed is individual and numerically one. But as regards the secondary substances, though it appears from the form of the name—when one speaks of man or animal—that a secondary substance likewise signifies a certain 'this', this is not really true; rather, it signifies a certain qualification—for the subject is not, as the primary substance is, one, but man and animal are said of many things. However, it does not signify simply a certain qualification, as white does. White signifies nothing but a qualification, whereas the species and the genus mark off the qualification of substance—they signify substance of a certain qualification. (One draws a wider boundary with the genus than with the species, for in speaking of animal one takes in more than in speaking of man.)

Another characteristic of substances is that there is nothing contrary to them. For what would be contrary to a primary substance? For example, there is nothing contrary to an individual man, nor yet is there anything contrary to man or to animal. This, however, is not peculiar to substance but holds of many other things also, for example, of quantity. For there is nothing contrary to four-foot or to ten or to anything of this kind—unless someone were to say that many is contrary to few or large to small; but still there is nothing contrary to any *definite* quantity.

Substance, it seems, does not admit of a more and a less. I do not mean that one substance is not more a substance than another (we have said that it is), but that any given substance is not called more, or less, that which it is. For example, if this substance is a man, it will not be more a man or less a man either than itself or than another man. For one man 4ᵇ1 is not more a man than another, as one pale thing is more pale than another and one beautiful thing more beautiful than another. Again, a thing is called more, or less, such-and-such than itself; for example, the body that is pale is called more pale now than before, and the one that is hot is called more, or less, hot. Substance, however, is not spoken of thus. For a man is not called more a man now than before, 5 nor is anything else that is a substance. Thus substance does not admit of a more and a less.

It seems most distinctive of substance that what 10 is numerically one and the same is able to receive contraries. In no other case could one bring forward anything, numerically one, which is able to receive contraries. For example, a colour which is numerically one and the same will not be black and white, nor will numerically one and the same action be bad 15 and good; and similarly with everything else that is not substance. A substance, however, numerically one and the same, is able to receive contraries. For example, an individual man—one and the same— becomes pale at one time and dark at another, and 20 hot and cold, and bad and good.

Nothing like this is to be seen in any other case, unless perhaps someone might object and say that statements and beliefs are like this. For the same 25 statement seems to be both true and false. Suppose, for example, that the statement that somebody is sitting is true; after he has got up this same statement will be false. Similarly with beliefs. Suppose you be- 30 lieve truly that somebody is sitting; after he has got up you will believe falsely if you hold the same belief about him. However, even if we were to grant this, there is still a difference in the *way* contraries

are received. For in the case of substances it is by themselves changing that they are able to receive contraries. For what has become cold instead of hot, or dark instead of pale, or good instead of bad, has changed (has altered); similarly in other cases too it is by itself undergoing change that each thing is able to receive contraries. Statements and beliefs, on the other hand, themselves remain completely unchangeable in every way; it is because the *actual* 35 *thing* changes that the contrary comes to belong to them. For the statement that somebody is sitting remains the same; it is because of a change in the actual thing that it comes to be true at one time and false at another. Similarly with beliefs. Hence at least 4ᵇ1 the *way* in which it is able to receive contraries— through a change in itself—would be distinctive of substance, even if we were to grant that beliefs and statements are able to receive contraries. However, this is not true. For it is not because they themselves 5 receive anything that statements and beliefs are said to be able to receive contraries, but because of what has happened to something else. For it is because the actual thing exists or does not exist that the statement is said to be true or false, not because it is able itself to receive contraries. No statement, in fact, or belief 10 is changed at all by anything. So, since nothing happens in them, they are not able to receive contraries. A substance, on the other hand, is said to be able to receive contraries because it itself receives con- 15 traries. For it receives sickness and health, and paleness and darkness; and because it itself receives the various things of this kind it is said to be able to receive contraries. It is, therefore, distinctive of substance that what is numerically one and the same is able to receive contraries. This brings to an end our discussion of substance.

Posterior Analytics (Analytica Posteriora)

Book I

1. All instruction given or received by way of argument proceeds from pre-existent knowledge. This becomes evident upon a survey of all the species of

such instruction. The mathematical sciences and all other speculative disciplines are acquired in this way, and so are the two forms of dialectical rea- 5 soning, *syllogistic* and *inductive*; for each of these latter makes use of old knowledge to impart new,

Reprinted from Aristotle's *Posterior Analytics*, translated by G. R. G. Mure by permission of Oxford University Press.

the syllogism assuming an audience that accepts its premises, induction exhibiting the universal as implicit in the clearly known particular. Again, the persuasion exerted by rhetorical arguments is in principle the same, since they use either example, a kind of induction, or enthymeme, a form of syllogism.

The pre-existent knowledge required is of two kinds. In some cases admission of the fact must be assumed, in others comprehension of the meaning of the term used, and sometimes both assumptions are essential. Thus, we assume that every predicate can be either truly affirmed or truly denied of any subject, and that 'triangle' means so and so; as regards 'unit' we have to make the double assumption of the meaning of the word and the existence of the thing. The reason is that these several objects are not equally obvious to us. Recognition of a truth may in some cases contain as factors both previous knowledge and also knowledge acquired simultaneously with that recognition—knowledge, this latter, of the particulars actually falling under the universal and therein already virtually known. For example, the student knew beforehand that the angles of every triangle are equal to two right angles; but it was only at the actual moment at which he was being led on to recognize this as true in the instance before him that he came to know 'this figure inscribed in the semicircle' to be a triangle. For some things (viz. the singulars finally reached which are not predicable of anything else as subject) are only learnt in this way, i. e. there is here no recognition through a middle of a minor term as subject to a major. Before he was led on to recognition or before he actually drew a conclusion, we should perhaps say that in a manner he knew, in a manner not.

If he did not in an unqualified sense of the term *know* the existence of this triangle, how could he *know* without qualification that its angles were equal to two right angles? No: clearly he *knows* not without qualification but only in the sense that he *knows* universally. If this distinction is not drawn, we are faced with the dilemma in the *Meno*: either a man will learn nothing or what he already knows; for we cannot accept the solution which some people offer. A man is asked, 'Do you, or do you not, know that every pair is even?' He says he does know it. The questioner then produces a particular pair, of the existence, and so *a fortiori* of the evenness, of which he was unaware. The solution which some people offer is to assert that they do not know that every pair is even, but only that everything which they

know to be a pair is even: yet what they know to be even is that of which they have demonstrated evenness, i. e. what they made the subject of their premiss, viz. not merely every triangle or number which they know to be such, but any and every number or triangle without reservation. For no premiss is ever couched in the form 'every number which you know to be such', or 'every rectilinear figure which you know to be such': the predicate is always construed as applicable to any and every instance of the thing. On the other hand, I imagine there is nothing to prevent a man in one sense knowing what he is learning, in another not knowing it. The strange thing would be, not if in some sense he knew what he was learning, but if he were to know it in that precise sense and manner in which he was learning it.

2. We suppose ourselves to possess unqualified scientific knowledge of a thing, as opposed to knowing it in the accidental way in which the sophist knows, when we think that we know the cause on which the fact depends, as the cause of that fact and of no other, and, further, that the fact could not be other than it is. Now that scientific knowing is something of this sort is evident—witness both those who falsely claim it and those who actually possess it, since the former merely imagine themselves to be, while the latter are also actually, in the condition described. Consequently the proper object of unqualified scientific knowledge is something which cannot be other than it is.

There may be another manner of knowing as well—that will be discussed later. What I now assert is that at all events we do know by demonstration. By demonstration I mean a syllogism productive of scientific knowledge, a syllogism, that is, the grasp of which is *eo ipso* such knowledge. Assuming then that my thesis as to the nature of scientific knowing is correct, the premisses of demonstrated knowledge must be true, primary, immediate, better known than and prior to the conclusion, which is further related to them as effect to cause. Unless these conditions are satisfied, the basic truths will not be 'appropriate' to the conclusion. Syllogism there may indeed be without these conditions, but such syllogism, not being productive of scientific knowledge, will not be demonstration. The premisses must be true: for that which is non-existent cannot be known—we cannot know, e.g., that the diagonal of a square is commensurate with its side. The premisses must be primary and indemonstrable; otherwise they will require demonstration in order to be known, since to have knowledge, if it be not accidental knowledge, of things which are demonstrable, means precisely to have a demonstration of them. The premises must be the causes of the conclusion, better known than it, and prior to it; its causes, since we possess scientific knowledge of a thing only when we know its cause; prior, in order to be causes; antecedently known, this antecedent knowledge being not our mere understanding of the meaning, but knowledge of the fact as well. Now 'prior' and 'better known' are ambiguous terms, for there is a difference between what is prior and better known in the order of being and what is prior and better known to man. I mean that objects nearer to sense are prior and better known to man; objects without qualification prior and better known are those further from sense. Now the most universal causes are furthest from sense and particular causes are nearest to sense, and they are thus exactly opposed to one another. In saying that the premises of demonstrated knowledge must be primary, I mean that they must be the 'appropriate' basic truths, for I identify primary premiss and basic truth. A 'basic truth' in a demonstration is an immediate proposition. An immediate proposition is one which has no other proposition prior to it. A proposition is either part of an enunciation, i. e. it predicates a single attribute of a single subject. If a proposition is dialectical, it assumes either part indifferently; if it is demonstrative, it lays down one part to the definite exclusion of the other because that part is true. The term 'enunciation' denotes either part of a contradiction indifferently. A contradiction is an opposition which of its own nature excludes a middle. The part of a contradiction which conjoins a predicate with a subject is an affirmation; the part disjoining them is a negation. I call an immediate basic truth of syllogism a 'thesis' when, though it is not susceptible of proof by the teacher, yet ignorance of it does not constitute a total bar to progress on the part of the pupil: one which the pupil must know if he is to learn anything whatever is an *axiom*. I call it an axiom because there are such truths and we give them the name of axioms *par excellence*. If a thesis assumes one part or the other of an enunciation, i. e. asserts either the existence or the non-existence of a subject, it is a hypothesis; if it does not so assert, it is a definition. Definition *is* a 'thesis' or a 'laying something down', since the arithmetician lays it down that to be a unit is to be quantitatively indivisible; but it is not a hypothesis, for to define

what a unit is is not the same as to affirm its existence.

Now since the required ground of our knowledge—i. e. of our conviction—of a fact is the possession of such a syllogism as we call demonstration, and the ground of the syllogism is the facts constituting its premises, we must not only know the primary premises—some if not all of them—beforehand, but know them better than the conclusion: for the cause of an attribute's inherence in a subject always itself inheres in the subject more firmly than that attribute; e. g. the cause of our loving anything is dearer to us than the object of our love. So since the primary premises are the cause of our knowledge—i. e. of our conviction—it follows that we know them better—that is, are more convinced of them—than their consequences, precisely because our knowledge of the latter is the effect of our knowledge of the premises. Now a man cannot believe in anything more than in the things he knows, unless he has either actual knowledge of it or something better than actual knowledge. But we are faced with this paradox if a student whose belief rests on demonstration has not prior knowledge; a man must believe in some, if not in all, of the basic truths more than in the conclusion. Moreover, if a man sets out to acquire the scientific knowledge that comes through demonstration, he must not only have a better knowledge of the basic truths and a firmer conviction of them than of the connexion which is being demonstrated: more than this, nothing must be more certain or better known to him than these basic truths in their character as contradicting the fundamental premises which lead to the opposed and erroneous conclusion. For indeed the conviction of pure science must be unshakable. . . .

19. As regards syllogism and demonstration, the definition of, and the conditions required to produce each of them, are now clear, and with that also the definition of, and the conditions required to produce, demonstrative knowledge, since it is the same as demonstration. As to the basic premises, how they become known and what is the developed state of knowledge of them is made clear by raising some preliminary problems.

We have already said that scientific knowledge through demonstration is impossible unless a man knows the primary immediate premises. But there are questions which might be raised in respect of the apprehension of these immediate premises: one might not only ask whether it is of the same kind as the apprehension of the conclusions, but also whether there is or is not scientific knowledge of both; or scientific knowledge of the latter, and of the former a different kind of knowledge; and, further, 25 whether the developed states of knowledge are not innate but come to be in us, or are innate but at first unnoticed. Now it is strange if we possess them from birth; for it means that we possess apprehensions more accurate than demonstration and fail to notice them. If on the other hand we acquire them and do not previously possess them, how could we apprehend and learn without a basis of pre-existence 30 knowledge? For that is impossible, as we used to find in the case of demonstration. So it emerges that neither can we possess them from birth, nor can they come to be in us if we are without knowledge of them to the extent of having no such developed state at all. Therefore we must possess a capacity of some sort, but not such as to rank higher in accuracy than these developed states. And this at least is an obvious characteristic of all animals, for they possess a 35 congenital discriminative capacity which is called sense-perception. But though sense-perception is innate in all animals, in some the sense-impression comes to persist, in others it does not. So animals in which this persistence does not come to be have either no knowledge at all outside the act of perceiving, or no knowledge of objects of which no impression persists; animals in which it does come into being have perception and can continue to retain the sense-impression in the soul: and when such persistence is frequently repeated a further distinction at 100ª once arises between those which out of the persistence of such sense-impressions develop a power of systematizing them and those which do not. So out of sense-perception comes to be what we call memory, and out of frequently repeated memories of the 5 same thing develops experience; for a number of memories constitute a single experience. From experience again—i. e. from the universal now stabilized in its entirety within the soul, the one beside the many which is a single identity within them all—originate the skill of the craftsman and the knowledge of the man of science, skill in the sphere of coming to be and science in the sphere of being.

We conclude that these states of knowledge are neither innate in a determinate form, nor developed from other higher states of knowledge, but from 10 sense-perception. It is like a rout in battle stopped by first one man making a stand and then another, until the original formation has been restored. The soul is so constituted as to be capable of this process.

Let us now restate the account given already, though with insufficient clearness. When one of a number of logically indiscriminable particulars has 15 made a stand, the earliest universal is present in the soul: for though the act of sense-perception is of the particular, its content is universal—is man, for example, not the man Callias. A fresh stand is made 100ᵇ among these rudimentary universals, and the process does not cease until the indivisible concepts, the true universals, are established: e. g. such and such a species of animal is a step towards the genus animal, which by the same process is a step towards a further generalization.

Thus it is clear that we must get to know the primary premisses by induction; for the method by which even sense-perception implants the universal is inductive. Now of the thinking states by which we 5 grasp truth, some are unfailingly true, others admit of error—opinion, for instance, and calculation, whereas scientific knowing and intuition are always true: further, no other kind of thought except intuition is more accurate than scientific knowledge, whereas primary premisses are more knowable than demonstrations, and all scientific knowledge is dis- 10 cursive. From these considerations it follows that there will be no scientific knowledge of the primary premisses, and since except intuition nothing can be truer than scientific knowledge, it will be intuition that apprehends the primary premisses—a result which also follows from the fact that demonstration cannot be the originative source of demonstration, nor, consequently, scientific knowledge of scientific knowledge. If, therefore, it is the only other kind of true thinking except scientific knowing, intuition will be the originative source of scientific knowl- 15 edge. And the originative source of science grasps the original basic premiss, while science as a whole is similarly related as originative source to the whole body of fact.

Physics

BOOK II

1. Of things that exist, some exist by nature, some
from other causes. By nature the animals and their
10 parts exist, and the plants and the simple bodies
(earth, fire, air, water)—for we say that these and
the like exist by nature.

All the things mentioned plainly differ from things
which are *not* constituted by nature. For each of them
has within itself a principle of motion and of stationariness (in respect of place, or of growth and de-
15 crease, or by way of alteration). On the other hand,
a bed and a coat and anything else of that sort, *qua*
receiving these designations—i.e. in so far as they
are products of art—have no innate impulse to
change. But in so far as they happen to be composed
of stone or of earth or of a mixture of the two, they
20 *do* have such an impulse, and just to that extent—
which seems to indicate that nature is a principle or
cause of being moved and of being at rest in that to
which it belongs primarily, in virtue of itself and not
accidentally.

I say 'not accidentally', because (for instance) a
man who is a doctor might himself be a cause of
health to himself. Nevertheless it is not in so far as
25 he is a patient that he possesses the art of medicine:
it merely has happened that the same man is doctor
and patient—and that is why these attributes are not
always found together. So it is with all other artificial products. None of them has in itself the principle of its own production. But while in some cases
30 (for instance houses and the other products of manual labour) that principle is in something else external to the thing, in others—those which may cause
a change in themselves accidentally—it lies in the
things themselves (but not in virtue of what they
are).

Nature then is what has been stated. Things have
a nature which have a principle of this kind. Each
of them is a substance; for it is a subject, and nature
is always in a subject.

35 The term 'according to nature' is applied to all
these things and also to the attributes which belong

to them in virtue of what they are, for instance the
property of fire to be carried upwards—which is not 193ª1
a nature nor has a nature but is by nature or according to nature.

What nature is, then, and the meaning of the terms
'by nature' and 'according to nature', has been
stated. *That* nature exists, it would be absurd to try
to prove; for it is obvious that there are many things
of this kind, and to prove what is obvious by what 5
is not is the mark of a man who is unable to distinguish what is self-evident from what is not. (This
state of mind is clearly possible. A man blind from
birth might reason about colours.) Presumably therefore such persons must be talking about words without any thought to correspond.

Some identify the nature or substance of a natural 10
object with that immediate constituent of it which
taken by itself is without arrangement, e.g. the wood
is the nature of the bed, and the bronze the nature
of the statue.

As an indication of this Antiphon points out that
if you planted a bed and the rotting wood acquired
the power of sending up a shoot, it would not be a
bed that would come up, but *wood* which shows that
the arrangement in accordance with the rules of the
art is merely an accidental attribute, whereas the sub- 15
stance is the other, which, further, persists continuously through the process.

But if the material of each of these objects has itself the same relation to something else, say bronze
(or gold) to water, bones (or wood) to earth and so
on, *that* (they say) would be their nature and sub- 20
stance. Consequently some assert earth, others fire
or air or water or some or all of these, to be the nature of the things that are. For whatever any one of
them supposed to have this character—whether one
thing or more than one thing—this or these he declared to be the whole of substance, all else being
its affections, states, or dispositions. Every such 25
thing they held to be eternal (for it could not pass
into anything else), but other things to come into being and cease to be times without number.

This then is one account of nature, namely that it

Reprinted from Aristotle's *Physics*, translated by R. P. Hardie & P. K. Gaye by permission of Oxford University Press.

is the primary underlying matter of things which have in themselves a principle of motion or change.

30   Another account is that nature is the shape or form which is specified in the definition of the thing.

For the word 'nature' is applied to what is according to nature and the natural in the same way as 'art' is applied to what is artistic or a work of art. We should not say in the latter case that there is anything artistic about a thing, if it is a bed only potentially, not yet having the form of a bed; nor should we call it a work of art. The same is true of natural compounds. What is potentially flesh or bone has
193ᵇ1 not yet its own nature, and does not exist by nature, until it receives the form specified in the definition, which we name in defining what flesh or bone is. Thus on the second account of nature, it would be the shape or form (not separable except in statement) of things which have in themselves a principle of
5 motion. (The combination of the two, e.g. man, is not nature but by nature.)

The form indeed is nature rather than the matter; for a thing is more properly said to be what it is when it exists in actuality than when it exists potentially. Again man is born from man but not bed from bed. That is why people say that the shape is not the nature of a bed, but the wood is—if the bed sprouted,
10 not a bed but wood would come up. But even if the shape *is* art, then on the same principle the shape of man is nature. For man is born from man.

Again, nature in the sense of a coming-to-be proceeds towards nature. For it is not like doctoring, which leads not to the art of doctoring but to health. Doctoring must start from the art, not lead to it. But
15 it is not in this way that nature is related to nature. What grows *qua* growing grows from something into something. Into what then does it grow? Not into that from which it arose but into that to which it tends. The shape then is nature.

Shape and nature are used in two ways. For the
20 privation too is in a way form. But whether in unqualified coming to be there is privation, i.e. a contrary, we must consider later.

2. We have distinguished, then, the different ways in which the term 'nature' is used.

The next point to consider is how the mathematician differs from the student of nature; for natural bodies contain surfaces and volumes, lines and
25 points, and these are the subject-matter of mathematics.

Further, is astronomy different from natural science or a department of it? It seems absurd that the

student of nature should be supposed to know the nature of sun or moon, but not to know any of their essential attributes, particularly as the writers on nature obviously do discuss their shape and whether 30 the earth and the world are spherical or not.

Now the mathematician, though he too treats of these things, nevertheless does not treat of them as the limits of a natural body; nor does he consider the attributes indicated as the attributes of such bodies. That is why he separates them; for in thought they are separable from motion, and it makes no difference, nor does any falsity result, if they are separated. The holders of the theory of Forms do the 35 same, though they are not aware of it; for they separate the objects of natural science, which are less 194ª1 separable than those of mathematics. This becomes plain if one tries to state in each of the two cases the definitions of the things and of their attributes. Odd and even, straight and curved, and likewise number, line, and figure, do not involve motion; not so flesh and bone and man—*these* are defined like snub nose, 5 not like curved.

Similar evidence is supplied by the more natural of the branches of mathematics, such as optics, harmonics, and astronomy. These are in a way the converse of geometry. While geometry investigates natural lines but not *qua* natural, optics investigates mathematical lines, but *qua* natural, not *qua* math- 10 ematical.

Since two sorts of thing are called nature, the form and the matter, we must investigate its objects as we would the essence of snubness, that is neither independently of matter nor in terms of matter only. Here too indeed one might raise a difficulty. Since there 15 are two natures, with which is the student of nature concerned? Or should he investigate the combination of the two? But if the combination of the two, then also each severally. Does it belong then to the same or to different sciences to know each severally?

If we look at the ancients, natural science would seem to be concerned with the *matter*. (It was only very slightly that Empedocles and Democritus touched on form and essence.)   20

But if on the other hand art imitates nature, and it is the part of the same discipline to know the form and the matter up to a point (e.g. the doctor has a knowledge of health and also of bile and phlegm, in which health is realized and the builder both of the form of the house and of the matter, namely that it 25 is bricks and beams, and so forth): if this is so, it would be the part of natural science also to know nature in both its senses.

Again, that for the sake of which, or the end, belongs to the same department of knowledge as the means. But the nature is the end or that for the sake of which. For if a thing undergoes a continuous 30 change toward some end, that last stage is actually that for the sake of which. (That is why the poet was carried away into making an absurd statement when he said 'he has the end for the sake of which he was born'. For not every stage that is last claims to be an end, but only that which is best.)

For the arts make their material (some simply 35 make it, others make it serviceable), and we use everything as if it was there for our sake. (We also are in a sense an end. 'That for the sake of which' may be taken in two ways, as we said in our work 194ᵇ1 *On Philosophy*.) The arts, therefore, which govern the matter and have knowledge are two, namely the art which uses the product and the art which directs the production of it. That is why the using art also is in a sense directive; but it differs in that it knows the form, whereas the art which is directive as be- 5 ing concerned with production knows the matter. For the helmsman knows and prescribes what sort of form a helm should have, the other from what wood it should be made and by means of what operations. In the products of art, however, we make the material with a view to the function, whereas in the products of nature the matter is there all along.

Again, matter is a relative thing—for different forms there is different matter.

10 How far then must the student of nature know the form or essence? Up to a point, perhaps, as the doctor must know sinew or the smith bronze (i.e. until he understands the purpose of each); and the student of nature is concerned only with things whose forms are separable indeed, but do not exist apart from matter. Man is begotten by man and by the sun as well. The mode of existence and essence of the separable 15 it is the business of first philosophy to define.

3. Now that we have established these distinctions, we must proceed to consider causes, their character and number. Knowledge is the object of our inquiry, and men do not think they know a thing till they have grasped the 'why' of it (which is to 20 grasp its primary cause). So clearly we too must do this as regards both coming to be and passing away and every kind of natural change, in order that, knowing their principles, we may try to refer to these principles each of our problems.

In one way, then, that out of which a thing comes to be and which persists, is called a cause, e.g. the 25 bronze of the statue, the silver of the bowl, and the genera of which the bronze and the silver are species.

In another way, the form or the archetype, i.e. the definition of the essence, and its genera, are called causes (e.g. of the octave the relation of 2:1, and generally number), and the parts in the definition.

Again, the primary source of the change or rest; 30 e.g. the man who deliberated is a cause, the father is cause of the child, and generally what makes of what is made and what changes of what is changed.

Again, in the sense of end or that for the sake of which a thing is done, e.g. health is the cause of walking about. ('Why is he walking about?' We say: 'To be healthy', and, having said that, we think we have assigned the cause.) The same is true also of 35 all the intermediate steps which are brought about through the action of something else as means towards the end, e.g. reduction of flesh, purging, 195ᵇ1 drugs, or surgical instruments are means towards health. All these things are for the sake of the end, though they differ from one another in that some are activities, others instruments.

This then perhaps exhausts the number of ways in which the term 'cause' is used.

As things are called causes in many ways, it follows that there are several causes of the same thing 5 (not merely accidentally), e.g. both the art of the sculptor and the bronze are causes of the statue. These are causes of the statue *qua* statue, not in virtue of anything else that it may be—only not in the same way, the one being the material cause, the other the cause whence the motion comes. Some things cause each other reciprocally, e.g. hard work causes fitness and *vice versa*, but again not in the same way, but the one as end, the other as the prin- 10 ciple of motion. Further the same thing is the cause of contrary results. For that which by its presence brings about one result is sometimes blamed for bringing about the contrary by its absence. Thus we ascribe the wreck of a ship to the absence of the pilot whose presence was the cause of its safety.

All the causes now mentioned fall into four fa- 15 miliar divisions. The letters are the causes of syllables, the material of artificial products, fire and the like of bodies, the parts of the whole, and the premisses of the conclusion, in the sense of 'that from which'. Of these pairs the one set are causes in the sense of what underlies, e.g. the parts, the other set 20 in the sense of essence—the whole and the combination and the form. But the seed and the doctor and the deliberator, and generally the maker, are all sources whence the change or stationariness originates, which the others are causes in the sense of the end or the good of the rest; for that for the sake of which tends to be what is best and the end of the things that lead up to it. (Whether we call it good or apparently good makes no difference.)

Such then is the number and nature of the kinds of cause.

Now the modes of causation are many, though when brought under heads they too can be reduced in number. For things are called causes in many ways and even within the same kind one may be prior to another; e.g. the doctor and the expert are causes of health, the relation 2:1 and number of the octave, and always what is inclusive to what is particular. Another mode of causation is the accidental and its genera, e.g. in one way Polyclitus, in another a sculptor is the cause of statue, because being Polyclitus and a sculptor are accidentally conjoined. Also the classes in which the accidental attribute is included; thus a man could be said to be the cause of a statue or, generally, a living creature. An accidental attribute too may be more or less remote, e.g. suppose that a pale man or a muscial man were said to be the cause of the statue.

All causes, both proper and accidental, may be spoken of either as potential or as actual; e.g. the cause of a house being built is either a house-builder or a house-builder building.

Similar distinctions can be made in the things of which the causes are causes, e.g. of this statue or of a statue or of an image generally, of this bronze or of bronze or of material generally. So too with the accidental attributes. Again we may use a complex expression for either and say, e.g., neither 'Polyclitus' nor a 'sculptor' but 'Polyclitus, the sculptor'.

All these various uses, however, come to six in number, under each of which again the usage is twofold. It is either what is particular or a genus, or an accidental attribute or a genus of that, and these either as a complex or each by itself; and all either as actual or as potential. The difference is this much, that causes which are actually at work and particular exist and cease to exist simultaneously with their effect, e.g. this healing person with this being-healed person and that housebuilding man with that being-built house; but this is not always true of potential causes—the house and the housebuilder do not pass away simultaneously.

In investigating the cause of each thing it is always necessary to seek what is most precise (as also in other things): thus a man builds because he is a builder, and a builder builds in virtue of his art of building. This last cause then is prior; and so generally.

Further, generic effects should be assigned to generic causes, particular effects to particular causes, e.g. statue to sculptor, this statue to this sculptor; and powers are relative to possible effects, actually operating causes to things which are actually being effected.

This must suffice for our account of the number of causes and the modes of causation.

4. But chance and spontaneity are also reckoned among causes: many things are said both to be and to come to be as a result of chance and spontaneity. We must inquire therefore in what manner chance and spontaneity are present among the causes enumerated, and whether they are the same or different, and generally what chance and spontaneity are.

Some people even question whether there are such things or not. They say that nothing happens by chance, but that everything which we ascribe to chance or spontaneity has some definite cause, e.g. coming by chance into the market and finding there a man whom one wanted but did not expect to meet is due to one's wish to go and buy in the market. Similarly, in other so-called cases of chance it is always possible, they maintain, to find something which is the cause; but not chance, for if chance were real, it would seem strange indeed, and the question might be raised, why on earth none of the wise men of old in speaking of the causes of generation and decay took account of chance; whence it would seem that they too did not believe that anything is by chance. But there is a further circumstance that is surprising. Many things both come to be and are by chance and spontaneity, and although all know that each of them can be ascribed to some cause (as the old argument said which denied chance), nevertheless they all speak of some of these things as happening by chance and others not. For this reason they ought to have at least referred to the matter in some way or other.

Certainly the early physicists found no place for chance among the causes which they recognized— love, strife, mind, fire, or the like. This is strange, whether they supposed that there is no such thing as chance or whether they thought there is but omitted to mention it—and that too when they sometimes

20 used it, as Empedocles does when he says that the air is not always separated into the highest region, but as it may chance. At any rate he says in his cosmogony that 'it happened to run that way at that time, but it often ran otherwise'. He tells us also that most of the parts of animals came to be by chance.

25 There are some who actually ascribe this heavenly sphere and all the worlds to spontaneity. They say that the vortex arose spontaneously, i.e. the motion that separated and arranged the universe in its present order. This statement might well cause surprise. For they are asserting that chance is not responsible for the existence or generation of animals

30 and plants, nature or mind or something of the kind being the cause of them (for it is not any chance thing that comes from a given seed but an olive from one kind and a man from another); and yet at the same time they assert that the heavenly sphere and the divinest of visible things arose spontaneously, having no such cause as is assigned to animals and

35 plants. Yet if this is so, it is a fact which deserves to be dwelt upon, and something might well have been said about it. For besides the other absurdities of the statement, it is the more absurd that people should make it when they see nothing coming to be

196ᵃ1 spontaneously in the heavens, but much happening by chance among the things which as they say are not due to chance; whereas we should have expected exactly the opposite.

5 Others there are who believe that chance is a cause, but that it is inscrutable to human intelligence, as being a divine thing and full of mystery.

Thus we must inquire what chance and spontaneity are, whether they are the same or different, and how they fit into our division of causes.

10 **5.** First then we observe that some things always come to pass in the same way, and others for the most part. It is clearly of neither of these that chance, or the result of chance, is said to be the cause—neither of that which is by necessity and always, nor of that which is for the most part. But as there is a third class of events besides these two—events which all

15 say are by chance—it is plain that there is such a thing as chance and spontaneity; for we know that things of this kind are due to chance and that things due to chance are of this kind.

Of things that come to be, some come to be for the sake of something, others not. Again, some of the former class are in accordance with intention, others not, but both are in the class of things which are for the sake of something. Hence it is clear that

even among the things which are outside what is 20 necessary and what is for the most part, there are some in connexion with which the phrase 'for the sake of something' is applicable. (Things that are for the sake of something include whatever may be done as a result of thought or of nature.) Things of this kind, then, when they come to pass accidentally are said to be by chance. For just as a thing is something either in virtue of itself or accidentally, so may it be a cause. For instance, the housebuilding fac- 25 ulty is in virtue of itself a cause of a house, whereas the pale or the musical is an accidental cause. That which is *per se* cause is determinate, but the accidental cause is indeterminable; for the possible attributes of an individual are innumerable. As we said, then, when a thing of this kind comes to pass among events which are for the sake of something, it is said to be spontaneous or by chance. (The dis- 30 tinction between the two must be made later—for the present it is sufficient if it is plain that both are in the sphere of things done for the sake of something.)

Example: A man is engaged in collecting subscriptions for a feast. He would have gone to such and such a place for the purpose of getting the money, if he had known. He actually went there for 35 another purpose, and it was only accidentally that he got his money by going there; and this was not due to the fact that he went there as a rule or necessarily, nor is the end effected (getting the money) a cause present in himself—it belongs to the class 197ᵃ1 of things that are objects of choice and the result of thought. It is when these conditions are satisfied that the man is said to have gone by chance. If he had chosen and gone for the sake of this—if he always or normally went there when he was collecting payments—he would not be said to have gone by chance. 5

It is clear then that chance is an accidental cause in the sphere of those actions for the sake of something which involve choice. Thought, then, and chance are in the same sphere, for choice implies thought.

It is necessary, no doubt, that the causes of what comes to pass by chance be indefinite; and that is why chance is supposed to belong to the class of the indefinite and to be inscrutable to man, and why it might be thought that, in a way, nothing occurs by 10 chance. For all these statements are correct, as might be expected. Things *do*, in a way, occur by chance, for they occur accidentally and chance is an accidental cause. But it is not the cause without qualification of anything; for instance, a housebuilder is the cause of a house; accidentally, a fluteplayer may 15 be so.

And the causes of the man's coming and getting the money (when he did not come for the sake of that) are innumerable. He may have wished to see somebody or been following somebody or avoiding somebody, or may have gone to see a spectacle. Thus to say that chance is unaccountable is correct. For an account is of what holds always or for the 20 most part, whereas chance belongs to a third type of event. Hence, since causes of this kind are indefinite, chance too is indefinite. (Yet in some cases one might raise the question whether *any* chance fact might be the cause of the chance occurrence, e.g. of health the fresh air or the sun's heat may be the cause, but having had one's hair cut *cannot*; for some accidental causes are more relevant to the effect than others.)

25 Chance is called good when the result is good, evil when it is evil. The terms 'good fortune' and 'ill fortune' are used when either result is of considerable magnitude. Thus one who comes within an ace of some great evil or great good is said to be fortunate or unfortunate. The mind affirms the presence of the attribute, ignoring the hair's breadth of 30 difference. Further, it is with reason that good fortune is regarded as unstable; for chance is unstable, as none of the things which result from it can hold always or for the most part.

Both are then, as I have said, accidental causes—both chance and spontaneity—in the sphere of things which are capable of coming to pass not simply, nor 35 for the most part and with reference to such of these as might come to pass for the sake of something.

6. They differ in that spontaneity is the wider. Every result of chance is from what is spontaneous, but not everything that is from what is spontaneous is from chance.

197ᵇ1 Chance and what results from chance are appropriate to agents that are capable of good fortune and of action generally. Therefore necessarily chance is in the sphere of actions. This is indicated by the fact that good fortune is thought to be the same, or nearly the same, as happiness, and happiness to be a kind 5 of action, since it is well-doing. Hence what is not capable of action cannot do anything by chance. Thus an inanimate thing or a beast or a child cannot do anything by chance, because it is incapable of choice; nor can good fortune or ill fortune be as-

cribed to them, except metaphorically, as Protarchus, for example, said that the stones of 10 which altars are made are fortunate because they are held in honour, while their fellows are trodden under foot. Even these things, however, can in a way be affected by chance, when one who is dealing with them does something to them by chance, but not otherwise.

The spontaneous on the other hand is found both in the beasts and in many inanimate objects. We say, for example, that the horse came spontaneously, be- 15 cause, though his coming saved him, he did not come for the sake of safety. Again, the tripod fell spontaneously, because, though it stood on its feet so as to serve for a seat, it did not fall so as to serve for a seat.

Hence it is clear that events which belong to the general class of things that may come to pass for the sake of something, when they come to pass not for the sake of what actually results, and have an external cause, may be described by the phrase 'from spontaneity'. These spontaneous events are said to 20 be from chance if they have the further characteristics of being the objects of choice and happening to agents capable of choice. This is indicated by the phrase 'in vain', which is used when one thing which is for the sake of another, does not result in it. For instance, taking a walk is for the sake of evacuation of the bowels; if this does not follow after walking, we say that we have walked in vain and that the walking was vain. This implies that what is natu- 25 rally for the sake of an end is in vain, when it does not effect the end for the sake of which it was the natural means—for it would be absurd for a man to say that he had bathed in vain because the sun was not eclipsed, since the one was not done for the sake of the other. Thus the spontaneous is even according to its derivation the case in which the thing itself happens in vain. The stone that struck the man 30 did not fall for the sake of striking him; therefore it fell spontaneously, because it might have fallen by the action of an agent and for the sake of striking. The difference between spontaneity and what results by chance is greatest in things that come to be by nature; for when anything comes to be contrary to nature, we do not say that it came to be by chance, but by spontaneity. Yet strictly this too is different 35 from the spontaneous proper; for the cause of the latter is external, that of the former internal.

We have now explained what chance is and what spontaneity is, and in what they differ from each 198ª1 other. Both belong to the mode of causation 'source of change', for either some natural or some intelligent agent is always the cause; but in this sort of causation the number of possible causes is infinite.

5 Spontaneity and chance are causes of effects which, though they might result from intelligence or nature, have in fact been caused by something accidentally. Now since nothing which is accidental is prior to what is *per se*, it is clear that no accidental cause can be prior to a cause *per se*. Spontaneity and chance, therefore, are posterior to intelligence and

10 nature. Hence, however true it may be that the heavens are due to spontaneity, it will still be true that intelligence and nature will be prior causes of this universe and of many things in it besides.

7. It is clear then that there are causes, and that the number of them is what we have stated. The number is the same as that of the things compre-

15 hended under the question 'why'. The 'why' is referred ultimately either, in things which do not involve motion, e.g. in mathematics, to the 'what' (to the definition of straight line or commensurable or the like); or to what initiated a motion, e.g. 'why did

20 they go to war?—because there had been a raid'; or we are inquiring 'for the sake of what?'—'that they may rule'; or in the case of things that come into being, we are looking for the matter. The causes, therefore, are these and so many in number.

Now, the causes being four, it is the business of the student of nature to know about them all, and if he refers his problems back to all of them, he will assign the 'why' in the way proper to his science—the matter, the form, the mover, that for the sake of

25 which. The last three often coincide; for the what and that for the sake of which are one, while the primary source of motion is the same in species as these. For man generates man—and so too, in general, with all things which cause movement by being themselves moved; and such as are not of this kind are no longer inside the province of natural science, for they cause motion not by possessing motion or a source of motion in themselves, but being

30 themselves incapable of motion. Hence there are three branches of study, one of things which are incapable of motion, the second of things in motion, but indestructible, the third of destructible things.

The question 'why', then, is answered by reference to the matter, to the form, and to the primary moving cause. For in respect of coming to be it is mostly in this last way that causes are investigated—

35 'what comes to be after what? what was the primary agent or patient?' and so at each step of the series.

Now the principles which cause motion in a natural way are two, of which one is not natural, as it has no principle of motion in itself. Of this kind is 198ᵇ1 whatever causes movement, not being itself moved, such as that which is completely unchangeable, the primary reality, and the essence of a thing, i.e. the form; for this is the end or that for the sake of which. Hence since nature is for the sake of something, we must know this cause also. We must explain the 'why' in all the senses of the term, namely, that from this 5 that will necessarily result ('from this' either without qualification or for the most part); that this must be so if that is to be so (as the conclusion presupposes the premisses); that this was the essence of the thing; and because it is better thus (not without qualification, but with reference to the substance in each case).

8. We must explain then first why nature belongs 10 to the class of causes which act for the sake of something; and then about the necessary and its place in nature, for all writers ascribe things to this cause, arguing that since the hot and the cold and the like are of such and such a kind, therefore certain things *necessarily* are and come to be—and if they mention 15 any other cause (one friendship and strife, another mind), it is only to touch on it, and then good-bye to it.

A difficulty presents itself: why should not nature work, not for the sake of something, nor because it is better so, but just as the sky rains, not in order to make the corn grow, but of necessity? (What is drawn up must cool, and what has been cooled must become water and descend, the result of this being that the corn grows.) Similarly if a man's crop is 20 spoiled on the threshing-floor, the rain did not fall for the sake of this—in order that the crop might be spoiled—but that result just followed. Why then should it not be the same with the parts in nature, e.g. that our teeth should come up of necessity—the front teeth sharp, fitted for tearing, the molars broad and useful for grinding down the food—since they did not arise for this end, but is was merely a coin- 25 cident result; and so with all other parts in which we suppose that there is purpose? Wherever then all the parts came about just what they would have been if they had come to be for an end, such things survived, being organized spontaneously in a fitting way; whereas those which grew otherwise perished 30 and continue to perish, as Empedocles says his 'man-faced ox-progeny' did.

Such are the arguments (and others of the kind) which may cause difficulty on this point. Yet it is impossible that this should be the true view. For teeth and all other natural things either invariably or for the most part come about in a given way; but of not one of the results of chance or spontaneity is this true. We do not ascribe to chance or mere coincidence the frequency of rain in winter, but frequent rain in summer we do; nor heat in summer but only if we have it in winter. If then, it is agreed that things are either the result of coincidence or for the sake of something, and these cannot be the result of coincidence or spontaneity, it follows that they must be for the sake of something; and that such things are all due to nature even the champions of the theory which is before us would agree. Therefore action for an end is present in things which come to be and are by nature.

Further, where there is an end, all the preceding steps are for the sake of that. Now surely as in action, so in nature; and as in nature, so it is in each action, if nothing interferes. Now action is for the sake of an end; therefore the nature of things also is so. Thus if a house, e.g., had been a thing made by nature, it would have been made in the same way as it is now by art; and if things made by nature were made not only by nature but also by art, they would come to be in the same way as by nature. The one, then, is for the sake of the other; and generally art in some cases completes what nature cannot bring to a finish, and in others imitates nature. If, therefore, artificial products are for the sake of an end, so clearly also are natural products. The relation of the later to the earlier items is the same in both.

This is most obvious in the animals other than man: they make things neither by art nor after inquiry or deliberation. That is why people wonder whether it is by intelligence or by some other faculty that these creatures work,—spiders, ants, and the like. By gradual advance in this direction we come to see clearly that in plants too that is produced which is conducive to the end—leaves, e.g. grow to provide shade for the fruit. If then it is both by nature and for an end that the swallow makes its nest and the spider its web, and plants grow leaves for the sake of the fruit and send their roots down (not up) for the sake of nourishment, it is plain that this kind of cause is operative in things which come to be and are by nature. And since nature is twofold, the matter and the form, of which the latter is the end, and since all the rest is for the sake of the end,

the form must be the cause in the sense of that for the sake of which.

Now mistakes occur even in the operations of art: the literate man makes a mistake in writing and the doctor pours out the wrong dose. Hence clearly mistakes are possible in the operations of nature also. If then in art there are cases in which what is rightly produced serves a purpose, and if where mistakes occur there was a purpose in what was attempted, only it was not attained, so must it be also in natural products, and monstrosities will be failures in the purposive effort. Thus in the original combinations the 'ox-progeny', if they failed to reach a determinate end must have arisen through the corruption of some principle, as happens now when the seed is defective.

Further, seed must have come into being first, and not straightway the animals: what was 'undifferentiated first' was seed.

Again, in plants too we find that for the sake of which, though the degree of organization is less. Were there then in plants also olive-headed vine-progeny, like the 'man-headed ox-progeny', or not? An absurd suggestion; yet there must have been, if there were such things among animals.

Moreover, among the seeds anything must come to be at random. But the person who asserts this entirely does away with nature and what exists by nature. For those things are natural which, by a continuous movement originated from an internal principle, arrive at some end: the same end is not reached from every principle; nor any chance end, but always the tendency in each is towards the same end, if there is no impediment.

The end and the means towards it may come about by chance. We say, for instance, that a stranger has come by chance, paid the ransom, and gone away, when he does so as if he had come for that purpose, though it was not for that that he came. This is accidental, for chance is an accidental cause, as I remarked before. But when an event takes place always or for the most part, it is not accidental or by chance. In natural products the sequence is invariable, if there is no impediment.

It is absurd to suppose that purpose is not present because we do not observe the agent deliberating. Art does not deliberate. If the ship-building art were in the wood, it would produce the same results by nature. If, therefore, purpose is present in art, it is present also in nature. The best illustration is a doctor doctoring himself: nature is like that.

It is plain then that nature is a cause, a cause that operates for a purpose.

9. As regards what is of necessity, we must ask whether the necessity is hypothetical, or simple as well. The current view places what is of necessity in the process of production, just as if one were to 200ᵃ1 suppose that the wall of a house necessarily comes to be because what is heavy is naturally carried downwards and what is light to the top, so that the stones and foundations take the lowest place, with earth above because it is lighter, and wood at the top of all as being the lightest. Whereas, though the wall 5 does not come to be *without* these, it is not *due* to these, except as its material cause: it comes to be for the sake of sheltering and guarding certain things. Similarly in all other things which involve that for the sake of which: the product cannot come to be without things which have a necessary nature, but it is not due to these (except as its material); it comes to be for an end. For instance, why is a saw such as 10 it is? To effect so-and-so and for the sake of so-and-so. This end, however, cannot be realized unless the saw is made of iron. It is, therefore, necessary for it to be of iron, if we are to have a saw and perform the operation of sawing. What is necessary then, is necessary on a hypothesis, not as an end. Necessity is in the matter, while that for the sake of which is in the definition.

15 Necessity in mathematics is in a way similar to necessity in things which come to be through the operation of nature. Since a straight line is what it is, it is necessary that the angles of a triangle should equal two right angles. But not conversely; though if the angles are *not* equal to two right angles, then the straight line is not what it is either. But in things which come to be for an end, the reverse is true. If the end is to exist or does exist, that also which pre-20 cedes it will exist or does exist; otherwise just as there, if the conclusion is not true, the principle will not be true, so here the end or that for the sake of which will not exist. For this too is itself a principle, but of the reasoning, not of the action. (In mathematics the principle is the principle of the reasoning only, as there is no action.) If then there is to be a house, such-and-such things must be made or be 25 there already or exist, or generally the matter relative to the end, bricks and stones if it is a house. But the end is not due to these except as the matter, nor will it come to exist because of them. Yet if they do not exist at all, neither will the house, or the saw—the former in the absence of stones, the latter in the

absence of iron—just as in the other case the principles will not be true, if the angles of. the triangle 30 are not equal to two right angles.

The necessary in nature, then, is plainly what we call by the name of matter, and the changes in it. Both causes must be stated by the student of nature, but especially the end; for that is the cause of the matter, not *vice versa*; and the end is that for the sake of which, and the principle starts from the definition or essence: as in artificial products, since a 200ᵇ1 house is of such-and-such a kind, certain things must *necessarily* come to be or be there already, or since health is this, these things must necessarily come to be or be there already, so too if man is this, then these; if these, then those. Perhaps the necessary is present also in the definition. For if one defines the operation of sawing as being a certain kind of di- 5 viding, then this cannot come about unless the saw has teeth of a certain kind; and these cannot be unless it is of iron. For in the definition too there are some parts that stand as matter.

BOOK III

1. Nature is a principle of motion and change, and it is the subject of our inquiry. We must therefore see that we understand what motion is; for if it were unknown, nature too would be unknown.

When we have determined the nature of motion, 15 our task will be to attack in the same way the terms which come next in order. Now motion is supposed to belong to the class of things which are continuous; and the infinite presents itself first in the continuous—that is how it comes about that the account of the infinite is often used in definitions of the continuous; for what is infinitely divisible is continu- 20 ous. Besides these, place, void, and time are thought to be necessary conditions of motion.

Clearly, then, for these reasons and also because the attributes mentioned are common to everything and universal, we must first take each of them in hand and discuss it. For the investigation of special attributes comes after that of the common attributes.

To begin then, as we said, with motion.   25

Some things are in fulfilment only, others in potentiality and in fulfilment—one being a 'this', another so much, another such and such, and similarly for the other categories of being. The term 'relative' is applied sometimes with reference to excess and defect, sometimes to agent and patient, and gener- 30 ally to what can move and what can be moved. For what can cause movement is relative to what can be moved, and *vice versa*.

There is no such thing as motion over and above the things. It is always with respect to substance or to quantity or to quality or to place that what changes changes. But it is impossible, as we assert, to find anything common to these which is neither 'this' nor 201ᵃ1 quantity nor quality nor any of the other predicates. Hence neither will motion and change have reference to something over and above the things mentioned; for there *is* nothing over and above them.

Now each of these belongs to all its subjects in either of two ways: namely, substance—the one is its form, the other privation; in quality, white and 5 black; in quantity, complete and incomplete. Similarly, in respect of locomotion, upwards and downwards or light and heavy. Hence there are as many types of motion or change as there are of being.

10 We have distinguished in respect of each class between what is in fulfilment and what is potentially; thus the fulfilment of what is potentially, as such, is motion—e.g. the fulfilment of what is alterable, as alterable, is alteration; of what is increasable and its opposite, decreasable (there is no common name for both), increase and decrease; of what can come to be and pass away, coming to be and passing away; of what can be carried along, locomotion.

That this is what motion is, is clear from what fol-15 lows: when what is buildable, in so far as we call it such, is in fulfilment, it is being built, and that is building. Similarly with learning, doctoring, rolling, jumping, ripening, aging.

The same thing can be both potential and fulfilled, 20 not indeed at the same time or not in the same respect, but e.g. potentially hot and actually cold. Hence such things will act and be acted on by one another in many ways: each of them will be capable at the same time of acting and of being acted upon. Hence, too, what effects motion as a natural agent can be moved: when a thing of this kind causes 25 motion, it is itself also moved. This, indeed, has led some people to suppose that every mover is moved. But this question depends on another set of arguments, and the truth will be made clear later. It *is* possible for a thing to cause motion, though it is itself incapable of being moved.

It is the fulfilment of what is potential when it is already fulfilled and operates not as itself but as 30 movable, that is motion. What I mean by 'as' is this: bronze is potentially a statue. But it is not the fulfilment of bronze as *bronze* which is motion. For to be bronze and to be a certain potentiality are not the same. If they were identical without qualification, i.e. in definition, the fulfilment of bronze as bronze *would* be motion. But they are not the same, as has been said. (This is obvious in contraries. To be capable of health and to be capable of illness are not the same; for if they were there would be no difference between being ill and being well. Yet the sub- 210ᵇ1 ject both of health and of sickness—whether it is humour or blood—is one and the same.)

We can distinguish, then, between the two—just as colour and visible are different—and clearly it is the fulfilment of what is potential as potential that is motion. 5

It is evident that this is motion, and that motion occurs just when the fulfilment itself occurs, and neither before nor after. For each thing is capable of being at one time actual, at another not. Take for instance the buildable: the actuality of the buildable 10 as buildable is the process of building. For the actuality must be either this or the house. But when there is a house, the buildable is no longer there. On the other hand, it *is* the buildable which is *being* built. Necessarily, then, the actuality is the process of building. But building is a kind of motion, and the same account will apply to the other kinds also. 15

2. The soundness of this definition is evident both when we consider the accounts of motion that the others have given, and also from the difficulty of defining it otherwise.

One could not easily put motion and change in another genus—this is plain if we consider where 20 some people put it: they identify motion with difference or inequality or not being; but such things are not necessarily moved, whether they are different or unequal or non-existent. Nor is change either to or from *these* rather than to or from their opposites.

The reason why they put motion into these genera is that it is thought to be something indefinite, and the principles in the second column are indefi- 25 nite because they are privative: none of them is either a 'this' or such or comes under any of the other categories. The reason why motion is thought to be indefinite is that it cannot be classed as a potentiality or as an actuality—a thing that is merely *capable* of having a certain size is not necessarily undergoing change, nor yet a thing that is *actually* of 30 a certain size, and motion is thought to be a sort of *actuality*, but incomplete, the reason for this view being that the potential whose actuality it is is incomplete. This is why it is hard to grasp what motion is. It is necessary to class it with privation or with potentiality or with simple actuality, yet none of these seems possible. There remains then the suggested mode of definition, namely that it is a sort of actuality, or actuality of the kind described, hard to grasp, but not incapable of existing.

Every mover too is moved, as has been said—every mover, that is, which is capable of motion, and whose immobility is rest (for when a thing is subject to motion its immobility is rest). For to act on the movable as such is just to move it. But this it does by contact, so that at the same time it is also acted on. Hence motion is the fulfilment of the movable as movable, the cause being contact with what can move, so that the mover is also acted on. The mover will always transmit a form, either a 'this' or such or so much, which, when it moves, will be the principle and cause of the motion, e.g. the actual man begets man from what is potentially man.

3. The solution of the difficulty is plain: motion is in the movable. It is the fulfilment of this potentiality by the action of that which has the power of causing motion; and the actuality of that which has the power of causing motion is not other than the actuality of the movable; for it must be the fulfilment of *both*. A thing is capable of causing motion because it *can* do this, it is a mover because it actually *does* it. But it is on the movable that it is capable of acting. Hence there is a single actuality of both alike, just as one to two and two to one are the same interval, and the steep ascent and the steep descent are one—for these are one and the same, although their definitions are not one. So it is with the mover and the moved.

This view has a dialectical difficulty. Perhaps it is necessary that there should be an actuality of the agent and of the patient. The one is agency and the other patiency; and the outcome and end of the one is an action, that of the other a passion. Since then they are both motions, we may ask: *in* what are they, if they are different? Either both are in what is acted on and moved, or the agency is in the agent and the patiency in the patient. (If we ought to call the latter also 'agency', the word would be used in two senses.)

Now, in the latter case, the motion will be in the mover, for the same account will hold of mover and moved. Hence either *every* mover will be moved, or, though having motion, it will not be moved.

If on the other hand both are in what is moved and acted on—both the agency and the patiency (e.g. both teaching and learning, though they are two, in the learner), then, first, the actuality of each will not be present *in* each, and, a second absurdity, a thing will have two motions at the same time. How will there be two alterations of quality in *one* subject towards *one* form? The thing is impossible: the actualization will be one.

But (someone will say) it is contrary to reason to suppose that there should be one identical actualization of two things which are different in kind. Yet there will be, if teaching and learning are the same, and agency and patiency. To teach will be the same as to learn, and to act the same as to be acted on—the teacher will necessarily be learning everything that he teaches, and the agent will be acted on. It is not absurd that the actualization of one thing should be in another. Teaching is the activity of a person who can teach, yet the operation is performed in something—it is not cut adrift from a subject, but is of one thing in another.

There is nothing to prevent two things having one and the same actualization (not the same in being, but related as the potential is to the actual).

Nor is it necessary that the teacher should learn, even if to act and to be acted on are one and the same, provided they are not the same in respect of the account which states their essence (as raiment and dress), but are the same in the sense in which the road from Thebes to Athens and the road from Athens to Thebes are the same, as has been explained above. For it is not things which are in any way the same that have all their attributes the same, but only those to be which is the same. But indeed it by no means follows from the fact that teaching is the same as learning, that to learn is the same as to teach, any more than it follows from the fact that there is one distance between two things which are at a distance from each other, that being here at a distance from there and being there at a distance from here are one and the same. To generalize, teaching is not the same as learning, or agency as patiency, in the full sense, though they belong to the same subject, the motion; for the actualization of this in that and the actualization of that through the action of this differ in definition.

What then motion is, has been stated both generally and particularly. It is not difficult to see how each of its types will be defined—alteration is the fulfilment of the alterable as alterable (or, more scientifically, the fulfilment of what can act and what can be acted on, as such)—generally and again in each particular case, building, healing. A similar definition will apply to each of the other kinds of motion.

On the Soul

10 **4.** Turning now to the part of the soul with which the soul knows and (whether this is separable from the others in definition only, or spatially as well) we have to inquire what differentiates this part, and how thinking can take place.

If thinking is like perceiving, it must be either a process in which the soul is acted upon by what is 15 capable of being thought, or a process different from but analogous to that. The thinking part of the soul must therefore be, while impassible, capable of receiving the form of an object; that is, must be potentially identical in character with its object without being the object. Thought must be related to what is thinkable, as sense is to what is sensible.

Therefore, since everything is a possible object of thought, mind in order, as Anaxagoras says, to dominate, that is, to know, must be pure from all ad-20 mixture; for the co-presence of what is alien to its nature is a hindrance and a block: it follows that it can have no nature of its own, other than that of having a certain capacity. Thus that in the soul which is called thought (by thought I mean that whereby the soul thinks and judges) is, before it thinks, not actually any real thing. For this reason it cannot reasonably be regarded as blended with the body: if so, 25 it would acquire some quality, e.g., warmth or cold, or even have an organ like the sensitive faculty: as it is, it has none. It was a good idea to call the soul 'the place of forms', though this description holds only of the thinking soul, and even this is the forms only potentially, not actually.

30 Observation of the sense-organs and their employment reveals a distinction between the impassibility of the sensitive faculty and that of the faculty of thought. After strong stimulation of a sense we are less able to exercise it than before, as e.g. in the case of a loud sound we cannot hear easily immediately 429ᵇ after, or in the case of a bright colour or a powerful odour we cannot see or smell, but in the case of thought thinking about an object that is highly thinkable renders it more and not less able afterwards to think of objects that are less thinkable: the reason is that while the faculty of sensation is dependent upon 5 the body, thought is separable from it.

When thought has become each thing in the way in which a man who actually knows is said to do so (this happens when he is now able to exercise the power on his own initiative), its condition is still one of potentiality, but in a different sense from the potentiality which preceded the acquisition of knowledge by learning or discovery; and thought is then able to think of itself.

Since we can distinguish between a magnitude 10 and what it is to be a magnitude, and between water and what it is to be water, and so in many other cases (though not in all; for in certain cases the thing and its form are identical), flesh and what it is to be flesh are discriminated either by different faculties, or by the same faculty in two different states; for flesh necessarily involves matter and is like what is snub-nosed, a *this* in a *this*. Now it is by means of the sensitive faculty that we discriminate the hot and the cold, i.e. the factors which combined in a cer-15 tain ratio constitute flesh: the essential character of flesh is apprehended by something different either wholly separate from the sensitive faculty or related to it as a bent line to the same line when it has been straightened out.

Again in the case of abstract objects what is straight is analogous to what is snub-nosed; for it necessarily implies a continuum: its constitutive essence is different, if we may distinguish between straightness and what is straight: let us take it to be two-ness. It must be apprehended, therefore, by a 20 different power or by the same power in a different state. To sum up, in so far as the realities it knows are capable of being separated from their matter, so it is also with the powers of thought.

The problem might be suggested: if thinking is a passive affection, then if thought is simple and impassible and has nothing in common with anything else, as Anaxagoras says, how can it come to think at all? For interaction between two factors is held to require a precedent community of nature between the factors. Again it might be asked, is thought a 25 possible object of thought to itself? For if thought is thinkable *per se* and what is thinkable is in kind one and the same, then either thought will belong to

Reprinted from Aristotle's *On the Soul*, translated by J. A. Smith (1956) by permission of Oxford University Press.

everything, or it will contain some element common to it with all other realities which makes them all thinkable.

30 Have not we already disposed of the difficulty about interaction involving a common element, when we said that thought is in a sense potentially whatever is thinkable, though actually it is nothing until it has thought? What it thinks must be in it just 430ᵃ as characters may be said to be on a writing-table on which as yet nothing actually stands written: this is exactly what happens with thought.

Thought is itself thinkable in exactly the same way as its objects are. For in the case of objects which involve no matter, what thinks and what is thought are identical; for speculative knowledge and its object are 5 identical. (Why thought is not always thinking we must consider later.) In the case of those which contain matter each of the objects of thought is only potentially present. It follows that while they will not have thought in them (for thought is a potentiality of them only in so far as they are capable of being disengaged from matter) thought may yet be thinkable.

10 **5.** Since in every class of things, as in nature as a whole, we find two factors involved, a matter which is potentially all the particulars included in the class, a cause which is productive in the sense that it makes them all (the latter standing to the former, as e.g. an art to its material), these distinct elements must likewise be found within the soul.

And in fact thought, as we have described it, is what it is by virtue of becoming all things, while 15 there is another which is what it is by virtue of making all things: this is a sort of positive state like light; for in a sense light makes potential colours into actual colours.

Thought in this sense of it is separable, impassible, unmixed, since it is in its essential nature activity (for always the active is superior to the passive factor, the originating force to the matter).

Actual knowledge is identical with its object: in the individual, potential knowledge is in time prior to actual knowledge, but absolutely it is not prior 20 even in time. It does not sometimes think and sometimes not think. When separated it is alone just what it is, and this alone is immortal and eternal (we do not remember because, while this is impassible, passive thought is perishable); and without this nothing thinks. 25

Metaphysics (Metaphysica)

BOOK A (I)

980ᵃ **1.** All men by nature desire to know. An indication of this is the delight we take in our senses; for even apart from their usefulness they are loved for 25 themselves; and above all others the sense of sight. For not only with a view to action, but even when we are not going to do anything, we prefer seeing (one might say) to everything else. The reason is that this, most of all the senses, makes us know and brings to light many differences between things.

By nature animals are born with the faculty of sensation, and from sensation memory is produced in some of them, though not in others. And therefore 980ᵇ the former are more intelligent and apt at learning than those which cannot remember; those which are incapable of hearing sounds are intelligent though they cannot be taught, e.g. the bee, and any other race of animals that may be like it; and those which besides memory have this sense of hearing can be taught.

The animals other than man live by appearances 25 and memories, and have but little of connected experience; but the human race lives also by art and reasonings. Now from memory experience is produced in men; for the several memories of the same thing produce finally the capacity for a single expe- 981ᵃ rience. And experience seems pretty much like science and art, but really science and art come to men *through* experience; for 'experience made art', as Polus says, 'but inexperience luck'. Now art arises when from many notions gained by experience one universal judgement about a class of objects is produced. For to have a judgement that when Callias 5 was ill of this disease this did him good, and similarly in the case of Socrates and in many individual

Reprinted from Aristotle's *Metaphysics*, translated by W. D. Ross by permission of Oxford University Press.

cases, is a matter of experience; but to judge that it has done good to all persons of a certain constitution, marked off in one class, when they were ill of this disease, e.g. to phlegmatic or bilious people when burning with fever—this is a matter of art.

With a view to action experience seems in no respect inferior to art, and men of experience succeed even better than those who have theory without experience. (The reason is that experience is knowledge of individuals, art of universals, and actions and productions are all concerned with the individual; for the physician does not cure *man*, except in an incidental way, but Callias or Socrates or some other called by some such individual name, who happens to be a man. If, then, a man has the theory without the experience, and recognizes the universal but does not know the individual included in this, he will often fail to cure; for it is the individual that is to be cured.) But yet we think that *knowledge* and *understanding* belong to art rather than to experience, and we suppose artists to be wiser than men of experience (which implies that Wisdom depends in all cases rather on knowledge); and this because the former know the cause, but the latter do not. For men of experience know that the thing is so, but do not know why, while the others know the 'why' and the cause. Hence we think also that the master-workers in each craft are more honourable and know in a truer sense and are wiser than the manual workers, because they know the causes of the things that are done (we think the manual workers are like certain lifeless things which act indeed, but act without knowing what they do, as fire burns—but while the lifeless things perform each of their functions by a natural tendency, the labourers perform them through habit); thus we view them as being wiser not in virtue of being able to act, but of having the theory for themselves and knowing the causes. And in general it is a sign of the man who knows and of the man who does not know, that the former can teach, and therefore we think art more truly knowledge than experience is; for artists can teach, and men of mere experience cannot.

Again, we do not regard any of the senses as Wisdom; yet surely these give the most authoritative knowledge of particulars. But they do not tell us the 'why' of anything—e.g. why fire is hot; they only say *that* it is hot.

At first he who invented any art whatever that went beyond the common perceptions of man was naturally admired by men, not only because there was something useful in the inventions, but because he was thought wise and superior to the rest. But as more arts were invented, and some were directed to the necessities of life, others to recreation, the inventors of the latter were naturally always regarded as wiser than the inventors of the former, because their branches of knowledge did not aim at utility. Hence when all such inventions were already established, the sciences which do not aim at giving pleasure or at the necessities of life were discovered, and first in the places where men first began to have leisure. This is why the mathematical arts were founded in Egypt; for there the priestly caste was allowed to be at leisure.

We have said in the *Ethics*[1] what the difference is between art and science and the other kindred faculties; but the point of our present discussion is this, that all men suppose what is called Wisdom to deal with the first causes and the principles of things; so that, as has been said before, the man of experience is thought to be wiser than the possessors of any sense-perception whatever, the artist wiser than the men of experience, the master-worker than the mechanic, and the theoretical kinds of knowledge to be more of the nature of Wisdom than the productive. Clearly then Wisdom is knowledge about certain principles and causes.

2. Since we are seeking this knowledge, we must inquire of what kind are the causes and the principles, the knowledge of which is Wisdom. If one were to take the notions we have about the wise man, this might perhaps make the answer more evident. We suppose first, then, that the wise man knows all things, as far as possible, although he has not knowledge of each of them in detail; secondly, that he who can learn things that are difficult, and not easy for man to know, is wise (sense-perception is common to all, and therefore easy and no mark of Wisdom); again, that he who is more exact and more capable of teaching the causes is wiser, in every branch of knowledge; and that of the sciences, also, that which is desirable on its own account and for the sake of knowing it is more of the nature of Wisdom than that which is desirable on account of its results, and the superior science is more of the nature of Wisdom than the ancillary; for the wise man must not be ordered but must order, and he must not obey another, but the less wise must obey *him*.

[1] 1139[b] 14-1141[b] 8.

20 Such and so many are the notions, then, which we have about Wisdom and the wise. Now of these characteristics that of knowing all things must belong to him who has in the highest degree universal knowledge; for he knows in a sense all the instances that fall under the universal. And these things, the most universal, are on the whole the hardest for men 25 to know; for they are farthest from the senses. And the most exact of the sciences are those which deal most with first principles; for those which involve fewer principles are more exact than those which involve additional principles, e. g. arithmetic than geometry. But the science which investigates causes is also *instructive*, in a higher degree, for the people who instruct us are those who tell the causes of 30 each thing. And understanding and knowledge pursued for their own sake are found most in the knowledge of that which is most knowable (for he who chooses to know for the sake of knowing will choose most readily that which is most truly knowledge, and 982ᵃ such is the knowledge of that which is most knowable); and the first principles and the causes are most knowable; for by reason of these, and from these, all other things come to be known, and not these by means of the things subordinate to them. And the science which knows to what end each thing must 5 be done is the most authoritative of the sciences, and more authoritative than any ancillary science; and this end is the good of that thing, and in general the supreme good in the whole of nature. Judged by all the tests we have mentioned, then, the name in question falls to the same science; this must be a science 10 that investigates the first principles and causes; for the good, i. e. the end, is one of the causes.

That it is not a science of production is clear even from the history of the earliest philosophers. For it is owing to their wonder that men both now begin and at first began to philosophize; they wondered originally at the obvious difficulties, then advanced little by little and stated difficulties about the greater 15 matters, e. g. about the phenomena of the moon and those of the sun and of the stars, and about the genesis of the universe. And a man who is puzzled and wonders thinks himself ignorant (whence even the lover of myth is in a sense a lover of Wisdom, for the myth is composed of wonders); therefore since they philosophized in order to escape from ignorance, evidently they were pursuing science in or-20 der to know, and not for any utilitarian end. And this is confirmed by the facts; for it was when almost all the necessities of life and the things that make for comfort and recreation had been secured, that such knowledge began to be sought. Evidently then we do not seek it for the sake of any other advantage; but as the man is free, we say, who exists for his 25 own sake and not for another's, so we pursue this as the only free science, for it alone exists for its own sake.

Hence also the possession of it might be justly regarded as beyond human power; for in many ways 30 human nature is in bondage, so that according to Simonides 'God alone can have this privilege', and it is unfitting that man should not be content to seek the knowledge that is suited to him. If, then, there 983ᵃ is something in what the poets say, and jealousy is natural to the divine power, it would probably occur in this case above all, and all who excelled in this knowledge would be unfortunate. But the divine power cannot be jealous (nay, according to the proverb, 'bards tell many a lie'), nor should any other science be thought more honourable than one of this sort. For the most divine science is also most 5 honourable; and this science alone must be, in two ways, most divine. For the science which it would be most meet for God to have is a divine science, and so is any science that deals with divine objects; and this science alone has both these qualities; for (1) God is thought to be among the causes of all things and to be a first principle, and (2) such a science either God alone can have, or God above all others. All the sciences, indeed, are more necessary 10 than this, but none is better.

Yet the acquisition of it must in a sense end in something which is the opposite of our original inquiries. For all men begin, as we said, by wondering that things are as they are, as they do about self- 15 moving marionettes, or about the solstices or the incommensurability of the diagonal of a square with the side; for it seems wonderful to all who have not yet seen the reason, that there is a thing which cannot be measured even by the smallest unit. But we must end in the contrary and, according to the proverb, the better state, as is the case in these instances too when men learn the cause; for there is nothing which would surprise a geometer so much as if the diagonal turned out to be commensurable. 20

We have stated, then, what is the nature of the science we are searching for, and what is the mark which our search and our whole investigation must reach.

3. Evidently we have to acquire knowledge of the original causes (for we say we know each thing only 25

when we think we recognize its first cause), and causes are spoken of in four senses. In one of these we mean the substance, i. e. the essence (for the 'why' is reducible finally to the definition, and the ultimate 30 'why' is a cause and principle); in another the matter or substratum, in a third the source of the change, and in a fourth the cause opposed to this, the purpose and 983ᵇ the good (for this is the end of all generation and change). We have studied these causes sufficiently in our work on nature,[2] but yet let us call to our aid those who have attacked the investigation of being and philosophized about reality before us. For obviously they too speak of certain principles and causes; to go over their views, then, will be of profit to the present inquiry, for we shall either find another kind of cause, 5 or be more convinced of the correctness of those which we now maintain.

Of the first philosophers, then, most thought the principles which were of the nature of matter were the only principles of all things. That of which all things that are consist, the first from which they come to be, the last into which they are resolved (the 10 substance remaining, but changing in its modifications), this they say is the element and this the principle of things, and therefore they think nothing is either generated or destroyed, since this sort of entity is always conserved, as we say Socrates neither comes to be absolutely when he comes to be beautiful or musical, nor ceases to be when he loses these 15 characteristics, because the substratum, Socrates himself, remains. Just so they say nothing else comes to be or ceases to be; for there must be some entity—either one or more than one—from which all other things come to be, it being conserved.

Yet they do not all agree as to the number and the nature of these principles. Thales, the founder of this 20 type of philosophy, says the principle is water (for which reason he declared that the earth rests on water), getting the notion perhaps from seeing that the nutriment of all things is moist, and that heat itself is generated from the moist and kept alive by it (and that from which they come to be is a principle of all 25 things). He got his notion from this fact, and from the fact that the seeds of all things have a moist nature, and that water is the origin of the nature of moist things.

Some think that even the ancients who lived long before the present generation, and first framed accounts of the gods, had a similar view of nature; for they made Ocean and Tethys the parents of creation, 30 and described the oath of the gods as being by water, to which they give the name of Styx; for what is oldest is most honourable, and the most honourable thing is that by which one swears. It may 984ᵃ perhaps be uncertain whether this opinion about nature is primitive and ancient, but Thales at any rate is said to have declared himself thus about the first cause. Hippo no one would think fit to include among these thinkers, because of the paltriness of his thought.

Anaximenes and Diogenes make air prior to wa- 5 ter, and the most primary of the simple bodies, while Hippasus of Metapontium and Heraclitus of Ephesus say this of fire, and Empedocles says it of the four elements (adding a fourth—earth—to those which have been named); for these, he says, always remain and do not come to be, except that they come to be 10 more or fewer, being aggregated into one and segregated out of one.

Anaxagoras of Clazomenae, who, though older than Empedocles, was later in his philosophical activity, says the principles are infinite in number; for he says almost all the things that are made of parts like themselves, in the manner of water or fire, are generated and destroyed in this way, only by aggregation and segregation, and are not in any other 15 sense generated or destroyed, but remain eternally.

From these facts one might think that the only cause is the so-called material cause; but as men thus advanced, the very facts opened the way for them and joined in forcing them to investigate the subject. However true it may be that all generation and destruction proceed from some one or (for that matter) from more elements, why does this happen and 20 what is the cause? For at least the substratum itself does not make itself change; e. g. neither the wood nor the bronze causes the change of either of them, nor does the wood manufacture a bed and the bronze a statue, but something else is the cause of the 25 change. And to seek this is to seek the second cause, as *we* should say—that from which comes the beginning of the movement. Now those who at the very beginning set themselves to this kind of inquiry, and said the substratum was one,[3] were not at all dissatisfied with themselves; but some at least of those who maintain it to be one[4]—as though defeated by 30 this search for the second cause—say the one and

---

[2]*Phys.* ii. 3, 7.

[3]Thales, Anaximenes, and Heraclitus.
[4]The Eleatics.

nature as a whole is unchangeable not only in respect of generation and destruction (for this is a primitive belief, and all agreed in it), but also of all 984ᵇ other change; and this view is peculiar to them. Of those who said the universe was one, then, none succeeded in discovering a cause of this sort, except perhaps Parmenides, and he only inasmuch as he supposes that there is not only one but also in some sense two causes. But for those who make more elements[5] it is more possible to state the second cause, 5 e. g. for those who make hot and cold, or fire and earth, the elements; for they treat fire as having a nature which fits it to move things, and water and earth and such things they treat in the contrary way.

When these men and the principles of this kind had had their day, as the latter were found inade-10 quate to generate the nature of things men were again forced by the truth itself, as we said,[6] to inquire into the next kind of cause. For it is not likely either that fire or earth or any such element should be the reason why things manifest goodness and beauty both in their being and in their coming to be, or that those thinkers should have supposed it was; nor again could it be right to entrust so great a matter to spontaneity and chance. When one man[7] said, then, that reason was present—as in animals, so 15 throughout nature—as the cause of order and of all arrangement, he seemed like a sober man in contrast with the random talk of his predecessors. We know that Anaxagoras certainly adopted these views, but Hermotimus of Clazomenae is credited with expressing them earlier. Those who thought thus stated that there is a principle of things which is at the same 20 time the cause of beauty, and that sort of cause from which things acquire movement.

4. One might suspect that Hesiod was the first to look for such a thing—or some one else who put 25 love or desire among existing things as a principle, as Parmenides, too, does; for he, in constructing the genesis of the universe, says:—

Love first of all the Gods she planned.

And Hesiod says:—

First of all things was chaos made, and then

Broad-breasted earth, . . .
And love, 'mid all the gods pre-
eminent,

which implies that among existing things there must 30 be from the first a cause which will move things and bring them together. How these thinkers should be arranged with regard to priority of discovery let us be allowed to decide later;[8] but since the contraries of the various forms of good were also perceived to be present in nature—not only order and the beau- 985ᵃ tiful, but also disorder and the ugly, and bad things in greater number than good, and ignoble things than beautiful—therefore another thinker introduced friendship and strife, each of the two the cause of one of these two sets of qualities. For if we were to 5 follow out the view of Empedocles, and interpret it according to its meaning and not to its lisping expression, we should find that friendship is the cause of good things, and strife of bad. Therefore, if we said that Empedocles in a sense both mentions, and is the first to mention, the bad and the good as principles, we should perhaps be right, since the cause of all goods is the good itself.

These thinkers, as we say, evidently grasped, and 10 to this extent, two of the causes which we distinguished in our work on nature[9]—the matter and the source of the movement—vaguely, however, and with no clearness, but as untrained men behave in fights; for they go round their opponents and often strike fine blows, but they do not fight on scientific 15 principles, and so too these thinkers do not seem to know what they say; for it is evident that, as a rule, they make no use of their causes except to a small extent. For Anaxagoras uses reason as a *deus ex machina* for the making of the world, and when he is at a loss to tell from what cause something necessarily is, then he drags reason in, but in all other cases ascribes events to anything rather than to reason.[10] And Empedocles, though he uses the causes 20 to a greater extent than this, neither does so sufficiently nor attains consistency in their use. At least, in many cases he makes love segregate things, and strife aggregate them. For whenever the universe is 25 dissolved into its elements by strife, fire is aggregated into one, and so is each of the other elements;

---

[5]The reference is probably to Empedocles.
[6]ᵃ18.
[7]Anaxagoras.

[8]The promise is not fulfilled.
[9]*Phys.* ii. 3, 7.
[10]Cf. Pl. *Phaedo*, 98 BC, *Laws*, 967 B–D.

but whenever again under the influence of love they come together into one, the parts must again be segregated out of each element.

Empedocles, then, in contrast with his predecessors, was the first to introduce the dividing of this 30 cause, not positing one source of movement, but different and contrary sources. Again, he was the first to speak of four material elements; yet he does not *use* four, but treats them as two only; he treats fire 985ᵇ by itself, and its opposites—earth, air, and water—as one kind of thing. We may learn this by study of his verses.

This philosopher then, as we say, has spoken of the principles in this way, and made them of this number. Leucippus and his associate Democritus say 5 that the full and the empty are the elements, calling the one being and the other non-being—the full and solid being being, the empty non-being (whence they say being no more is than non-being, because the solid no more is than the empty); and they make 10 these the material causes of things. And as those who make the underlying substance one generate all other things by its modifications, supposing the rare and the dense to be the sources of the modifications, in the same way these philosophers say the differences in the elements are the causes of all other qualities. These differences, they say, are three—shape and 15 order and position. For they say the real is differentiated only by 'rhythm' and 'inter-contact' and 'turning'; and of these rhythm is shape, inter-contact is order, and turning is position; for A differs from N in shape, AN from NA in order, Ⅎ from H in position. The question of movement—whence or how it is to belong to things—these thinkers, like the others, lazily neglected.

20   Regarding the two causes, then, as we say, the inquiry seems to have been pushed thus far by the early philosophers.

5. Contemporaneously with these philosophers 25 and before them, the so-called Pythagoreans, who were the first to take up mathematics, not only advanced this study, but also having been brought up in it they thought its principles were the principles of all things. Since of these principles numbers are by nature the first, and in numbers they seemed to see many resemblances to the things that exist and come into being—more than in fire and earth and water (such and such a modification of numbers being justice, another being soul and reason, an- 30 other being opportunity—and similarly almost all other things being numerically expressible); since,

again, they saw that the modifications and the ratios of the musical scales were expressible in numbers;—since, then, all other things seemed in their whole nature to be modelled on numbers, and num- 986ᵃ bers seemed to be the first things in the whole of nature, they supposed the elements of numbers to be the elements of all things, and the whole heaven to be a musical scale and a number. And all the properties of numbers and scales which they could 5 show to agree with the attributes and parts and the whole arrangement of the heavens, they collected and fitted into their scheme; and if there was a gap anywhere, they readily made additions so as to make their whole theory coherent. E. g. as the number 10 is thought to be perfect and to comprise the whole nature of numbers, they say that 10 the bodies which move through the heavens are ten, but as the visible bodies are only nine, to meet this they invent a tenth—the 'counter-earth'. We have discussed these matters more exactly elsewhere.[11]

But the object of our review is that we may learn from these philosophers also what they suppose to be the principles and how these fall under the causes we have named. Evidently, then, these thinkers also consider that number is the principle both as matter 15 for things and as forming both their modifications and their permanent states, and hold that the elements of number are the even and the odd, and that of these the latter is limited, and the former unlimited; and that the One proceeds from both of these (for it is both even and odd), and number from the One; and that the whole heaven, as has been said, is 20 numbers.

Other members of this same school say there are ten principles, which they arrange in two columns of cognates—limit and unlimited, odd and even, one and plurality, right and left, male and female, rest- 25 ing and moving, straight and curved, light and darkness, good and bad, square and oblong. In this way Alcmaeon of Croton seems also to have conceived the matter, and either he got this view from them or they got it from him; for he expressed himself sim- 30 ilarly to them. For he says most human affairs go in pairs, meaning not definite contrarieties such as the Pythagoreans speak of, but any chance contrarieties, e. g. white and black, sweet and bitter, good and bad, great and small. He threw out indefinite suggestions about the other contrarieties, but the Pythagoreans

[11]*De Caelo*, ii. 13.

986ᵇ declared both how many and which their contrarieties are.

From both these schools, then, we can learn this much, that the contraries are the principles of things; and how many these principles are and which they are, we can learn from one of the two schools. But how these principles can be brought together under 5 the causes we have named has not been clearly and articulately stated by them; they seem, however, to range the elements under the head of matter; for out of these as immanent parts they say substance is composed and moulded.

From these facts we may sufficiently perceive the meaning of the ancients who said the elements of nature were more than one; but there are some who 10 spoke of the universe as if it were one entity, though they were not all alike either in the excellence of their statement or in its conformity to the facts of nature. The discussion of them is in no way appropriate to our present investigation of causes, for they do not, like some of the natural philosophers, assume being to be one and yet generate it out of the one as out of 15 matter, but they speak in another way; those others add change, since they generate the universe, but these thinkers say the universe is unchangeable. Yet *this* much is germane to the present inquiry: Parmenides seems to fasten on that which is one in definition, Melissus on that which is one in matter, for which reason the former says that it is limited, the latter that 20 it is unlimited; while Xenophanes, the first of these partisans of the One (for Paramenides is said to have been his pupil), gave no clear statement, nor does he seem to have grasped the nature of either of these causes, but with reference to the whole material universe he says the One is God. Now these thinkers, as 25 we said, must be neglected for the purposes of the present inquiry—two of them entirely, as being a little too naïve, viz. Xenophanes and Melissus; but Parmenides seems in places to speak with more insight. For, claiming that, besides the existent, nothing nonexistent exists, he thinks that of necessity one thing 30 exists, viz. the existent and nothing else (on this we have spoken more clearly in our work on nature),[12] but being forced to follow the observed facts, and supposing the existence of that which is one in definition, but more than one according to our sensations, he now posits two causes and two principles, calling them hot and cold, i. e. fire and earth; and of these

he ranges the hot with the existent, and the other with 987ᵃ the nonexistent.

From what has been said, then, and from the wise men who have now sat in council with us, we have got thus much—on the one hand from the earliest philosophers, who regard the first principle as cor- 5 poreal (for water and fire and such things are bodies), and of whom some suppose that there is one corporeal principle, others that there are more than one, but both put these under the head of matter; and on the other hand from some who posit both this cause and besides this the source of movement, which we have got from some as single and from others as twofold.

Down to the Italian school, then, and apart from it, philosophers have treated these subjects rather ob- 10 scurely, except that, as we said, they have in fact used two kinds of cause, and one of these—the source of movement—some treat as one and others as two. But the Pythagoreans have said in the same way that there are two principles, but added this 15 much, which is peculiar to them, that they thought that finitude and infinity were not attributes of certain other things, e. g. of fire or earth or anything else of this kind, but that infinity itself and unity itself were the substance of the things of which they are predicated. This is why number was the substance of all things. On this subject, then, they ex- 20 pressed themselves thus; and regarding the question of essence they began to make statements and definitions, but treated the matter too simply. For they both defined superficially and thought that the first subject of which a given definition was predicable was the substance of the thing defined, as if one supposed that 'double' and '2' were the same, because 2 is the first thing of which 'double' is predicable. But surely to be double and to be 2 are not the same; 25 if they are, one thing will be many—a consequence which they actually drew. From the earlier philosophers, then, and from their successors we can learn thus much.

6. After the systems we have named came the philosophy of Plato, which in most respects followed these thinkers, but had peculiarities that distin- 30 guished it from the philosophy of the Italians. For, having in his youth first become familiar with Cratylus and with the Heraclitean doctrines (that all sensible things are ever in a state of flux and there is no knowledge about them), these views he held even 987ᵇ in later years. Socrates, however, was busying himself about ethical matters and neglecting the world

---

¹²*Phys.* i. 3.

of nature as a whole but seeking the universal in these ethical matters, and fixed thought for the first time on definitions; Plato accepted his teaching, but held that the problem applied not to sensible things 5 but to entities of another kind—for this reason, that the common definition could not be a definition of any sensible thing, as they were always changing. Things of this other sort, then, he called Ideas, and sensible things, he said, were all named after these, and in virtue of a relation to these; for the many existed by participation in the Ideas that have the same 10 name as they. Only the name 'participation' was new; for the Pythagoreans say that things exist by 'imitation' of numbers, and Plato says they exist by participation, changing the name. But what the participation or the imitation of the Forms could be they left an open question.

Further, besides sensible things and Forms he says 15 there are the objects of mathematics, which occupy an intermediate position, differing from sensible things in being eternal and unchangeable, from Forms in that there are many alike, while the Form itself is in each case unique.

Since the Forms were the causes of all other things, he thought their elements were the elements 20 of all things. As matter, the great and the small were principles; as essential reality, the One; for from the great and the small, by participation in the One, come the Numbers.

But he agreed with the Pythagoreans in saying that the One is substance and not a predicate of something else; and in saying that the Numbers are the 25 causes of the reality of other things he agreed with them; but positing a dyad and constructing the infinite out of great and small, instead of treating the infinite as one, is peculiar to him; and so is his view that the Numbers exist apart from sensible things, while *they* say that the things themselves are Numbers, and do not place the objects of mathematics between Forms and sensible things. His divergence 30 from the Pythagoreans in making the One and the Numbers separate from things, and his introduction of the Forms, were due to his inquiries in the region of definitions (for the earlier thinkers had no tincture of dialectic), and his making the other entity besides the One a dyad was due to the belief that the numbers, except those which were prime, could be neatly produced out of the dyad as out of some plastic material.

988ᵃ   Yet what *happens* is the contrary; the theory is not a reasonable one. For they make many things

out of the matter, and the form generates only once, but what we observe is that one table is made from one matter, while the man who applies the form, though he is one, makes many tables. And the rela- 5 tion of the male to the female is similar; for the latter is impregnated by one copulation, but the male impregnates many females; yet these are analogues of those first principles.

Plato, then, declared himself thus on the points in question; it is evident from what has been said that he has used only two causes, that of the essence and the material cause (for the Forms are the causes of the essence of all other things, and the One is the 10 cause of the essence of the Forms); and it is evident what the underlying matter is, of which the Forms are predicated in the case of sensible things, and the One in the case of Forms, viz. that this is a dyad, the great and the small. Further, he has assigned the cause of good and that of evil to the elements, one to each of the two, as we say some of his predeces- 15 sors sought to do, e. g. Empedocles and Anaxagoras.

7. Our review of those who have spoken about first principles and reality and of the way in which they have spoken, has been concise and summary; 20 but yet we have learnt *this* much from them, that of those who speak about 'principle' and 'cause' no one has mentioned any principle except those which have been distinguished in our work on nature, but all evidently have some inkling of *them*, though only vaguely. For some speak of the first principle as matter, whether they suppose one or more first principles, and whether they suppose this to be a body or to be incorporeal; e. g. Plato spoke of the great and 25 the small, the Italians of the infinite, Empedocles of fire, earth, water, and air, Anaxagoras of the infinity of things composed of similar parts. These, then, have all had a notion of this kind of cause, and so have all who speak of air or fire or water, or something denser than fire and rarer than air; for some have said the prime element is of this kind.   30

These thinkers grasped this cause only; but certain others have mentioned the source of movement, e. g. those who make friendship and strife, or reason, or love, a principle.

The essence, i. e. the substantial reality, no one has expressed distinctly. It is hinted at chiefly by 35 those who believe in the Forms; for they do not suppose either that the Forms are the matter of sensible 988ᵇ things, and the One the matter of the Forms, or that they are the source of movement (for they say these are causes rather of immobility and of being at rest), but they furnish the Forms as the essence of every other thing, and the One as the essence of the Forms.

That for whose sake actions and changes and movements take place, they assert to be a cause in a way, but not in this way, i. e. not in the way in which it is its *nature* to be a cause. For those who speak of reason or friendship class these causes as goods; they do not speak, however, as if anything that exists either existed or came into being for the same of these, but as if movements started from these. In the same way those who say the One or the existent is the good, say that it is the cause of substance, but not that substance either is or comes to be for the sake of this. Therefore it turns out that in a sense they both say and do not say the good is a cause; for they do not call it a cause *qua* good but only incidentally.

All these thinkers, then, as they cannot pitch on another cause, seem to testify that we have determined rightly both how many and of what sort the causes are. Besides this it is plain that when the causes are being looked for, either all four must be sought thus or they must be sought in one of these four ways. Let us next discuss the possible difficulties with regard to the way in which each of these thinkers has spoken, and with regard to his situation relatively to the first principles.

8. Those, then, who say the universe is one and posit one kind of thing as matter, and as corporeal matter which has spatial magnitude, evidently go astray in many ways. For they posit the elements of bodies only, not of incorporeal things, though there are also incorporeal things. And in trying to state the causes of generation and destruction, and in giving a physical account of all things, they do away with the cause of movement. Further, they err in not positing the substance, i. e. the essence, as the cause of anything, and besides this in lightly calling any of the simple bodies except earth the first principle, without inquiring how they are produced out of one another,—I mean fire, water, earth, and air. For some things are produced out of each other by combination, others by separation, and this makes the greatest difference to their priority and posteriority. For (1) in a way the property of being most elementary of all would seem to belong to the first thing from which they are produced by combination, and this property would belong to the most fine-grained and subtle of bodies. For this reason those who make fire the principle would be most in agreement with

this argument. But each of the other thinkers agrees that the element of corporeal things is of this sort. At least none of those who named one element claimed that earth was the element, evidently because of the coarseness of its grain. (Of the other three elements each has found some judge on its side; for some maintain that fire, others that water, others that air is the element. Yet why, after all, do they not name earth also, as most men do? For people say all things are earth. And Hesiod says earth was produced first of corporeal things; so primitive and popular has the opinion been.) According to this argument, then, no one would be right who either says the first principle is any of the elements other than fire, or supposes it to be denser than air but rarer than water. But (2) if that which is later in generation is prior in nature, and that which is concocted and compounded is later in generation, the contrary of what we have been saying must be true—water must be prior to air, and earth to water.

So much, then, for those who posit one cause such as we mentioned; but the same is true if one supposes more of these, as Empedocles says the matter of things is four bodies. For he too is confronted by consequences some of which are the same as have been mentioned, while others are peculiar to him. For we see these bodies produced from one another, which implies that the same body does not always remain fire or earth (we have spoken about this in our works on nature[13]); and regarding the cause of movement and the question whether we must posit one or two, he must be thought to have spoken neither correctly nor altogether plausibly. And in general, change of quality is necessarily done away with for those who speak thus, for on their view cold will not come from hot nor hot from cold. For if it did there would be something that accepted the contraries themselves, and there would be some one entity that became fire and water, which Empedocles denies.

As regards Anaxagoras, if one were to suppose that he said there were two elements, the supposition would accord thoroughly with an argument which Anaxagoras himself did not state articulately, but which he must have accepted if any one had led him on to it. True, to say that in the beginning all things were mixed is absurd both on other grounds and because it follows that they must have existed before in an unmixed form, and because nature does

---

[13]*De Caelo*, iii. 7.

not allow any chance thing to be mixed with any chance thing, and also because on this view modifications and accidents could be separated from substances (for the same things which are mixed can be separated); yet if one were to follow him up, piecing together what he means, he would perhaps be seen to be somewhat modern in his views. For when nothing was separated out, evidently nothing could be truly asserted of the substance that then existed. I mean, e. g., that it was neither white nor black, nor grey nor any other colour, but of necessity colourless; for if it had been coloured, it would have had one of these colours. And similarly, by this same argument, it was flavourless, nor had it any similar attribute; for it could not be either of any quality or of any size, nor could it be any definite kind of thing. For if it were, one of the particular forms would have belonged to it, and this is impossible, since all were mixed together; for the particular form would necessarily have been already separated out, but he says all were mixed except reason, and this alone was unmixed and pure. From this it follows, then, that he must say the principles are the One (for this is simple and unmixed) and the Other, which is of such a nature as we suppose the indefinite to be before it is defined and partakes of some form. Therefore, while expressing himself neither rightly nor clearly, he means something like what the later thinkers say and what is now more clearly seen to be the case.

But these thinkers are, after all, at home only in arguments about generation and destruction and movement; for it is practically only of this sort of substance that they seek the principles and the causes. But those who extend their vision to all things that exist, and of existing things suppose some to be perceptible and others not perceptible evidently study both classes, which is all the more reason why one should devote some time to seeing what is good in their views and what bad from the standpoint of the inquiry we have now before us.

The 'Pythagoreans' treat of principles and elements stranger than those of the physical philosophers (the reason is that they got the principles from non-sensible things, for the objects of mathematics, except those of astronomy, are of the class of things without movement); yet their discussions and investigations are all about nature; for they generate the heavens, and with regard to their parts and attributes and functions they observe the phenomena, and use up the principles and the causes in explaining these, which implies that they agree with the others, the physical philosophers, that the *real* is just all that which is perceptible and contained by the so-called 'heavens'. But the causes and the principles which they mention are, as we said, sufficient to act as steps even up to the higher realms of reality, and are more suited to these than to theories about nature. They do not tell us at all, however, how there can be movement if limit and unlimited and odd and even are the only things assumed, or how without movement and change there can be generation and destruction, or the bodies that move through the heavens can do what they do.

Further, if one either granted them that spatial magnitude consists of these elements, or this were proved, still how would some bodies be light and others have weight? To judge from what they assume and maintain they are speaking no more of mathematical bodies than of perceptible; hence they have said nothing whatever about fire or earth or the other bodies of this sort, I suppose because they have nothing to say which applies *peculiarly* to perceptible things.

Further, how are we to combine the beliefs that the attributes of number, and number itself, are causes of what exists and happens in the heavens both from the beginning and now, and that there is no other number than this number out of which the world is composed? When in one particular region they place opinion and opportunity, and, a little above or below, injustice and decision or mixture, and allege, as proof, that each of these is a number, and that there happens to be already in this place a plurality of the extended bodies composed of numbers, because these attributes of number attach to the various places—this being so, is this number, which we must suppose each of these abstractions to be, the same number which is exhibited in the material universe, or is it another than this? Plato says it is different; yet even he thinks that both these bodies and their causes are numbers, but that the *intelligible* numbers are causes, while the others are *sensible.*

9. Let us leave the Pythagoreans for the present; for it is enough to have touched on them as much as we have done. But as for those who posit the Ideas as causes, firstly, in seeking to grasp the causes of the things around us, they introduced others equal in number to these, as if a man who wanted to count things thought he would not be able to do it while they were few, but tried to count them when he had added to their number. For the Forms are practically equal to—or not fewer than—the things, in trying to explain which these thinkers proceeded from them to the Forms. For to each thing there answers an entity which has the same name and exists apart from the substances, and so also in the case of all other groups there is a one over many, whether the many are in this world or are eternal.

Further, of the ways in which we prove that the Forms exist, none is convincing; for from some no inference necessarily follows, and from some arise Forms even of things of which we think there are no Forms. For according to the arguments from the existence of the sciences there will be Forms of all things of which there are sciences, and according to the 'one over many' argument there will be Forms even of negations, and according to the argument that there is an object for thought even when the thing has perished, there will be Forms of perishable things; for we have an image of these. Further, of the more accurate arguments, some lead to Ideas of relations, of which we say there is no independent class, and other introduce the 'third man'.

And in general the arguments for the Forms destroy the things for whose existence we are more zealous than for the existence of the Ideas; for it follows that not the dyad but number is first, i. e. that the relative is prior to the absolute—besides all the other points on which certain people by following out the opinions held about the Ideas have come into conflict with the principles of the theory.

Further, according to the assumption on which our belief in the Ideas rests, there will be Forms not only of substances but also of many other things (for the concept is single not only in the case of substances but also in the other cases, and there are sciences not only of substance but also of other things, and a thousand other such difficulties confront them). But according to the necessities of the case and the opinions held about the Forms, if Forms can be shared in there must be Ideas of substances only. For they are not shared in incidentally, but a thing must share in its Form as in something not predicated of a subject (by 'being shared in incidentally' I mean that e. g. if a thing shares in 'double itself', it shares also in 'eternal', but incidentally; for 'eternal' happens to be predicable of the 'double'). Therefore the Forms will be substance; but the same terms indicate substance in this and in the ideal world (or what will be the meaning of saying that there is something apart from the particulars—the one over many?). And if the Ideas and the particulars that share in them have the same form, there will be something common to these; for why should '2' be one and the same in the perishable 2's or in those which are many but eternal, and not the same in the '2 itself' as in the particular 2? But if they have not the same form, they must have only the name in common, and it is as if one were to call both Callias and a wooden image a 'man', without observing any community between them.[14]

Above all one might discuss the question what on earth the Forms contribute to sensible things, either to those that are eternal or to those that come into being and cease to be. For they cause neither movement nor any change in them. But again they help in no wise either towards the knowledge of the other things (for they are not even the substance of these, else they would have been in them), or towards their being, if they are not *in* the particulars which share in them; though if they were, they might be thought to be causes, as white causes whiteness in a white object by entering into its composition. But this argument, which first Anaxagoras and later Eudoxus and certain others used, is very easily upset; for it is not difficult to collect many insuperable objections to such a view.

But, further, all other things cannot come from the Forms in any of the usual senses of 'from'. And to say that they are patterns and the other things share in them is to use empty words and poetical metaphors. For what is it that works, looking to the Ideas? And anything can either be, or become, like another without being copied from it, so that whether Socrates exists or not a man like Socrates might come to be; and evidently this might be so even if Socrates were eternal. And there will be several patterns of the same thing, and therefore several Forms; e. g. 'animal' and 'two-footed' and also 'man himself' will be Forms of man. Again, the Forms are patterns not only of sensible things, but of Forms themselves also; i. e. the genus, as genus of various species, will be so; therefore the same thing will be pattern and copy.

Again, it would seem impossible that the substance and that of which it is the substance should exist apart; how, therefore, could the Ideas, being the substances of things, exist apart? In the *Phaedo*[15] the case is stated in this way—that the Forms are causes both of being and of becoming; yet when the

---

[14]With 990[b] 2–991[a] 8 Cf. xiii. 1078[b] 34–1079[b] 3.
[15]IQQ C–E.

5 Forms exist, still the things that share in them do not come into being, unless there is something to originate movement; and many other things come into being (e. g. a house or a ring) of which we say there are no Forms. Clearly, therefore, even the other things can both be and come into being owing to such causes as produce the things just mentioned.[16]

Again, if the Forms are numbers, how can they 10 be causes? Is it because existing things are other numbers, e. g. one number is man, another is Socrates, another Callias? Why then are the one set of numbers causes of the other set? It will not make any difference even if the former are eternal and the latter are not. But if it is because things in this sensible world (e. g. harmony) are ratios of numbers, evidently the things between which they are ratios 15 are some one class of things. If, then, this—the matter—is some definite thing, evidently the numbers themselves too will be ratios of something to something else. E. g. if Callias is a numerical ratio between fire and earth and water and air, his Idea also will be a number of certain other underlying things; and man-himself, whether it is a number in a sense or not, will still be a numerical ratio of certain things and not a number proper, nor will it be a kind of 20 number merely because it is a numerical ratio.

Again, from many numbers one number is produced, but how can one Form come from many Forms? And if the number comes not from the many numbers themselves but from the units in them, e. g. in 10,000, how is it with the units? If they are 25 specifically alike, numerous absurdities will follow, and also if they are not alike (neither the units in one number being themselves like one another nor those in other numbers being all like to all); for in what will they differ, as they are without quality? This is not a plausible view, nor is it consistent with our thought on the matter.

Further, they must set up a second kind of number (with which arithmetic deals), and all the objects which are called 'intermediate' by some thinkers; and how do these exist or from what principles do they proceed? Or why must they be intermediate be-30 tween the things in this sensible world and the things-themselves?

Further, the units in 2 must each come from a prior 2; but this is impossible.

Further, why is a number, when taken all together, 992ª one?

Again, besides what has been said, if the units are *diverse* the Platonists should have spoken like those who say there are four, or two, elements; for each of these thinkers gives the name of element not to that which is common, e. g. to body, but to fire and 5 earth, whether there is something common to them, viz. body, or not. But in fact the Platonists speak as if the One were *homogeneous* like fire or water; and if this is so, the numbers will not be substances. Evidently, if there is a One-itself and this is a first principle, 'one' is being used in more than one sense; for otherwise the theory is impossible.

When we wish to reduce substances to their prin-10 ciples, we state that lines come from the short and long (i. e. from a kind of small and great), and the plane from the broad and narrow, and body from the deep and shallow. Yet how then can either the plane contain a line, or the solid a line or a plane? For the broad and narrow is a different class from the deep and shallow. Therefore, just as number is not pre-15 sent in these, because the many and few are different from these, evidently no other of the higher classes will be present in the lower. But again the broad is not a genus which includes the deep, for then the solid would have been a species of plane.[17] Further, from what principle will the presence of the *points* in the line be derived? Plato even used to object to this class of things as being a geometrical fiction. He gave the name of principle of the line—and 20 this he often posited—to the indivisible lines. Yet these must have a limit; therefore the argument from which the existence of the line follows proves also the existence of the point.

In general, though philosophy seeks the cause of perceptible things, we have given this up (for we say 25 nothing of the cause from which change takes its start), but while we fancy we are stating the substance of perceptible things, we assert the existence of a second class of substances, while our account of the way in which they are the substances of perceptible things is empty talk; for 'sharing', as we said before,[18] means nothing.

Nor have the Forms any connexion with what we see to be the cause in the case of the arts, that for 30 whose sake both all mind and the whole of nature are operative[19]—with this cause which we assert to be one of the first principles; but mathematics has

---

[16]With 991ª 8–ᵇ 9 Cf. xiii. 1079ᵇ 12–1080ª 8.

[17]With 992ª 10–19 Cf. xiii. 1085ª 9–19.

[18]991ª 20–22.

[19]*sc.* the final cause.

come to be identical with philosophy for modern thinkers, though they say that it should be studied for the sake of other things.[20]

992ᵇ   Further, one might suppose that the substance which according to them underlies as matter is too mathematical, and is a predicate and differentia of the substance, i. e. of the matter, rather than than matter itself; i. e. *the great and the small* are like *the rare and the dense* which the 5 physical philosophers speak of, calling these the primary differentiae of the substratum; for these are a kind of excess and defect. And regarding movement, if the great and the small are to *be* movement, evidently the Forms will be moved; but if they are not to be movement, whence did movement come? The whole study of nature has been annihilated.

And what is thought to be easy—to show that all 10 things are one—is not done; for what is proved by the method of setting out instances[21] is not that all things are one but that there is a One-itself,—if we grant all the assumptions. And not even this follows, if we do not grant that the universal is a genus; and this in some cases it cannot be.

Nor can it be explained either how the lines and planes and solids that come after the numbers exist 15 or can exist, or what significance they have; for these can neither be Forms (for they are not numbers), nor the intermediates (for those are the objects of mathematics), nor the perishable things. This is evidently a distinct fourth class.

In general, if we search for the elements of existing things without distinguishing the many senses in which things are said to exist, we cannot find them, especially if the search for the elements of which 20 things are made is conducted in this manner. For it is surely impossible to discover what 'acting' or 'being acted on', or 'the straight', is made of, but if elements can be discovered at all, it is only the elements of substances; therefore either to seek the elements of all existing things or to think one has them is incorrect.

And how could we *learn* the elements of all things? Evidently we cannot start by knowing any-25 thing before. For as he who is learning geometry, though he may know other things before, knows none of the things with which the science deals and about which he is to learn, so is it in all other cases. Therefore if there is a science of all things, such as some assert to exist, he who is learning this will know nothing before. Yet all learning is by means of premisses which are (either all or some of them) 30 known before—whether the learning be by demonstration or by definitions; for the elements of the definition must be known before and be familiar; and learning by induction proceeds similarly. But again, if the science were actually innate, it were strange that we are unaware of our possession of the great-993ᵃ est of sciences.

Again, how is one to *come to know* what all things are made of, and how is this to be made *evident*? This also affords a difficulty; for there might be a conflict of opinion, as there is about certain syllables; some say *za* is made out of *s* and *d* and *a*, while 5 others say it is a distinct sound and none of those that are familiar.

Further, how could we know the objects of sense without having the sense in question? Yet we ought to, if the elements of which all things consist, as complex sounds consist of the elements proper to 10 sound, are the same.

10. It is evident, then, even from what we have said before, that all men seem to seek the causes named in the *Physics*,[22] and that we cannot name any beyond these; but they seek these vaguely; and though in a sense they have all been described before, in a sense they have not been described at all. For the earliest philosophy is, on all subjects, like 15 one who lisps, since it is young and in its beginnings. For even Empedocles says bone exists by virtue of the ratio in it. Now this is the essence and the substance of the thing. But it is similarly necessary that flesh and each of the other tissues should be the ratio of its elements, or that not one of them should; for it is on account of this that both flesh 20 and bone and everything else will exist, and not on account of the matter, which *he* names—fire and earth and water and air. But while he would necessarily have agreed if another had said this, he has not said it clearly.

On these questions our views have been expressed before; but let us return to enumerate the difficulties that might be raised on these same points; for 25 perhaps we may get from them some help towards our later difficulties. . . .

---

[20]Cf. Plato, *Rep.* vii. 531 D, 533 B–E.

[21]For this Platonic method Cf. vii. 1031ᵇ 21, xiii. 1086ᵇ 9, xiv. 1090ᵃ 17.

[22]ii. 3, 7.

BOOK Λ (XII)

1. The subject of our inquiry is substance; for the principles and the causes we are seeking are those of substances. For if the universe is of the nature of a whole, substance is its first part; and if it coheres merely by virtue of serial succession, on this view also substance is first, and is succeeded by quality, and then by quantity. At the same time these latter are not even being in the full sense, but are qualities and movements of it—or else even the not-white and the not-straight would be being; at least we say even these *are*, e. g. 'there is a not-white'.[23] Fur-
25 ther, none of the categories other than substance can exist apart. And the early philosophers also in practice testify to the primacy of substance; for it was of substance that they sought the principles and elements and causes. The thinkers of the present[24] day tend to rank universals as substances (for genera are universals, and these they tend to describe as principles and substances, owing to the abstract nature of their inquiry); but the thinkers of old ranked particular things as substances, e. g. fire and earth, not what is common to both, body.

30 There are three kinds of substance—one that is sensible (of which one subdivision is eternal and another is perishable; the latter is recognized by all men, and includes e. g. plants and animals), of which we must grasp the elements, whether one or many;
35 and another that is immovable, and this certain thinkers assert to be capable of existing apart, some dividing it into two, others identifying the Forms and the objects of mathematics, and others positing, of these two, only the objects of mathematics.[25] The former two kinds of substance are the subject of
1069b physics (for they imply movement); but the third kind belongs to another science, if there is no principle common to it and to the other kinds.

2. Sensible substance is changeable. Now if change proceeds from opposites or from intermediates, and not from all opposites (for the voice is not-
5 white [but it does not therefore change to white]), but from the contrary, there must be something underlying which changes into the contrary state; for the *contraries* do not change. Further, something

persists, but the contrary does not persist; there is, then, some third thing besides the contraries, viz. the matter. Now since changes are of four kinds—either in respect of the 'what' or of the quality or of the 10 quantity or of the place, and change in respect of 'thisness' is simple generation and destruction, and change in quantity is increase and diminution, and change in respect of an affection is alteration, and change of place is motion, changes will be from given states into those contrary to them in these several respects. The matter, then, which changes must 15 be capable of both states. And since that which 'is' has two senses, we must say that everything changes from that which is potentially to that which is actually, e. g. from potentially white to actually white, and similarly in the case of increase and diminution. Therefore not only can a thing come to be, incidentally, out of that which is not, but also all things come to be out of that which is, but is potentially, and is not actually. And this is the 'One' of Anaxago- 20 ras; for instead of 'all things were together'—and the 'Mixture' of Empedocles and Anaximander and the account given by Democritus—it is better to say 'all things were together potentially but not actually'. Therefore these thinkers seem to have had some notion of matter. Now all things that change have matter, but different matter; and of eternal things those which are not generable but are mov- 25 able in space have matter—not matter for generation, however, but for motion from one place to another.

One might raise the question from what sort of non-being generation proceeds; for 'non-being' has three senses. If, then, one form of nonbeing exists potentially, still it is not by virtue of a potentiality for any and every thing, but different things come from different things; nor is it satisfactory to say that 'all things were together'; for they differ in their 30 matter, since otherwise why did an infinity of things come to be, and not one thing? For 'reason' is one, so that if matter also were one, that must have come to be in actuality which the matter was in potency.[26] The causes and the principles, then, are three, two being the pair of contraries of which one is definition and form and the other is privation, and the third being the matter.

3. Note, next, that neither the matter nor the form comes to be—and I mean the last matter and form. 35 For everything that changes is something and is

---

[23]This is an implication of the ordinary type of judgement, '*x* is not white'.

[24]The Platonists.

[25]The three views appear to have been held respectively by Plato, Xenocrates, and Speusippus.

[26]*sc.* an undifferentiated unity.

changed by something and into something. That by 1070ᵃ which it is changed is the immediate mover; that which is changed, the matter; that into which it is changed, the form. The process, then, will go on to infinity, if not only the bronze comes to be round but also the round or the bronze comes to be; therefore there must be a stop.

Note, next, that each substance comes into being out of something that shares its name. (Natural objects and other things both rank as substances.) For things come into being either by art or by nature or by luck or by spontaneity. Now art is a principle of movement in something other than the thing moved, nature is a principle in the thing itself (for man begets man), and the other causes are privations of these two.

There are three kinds of substance—the matter, which is a 'this' in appearance (for all things that are characterized by contact and not by organic unity are matter and substratum, e. g. fire, flesh, head; for these are all matter, and the last matter is the matter of that which is in the full sense substance); the nature, which is a 'this' or positive state towards which movement takes place; and again, thirdly, the particular substance which is composed of these two, e. g. Socrates or Callias. Now in some cases the 'this' does not exist apart from the composite substance, e. g. the form of house does not so exist, unless the art of building exists apart (nor is there generation and destruction of these forms, but it is in another way that the house apart from its matter, and health, and all ideals of art, exist and do not exist); but if the 'this' exists apart from the concrete thing, it is only in the case of natural objects. And so Plato was not far wrong when he said that there are as many Forms as there are kinds of natural object (if there *are* Forms distinct from the things of this earth). The moving causes exist as things preceding the effects, but causes in the sense of definitions are simultaneous with their effects. For when a man is healthy, then health also exists; and the shape of a bronze sphere exists at the same time as the bronze sphere. (But we must examine whether any form also survives afterwards. For in some cases there is nothing to prevent this; e. g. the soul may be of this sort—not all soul but the reason; for presumably it is impossible that *all* soul should survive.) Evidently then there is no necessity, on this ground at least, for the existence of the Ideas. For man is begotten by man, a given man by an individual father; and similarly in the arts; for the medical art is the formal cause of health.

4. The causes and the principles of different things are in a sense different, but in a sense, if one speaks universally and analogically, they are the same for all. For one might raise the question whether the principles and elements are different or the same for substances and for relative terms, and similarly in the case of each of the categories. But it would be paradoxical if they were the same for all. For then from the same elements will proceed relative terms and substances. What then will this 1070ᵇ common element be? For (1) (*a*) there is nothing common to and distinct from substance and the other categories, viz. those which are predicated; but an element is prior to the things of which it is an element. But again (*b*) substance is not an element in relative terms, nor is any of these an element in substance. Further, (2) how can all things have the same elements? For none of the elements can be the same as that which is composed of elements, e. g. *b* or *a* cannot be the same as *ba*. (None, therefore, of the intelligibles, e. g. being or unity, is an element; for these are predicable of each of the compounds as well.) None of the elements, then, will be either a substance or a relative term; but it must be one or other. All things, then, have not the same elements.

Or, as we are wont to put it, in a sense they have and in a sense they have not; e. g. perhaps the elements of perceptible bodies are, as *form*, the hot, and in another sense the cold, which is the *privation*; and, as *matter*, that which directly and of itself potentially has these attributes; and substances comprise both these and the things composed of these, of which these are the principles, or any unity which is produced out of the hot and the cold, e. g. flesh or bone; for the product must be different from the elements. These things then have the same elements and principles (though specifically different things have specifically different elements); but *all* things have not the same elements in this sense, but only analogically; i. e. one might say that there are three principles—the firm, the privation, and the matter. But each of these is different for each class; e. g. in colour they are white, black, and surface, and in day and night they are light, darkness, and air.

Since not only the elements present in a thing are causes, but also something external, i. e. the moving cause, clearly while 'principle' and 'element' are different both are causes, and 'principle' is divided into these two kinds[27] and that which acts as pro-

---

[27]i. e. the principles which are elements and those which are not.

ducing movement or rest is a principle and a sub-
25 stance. Therefore analogically there are three elements, and four causes and principles; but the elements are different in different things, and the
proximate moving cause is different for different
things. Health, disease, body; the moving cause is
the medical art. Form, disorder of a particular kind,
30 bricks; the moving cause is the building art. And
since the moving cause in the case of natural things
is—for man, for instance, man, and in the products
of thought the form or its contrary, there will be in
a sense three causes, while in a sense there are four.
For the medical art is in some sense health, and the
building art is the form of the house, and man begets
man;[28] further, besides these there is that which as
35 first of all things moves all things.

5. Some things can exist apart and some cannot,
and it is the former that are substances. And therefore all things have the same causes,[29] because,
1071a without substances, modifications and movements
do not exist. Further, these causes will probably be
soul and body, or reason and desire and body.

5   And in yet another way, analogically identical
things are principles, i. e. actuality and potency; but
these also are not only different for different things
but also apply in different ways to them. For in some
cases the same thing exists at one time actually and
at another potentially, e. g. wine or flesh or man does
so. (And these two fall under the above-named
causes.[30] For the form exists actually, if it can exist
apart, and so does the complex of form and matter,
10 and the privation, e. g. darkness or disease; but the
matter exists potentially; for this is that which can
become qualified either by the form or by the privation.) But the distinction of actuality and potentiality applies in another way to cases where the matter of cause and of effect is not the same, in some
of which cases the form is not the same but different; e. g. the cause of man is (1) the elements in man
15 (viz. fire and earth as matter, and the peculiar form),
and further (2) something else outside, i. e. the father, and (3) besides these the sun and its oblique
course, which are neither matter nor form nor privation of man nor of the same species with him, but
moving causes.

Further, one must observe that some causes can
be expressed in universal terms, and some cannot.
The proximate principles of all things are the 'this'
which is proximate in actuality, and another which
is proximate in potentiality.[31] The universal causes,
then, of which we spoke[32] do not *exist*. For it is the 20
individual that is the originative principle of the individuals. For while man is the originative principle
of man universally, there *is* no universal man, but
Peleus is the originative principle of Achilles, and
your father of you, and this particular *b* of this particular *ba*, though *b* in general is the originative principle of *ba* taken without qualification.

Further, if the causes of substances are the causes
of all things, yet different things have different
causes and elements, as was said[33]; the causes of 25
things that are not in the same class, e. g. of colours
and sounds, of substances and quantities, are different except in an analogical sense; and those of
things in the same species are different, not in
species, but in the sense that the causes of different individuals are different, your matter and form
and moving cause being different from mine, while
in their universal definition they are the same. And
if we inquire what are the principles or elements 30
of substances and relations and qualities—whether
they are the same or different—clearly when the
names of the causes are used in several senses the
causes of each are the same, but when the senses
are distinguished the causes are not the same but
different, except that in the following senses the
causes of all are the same. They are (1) the same
or analogous in this sense, that matter, form, privation, and the moving cause are common to all
things; and (2) the causes of substances may be
treated as causes of all things in this sense, that
when substances are removed all things are removed; further, (3) that which is first in respect of 35
complete reality is the cause of all things. But in
another sense there are different first causes, viz.
all the contraries which are neither generic nor ambiguous terms; and, further, the matters of different things are different. We have stated, then, what 1071b
are the principles of sensible things and how many

---

[28]i. e. the efficient cause is identical with the formal.

[29]i. e. the causes of substance are the causes of all things.

[30]i. e. the division into potency and actuality stands in a definite relation to the previous division into matter, form, and privation.

[31]e. g. the proximate causes of a child are the individual father (who
on Aristotle's view is the efficient and contains the formal cause) and
the germ contained in the individual mother (which is the material
cause).

[32]In l. 17.

[33]In 1070b 17.

they are, and in what sense they are the same and in what sense different.

6. Since there were[34] three kinds of substance, two of them physical and one unmovable, regarding the latter we must assert that it is necessary that there should be an eternal unmovable substance. For substances are the first of existing things, and if they are all destructible, all things are destructible. But it is impossible that movement should either have come into being or cease to be (for it must always have existed), or that time should. For there could not be a before and an after if time did not exist. Movement also is continuous, then, in the sense in which time is; for time is either the same thing as movement or an attribute of movement. And there is no continuous movement except movement in place, and of this only that which is circular is continuous.

But if there is something which is capable of moving things or acting on them, but is not actually doing so, there will not necessarily be movement; for that which has a potency need not exercise it. Nothing, then, is gained even if we suppose eternal substances, as the believers in the Forms do, unless there is to be in them some principle which can cause change; nay, even this is not enough, nor is another substance besides the Forms enough; for if it is not to *act*, there will be no movement. Further, even if it acts, this will not be enough, if its essence is potency; for there will not be *eternal* movement, since that which is potentially may possibly not be. There must, then, be such a principle, whose very essence is actuality. Further, then, these substances must be without matter; for they must be eternal, if *anything* is eternal. Therefore they must be actuality.

Yet there is a difficulty; for it is thought that everything that acts is able to act, but that not everything that is able to act acts, so that the potency is prior. But if this is so, nothing that is need be; for it is possible for all things to be capable of existing but not yet to exist.

Yet if we follow the theologians who generate the world from night, or the natural philosophers who say that 'all things were together',[35] the same impossible result ensues. For how will there be movement, if there is no actually existing cause? Wood will surely not move itself—the carpenter's art must act on it; nor will the menstrual blood nor the earth

set themselves in motion, but the seeds must act on the earth and the *semen* on the menstrual blood.

This is why some suppose eternal actuality—e. g. Leucippus[36] and Plato[37]; for they say there is always movement. But why and what this movement is they do not say, nor, if the world moves in this way or that, do they tell us the cause of its doing so. Now nothing is moved at random, but there must always be something present to move it; e. g. as a matter of fact a thing moves in one way by nature, and in another by force or through the influence of reason or something else. (Further, what sort of movement is primary? This makes a vast difference.) But again for Plato, at least, it is not permissible to name here that which he sometimes supposes to be the source of movement—that which moves itself;[38] for the soul is later, and coeval with the heavens, according to his account.[39] To suppose potency prior to actuality, then, is in a sense right, and in a sense not; and we have specified these senses.[40] That actuality is prior is testified by Anaxagoras (for his 'reason' is actuality) and by Empedocles in his doctrine of love and strife, and by those who say that there is always movement, e.g. Leucippus. Therefore chaos or night did not exist for an infinite time, but the same things have always existed (either passing through a cycle of changes or obeying some other law), since actuality is prior to potency. If, then, there is a constant cycle, something must always remain,[41] acting in the same way. And if there is to be generation and destruction, there must be something else[42] which is always acting in different ways. This must, then, act in one way in virtue of itself, and in another in virtue of something else—either of a third agent, therefore, or of the first. Now it must be in virtue of the first. For otherwise this again causes the motion both of the second agent and of the third. Therefore it is better to say 'the first'. For it was the cause of eternal uniformity; and something else is the cause of variety, and evidently both together are the cause of eternal variety. This, accordingly, is the character which the motions actually exhibit. What need then is there to seek for other principles?

---

[34]Cf. 1069[a] 30.

[35]Anaxagoras.

[36]Cf. *De Caelo*, iii. 300[b] 8.

[37]Cf. *Timaeus*, 30 A.

[38]Cf. *Phaedrus*, 245 c; *Laws*, 894 E.

[39]Cf. *Timaeus*, 34 B.

[40]Cf. 1071[b] 22–26.

[41]i. e. the sphere of the fixed stars.

[42]i. e. the sun. Cf. *De Gen. et Corr.* ii. 336[a] 23 ff.

7. Since (1) this is a possible account of the matter, and (2) if it were not true, the world would have proceeded out of night and 'all things together' and out of non-being, these difficulties may be taken as 20 solved. There is, then, something which is always moved with an unceasing motion, which is motion in a circle; and this is plain not in theory only but in fact. Therefore the first heaven[43] must be eternal. There is therefore also something which moves 25 it. And since that which is moved and moves is intermediate, there is something which moves without being moved, being eternal, substance, and actuality. And the object of desire and the object of thought move in this way; they move without being moved. The primary objects of desire and of thought are the same. For the apparent good is the object of appetite, and the real good is the primary object of rational wish. But desire is consequent on opinion rather than opinion on desire; for the think-30 ing is the starting-point. And thought is moved by the object of thought, and one of the two columns of opposites is in itself the object of thought; and in this, substance is first, and in substance, that which is simple and exists actually. (The one and the simple are not the same; for 'one' means a measure, but 'simple' means that the thing itself has a certain nature.) But the beautiful, also, and that which is in itself desirable are in the same column; 35 and the first in any class is always best, or analogous to the best.

1072ᵇ   That a final cause may exist among unchangeable entities is shown by the distinction of its meanings. For the final cause is (a) some being for whose good an action is done, and (b) something at which the action aims; and of these the latter exists among unchangeable entities though the former does not. The final cause, then, produces motion as being loved, but all other things move by being moved.

Now if something is moved it is capable of being otherwise than as it is. Therefore if its actuality is 5 the primary form of spatial motion, then in so far as it is subject to change, in this respect it is capable of being otherwise—in place, even if not in substance. But since there is something which moves while itself unmoved, existing actually, this can in no way be otherwise than as it is. For motion in space is the first of the kinds of change, and motion 10 in a circle the first kind of spatial motion; and this

the first mover produces.[44] The first mover, then, exists of necessity; and in so far as it exists by necessity, its mode of being is good, and it is in this sense a first principle. For the necessary has all these senses—that which is necessary perforce because it is contrary to the natural impulse, that without which the good is impossible, and that which cannot be otherwise but can exist only in a single way.

On such a principle, then, depend the heavens and the world of nature. And it is a life such as the best which we enjoy, and enjoy for but a short time (for it is ever in this state, which we cannot be), since its 15 actuality is also pleasure. (And for this reason[45] are waking, perception, and thinking most pleasant, and hopes and memories are so on account of these.) And thinking in itself deals with that which is best in itself, and that which is thinking in the fullest sense with that which is best in the fullest sense. And thought thinks on itself because it shares the 20 nature of the object of thought; for it becomes an object of thought in coming into contact with and thinking its objects, so that thought and object of thought are the same. For that which is capable of receiving the object of thought, i. e. the essence, is thought. But it is active when it possesses this object. Therefore the possession rather than the receptivity is the divine element which thought seems to contain, and the act of contemplation is what is most pleasant and best. If, then, God is always in that good state in which we sometimes are, this compels our wonder; and if in a better this compels it yet more. And God is in a better state. And life also belongs 25 to God; for the actuality of thought is life, and God is that actuality; and God's self-dependent actuality is life most good and eternal. We say therefore that God is a living being, eternal, most good, so that life and duration continuous and eternal belong to God; 30 for this is God.

Those who suppose, as the Pythagoreans and Speusippus do, that supreme beauty and goodness are not present in the beginning, because the beginnings both of plants and of animals are causes, but beauty and completeness are in the effects of these, are wrong in their opinion. For the seed comes from 35 other individuals which are prior and complete, and

---

[43]i. e. the outer sphere of the universe, that in which the fixed stars are set.

[44]If it had any movement, it would have the first. But it produces this and therefore cannot share in it; for if it did, we should have to look for something that is prior to the first mover and imparts this motion to it.

[45]sc. because they are activities or actualities.

the first thing is not seed but the complete being; e. g. we must say that before the seed there is a 1073ᵃ man—not the man produced from the seed, but another from whom the seed comes.

It is clear then from what has been said that there is a substance which is eternal and unmovable and separate from sensible things. It has been shown also 5 that this substance cannot have any magnitude, but is without parts and indivisible (for it produces movement through infinite time, but nothing finite has infinite power; and, while every magnitude is either infinite or finite, it cannot, for the above rea- 10 son, have finite magnitude, and it cannot have infinite magnitude because there is no infinite magnitude at all). But it has also been shown that it is impassive and unalterable; for all the other changes are posterior to change of place.

8. It is clear, then, why these things are as they are. But we must not ignore the question whether we have to suppose one such substance or more than 15 one, and if the latter, how many; we must also mention, regarding the opinions expressed by others, that they have said nothing about the number of the substances that can even be clearly stated. For the theory of Ideas has no special discussion of the subject; for those who speak of Ideas say the Ideas are numbers, and they speak of numbers now as unlimited, now as limited by the number 10; but as for the rea- 20 son why there should be just so many numbers, nothing is said with any demonstrative exactness. We however must discuss the subject, starting from the presuppositions and distinctions we have mentioned. The first principle or primary being is not movable either in itself or accidentally, but produces the pri- 25 mary eternal and single movement. But since that which is moved must be moved by something, and the first mover must be in itself unmovable, and eternal movement must be produced by something eternal and a single movement by a single thing, and since we see that besides the simple spatial movement of the universe, which we say the first and unmovable substance produces, there are other spatial 30 movements—those of the planets—which are eternal (for a body which moves in a circle is eternal and unresting; we have proved these points in the physical treatises), each of *these* movements also must be caused by a substance both unmovable in itself and eternal. For the nature of the stars[46] is eter-

nal just because it is a certain kind of substance, and the mover is eternal and prior to the moved, and that which is prior to a substance must be a substance. Evidently, then, there must be substances which are 35 of the same number as the movements of the stars, and in their nature eternal, and in themselves unmovable, and without magnitude, for the reason before mentioned.[47]

That the movers are substances, then, and that one 1073ᵇ of these is first and another second according to the same order as the movements of the stars, is evident. But in the number of the movements we reach a problem which must be treated from the standpoint of that one of the mathematical sciences which is most akin to philosophy—viz. of astronomy; for this 5 science speculates about substance which is perceptible but eternal, but the other mathematical sciences, i. e. arithmetic and geometry, treat of no substance. That the movements are more numerous than the bodies that are moved is evident to those who have given even moderate attention to the matter; for each of the planets has more than one movement. But as to the actual number of these movements, we 10 now—to give some notion of the subject—quote what some of the mathematicians say, that our thought may have some definite number to grasp; but, for the rest, we must partly investigate for ourselves, partly learn from other investigators, and if 15 those who study this subject form an opinion contrary to what we have now stated, we must esteem both parties indeed, but follow the more accurate.

Eudoxus supposed that the motion of the sun or of the moon involves, in either case, three spheres, of which the first is the sphere of the fixed stars, and the second moves in the circle which runs along the middle of the zodiac, and the third in the circle which 20 is inclined across the breadth of the zodiac; but the circle in which the moon moves is inclined at a greater angle than that in which the sun moves. And the motion of the planets involves, in each case, four spheres, and of these also the first and second are the same as the first two mentioned above (for the sphere of the fixed stars is that which moves all the 25 other spheres, and that which is placed beneath this and has its movement in the circle which bisects the zodiac is common to all), but the *poles* of the third sphere of each planet are in the circle which bisects the zodiac, and the motion of the fourth sphere is in the circle which is inclined at an angle to the equa-

---

[46]This is to be understood as a general term including both fixed stars and planets.

[47]Cf. ll. 5–11.

tor of the third sphere; and the poles of the third
30 sphere are different for each of the other planets, but
those of Venus and Mercury are the same.

Callippus made the position of the spheres the
same as Eudoxus did, but while he assigned the same
number as Eudoxus did to Jupiter and to Saturn, he
35 thought two more spheres should be added to the
sun and two to the moon, if one is to explain the observed facts; and one more to each of the other planets.

But it is necessary, if all the spheres combined are
to explain the observed facts, that for each of the
planets there should be other spheres (one fewer than
1074ᵃ those hitherto assigned) which counteract those already mentioned and bring back to the same position the outermost sphere of the star which in each
case is situated below[48] the star in question; for only
thus can all the forces at work produce the observed
5 motion of the planets. Since, then, the spheres involved in the movement of the planets themselves
are—eight for Saturn and Jupiter and twenty-five for
the others, and of these only those involved in the
movement of the lowest-situated planet need not be
counteracted, the spheres which counteract those of
the outermost two planets will be six in number, and
the spheres which counteract those of the next four
planets will be sixteen; therefore the number of all
10 the spheres—both those which move the planets and
those which counteract these—will be fifty-five.
And if one were not to add to the moon and to the
sun the movements we mentioned, the whole set of
spheres will be forty-seven in number.

Let this, then, be taken as the number of the
spheres, so that the unmovable substances and prin-
15 ciples also may probably be taken as just so many;
the assertion of *necessity* must be left to more powerful thinkers. But if there can be no spatial movement which does not conduce to the moving of a
star, and if further every being and every substance
which is immune from change and in virtue of itself
has attained to the best must be considered an end,
there can be no other being apart from these we have
20 named, but this must be the number of the substances. For if there are others, they will cause
change as being a final cause of movement; but there
cannot *be* other movements besides those mentioned. And it is reasonable to infer this from a con-
25 sideration of the bodies that are moved; for if every-

thing that moves is for the sake of that which is
moved, and every movement belongs to something
that is moved, no movement can be for the sake of
itself or of another movement, but all the movements
must be for the sake of the stars. For if there is to
be a movement for the sake of a movement, this latter also will have to for the sake of something else;
so that since there cannot be an infinite regress, the 30
end of every movement will be one of the divine
bodies which move through the heaven.

(Evidently there is but one heaven. For if there
are many heavens as there are many men, the moving principles, of which each heaven will have one,
will be one in form but in *number* many. But all
things that are many in number have matter; for one
and the same definition, e. g. that of man, applies to 35
many things, while Socrates is one. But the primary
essence has not matter; for it is complete reality. So
the unmovable first mover is one both in definition
and in number; so too, therefore, is that which is
moved always and continuously; therefore there is
one heaven alone.)

Our forefathers in the most remote ages have 1074ᵇ
handed down to their posterity a tradition, in the
form of a myth, that these bodies are gods and that
the divine encloses the whole of nature. The rest of
the tradition has been added later in mythical form
with a view to the persuasion of the multitude and
to its legal and utilitarian expediency; they say these 5
gods are in the form of men or like some of the other
animals, and they say other things consequent on
and similar to these which we have mentioned. But
if one were to separate the first point from these additions and take it alone—that they thought the first
substances to be gods, one must regard this as an inspired utterance, and reflect that, while probably 10
each art and each science has often been developed
as far as possible and has again perished, these opinions, with others, have been preserved until the present like relics of the ancient treasure. Only thus far,
then, is the opinion of our ancestors and of our earliest predecessors clear to us.

9. The nature of the divine thought involves cer- 15
tain problems; for while thought is held to be the
most divine of things observed by us, the question
how it must be situated in order to have that character involves difficulties. For if it thinks of nothing, what is there here of dignity? It is just like one
who sleeps. And if it thinks, but this depends on
something else, then (since that which is its substance is not the act of thinking, but a potency) it 20

---

[48]i. e. inwards from, the universe being thought of as a system of concentric spheres encircling the earth.

cannot be the best substance; for it is through thinking that its value belongs to it. Further, whether its substance is the faculty of thought or the act of thinking, what does it think of? Either of itself or of something else; and if of something else, either of the same thing always or of something different. Does it matter, then, or not, whether it thinks of the good 25 or of any chance thing? Are there not some things about which it is incredible that it should think? Evidently, then, it thinks of that which is most divine and precious, and it does not change; for change would be change for the worse, and this would be already a movement. First, then, if 'thought' is not the act of thinking but a potency, it would be reasonable to suppose that the continuity of its thinking is wearisome to it. Secondly, there would evidently be something else more precious than 30 thought, viz. that which is thought of. For both thinking and the act of thought will belong even to one who thinks of the worst thing in the world, so that if this ought to be avoided (and it ought, for there are even some things which it is better not to see than to see), the act of thinking cannot be the best of things. Therefore it must be of itself that the divine thought thinks (since it is the most excellent of things), and its thinking is a thinking on thinking.

35 But evidently knowledge and perception and opinion and understanding have always something else as their object, and themselves only by the way. Further, if thinking and being thought of are different, in respect of which does goodness belong to thought? For to *be* an act of thinking and to *be* an object of thought are not the same thing. We answer 1075ᵃ that in some cases the knowledge is the object. In the productive sciences it is the substance or essence of the object, matter omitted, and in the theoretical sciences the definition or the act of thinking is the object. Since, then, thought and the object of thought are not different in the case of things that have not matter, the divine thought and its object will be the same, i. e. the thinking will be one with the object of its thought.

5 A further question is left—whether the object of the divine thought is composite; for if it were, thought would change in passing from part to part of the whole. We answer that everything which has not matter is indivisible—as human thought, or rather the thought of composite beings, is in a certain period of time (for it does not possess the good 10 at this moment or at that, but its best, being something *different* from it, is attained only in a whole

period of time), so throughout eternity is the thought which has *itself* for its object.

10. We must consider also in which of two ways the nature of the universe contains the good and the highest good, whether as something separate and by itself, or as the order of the parts. Probably in both ways, as an army does; for its good is found both in its order and in its leader, and more in the latter; for 15 he does not depend on the order but it depends on him. And all things are ordered together somehow, but not all alike—both fishes and fowls and plants; and the world is not such that one thing has nothing to do with another, but they are connected. For all are ordered together to one end, but it is as in a house, where the freemen are least at liberty to act at random, but all things or most things are already ordained for them, while the slaves and the animals do little for the common good, and for the most part 20 live at random; for this is the sort of principle that constitutes the nature of each. I mean, for instance, that all must at least come to be dissolved into their elements,[49] and there are other functions similarly in which all share for the good of the whole.

We must not fail to observe how many impossi- 25 ble or paradoxical results confront those who hold different views from our own, and what are the views of the subtler thinkers, and which views are attended by fewest difficulties. All make all things out of contraries. But neither 'all things' nor 'out of contraries' is right; nor do these thinkers tell us how all the things in which the contraries are present can be made out of the contraries; for contraries are not 30 affected by one another. Now for us this difficulty is solved naturally by the fact that there is a third element.[50] These thinkers however make one of the two contraries matter; this is done for instance by those who make the unequal matter for the equal, or the many matter for the one. But this also is refuted in the same way; for the one matter which underlies any pair of contraries is contrary to nothing. Further, all things, except the one, will, on the view we are criticizing, partake of evil; for the bad itself is one 35 of the two elements. But the other school does not treat the good and the bad even as principles; yet in all things the good is in the highest degree a principle. The school we first mentioned is right in saying that is is a principle, but *how* the good is a prin-

---

[49]*sc.* in order that higher forms of being may be produced by new combinations of the elements.

[50]i. e. the substratum.

ciple they do not say—whether as end or as mover or as form.

1075ᵇ Empedocles also has a paradoxical view; for he identifies the good with love, but this is a principle both as mover (for it brings things together) and as matter (for it is part of the mixture). Now even if it 5 happens that the same thing is a principle both as matter and as mover, still the being, at least, of the two is not the same. In which respect then is love a principle? It is paradoxical also that strife should be imperishable; the nature of his 'evil' is just strife.

Anaxagoras makes the good a motive principle; for his 'reason' moves things. But it moves them for an end, which must be something other than it, except according to *our* way of stating the case; for, on our view, the medical art is in a sense health. It 10 is paradoxical also not to suppose a contrary to the good, i. e. to reason. But all who speak of the contraries make no use of the contraries, unless we bring their views into shape. And why some things are perishable and others imperishable, no one tells us; for they make all existing things out of the same 15 principles. Further, some make existing things out of the non-existent; and others to avoid the necessity of this make all things one.

Further, why should there always be becoming, and what is the cause of becoming?—this no one tells us. And those who suppose two principles must suppose another, a superior principle, and so must those who believe in the Forms; for why did things come to participate, or why do they participate, in 20 the Forms? And all other thinkers[51] are confronted by the necessary consequence that there is something contrary to Wisdom, i. e. to the highest knowledge; but *we* are not. For there is nothing contrary to that which is primary; for all contraries have matter, and things that have matter exist only poten-

tially; and the ignorance which is contrary to any knowledge leads to an object contrary to the object of the knowledge; but what is primary has no contrary.

Again, if besides sensible things no others exist, 25 there will be no first principle, no order, no becoming, no heavenly bodies, but each principle will have a principle before it, as in the accounts of the theologians and all the natural philosophers. But if the Forms or the numbers are to exist, they will be causes of nothing; or if not that, at least not of movement. Further, how is extension, i. e. a *continuum*, to be produced out of unextended parts? For number will not, either as mover or as form, produce a *continuum*. But again there cannot be any *contrary* 30 that is also essentially a productive or moving principle; or it would be possible not to be.[52] Or at least its action would be posterior to its potency. The world, then, would not be eternal. But it is; one of these premisses, then, must be denied. And we have said how this must be done. Further, in virtue of 35 what the numbers, or the soul and the body, or in general the form and the thing, are one—of this no one tells us anything; nor can any one tell, unless he says, as we do, that the mover makes them one. And those who say mathematical number is first and go on to generate one kind of substance after another and give different principles for each, make the sub- 1076ᵃ stance of the universe a mere series of episodes (for one substance has no influence on another by its existence or non-existence), and they give us many governing principles; but the world refuses to be governed badly.

'The rule of many is not good; one ruler let there be.'

---

[51]The special reference is to Plato; Cf. *Rep*. 477.

[52]Since contraries must contain matter, and matter implies potentiality and contingency.

Nicomachean Ethics

BOOK I

1094ª1 **1.** Every art and every inquiry, and similarly every action and choice, is thought to aim at some good; and for this reason the good has rightly been declared to be that at which all things aim. But a certain difference is found among ends; some are activities, others are products apart from the activities that produce them. Where there are ends apart from 5 the actions, it is the nature of the products to be better than the activities. Now, as there are many actions, arts, and sciences, their ends also are many; the end of the medical art is health, that of ship-building a vessel, that of strategy victory, that of eco-10 nomics wealth. But where such arts fall under a single capacity—as bridle-making and the other arts concerned with the equipment of horses fall under the art of riding, and this and every military action under strategy, in the same way other arts fall under yet others—in all of these the ends of the master arts are to be preferred to all the subordinate ends; for it is for the sake of the former that the latter are 15 pursued. It makes no difference whether the activities themselves are the ends of the actions, or something else apart from the activities, as in the case of the sciences just mentioned.

2. If, then, there is some end of the things we do, which we desire for its own sake (everything else being desired for the sake of this), and if we do not 20 choose everything for the sake of something else (for at that rate the process would go on to infinity, so that our desire would be empty and vain), clearly this must be the good and the chief good. Will not the knowledge of it, then, have a great influence on 25 life? Shall we not, like archers who have a mark to aim at, be more likely to hit upon what we should? If so, we must try, in outline at least, to determine what it is, and of which of the sciences or capacities it is the object. It would seem to belong to the most authoritative art and that which is most truly 1094ᵇ1 the master art. And politics appears to be of this nature; for it is this that ordains which of the sciences should be studied in a state, and which each class of citizens should learn and up to what point they should learn them; and we see even the most highly esteemed of capacities to fall under this, e.g. strategy, economics, rhetoric; now, since politics uses the rest of the sciences, and since, again, it legislates as to what we are to do and what we are to abstain from, the end of this science must include those of 5 the others, so that this end must be the good for man. For even if the end is the same for a single man and for a state, that of the state seems at all events something greater and more complete both to attain and to preserve; for though it is worth while to attain the end merely for one man, it is finer and more god-like to attain it for a nation or for city-states. These, 10 then, are the ends at which our inquiry, being concerned with politics, aims.

3. Our discussion will be adequate if it has as much clearness as the subject-matter admits of; for precision is not to be sought for alike in all discussions, any more than in all the products of the crafts. Now fine and just actions, which political science investigates, exhibit much variety and fluctuation, so that they may be thought to exist only by con-15 vention, and not by nature. And goods also exhibit a similar fluctuation because they bring harm to many people; for before now men have been undone by reason of their wealth, and others by reason of their courage. We must be content, then, in speaking of such subjects and with such premises to in-20 dicate the truth roughly and in outline, and in speaking about things which are only for the most part true and with premises of the same kind to reach conclusions that are no better. In the same spirit, therefore, should each of our statements be *received*; for it is the mark of an educated man to look for precision in each class of things just so far as the nature of the subject admits: it is evidently equally 25 foolish to accept probable reasoning from a mathematician and to demand from a rhetorician demonstrative proofs.

Now each man judges well the things he knows, and of these he is a good judge. And so the man who has been educated in a subject is a good judge of 1095ª1

Reprinted from Aristotle's *Nicomachean Ethics*, translated by W. D. Ross by permission of Oxford University Press.

that subject, and the man who has received an all-round education is a good judge in general. Hence a young man is not a proper hearer of lectures on political science; for he is inexperienced in the actions that occur in life, but its discussions start from these and are about these; and, further, since he tends to follow his passions, his study will be vain and un-5 profitable, because the end aimed at is not knowledge but action. And it makes no difference whether he is young in years or youthful in character; the defect does not depend on time, but on his living and pursuing each successive object as passion directs. For to such persons, as to the incontinent, knowledge brings no profit; but to those who desire and act in accordance with a rational principle knowl-10 edge about such matters will be of great benefit.

These remarks about the student, the way in which our statements should be received, and the purpose of the inquiry, may be taken as our preface.

4. Let us resume our inquiry and state, in view of the fact that all knowledge and choice aims at some 15 good, what it is that we say political science aims at and what is the highest of all goods achievable by action. Verbally there is very general agreement; for both the general run of men and people of superior refinement say that it is happiness, and identify living well and faring well with being happy; but with regard to what happiness is they differ, and the many do not give the same account as the wise. For the former think it is some plain and obvious thing, like pleasure, wealth, or honour; they differ, however, 20 from one another—and often even the same man identifies it with different things, with health when he is ill, with wealth when he is poor; but, conscious of their ignorance, they admire those who proclaim some great thing that is above their comprehension. Now some thought that apart from these many goods 25 there is another which is good in itself and causes the goodness of all these as well. To examine all the opinions that have been held would no doubt be somewhat fruitless: it is enough to examine those that are most prevalent or that seem to have some 30 reason in their favour.

Let us not fail to notice, however, that there is a difference between arguments from and those to the first principles. For Plato, too, was right in raising this question and asking, as he used to do, 'are we on the way from or to the first principles?' There is a difference, as there is in a race-course between the course from the judges to the turning-point and the way back. For, while we must begin with what is familiar, things are so in two ways—some to us, some without qualification. Presumably, then, we must begin with things familiar to us. Hence any one who is to listen intelligently to lectures about what 1095ʰ1 is noble and just and, generally, about the subjects of political science must have been brought up in good habits. For the facts are the starting-point, and if they are sufficiently plain to him, he will not need 5 the reason as well; and the man who has been well brought up has or can easily get starting-points. And as for him who neither has nor can get them, let him hear the words of Hesiod:[1]

Far best is he who knows all things himself;   10
Good, he that hearkens when men counsel right;
But he who neither knows, nor lays to heart
Another's wisdom, is a useless wight.

5. Let us, however, resume our discussion from the point at which we digressed. To judge from the lives that men lead, most men, and men of the most vulgar type, seem (not without some reason) to identify the good, or happiness, with pleasure; which is 15 the reason why they love the life of enjoyment. For there are, we may say, three prominent types of life—that just mentioned, the political, and thirdly the contemplative life. Now the mass of mankind are evidently quite slavish in their tastes, preferring a life suitable to beasts, but they get some reason for 20 their view from the fact that many of those in high places share the tastes of Sardanapallus. But people of superior refinement and of active disposition identify happiness with honour; for this is, roughly speaking, the end of the political life. But it seems too superficial to be what we are looking for, since it is thought to depend on those who bestow honour 25 rather than on him who receives it, but the good we divine to be something of one's own and not easily taken from one. Further, men seem to pursue honour in order that they may be assured of their merit; at least it is by men of practical wisdom that they seek to be honoured, and among those who know them, and on the ground of their excellence; clearly, 30 then, according to them, at any rate, excellence is better. And perhaps one might even suppose this to be, rather than honour, the end of the political life. But even this appears somewhat incomplete; for possession of excellence seems actually compatible with being asleep, or with lifelong inactivity, and,

[1]*Works and Days* 293–7.

further, with the greatest sufferings and misfortunes; but a man who was living so no one would call 1096ᵃ1 happy, unless he were maintaining a thesis at all costs. But enough of this; for the subject has been sufficiently treated even in ordinary discussions. Third comes the contemplative life, which we shall 5 consider later.

The life of money-making is one undertaken under compulsion, and wealth is evidently not the good we are seeking; for it is merely useful and for the sake of something else. And so one might rather take the aforenamed objects to be ends; for they are loved for themselves. But it is evident that not even these are ends—although many arguments have been thrown away in support of them. Let us then dismiss 10 them.

6. We had perhaps better consider the universal good and discuss thoroughly what is meant by it, although such an inquiry is made an uphill one by the fact that the Forms have been introduced by friends of our own. Yet it would perhaps be thought to be better, indeed to be our duty, for the sake of maintaining the truth even to destroy what touches us 15 closely, especially as we are philosophers; for, while both are dear, piety requires us to honour truth above our friends.

The men who introduced this doctrine did not posit Ideas of classes within which they recognized priority and posteriority (which is the reason why they did not maintain the existence of an Idea embracing all numbers); but things are called good both 20 in the category of substance and in that of quality and in that of relation, and that which is *per se*, i.e. substance, is prior in nature to the relative (for the latter is like an offshoot and accident of what is); so that there could not be a common Idea set over all these goods. Further, since things are said to be good in as many ways as they are said to be (for things are called good both in the category of substance, as 25 God and reason, and in quality, e.g. the virtues, and in quantity, e.g. that which is moderate, and in relation, e.g. the useful, and in time, e.g. the right opportunity, and in place, e.g. the right locality and the like), clearly the good cannot be something universally present in all cases and single; for then it would not have been predicated in all the categories but in one only. Further, since of the things answering to 30 one Idea there is one science, there would have been one science of all the goods; but as it is there are many sciences even of the things that fall under one category, e.g. of opportunity (for opportunity in war

is studied by strategy and in disease by medicine), and the moderate in food is studied by medicine and in exercise by the science of gymnastics. And one might ask the question, what in the world they *mean* by 'a thing itself', if in man himself and in a particular man the account of man is one and the same. For in so far as they are men, they will in no respect 1096ᵇ1 differ; and if this is so, neither will there be a difference in so far as they are good. But again it will not be good any the more for being eternal, since that which lasts long is no whiter than that which perishes in a day. The Pythagoreans seem to give a more plausible account of the good, when they place the one in the column of goods; and it is they that 5 Speusippus seems to have followed.

But let us discuss these matters elsewhere; an objection to what we have said, however, may be discerned in the fact that the Platonists have not been speaking about *all* goods, and that the goods that are 10 pursued and loved for themselves are called good by reference to a single Form, while those which tend to produce or to preserve these somehow or to prevent their contraries are called so by reference to these, and in a different sense. Clearly, then, goods must be spoken of in two ways, and some must be good in themselves, the others by reason of these. Let us separate, then, things good in themselves from 15 things useful, and consider whether the former are called good by reference to a single Idea. What sort of goods would one call good in themselves? Is it those that are pursued even when isolated from others, such as intelligence, sight, and certain pleasures and honours? Certainly, if we pursue these also for the sake of something else, yet one would place them among things good in themselves. Or is nothing other than the Idea good in itself? In that case the Form will be empty. But if the things we have named 20 are also things good in themselves, the account of the good will have to appear as something identical in them all, as that of whiteness is identical in snow and in white lead. But of honour, wisdom, and pleasure, just in respect of their goodness, the accounts are distinct and diverse. The good, therefore, is not 25 something common answering to one Idea.

But then in what way are things called good? They do not seem to be like the things that only chance to have the same name. Are goods one, then, by being derived from one good or by all contributing to one good, or are they rather one by analogy? Certainly as sight is in the body, so is reason in the soul, and so on in other cases. But perhaps these subjects 30 had better be dismissed for the present; for perfect precision about them would be more appropriate to another branch of philosophy. And similarly with regard to the Idea; even if there is some one good which is universally predictable of goods or is capable of separate and independent existence, clearly 1097ªl it could not be achieved or attained by man; but we are now seeking something attainable. Perhaps, however, some one might think it worth while to have knowledge of it with a view to the goods that *are* attainable and achievable; for having this as a sort of pattern we shall know better the goods that are good for us, and if we know them shall attain them. This argument has some plausibility, but seems to clash with the procedure of the sciences; 5 for all of these, though they aim at some good and seek to supply the deficiency of it, leave on one side the knowledge of *the* good. Yet that all the exponents of the arts should be ignorant of, and should not even seek, so great an aid is not probable. It is hard, too, to see how a weaver or a carpenter will be benefited in regard to his own craft by knowing this 'good itself', or how the man who has viewed the Idea itself will be a better doctor or general 10 thereby. For a doctor seems not even to study health in this way, but the health of man, or perhaps rather the health of a particular man; for it is individuals that he is healing. But enough of these topics.

15 **7.** Let us again return to the good we are seeking, and ask what it can be. It seems different in different actions and arts; it is different in medicine, in strategy, and in the other arts likewise. What then is the good of each? Surely that for whose sake everything else is done. In medicine this is health, in strategy victory, in architecture a house, in any other 20 sphere something else, and in every action and choice the end; for it is for the sake of this that all men do whatever else they do. Therefore, if there is an end for all that we do, this will be the good achievable by action, and if there are more than one, these will be the goods achievable by action.

So the argument has by a different course reached the same point; but we must try to state this even more clearly. Since there are evidently more than 25 one end, and we choose some of these (e.g. wealth, flutes, and in general instruments) for the sake of something else, clearly not all ends are complete ends; but the chief good is evidently something complete. Therefore, if there is only one complete end, this will be what we are seeking, and if there are more than one, the most complete of these will be

what we are seeking. Now we call that which is in 30 itself worthy of pursuit more complete than that which is worthy of pursuit for the sake of something else, and that which is never desirable for the sake of something else more complete than the things that are desirable both in themselves and for the sake of that other thing, and therefore we call complete without qualification that which is always desirable in itself and never for the sake of something else.

Now such a thing happiness, above all else, is held to be; for this we choose always for itself and never 1097ᵇl for the sake of something else, but honour, pleasure, reason, and every excellence we choose indeed for themselves (for if nothing resulted from them we should still choose each of them), but we choose them also for the sake of happiness, judging that through them we shall be happy. Happiness, on the 5 other hand, no one chooses for the sake of these, nor, in general, for anything other than itself.

From the point of view of self-sufficiency the same result seems to follow; for the complete good is thought to be self-sufficient. Now by self-sufficient we do not mean that which is sufficient for a man by himself, for one who lives a solitary life, but also for parents, children, wife, and in general for 10 his friends and fellow citizens, since man is sociable by nature. But some limit must be set to this; for if we extend our requirement to ancestors and de- 15 scendants and friends' friends we are in for an infinite series. Let us examine this question, however, on another occasion; the self-sufficient we now define as that which when isolated makes life desirable and lacking in nothing; and such we think happiness to be; and further we think it most desirable of all things, without being counted as one good thing among others—if it were so counted it would clearly be made more desirable by the addition of even the least of goods; for that which is added becomes an excess of goods, and of goods the greater is always more desirable. Happiness, then, is some- 20 thing complete and self-sufficient, and is the end of action.

Presumably, however, to say that happiness is the chief good seems a platitude, and a clearer account of what it is is still desired. This might perhaps be given, if we could first ascertain the function of man. 25 For just as for a flute-player, a sculptor, or any artist, and, in general, for all things that have a function or activity, the good and the 'well' is thought to reside in the function, so would it seem to be for man, if he has a function. Have the carpenter, then, and the

tanner certain functions or activities, and has man
30 none? Is he naturally functionless? Or as eye, hand,
foot, and in general each of the parts evidently has
a function, may one lay it down that man similarly
has a function apart from all these? What then can
1098ª1 this be? Life seems to be common even to plants,
but we are seeking what is preculiar to man. Let us
exclude, therefore, the life of nutrition and growth.
Next there would be a life of perception, but *it* also
seems to be common even to the horse, the ox, and
every animal. There remains, then, an active life of
the element that has a rational principle (of this, one
part has such a principle in the sense of being obedient to one, the other in the sense of possessing one
5 and exercising thought); and as this too can be taken
in two ways, we must state that life in the sense of
activity is what we mean; for this seems to be the
more proper sense of the term. Now if the function
of man is an activity of soul in accordance with, or
not without, rational principle, and if we say a so-
and-so and a good so-and-so have a function which
is the same in kind, e.g. a lyre-player and a good
lyre-player, and so without qualification in all cases,
eminence in respect of excellence being added to the
10 function (for the function of a lyre-player is to play
the lyre, and that of a good lyre-player is to do so
well): if this is the case, [and we state the function
of man to be a certain kind of life, and this to be an
activity or actions of the soul implying a rational
principle, and the function of a good man to be the
good and noble performance of these, and if any action is well performed when it is performed in accordance with the appropriate excellence: if this is
the case,]² human good turns out to be activity of
15 soul in conformity with excellence, and if there are
more than one excellence, in conformity with the
best and most complete.

But we must add 'in a complete life'. For one
swallow does not make a summer, nor does one day;
and so too one day, or a short time, does not make
a man blessed and happy.

20 Let this serve as an outline of the good; for we
must presumably first sketch it roughly, and then
later fill in the details. But it would seem that any
one is capable of carrying on and articulating what
has once been well outlined, and that time is a good
discoverer or partner in such a work; to which facts
the advances of the arts are due; for any one can add
25 what is lacking. And we must also remember what

has been said before, and not look for precision in
all things alike, but in each class of things such precision as accords with the subject-matter, and so
much as is appropriate to the inquiry. For a carpenter and a geometer look for right angles in different
ways; the former does so in so far as the right angle is useful for his work, while the latter inquires 30
what it is or what sort of thing it is; for he is a spectator of the truth. We must act in the same way, then,
in all other matters as well, that our main task may
not be subordinated to minor qustions. Nor must we
demand the cause in all matters alike; it is enough 1098ᵇ1
in some cases that the *fact* be well established, as in
the case of the first principles; the fact is a primary
thing or first principle. Now of first principles we
see some by induction, some by perception, some
by a certain habituation, and others too in other
ways. But each set of principles we must try to investigate in the natural way, and we must take pains
to determine them correctly, since they have a great 5
influence on what follows. For the beginning is
thought to be more than half of the whole, and many
of the questions we ask are cleared up by it.

8. We must consider it, however, in the light not
only of our conclusion and our premisses, but also 10
of what is commonly said about it; for with a true
view all the facts harmonize, but with a false one
they³ soon clash. Now goods have been divided into
three classes, and some are described as external,
others as relating to soul or to body; and we call 15
those that relate to soul most properly and truly
goods. But we are positing actions and activities relating to soul.⁴ Therefore our account must be sound,
at least according to this view, which is an old one
and agreed on by philosophers. It is correct also in
that we identify the end with certain actions and activities; for thus it falls among goods of the soul and
not among external goods. Another belief which har- 20
monizes with our account is that the happy man lives
well and fares well; for we have practically defined
happiness as a sort of living and faring well. The
characteristics that are looked for in happiness seem
also, all of excellence, some with practical wisdom,
others with a kind of philosophic wisdom, others
with these, or one of these, accompanied by plea- 25
sure or not without pleasure; while others include
also external prosperity. Now some of these views
have been held by many men and men of old, oth-

---

²Excised by Bywater.

³Omitting τἀληθές.
⁴Omitting ψυχικάς.

ers by a few persons; and it is not probable that either of these should be entirely mistaken, but rather that they should be right in at least some one respect or even in most respects.

30 With those who identify happiness with excellence or some one excellence our account is in harmony; for to excellence belongs activity in accordance with excellence. But it makes, perhaps, no small difference whether we place the chief good in possession or in use, in state or in activity. For the 1099ª1 state may exist without producing any good result, as in a man who is asleep or in some other way quite inactive, but the activity cannot; for one who has the activity will of necessity be acting, and acting well. And as in the Olympic Games it is not the most beautiful and the strongest that are crowned but those who compete (for it is some of these that are victo-5 rious), so those who act rightly win the noble and good things in life.

5 Their life is also in itself pleasant. For pleasure is a state of soul, and to each man that which he is said 10 to be a lover of is pleasant; e.g. not only is a horse pleasant to the lover of horses, and a spectacle to the lover of sights, but also in the same way just acts are pleasant to the lover of justice and in general excellent acts to the lover of excellence. Now for most men their pleasures are in conflict with one another because these are not by nature pleasant, but the lovers of what is noble find pleasant the things that are by nature pleasant; and excellence actions are such, so that these are pleasant for such men as well 15 as in their own nature. Their life, therefore, has no further need of pleasure as a sort of adventitious charm, but has its pleasure in itself. For, besides what we have said, the man who does not rejoice in noble actions is not even good; since no one would call a man just who did not enjoy acting justly, nor 20 any man liberal who did not enjoy liberal actions; and similarly in all other cases. If this is so, excellent actions must be in themselves pleasant. But they are also *good* and *noble*, and have each of these attributes in the highest degree, since the good man judges well about these attributes and he judges in the way we have described. Happiness then is the best, noblest, and most pleasant thing, and these 25 attributes are not severed as in the inscription at Delos—

Most noble is that which is justest, and best is health;
But pleasantest is it to win what we love.

For all these properties belong to the best activities; 30 and these, or one—the best—of these, we identify with happiness.

Yet evidently, as we said, it needs the external goods as well; for it is impossible, or not easy, to do noble acts without the proper equipment. In many 1099ᵇ1 actions we use friends and riches and political power as instruments; and there are some things the lack of which takes the lustre from blessedness, as good birth, satisfactory children, beauty; for the man who is very ugly in appearance or ill-born or solitary and childless is hardly happy, and perhaps a man would be still less so if he had thoroughly bad children or friends or had lost good children or friends by death. 5 As we said, then, happiness seems to need this sort of prosperity in addition; for which reason some identify happiness with good fortune, though others identify it with excellence.

9. For this reason also the question is asked, 10 whether happiness is to be acquired by learning or by habituation or some other sort of training, or comes in virtue of some divine providence or again by chance. Now if there is *any* gift of the gods to men, it is reasonable that happiness should be god-given, and most surely god-given of all human things inasmuch as it is the best. But this question would perhaps be more appropriate to another inquiry; happiness seems, however, even if it is not god-sent but comes as a result of excellence and 15 some process of learning or training, to be among the most godlike things; for that which is the prize and end of excellence seems to be the best thing and something godlike and blessed.

It will also on this view be very generally shared; for all who are not maimed as regards excellence may win it by a certain kind of study and care. But if it is better to be happy thus than by chance, it is reasonable that the facts should be so, since everything that depends on the action of nature is by na-20 ture as good as it can be, and similarly everything that depends on art or any cause, and especially if it depends on the best of all causes. To entrust to chance what is greatest and most noble would be a very defective arrangement.

The answer to the question we are asking is plain 25 also from the definition[5]; for it has been said to be a certain kind of activity of soul. Of the remaining goods, some are necessary and others are naturally co-operative and useful as instruments. And this will

[5]Omitting κατ᾽ ἀρετήν.

be found to agree with what we said at the outset; for we stated the end of political science to be the best end, and political science spends most of its
30 pains on making the citizens to be of a certain character, viz. good and capable of noble acts.

It is natural, then, that we call neither ox nor horse
1100ᵃ1 nor any other of the animals happy; for none of them is capable of sharing in such activity. For this reason also a boy is not happy; for he is not yet capable of such acts, owing to his age; and boys who are called happy are being congratulated by reason of the hopes we have for them. For there is required, as we said, not only complete excellence but also a
5 complete life, since many changes occur in life, and all manner of chances, and the most prosperous may fall into great misfortunes in old age, as is told of Priam in the Trojan Cycle; and one who has experienced such chances and has ended wretchedly no one calls happy.

10 **10.** Must no one at all, then, be called happy while he lives; must we, as Solon says, see the end? Even if we are to lay down this doctrine, is it also the case that a man is happy when he is *dead*? Or is not this
15 quite absurd, especially for us who say that happiness is an activity? But if we do not call the dead man happy, and if Solon does not mean this, but that one can then safely *call* a man blessed as being at last beyond evils and misfortunes, this also affords matter for discussion; for both evil and good are thought to exist for a dead man, as much as for one who is alive but not aware of them; e.g. honours and
20 dishonours and the good or bad fortunes of children and in general of descendants. And this also presents a problem; for though a man has lived blessedly up to old age and has had a death worthy of his life,
25 many reverses may befall his descendants—some of them may be good and attain the life they deserve, while with others the opposite may be the case; and clearly too the degrees of relationship between them and their ancestors may vary indefinitely. It would be odd, then, if the dead man were to share in these changes and become at one time happy, at another wretched; while it would also be odd if the fortunes
30 of the descendants did not for *some* time have *some* effect on the happiness of their ancestors.

But we must return to our first difficulty; for perhaps by a consideration of it our present problem might be solved. Now if we must see the end and only then call a man blessed, not as being blessed but as having been so before, surely it is odd that when he is happy the attribute that belongs to him

is not to be truly predicated of him because we do not wish to call living men happy, on account of the changes that may befall them, and because we have assumed happiness to be something permanent and by no means easily changed, while a single man may 1100ᵇ1 suffer many turns of fortune's wheel. For clearly if we were to follow his fortunes, we should often call the same man happy and again wretched, making the happy man out to be a 'chameleon and insecurely based'. Or is this following his fortunes quite 5 wrong? Success or failure in life does not depend on these, but human life, as we said, needs these as well, while excellent activities or their opposites are what 10 determine happiness or the reverse.

The question we have now discussed confirms our definition. For no function of man has so much permanence as excellent activities (these are thought to be more durable even than knowledge), and of these 15 themselves the most valuable are more durable because those who are blessed spend their life most readily and most continuously in these; for this seems to be the reason why we do not forget them. The attribute in question, then, will belong to the happy man, and he will be happy throughout his life; for always, or by preference to everything else, he will do and contemplate what is excellent, and he will bear the chances of life most nobly and alto- 20 gether decorously, if he is 'truly good' and 'foursquare beyond reproach'.

Now many events happen by chance, and events differing in importance; small pieces of good fortune or of its opposite clearly do not weigh down 25 the scales of life one way or the other, but a multitude of great events if they turn out well will make life more blessed (for not only are they themselves such as to add beauty to life, but the way a man deals with them may be noble and good), while if they turn out ill they crush and maim blessedness; for 30 they both bring pain with them and hinder many activities. Yet even in these nobility shines through, when a man bears with resignation many great misfortunes, not through insensibility to pain but through nobility and greatness of soul.

If activities are, as we said, what determines the character of life, no blessed man can become miserable; for he will never do the acts that are hateful and mean. For the man who is truly good and wise, we think, bears all the chances of life becomingly 1101ᵃ1 and always makes the best of circumstances, as a good general makes the best military use of the army at his command and a shoemaker makes the best shoes out of the hides that are given him; and so with all other craftsmen. And if this is the case, the happy man can never become miserable—though he will not reach *blessedness*, if he meet with fortunes like those of Priam.

Nor, again, is he many-coloured and changeable; for neither will he be moved from his happy state easily or by any ordinary misadventures, but only by many great ones, nor, if he has had many great misadventures, will he recover his happiness in a short time, but if at all, only in a long and complete one in which he has attained many splendid successes.

Why then should we not say that he is happy who is active in conformity with complete excellence and is sufficiently equipped with external goods, not for some chance period but throughout a complete life? Or must we add 'and who is destined to live thus and die as befits his life'? Certainly the future is obscure to us, while happiness, we claim, is an end and something in every way final. If so, we shall call blessed those among living men in whom these conditions are, and are to be, fulfilled—but blessed *men*. So much for these questions.

11. That the fortunes of descendants and of all a man's friends should not affect his happiness at all seems a very unfriendly doctrine, and one opposed to the opinions men hold; but since the events that happen are numerous and admit of all sorts of difference, and some come more near to us and others less so, it seems a long—indeed an endless—task to discuss each in detail; a general outline will perhaps suffice. If, then, as some of a man's own misadventures have a certain weight and influence on life while others are, as it were, lighter, so too there are differences among the misadventures of all our friends, and it makes a difference whether the various sufferings befall the living or the dead (much more even than whether lawless and terrible deeds are presupposed in a tragedy or done on the stage), this difference also must be taken into account; or rather, perhaps, the fact that doubt is felt whether the dead share in any good or evil. For it seems, from these considerations, that even if anything whether good or evil penetrates to them, it must be something weak and negligible, either in itself or for them, or if not, at least it must be such in degree and kind as not to make happy those who are not happy nor to take away their blessedness from those who are. The good or bad fortunes of friends, then, seem to have some effects on the dead, but effects of such

a kind and degree as neither to make the happy unhappy nor to produce any other change of the kind.

12. These questions having been answered, let us consider whether happiness is among the things that are praised or rather among the things that are prized; for clearly it is not to be placed among *potentialities*. Everything that is praised seems to be praised because it is of a certain kind and is related somehow to something else; for we praise the just or brave man and in general both the good man and excellence itself because of the actions and functions involved, and we praise the strong man, the good runner, and so on, because he is of a certain kind and is related in a certain way to something good and important. This is clear also from the praises of the gods; for it seems absurd that the gods should be referred to our standard, but this is done because praise involves a reference, as we said, to something else. But if praise is for things such as we have described, clearly what applies to the best things is not praise, but something greater and better, as is indeed obvious; for what we do to the gods and the most godlike of men is to call them blessed and happy. And so too with good things; no one praises happiness as he does justice, but rather calls it blessed, as being something more divine and better.

Eudoxus also seems to have been right in his method of advocating the supremacy of pleasure; he thought that the fact that, though a good, it is not praised indicated it to be better than the things that are praised, and that this is what God and the good are; for by reference to these all other things are judged. Praise is appropriate to excellence; for as a result of excellence men tend to do noble deeds (*encomia* are bestowed on acts, whether of the body or of the soul—but perhaps nicety in these matters is more proper to those who have made a study of encomia); but to us it is clear from what has been said that happiness is among the things that are prized and complete. It seems to be so also from the fact that it is a first principle; for it is for the sake of this that we all do everything else, and the first principle and cause of goods is, we claim, something prized and divine.

13. Since happiness is an activity of soul in accordance with complete excellence, we must consider the nature of excellence; for perhaps we shall thus see better the nature of happiness. The true student of politics, too, is thought to have studied this above all things; for he wishes to make his fellow citizens good and obedient to the laws. As an ex-

10 ample of this we have the lawgivers of the Cretans and the Spartans, and any others of the kind that there may have been. And if this inquiry belongs to political science, clearly the pursuit of it will be in accordance with our original plan. But clearly the excellence we must study is human excellence; for 15 the good we were seeking was human good and the happiness human happiness. By human excellence we mean not that of the body but that of the soul; and happiness also we call an activity of soul. But if this is so, clearly the student of politics must know somehow the facts about soul, as the man who is to heal the eyes must know about the whole body also; 20 and all the more since politics is more prized and better than medicine; but even among doctors the best educated spend much labour on acquiring knowledge of the body. The student of politics, then, must study the soul, and must study it with these objects in view, and do so just to the extent which is sufficient for the questions we are discussing; for further precision is perhaps something more labori-25 ous than our purposes require.

Some things are said about it, adequately enough, even in the discussions outside our school, and we must use these; e.g. that one element in the soul is irrational and one has a rational principle. Whether these are separated as the parts of the body or of 30 anything divisible are, or are distinct by definition but by nature inseparable, like convex and concave in the circumference of a circle, does not affect the present question.

Of the irrational element one division seems to be widely distributed, and vegetative in its nature, 1102ᵇ1 I mean that which causes nutrition and growth; for it is this kind of power of the soul that one must assign to all nurslings and to embryos, and this same power to full-grown creatures; this is more reasonable than to assign some different power to 5 them. Now the excellence of this seems to be common to all and not specifically human; for this part or faculty seems to function most in sleep, while goodness and badness are least manifest in sleep (whence comes the saying that the happy are not better off than the wretched for half their lives; and this happens naturally enough, since sleep is an inactivity of the soul in that respect in which it is called good or bad), unless perhaps to a small extent some of the movements actually penetrate, and in this respect the dreams of good men are bet-10 ter than those of ordinary people. Enough of this subject, however; let us leave the nutritive faculty

alone, since it has by its nature no share in human excellence.

There seems to be also another irrational element in the soul—one which in a sense, however, shares in a rational principle. For we praise the reason of the 15 continent man and of the incontinent, and the part of their soul that has reason, since it urges them aright and towards the best objects; but there is found in them also another natural element beside reason, which fights against and resists it. For exactly as paralysed limbs when we choose to move them to the right turn on the contrary to the left, so is it with the soul; the impulses of incontinent people move in con-trary directions. But while in the body we see that 20 which moves astray, in the soul we do not. No doubt, however, we must none the less suppose that in the soul too there is something beside reason, resisting and opposing it. In what sense it is distinct from the other elements does not concern us. Now even this seems to have a share in reason, as we said; at any 25 rate in the continent man it obeys reason—and pre-sumably in the temperate and brave man it is still more obedient; for in them it speaks, on all matters, with the same voice as reason.

Therefore the irrational element also appears to be two-fold. For the vegetative element in no way 30 shares in reason, but the appetitive and in general the desiring element in a sense shares in it, in so far as it listens to and obeys it; this is the sense in which we speak of paying heed to one's father or one's friends, not that in which we speak of 'the rational' 1103ª1 in mathematics.[6] That the irrational element is in some sense persuaded by reason is indicated also by the giving of advice and by all reproof and exhor-tation. And if this element also must be said to have reason, that which has reason also will be twofold, one subdivision having it in the strict sense and in itself, and the other having a tendency to obey as one does one's father.

Excellence too is distinguished into kinds in ac-cordance with this difference; for we say that some 5 excellences are intellectual and others moral,[7] philo-sophic wisdom and understanding and practical wis-dom being intellectual, liberality and temperance moral. For in speaking about a man's character we do not say that he is wise or has understanding but

[6]Λόγον ἔχειν means (i) 'possess reason', (ii) 'pay heed to', 'obey', (iii) 'be rational' (in the mathematical sense).

[7]'Moral', here and hereafter, is used in the archaic sense of 'pertain-ing to character or *mores*'.

that he is good-tempered or temperate; yet we praise
10 the wise man also with respect to his state; and of
states we call those which merit praise excellences.

BOOK II

1. Excellence, then, being of two kinds, intellectual and moral, intellectual excellence in the main
15 owes both its birth and its growth to teaching (for
which reason it requires experience and time), while
moral excellence comes about as a result of habit,
whence also its name is one that is formed by a slight
20 variation from the word for 'habit'.[8] From this it is
also plain that none of the moral excellences arises
in us by nature; for nothing that exists by nature can
form a habit contrary to its nature. For instance the
stone which by nature moves downwards cannot be
habituated to move upwards, not even if one tries to
train it by throwing it up ten thousand times; nor can
fire be habituated to move downwards, nor can anything else that by nature behaves in one way be
trained to behave in another. Neither by nature, then,
nor contrary to nature do excellences arise in us;
rather we are adapted by nature to receive them, and
25 are made perfect by habit.

Again, of all the things that come to us by nature
we first acquire the potentiality and later exhibit the
activity (this is plain in the case of the senses; for it
was not by often seeing or often hearing that we got
these senses, but on the contrary we had them before we used them, and did not come to have them
30 by using them); but excellences we get by first exercising them, as also happens in the case of the arts
as well. For the things we have to learn before we
can do, we learn by doing, e.g. men become builders
by building and lyre-players by playing the lyre; so
1103b1 too we become just by doing just acts, temperate by
doing temperate acts, brave by doing brave acts.

This is confirmed by what happens in states; for
legislators make the citizens good by forming habits
in them, and this is the wish of every legislator; and
5 those who do not effect it miss their mark, and it is
in this that a good constitution differs from a bad one.

Again, it is from the same causes and by the same
10 means that every excellence is both produced and
destroyed, and similarly every art; for it is from playing the lyre that both good and bad lyre-players are
produced. And the corresponding statement is true

of builders and of all the rest; men will be good or
bad builders as a result of building well or badly.
For if this were not so, there would have been no
need of a teacher, but all men would have been born
good or bad at their craft. This, then, is the case with
the excellences also; by doing the acts that we do in
our transactions with other men we become just or
unjust, and by doing the acts that we do in the pres- 15
ence of danger, and being habituated to feel fear or
confidence, we become brave or cowardly. The
same is true of appetites and feelings of anger; some
men become temperate and good-tempered, others
self-indulgent and irascible, by behaving in one way
or the other in the appropriate circumstances. Thus, 20
in one word, states arise out of like activities. This
is why the activities we exhibit must be of a certain
kind; it is because the states correspond to the differences between these. It makes no small difference, then, whether we form habits of one kind or
of another from our very youth; it makes a very great 25
difference, or rather *all* the difference.

2. Since, then, the present inquiry does not aim
at theoretical knowledge like the others (for we are
inquiring not in order to know what excellence is,
but in order to become good, since otherwise our inquiry would have been of no use), we must examine the nature of actions, namely how we ought to 30
do them; for these determine also the nature of the
states that are produced, as we have said. Now, that
we must[9] act according to right reason is a common
principle and must be assumed—it will be discussed
later, i.e. both what it is, and how it is related to the 1104a1
other excellences. But this must be agreed upon beforehand, that the whole account of matters of conduct must be given in outline and not precisely, as
we said at the very beginning that the accounts we
demand must be in accordance with the subject-matter; matters concerned with conduct and questions
of what is good for us have no fixity, any more than
matters of health. The general account being of this 5
nature, the account of particular cases is yet more
lacking in exactness; for they do not fall under any
art or set of precepts, but the agents themselves must
in each case consider what is appropriate to the occasion, as happens also in the art of medicine or of
navigation.

But though our present account is of this nature 10
we must give what help we can. First, then, let us
consider this, that it is the nature of such things to

---

[8]ἠθική from ἔθις.

[9]Reading πράττειν δεῖν.

be destroyed by defect and excess, as we see in the case of strength and of health (for to gain light on things imperceptible we must use the evidence of 15 sensible things); both excessive and defective exercise destroys the strength, and similarly drink or food which is above or below a certain amount destroys the health, while that which is proportionate both produces and increases and preserves it. So too is it, then, in the case of temperance and courage 20 and the other excellences. For the man who flies from and fears everything and does not stand his ground against anything becomes a coward, and the man who fears nothing at all but goes to meet every danger becomes rash; and similarly the man who indulges in every pleasure and abstains from none becomes self-indulgent, while the man who shuns every pleasure, as boors do, becomes in a way in-25 sensible; temperance and courage, then, are destroyed by excess and defect, and preserved by the mean.

But not only are the sources and causes of their origination and growth the same as those of their destruction, but also the sphere of their activity will be 30 the same; for this is also true of the things which are more evident to sense, e.g. of strength; it is produced by taking much food and undergoing much exertion, and it is the strong man that will be most able to do these things. So too is it with the excellences; by abstaining from pleasures we become temperate, and it is when we have become so that we are most able to abstain from them; and similarly too in the case of courage; for by being habituated to despise things 1104ᵃ1 that are terrible and to stand our ground against them we become brave, and it is when we have become so that we shall be most able to stand our ground against them.

3. We must take as a sign of states the pleasure 5 or pain that supervenes on acts; for the man who abstains from bodily pleasures and delights in this very fact is temperate, while the man who is annoyed at it is self-indulgent, and he who stands his ground 10 against things that are terrible and delights in this or at least is not pained is brave, while the man who is pained is a coward. For moral excellence is concerned with pleasures and pains; it is on account of pleasure that we do bad things, and on account of pain that we abstain from noble ones. Hence we ought to have been brought up in a particular way from our very youth, as Plato says, so as both to delight in and to be pained by the things that we ought; for this is the right education.

Again, if the excellences are concerned with actions and passions, and every passion and every ac-15 tion is accompanied by pleasure and pain, for this reason also excellence will be concerned with pleasures and pains. This is indicated also by the fact that punishment is inflicted by these means; for it is a kind of cure, and it is the nature of cures to be effected by contraries.

Again, as we said but lately, every state of soul has a nature relative to and concerned with the kind 20 of things by which it tends to be made worse or better; but it is by reason of pleasures and pains that men become bad, by pursuing and avoiding these—either the pleasures and pains they ought not or when they ought not or as they ought not, or by going wrong in one of the other similar ways that reason can distinguish. Hence men even define the excel-25 lences as certain states of impassivity and rest; not well, however, because they speak absolutely, and do not say 'as one ought' and 'as one ought not' and 'when one ought or ought not', and the other things that may be added. We assume, then, that this kind of excellence tends to do what is best with regard to pleasures and pains, and badness does the contrary.

The following facts also may show us that they are concerned with these same things. There being 30 three objects of choice and three of avoidance, the noble, the advantageous, the pleasant, and their contraries, the base, the injurious, the painful, about all of these the good man tends to go right and the bad man to go wrong, and especially about pleasure; for this is common to the animals, and also it accompanies all objects of choice; for even the noble and the advantagenous appear pleasant. 1105ᵃ1

Again, it has grown up with us all from our infancy; this is why it is difficult to rub off this passion, engrained as it is in our life. And we measure even our actions, some of us more and others less, 5 by pleasure and pain. For this reason, then, our whole inquiry must be about these; for to feel delight and pain rightly or wrongly has no small effect on our actions.

Again, it is harder to fight with pleasure than with anger, to use Heraclitus' phrase, but both art and excellence are always concerned with what is harder; 10 for even the good is better when it is harder. Therefore for this reason also the whole concern both of excellence and of political science is with pleasures and pains; for the man who uses these well will be good, he who uses them badly bad.

That excellence, then, is concerned with pleasures 15

and pains, and that by the acts from which it arises it is both increased and, if they are done differently, destroyed, and that the acts from which it arose are those in which it actualizes itself—let this be taken as said.

4. The question might be asked, what we mean by saying that we must become just by doing just acts, and temperate by doing temperate acts; for if men do just and temperate acts, they are already just and temperate, exactly as, if they do what is grammatical or musical they are proficient in grammar and music.

Or is this not true even of the arts? It is possible to do something grammatical either by chance or under the guidance of another. A man will be proficient in grammar, then, only when he has both done something grammatical and done it grammatically; and this means doing it in accordance with the grammatical knowledge in himself.

Again, the case of the arts and that of the excellences are not similar; for the products of the arts have their goodness in themselves, so that it is enough that they should have a certain character, but if the acts that are in accordance with the excellences have themselves a certain character it does not follow that they are done justly or temperately. The agent also must be in a certain condition when he does them; in the first place he must have knowledge, secondly he must choose the acts, and choose them for their own sakes, and thirdly his action must proceed from a firm and unchangeable character. These are not reckoned in as conditions of the possession of the arts, except the bare knowledge; but as a condition of the possession of the excellences, knowledge has little or no weight, while the other conditions count not for a little but for everything, i.e. the very conditions which result from often doing just and temperate acts.

Actions, then, are called just and temperate when they are such as the just or the temperate man would do; but it is not the man who does these that is just and temperate, but the man who also does them *as* just and temperate men do them. It is well said, then, that it is by doing just acts that the just man is produced, and by doing temperate acts the temperate man; without doing these no one would have even a prospect of becoming good.

But most people do not do these, but take refuge in theory and think they are being philosophers and will become good in this way, behaving somewhat like patients who listen attentively to their doctors, but do none of the things they are ordered to do. As the latter will not be made well in body by such a course of treatment, the former will not be made well in soul by such a course of philosophy.

5. Next we must consider what excellence is. Since things that are found in the soul are of three kinds—passions, faculties, states—excellence must be one of these. By passions I mean appetite, anger, fear, confidence, envy, joy, love, hatred, longing, emulation, pity, and in general the feelings that are accompanied by pleasure or pain; by faculties the things in virtue of which we are said to be capable of feeling these, e.g. of becoming angry or being pained or feeling pity; by states the things in virtue of which we stand well or badly with reference to the passions, e.g. with reference to anger we stand badly if we feel it violently or too weakly, and well if we feel it moderately; and similarly with reference to the other passions.

Now neither the excellences nor the vices are *passions*, because we are not called good or bad on the ground of our passions, but are so called on the ground of our excellences and our vices, and because we are neither praised nor blamed for our passions (for the man who feels fear or anger is not praised, nor is the man who simply feels anger blamed, but the man who feels it in a certain way), but for our excellences and our vices we *are* praised or blamed.

Again, we feel anger and fear without choice, but the excellences are choices or involve choice. Further, in respect of the passions we are said to be moved, but in respect of the excellences and the vices we are said not to be moved but to be disposed in a particular way.

For these reasons also they are not *faculties* 1; for we are neither called good nor bad, nor praised nor blamed, for the simple capacity of feeling the passions; again, we have the faculties by nature, but we are not made good or bad by nature; we have spoken of this before.

If, then, the excellences are neither passions nor faculties, all that remains is that they should be *states*.

Thus we have stated what excellence is in respect of its genus.

6. We must, however, not only describe it as a state, but also say what sort of state it is. We may remark, then, that every excellence both brings into good condition the thing of which it is the excellence and makes the work of that thing be done well;

20 e.g. the excellence of the eye makes both the eye and its work good; for it is by the excellence of the 20 eye that we see well. Similarly the excellence of the horse makes a horse both good in itself and good at running and at carrying its rider and at awaiting the attack of the enemy. Therefore, if this is true in every case, the excellence of man also will be the state which makes a man good and which makes him do his own work well.

How this is to happen we have stated already, but 25 it will be made plain also by the following consideration of the nature of excellence. In everything that is continuous and divisible it is possible to take more, less, or an equal amount, and that either in terms of the thing itself or relatively to us; and the equal is an intermediate between excess and defect. 30 By the intermediate in the object I mean that which is equidistant from each of the extremes, which is one and the same for all men; by the intermediate relatively to us that which is neither too much nor too little—and this is not one, nor the same for all. For instance, if ten is many and two is few, six is intermediate, taken in terms of the object; for it exceeds and is exceeded by an equal amount; this is intermediate according to arithmetical proportion. 35 But the intermediate relatively to us is not to be taken so; if ten pounds are too much for a particular person to eat and two too little, it does not follow that the trainer will order six pounds; for this also is perhaps too much for the person who is to take it, or 1106ᵇ1 too little—too little for Milo, too much for the beginner in athletic exercises. The same is true of running and wrestling. Thus a master of any art avoids excess and defect, but seeks the intermediate and chooses this—the intermediate not in the object but 5 relatively to us.

If it is thus, then, that every art does its work well—by looking to the intermediate and judging its works by this standard (so that we often say of good 10 works of the art that it is not possible either to take away or to add anything, implying that excess and defect destroy the goodness of works of art, while the mean preserves it; and good artists, as we say, look to this in their work), and if, further, excellence 15 is more exact and better than any art, as nature also is, then it must have the quality of aiming at the intermediate. I mean moral excellence; for it is this that is concerned with passions and actions, and in these there is excess, defect, and the intermediate. For instance, both fear and confidence and appetite 20 and anger and pity and in general pleasure and pain

may be felt both too much and too little, and in both cases not well; but to feel them at the right times, with reference to the right objects, towards the right people, with the right aim, and in the right way, is what is both intermediate and best, and this is characteristic of excellence. Similarly with regard to actions also there is excess, defect, and the intermediate. Now excellence is concerned with passions and 25 actions, in which excess is a form of failure, and so is defect, while the intermediate is praised and is a form of success; and both these things are characteristics of excellence. Therefore excellence is a kind of mean, since it aims at what is intermediate.

Again, it is possible to fail in many ways (for evil belongs to the class of the unlimited, as the 30 Pythagoreans conjectured, and good to that of the limited), while to succeed is possible only in one way (for which reason one is easy and the other difficult—to miss the mark easy, to hit it difficult); for these reasons also, then, excess and defect are characteristic of vice, and the mean of excellence;

For men are good in but one way, but bad in many. 35

Excellence, then, is a state concerned with choice, 1107ᵃ1 lying in a mean relative to us, this being determined by reason and in the way in[10] which the man of practical wisdom would determine it. Now it is a mean between two vices, that which depends on excess and that which depends on defect; and again it is a mean because the vices respectively fall short of or 5 exceed what is right in both passions and actions, while excellence both finds and chooses that which is intermediate. Hence in respect of its substance and the account which states its essence is a mean, with regard to what is best and right it is an extreme.

But not every action nor every passion admits of a mean; for some have names that already imply 10 badness, e.g. spite, shamelessness, envy, and in the case of actions adultery, theft, murder; for all of these and suchlike things imply by their names that they are themselves bad, and not the excesses or deficiencies of them. It is not possible, then, ever to be right with regard to them; one must always be wrong. Nor does goodness or badness with regard 15 to such things depend on committing adultery with the right woman, at the right time, and in the right way, but simply to do any of them is to go wrong. It would be equally absurd, then, to expect that in unjust, cowardly, and self-indulgent action there 20 should be a mean, an excess, and a deficiency; for

---

[10]Reading ὡς ἄν.

at that rate there would be a mean of excess and of deficiency, an excess of excess, and a deficiency of deficiency. But as there is no excess and deficiency of temperance and courage because what is intermediate is in a sense an extreme, so too of the actions we have mentioned there is no mean nor any
25 excess and deficiency, but however they are done they are wrong; for in general there is neither a mean of excess and deficiency, nor excess and deficiency of a mean.

7. We must, however, not only make this general statement, but also apply it to the individual facts. For among statements about conduct those which
30 are general apply more widely, but those which are particular are more true, since conduct has to do with individual cases, and our statements must harmonize with the facts in these cases. We may take these cases from the diagram. With regard to feelings of fear and confidence courage is the mean; of the peo-
1107ᵇ1 ple who exceed, he who exceeds in fearlessness has no name (many of the states have no name), while the man who exceeds in confidence is rash, and he who exceeds in fear and falls short in confidence is a coward. With regard to pleasures and pains—not all of them, and not so much with regard to the
5 pains—the mean is temperance, the excess self-indulgence. Persons deficient with regard to the pleasures are not often found; hence such persons also have received no name. But let us call them 'insensible'.

With regard to giving and taking of money the mean is liberality, the excess and the defect prodi-
10 gality and meanness. They exceed and fall short in contrary ways to one another;[11] The prodigal exceeds in spending and falls short in taking, while the mean man exceeds in taking and falls short in spend-
15 ing. (At present we are giving a mere outline or summary, and are satisfied with this; later these states will be more exactly determined.) With regard to money there are also other dispositions—a mean, magnificence (for the magnificent man differs from the liberal man; the former deals with large sums, the latter with small ones), an excess, tastelessness and vulgarity, and a deficiency, niggardliness; these
20 differ from the states opposed to liberality, and the mode of their difference will be stated later.

With regard to honour and dishonour the mean is proper pride, the excess is known as a sort of empty vanity, and the deficiency is undue humility; and as

we said liberality was related to magnificence, dif-
25 fering from it by dealing with small sums, so there is a state similarly related to proper pride, being concerned with small honours while that is concerned with great. For it is possible to desire small honours[12] as one ought, and more than one ought, and less, and the man who exceeds in his desires is called ambitious, the man who falls short unambitious,
30 while the intermediate person has no name. The dispositions also are nameless, except that that of the ambitious man is called ambition. Hence the people who are at the extremes lay claim to the middle place; and we ourselves sometimes call the intermediate person ambitious and sometimes unambitious, and sometimes praise the ambitious man and
1108ᵃ1 sometimes the unambitious. The reason of our doing this will be stated in what follows; but now let us speak of the remaining states according to the method which has been indicated.

With regard to anger also there is an excess, a deficiency, and a mean. Although they can scarcely be said to have names, yet since we call the intermedi-
5 ate person good-tempered let us call the mean good temper; of the persons at the extremes let the one who exceeds be called irascible, and his vice irascibility, and the man who falls short an inirascible sort of person, and the deficiency inirascibility.

There are also three other means, which have a
10 certain likeness to one another, but differ from one another: for they are all concerned with intercourse in words and actions, but differ in that one is concerned with truth in this sphere, the other two with pleasantness; and of this one kind is exhibited in giving amusement, the other in all the circumstances of life. We must therefore speak of these too, that we
15 may the better see that in all things the mean is praiseworthy, and the extremes neither praiseworthy nor right, but worthy of blame. Now most of these states also have no names, but we must try, as in the other cases, to invent names ourselves so that we may be clear and easy to follow. With regard to truth, then, the intermediate is a truthful sort of person and
20 the mean may be called truthfulness, while the pretence which exaggerates is boastfulness and the person characterized by it a boaster, and that which understates is mock modesty and the person characterized by it mock-modest. With regard to pleasantness in the giving of amusement the intermediate person is ready-witted and the disposition

[11]Reading ἐναντίως δὲ αὐτοῖς.

[12]Reading μικρᾶς τιμῆς.

25 ready wit, the excess is buffoonery and the person characterized by it a buffoon, while the man who falls short is a sort of boor and his state is boorishness. With regard to the remaining kind of pleasantness, that which is exhibited in life in general, the man who is pleasant in the right way is friendly and the mean is friendliness, while the man who exceeds is an obsequious person if he has no end in view, a flatterer if he is aiming at his own advantage, and the man who falls short and is unpleasant in all cir-
30 cumstances is a quarrelsome and surly sort of person.

There are also means in the passions and concerned with the passions; since shame is not an excellence, and yet praise is extended to the modest man. For even in these matters one man is said to be intermediate, and another to exceed, as for instance the bashful man who is ashamed of everything; while he who falls short or is not ashamed of
1108b1 anything at all is shameless, and the intermediate person is modest. Righteous indignation is a mean between envy and spite, and these states are concerned with the pain and pleasure that are felt at the fortunes of our neighbours; the man who is characterized by righteous indignation is pained at undeserved good fortune, the envious man, going beyond him, is pained at all good fortune, and the spiteful
5 man falls so far short of being pained that he even rejoices. But these states there will be an opportunity of describing elsewhere; with regard to justice, since it has not one simple meaning, we shall, after describing the other states, distinguish its two kinds
10 and say how each of them is a mean; and similarly we shall treat also of the rational excellences.

8. There are three kinds of disposition, then, two of them vices, involving excess and deficiency and one an excellence, viz. the mean, and all are in a
15 sense opposed to all; for the extreme states are contrary both to the intermediate state and to each other, and the intermediate to the extremes; as the equal is greater relatively to the less, less relatively to the greater, so the middle states are excessive relatively to the deficiencies, deficient relatively to the ex-
20 cesses, both in passions and in actions. For the brave man appears rash relatively to the coward, and cowardly relatively to the rash man; and similarly the temperate man appears self-indulgent relatively to the insensible man, insensible relatively to the self-indulgent, and the liberal man prodigal relatively to the mean man, mean relatively to the prodigal. Hence also the people at the extremes push the in-

termediate man each over to the other, and the brave man is called rash by the coward, cowardly by the 25 rash man, and correspondingly in the other cases.

These states being thus opposed to one another, the greatest contrariety is that of the extremes to each other, rather than to the intermediate; for these are further from each other than from the intermediate, as the great is further from the small and the small 30 from the great than both are from the equal. Again, to the intermediate some extremes show a certain likeness, as that of rashness to courage and that of prodigality to liberality; but the extremes show the greatest unlikeness to each other; now contraries are defined as the things that are furthest from each other, so that things that are further apart are more contrary. 1109a1

To the mean in some cases the deficiency, in some the excess is more opposed; e.g. it is not rashness, which is an excess, but cowardice, which is a deficiency, that is more opposed to courage, and not insensibility, which is a deficiency, but self-indulgence, which is an excess, that is more opposed to temperance. This happens from two reasons, one be- 5 ing drawn from the thing itself; for because one extreme is nearer and liker to the intermediate, we oppose not this but rather its contrary to the intermediate. E.g., since rashness is thought liker and nearer to courage, and cowardice more unlike, 10 we oppose rather the latter to courage; for things that are further from the intermediate are thought more contrary to it. This, then, is one cause, drawn from the thing itself; another is drawn from ourselves; for the things to which we ourselves more naturally tend seem more contrary to the intermediate. For instance, we ourselves tend more naturally to pleasures, and hence are more easily carried away to- 15 wards self-indulgence than towards propriety. We describe as contrary to the mean, then, the states into which we are more inclined to lapse; and therefore self-indulgence, which is an excess, is the more contrary to temperance. 20

9. That moral excellence is a mean, then, and in what sense it is so, and that it is a mean between two vices, the one involving excess, the other deficiency, and that it is such because its character is to aim at what is intermediate in passions and in actions, has been sufficiently stated. Hence also it is no easy task to be good. For in everything it is no 25 easy task to find the middle, e.g. to find the middle of a circle is not for every one but for him who knows; so, too, any one can get angry—that is easy—or give or spend money; but to do this to the right person, to the right extent, at the right time, with the right aim, and in the right way, *that* is not for every one, nor is it easy; that is why goodness 30 is both rare and laudable and noble.

Hence he who aims at the intermediate must first depart from what is the more contrary to it, as Calypso advises—

Hold the ship out beyond that surf and spray.[13]

For of the extremes one is more erroneous, one less so; therefore, since to hit the mean is hard in the extreme, we must as a second best, as people say, take 1109ᵇ1 the least of the evils; and this be done best in the way we describe.

But we must consider the things towards which we ourselves also are easily carried away; for some of us tend to one thing, some to another; and this will be recognizable from the pleasure and the pain we feel. We must drag ourselves away to the con-5 trary extreme; for we shall get into the intermediate state by drawing well away from error, as people do in straightening sticks that are bent.

Now in everything the pleasant or pleasure is most to be guarded against; for we do not judge it impartially. We ought, then, to feel towards pleasure as the elders of the people felt towards Helen, and in all circumstances repeat their saying; for if we 10 dismiss pleasure thus we are less likely to go astray. It is by doing this, then, (to sum the matter up) that we shall best be able to hit the mean.

But this is no doubt difficult, and especially in in-15 dividual cases; for it is not easy to determine both how and with whom and on what provocation and how long one should be angry; for we too sometimes praise those who fall short and call them goodtempered, but sometimes we praise those who get angry and call them manly. The man, however who 20 deviates little from goodness is not blamed, whether he do so in the direction of the more or of the less, but only the man who deviates more widely; for *he* does not fail to be noticed. But up to what point and to what extent a man must deviate before he becomes blameworthy it is not easy to determine by reasoning, any more than anything else that is perceived by the senses; such things depend on particular facts, and the decision rests with perception. So much, then, makes it plain that the intermediate state

[13]*Odyssey* XII 219.

is in all things to be praised, but that we must incline sometimes towards the excess, sometimes to-25 wards the deficiency; for so shall we most easily hit the mean and what is right.

BOOK III

1. Since excellence is concerned with passions 30 and actions, and on voluntary passions and actions praise and blame are bestowed, on those that are involuntary forgiveness, and sometimes also pity, to distinguish the voluntary and the involuntary is presumably necessary for those who are studying excellence and useful also for legislators with a view to the assigning both of honours and of punishments.

Those things, then, are thought involuntary, which take place under compulsion or owing to ignorance; 1110ᵃ1 and that is compulsory of which the moving principle is outside, being a principle in which nothing is contributed by the person who acts or is acted upon, e.g. if he were to be carried somewhere by a wind, or by men who had him in their power.

But with regard to the things that are done from fear of greater evils or for some noble object (e.g. 5 if a tyrant were to order one to do something base, having one's parents and children in his power, and if one did the action they were to be saved, but otherwise would be put to death), it may be debated whether such actions are involuntary or voluntary. 10 Something of the sort happens also with regard to the throwing of goods overboard in a storm; for in the abstract no one throws goods away voluntarily, but on condition of its securing the safety of him-15 self and his crew any sensible man does so. Such actions, then, are mixed, but are more like voluntary actions; for they are worthy of choice at the time when they are done, and the end of an action is relative to the occasion. Both the terms, then, 'voluntary' and 'involuntary', must be used with reference to the moment of action. Now the man acts voluntarily; for the principle that moves the instrumental parts of the body in such actions is in him, and the things of which the moving principle is in a man himself are in his power to do or not to do. Such actions, therefore, are voluntary, but in the abstract perhaps involuntary; for no one would choose any such act in itself.

For such actions men are sometimes even praised, 20 when they endure something base or painful in return for great and noble objects gained; in the opposite case they are blamed, since to endure the greatest indignities for no noble end or for a trifling end is the mark of an inferior person. On some actions praise indeed is not bestowed, but forgiveness is, when one does what he ought not under pressure which overstrains human nature and which no one could withstand. But some acts, perhaps, we cannot be forced to do, but ought rather to face death after the most fearful sufferings; for the things that forced Euripides' Alcmaeon to slay his mother seem absurd. It is difficult sometimes to determine what should be chosen at what cost, and what should be endured in return for what gain, and yet more difficult to abide by our decisions; for as a rule what is expected is painful, and what we are forced to do is base, whence praise and blame are bestowed on those who have been compelled or have not.

What sort of acts, then, should be called compulsory? We answer that without qualification actions are so when the cause is in the external circumstances and the agent contributes nothing. But the things that in themselves are involuntary, but now and in return for these gains are worthy of choice, and whose moving principle is in the agent, are in themselves involuntary, but now and in return for these gains voluntary. They are more like voluntary acts; for actions are in the class of particulars, and the particular acts here are voluntary. What sort of things are to be chosen in return for what it is not easy to state; for there are many differences in the particular cases.

But if some one were to say that pleasant and noble objects have a compelling power, forcing us from without, all acts would be for him compulsory; for it is for these objects that all men do everything they do. And those who act under compulsion and unwillingly act with pain, but those who do acts for their pleasantness and nobility do them with pleasure; it is absurd to make external circumstances responsible, and not oneself, as being easily caught by such attractions, and to make oneself responsible for noble acts but the pleasant objects responsible for base acts. The compulsory, then, seems to be that whose moving principle is outside, the person compelled contributing nothing.

Everything that is done by reason of ignorance is *non*-voluntary; it is only what produces pain and regret that is *in*voluntary. For the man who has done something owing to ignorance, and feels not the least vexation at his action, has not acted voluntarily, since he did not know what he was doing, nor yet involuntarily, since he is not pained. Of people, then, who act by reason of ignorance he who regrets is thought an involuntary agent, and the man who does not regret may, since he is different, be called a non-voluntary agent; for, since he differs from the other, it is better that he should have a name of his own.

Acting by reason of ignorance seems also to be different from acting *in* ignorance; for the man who is drunk or in a rage is thought to act as a result not of ignorance but of one of the causes mentioned, yet not knowingly but in ignorance.

Now every wicked man is ignorant of what he ought to do and what he ought to abstain from, and error of this kind makes men unjust and in general bad; but the term 'involuntary' tends to be used not if a man is ignorant of what is to his advantage— for it is not ignorance in choice that makes action involuntary (it makes men wicked), nor ignorance of the universal (for *that* men are *blamed*), but ignorance of particular circumstances of the action and the objects with which it is concerned. For it is on these that both pity and forgiveness depend, since the person who is ignorant of any of these acts involuntarily.

Perhaps it is just as well, therefore, to determine their nature and number. A man may be ignorant, then, of who he is, what he is doing, what or whom he is acting on, and sometimes also what (e.g. what instrument) he is doing it with, and to what (e.g. for safety), and how he is doing it (e.g. whether gently or violently). Now of all of these no one could be ignorant unless he were mad, and evidently also he could not be ignorant of the agent; for how could he not know himself? But of what he is doing a man might be ignorant, as for instance people say 'it slipped out of their mouths as they were speaking',[14] or 'they did not know it was a secret', as Aeschylus said of the mysteries, or a man might say he 'let it go off when he merely wanted to show its working', as the man did with the catapult. Again, one might think one's son was an enemy, as Merope did, or that a pointed spear had a button on it, or that a stone was pumice-stone; or one might give a man a draught to save him, and really kill him; or one might want to touch a man, as people do in sparring, and really strike him. The ignorance may relate, then, to any of these things, i.e. of the circumstances of the action, and the man who was ignorant of any of these is thought to have acted involuntarily, and especially

_____
[14]Reading λέγοντας . . . αὐτούς.

if he was ignorant on the most important points; and these are thought to be what[15] he is doing and with 20 what aim. Further,[16] the doing of an act that is called involuntary in virtue of ignorance of this sort must be painful and involve regret.

Since that which is done under compulsion or by reason of ignorance is involuntary, the voluntary would seem to be that of which the moving principle is in the agent himself, he being aware of the 25 particular circumstances of the action. Presumably acts done by reason of anger or appetite are not rightly called involuntary. For in the first place, on that showing none of the other animals will act voluntarily, nor will children; and secondly, is it meant that we do not do voluntarily *any* of the acts that are due to appetite or anger, or that we do the noble acts voluntarily and the base acts involuntarily? Is not this absurd, when one and the same thing is the cause? But it would surely be odd to describe as involuntary the things one ought to desire; and we 30 ought both to be angry at certain things and to have an appetite for certain things, e.g. for health and for learning. Also what is involuntary is thought to be painful, but what is in accordance with appetite is thought to be pleasant. Again, what is the difference in respect of involuntariness between errors committed upon calculation and those committed in anger? Both are to be avoided, but the irrational pas-1111b1 sions are thought not less human than reason is, and therefore also the actions which proceed from anger or appetite are the man's actions. It would be odd, then, to treat them as involuntary.

2. Both the voluntary and the involuntary having been delimited, we must next discuss choice; for it is thought to be most closely bound up with excel-5 lence and to discriminate characters better than actions do.

Choice, then, seems to be voluntary, but not the same thing as the voluntary; the latter extends more widely. For both children and the other animals share in voluntary action, but not in choice, and acts done on the spur of the moment we describe as vol-10 untary, but not as chosen.

Those who say it is appetite or anger or wish or a kind of opinion do not seem to be right. For choice is not common to irrational creatures as well, but appetite and anger are. Again, the incontinent man acts with appetite, but not with choice; while the conti-

nent man on the contrary acts with choice, but not with appetite. Again, appetite is contrary to choice, 15 but not appetite to appetite. Again, appetite relates to the pleasant and the painful, choice neither to the painful nor to the pleasant.

Still less is it anger; for acts due to anger are thought to be less than any other objects of choice.

But neither is it wish, though it seems near to it; 20 for choice cannot relate to impossibles, and if any one said he chose them he would be thought silly; but there may be a wish even for impossibles, e.g. for immortality. And wish may relate to things that could in no way be brought about by one's own ef-25 forts, e.g. that a particular actor or athlete should win in a competition; but no one chooses such things, but only the things that he thinks could be brought about by his own efforts. Again, wish relates rather to the end, choice to what contributes to the end; for instance, we wish to be healthy, but we choose the acts which will make us healthy, and we wish to be happy and say we do, but we cannot well say we choose to be so; for, in general, choice seems to re-30 late to the things that are in our own power.

For this reason, too, it cannot be opinion; for opinion is thought to relate to all kinds of things, no less to eternal things and impossible things than to things in our own power; and it is distinguished by its falsity or truth, not by its badness or goodness, while choice is distinguished rather by these.

Now with opinion in general perhaps no one really says it is identical. But it is not identical even 1112a1 with any kind of opinion; for by choosing what is good or bad we are men of a certain character, which we are not by holding certain opinions. And we choose to get or avoid something good or bad, but we have opinions about what a thing is or whom it is good for or how it is good for him; we can hardly be said to opine to get or avoid anything. And choice is praised for being related to the right object rather 5 than for being rightly related to it, opinion for being truly related to its object. And we choose what we best know to be good, but we opine what we do not know at all; and it is not the same people that are thought to make the best choices and to have the best opinions, but some are thought to have fairly good opinions, but by reason of vice to choose what 10 they should not. If opinion precedes choice or accompanies it, that makes no difference; for it is not this that we are considering, but whether it is *identical* with some kind of opinion.

What, then, or what kind of thing is it, since it is

[15]Reading δοκεῖ ὃ καὶ οὗ ἕνεκα.

[16]Reading δέ.

none of the things we have mentioned? It seems to be voluntary, but not all that is voluntary to be an object of choice. Is it, then, what has been decided on by previous deliberation? For choice involves 15 reason and thought. Even the name seems to suggest that it is what is chosen before other things.[17]

3. Do we deliberate about everything, and is everything a possible subject of deliberation, or is deliberation impossible about some things? We ought presumably to call not what a fool or a mad-20 man would deliberate about, but what a sensible man would deliberate about, a subject of deliberation. Now about eternal things no one deliberates, e.g. about the universe or the incommensurability of the 25 diagonal and the side of a square. But no more do we deliberate about the things that involve movement but always happen in the same way, whether of necessity or by nature or from any other cause, e.g. the solstices and the risings of the stars; nor about things that happen now in one way, now in another, e.g. droughts and rains; nor about chance events, like the finding of treasure. But we do not deliberate even about all human affairs; for instance, no Spartan deliberates about the best constitution for 30 the Scythians. For none of these things can be brought about by our own efforts.

We deliberate about things that are in our power and can be done; and these are in fact what is left. For nature, necessity, and chance are thought to be 1112ᵇ1 causes, and also thought and everything that depends on man. Now every class of men deliberates about the things that can be done by their own efforts. And in the case of exact and self-contained sciences there is no deliberation, e.g. about the letters of the alphabet (for we have no doubt how they should be written); but the things that are brought about by our own efforts, but not always in the same way, are the things about which we deliberate, e.g. questions of 5 medical treatment or of money-making. And we do so more in the case of the art of navigation than in that of gymnastics, inasmuch as it has been less exactly worked out, and again about other things in the same ratio, and more also in the case of the arts than in that of the sciences; for we have more doubt about the former. Deliberation is concerned with things that happen in a certain way for the most part, but in which the event is obscure, and with things in 10 which it is indeterminate. We call in others to aid

us in deliberation on important questions, distrusting ourselves as not being equal to deciding.

We deliberate not about ends but about what contributes to ends. For a doctor does not deliberate whether he shall heal, nor an orator whether he shall convince, nor a statesman whether he shall produce 15 law and order, nor does any one else deliberate about his end. Having set the end they consider how and by what means it is to be attained; and if it seems to be produced by several means they consider by which it is most easily and best produced, while if it is achieved by one only they consider how it will be achieved by this and by what means *this* will be achieved, till they come to the first cause, which in the order of discovery is last. For the person who deliberates seems to inquire and analyse in the way 20 described as though he were analysing a geometrical construction (not all inquiry appears to be deliberation—for instance mathematical inquiries—but all deliberation is inquiry), and what is last in the order of analysis seems to be first in the order of becoming. And if we come on an impossibility, we give up the search, e.g. if we need money and this cannot be got; but if a thing appears possible we 25 try to do it. By 'possible' things I mean things that might be brought about by our own efforts; and these in a sense include things that can be brought about by the efforts of our friends, since the moving principle is in ourselves. The subject of investigation is sometimes the instruments, sometimes the use of them; and similarly in the other cases—sometimes the means, sometimes the mode of using it or the means of bringing it about. It seems, then, as has 30 been said, that man is a moving principle of actions; now deliberation is about the things to be done by the agent himself, and actions are for the sake of things other than themselves. For the end cannot be a subject of deliberation, but only what contributes to the ends; nor indeed can the particular facts be a subject of it, as whether this is bread or has been 1113ᵃ1 baked as it should; for these are matters of perception. If we are to be always deliberating, we shall have to go on to infinity.

The same thing is deliberated upon and is chosen, except that the object of choice is already determinate, since it is that which has been decided upon as a result of deliberation that is the object of choice. 5 For every one ceases to inquire how he is to act when he has brought the moving principle back to himself and to the ruling part of himself; for this is what chooses. This is plain also from the ancient consti-

---

[17] ‘προαίρεσις’ connected with ‘πρὸ ἑτέρων αἱρετόν’.

tutions, which Homer represented; for the kings announced their choices to the people. The object of choice being one of the things in our own power 10 which is desired after deliberation, choice will be deliberate desire of things in our own power; for when we have decided as a result of deliberation, we desire in accordance with our deliberation.

We may take it, then, that we have described choice in outline, and stated the nature of its objects and the fact that it is concerned with what contributes to the ends.

15 **4.** That *wish* is for the end has already been stated; some think it is for the good, others for the apparent good. Now those who say that the good is the object of wish must admit in consequence that that which the man who does not choose aright wishes for is not an object of wish (for if it is to be so, it 20 must also be good; but it was, if it so happened, bad); while those who say the apparent good is the object of wish must admit that there is no natural object of wish, but only what seems so to each man. Now different things appear so to different people, and, if it so happens, even contrary things.

If these consequences are unpleasing, are we to say that absolutely and in truth the good is the object of wish, but for each person the apparent good; 25 that that which is in truth an object of wish is an object of wish to the good man, while any chance thing may be so to the bad man, as in the case of bodies also the things that are in truth wholesome are wholesome for bodies which are in good condition, while for those that are diseased other things are wholesome—or bitter or sweet or hot or heavy, and so on; since the good man judges each class of things rightly, and in each the truth appears to him? For 30 each state of character has its own ideas of the noble and the pleasant, and perhaps the good man differs from others most by seeing the truth in each class of things, being as it were the norm and measure of them. In most things the error seems to be due to pleasure; for it appears a good when it is not. We therefore choose the pleasant as a good, and 1113ᵇ1 avoid pain as an evil.

5. The end, then, being what we wish for, the things contributing to the end what we deliberate 5 about and choose, actions concerning the latter must be according to choice and voluntary. Now the exercise of the excellences is concerned with these. Therefore excellence also is in our own power, and so too vice. For where it is in our power to act it is also in our power not to act, and *vice versa*; so that,

if to act, where this is noble, is in our power, not to act, which will be base, will also be in our power, and if not to act, where this is noble, is in our power, to act, which will be base, will also be in our power. 10 Now if it is in our power to do noble or base acts, and likewise in our power not to do them, and this was what being good or bad meant, then it is in our power to be virtuous or vicious.

The saying that 'no one is voluntarily wicked nor 15 involuntarily blessed' seems to be partly false and partly true; for no one is involuntarily blessed, but wickedness *is* voluntary. Or else we shall have to dispute what has just been said, at any rate, and deny that man is a moving principle or begetter of his actions as of children. But if these facts are evident 20 and we cannot refer actions to moving principles other than those in ourselves, the acts whose moving principles are in us must themselves also be in our power and voluntary.

Witness seems to be borne to this both by individuals in their private capacity and by legislators themselves; for these punish and take vengeance on those who do wicked acts (unless they have acted under compulsion or as a result of ignorance for which they are not themselves responsible), while 25 they honour those who do noble acts, as though they meant to encourage the latter and deter the former. But no one is encouraged to do the things that are neither in our power nor voluntary; it is assumed that there is no gain in being persuaded not to be hot or in pain or hungry or the like, since we shall experience these feelings none the less. Indeed, we punish a man for his very ignorance, if he is thought responsible for the ignorance, as when penalties are doubled in the case of drunkenness; for the moving principle is in the man himself, since he had the 30 power of not getting drunk and his getting drunk was the cause of his ignorance. And we punish those who are ignorant of anything in the laws that they ought to know and that is not difficult, and so too in the case of anything else that they are thought to be ig- 1114ᵃ1 norant of through carelessness; we assume that it is in their power not to be ignorant, since they have the power of taking care.

But perhaps a man is the kind of man not to take care. Still they are themselves by their slack lives responsible for becoming men of that kind, and men 5 are themselves responsible for being unjust or self-indulgent, in that they cheat or spend their time in drinking bouts and the like; for it is activities exercised on particular objects that make the corresponding character. This is plain from the case of people training for any contest or action; they practise the activity the whole time. Now not to know that it is from the exercise of activities on particular objects that states of character are produced is 10 the mark of a thoroughly senseless person. Again, it is irrational to suppose that a man who acts unjustly does not wish to be unjust or a man who acts self-indulgently to be self-indulgent. But if without being ignorant a man does the things which will make him unjust, he will be unjust voluntarily. Yet it does not follow that if he wishes he will cease to be un-15 just and will be just. For neither does the man who is ill become well on those terms—although[18] he may, perhaps, be ill voluntarily, through living incontinently and disobeying his doctors. In that case it was *then* open to him not to be ill, but not now, when he has thrown away his chance, just as when you have let a stone go it is too late to recover it; but yet it was in your power to throw it, since the moving principle was in you. So, too, to the unjust 20 and to the self-indulgent man it was open at the beginning not to become men of this kind, and so they are such voluntarily; but now that they have become so it is not possible for them not to be so.

But not only are the vices of the soul voluntary, but those of the body also for some men, whom we accordingly blame; while no one blames those who are ugly by nature, we blame those who are so owing to want of exercise and care. So it is, too, with 25 respect to weakness and infirmity; no one would reproach a man blind from birth or by disease or from a blow, but rather pity him, while every one would blame a man who was blind from alcoholism or some other form of self-indulgence. Of vices of the body, then, those in our own power are blamed, those not in our power are not. And if this be so, in 30 the other cases also the vices that are blamed must be in our own power.

Now some one may say that all men aim at the apparent good, but have no control over how things appear to him; but the end appears to each man in 1114ᵇ1 a form answering to his character. We reply that if each man is somehow responsible for the state he is in, he will also be himself somehow responsible for how things appear; but if not, no one is responsible for his own evildoing, but everyone does evil acts 5 through ignorance of the end, thinking that by these he will get what is best, and the aiming at the end

is not self-chosen but one must be born with an eye, as it were, by which to judge rightly and choose what is truly good, and he is well endowed by nature who is well endowed with this. For it is what is greatest and most noble, and what we cannot get or learn from another, but must have just such as it was when 10 given us at birth, and to be well and nobly endowed with this will be complete and true natural endowment. If this is true, then, how will excellence be more voluntary than vice? To both men alike, the good and the bad, the end appears and is fixed by nature or however it may be, and it is by referring everything else to this that men do whatever they 15 do.

Whether, then, it is not by nature that the end appears to each man such as it does appear, but something also depends on him, or the end is natural but because the good man does the rest voluntarily excellence is voluntary, vice also will be none the less voluntary; for in the case of the bad man there is 20 equally present that which depends on himself in his actions even if not in his end. If, then, as is asserted, the excellences are voluntary (for we are ourselves somehow part-causes of our states of character, and it is by being persons of a certain kind that we assume the end to be so and so), the vices also will be 25 voluntary; for the same is true of them.

With regard to the excellences in *general* we have stated their genus in outline, viz. that they are means and that they are states, and that they tend by their own nature to the doing of the acts by which they are produced, and that they are in our power and 30 voluntary, and act as right reason prescribes. But actions and states are not voluntary in the same way; for we are masters of our actions from the beginning right to the end, if we know the particular facts, but though we control the beginning of our states the gradual progress is not obvious, any more than 1115ᵃ1 it is in illnesses; because it was in our power, however, to act in this way or not in this way, therefore the states are voluntary.

Let us take up the several excellences, however, and say which they are and what sort of things they are concerned with and how they are concerned with 5 them; at the same time it will become plain how many they are. And first let us speak of courage.

6. That it is a mean with regard to fear and confidence has already been made evident; and plainly the things we fear are terrible things, and these are, to speak without qualification, evils; for which reason people even define fear as expectation of evil.

[18]Reading καίτοι εἰ

10 Now we fear all evils, e.g. disgrace, poverty, disease, friendlessness, death, but the brave man is not thought to be concerned with all; for to fear some things is even right and noble, and it is base not to fear them—e.g. disgrace; he who fears this is good and modest, and he who does not is shameless. He 15 is, however, by some people called brave, by an extension of the word; for he has in him something which is like the brave man, since the brave man also is a fearless person. Poverty and disease we perhaps ought not to fear, nor in general the things that do not proceed from vice and are not due to a man himself. But not even the man who is fearless of these is brave. Yet we apply the word to him also 20 in virtue of a similarity; for some who in the dangers of war are cowards are liberal and are confident in face of the loss of money. Nor is a man a coward if he fears insult to his wife and children or envy or anything of the kind; nor brave if he is confident when he is about to be flogged. With what sort of terrible things, then, is the brave man con- 25 cerned? Surely with the greatest; for no one is more likely than he to stand his ground against what is dreadful. Now death is the most terrible of all things; for it is the end, and nothing is thought to be any longer either good or bad for the dead. But the brave man would not seem to be concerned even with death in *all* circumstances, e.g. at sea or in disease. In what circumstances, then? Surely in the noblest. Now such deaths are those in battle; for these take place in the greatest and noblest danger. And this 30 agrees with the ways in which honours are bestowed in city-states and at the courts of monarchs. Properly, then, he will be called brave who is fearless in face of a noble death, and of all emergencies that involve death; and the emergencies of war are in the highest degree of this kind. Yet at sea also, and in disease, the brave man is fearless, but not in the same 1115ᵇ1 way as the seamen; for he has given up hope for safety, and is disliking the thought of death in this shape, while they are hopeful because of their experience. At the same time, we show courage in situations where there is the opportunity of showing prowess or where death is noble; but in these forms 5 of death neither of these conditions is fulfilled.

7. What is terrible is not the same for all men; but we say there are things terrible even beyond human strength. These, then, are terrible to every one—at least to every sensible man; but the terrible things that are *not* beyond human strength differ in 10 magnitude and degree, and so too do the things that

inspire confidence. Now the brave man is as dauntless as man may be. Therefore, while he will fear even the things that are not beyond human strength, he will fear them as he ought and as reason directs, and[19] he will face them for the sake of what is noble; for this is the end of excellence. But it is possible to fear these more, or less, and again to fear things that are not terrible as if they were. Of the 15 faults that are committed one consists in fearing what one should not, another in fearing as we should not, another in fearing when we should not, and so on; and so too with respect to the things that inspire confidence. The man, then, who faces and who fears the right things and with the right aim, in the right way and at the right time, and who feels confidence under the corresponding conditions, is brave; for the brave man feels and acts according to the merits of the case and in whatever way reason directs. Now 20 the end of every activity is conformity to the corresponding state. This is true, therefore, of the brave man as well as of others. But courage is noble.[20] Therefore the end also is noble; for each thing is defined by its end. Therefore it is for a noble end that the brave man endures and acts as courage directs.

Of those who go to excess he who exceeds in fearlessness has no name (we have said previously that many states have no names), but he would be a sort of madman or insensible person if he feared nothing, neither earthquakes nor the waves, as they say 25 the Celts do not; while the man who exceeds in confidence about what really is terrible is rash. The rash man, however, is also thought to be boastful and only a pretender to courage; at all events, as the brave man *is* with regard to what is terrible, so the rash man wishes to *appear*; and so he imitates him 30 in situations where he can. Hence also most of them are a mixture of rashness and cowardice; for, while in these situations they display confidence, they do not hold their ground against what is really terrible. The man who exceeds in fear is a coward; for he fears both what he ought not and as he ought not, and all the similar characterizations attach to him. He is lacking also in confidence; but he is more con- 1116ᵃ1 spicuous for his excess of fear in painful situations. The coward, then, is a despairing sort of person; for he fears everything. The brave man, on the other hand, has the opposite disposition; for confidence is the mark of a hopeful disposition. The coward, the

---

[19]Reading ὡς ὁ λόγος, ὑπομενεῖ τε.

[20]Reading ἀνδρείῳ δή · ἠδ' ἀνδρεία.

rash man, and the brave man, then, are concerned with the same objects but are differently disposed 5 towards them; for the first two exceed and fall short, while the third holds the middle, which is the right, position; and rash men are precipitate, and wish for dangers beforehand but draw back when they are in them, while brave men are keen in the moment of action, but quiet beforehand.

10 As we have said, then, courage is a mean with respect to things that inspire confidence or fear, in the circumstances that have been stated; and it chooses or endures things because it is noble to do so, or because it is base not to do so. But to die to escape from poverty or love or anything painful is not the mark of a brave man, but rather of a coward; for it is softness to fly from what is troublesome, and such 15 a man endures death not because it is noble but to fly from evil.

8. Courage, then, is something of this sort, but the name is also applied to five other kinds. (1) First comes political courage; for this is most like true courage. Citizens seem to face dangers because of 20 the penalties imposed by the laws and the reproaches they would otherwise incur, and because of the honours they win by such action; and therefore those peoples seem to be bravest among whom cowards are held in dishonour and brave men in honour. This is the kind of courage that Homer depicts, e.g. in Diomede and in Hector:

> First will Polydamas be to heap reproach on
> me then.[21]

and

25 For Hector one day 'mid the Trojans shall utter
> his vaulting harangue:
> "Afraid was Tydeides, and fled from my face,"[22]

This kind of courage is most like that which we described earlier, because it is due to excellence; for it is due to shame and to desire of a noble object 30 (i.e. honour) and avoidance of disgrace, which is ignoble. One might rank in the same class even those who are compelled by their rulers; but they are inferior, inasmuch as they act not from shame but from fear, and to avoid not what is disgraceful but what

is painful; for their masters compel them, as Hector does:

> But if I shall spy any dastard that cowers far
> from the fight,
> Vainly will such an one hope to escape from   35
> the dogs.[23]

And those who give them their posts, and beat them if they retreat, do the same, and so do those who 1116^b1 draw them up with trenches or something of the sort behind them; all of these apply compulsion. But one ought to be brave not under compulsion but because it is noble to be so.

(2) Experience with regard to particular facts is also thought to be courage; this is indeed the reason why Socrates thought courage was knowledge. 5 Other people exhibit this quality in other dangers, and soldiers exhibit it in the dangers of war; for there seem to be many empty alarms in war, of which these have had the most comprehensive experience; therefore they seem brave, because the others do not know the nature of the facts. Again, their experience makes them most capable of doing without being done to, since they can use their arms and have the kind that are likely to be best both for doing and for not being done to; therefore they fight like armed 10 men against unarmed or like trained athletes against amateurs; for in such contests too it is not the bravest men that fight best, but those who are strongest and have their bodies in the best condition. Soldiers turn 15 cowards, however, when the danger puts too great a strain on them and they are inferior in numbers and equipment; for they are the first to fly, while citizen-forces die at their posts, as in fact happened at the temple of Hermes. For to the latter flight is disgraceful and death is preferable to safety on those terms; while the former from the very beginning 20 faced the danger on the assumption that they were stronger, and when they know the facts they fly, fearing death more than disgrace; but the brave man is not that sort of person.

(3) Passion also is sometimes reckoned as courage; those who act from passion, like wild beasts rushing at those who have wounded them, are 25 thought to be brave, because brave men also are passionate; for passion above all things is eager to rush on danger, and hence Homer's 'put strength into his passion' and 'aroused their spirit and passion' and

[21]*Iliad* XXII 100.
[22]*Iliad* VIII 148.

[23]See *Iliad* II 391; XV 348.

'bitter spirit in his nostrils' and 'his blood boiled'.[24]
For all such expressions seem to indicate the stir-
30 ring and onset of passion. Now brave men act for
the sake of the noble, but passion aids them; while
wild beasts act under the influence of pain; for they
attack because they have been wounded or because
they are afraid, since if they are in a forest they do
35 not come near one. Thus they are not brave because,
driven by pain and passion, they rush on danger
without foreseeing any of the perils, since at that rate
1117ᵃ1 even asses would be brave when they are hungry;
for blows will not drive them from their food; and
lust also makes adulterers do many daring things.
[Those creatures are not brave, then, which are
driven on to danger by pain or passion.][25] The
courage that is due to passion seems to be the most
5 natural, and to be courage if choice and aim be
added.

Men, then, as well as beasts, suffer pain when they
are angry, and are pleased when they exact their revenge; those who fight for these reasons, however,
are pugnacious but not brave; for they do not act for
the sake of the noble nor as reason directs, but from
feeling; they have, however, something akin to
courage.

10　(4) Nor are sanguine people brave; for they are
confident in danger only because they have con-
quered often and against many foes. Yet they closely
resemble brave men, because both are confident; but
brave men are confident for the reasons stated earlier, while these are so because they think they are
the strongest and can suffer nothing. (Drunken men
15 also behave in this way; they become sanguine).
When their adventures do not succeed, however,
they run away; but it was the mark of a brave man
to face things that are, and seem, terrible for a man,
because it is noble to do so and disgraceful not to
do so. Hence also it is thought the mark of a braver
man to be fearless and undisturbed in sudden alarms
20 than to be so in those that are foreseen; for it must
have proceeded more from a state of character, because less from preparation; for acts that are foreseen may be chosen by calculation and reason, but
sudden actions in accordance with one's state of
character.

(5) People who are ignorant also appear brave,
and they are not far removed from those of a san-

guine temper, but are inferior inasmuch as they have
no self-reliance while these have. Hence also the
sanguine hold their ground for a time; but those who 25
have been deceived fly if they know or suspect that
things are different as happened to the Argives when
they fell in with the Spartans and took them for Sicy-
onians.

9. We have, then, described the character both of
brave men and of those who are thought to be brave.

Though courage is concerned with confidence and 30
fear, it is not concerned with both alike, but more
with the things that inspire fear; for he who is undisturbed in face of these and bears himself as he should
towards these is more truly brave than the man who
does so towards the things that inspire confidence.
It is for facing what is painful, then, as has been said,
that men are called brave. Hence also courage involves pain, and is justly praised; for it is harder to
face what is painful than to abstain from what is
pleasant. Yet the end which courage sets before it 1117ᵇ1
would seem to be pleasant, but to be concealed by
the attending circumstances, as happens also in athletic contests; for the end at which boxers aim is
pleasant—the crown and the honours—but the 5
blows they take are distressing to flesh and blood,
and painful, and so is their whole exertion; and because the blows and the exertions are many the end,
which is but small, appears to have nothing pleasant in it. And so, if the case of courage is similar,
death and wounds will be painful to the brave man
and against his will, but he will face them because
it is noble to do so or because it is base not to do 10
so. And the more he is possessed of excellence in
its entirety and the happier he is, the more he will
be pained at the thought of death; for life is best
worth living for such a man, and he is knowingly
losing the greatest goods, and this is painful. But he
is none the less brave, and perhaps all the more so, 15
because he chooses noble deeds of war at that cost.
It is not the case, then, with all the excellences that
the exercise of them is pleasant, except in so far as
it reaches its end. But it is quite possible that the
best soldiers may be not men of this sort but those
who are less brave but have no other good; for these
are ready to face danger, and they sell their life for 20
trifling gains.

So much, then, for courage; it is not difficult to
grasp its nature in outline, at any rate, from what has
been said.

10. After courage let us speak of temperance; for
these seem to be the excellences of the irrational

---

[24]See *Iliad* V 470; XI 11; XVI 529; *Odyssey* XXIV 318.
[25]Excised in Bywater.

25 parts. We have said that temperance is a mean with regard to pleasures (for it is less, and not in the same way, concerned with pains); self-indulgence also is manifested in the same sphere. Now, therefore, let us determine with what sort of pleasures they are concerned. We may assume the distinction between bodily pleasures and those of the soul, such as love 30 of honour and love of learning; for the lover of each of these delights in that of which he is a lover, the body being in no way affected, but rather the mind; but men who are concerned with such pleasures are called neither temperate nor self-indulgent. Nor, again, are those who are concerned with the other pleasures that are not bodily; for those who are fond of hearing and telling stories and who spend their days on anything that turns up are called gossips, but not self-indulgent, nor are those who are pained 1118ᵃ1 at the loss of money or of friends.

Temperance must be concerned with bodily pleasures, but not all even of these; for those who delight in objects of vision, such as colours and shapes and painting, are called neither temperate nor self-indulgent; yet it would seem possible to delight even 5 in these either as one should or to excess or to a deficient degree.

And so too is it with objects of hearing; no one calls those who delight extravagantly in music or acting self-indulgent, nor those who do so as they ought temperate.

Nor do we apply these names to those who delight in odour, unless it be incidentally; we do not 10 call those self-indulgent who delight in the odour of apples or roses or incense, but rather those who delight in the odour of unguents or of dainty dishes; for self-indulgent people delight in these because these remind them of the objects of their appetite. And one may see even other people, when they are hungry, delighting in the smell of food; but to de- 15 light in this kind of thing is the mark of the self-indulgent man; for these are objects of appetite to him.

Nor is there in animals other than man any pleasure connected with these senses except incidentally. For dogs do not delight in the scent of hares, but in the eating of them, but the scent told them the hares were there; nor does the lion delight in the lowing 20 of the ox, but in eating it; but he perceived by the lowing that it was near, and therefore appears to delight in the lowing; and similarly he does not delight because he sees 'a stag or a wild goat',²⁶ but be-

²⁶*Iliad* III 24.

cause he is going to make a meal of it. Temperance and self-indulgence, however, are concerned with the kind of pleasures that the other animals share in, which therefore appear slavish and brutish; these are touch and taste. But even of taste they appear to 25 make little or no use; for the business of taste is the discriminating of flavours, which is done by wine-tasters and people who season dishes; but they hardly take pleasure in making these discriminations, or at least self-indulgent people do not, but in the actual enjoyment, which in all cases comes through touch, both in the case of good and in that of drink and in that of sexual intercourse. This is 30 why a certain gourmand prayed that his throat might become longer than a crane's, implying that it was the contact that he took pleasure in. Thus the sense 1118ᵇ1 with which self-indulgence is connected is the most widely shared of the senses; and self-indulgence would seem to be justly a matter of reproach, because it attaches to us not as men but as animals. To delight in such things, then, and to love them above all others, is brutish. For even of the pleasures of touch the most liberal have been eliminated, e.g. those produced in the gymnasium by rubbing and 5 by the consequent heat; for the contact characteristic of the self-indulgent man does not affect the whole body but only certain parts.

11. Of the appetites some seem to be common, others to be peculiar to individuals and acquired; e.g. the appetite for food is natural; since every one who is without it craves for food or drink, and sometimes for both, and for love also (as Homer says) if he is 10 young and lusty; but not every one craves for this or that kind of nourishment or love, nor for the same things. Hence such craving appears to be our very own. Yet it has of course something natural about it; for different things are pleasant to different kinds of people, and some things are more pleasant to every one than chance objects. Now in the natural 15 appetites few go wrong, and only in one direction, that of excess; for to eat or drink whatever offers itself till one is surfeited is to exceed the natural amount, since natural appetite is the replenishment of one's deficiency. Hence these people are called belly-gods, this implying that they fill their belly be- 20 yond what is right. It is people of entirely slavish character that become like this. But with regard to the pleasures peculiar to individuals many people go wrong and in many ways. For while the people who are fond of so and so are so called because they delight either in the wrong things, or more than most people do, or in the wrong way, the self-indulgent exceed in all three ways; they both delight in some things that they ought not to delight in (since they are hateful), and if one ought to delight in some of the things they delight in, they do so more than one ought and than most men do.

Plainly, then, excess with regard to pleasures is self-indulgence and is culpable; with regard to pains one is not, as in the case of courage, called temperate for facing them or self-indulgent for not doing so, but the self-indulgent man is so called because he is pained more than he ought at not getting pleasant things (even his pain being caused by pleasure), and the temperate man is so called because he is not pained at the absence of what is pleasant and at his abstinence from it.

1119ª1 The self-indulgent man, then, craves for all pleasant things or those that are most pleasant, and is led by his appetite to choose these at the cost of everything else; hence he is pained both when he fails to get them and when he is craving for them (for appetite involves pain); but it seems absurd to be pained for the sake of pleasure. People who fall short with regard to pleasures and delight in them less than they should are hardly found; for such insensibility is not human. Even the other animals distinguish different kinds of food and enjoy some and not others; and if there is any one who finds nothing pleasant and nothing more attractive than anything else, he must be something quite different from a man; this sort of person has not received a name because he hardly occurs. The temperate man occupies a middle position with regard to these objects. For he neither enjoys the things that the self-indulgent man enjoys most—but rather dislikes them—nor in general the things that he should not, nor anything of this sort to excess, nor does he feel pain or craving when they are absent, or does so only to a moderate degree, and not more than he should, nor when he should not, and so on; but the things that, being pleasant, make for health or for good condition, he will desire moderately and as he should, and also other pleasant things if they are not hindrances to these ends, or contrary to what is noble, or beyond his means. For he who neglects these conditions loves such pleasures more than they are worth, but the temperate man is not that sort of person, but the sort of person that right reason prescribes.

12. Self-indulgence is more like a voluntary state than cowardice. For the former is actuated by pleasure, the latter by pain, of which the one is to be cho-

sen and the other to be avoided; and pain upsets and destroys the nature of the person who feels it, while pleasure does nothing of the short. Therefore self-indulgence is more voluntary. Hence also it is more a matter of reproach; for it is easier to become accustomed to its objects, since there are many things of this sort in life, and the process of habituation to them is free from danger, while with terrible objects the reverse is the case. But cowardice would seem to be voluntary in a different degree from its particular manifestations; for it is itself painless, but in these we are upset by pain, so that we even throw down our arms and disgrace ourselves in other ways; hence our acts are even thought to be done under compulsion. For the self-indulgent man, on the other hand, the particular acts are voluntary (for he does them with craving and desire), but the whole state is less so; for no one craves to be self-indulgent.

The name self-indulgence is applied also to childish faults; for they bear a certain resemblance to what we have been considering. Which is called after which, makes no difference to our present purpose; plainly, however, the later is called after the earlier. The transference of the name seems not a bad one; for that which desires what is base and which develops quickly ought to be kept in a chastened condition,[27] and these characteristics belong above all to appetite and to the child, since children in fact live at the beck and call of appetite, and it is in them that the desire for what is pleasant is strongest. If, then, it is not going to be obedient and subject to the ruling principle, it will go to great lengths; for in an irrational being the desire for pleasure is insatiable and tries every source of gratification, and the exercise of appetite increases its innate force, and if appetites are strong and violent they even expel the power of calculation. Hence they should be moderate and few, and should in no way oppose reason—and this is what we call an obedient and chastened state—and as the child should live according to the direction of his tutor, so the appetitive element should live according to reason. Hence the appetitive element in a temperate man should harmonize with reason; for the noble is the mark at which both aim, and the temperate man craves for the things he ought, as he ought, and when he ought; and this is what reason directs.

Here we conclude our account of temperance.

---

[27] ἀκόλαστος ('self-indulgent') is connected with κολάζειν ('chasten,' 'punish').

BOOK X

30   **6.** Now that we have spoken of the excellences, the forms of friendship, and the varieties of pleasure, what remains is to discuss in outline the nature of happiness, since this is what we state the end of human nature to be. Our discussion will be the more concise if we first sum up what we have said already. We said, then, that it is not a state; for if it were it might belong to some one who was asleep throughout his life, living the life of a plant, or, again, to some one who was suffering the greatest
1176ʰ1 misfortunes. If these implications are unacceptable, and we must rather class happiness as an activity, as we have said before, and if some activities are necessary and desirable for the sake of something else, while others are so in themselves, evidently happiness must be placed among those desirable in themselves, not among those desirable for the sake of something else; for happiness does not lack any-
5 thing, but is self-sufficient. Now those activities are desirable in themselves from which nothing is sought beyond the activity. And of this nature excellent actions are thought to be; for to do noble and good deeds is a thing desirable for its own sake.

Pleasant amusements also are thought to be of this nature; we choose them not for the sake of other
10 things; for we are injured rather than benefited by them, since we are led to neglect our bodies and our property. But most of the people who are deemed happy take refuge in such pastimes, which is the reason why those who are ready-witted at them are highly esteemed at the courts of tyrants; they make themselves pleasant companions in the tyrant's favourite pursuits, and that is the sort of man they
15 want. Now these things are thought to be of the nature of happiness because people in despotic positions spend their leisure in them, but perhaps such people prove nothing; for excellence and thought, from which good activities flow, do not depend on despotic position; nor, if these people, who have never tasted pure and generous pleasure, take refuge in the bodily pleasures, should these for that reason
20 be thought more desirable; for boys, too, think the things that are valued among themselves are the best. It is to be expected, then, that, as different things seem valuable to boys and to men, so they should to bad men and to good. Now, as we have often
25 maintained, those things are both valuable and pleasant which are such to the good man; and to each man the activity in accordance with his own state is

most desirable, and, therefore, to the good man that which is in accordance with excellence. Happiness, therefore, does not lie in amusement; it would, in-
30 deed, be strange if the end were amusement, and one were to take trouble and suffer hardship all one's life in order to amuse oneself. For, in a word, everything that we choose we choose for the sake of something else—except happiness, which is an end. Now to exert oneself and work for the sake of amusement seems silly and utterly childish. But to amuse oneself in order that one may exert oneself, as Anacharsis puts it, seems right; for amusement is a sort of relaxation, and we need relaxation because we cannot work continuously. Relaxation, then, is not an 1177ª1 end; for it is taken for the sake of activity.

The happy life is thought to be one of excellence; now an excellent life requires exertion, and does not consist in amusement. And we say that serious things are better than laughable things and those connected with amusement, and that the activity of the 5 better of any two things—whether it be two parts or two men—is the better; but the activity of the better is *ipso facto* superior and more of the nature of happiness. And any chance person—even a slave—can enjoy the bodily pleasures no less than the best man; but no one assigns to a slave a share in happiness—unless he assigns to him also a share in human life. For happiness does not lie in such occu- 10 pations, but, as we have said before, in excellent activities.

7. If happiness is activity in accordance with excellence, it is reasonable that it should be in accordance with the highest excellence; and this will be that of the best thing in us. Whether it be intellect 15 or something else that is this element which is thought to be our natural ruler and guide and to take thought of things noble and divine, whether it be itself also divine or only the most divine element in us, the activity of this in accordance with its proper excellence will be complete happiness. That this activity is contemplative we have already said.

Now this would seem to be in agreement both with what we said before and with the truth. For this ac- 20 tivity is the best (since not only is intellect the best thing in us, but the objects of intellect are the best of knowable objects); and, secondly, it is the most continuous, since we can contemplate truth more continuously than we can *do* anything. And we think happiness has pleasure mingled with it, but the activity of wisdom is admittedly the pleasantest of ex- 25 cellent activities; at all events philosophy is thought to offer pleasures marvellous for their purity and their enduringness, and it is to be expected that those who know will pass their time more pleasantly than those who inquire. And the self-sufficiency that is spoken of must belong most to the contemplative 30 activity. For while a wise man, as well as a just man and the rest, needs the necessaries of life, when they are sufficiently equipped with things of that sort the just man needs people towards whom and with whom he shall act justly, and the temperate man, the brave man, and each of the others is in the same case, but the wise man, even when by himself, can contemplate truth, and the better the wiser he is; he can perhaps do so better if he has fellow-workers, 1177ᵇ1 but still he is the most self-sufficient. And this activity alone would seem to be loved for its own sake; for nothing arises from it apart from the contemplating, while from practical activities we gain more 5 or less apart from the action. And happiness is thought to depend on leisure; for we are busy that we may have leisure, and make war that we may live in peace. Now the activity of the practical excellences is exhibited in political or military affairs, but the actions concerned with these seem to be un-10 leisurely. Warlike actions are completely so (for no one chooses to be at war, or provokes war, for the sake of being at war; any one would seem absolutely murderous if he were to make enemies of his friends in order to bring about battle and slaughter); but the action of the statesman is also unleisurely, and— apart from the political action itself—aims at despotic power and honours, or at all events happiness, for him and his fellow citizens—a happiness different from political action, and evidently sought 15 as being different. So if among excellent actions political and military actions are distinguished by nobility and greatness, and these are unleisurely and aim at an end and are not desirable for their own sake, but the activity of intellect, which is contemplative, seems both to be superior in worth and to aim at no end beyond itself, and to have its pleasure proper to itself (and this augments the activity), and 20 the self-sufficiency, leisureliness, unweariedness (so far as this is possible for man), and all the other attributes ascribed to the blessed man are evidently those connected with this activity, it follows that this will be the complete happiness of man, if it be allowed a complete term of life (for none of the at-25 tributes of happiness is *in*complete).

But such a life would be too high for man; for it is not in so far as he is man that he will live so, but in so far as something divine is present in him; and by so much as this is superior to our composite nature is its activity superior to that which is the exercise of the other kind of excellence. If intellect is 30 divine, then, in comparison with man, the life according to it is divine in comparison with human life. But we must not follow those who advise us, being men, to think of human things, and, being mortal, of mortal things, but must, so far as we can, make ourselves immortal, and strain every nerve to live in accordance with the best thing in us; for even if it 1178ᵃ1 be small in bulk, much more does it in power and worth surpass everything. This would seem, too, to be each man himself, since it is the authoritative and better part of him. It would be strange, then, if he were to choose not the life of himself but that of something else. And what we said before will apply 5 now; that which is proper to each thing is by nature best and most pleasant for each thing; for man, therefore, the life according to intellect is best and pleasantest, since intellect more than anything else *is* man. This life therefore is also the happiest.

8. But in a secondary degree the life in accordance with the other kind of excellence is happy; for the activities in accordance with this befit our hu-10 man estate. Just and brave acts, and other excellent acts, we do in relation to each other, observing what is proper to each with regard to contracts and services and all manner of actions and with regard to passions; and all of these seem to be human. Some of them seem even to arise from the body, and excellence of character to be in many ways bound up 15 with the passions. Practical wisdom, too, is linked to excellence of character, and this to practical wisdom, since the principles of practical wisdom are in accordance with the moral excellences and rightness in the moral excellences is in accordance with prac-20 tical wisdom. Being connected with the passions also, the moral excellences must belong to our composite nature; and the excellences of our composite nature are human; so, therefore, are the life and the happiness which correspond to these. The excellence of the intellect is a thing apart; we must be content to say this much about it, for to describe it precisely is a task greater than our purpose requires. It would seem, however, also to need external equipment but little, or less than moral excellence does. Grant that 25 both need the necessaries, and do so equally, even if the statesman's work is the more concerned with the body and things of that sort; for there will be little difference there; but in what they need for the exercise of their activities there will be much difference. The liberal man will need money for the doing of his liberal deeds, and the just man too will need it for the returning of services (for wishes are 30 hard to discern, and even people who are not just pretend to wish to act justly); and the brave man will need power if he is to accomplish any of the acts that correspond to his excellence, and the temperate man will need opportunity; for how else is either he or any of the others to be recognized? It is debated, too, whether the choice or the deed is more essential to excellence, which is assumed to involve both; it is surely clear that its completion involves both; 1178ᵇ1 but for deeds many things are needed, and more, the greater and nobler the deeds are. But the man who is contemplating the truth needs no such thing, at least with a view to the exercise of his activity; indeed they are, one may say, even hindrances, at all events to his contemplation; but in so far as he is a 5 man and lives with a number of people, he chooses to do excellent acts; he will therefore need such aids to living a human life.

But that complete happiness is a contemplative activity will appear from the following consideration as well. We assume the gods to be above all other beings blessed and happy; but what sort of ac- 10 tions must we assign to them? Acts of justice? Will not the gods seem absurd if they make contracts and return deposits, and so on? Acts of a brave man, then, confronting dangers and running risks because it is noble to do so? Or liberal acts? To whom will 15 they give? It will be strange if they are really to have money or anything of the kind. And what would their temperate acts be? Is not such praise tasteless, since they have no bad appetites? If we were to run through them all, the circumstances of action would be found trivial and unworthy of gods. Still, every one supposes that they *live* and therefore that they are active; we cannot suppose them to sleep like Endymion. Now if you take away from a living be- 20 ing action, and still more production, what is left but contemplation? Therefore the activity of God, which surpasses all others in blessedness, must be contemplative; and of human activities, therefore, that which is most akin to this must be most of the nature of happiness.

This is indicated, too, by the fact that the other animals have no share in happiness, being com- 25 pletely deprived of such activity. For while the whole life of the gods is blessed, and that of men too in so far as some likeness of such activity be-

longs to them, none of the other animals is happy, since they in no way share in contemplation. Happiness extends, then, just so far as contemplation does, and those to whom contemplation more fully belongs are more truly happy, not accidentally, but in virtue of the contemplation; for this is in itself 30 precious. Happiness, therefore, must be some form of contemplation.

But, being a man, one will also need external prosperity; for our nature is not self sufficient for the purpose of contemplation, but our body also must be healthy and must have food and other attention. Still, we must not think that the man who is to be 1179ᵃ1 happy will need many things or great things, merely because he cannot be blessed without external goods; for self-sufficiency and action do not depend on excess, and we can do noble acts without ruling earth and sea; for even with moderate advantages one can act excellently (this is manifest enough; for private persons are thought to do worthy acts no less than despots—indeed even more); and it is enough that we should have so much as that; for the life of 5 the man who is active in accordance with excellence will be happy. Solon, too, was perhaps sketching well the happy man when he described him as moderately furnished with externals but as having done (as Solon thought) the noblest acts, and lived temperately; for one can with but moderate possessions do what one ought. Anaxagoras also seems to have 10 supposed the happy man not to be rich nor a despot, when he said that he would not be surprised if the happy man were to seem to most people a strange person; for they judge by externals, since these are 15 all they perceive. The opinions of the wise seem, then, to harmonize with our arguments. But while even such things carry some conviction, the truth in practical matters is discerned from the facts of life; for these are the decisive factor. We must therefore survey what we have already said, bringing it to the 20 test of the facts of life, and if it harmonizes with the facts we must accept it, but if it clashes with them we must suppose it to be mere theory. Now he who exercises his intellect and cultivates it seems to be both in the best state and most dear to the gods. For if the gods have any care for human affairs, as they are thought to have, it would be reasonable both that 25 they should delight in that which was best and most akin to them (i.e. intellect) and that they should reward those who love and honour this most, as caring for the things that are dear to them and acting both rightly and nobly. And that all these attributes 30 belong most of all to the wise man is manifest. He, therefore, is the dearest to the gods. And he who is that will presumably be also the happiest; so that in this way too the wise man will more than any other be happy.

9. If these matters and the excellences, and also friendship and pleasure, have been dealt with sufficiently in outline, are we to suppose that our programme has reached its end? Surely, as is said, where there are things to be done the end is not to survey and recognize the various things, but rather to do them; with regard to excellence, then, it is not enough to know, but we must try to have and use it, or try any other way there may be of becoming good. Now if arguments were in themselves enough to make men good, they would justly, as Theognis says, have won very great rewards, and such rewards should have been provided; but as things are, while they seem to have power to encourage and stimulate the generous-minded among the young, and to make a character which is gently born, and a true lover of what is noble, ready to be possessed by excellence, they are not able to encourage the many to nobility and goodness. For these do not by nature obey the sense of shame, but only fear, and do not abstain from bad acts because of their baseness but through fear of punishment; living by passion they pursue their own pleasures and the means to them, and avoid the opposite pains, and have not even a conception of what is noble and truly pleasant, since they have never tasted it. What argument would remould such people? It is hard, if not impossible, to remove by argument the traits that have long since been incorporated in the character; and perhaps we must be content if, when all the influences by which we are thought to become good are present, we get some tincture of excellence.

Now some think that we are made good by nature, others by habituation, others by teaching. Nature's part evidently does not depend on us, but as a result of some divine causes is present in those who are truly fortunate; while argument and teaching, we may suspect, are not powerful with all men, but the soul of the student must first have been cultivated by means of habits for noble joy and noble hatred, like earth which is to nourish the seed. For he who lives as passion directs will not hear argument that dissuades him, nor understand it if he does; and how can we persuade one in such a state to change his ways? And in general passion seems to yield not to argument but to force. The character,

then, must somehow be there already with a kinship to excellence, loving what is noble and hating what is base.

But it is difficult to get from youth up a right training for excellence if one has not been brought up under right laws; for to live temperately and hardily is not pleasant to most people, especially when they are young. For this reason their nurture and occupations should be fixed by law; for they will not be painful when they have become customary. But it is surely not enough that when they are young they should get the right nurture and attention; since they must, even when they are grown up, practise and be habituated to them, we shall need laws for this as well, and generally speaking to cover the whole of life; for most people obey necessity rather than argument, and punishments rather than what is noble.

This is why some think that legislators ought to stimulate men to excellence and urge them forward by the motive of the noble, on the assumption that those who have been well advanced by the formation of habits will attend to such influences; and that punishments and penalties should be imposed on those who disobey and are of inferior nature, while the incurably bad should be completely banished. A good man (they think), since he lives with his mind fixed on what is noble, will submit to argument, while a bad man, whose desire is for pleasure, is corrected by pain like a beast of burden. This is, too, why they say the pains inflicted should be those that are most opposed to the pleasures such men love.

However that may be, if (as we have said) the man who is to be good must be well trained and habituated, and go on to spend his time in worthy occupations and neither willingly nor unwillingly do bad actions, and if this can be brought about if men live in accordance with a sort of intellect and right order, provided this has force,—if this be so, the paternal command indeed has not the required force or compulsive power (nor in general has the command of one man, unless he be a king or something similar), but the law *has* compulsive power, while it is at the same time an account proceeding from a sort of practical wisdom and intellect. And while people hate *men* who oppose their impulses, even if they oppose them rightly, the law in its ordaining of what is good is not burdensome.

In the Spartan state alone, or almost alone, the legislator seems to have paid attention to questions of nurture and occupations; in most states such matters have been neglected, and each man lives as he pleases, Cyclops-fashion, 'to his own wife and children dealing law'.[28] Now it is best that there should be a public and proper care for such matters; but if they are neglected by the community it would seem right for each man to help his children and friends towards excellence, and that they should be able or at least choose, to do this.[29]

It would seem from what has been said that he can do this better if he makes himself capable of legislating. For public care is plainly effected by laws, 1180ᵇ1 and good care by good laws; whether written or unwritten would seem to make no difference, nor whether they are laws providing for the education of individuals or of groups—any more than it does in the case of music or gymnastics and other such pursuits. For as in cities laws and character have force, so in households do the injunctions and the habits of the father, and these have even more because of the tie of blood and the benefits he confers; for the children start with a natural affection and disposition to obey. Further, individual education has an advantage over education in common, as individual medical treatment has; for while in general rest and abstinence from food are good for a man in a fever, for a particular man they may not be; and a boxer presumably does not prescribe the same style of fighting to all his pupils. It would seem, then, that the detail is worked out with more precision if the care is particular to individuals; for each person is more likely to get what suits his case.

But individuals[30] can be best cared for by a doctor or gymnastic instructor or any one else who has the universal knowledge of what is good for every one or for people of a certain kind (for the sciences both are said to be, and are, concerned with what is common); not but what some particular detail may perhaps be well looked after by an unscientific person, if he has studied accurately in the light of experience what happens in each case, just as some pople seem to be their own best doctors, though they could give no help to any one else. None the less, it will perhaps be agreed that if a man does wish to become master of an art or science he must go to the universal, and come to know it as well as possible; for, as we have said, it is with this that the sciences are concerned.

And surely he who wants to make men, whether many or few, better by his care must try to become capable of legislating, if it is through laws that we can become good. For to get anyone whatever—anyone who is put before us—into the right condition is not for the first chance comer; if anyone can do it, it is the man who knows, just as in medicine and all other matters which give scope for care and practical wisdom.

Must we not, then, next examine whence or how one can learn how to legislate? Is it, as in all other cases, from statesmen? Certainly it was thought to be a part of statesmanship. Or is a difference apparent between statesmanship and the other sciences and faculties? In the others the same people are found offering to teach the faculties and practising them, e.g. doctors or painters; but while the sophists profess to teach politics, it is practised not by any of them but by the politicians, who would seem to 1181ᵃ1 do so by dint of a certain faculty and experience rather than of thought; for they are not found either writing or speaking about such matters (though it were a nobler occupation perhaps than composing speeches for the law-courts and the assembly), nor again are they found to have made statesmen of their own sons or any other of their friends. But it was to be expected that they should if they could; for there is nothing better than such a skill that they could have left to their cities, or could choose to have for themselves, or, therefore, for those dearest to them. Still, experience seems to contribute not a little; else they could not have become politicians by familiarity with politics; and so it seems that those who aim at knowing about the art of politics need experience as well.

But those of the sophists who profess the art seem to be very far from teaching it. For, to put the matter generally, they do not even know what kind of thing it is nor what kinds of things it is about; otherwise they would not have classed it as identical with rhetoric or even inferior to it, nor have thought it easy to legislate by collecting the laws that are thought well of; they say it is possible to select the best laws, as though even the selection did not demand intelligence and as though right judgement were not the greatest thing, as in matters of music. For while people experienced in any department judge rightly the works produced in it, and understand by what means or how they are achieved, and what harmonizes with what, the inexperienced must be content if they do not fail to see whether the work has been well or ill made—as in the case of painting. Now laws are as it were the works of the political art; how then can one learn from them to be a legislator, or judge which are best? Even medical men do not seem to be made by a study of textbooks. Yet people try, at any rate, to state not only the treatments, but also how particular classes of people can be cured and should be treated—distinguishing the various states; but while this seems useful to experienced people, to the ignorant it is valueless. Surely, then, while collections of laws, and of constitutions also, may be serviceable to those who can study them and judge what is good or bad and what enactments suit what circumstances, those who go through such collections without a practised faculty will not have right judgement (unless it be spontaneous), though they may perhaps become more intelligent in such matters.

Now our predecessors have left the subject of legislation to us unexamined; it is perhaps best, therefore, that we should ourselves study it, and in general study the question of the constitution, in order to complete to the best of our ability the philosophy of human nature. First, then, if anything has been said well in detail by earlier thinkers, let us try to review it; then in the light of the constitutions we have collected let us study what sorts of influence preserve and destroy states, and what sorts preserve or destroy the particular kinds of constitution, and to what causes it is due that some are well and others ill administered. When these have been studied we shall perhaps be more likely to see which constitution is best, and how each must be ordered, and what laws and customs it must use. Let us make a beginning of our discussion.

Politics

BOOK I

1. Every state is a community of some kind, and every community is established with a view to some good; for everyone always acts in order to obtain that which they think good. But, if all communities aim at some good, the state or political community, which is the highest of all, and which embraces all the rest, aims at good in a greater degree than any other, and at the highest good.

Some people think that qualifications of a statesman, king, householder, and master are the same, and that they differ, not in kind, but only in the number of their subjects. For example, the ruler over a few is called a master; over more, the manager of a household; over a still larger number, a statesman or king, as if there were no difference between a great household and a small state. The distinction which is made between the king and the statesman is as follows: When the government is personal, the ruler is a king; when, according to the rules of the political science, the citizens rule and are ruled in turn, then he is called a statesman.

But all this is a mistake, as will be evident to any one who considers the matter according to the method which has hitherto guided us. As in other departments of science, so in politics, the compound should always be resolved into the simple elements or least parts of the whole. We must therefore look at the elements of which the state is composed, in order that we may see in what the different kinds of rule differ from one another, and whether any scientific result can be attained about each one of them.

2. He who thus considers things in their first growth and origin, whether a state or anything else, will obtain the clearest view of them. In the first place there must be a union of those who cannot exist without each other; namely, of male and female, that the race may continue (and this is a union which is formed, not of choice, but because, in common with other animals and with plants, mankind have a natural desire to leave behind them an image of themselves), and of natural ruler and subject, that both may be preserved. For that which can foresee by the exercise of mind is by nature lord and master, and that which can with its body give effect to such foresight is a subject, and by nature a slave; hence master and slave have the same interest. Now nature has distinguished between the female and the slave. For she is not niggardly, like the smith who fashions the Delphian knife for many uses; she makes each thing for a single use, and every instrument is best made when intended for one and not for many uses. But among barbarians no distinction is made between women and slaves, because there is no natural ruler among them: they are a community of slaves, male and female. That is why the poets say,—

> It is meet that Hellenes should rule over
> barbarians;

as if they thought that the barbarian and the slave were by nature one.

Out of these two relationships the first thing to arise is the family, and Hesiod is right when he says,—

> First house and wife and an ox for the plough,

for the ox is the poor man's slave. The family is the association established by nature for the supply of men's everyday wants, and the members of it are called by Charondas, 'companions of the cupboard', and by Epimenides the Cretan, 'companions of the manger'. But when several families are united, and the association aims at something more than the supply of daily needs, the first society to be formed is the village. And the most natural form of the village appears to be that of a colony from the family, composed of the children and grandchildren, who are said to be 'suckled with the same milk'. And this is the reason why Hellenic states were originally governed by kings; because the Hellenes were under royal rule before they came together, as the barbarians still are. Every family is ruled by the eldest, and therefore in the colonies of the family the kingly form of government prevailed because they were of the same blood. As Homer says:

> Each one gives law to his children and to
> his wives.

For they lived dispersedly, as was the manner in ancient times. That is why men say that the Gods have a king, because they themselves either are or were in ancient times under the rule of a king. For they imagine not only the forms of the Gods but their ways of life to be like their own.

When several villages are united in a single complete community, large enough to be nearly or quite self-sufficing, the state comes into existence, originating in the bare needs of life, and continuing in existence for the sake of a good life. And therefore, if the earlier forms of society are natural, so is the state, for it is the end of them, and the nature of a thing is its end. For what each thing is when fully developed, we call its nature, whether we are speaking of a man, a horse, or a family. Besides, the final cause and end of a thing is the best, and to be self-sufficing is the end and the best.

Hence it is evident that the state is a creation of nature, and that man is by nature a political animal. And he who by nature and not by mere accident is without a state, is either a bad man or above humanity; he is like the

> Tribeless, lawless, heartless one,

whom Homer denounces—the natural outcast is forthwith a lover of war; he may be compared to an isolated piece at draughts.

Now, that man is more of a political animal than bees or any other gregarious animals is evident. Nature, as we often say, makes nothing in vain, and man is the only animal who has the gift of speech. And whereas mere voice is but an indication of pleasure or pain, and is therefore found in other animals (for their nature attains to the perception of pleasure and pain and the intimation of them to one another, and no further), the power of speech is intended to set forth the expedient and inexpedient, and therefore likewise the just and the unjust. And it is a characteristic of man that he alone has any sense of good and evil, of just and unjust, and the like, and the association of living beings who have this sense makes a family and a state.

Further, the state is by nature clearly prior to the family and to the individual, since the whole is of necessity prior to the part; for example, if the whole body be destroyed, there will be no foot or hand, except homonymously, as we might speak of a stone hand; for when destroyed the hand will be no better than that. But things are defined by their function and power; and we ought not to say that they are the same when they no longer have their proper quality, but only that they are homonymous. The proof that the state is a creation of nature and prior to the individual is that the individual, when isolated, is not self-sufficing; and therefore he is like a part in relation to the whole. But he who is unable to live in society, or who has no need because he is suffi-

cient for himself, must be either a beast or a god: he
is no part of a state. A social instinct is implanted
in all men by nature, and yet he who first founded
the state was the greatest of benefactors. For man,
when perfected, is the best of animals, but, when
separated from law and justice, he is the worst of
all; since armed injustice is the more dangerous, and
he is equipped at birth with arms, meant to be used
by intelligence and excellence, which he may use
for the worst ends. That is why, if he has not excellence, he is the most unholy and the most savage
of animals, and the most full of lust and gluttony.
But justice is the bond of men in states; for the administration of justice, which is the determination of
what is just, is the principle of order in political society.

1253ᵇ   **3.** Seeing then that the state is made up of households, before speaking of the state we must speak of
the management of the household. The parts of
household management correspond to the persons
who compose the household, and a complete household consists of slaves and freemen. Now we should
begin by examining everything in its fewest possible elements; and the first and fewest possible parts
of a family are master and slave, husband and wife,
father and children. We have therefore to consider
what each of these three relations is and ought to
be:—I mean the relation of master and servant, the
marriage relation (the conjunction of man and wife
has no name of its own), and thirdly, the paternal
relation (this also has no proper name). And there is
another element of a household, the so-called art of
getting wealth, which, according to some, is identical with household management, according to others, a principal part of it; the nature of this art will
also have to be considered by us.

Let us first speak of master and slave, looking to
the needs of practical life and also seeking to attain
some better theory of their relation than exists at present. For some are of the opinion that the rule of a
master is a science, and that the management of a
household, and the mastership of slaves, and the political and royal rule, as I was saying at the outset,
are all the same. Others affirm that the rule of a master over slaves is contrary to nature, and that the distinction between slave and freeman exists by convention only, and not by nature; and being an
interference with nature is therefore unjust.

4. Property is a part of the household, and the art
of acquiring property is a part of the art of managing the household; for no man can live well, or in-

deed live at all, unless he is provided with necessaries. And as in the arts which have a definite sphere
the workers must have their own proper instruments
for the accomplishment of their work, so it is in the
management of a household. Now instruments are
of various sorts; some are living, others lifeless; in
the rudder, the pilot of a ship has a lifeless, in the
look-out man, a living instrument; for in the arts the
servant is a kind of instrument. Thus, too, a possession is an instrument for maintaining life. And so,
in the arrangement of the family, a slave is a living
possession, and property a number of such instruments; and the servant is himself an instrument for
instruments. For if every instrument could accomplish its own work, obeying or anticipating the will
of others, like the statues of Daedalus, or the tripods
of Hephaestus, which, says the poet,

> of their own accord entered the assembly of
> the Gods;

if, in like manner, the shuttle would weave and the 1254ᵃ
plectrum touch the lyre, chief workmen would not
want servants, nor masters slaves. Now the instruments commonly so called are instruments of production, whilst a possession is an instrument of action. From a shuttle we get something else besides
the use of it, whereas of a garment or of a bed there
is only the use. Further, as production and action are
different in kind, and both require instruments, the
instruments which they employ must likewise differ
in kind. But life is action and not production, and
therefore the slave is the minister of action. Again,
a possession is spoken of as a part is spoken of; for
the part is not only a part of something else, but
wholly belongs to it; and this is also true of a possession. The master is only the master of the slave;
he does not belong to him, whereas the slave is not
only the slave of his master, but wholly belongs to
him. Hence we see what is the nature and office of
a slave; he who is by nature not his own but another's man, is by nature a slave; and he may be said
to be another's man who, being a slave, is also a
possession. And a possession may be defined as an
instrument of action, separable from the possessor.

5. But is there any one thus intended by nature to
be a slave, and for whom such a condition is expedient and right, or rather is not all slavery a viola-
tion of nature?

There is no difficulty in answering this question,
on grounds both of reason and of fact. For that some

should rule and others be ruled is a thing not only necessary, but expedient; from the hour of their birth, some are marked out for subjection, others for rule.

And there are many kinds both of rulers and subjects (and that rule is the better which is exercised over better subjects—for example, to rule over men is better than to rule over wild beasts; for the work is better which is executed by better workmen, and where one man rules and another is ruled, they may be said to have a work); for in all things which form a composite whole and which are made up of parts, whether continuous or discrete, a distinction between the ruling and the subject element comes to light. Such a duality exists in living creatures, originating from nature as a whole; even in things which have no life there is a ruling principle, as in a musical mode. But perhaps this is matter for a more popular investigation. A living creature consists in the first place of soul and body, and of these two, the one is by nature the ruler and the other the sub-1254ʰ ject. But then we must look for the intentions of nature in things which retain their nature, and not in things which are corrupted. And therefore we must study the man who is in the most perfect state both of body and soul, for in him we shall see the true relation of the two; although in bad or corrupted natures the body will often appear to rule over the soul, because they are in an evil and unnatural condition. At all events we may firstly observe in living creatures both a despotical and a constitutional rule; for the soul rules the body with a despotical rule, whereas the intellect rules the appetites with a constitutional and royal rule. And it is clear that the rule of the soul over the body, and of the mind and the rational element over the passionate, is natural and expedient; whereas the equality of the two or the rule of the inferior is always hurtful. The same holds good of animals in relation to men; for tame animals have a better nature than wild and all tame animals are better off when they are ruled by man; for then they are preserved. Again, the male is by nature superior, and the female inferior; and the one rules, and the other is ruled; this principle, of necessity, extends to all mankind. Where then there is such a difference as that between soul and body, or between men and animals (as in the case of those whose business is to use their body, and who can do nothing better), the lower sort are by nature slaves, and it is better for them as for all inferiors that they should be under the rule of a master. For he who can be,

and therefore is, another's, and he who participates in reason enough to apprehend, but not to have, is a slave by nature. Whereas the lower animals cannot even apprehend reason; they obey their passions. And indeed the use made of slaves and of tame animals is not very different; for both with their bodies minister to the needs of life. Nature would like to distinguish between the bodies of freemen and slaves, making the one strong for servile labour, the other upright, and although useless for such services, useful for political life in the arts both of war and peace. But the opposite often happens—that some have the souls and others have the bodies of freemen. And doubtless if men differed from one another in the mere forms of their bodies as much as the statues of the Gods do from men, all would acknowledge that the inferior class should be slaves of the superior. And if this is true of the body, how much more just that a similar distinction should exist in the soul? But the beauty of the body is seen, whereas the beauty of the soul is not seen. It is clear, then, that some men are by nature free, and others slaves, and that for these latter slavery is both expedient and 1255ᵃ right.

6. But that those who take the opposite view have in a certain way right on their side, may be easily seen. For the words slavery and slave are used in two senses. There is a slave or slavery by convention as well as by nature. The convention is a sort of agreement—the convention by which whatever is taken in war is supposed to belong to the victors. But this right many jurists impeach, as they would an orator who brought forward an unconstitutional measure; they detest the notion that, because one man has the power of doing violence and is superior in brute strength, another shall be his slave and subject. Even among philosophers there is a difference of opinion. The origin of the dispute, and what makes the views invade each other's territory, is as follows: in some sense excellence, when furnished with means, has actually the greatest power of exercising force: and as superior power is only found where there is superior excellence of some kind, power seems to imply excellence, and the dispute to be simply one about justice (for it is due to one party identifying justice with goodwill, while the other identifies it with the mere rule of the stronger). If these views are thus set out separately, the other views have no force or plausibility against the view that the superior in excellence ought to rule, or be master. Others, clinging, as they think, simply to a

principle of justice (for convention is a sort of justice), assume that slavery in accordance with the custom of war is just, but at the same moment they deny this. For what if the cause of the war be unjust? And again, no one would ever say that he is a slave who is unworthy to be a slave. Were this the case, men of the highest rank would be slaves and the children of slaves if they or their parents chanced to have been taken captive and sold. That is why people do not like to call themselves slaves, but confine the term to foreigners. Yet, in using this language, they really mean the natural slave of whom we spoke at first; for it must be admitted that some are slaves everywhere, others nowhere. The same principle applies to nobility. People regard themselves as noble everywhere, and not only in their own country, but they deem foreigners noble only when at home, thereby implying that there are two sorts of nobility and freedom, the one absolute, the other relative. The Helen of Theodectes says:

Who would presume to call me servant who am on both sides sprung from the stem of the Gods?

1255ᵇ What does this mean but that they distinguish freedom and slavery, noble and humble birth, by the two principles of good and evil? They think that as men and animals beget men and animals, so from good men a good man springs. Nature intends to do this often but cannot.

We see then that there is some foundation for this difference of opinion, and that all are not either slaves by nature or freemen by nature, and also that there is in some cases a marked distinction between the two classes, rendering it expedient and right for the one to be slaves and the others to be masters: the one practising obedience, the others exercising the authority and lordship which nature intended them to have. The abuse of this authority is injurious to both; for the interests of part and whole, of body and soul, are the same, and the slave is a part of the master, a living but separated part of his bodily frame. Hence, where the relation of master and slave between them is natural they are friends and have a common interest, but where it rests merely on convention and force the reverse is true.

7. The previous remarks are quite enough to show that the rule of a master is not a constitutional rule, and that all the different kinds of rule are not, as some affirm, the same as each other. For there is one rule exercised over subjects who are by nature free, another over subjects who are by nature slaves. The rule of a household is a monarchy, for every house is under one head: whereas constitutional rule is a government of freemen and equals. The master is not called a master because he has science, but because he is of a certain character, and the same remark applies to the slave and the freeman. Still there may be a science for the master and a science for the slave. The science of the slave would be such as the man of Syracuse taught, who made money by instructing slaves in their ordinary duties. And such a knowledge may be carried further, so as to include cookery and similar menial arts. For some duties are of the more necessary, others of the more honourable sort; as the proverb says, 'slave before slave, master before master'. But all such branches of knowledge are servile. There is likewise a science of the master, which teaches the use of slaves; for the master as such is concerned, not with the acquisition, but with the use of them. Yet this science is not anything great or wonderful; for the master need only know how to order that which the slave must know how to execute. Hence those who are in a position which places them above toil have stewards who attend to their households while they occupy themselves with philosophy or with politics. But the art of acquiring slaves, I mean of justly acquiring them, differs both from the art of the master and the art of slave, being a species of hunting or war. Enough of the distinction between master and slave.

8. Let us now inquire into property generally, and 1256ᵃ into the art of getting wealth, in accordance with our usual method, for a slave has been shown to be a part of property. The first question is whether the art of getting wealth is the same as the art of managing a household or a part of it, or instrumental to it; and if the last, whether in the way that the art of making shuttles is instrumental to the art of weaving, or in the way that the casting of bronze is instrumental to the art of the statuary, for they are not instrumental in the same way, but the one provides tools and the other material; and by material I mean the substratum out of which any work is made; thus wool is the material of the weaver, bronze of the statuary. Now it is easy to see that the art of household management is not identical with the art of getting wealth, for the one uses the material which the other provides. For the art which uses household stores can be no other than the art of household management. There is, however, a doubt whether the art

of getting wealth is a part of household management or a distinct art. If the getter of wealth has to consider whence wealth and property can be procured, but there are many sorts of property and riches, then are husbandry, and the care and provision of food in general, parts of the art of household management or distinct arts? Again, there are many sorts of food, and therefore there are many kinds of lives both of animals and men; they must all have food, and the differences in their food have made differences in their ways of life. For of beasts, some are gregarious, others are solitary; they live in the way which is best adapted to sustain them, accordingly as they are carnivorous or herbivorous or omnivorous: and their habits are determined for them by nature with regard to their ease and choice of food. But the same things are not naturally pleasant to all of them; and therefore the lives of carnivorous or herbivorous animals further differ among themselves. In the lives of men too there is a great difference. The laziest are shepherds, who lead an idle life, and get their subsistence without trouble from tame animals; their flocks having to wander from place to place in search of pasture, they are compelled to follow them, cultivating a sort of living farm. Others support themselves by hunting, which is of different kinds. Some, for example, are brigands, others, who dwell near lakes or marshes or rivers or a sea in which there are fish, are fishermen, and others live by the pursuit of birds or wild beasts. The greater number obtain a living from the cultivated fruits of the soil. Such are the modes of subsistence which prevail among those whose industry springs up of itself, and whose food is not acquired by exchange and retail trade—there is the shepherd, the husbandman, the 1256^b brigand, the fisherman, the hunter. Some gain a comfortable maintenance out of two employments, eking out the deficiencies of one of them by another: thus the life of a shepherd may be combined with that of a brigand, the life of a farmer with that of a hunter. Other modes of life are similarly combined in any way which the needs of men may require. Property, in the sense of a bare livelihood, seems to be given by nature herself to all, both when they are first born, and when they are grown up. For some animals bring forth, together with their offspring, so much food as will last until they are able to supply themselves; of this the vermiparous or oviparous animals are an instance; and the viviparous animals have up to a certain time a supply of food for their young in themselves, which is called milk. In like manner we may infer that, after the birth of animals, plants exist for their sake, and that the other animals exist for the sake of man, the tame for use and food, the wild, if not all, at least the greater part of them, for food, and for the provision of clothing and various instruments. Now if nature makes nothing incomplete, and nothing in vain, the inference must be that she has made all animals for the sake of man. And so, from one point of view, the art of war is a natural art of acquisition, for the art of acquisition includes hunting, an art which we ought to practise against wild beasts, and against men who, though intended by nature to be governed, will not submit; for war of such a kind is naturally just.

Of the art of acquisition then there is one kind which by nature is a part of the management of a household, in so far as the art of household management must either find ready to hand, or itself provide, such things necessary to life, and useful for the community of the family or state, as can be stored. They are the elements of true riches; for the amount of property which is needed for a good life is not unlimited, although Solon in one of his poems says that

No bound to riches has been fixed for man.

But there is a boundary fixed, just as there is in the other arts; for the instruments of any art are never unlimited, either in number or size, and riches may be defined as a number of instruments to be used in a household or in a state. And so we see that there is a natural art of acquisition which is practised by managers of households and by statesmen, and the reason for this.

9. There is another variety of the art of acquisi- 1257^a tion which is commonly and rightly called an art of wealth-getting, and has in fact suggested the notion that riches and property have no limit. Being nearly connected with the preceding, it is often identified with it. But though they are not very different, neither are they the same. The kind already described is given by nature, the other is gained by experience and art.

Let us begin our discussion of the question with the following considerations. Of everything which we possess there are two uses: both belong to the thing as such, but not in the same manner, for one is the proper, and the other the improper use of it. For example, a shoe is used for wear, and is used for exchange; both are uses of the shoe. He who gives a shoe in exchange for money or food to him who wants one, does indeed use the shoe as a shoe, but this is not its proper use, for a shoe is not made to be an object of barter. The same may be said of all possessions, for the art of exchange extends to all of them, and it arises at first from what is natural, from the circumstance that some have too little, others too much. Hence we may infer that retail trade is not a natural part of the art of getting wealth; had it been so, men would have ceased to exchange when they had enough. In the first community, indeed, which is the family, this art is obviously of no use, but it begins to be useful when the society increases. For the members of the family originally had all things in common; later, when the family divided into parts, the parts shared in many things, and different parts in different things, which they had to give in exchange for what they wanted, a kind of barter which is still practised among barbarous nations who exchange with one another the necessaries of life and nothing more; giving and receiving wine, for example, in exchange for corn, and the like. This sort of barter is not part of the wealth-getting art and is not contrary to nature, but is needed for the satisfaction of men's natural wants. The other form of exchange grew, as might have been inferred, out of this one. When the inhabitants of one country became more dependent on those of another, and they imported what they needed, and exported what they had too much of, money necessarily came into use. For the various necessaries of life are not easily carried about, and hence men agreed to employ in their dealings with each other something which was intrinsically useful and easily applicable to the purposes of life, for example, iron, silver, and the like. Of this the value was at first measured simply by size and weight, but in process of time they put a stamp upon it, to save the trouble of weighing and to mark the value.

1257b   When the use of coin had once been discovered, out of the barter of necessary articles arose the other art of wealth-getting, namely, retail trade; which was at first probably a simple matter, but became more complicated as soon as men learned by experience whence and by what exchanges the greatest profit might be made. Originating in the use of coin, the art of getting wealth is generally thought to be chiefly concerned with it, and to be the art which produces riches and wealth, having to consider how they may be accumulated. Indeed, riches is assumed by many to be only a quantity of coin, because the arts of getting wealth and retail trade are concerned with coin. Others maintain that coined money is a mere sham, a thing not natural, but conventional only, because, if the users substitute another commodity for it, it is worthless, and because it is not useful as a means to any of the necessities of life, and, indeed, he who is rich in coin may often be in want of necessary food. But how can that be wealth of which a man may have a great abundance and yet perish with hunger, like Midas in the fable, whose insatiable prayer turned everything that was set before him into gold?

Hence men seek after a better notion of riches and of the art of getting wealth, and they are right. For natural riches and the natural art of wealth-getting are a different thing; in their true form they are part of the management of a household; whereas retail trade is the art of producing wealth, not in every way, but by exchange. And it is thought to be concerned with coin; for coin is the unit of exchange and the limit of it. And there is no bound to the riches which spring from this art of wealth-getting. As in the art of medicine there is no limit to the pursuit of health, and as in the other arts there is no limit to the pursuit of their several ends, for they aim at accomplishing their ends to the uttermost (but of the means there is a limit, for the end is always the limit), so, too, in this art of wealth-getting there is no limit of the end, which is riches of the spurious kind, and the acquisition of wealth. But the art of wealth-getting which consists in household management, on the other hand, has a limit; the unlimited acquisition of wealth is not its business. And, therefore, from one point of view, all riches must have a limit; nevertheless, as a matter of fact, we find the opposite to be the case; for all getters of wealth increase their hoard of coin without limit. The source of the confusion is the near connexion between the two kinds of wealth-getting; in both, the instrument is the same, although the use is different, and so they pass into one another; for each is a use of the same property, but with a difference: accumulation is the end in the one case, but there is a further end in the other. Hence some persons are led to believe that getting wealth is the object of household management, and 1258a the whole idea of their lives is that they ought either to increase their money without limit, or at any rate not to lose it. The origin of this disposition in men is that they are intent upon living only, and not upon living well; and, as their desires are unlimited, they also desire that the means of gratifying them should be without limit. Those who do aim at a good life seek the means of obtaining bodily pleasures; and, since the enjoyment of these appears to depend on property, they are absorbed in getting wealth: and so there arises the second species of wealth-getting. For, as their enjoyment is in excess, they seek an art which produces the excess of enjoyment; and, if they are not able to supply their pleasures by the art of getting wealth, they try other causes, using in turn every faculty in a manner contrary to nature. The quality of courage, for example, is not intended to make wealth, but to inspire confidence; neither is this the aim of the general's or of the physician's art; but the one aims at victory and the other at health. Nevertheless, some men turn every quality or art into a means of getting wealth; this they conceive to be the end, and to the promotion of the end they think all things must contribute.

Thus, then, we have considered the art of wealth-getting which is unnecessary, and why men want it; and also the necessary art of wealth-getting, which we have seen to be different from the other, and to be a natural part of the art of managing a household, concerned with the provision of food, not, however, like the former kind, unlimited, but having a limit.

10. And we have found the answer to our original question, Whether the art of getting wealth is the business of the manager of a household and of the statesman or not their business?—viz. that wealth is presupposed by them. For as political science does not make men, but takes them from nature and uses them, so too nature provides them with earth or sea or the like as a source of food. At this stage begins the duty of the manager of a household, who has to order the things which nature supplies—he may be compared to the weaver who has not to make but to use wool, and to know, too, what sort of wool is good and serviceable or bad and unserviceable. Were this otherwise, it would be difficult to see why the art of getting wealth is a part of the management of a household and the art of medicine not; for surely the members of a household must have health just as they must have life or any other necessity. The answer is that as from one point of view the master of the house and the ruler of the state have to consider about health, from another point of view not they but the physician has to; so in one way the art of household management, in another way the subordinate art, has to consider about wealth. But, strictly speaking, as I have already said, the means of life must be provided beforehand by nature; for

the business of nature is to furnish food to that which is born, and the food of the offspring is always what remains over of that from which it is produced. That is why the art of getting wealth out of fruits and animals is always natural.

There are two sorts of wealth-getting, as I have said; one is a part of household management, the other is retail trade: the former is necessary and honourable, while that which consists in exchange is justly censured; for it is unnatural, and a mode by which men gain from one another. The most hated 1258ᵇ sort, and with the greatest reason, is usury, which makes a gain out of money itself, and not from the natural object of it. For money was intended to be used in exchange, but not to increase at interest. And this term interest, which means the birth of money from money, is applied to the breeding of money because the offspring resembles the parent. That is why of all modes of getting wealth this is the most unnatural.

11. Enough has been said about the theory of wealth-getting; we will now proceed to the practical part. Such things may be studied by a free man, but will only be practised from necessity. The useful parts of wealth-getting are, first, the knowledge of live-stock—which are most profitable, and where, and how—as for example, what sort of horses or sheep or oxen or any other animals are most likely to give a return. A man ought to know which of these pay better than others, and which pay best in particular places, for some do better in one place and some in another. Secondly, husbandry, which may be either tillage or planting, and the keeping of bees and of fish, or fowl, or of any animals which may be useful to man. These are the divisions of the true or proper art of wealth-getting and come first. Of the other, which consists in exchange, the first and most important division is commerce (of which there are three kinds—ship-owning, the conveyance of goods, exposure for sale—these again differing as they are safer or more profitable), the second is usury, the third, service for hire—of this, one kind is employed in the mechanical arts, the other in unskilled and bodily labour. There is still a third sort of wealth-getting intermediate between this and the first or natural mode which is partly natural, but is also concerned with exchange, viz. the industries that make their profit from the earth, and from things growing from the earth which, although they bear no fruit, are nevertheless profitable; for example, the cutting of timber and all mining. The art of mining itself has many branches, for there are various kinds of things dug out of the earth. Of the several divisions of wealth-getting I now speak generally; a minute consideration of them might be useful in practice, but it would be tiresome to dwell upon them at greater length now.

Those occupations are most truly arts in which there is the least element of chance; they are the meanest in which the body is most maltreated, the most servile in which there is the greatest use of the body, and the most illiberal in which there is the least need of excellence.

Works have been written upon these subjects by various persons; for example, by Chares the Parian, and Apollodorus the Lemnian, who have treated of Tillage and Planting, while others have treated of other branches; anyone who cares for such matters may refer to their writings. It would be well also to collect the scattered stories of the ways in which individuals have succeeded in amassing a fortune; for all this is useful to persons who value the art of getting wealth. There is the anecdote of Thales the Milesian and his financial scheme, which involves a principle of universal application, but is attributed to him on account of his reputation for wisdom. He was reproached for his poverty, which was supposed to show that philosophy was of no use. According to the story, he knew by his skill in the stars while it was yet winter that there would be a great harvest of olives in the coming year; so, having a little money, he gave deposits for the use of all the olive-presses in Chios and Miletus, which he hired at a low price because no one bid against him. When the harvest-time came, and many were wanted all at once and of a sudden, he let them out at any rate which he pleased, and made a quantity of money. Thus he showed the world that philosophers can easily be rich if they like, but that their ambition is of another sort. He is supposed to have given a striking proof of his wisdom, but, as I was saying, his scheme for getting wealth is of universal application, and is nothing but the creation of a monopoly. It is an art often practised by cities when they are in want of money; they make a monopoly of provisions.

There was a man of Sicily, who, having money deposited with him, bought up all the iron from the iron mines; afterwards, when the merchants from their various markets came to buy, he was the only seller, and without much increasing the price he gained 200 per cent. Which when Dionysius heard, he told him that he might take away his money, but that he must not remain at Syracuse, for he thought that the man had discovered a way of making money which was injurious to his own interests. He made the same discovery as Thales; they both contrived to create a monopoly for themselves. And statesmen as well ought to know these things; for a state is often as much in want of money and of such schemes for obtaining it as a household, or even more so; hence some public men devote themselves entirely to finance.

12. Of household management we have seen that there are three parts—one is the rule of a master over slaves, which has been discussed already, another of a father, and the third of a husband. A husband and father, we saw, rules over wife and children, both free, but the rule differs, the rule over his children being a royal, over his wife a constitutional rule. For although there may be exceptions to the order of nature, the male is by nature fitter for command than the female, just as the elder and full-grown is superior to the younger and more immature. But in most constitutional states the citizens rule and are ruled by turns, for the idea of a constitutional state implies that the natures of the citizens are equal, and do not differ at all. Nevertheless, when one rules and the other is ruled we endeavour to create a difference of outward forms and names and titles of respect, which may be illustrated by the saying of Amasis about his foot-pan. The relation of the male to the female is always of this kind. The rule of a father over his children is royal, for he rules by virtue both of love and of the respect due to age, exercising a kind of royal power. And therefore Homer has appropriately called Zeus 'father of Gods and men', because he is the king of them all. For a king is the natural superior of his subjects, but he should be of the same kin or kind with them, and such is the relation of elder and younger, of father and son.

13. Thus it is clear that household management attends more to men than to the acquisition of inanimate things, and to human excellence more than to the excellence of property which we call wealth, and to the excellence of freemen more than to the excellence of slaves. A question may indeed be raised, whether there is any excellence at all in a slave beyond those of an instrument and of a servant—whether he can have the excellences of temperance, courage, justice, and the like; or whether slaves possess only bodily services. And, whichever way we answer the question, a difficulty arises; for, if they have excellence, in what will they differ from freemen? On the other hand, since they are men and share in rational principle, it seems absurd to say that they have no excellence. A similar question may be raised about women and children, whether they too have excellences; ought a woman to be temperate and brave and just, and is a child to be called temperate, and intemperate, or not? So in general we may ask about the natural ruler, and the natural subject, whether they have the same or different excellences. For if a noble nature is equally required in both, why should one of them always rule, and the other always be ruled? Nor can we say that this is a question of degree, for the difference between ruler and subject is a difference of kind, which the difference of more and less never is. Yet how strange is the supposition that the one ought, and that the 1260ª other ought not, to have excellence! For if the ruler is intemperate and unjust, how can he rule well? if the subject, how can he obey well? If he is licentious and cowardly, he will certainly not do what is fitting. It is evident, therefore, that both of them must have a share of excellence, but varying as natural subjects also vary among themselves. Here the very constitution of the soul has shown us the way; in it one part naturally rules, and the other is subject, and the excellence of the ruler we maintain to be different from that of the subject—the one being the excellence of the rational, and the other of the irrational part. Now, it is obvious that the same principle applies generally, and therefore almost all things rule and are ruled according to nature. But the kind of rule differs—the freeman rules over the slave after another manner from that in which the male rules over the female, or the man over the child; although the parts of the soul are present in all of them, they are present in different degrees. For the slave has no deliberative faculty at all; the woman has, but it is without authority, and the child has, but it is immature. So it must necessarily be supposed to be with the excellences of character also; all should partake of them, but only in such manner and degree as is required by each for the fulfilment of his function. Hence the ruler ought to have excellence of character in perfection, for his function, taken absolutely, demands a master artificer, and reason is such an artificer; the subjects, on the other hand, require only that measure of excellence which is proper to each of them. Clearly, then, excellence of character belongs to all of them; but the temperance of a man and of a woman, or the courage and justice of a man

and of a woman, are not, as Socrates maintained, the same; the courage of a man is shown in commanding, of a woman in obeying. And this holds of all other excellences, as will be more clearly seen if we look at them in detail, for those who say generally that excellence consists in a good disposition of the soul, or in doing rightly, or the like, only deceive themselves. Far better than such definitions is the mode of speaking of those who, like Gorgias, enumerate the excellences. All classes must be deemed to have their special attributes; as the poet says of women,

> Silence is a woman's glory,

but this is not equally the glory of man. The child is imperfect, and therefore obviously his excellence is not relative to himself alone, but to the perfect man and to his teacher, and in like manner the excellence of the slave is relative to a master. Now we determined that a slave is useful for the wants of life, and therefore he will obviously require only so 1260ᵇ much excellence as will prevent him from failing in his function through cowardice or lack of self-control. Someone will ask whether, if what we are saying is true, excellence will not be required also in the artisans, for they often fail in their work through the lack of self-control. But is there not a great difference in the two cases? For the slave shares in his master's life; the artisan is less closely connected with him, and only attains excellence in proportion as he becomes a slave. The meaner sort of mechanic has a special and separate slavery; and whereas the slave exists by nature, not so the shoemaker or other artisan. It is manifest, then, that the master ought to be the source of such excellence in the slave, and not a mere possessor of the art of mastership which trains the slave in his functions. That is why they are mistaken who forbid us to converse with slaves and say that we should employ command only, for slaves stand even more in need of admonition than children.

So much for this subject; the relations of husband and wife, father and child, their several excellences, what in their intercourse with one another is good, and what is evil, and how we may pursue the good and escape the evil, will have to be discussed when we speak of the different forms of government. For, inasmuch as every family is a part of a state, and these relationships are the parts of a family, and the excellence of the part must have regard to the excellence of the whole, women and children must be trained by education with an eye to the constitution, if the excellences of either of them are supposed to make any difference in the excellences of the state. And they must make a difference: for the children grow up to be citizens, and half the free persons in a state are women.

Of these matters, enough has been said; of what remains, let us speak at another time. Regarding, then, our present inquiry as complete, we will make a new beginning. And, first, let us examine the various theories of a perfect state.

BOOK II

1. Our purpose is to consider what form of political community is best of all for those who are most able to realize their ideal of life. We must therefore examine not only this but other constitutions, both such as actually exist in well-governed states, and any theoretical forms which are held in esteem, so that what is good and useful may be brought to light. And let no one suppose that in seeking for something beyond them we are anxious to make a sophistical display at any cost; we only undertake this inquiry because all the constitutions which now exist are faulty.

We will begin with the natural beginning of the subject. The members of a state must either have all things or nothing in common, or some things in common and some not. That they should have nothing in common is clearly impossible, for the constitution is a community, and must at any rate have a common place—one city will be in one place, and the citizens are those who share in that one city. But should a well-ordered state have all things, as far as may be, in common, or some only and not others? For the citizens might conceivably have wives and children and property in common, as Socrates proposes in the Republic of Plato. Which is better, our present condition, or one conforming to the law laid down in the Republic?

2. There are many difficulties in the community of women. And the principle on which Socrates rests the necessity of such an institution evidently is not established by his arguments. Further, as a means to the end which he ascribes to the state, the scheme, taken literally, is impracticable, and how we are to interpret it is nowhere precisely stated. I am speaking of the supposition from which the argument of

Socrates proceeds, that it is best for the whole state to be as unified as possible. Is it not obvious that a state may at length attain such a degree of unity as to be no longer a state?—since the nature of a state is to be a plurality, and in tending to greater unity, from being a state, it becomes a family, and from being a family, an individual; for the family may be said to be more one than the state, and the individual than the family. So that we ought not to attain this greatest unity even if we could, for it would be the destruction of the state. Again, a state is not made up only of so many men, but of different kinds of men; for similars do not constitute a state. It is not like a military alliance. The usefulness of the latter depends upon its quantity even where there is no difference in quality (for mutual protection is the end aimed at), just as a greater weight depresses the scale more (in like manner, a state differs from a nation, when the nation has not its population organized in villages, but lives an Arcadian sort of life); but the elements out of which a unity is to be formed differ in kind. That is why the principle of reciprocity, as I have already remarked in the Ethics, is the salvation of states. Even among freemen and equals this is a principle which must be maintained, for they cannot all rule together, but must change at the end of a year or some other period of time or in some order of succession. The result is that upon this plan they all govern; just as if shoemakers and carpenters were to exchange their occupations, and the same persons did not always continue shoemakers and carpenters. And since it is better that this should be so in politics as well, it is clear that while there should be continuance of the same persons in power where this is possible, yet where this is not possible by reason of the natural equality of the citizens, and at the same time it is just that all should share in the government (whether to govern be a good thing or a bad),—in these cases this is imitated. Thus the one party rules and the others are ruled in turn, as if they were no longer the same persons. In like manner when they hold office there is a variety in the offices held. Hence it is evident that a city is not by nature one in that sense which some persons affirm; and that what is said to be the greatest good of cities is in reality their destruction; but surely the good of things must be that which preserves them. Again, from another point of view, this extreme unification of the state is clearly not good; for a family is more self-suffing than an individual, and a city than a family, and a city only comes into being when the community is large enough to be self-sufficing. If then self-sufficiency is to be desired, the lesser degree of unity is more desirable than the greater.

3. But, even supposing that it were best for the community to have the greatest degree of unity, this unity is by no means proved to follow from the fact of all men saying 'mine' and 'not mine' at the same instant of time, which, according to Socrates, is the sign of perfect unity in a state. For the word 'all' is ambiguous. If the meaning be that every individual says 'mine' and 'not mine' at the same time, then perhaps the result at which Socrates aims may be in some degree accomplished; each man will call the same person his own son and the same person his own wife, and so of his property and of all that falls to his lot. This, however, is not the way in which people would speak who had their wives and children in common; they would say 'all' but not 'each'. In like manner their property would be described as belonging to them, not severally but collectively. There is an obvious fallacy in the term 'all': like some other words, 'both', 'odd', 'even', it is ambiguous, and even in abstract argument becomes a source of logical puzzles. That all persons call the same thing mine in the sense in which each does so may be a fine thing, but it is impracticable; or if the words are taken in the other sense, such a unity in no way conduces to harmony. And there is another objection to the proposal. For that which is common to the greatest number has the least care bestowed upon it. Everyone thinks chiefly of his own, hardly at all of the common interest; and only when he is himself concerned as an individual. For besides other considerations, everybody is more inclined to neglect something which he expects another to fulfil; as in families many attendants are often less useful than a few. Each citizen will have a thousand sons who will not be his sons individually, but anybody will be equally the son of anybody, and will therefore be neglected by all alike. Further, upon this principle, every one will use the word 'mine' of one who is prospering or the reverse, however small a fraction he may himself be of the whole number; the same boy will be my son, so and so's son, the son of each of the thousand, or whatever be the number of the citizens; and even about this he will not be positive; for it is impossible to know who chanced to have a child, or whether, if one came into existence, it has survived. But which is better—for each to say 'mine' in this way, making a man the same relation to two thousand or ten thousand citizens, or

1262ª

to use the word 'mine' as it is now used in states? For usually the same person is called by one man his own son whom another calls his own brother or cousin or kinsman—blood relation or connexion by marriage—either of himself or of some relation of his, and yet another his clansman or tribesman; and how much better it is to be the real cousin of somebody than to be a son after Plato's fashion! Nor is there any way of preventing brothers and children and fathers and mothers from sometimes recognizing one another; for children are born like their parents, and they will necessarily be finding indications of their relationship to one another. Geographers declare such to be the fact; they say that in part of Upper Libya, where the women are common, nevertheless the children who are born are assigned to their respective fathers on the ground of their likeness. And some women, like the females of other animals—for example, mares and cows—have a strong tendency to produce offspring resembling their parents, as was the case with the Pharsalian mare called Honest Wife.

4. Other difficulties, against which it is not easy for the authors of such a community to guard, will be assaults and homicides, voluntary as well as involuntary, quarrels and slanders, all of which are most unholy acts when committed against fathers and mothers and near relations, but not equally unholy when there is no relationship. Moreover, they are much more likely to occur if the relationship is unknown than if it is known and, when they have occurred, the customary expiations of them can be made if the relationship is known, but not otherwise. Again, how strange it is that Socrates, after having made the children common, should hinder lovers from carnal intercourse only, but should permit love and familiarities between father and son or between brother and brother, than which nothing can be more unseemly, since even without them love of this sort is improper. How strange, too, to forbid intercourse for no other reason than the violence of the pleasure, as though the relationship of father and son or of brothers with one another made no difference.

This community of wives and children seems better suited to the husbandmen than to the guardians, for if they have wives and children in common, they 1262ᵇ will be bound to one another by weaker ties, as a subject class should be, and they will remain obedient and not rebel. In a word, the result of such a law would be just the opposite of that which good laws ought to have, and the intention of Socrates in making these regulations about women and children would defeat itself. For friendship we believe to be the greatest good of states and what best preserves them against revolutions; and Socrates particularly praises the unity of the state which seems and is said by him to be created by friendship. But the unity which he commends would be like that of the lovers in the Symposium, who, as Aristophanes says, desire to grow together in the excess of their affection, and from being two to become one, in which case one or both would certainly perish. Whereas in a state having women and children common, love will be diluted; and the father will certainly not say 'my son', or the son 'my father'. As a little sweet wine mingled with a great deal of water is imperceptible in the mixture, so, in this sort of community, the idea of relationship which is based upon these names will be lost; there is no reason why the so-called father should care about the son, or the son about the father, or brothers about one another. Of the two qualities which chiefly inspire regard and affection—that a thing is your own and that it is precious—neither can exist in such a state as this.

Again, the transfer of children as soon as they are born from the rank of husbandmen or of artisans to that of guardians, and from the rank of guardians into a lower rank, will be very difficult to arrange; the givers or transferrers cannot but know whom they are giving and transferring, and to whom. And the previously mentioned assaults, unlawful loves, homicides, will happen more often among them; for they will no longer call the members of the class they have left brothers, and children, and fathers, and mothers, and will not, therefore, be afraid of committing any crimes by reason of consanguinity. Touching the community of wives and children, let this be our conclusion.

5. Next let us consider what should be our arrangements about property: should the citizens of the perfect state have their possessions in common or not? This question may be discussed separately from the enactments about women and children. Even supposing that the women and children belong to individuals, according to the custom which is at present universal, may there not be an advantage in 1263ᵃ having and using possessions in common? E.g. (1) the soil may be appropriated, but the produce may be thrown for consumption into the common stock; and this is the practice of some nations. Or (2), the soil may be common, and may be cultivated in common, but the produce divided among individu-

als for their private use; this is a form of common property which is said to exist among certain foreigners. Or (3), the soil and the produce may be alike common.

When the husbandmen are not the owners, the case will be different and easier to deal with; but when they till the ground for themselves the question of ownership will give a world of trouble. If they do not share equally in enjoyments and toils, those who labour much and get little will necessarily complain of those who labour little and receive or consume much. But indeed there is always a difficulty in men living together and having all human relations in common, but especially in their having common property. The partnerships of fellow-travellers are an example to the point; for they generally fall out over everyday matters and quarrel about any trifle which turns up. So with servants: we are most liable to take offence at those with whom we most frequently come into contact in daily life.

These are only some of the disadvantages which attend the community of property; the present arrangement, if improved as it might be by good customs and laws, would be far better, and would have the advantages of both systems. Property should be in a certain sense common, but, as a general rule, private; for, when everyone has a distinct interest, men will not complain of one another, and they will make more progress, because everyone will be attending to his own business. And yet by reason of goodness, and in respect of use, 'Friends', as the proverb says, 'will have all things common'. Even now there are traces of such a principle, showing that it is not impracticable, but, in well-ordered states, exists already to a certain extent and may be carried further. For, although every man has his own property, some things he will place at the disposal of his friends, while of others he shares the use with them. The Lacedaemonians, for example, use one another's slaves, and horses, and dogs, as if they were their own; and when they lack provisions on a journey, they appropriate what they find in the fields throughout the country. It is clearly better that property should be private, but the use of it common; and the special business of the legislator is to create in men this benevolent disposition. Again, how im- 1263ᵇ measurably greater is the pleasure, when a man feels a thing to be his own; for surely the love of self is a feeling implanted by nature and not given in vain, although selfishness is rightly censured; this, however, is not the mere love of self, but the love of self in excess, like the miser's love of money; for all, or almost all, men love money and other such objects in a measure. And further, there is the greatest pleasure in doing a kindness or service to friends or guests or companions, which can only be rendered when a man has private property. These advantages are lost by excessive unification of the state. The exhibition of two excellences, besides, is visibly annihilated in such a state: first, temperance towards women (for it is an honourable action to abstain from another's wife for temperance sake); secondly, liberality in the matter of property. No one, when men have all things in common, will any longer set an example of liberality or do any liberal action; for liberality consists in the use which is made of property.

Such legislation may have a specious appearance of benevolence; men readily listen to it, and are easily induced to believe that in some wonderful manner everybody will become everybody's friend—especially when someone is heard denouncing the evils now existing in states, suits about contracts, convictions for perjury, flatteries of rich men and the like, which are said to arise out of the possession of private property. These evils, however, are due not to the absence of communism but to wickedness. Indeed, we see that there is much more quarrelling among those who have all things in common, though there are not many of them when compared with the vast numbers who have private property.

Again, we ought to reckon not only the evils from which the citizens will be saved, but also the advantages which they will lose. The life which they are to lead appears to be quite impracticable. The error of Socrates must be attributed to the false supposition from which he starts. Unity there should be, both of the family and of the state, but in some respects only. For there is a point at which a state may attain such a degree of unity as to be no longer a state, or at which, without actually ceasing to exist, it will become an inferior state, like harmony passing into unison, or rhythm which has been reduced to a single foot. The state, as I was saying, is a plurality, which should be united and made into a community by education; and it is strange that the author of a system of education which he thinks will make the state virtuous, should expect to improve his citizens by regulations of this sort, and not by philosophy or by customs and laws, like those which prevail at Sparta and Crete respecting common

meals, whereby the legislator has made property common. Let us remember that we should not disregard the experience of ages; in the multitude of years these things, if they were good, would certainly not have been unknown; for almost everything has been found out, although sometimes they are not put together; in other cases men do not use the knowledge which they have. Great light would be thrown on this subject if we could see such a form of government in the actual process of construction; for the legislator could not form a state at all without distributing and dividing its constituents into associations for common meals, and into phratries and tribes. But all this legislation ends only in forbidding agriculture to the guardians, a prohibition which the Lacedaemonians try to enforce already. 1264ᵃ

But, indeed, Socrates has not said, nor is it easy to decide, what in such a community will be the general form of the state. The citizens who are not guardians are the majority, and about them nothing has been determined: are the husbandmen, too, to have their property in common? Or is each individual to have his own? and are their wives and children to be individual or common? If, like the guardians, they are to have all things in common, in what do they differ from them, or what will they gain by submitting to their government? Or upon what principle would they submit, unless indeed the governing class adopt the ingenious policy of the Cretans, who give their slaves the same institutions as their own, but forbid them gymnastic exercises and the possession of arms. If, on the other hand, the inferior classes are to be like other cities in respect of marriage and property, what will be the form of the community? Must it not contain two states in one, each hostile to the other? He makes the guardians into a mere occupying garrison, while the husbandmen and artisans and the rest are real citizens. But if so the suits and quarrels, and all the evils which Socrates affirms to exist in other states, will exist equally among them. He says indeed that, having so good an education, the citizens will not need many laws, for example laws about the city or about the markets; but then he confines his education to the guardians. Again, he makes the husbandmen owners of the property upon condition of their paying a tribute. But in that case they are likely to be much more unmanageable and conceited than the Helots, or Penestae, or slaves in general. And whether community of wives and property be necessary for the lower equally with the higher class or not, and the questions akin to this, what will be the education, form of government, laws of the lower class, Socrates has nowhere determined: neither is it easy to discover this, nor is their character of small importance if the common life of the guardians is to be maintained.

Again, if Socrates make the women common, and retains private property, the men will see to the fields, but who will see to the house? And who will do so if the agricultural class have both their property and their wives in common? Once more: it is absurd to argue, from the analogy of animals, that men and women should follow the same pursuits, for animals have not to manage a household. The government, too, as constituted by Socrates, contains elements of danger; for he makes the same persons always rule. And if this is often a cause of disturbance among the meaner sort, how much more among high-spirited warriors? But that the persons whom he makes rulers must be the same is evident; for the gold which the God mingles in the souls of men is not at one time given to one, at another time to another, but always to the same: as he says, God mingles gold in some, and silver in others, from their very birth; but brass and iron in those who are meant to be artisans and husbandmen. Again, he deprives the guardians even of happiness, and says that the legislator ought to make the whole state happy. But the whole cannot be happy unless most, or all, or some of its parts enjoy happiness. In this respect happiness is not like the even principle in numbers, which may exist only in the whole, but in neither of the parts; not so happiness. And if the guardians are not happy, who are? Surely not the artisans, or the common people. The Republic of which Socrates discourses has all these difficulties, and others quite as great.

6. The same, or nearly the same, objections apply to Plato's later work, the Laws, and therefore we had better examine briefly the constitution which is therein described. In the Republic, Socrates has definitely settled in all a few questions only; such as the community of women and children, the community of property, and the constitution of the state. The population is divided into two classes—one of husbandmen, and the other of warriors; from this latter is taken a third class of counsellors and rulers of the state. But Socrates has not determined whether the husbandmen and artisans are to have a share in the government, and whether they, too, are to carry arms and share in the military service, or not. He

1265ª

certainly thinks that the women ought to share in the education of the guardians, and to fight by their side. The remainder of the work is filled up with digressions foreign to the main subject, and with discussions about the education of the guardians. In the Laws there is hardly anything but laws; not much is said about the constitution. This, which he had intended to make more of the ordinary type, he gradually brings round to the other form. For with the exception of the community of women and property, he supposes everything to be the same in both states; there is to be the same education; the citizens of both are to live free from servile occupations, and there are to be common meals in both. The only difference is that the Laws, the common meals are extended to women, and the warriors number 5000, but in the Republic only 1000.

The discourses of Socrates are never commonplace; they always exhibit grace and originality and thought; but perfection in everything can hardly be expected. We must not overlook the fact that the number of 5000 citizens, just now mentioned, will require a territory as large as Babylon, or some other huge site, if so many persons are to be supported in idleness, together with their women and attendants, who will be a multitude many times as great. In framing an ideal we may assume what we wish, but should avoid impossibilities.

It is said that the legislator ought to have his eye directed to two points—the people and the country. But neighbouring countries also must not be forgotten by him, firstly because the state for which he legislates is to have a political and not an isolated life. For a state must have such a military force as will be serviceable against her neighbours, and not merely useful at home. Even if such a life is not accepted, either for individuals or states, still a city should be formidable to enemies, whether invading or retreating.

There is another point: Should not the amount of property be defined in some way which differs from this by being clearer? For Socrates says that a man should have so much property as will enable him to live temperately, which is only a way of saying to live well; this is too general a conception. Further, a man may live temperately and yet miserably. A better definition would be that a man must have so much property as will enable him to live not only temperately but liberally; if the two are parted, liberality will combine with luxury; temperance will be associated with toil. For liberality and temperance are the only eligible qualities which have to do with the use of property. A man cannot use property with mildness or courage, but temperately and liberally he may; and therefore the practice of these excellences is inseparable from property. There is an absurdity, too, in equalizing the property and not regulating the number of citizens; the population is to remain unlimited, and he thinks that it will be sufficiently equalized by a certain number of marriages being unfruitful, however many are born to others, because he finds this to be the case in existing states. But greater care will be required than now; for among ourselves, whatever may be the number of citizens, the property is always distributed among them, and therefore no one is in want; but, if the property were incapable of division as in the Laws, the supernumeraries, whether few or many, would get nothing. One would have thought that it was even more necessary to limit population than property; and that the limit should be fixed by calculating the chances of mortality in the children, and of sterility in married persons. The neglect of this subject, which in existing states is so common, is a never-failing cause of poverty among the citizens; and poverty is the parent of revolution and crime. Pheidon the Corinthian, who was one of the most ancient legislators, thought that the families and the number of citizens ought to remain the same, although originally all the lots may have been of different sizes; but in the Laws the opposite principle is maintained. What in our opinion is the right arrangement will have to be explained hereafter.

There is another omission in the Laws: Socrates does not tell us how the rulers differ from their subjects; he only says that they should be related as the warp and the woof, which are made out of different wools. He allows that a man's whole property may be increased fivefold, but why should not his land also increase to a certain extent? Again, will the good management of a household be promoted by his arrangement of homesteads? for he assigns to each individual two homesteads in separate places, and it is difficult to live in two houses.

The whole system of government tends to be neither democracy nor oligarchy, but something in a mean between them, which is usually called a polity, and is composed of the heavy-armed soldiers. Now, if he intended to frame a constitution which would suit the greatest number of states, he was very likely right, but not if he meant to say that this constitutional form came nearest to his first state; for many would prefer the Lacedaemonian, or, possibly, some other more aristocratic government. Some, indeed, say that the best constitution is a combination of all existing forms, and they praise the Lacedaemonian because it is made up of oligarchy, monarchy, and democracy, the king forming the monarchy, and the council of elders the oligarchy, while the democratic element is represented by the Ephors; for the Ephors are selected from the people. Others, however, declare the Ephorate to be a tyranny, and find the element of democracy in the common meals and in the habits of daily life. In the Laws it is maintained that the best constitution is made up of democracy and tyranny, which are either not constitutions at all, or are the worst of all. But they are nearer the truth who combined many forms; for the constitution is better which is made up of more numerous elements. The constitution proposed in the Laws has no element of monarchy at all; it is nothing but oligarchy and democracy, leaning rather to oligarchy. This is seen in the mode of appointing magistrates; for although the appointment of them by lot from among those who have been already selected combines both elements, the way in which the rich are compelled by law to attend the assembly and vote for magistrates or discharge other political duties, while the rest may do as they like, and the endeavour to have the greater number of the magistrates appointed out of the richer classes and the highest officers selected from those who have the greatest incomes, both these are oligarchical features. The oligarchical principle prevails also in the choice of the council, for all are compelled to choose, but the compulsion extends only to the choice out of the first class, and of an equal number out of the second class and out of the third class, but not in this latter case to all the voters but to those from the third or fourth class; and the selection of candidates out of the fourth class is only compulsory on the first and second. Then, from the persons so chosen, he says that there ought to be an equal number of each class selected. Thus a preponderance will be given to the better sort of people, who have the larger incomes, because some of the lower classes, not being compelled, will not vote. These considerations, and others which will be adduced when the time comes for examining similar constitutions, tend to show that states like Plato's should not be composed of democracy and monarchy. There is also a danger in electing the magistrates out of a body who are themselves elected; for, if but a small number choose to combine, the elections will always go as they desire. Such is the constitution which is described in the Laws. . . .

BOOK III

1. He who would inquire into the essence and attributes of various kinds of government must first of all determine what a state is. At present this is a disputed question. Some say that the state has done a certain act; others, not the state, but the oligarchy or the tyrant. And the legislator or statesman is concerned entirely with the state, a government being an arrangement of the inhabitants of a state. But a state is composite, like any other whole made up of many parts—these are the citizens, who compose it. 1275ᵃ It is evident, therefore, that we must begin by asking, Who is the citizen, and what is the meaning of the term? For here again there may be a difference of opinion. He who is a citizen in a democracy will often not be a citizen in an oligarchy. Leaving out of consideration those who have been made citizens, or who have obtained the name of citizen in any other accidental manner, we may say, first, that a citizen is not a citizen because he lives in a certain place, for resident aliens and slaves share in the place; nor is he a citizen who has legal rights to the extent of suing and being sued; for this right may be enjoyed under the provisions of a treaty. Resident aliens in many places do not possess even such rights completely, for they are obliged to have a patron, so that they do but imperfectly participate in the community, and we call them citizens only in a qualified sense, as we might apply the term to children who are too young to be on the register, or to old men who have been relieved from state duties. Of these we do not say quite simply that they are citizens, but add in the one case that they are not of age, and in the other, that they are past the age, or something of that sort; the precise expression is immaterial, for our meaning is clear. Similar difficulties to those which I have mentioned may be raised and answered about disfranchised citizens and about exiles. But the citizen whom we are seeking to define is a citizen in the strictest sense, against whom no such exception can be taken, and his special characteristic is that he shares in the administration of justice, and in offices. Now of offices some are discontinuous, and the same persons are not allowed to hold them twice, or can only hold them after a fixed interval; others have no limit of time—for example, the office of juryman or member of the assembly. It may, indeed, be argued that these are not magistrates at all, and that their functions give them no share in the government. But surely it is ridiculous to say that those who have the supreme power do not govern. Let us not dwell further upon this, which is a purely verbal question; what we want is a common term including both juryman and member of the assembly. Let us, for the sake of distinction, call it 'indefinite office', and we will assume that those who share in such office are citizens. This is the most comprehensive definition of a citizen, and best suits all those who are generally so called.

But we must not forget that things of which the underlying principles differ in kind, one of them being first, another second, another third, have, when regarded in this relation, nothing, or hardly anything, worth mentioning in common. Now we see that gov- 1275ᵇ ernments differ in kind, and that some of them are prior and that others are posterior; those which are faulty or perverted are necessarily posterior to those which are perfect. (What we mean by perversion will be hereafter explained.) The citizen then of necessity differs under each form of government; and our definition is best adapted to the citizen of a democracy; but not necessarily to other states. For in some states the people are not acknowledged, nor have they any regular assembly, but only extraordinary ones; and law-suits are distributed by sections among the magistrates. At Lacedaemon, for instance, the Ephors determine suits about contracts, which they distribute among themselves, while the elders are judges of homicide, and other causes are decided by other magistrates. A similar principle prevails at Carthage; there certain magistrates decide all causes. We may, indeed, modify our definition of the citizen so as to include these states. In them it is the holder of a definite, not an indefinite office, who is juryman and member of the assembly, and to some or all such holders of definite offices is reserved the right of deliberating or judging about some things or about all things. The conception of the citizen now begins to clear up.

He who has the power to take part in the deliberative or judicial administration of any state is said by us to be a citizen of that state; and, speaking generally, a state is a body of citizens suffing for the purposes of life.

2. But in practice a citizen is defined to be one of whom both the parents are citizens (and not just one, i.e. father or mother); others insist on going further back; say to two or three or more ancestors. This is a short and practical definition; but there are some who raise the further question of how this third of fourth ancestor came to be a citizen. Gorgias of Leontini, partly because he was in a difficulty, partly in irony, said that mortars are what is made by the mortar-makers, and the citizens of Larissa are those who are made by the magistrates; for it is their trade to 'make Larissaeans'. Yet the question is really simple, for, if according to the definition just given they shared in the government, they were citizens. This is a better definition that the other. For the words, 'born of a father or mother who is a citizen', cannot possibly apply to the first inhabitants or founders of a state.

There is a greater difficulty in the case of those who have been made citizens after a revolution, as by Cleisthenes at Athens after the expulsion of the tyrants, for he enrolled in tribes many metics, both 1276ᵃ strangers and slaves. The doubt in these cases is, not who is, but whether he who is ought to be a citizen; and there will still be a further doubt, whether he who ought not to be a citizen, is one in fact, for what ought not to be is what is false. Now, there are some who hold office, and yet ought not to hold office, whom we describe as ruling, but ruling unjustly. And the citizen was defined by the fact of his holding some kind of rule or office—he who holds a certain sort of office fulfils our definition of a citizen. It is evident, therefore, that the citizens about whom the doubt has arisen must be called citizens.

3. Whether they ought to be so or not is a question which is bound up with the previous inquiry. For a parallel question is raised respecting the state, whether a certain act is or is not an act of the state; for example, in the transition from an oligarchy or a tyranny to a democracy. In such cases persons refuse to fulfil their contracts or any other obligations, on the ground that the tyrant and not the state, contracted them; they argue that some constitutions are established by force, and not for the sake of the common good. But this would apply equally to democracies, and then the acts of the democracy will be neither more nor less acts of the state in question than those of an oligarchy or of a tyranny. This question runs up into another:—on what principle shall we ever say that the state is the same, or different? It would be a very superficial view which considered only the place and the inhabitants (for the soil and the population may be separated, and some of

the inhabitants may live in one place and some in another). This, however, is not a very serious difficulty; we need only remark that the word 'state' is ambiguous.

It is further asked: When are men, living in the same place, to be regarded as a single city—what is the limit? Certainly not the wall of the city, for you might surround all Peloponnesus with a wall. Babylon, we may say, is like this, and every city that has the compass of a nation rather than a city; Babylon, they say, had been taken for three days before some part of the inhabitants become aware of the fact. This difficulty may, however, with advantage be deferred to another occasion; the statesman has to consider the size of the state, and whether it should consist of more than one race or not.

Again, shall we say that while the race of inhabitants remains the same, the city is also the same, although the citizens are always dying and being born, as we call rivers and fountains the same, although the water is always flowing away and more coming? Or shall we say that the generations of men, 1276ᵇ like the rivers, are the same, but that the state changes? For, since the state is a partnership, and is a partnership of citizens in a constitution, when the form of the government changes, and becomes different, then it may be supposed that the state is no longer the same, just as a tragic differs from a comic chorus, although the members of both may be identical. And in this manner we speak of every union or composition of elements as different when the form of their composition alters; for example, a scale containing the same sounds is said to be different, accordingly as the Dorian or the Phrygian mode is employed. And if this is true it is evident that the sameness of the state consists chiefly in the sameness of the constitution, and it may be called or not called by the same name, whether the inhabitants are the same or entirely different. It is quite another question, whether a state ought or ought not to fulfil engagements when the form of government changes.

4. There is a point nearly allied to the preceding: Whether the excellence of a good man and a good citizen is the same or not. But before entering on this discussion, we must certainly first obtain some general notion of the excellence of the citizen. Like the sailor, the citizen is a member of a community. Now, sailors have different functions, for one of them is a rower, another a pilot, and a third a lookout man, a fourth is described by some similar term;

and while the precise definition of each individual's excellence applies exclusively to him, there is, at the same time, a common definition applicable to them all. For they have all of them a common object, which is safety in navigation. Similarly, one citizen differs from another, but the salvation of the community is the common business of them all. This community is the constitution; the excellence of the citizen must therefore be relative to the constitution of which he is a member. If, then, there are many forms of government, it is evident that there is not one single excellence of the good citizen which is perfect excellence. But we say that the good man is he who has one single excellence which is perfect excellence. Hence it is evident that the good citizen need not of necessity possess the excellence which makes a good man.

The same question may also be approached by another road, from a consideration of the best constitution. If the state cannot be entirely composed of good men, and yet each citizen is expected to do his own business well, and must therefore have excellence, still, inasmuch as all the citizens can-1277ª not be alike, the excellence of the citizen and of the good man cannot coincide. All must have the excellence of the good citizen—thus, and thus only, can the state be perfect; but they will not have the excellence of a good man, unless we assume that in the good state all the citizens must be good.

Again, the state, as composed of unlikes, may be compared to the living being: as the first elements into which a living being is resolved are soul and body, as soul is made up of rational principle and appetite, the family of husband and wife, property of master and slave, so of all these, as well as other dissimilar elements, the state is composed; and therefore the excellence of all the citizens cannot possibly be the same, any more than the excellence of the leader of a chorus is the same as that of the performer who stands by his side. I have said enough to show why the two kinds of excellence cannot be absolutely the same.

But will there then be no case in which the excellence of the good citizen and the excellence of the good man coincide? To this we answer that the good ruler is a good and wise man, but the citizen need not be wise. And some persons say that even the education of the ruler should be of a special kind; for are not the children of kings instructed in riding and military exercises? As Euripides says:

No subtle arts for me, but what the state requires.

As though there were a special education needed for a ruler. If the excellence of a good ruler is the same as that of a good man, and we assume further that the subject is a citizen as well as the ruler, the excellence of the good citizen and the excellence of the good man cannot be absolutely the same, although in some cases they may; for the excellence of a ruler differs from that of a citizen. It was the sense of this difference which made Jason say that 'he felt hungry when he was not a tyrant', meaning that he could not endure to live in a private station. But, on the other hand, it may be argued that men are praised for knowing both how to rule and how to obey, and he is said to be a citizen of excellence who is able to do both well. Now if we suppose the excellence of a good man to be that which rules, and the excellence of the citizen to include ruling and obeying, it cannot be said that they are equally worthy of praise. Since, then, it is sometimes thought that the ruler and the ruled must learn different things and not the same, but that the citizen must know and share in them both, the inference is obvious. There is, indeed, the rule of a master, which is concerned with menial offices—the master need not know how to perform these, but may employ others in the execution of them: the other would be degrading; and by the other I mean the power actually to do menial duties, which vary much in character and are executed by various classes of slaves, such, for example, as handicraftsmen, who, as their name signifies, live by the labour of their hands—under these the mechanic is included. Hence in ancient 1277ᵇ times, and among some nations, the working classes had no share in the government—a privilege which they only acquired under extreme democracy. Certainly the good man and the statesman and the good citizen ought not to learn the crafts of inferiors except for their own occasional use; if they habitually practise them, there will cease to be a distinction between master and slave.

But there is a rule of another kind, which is exercised over freemen and equals by birth—a constitutional rule, which the ruler must learn by obeying, as he would learn the duties of a general of cavalry by being under the orders of a general of cavalry, or the duties of a general of infantry by being under the orders of a general of infantry, and by having had the command of a regiment and of a company. It has been well said that he who has never learned to obey cannot be a good commander. The excellence of the two is not the same, but the good citizen ought to be capable of both; he should know how to govern like a freeman, and how to obey like a freeman—these are the excellences of a citizen. And, although the temperance and justice of a ruler are distinct from those of a subject, the excellence of a good man will include both; for the excellence of the good man who is free and also a subject, e.g. his justice, will not be one but will comprise distinct kinds, the one qualifying him to rule, the other to obey, and differing as the temperance and courage of men and women differ. For a man would be thought a coward if he had no more courage than a courageous woman, and a woman would be thought loquacious if she imposed no more restraint on her conversation than the good man; and indeed their part in the management of the household is different, for the duty of the one is to acquire, and of the other to preserve. Practical wisdom is the only excellence peculiar to the ruler: it would seem that all other excellences must equally belong to ruler and subject. The excellence of the subject is certainly not wisdom, but only true opinion; he may be compared to the maker of the flute, while his master is like the flute-player or user of the flute.

From these considerations may be gathered the answer to the question, whether the excellence of the good man is the same as that of the good citizen, or different, and how far the same, and how far different.

5. There still remains one more question about the citizen: Is he only a true citizen who has a share of office, or is the mechanic to be included? If they who hold no office are to be deemed citizens, not every citizen can have this excellence; for this man is a citizen. And if none of the lower class are citizens, in which part of the state are they to be placed? For they are not resident aliens, and they are not foreigners. May we not reply, that as far as this objection goes there is no more absurdity in excluding them than in excluding slaves and freedmen from any of the above-mentioned classes? It must be admitted that we cannot consider all those to be citizens who are necessary to the existence of the state; for example, children are not citizens equally with grown-up men, who are citizens absolutely, but children, not being grown up, are only citizens on a certain assumption. In ancient times, and among some nations, the artisan class were slaves or foreigners, and therefore the majority of them are so now. The

best form of state will not admit them to citizenship; but if they are admitted, then our definition of the excellence of a citizen will not apply to every citizen, nor to every free man as such, but only to those who are freed from necessary services. The necessary people are either slaves who minister to the wants of individuals, or mechanics and labourers who are the servants of the community. These reflections carried a little further will explain their position; and indeed what has been said already is of itself, when understood, explanation enough.

Since there are many forms of government there must be many varieties of citizens, and especially of citizens who are subjects; so that under some governments the mechanic and the labourer will be citizens, but not in others, as, for example, in so-called aristocracies, if there are any, in which honours are given according to excellence and merit; for no man can practise excellence who is living the life of a mechanic or labourer. In oligarchies the qualification for office is high, and therefore no labourer can ever be a citizen; but a mechanic may, for an actual majority of them are rich. At Thebes there was a law that no man could hold office who had not retired from business for ten years. But in many states the law goes to the length of admitting aliens; for in some democracies a man is a citizen though his mother only be a citizen; and a similar principle is applied to illegitimate children among many. Nevertheless they make such people citizens because of the dearth of legitimate citizens (for they introduce this sort of legislation owing to lack of population); so when the number of citizens increases, first the children of a male or a female slave are excluded; then those whose mothers only are citizens; and at last the right of citizenship is confined to those whose fathers and mothers are both citizens.

Hence, as is evident, there are different kinds of citizens; and he is a citizen in the fullest sense who shares in the honours of the state. Compare Homer's words 'like some dishonoured stranger'; he who is excluded from the honours of the state is no better than an alien. But when this exclusion is concealed, then its object is to deceive their fellow inhabitants.

As to the question whether the excellence of the 1278ᵇ good man is the same as that of the good citizen, the considerations already adduced prove that in some states the good man and the good citizen are the same, and in others different. When they are the same it is not every citizen who is a good man, but only the statesman and those who have or may have, alone or in conjunction with others, the conduct of public affairs.

6. Having determined these questions, we have next to consider whether there is only one form of government or many, and if many, what they are, and how many, and what are the differences between them.

A constitution is the arrangement of magistracies in a state, especially of the highest of all. The government is everywhere sovereign in the state, and the constitution is in fact the government. For example, in democracies the people are supreme, but in oligarchies, the few; and, therefore, we say that these two constitutions also are different: and so in other cases.

First, let us consider what is the purpose of a state, and how many forms of rule there are by which human society is regulated. We have already said, in the first part of this treatise, when discussing household management and the rule of a master, that man is by nature a political animal. And therefore, men, even when they do not require one another's help, desire to live together; not but that they are also brought together by their common interests in so far as they each attain to any measure of well-being. This is certainly the chief end, both of individuals and of states. And mankind meet together and maintain the political community also for the sake of mere life (in which there is possibly some noble element so long as the evils of existence do not greatly overbalance the good). And we all see that men cling to life even at the cost of enduring great misfortune, seeming to find in life a natural sweetness and happiness.

There is no difficulty in distinguishing the various kinds of rule; they have been often defined already in our popular discussions. The rule of a master, although the slave by nature and the master by nature have in reality the same interests, is nevertheless exercised primarily with a view to the interest of the master, but accidentally considers the slave, since, if the slave perish, the rule of the master perishes with him. On the other hand, the government of a wife and children and of a household, which we have called household management, is exercised in the first instance for the good of the governed or for the common good of both parties, but essentially for the good of the governed, as we see to be the case in medicine, gymnastic, and the arts in general, which are only accidentally concerned with the good of the artists themselves. For there is

1279ª

no reason why the trainer may not sometimes practise gymnastics, and the helmsman is always one of the crew. The trainer or the helmsman considers the good of those committed to his care. But, when he is one of the persons taken care of, he accidentally participates in the advantage, for the helmsman is also a sailor, and the trainer becomes one of those in training. And so in politics: when the state is framed upon the principle of equality and likeness, the citizens think that they ought to hold office by turns. Formerly, as is natural, everyone would take his turn of service; and then again, somebody else would look after this interest, just as he, while in office, had looked after theirs. But nowadays, for the sake of the advantage which is to be gained from the public revenues and from office, men want to be always in office. One might imagine that the rulers, being sickly, were only kept in health while they continued in office; in that case we may be sure that they would be hunting after places. The conclusion is evident: that governments which have a regard to the common interest are constituted in accordance with strict principles of justice, and are therefore true forms; but those which regard only the interest of the rulers are all defective and perverted forms, for they are despotic, whereas a state is a community of freemen.

7. Having determined these points, we have next to consider how many forms of government there are, and what they are; and in the first place what are the true forms, for when they are determined the perversions of them will at once be apparent. The words constitution and government have the same meaning, and the government, which is the supreme authority in states, must be in the hands of one, or of a few, or of the many. The true forms of government, therefore, are those in which the one, or the few, or the many, govern with a view to the common interest; but governments which rule with a view to the private interest, whether of the one, or of the few, or of the many, are perversions. For the members of a state, if they are truly citizens, ought to participate in its advantages. Of forms of government in which one rules, we call that which regards the common interest, kingship; that in which more than one, but not many, rule, aristocracy; and it is so called, either because the rulers are the best men, or because they have at heart the best interests of the state and of the citizens. But when the many administer the state for the common interest, the government is called by the generic name—a con-

1279ᵇ stitution. And there is a reason for this use of language. One man or a few may excel in excellence; but as the number increases it becomes more difficult for them to attain perfection in every kind of excellence, though they may in military excellence, for this is found in the masses. Hence in a constitutional government the fighting-men have the supreme power, and those who possess arms are the citizens.

Of the above-mentioned forms, the perversions are as follows:—of kingship, tyranny; of aristocracy, oligarchy; of constitutional government, democracy. For tyranny is a kind of monarchy which has in view the interest of the monarch only; oligarchy has in view the interest of the wealthy; democracy, of the needy: none of them the common good of all.

8. But there are difficulties about these forms of government, and it will therefore be necessary to state a little more at length the nature of each of them. For he who would make a philosophical study of the various sciences, and is not only concerned with practice, ought not to overlook or omit anything, but to set forth the truth in every particular. Tyranny, as I was saying, is monarchy exercising the rule of a master over the political society; oligarchy is when men of property have the government in their hands; democracy, the opposite, when the indigent, and not the men of property, are the rulers. And here arises the first of our difficulties, and it relates to the distinction just drawn. For democracy is said to be the government of the many. But what if the many are men of property and have the power in their hands? In like manner oligarchy is said to be the government of the few; but what if the poor are fewer than the rich, and have the power in their hands because they are stronger? In these cases the distinction which we have drawn between these different forms of government would no longer hold good.

Suppose, once more, that we add wealth to the few and poverty to the many, and name the governments accordingly—an oligarchy is said to be that in which the few and the wealthy, and a democracy that in which the many and the poor are the rulers—there will still be a difficulty. For, if the only forms of government are the ones already mentioned, how shall we describe those other governments also just mentioned by us, in which the rich are the more numerous and the poor are the fewer, and both govern in their respective states?

The argument seems to show that, whether in oligarchies or in democracies, the number of the governing body, whether the greater number, as in a democracy, or the smaller number, as in an oligarchy, is an accident due to the fact that the rich everywhere are few, and the poor numerous. But if so, there is a misapprehension of the causes of the difference between them. For the real difference be- 1280ᵃ tween democracy and oligarchy is poverty and wealth. Wherever men rule by reason of their wealth, whether they be few or many, that is an oligarchy, and where the poor rule, that is a democracy. But in fact the rich are few and the poor many; for few are well-to-do, whereas freedom is enjoyed by all, and wealth and freedom are the grounds on which the two parties claim power in the state.

9. Let us begin by considering the common definitions of oligarchy and democracy, and what is oligarchical and democratic justice. For all men cling to justice of some kind, but their conceptions are imperfect and they do not express the whole idea. For example, justice is thought by them to be, and is, equality—not, however, for all, but only for equals. And inequality is thought to be, and is, justice; neither is this for all, but only for unequals. When the persons are omitted, then men judge erroneously. The reason is that they are passing judgement on themselves, and most people are bad judges in their own case. And whereas justice implies a relation to persons as well as to things, and a just distribution, as I have already said in the Ethics, implies the same ratio between the persons and between the things, they agree about the equality of the things, but dispute about the equality of the persons, chiefly for the reason which I have just given—because they are bad judges in their own affairs; and secondly, because both the parties to the argument are speaking of a limited and partial justice, but imagine themselves to be speaking of absolute justice. For the one party, if they are unequal in one respect, for example wealth, consider themselves to be unequal in all; and the other party, if they are equal in one respect, for example free birth, consider themselves to be equal in all. But they leave out the capital point. For if men met and associated out of regard to wealth only, their share in the state would be proportioned to their property, and the oligarchical doctrine would then seem to carry the day. It would not be just that he who paid one mina should have the same share of a hundred minae, whether of the principal or of the profits, as he who paid the remaining ninety-nine. But a state exists for the sake of a good life, and not for the sake of life only: if life only were the object, slaves and brute animals might form a state, but they cannot, for they have no share in happiness or in a life based on choice. Nor does a state exist for the sake of alliance and security from injustice, nor yet for the sake of exchange and mutual intercourse; for then the Tyrrhenians and the Carthaginians, and all who have commercial treaties with one another, would be the citizens of one state. True, they have agreements about imports, and engagements that they will do no wrong to one another, and written articles of alliance. But there are no magistracies common to the contracting parties; different states have each their own magistracies. Nor does one state take care that the citizens of the other are such as they ought to be, nor see that those who come under the terms of the treaty do no wrong or wickedness at all, but only that they do no injustice to one another. Whereas, those who care for good government take into consideration political 1280ᵇ excellence and defect. Whence it may be further inferred that excellence must be the care of a state which is truly so called, and not merely enjoys the name: for without this end the community becomes a mere alliance which differs only in place from alliances of which the members live apart; and law is only a convention, 'a surety to one another of justice', as the sophist Lycophron says, and has no real power to make the citizens good and just.

This is obvious; for suppose distinct places, such as Corinth and Megara, to be brought together so that their walls touched, still they would not be one city, not even if the citizens had the right to intermarry, which is one of the rights peculiarly characteristic of states. Again, if men dwelt at a distance from one another, but not so far off as to have no intercourse, and there were laws among them that they should not wrong each other in their exchanges, neither would this be a state. Let us suppose that one man is a carpenter, another a farmer, another a shoemaker, and so on, and that their number is ten thousand: nevertheless, if they have nothing in common but exchange, alliance, and the like, that would not constitute a state. Why is this? Surely not because they are at a distance from one another; for even supposing that such a community were to meet in one place, but that each man had a house of his own, which was in a manner his state, and that they made alliance with one another, but only against evildoers; still an accurate thinker would not deem this to be a state, if their intercourse with one another

was of the same character after as before their union. It is clear then that a state is not a mere society, having a common place, established for the prevention of mutual crime and for the sake of exchange. These are conditions without which a state cannot exist; but all of them together do not constitute a state, which is a community of families and aggregations of families in well-being, for the sake of a perfect and self-sufficing life. Such a community can only be established among those who live in the same place and intermarry. Hence there arise in cities family connexions, brotherhoods, common sacrifices, amusements which draw men together. But these are created by friendship, for to choose to live together is friendship. The end of the state is the good life, and these are the means towards it. And the state is the union of families and villages in a perfect and self-sufficing life, by which we mean a happy and 1281ᵃ honourable life.

Our conclusion, then, is that political society exists for the sake of noble actions, and not of living together. Hence they who contribute most to such a society have a greater share in it than those who have the same or a greater freedom or nobility of birth but are inferior to them in political excellence; or than those who exceed them in wealth but are surpassed by them in excellence.

From what has been said it will be clearly seen that all the partisans of different forms of government speak of a part of justice only.

10. There is also a doubt as to what is to be the supreme power in the state:—Is it the multitude? Or the wealthy? Or the good? Or the one best man? Or a tyrant? Any of these alternatives seems to involve disagreeable consequences. If the poor, for example, because they are more in number, divide among themselves the property of the rich—is not this unjust? No, by heaven (will be the reply), for the supreme authority justly willed it. But if this is not extreme injustice, what is? Again, when in the first division all has been taken, and the majority divide anew the property of the minority, is it not evident, if this goes on, that they will ruin the state? Yet surely, excellence is not the ruin of those who possess it, nor is justice destructive of a state; and therefore this law of confiscation clearly cannot be just. If it were, all the acts of a tyrant must of necessity be just; for he only coerces other men by superior power, just as the multitude coerce the rich. But is it just then that the few and the wealthy should be the rulers? And what if they, in like manner, rob and plunder the people—is this just? If so, the other case will likewise be just. But there can be no doubt that all these things are wrong and unjust.

. Then ought the good to rule and have supreme power? But in that case everybody else, being excluded from power, will be dishonoured. For the offices of a state are posts of honour; and if one set of men always hold them, the rest must be deprived of them. Then will it be well that the one best man should rule? That is still more oligarchical, for the number of those who are dishonoured is thereby increased. Someone may say that it is bad in any case for a man, subject as he is to all the accidents of human passion, to have the supreme power, rather than the law. But what if the law itself be democratic or oligarchical, how will that help us out of our difficulties? Not at all; the same consequences will follow.

11. Most of these questions may be reserved for another occasion. The principle that the multitude ought to be in power rather than the few best might seem to be solved and to contain some difficulty and 1281ᵇ perhaps even truth. For the many, of whom each individual is not a good man, when they meet together may be better than the few good, if regarded not individually but collectively, just as a feast to which many contribute is better than a dinner provided out of a single purse. For each individual among the many has a share of excellence and practical wisdom, and when they meet together, just as they become in a manner one man, who has many feet, and hands, and senses, so too with regard to their character and thought. Hence the many are better judges than a single man of music and poetry; for some understand one part, and some another, and among them they understand the whole. There is a similar combination of qualities in good men, who differ from any individual of the many, as the beautiful are said to differ from those who are not beautiful, and works of art from realities, because in them the scattered elements are combined, although, if taken separately, the eye of one person or some other feature in another person would be fairer than in the picture. Whether this principle can apply to every democracy, and to all bodies of men, is not clear. Or rather, by heaven, in some cases it is impossible to apply; for the argument would equally hold about brutes; and wherein, it will be asked, do some men differ from brutes? But there may be bodies of men about whom our statement is nevertheless true. And if so, the difficulty which has been already raised,

and also another which is akin to it—viz. what power should be assigned to the mass of freemen and citizens, who are not rich and have no personal merit— are both solved. There is still a danger in allowing them to share the great offices of state, for their folly will lead them into error, and their dishonesty into crime. But there is a danger also in not letting them share, for a state in which many poor men are excluded from office will necessarily be full of enemies. The only way of escape is to assign to them some deliberative and judicial functions. For this reason Solon and certain other legislators give them the power of electing to offices, and of calling the magistrates to account, but they do not allow them to hold office singly. When they meet together their perceptions are quite good enough, and combined with the better class they are useful to the state (just as impure food when mixed with what is pure sometimes makes the entire mass more wholesome than a small quantity of the pure would be), but each individual, left to himself, forms an imperfect judgement. On the other hand, the popular form of government involves certain difficulties. In the first place, it might be objected that he who can judge of the healing of a sick man would be one who could himself heal his disease, and make him whole—that is, in other words, the physician; and so in all professions and arts. As, then, the physician ought to be called to account by physicians, so ought men in 1282ᵃ general to be called to account by their peers. But physicians are of three kinds:—there is the ordinary practitioner, and there is the master physician, and thirdly the man educated in the art: in all arts there is such a class; and we attribute the power of judging to them quite as much as to professors of the art. Secondly, does not the same principle apply to elections? For a right election can only be made by those who have knowledge; those who know geometry, for example, will choose a geometrician rightly, and those who know how to steer, a pilot; and, even if there be some occupations and arts in which private persons share in the ability to choose, they certainly cannot choose better than those who know. So that, according to this argument, neither the election of magistrates, nor the calling of them to account, should be entrusted to the many. Yet possibly these objections are to a great extent met by our old answer, that if the people are not utterly degraded, although individually they may be worse judges than those who have special knowledge, as a body they are as good or better. Moreover, there are some arts whose products are not judged of solely, or best, by the artists themselves, namely those arts whose products are recognized even by those who do not possess the art; for example, the knowledge of the house is not limited to the builder only; the user, or, in other words, the master, of the house will actually be a better judge than the builder, just as the pilot will judge better of a rudder than the carpenter, and the guest will judge better of a feast than the cook.

This difficulty seems now to be sufficiently answered, but there is another akin to it. That inferior persons should have authority in greater matters than the good would appear to be a strange thing, yet the election and calling to account of the magistrates is the greatest of all. And these, as I was saying, are functions which in some states are assigned to the people, for the assembly is supreme in all such matters. Yet persons of any age, and having but a small property qualification, sit in the assembly and deliberate and judge, although for the great officers of state, such as treasurers and generals, a high qualification is required. This difficulty may be solved in the same manner as the preceding, and the present practice of democracies may be really defensible. For the power does not reside in the juryman, or counsellor, or member of the assembly, but in the court, and the council, and the assembly, of which the aforesaid individuals—counsellor, assemblyman, juryman—are only parts or members. And for this reason the many may claim to have a higher authority than the few; for the people, and the council, and the courts consist of many persons, and their property collectively is greater than the property of one or of a few individuals holding great offices. But enough of this.

The discussion of the first question shows nothing so clearly as that laws, when good, should be 1282ᵇ supreme; and that the magistrate or magistrates should regulate those matters only on which the laws are unable to speak with precision owing to the difficulty of any general principle embracing all particulars. But what are good laws has not yet been clearly explained; the old difficulty remains. The goodness or badness, justice or injustice, of laws varies of necessity with the constitutions of states. This, however, is clear, that the laws must be adapted to the constitutions. But, if so, true forms of government will of necessity have just laws, and perverted forms of government will have unjust laws.

12. In all sciences and arts the end is a good, and the greatest good and in the highest degree a good in the most authoritative of all—this is the political science of which the good is justice, in other words, the common interest. All men think justice to be a sort of equality; and to a certain extent they agree with what we have said in our philosophical works about ethics. For they say that what is just is just for someone and that it should be equal for equals. But there still remains a question: equality or inequality of what? Here is a difficulty which calls for political speculation. For very likely some persons will say that offices of state ought to be unequally distributed according to superior excellence, in whatever respect, of the citizen, although there is no other difference between him and the rest of the community; for those who differ in any one respect have different rights and claims. But, surely, if this is true, the complexion or height of a man, or any other advantage, will be a reason for his obtaining a greater share of political rights. The error here lies upon the surface, and may be illustrated from the other arts and sciences. When a number of flute-players are equal in their art, there is no reason why those of them who are better born should have better flutes given to them; for they will not play any better on the flute, and the superior instrument should be reserved for him who is the superior artist. If what I am saying is still obscure, it will be made clearer as 1283ᵃ we proceed. For if there were a superior flute-player who was far inferior in birth and beauty, although either of these may be a greater good than the art of flute-playing and may excel flute-playing in a greater ratio than he excels the others in his art, still he ought to have the best flutes given to him, unless the advantages of wealth and birth contribute to excellence in flute-playing, which they do not. Moreover, upon this principle any good may be compared with any other. For if a given height may be measured against wealth and against freedom, height in general may be so measured. Thus if A excels in height more than B in excellence, even if excellence in general excels height still more, all goods will be comparable; for if a certain amount is better than some other, it is clear that some other will be equal. But since no such comparison can be made, it is evident that there is good reason why in politics men do not ground their claim to office on every sort of inequality. For if some be slow, and others swift, that is no reason why the one should have little and the others much; it is in gymnastic contests that such excellence is rewarded. Whereas the rival claims of candidates for office can only be based on the possession of elements which enter into the composition of a state. And therefore the well-born, or freeborn, or rich, may with good reason claim office; for holders of offices must be freemen and tax-payers: a state can be no more composed entirely of poor men than entirely of slaves. But if wealth and freedom are necessary elements, justice and valour are equally so; for without the former qualities a state cannot exist at all, without the latter not well.

BOOK VII

1323ᵃ **1.** He who would duly inquire about the best form of a state ought first to determine which is the most eligible life; while this remains uncertain the best form of the state must also be uncertain; for, in the natural order of things, those men may be expected to lead the best life who are governed in the best manner of which their circumstances admit. We ought therefore to ascertain, first of all, which is the most generally eligible life, and then whether the same life is or is not best for the state and for individuals.

Assuming that enough has been already said in discussions outside the school concerning the best life, we will now only repeat what is contained in them. Certainly no one will dispute the propriety of that partition of goods which separates them into three classes, viz. external goods, goods of the body, and goods of the soul, or deny that the happy man must have all three. For no one would maintain that he is happy who has not in him a particle of courage or temperance or justice or practical wisdom, who is afraid of every insect which flutters past him, and will commit any crime, however great, in order to gratify his lust for meat or drink, who will sacrifice his dearest friend for the sake of half a farthing, and is as feeble and false in mind as a child or a madman. These propositions are almost universally acknowledged as soon as they are uttered, but men differ about the degree or relative superiority of this or that good. Some think that a very moderate amount of excellence is enough, but set no limit to their desires for wealth, property, power, reputation, and the 1323ᵇ like. To them we shall reply by an appeal to facts, which easily prove that mankind does not acquire or preserve the excellences by the help of external goods, but external goods by the help of the excellences, and that happiness, whether consisting in pleasure or excellence, or both, is more often found

with those who are most highly cultivated in their mind and in their character, and have only a moderate share of external goods, than among those who possess external goods to a useless extent but are deficient in higher qualities; and this is not only a matter of experience, but, if reflected upon, will easily appear to be in accordance with reason. For, whereas external goods have a limit, like any other instrument, and all things useful are useful for a purpose, and where there is too much of them they must either do harm, or at any rate be of no use, to their possessors, every good of the soul, the greater it is, is also of greater use, if the epithet useful as well as noble is appropriate to such subjects. No proof is required to show that the best state of one thing in relation to another corresponds in degree of excellence to the interval between the natures of which we say that these very states are states: so that, if the soul is more noble than our possessions or our bodies, both absolutely and in relation to us, it must be admitted that the best state of either has a similar ratio to the other. Again, it is for the sake of the soul that goods external and goods of the body are desirable at all, and all wise men ought to choose them for the sake of the soul, and not the soul for the sake of them.

Let us acknowledge then that each one has just so much of happiness as he has of excellence and wisdom, and of excellent and wise action. The gods are a witness to us of this truth, for they are happy and blessed, not by reason of any external good, but in themselves and by reason of their own nature. And herein of necessity lies the difference between good fortune and happiness; for external goods come of themselves, and chance is the author of them, but no one is just or temperate by or through chance. In like manner, and by a similar train of argument, the happy state may be shown to be that which is best and which acts rightly; and it cannot act rightly without doing right actions, and neither individual nor state can do right actions without excellence and wisdom. Thus the courage, justice, and wisdom of a state have the same form and nature as the qualities which give the individual who possesses them the name of just, wise or temperate.

This much may suffice by way of preface: for I could not avoid touching upon these questions, neither could I go through all the arguments affecting them; these are the business of another science.

Let us assume then that the best life, both for individuals and states, is the life of excellence, when 1324ᵃ excellence has external goods enough for the performance of good actions. If there are any who dispute our assertion, we will in this treatise pass them over, and consider their objections hereafter.

2. There remains to be discussed the question, whether the happiness of the individual is the same as that of the state, or different. Here again there can be no doubt—no one denies that they are the same. For those who hold that the well-being of the individual consists in his wealth, also think that riches make the happiness of the whole state, and those who value most highly the life of a tyrant deem that city the happiest which rules over the greatest number; while they who approve an individual for his excellence say that the more excellent a city is, the happier it is. Two points here present themselves for consideration: first, which is the more desirable life, that of a citizen who is a member of a state, or that of an alien who has no political ties; and again, which is the best form of constitution or the best condition of a state, either on the supposition that political privileges are desirable for all, or for a majority only? Since the good of the state and not of the individual is the proper subject of political thought and speculation, and we are engaged in a political discussion, while the first of these two points has a secondary interest for us, the latter will be the main subject of our inquiry.

Now it is evident that that form of government is best in which every man, whoever he is, can act best and live happily. But even those who agree in thinking that the life of excellence is the most desirable raise a question, whether the life of business and politics is or is not more desirable than one which is wholly independent of external goods, I mean than a contemplative life, which by some is maintained to be the only one worthy of a philosopher. For these two lives—the life of the philosopher and the life of the statesman—appear to have been preferred by those who have been most keen in the pursuit of excellence, both in our own and in other ages. Which is the better is a question of no small moment; for the wise man, like the wise state, will necessarily regulate his life according to the best end. There are some who think that while a despotic rule over others is the greatest injustice, to exercise a constitutional rule over them, even though not unjust, is a great impediment to a man's individual well-being. Others take an opposite view; they maintain that the true life of man is the practical and political, and that every excellence admits of being practised, quite

as much by statesmen and rulers as by private individuals. Others, again, are of the opinion that arbitrary and tyrannical rule alone makes for happiness; indeed, in some states the entire aim both of the laws and of the constitution is to give men despotic power over their neighbours. And, therefore, although in most cities the laws may be said generally to be in a chaotic state, still, if they aim at anything, they aim at the maintenance of power: thus in Lacedaemon and Crete the system of education and the greater part of the laws are framed with a view to war. And in all nations which are able to gratify their ambition military power is held in esteem, for example among the Scythians and Persians and Thracians and Celts. In some nations there are even laws tending to stimulate the warlike virtues, as at Carthage, where we are told that men obtain the honour of wearing as many armlets as they have served campaigns. There was once a law in Macedonia that he who had not killed an enemy should wear a halter, and among the Scythians no one who had not slain his man was allowed to drink out of the cup which was handed round at a certain feast. Among the Iberians, a warlike nation, the number of enemies whom a man has slain is indicated by the number of obelisks which are fixed in the earth round his tomb; and there are numerous practices among other nations of a like kind, some of them established by law and others by custom. Yet to a reflecting mind it must appear very strange that the statesman should be always considering how he can dominate and tyrannize over others, whether they are willing or not. How can that which is not even lawful be the business of the statesman or the legislator? Unlawful it certainly is to rule without regard to justice, for there may be might where there is no right. The other arts and sciences offer no parallel; a physician is not expected to persuade or coerce his patients, nor a pilot the passengers in his ship. Yet most men appear to think that the art of despotic government is statesmanship, and what men affirm to be unjust and inexpedient in their own case they are not ashamed of practising towards others; they demand just rule for themselves, but where other men are concerned they care nothing about it. Such behaviour is irrational; unless the one party is, and the other is not, born to serve, in which case men have a right to command, not indeed all their fellows, but only those who are intended to be subjects; just as we ought not to hunt men, whether for food or sacrifice, but only those animals which may be hunted for food or sacrifice, that is to say, such wild animals as are eatable. And surely there may 1325ᵃ be a city happy in isolation, which we will assume to be well-governed (for it is quite possible that a city thus isolated might be well-administered and have good laws); but such a city would not be constituted with any view to war or the conquest of enemies—all that sort of thing must be excluded. Hence we see very plainly that warlike pursuits, although generally to be deemed honourable, are not the supreme end of all things, but only means. And the good lawgiver should inquire how states and races of men and communities may participate in a good life, and in the happiness which is attainable by them. His enactments will not be always the same; and where there are neighbours he will have to see what sort of studies should be practised in relation to their several characters, or how the measures appropriate in relation to each are to be adopted. The end at which the best form of government should aim may be properly made a matter of future consideration.

3. Let us now address those who, while they agree that the life of excellence is the most desirable, differ about the manner of practising it. For some renounce political power, and think that the life of the freeman is different from the life of the statesman and the best of all; but others think the life of the statesman best. The argument of the latter is that he who does nothing cannot do well, and that acting well is identical with happiness. To both we say: 'you are partly right and partly wrong.' The first class are right in affirming that the life of the freeman is better than the life of the despot; for there is nothing noble in having the use of a slave, in so far as he is a slave; or in issuing commands about necessary things. But it is an error to suppose that every sort of rule is despotic like that of a master over slaves, for there is as great a difference between rule over freemen and rule over slaves as there is between slavery by nature and freedom by nature, about which I have said enough at the commencement of this treatise. And it is equally a mistake to place inactivity above action, for happiness is activity, and the actions of the just and wise are the realization of much that is noble.

But perhaps someone, accepting these premises, may still maintain that supreme power is the best of all things, because the possessors of it are able to perform the greatest number of noble actions. If so, the man who is able to rule, instead of giving up

anything to his neighbour, ought rather to take away his power; and the father should care nothing for his son, nor the son for his father, nor friend for friend; they should not bestow a thought on one another in comparison with this higher object, for the best is the most desirable and 'acting well' is the best. There might be some truth in such a view if we assume that robbers and plunderers attain the chief good. But this can never be; their hypothesis is false. For the actions of a ruler cannot really be honourable, unless he is as much superior to other men as a man 1325ᵇ is to a woman, or a father to his children, or a master to his slaves. And therefore he who violates the law can never recover by any success, however great, what he has already lost in departing from excellence. For equals the honourable and the just consist in sharing alike, as is just and equal. But that the unequal should be given to equals, and the unlike to those who are like, is contrary to nature, and nothing which is contrary to nature is good. If, therefore, there is anyone superior in excellence and in the power of performing the best actions, he is the man we ought to follow and obey, but he must have the capacity for action as well as excellence.

If we are right in our view, and happiness is assumed to be acting well, the active life will be the best, both for every city collectively, and for individuals. Not that a life of action must necessarily have relation to others, as some persons think, nor are those ideas only to be regarded as practical which are pursued for the sake of practical results, but much more the thoughts and contemplations which are independent and complete in themselves; since acting well, and therefore a certain kind of action, is an end, and even in the case of external actions the directing mind is most truly said to act. Neither, again, is it necessary that states which are cut off from others and choose to live alone should be inactive; for activity, as well as other things, may take place by sections; there are many ways in which the sections of a state act upon one another. The same thing is equally true of every individual. If this were otherwise, the gods and the universe, who have no external actions over and above their own energies, would be far enough from perfection. Hence it is evident that the same life is best for each individual, and for states and for mankind collectively.

13. Returning to the constitution itself, let us seek 1331ᵇ to determine out of what and what sort of elements the state which is to be happy and well-governed should be composed. There are two things in which

all well-being consists: one of them is the choice of a right end and aim of action, and the other the discovery of the actions which contribute towards it; for the means and the end may agree or disagree. Sometimes the right end is set before men, but in practice they fail to attain it; in other cases they are successful in all the contributory factors, but they propose to themselves a bad end; and sometimes they fail in both. Take, for example, the art of medicine; physicians do not always understand the nature of health, and also the means which they use may not effect the desired end. In all arts and sciences both the end and the means should be equally within our control.

The happiness and well-being which all men manifestly desire, some have the power of attaining, but 1332ᵃ to others, from some accident or defect of nature, the attainment of them is not granted; for a good life requires a supply of external goods, in a less degree when men are in a good state, in a greater degree when they are in a lower state. Others again, who possess the conditions of happiness, go utterly wrong from the first in the pursuit of it. But since our object is to discover the best form of government, that, namely, under which a city will be best governed, and since the city is best governed which has the greatest opportunity of obtaining happiness, it is evident that we must clearly ascertain the nature of happiness.

We maintain, and have said in the Ethics, if the arguments there adduced are of any value, that happiness is the realization and perfect exercise of excellence, and this not conditional, but absolute. And I use the term 'conditional' to express that which is indispensable, and 'absolute' to express that which is good in itself. Take the case of just actions; just punishments and chastisements do indeed spring from a good principle, but they are good only because we cannot do without them—it would be better that neither individuals nor states should need anything of the sort—but actions which aim at honour and advantage are absolutely the best. The conditional action is only the choice of a lesser evil; whereas these are the foundation and creation of good. A good man may make the best even of poverty and disease, and the other ills of life; but he can only attain happiness under the opposite conditions (for this also has been determined in the Ethics, that the good man is he for whom, because he is excellent, the things that are absolutely good are good; it is also plain that his use of these goods must be

excellent and in the absolute sense good). This makes men fancy that external goods are the cause of happiness, yet we might as well say that a brilliant performance on the lyre was to be attributed to the instrument and not to the skill of the performer.

It follows then from what has been said that some things the legislator must find ready to his hand in a state, others he must provide. And therefore we can only say: may our state be constituted in such a manner as to be blessed with the goods of which fortune disposes (for we acknowledge her power): whereas excellence and goodness in the state are not a matter of chance but the result of knowledge and choice. A city can be excellent only when the citizens who have a share in the government are excellent, and in our state all the citizens share in the government; let us then inquire how a man becomes excellent. For even if we could suppose the citizen body to be excellent, without each of them being so, yet the latter would be better, for in the excellence of each the excellence of all is involved.

There are three things which make men good and excellent; these are nature, habit, reason. In the first place, every one must be born a man and not some 1332ᵇ other animal; so, too, he must have a certain character, both of body and soul. But some qualities there is no use in having at birth, for they are altered by habit, and there are some gifts which by nature are made to be turned by habit to good or bad. Animals lead for the most part a life of nature, although in lesser particulars some are influenced by habit as well. Man has reason, in addition, and man only. For this reason nature, habit, reason must be in harmony with one another; for they do not always agree; men do many things against habit and nature, if reason persuades them that they ought. We have already determined what natures are likely to be most easily moulded by the hands of the legislator. All else is the work of education; we learn some things by habit and some by instruction.

14. Since every political society is composed of rulers and subjects, let us consider whether the relations of one to the other should interchange or be permanent. For the education of the citizens will necessarily vary with the answer given to this question. Now, if some men excelled others in the same degree in which gods and heroes are supposed to excel mankind in general (having in the first place a great advantage even in their bodies, and secondly in their minds), so that the superiority of the governors was undisputed and patient to their subjects, it would clearly be better that once for all the one class should rule and the others serve. But since this is unattainable, and kings have no marked superiority over their subjects, such as Scylax affirms to be found among the Indians, it is obviously necessary on many grounds that all the citizens alike should take their turn of governing and being governed. Equality consists in the same treatment of similar persons, and no government can stand which is not founded upon justice. For if the government is unjust everyone in the country unites with the governed in the desire to have a revolution, and it is an impossibility that the members of the government can be so numerous as to be stronger than all their enemies put together. Yet that governors should be better than their subjects is undeniable. How all this is to be effected, and in what way they will respectively share in the government, the legislator has to consider. The subject has been already mentioned. Nature herself has provided the distinction when she made a difference between old and young within the same species, of whom she fitted the one to govern and the other to be governed. No one takes offence at being governed when he is young, nor does he think himself better than his governors, especially if he will enjoy the same privilege when he reaches the required age.

1333ª   We conclude that from one point of view governors and governed are identical, and from another different. And therefore their education must be the same and also different. For he who would learn to command well must, as men say, first of all learn to obey. As I observed in the first part of this treatise, there is one rule which is for the sake of the rulers and another rule which is for the sake of the ruled; the former is a despotic, the latter a free government. Some commands differ not in the thing commanded, but in the intention with which they are imposed. That is why many apparently menial offices are an honour to the free youth by whom they are performed; for actions do not differ as honourable or dishonourable in themselves so much as in the end and intention of them. But since we say that the excellence of the citizen and ruler is the same as that of the good man, and that the same person must first be a subject and then a ruler, the legislator has to see that they become good men, and by what means this may be accomplished, and what is the end of the perfect life.

Now the soul of man is divided into two parts, one of which has a rational principle in itself, and the other, not having a rational principle in itself, is able to obey such a principle. And we call a man in any way good because he has the excellences of these two parts. In which of them the end is more likely to be found is no matter of doubt to those who adopt our division; for in the world both of nature and of art the inferior always exists for the sake of the superior, and the superior is that which has a rational principle. This principle, too, in our ordinary way of making the division, is divided into two kinds, for there is a practical and a speculative principle. This part, then, must evidently be similarly divided. And there must be a corresponding division of actions; the actions of the naturally better part are to be preferred by those who have it in their power to attain to two out of the three or to all, for that is always to everyone the most desirable which is the highest attainable by him. The whole of life is further divided into two parts, business and leisure, war and peace, and of actions some aim at what is necessary and useful, and some at what is honourable. And the preference given to one or the other class of actions must necessarily be like the preference given to one or other part of the soul and its actions over the other; there must be war for the sake of peace, business for the sake of leisure, things useful and necessary for the sake of things honourable. All these points the statesman should keep in view when he frames his laws; he should consider the parts of the soul and their functions, and above all the better and the end; he should also remember the diversities of human lives and actions. For men must be able to engage in business and go to war, but leisure 1333ᵇ and peace are better; they must do what is necessary and indeed what is useful, but what is honourable is better. On such principles children and persons of every age which requires education should be trained. Whereas even the Greeks of the present day who are reputed to be best governed, and the legislators who gave them their constitutions, do not appear to have framed their governments with a regard to the best end, or to have given them laws and education with a view to all the excellences, but in a vulgar spirit have fallen back on those which promised to be more useful and profitable. Many modern writers have taken a similar view: they commend the Lacedaemonian constitution, and praise the legislator for making conquest and war his sole aim, a doctrine which may be refuted by argument and has long ago been refuted by facts. For most men desire empire in the hope of accumulating the goods of fortune; and on this ground Thibron and all those who have written about the Lacedaemonian constitution have praised their legislator, because the Lacedaemonians, by being trained to meet dangers, gained great power. But surely they are not a happy people now that their empire has passed away, nor was their legislator right. How ridiculous is the result, if, while they are continuing in the observance of his laws and no one interferes with them, they have lost the better part of life! These writers further err about the sort of government which the legislator should approve, for the government of freemen is nobler and implies more excellence than despotic government. Neither is a city to be deemed happy or a legislator to be praised because he trains his citizens to conquer and obtain dominion over their neighbours, for there is great harm in this. On a similar principle any citizen who could, should obviously try to obtain the power in his own state— the crime which the Lacedaemonians accuse king Pausanias of attempting, although he had such great honour already. No such principle and no law having this object is either statesmanlike or useful or right. For the same things are best both for individuals and for states, and these are the things which 1334ᵃ the legislator ought to implant in the minds of his citizens. Neither should men study war with a view to the enslavement of those who do not deserve to be enslaved; but first of all they should provide against their own enslavement, and in the second place obtain empire for the good of the governed, and not for the sake of exercising a general despotism, and in the third place they should seek to be masters only over those who deserve to be slaves. Facts, as well as arguments, prove that the legislator should direct all his military and other measures to the provision of leisure and the establishment of peace. For most of these military states are safe only while they are at war, but fall when they have acquired their empire; like unused iron they lose their edge in time of peace. And for this the legislator is to blame, he never having taught them how to lead the life of peace.

15. Since the end of individuals and of states is the same, the end of the best man and of the best constitution must also be the same; it is therefore evident that there ought to exist in both of them the excellences of leisure; for peace, as has been often repeated, is the end of war, and leisure of toil. But leisure and cultivation may be promoted not only by those excellences which are practised in leisure,

but also by some of those which are useful to business. For many necessaries of life have to be supplied before we can have leisure. Therefore a city must be temperate and brave, and able to endure: for truly, as the proverb says, 'There is no leisure for slaves,' and those who cannot face danger like men are the slaves of any invader. Courage and endurance are required for business and philosophy for leisure, temperance and justice for both, and more especially in times of peace and leisure, for war compels men to be just and temperate, whereas the enjoyment of good fortune and the leisure which comes with peace tend to make them insolent. Those then who seem to be the best-off and to be in the possession of every good, have special need of justice and temperance—for example, those (if such there be, as the poets say) who dwell in the Islands of the Blest; they above all will need philosophy and temperance and justice, and all the more the more leisure they have, living in the midst of abundance. There is no difficulty in seeing why the state that would be happy and good ought to have these excellences. If it is disgraceful in men not to be able to use the goods of life, it is peculiarly disgraceful not to be able to use them in time of leisure—to show excellent qualities in action and war, and when they have peace and leisure to be no better than slaves. That is why we should not practise excellence after the manner of the Lacedaemonians. For they, while agreeing with other men in their conception of the highest goods, differ from the rest of mankind in thinking that they are to be obtained by the practice of a single excellence. And since these goods and the enjoyment 1334ᵇ of them are greater than the enjoyment derived from the excellences . . . and that for its own sake, is evident from what has been said; we must now consider how and by what means it is to be attained.

We have already determined that nature and habit and reason are required, and, of these, the proper nature of the citizens has also been defined by us. But we have still to consider whether the training of early life is to be that of reason or habit, for these two must accord, and when in accord they will then form the best of harmonies. Reason may be mistaken and fail in attaining the highest ideal of life, and there may be a like influence of habit. Thus much is clear in the first place, that, as in all other things, birth implies an antecedent beginning, and that there are beginnings whose end is relative to a further end. Now, in men reason and mind are the end towards which nature strives, so that the birth and training in custom of the citizens ought to be ordered with a view to them. In the second place, as the soul and body are two, we see also that there are two parts of the soul, the rational and the irrational, and two corresponding states—reason and appetite. And as the body is prior in order of generation to the soul, so the irrational is prior to the rational. The proof is that anger and wishing and desire are implanted in children from their very birth, but reason and understanding are developed as they grow older. For this reason, the care of the body ought to precede that of the soul, and the training of the appetitive part should follow: none the less our care of it must be for the sake of the reason, and our care of the body for the sake of the soul.

Chapter 4

EPICURUS

Epicurus (341–271 B.C.), a Greek philosopher who was born on the isle of Samos, lived much of his life in Athens, where he founded his very successful school of philosophy, called the "Garden." He was influenced by the materialist Democritus (460–370 B.C.), who is the first philosopher known to believe that the world is made up of atoms. Epicurus added the concept of the "swerve" to atomic theory. Atoms cannot move in parallel lines, otherwise there would be no combinations or changes in bodies. So there must be infinitesimal swerves in their motion, causing collisions and combinations. Only a few fragments of Epicurus's writings are extant.

Epicurus identified good with pleasure and evil with pain. This doctrine (repeated later by Jeremy Bentham [1748–1832]) is called *hedonism* (from the Greek word for pleasure). But contrary to popular opinion, Epicurus was not what "Epicureanism" stands for today, a sensuous, profligate life style or gourmet tastes. Quite the opposite. Epicurus believed that the true life of pleasure consisted in an attitude of imperturbable emotional calm which needed only simple pleasures, a healthy diet, a prudent moral life (based on contractual agreement), and good friends. Prudence must constrain pleasure. Since only good or bad sensations (pleasures or pains) should concern us, and death is not a sensation, we should not fear death.

FOR FURTHER READING:

Long, A. A. *Hellenistic Philosophy: Stoics, Epicureans, Sceptics,* 2nd ed. (University of California Press, 1985).

Long, A. A. and D. N. Sedley, eds. *The Hellenistic Philosophers.* (Cambridge University Press, 1987).

Lucretius. *One the Nature of the Universe,* trans. R. E. Latham. (Penguin Books, 1951).

Rist, John M. *Epicurus: An Introduction.* (Cambridge University Press, 1972).

Saunders, Jason, ed. *Greek and Roman Philosophy After Aristotle.* (Macmillan, 1966).

Letter to Menoeceus

EPICURUS TO MENOECEUS

Let no one when young delay to study philosophy, nor when he is old grow weary of his study. For no one can come too early or too late to secure the health of his soul. And the man who says that the age for philosophy has either not yet come or has gone by is like the man who says that the age for happiness is not yet come to him, or has passed away. Wherefore both when young and old a man must study philosophy, that as he grows old he may be young in blessings through the grateful recollection of what has been, and that in youth he may be old as well, since he will know no fear of what is to come. We must then meditate on the things that make our happiness, seeing that when that is with us we have all, but when it is absent we do all to win it.

The things which I used unceasingly to commend to you, these do and practise, considering them to be the first principles of the good life. First of all believe that god is a being immortal and blessed, even as the common idea of a god is engraved on men's minds, and do not assign to him anything alien to his immortality or ill-suited to his blessedness: but believe about him everything that can uphold his blessedness and immortality. For gods there are, since the knowledge of them is by clear vision. But they are not such as the many believe them to be: for indeed they do not consistently represent them as they believe them to be. And the impious man is not he who denies the gods of the many, but he who attaches to the gods the beliefs of the many. For the statements of the many about the gods are not conceptions derived from sensation, but false suppositions, according to which the greatest misfortunes befall the wicked and the greatest blessings the good by the gift of the gods. For men being accustomed always to their own virtues welcome those like themselves, but regard all that is not of their nature as alien.

Become accustomed to the belief that death is nothing to us. For all good and evil consists in sensation, but death is deprivation of sensation. And therefore a right understanding that death is nothing to us makes the mortality of life enjoyable, not because it adds to it an infinite span of time, but because it takes away the craving for immortality. For there is nothing terrible in life for the man who has truly comprehended that there is nothing terrible in not living. So that the man speaks but idly who says that he fears death not because it will be painful when it comes, but because it is painful in anticipation. For that which gives no trouble when it comes, is but an empty pain in anticipation. So death, the most terrifying of ills, is nothing to us, since so long as we exist, death is not with us; but when death comes, then we do not exist. It does not then concern either the living or the dead, since for the former it is not, and the latter are no more.

But the many at one moment shun death as the greatest of evils, at another yearn for it as a respite from the evils in life. But the wise man neither seeks to escape life nor fears the cessation of life, for neither does life offend him nor does the absence of life seem to be any evil. And just as with food he does not seek simply the larger share and nothing else, but rather the most pleasant, so he seeks to enjoy not the longest period of time, but the most pleasant.

And he who counsels the young man to live well, but the old man to make a good end, is foolish, not merely because of the desirability of life, but also because it is the same training which teaches to live well and to die well. Yet much worse still is the man who says it is good not to be born, but

"once born make haste to pass the gates of
    Death." [*Theognis, 427*]

For if he says this from conviction why does he not pass away out of life? For it is open to him to do so, if he had firmly made up his mind to this. But if he speaks in jest, his words are idle among men who cannot receive them.

We must then bear in mind that the future is neither ours, nor yet wholly not ours, so that we may not altogether expect it as sure to come, nor abandon hope of it, as if it will certainly not come.

Reprinted from *The Extant Remains,* translated by Cyril Bailey (1926) by permission of Oxford University Press.

We must consider that of desires some are natural, others vain, and of the natural some are necessary and others merely natural; and of the necessary some are necessary for happiness, others for the repose of the body, and others for very life. The right understanding of these facts enables us to refer all choice and avoidance to the health of the body and the soul's freedom from disturbance, since this is the aim of the life of blessedness. For it is to obtain this end that we always act, namely, to avoid pain and fear. And when this is once secured for us, all the tempest of the soul is dispersed, since the living creature has not to wander as though in search of something that is missing, and to look for some other thing by which he can fulfil the good of the soul and the good of the body. For it is then that we have need of pleasure, when we feel pain owing to the absence of pleasure; but when we do not feel pain, we no longer need pleasure. And for this cause we call pleasure the beginning and end of the blessed life. For we recognize pleasure as the first good innate in us, and from pleasure we begin every act of choice and avoidance, and to pleasure we return again, using the feeling as the standard by which we judge every good.

And since pleasure is the first good and natural to us, for this very reason we do not choose every pleasure, but sometimes we pass over many pleasures, when greater discomfort accrues to us as the result of them: and similarly we think many pains better than pleasures, since a greater pleasure comes to us when we have endured pains for a long time. Every pleasure then because of its natural kinship to us is good, yet not every pleasure is to be chosen: even as every pain also is an evil, yet not all are always of a nature to be avoided. Yet by a scale of comparison and by the consideration of advantages and disadvantages we must form our judgement on all these matters. For the good on certain occasions we treat as bad, and conversely the bad as good.

And again independence of desire we think a great good—not that we may at all times enjoy but a few things, but that, if we do not possess many, we may enjoy the few in the genuine persuasion that those have the sweetest pleasure in luxury who least need it, and that all that is natural is easy to be obtained, but that which is superfluous is hard. And so plain savours bring us a pleasure equal to a luxurious diet, when all the pain due to want is removed; and bread and water produce the highest pleasure, when one who needs them puts them to his lips. To grow ac-customed therefore to simple and not luxurious diet gives us health to the full, and makes a man alert for the needful employments of life, and when after long intervals we approach luxuries, disposes us better towards them, and fits us to be fearless of fortune.

When, therefore, we maintain that pleasure is the end, we do not mean the pleasures of profligates and those that consist in sensuality, as is supposed by some who are either ignorant or disagree with us or do not understand, but freedom from pain in the body and from trouble in the mind. For it is not continuous drinkings and revellings, nor the satisfaction of lusts, nor the enjoyment of fish and other luxuries of the wealthy table, which produce a pleasant life, but sober reasoning, searching out the motives for all choice and avoidance, and banishing mere opinions, to which are due the greatest disturbance of the spirit.

Of all this the beginning and the greatest good is prudence. Wherefore prudence is a more precious thing even than philosophy: for from prudence are sprung all the other virtues, and it teaches us that it is not possible to live pleasantly without living prudently and honourably and justly, nor, again, to live a life of prudence, honour, and justice without living pleasantly. For the virtues are by nature bound up with the pleasant life, and the pleasant life is inseparable from them. For indeed who, think you, is a better man than he who holds reverent opinions concerning the gods, and is at all times free from fear of death, and has reasoned out the end ordained by nature? He understands that the limit of good things is easy to fulfil and easy to attain, whereas the course of ills is either short in time or slight in pain: he laughs at destiny, whom some have introduced as the mistress of all things. He thinks that with us lies the chief power in determining events, some of which happen by necessity and some by chance, and some are within our control; for while necessity cannot be called to account, he sees that chance is inconstant, but that which is in our control is subject to no master, and to it are naturally attached praise and blame. For, indeed, it were better to follow the myths about the gods than to become a slave to the destiny of the natural philosophers: for the former suggests a hope of placating the gods by worship, whereas the latter involves a necessity which knows no placation. As to chance, he does not regard it as a god as most men do (for in a god's acts there is no disorder), nor as an uncertain cause of all things: for he does not believe that good and evil are given by chance to man for the framing of a blessed life, but that opportunities for great good and great evil are afforded by it. He therefore thinks it better to be unfortunate in reasonable action than to prosper in unreason. For it is better in a man's actions that what is well chosen should fail, rather than that what is ill chosen should

be successful owing to chance.

Meditate therefore on these things and things akin to them night and day by yourself, and with a companion like to yourself, and never shall you be disturbed waking or asleep, but you shall live like a god among men. For a man who lives among immortal blessings is not like to a mortal being.

Principal Doctrines

I. The blessed and immortal nature knows no trouble itself nor causes trouble to any other, so that it is never constrained by anger or favour. For all such things exist only in the weak.

II. Death is nothing to us: for that which is dissolved is without sensation; and that which lacks sensation is nothing to us.

III. The limit of quantity in pleasures is the removal of all that is painful. Wherever pleasure is present, as long as it is there, there is neither pain of body nor of mind, nor of both at once.

IV. Pain does not last continuously in the flesh, but the acutest pain is there for a very short time, and even that which just exceeds the pleasure in the flesh does not continue for many days at once. But chronic illnesses permit a predominance of pleasure over pain in the flesh.

V. It is not possible to live pleasantly without living prudently and honourably and justly, nor again to live a life of prudence, honour, and justice without living pleasantly. And the man who does not possess the pleasant life, is not living prudently and honourably and justly, and the man who does not possess the virtuous life, cannot possibly live pleasantly.

VI. To secure protection from men anything is a natural good, by which you may be able to attain this end.

VII. Some men wished to become famous and conspicuous, thinking that they would thus win for themselves safety from other men. Wherefore if the life of such men is safe, they have obtained the good which nature craves; but if it is not safe, they do not

possess that for which they strove at first by the instinct of nature.

VIII. No pleasure is a bad thing in itself: but the means which produce some pleasures bring with them disturbances many times greater than the pleasures.

IX. If every pleasure could be intensified so that it lasted and influenced the whole organism or the most essential parts of our nature, pleasures would never differ from one another.

X. If the things that produce the pleasures of profligates could dispel the fears of the mind about the phenomena of the sky and death and its pains, and also teach the limits of desires and of pains, we should never have cause to blame them: for they would be filling themselves full with pleasures from every source and never have pain of body or mind, which is the evil of life.

XI. If we were not troubled by our suspicions of the phenomena of the sky and about death, fearing that it concerns us, and also by our failure to grasp the limits of pains and desires, we should have no need of natural science.

XII. A man cannot dispel his fear about the most important matters if he does not know what is the nature of the universe but suspects the truth of some mythical story. So that without natural science it is not possible to attain our pleasures unalloyed.

XIII. There is no profit in securing protection in relation to men, if things above and things beneath the earth and indeed all in the boundless universe remain matters of suspicion.

XIV. The most unalloyed source of protection from men, which is secured to some extent by a cer-

Reprinted from *The Extant Remains*, translated by Cyril Bailey (1926) by permission of Oxford University Press.

tain force of expulsion, is in fact the immunity which results from a quiet life and the retirement from the world.

XV. The wealth demanded by nature is both limited and easily procured; that demanded by idle imaginings stretches on to infinity.

XVI. In but few things chance hinders a wise man, but the greatest and most important matters reason has ordained and throughout the whole period of life does and will ordain.

XVII. The just man is most free from trouble, the unjust most full of trouble.

XVIII. The pleasure in the flesh is not increased, when once the pain due to want is removed, but is only varied: and the limit as regards pleasure in the mind is begotten by the reasoned understanding of these very pleasures and of the emotions akin to them, which used to cause the greatest fear to the mind.

XIX. Infinite time contains no greater pleasure than limited time, if one measures by reason the limits of pleasure.

XX. The flesh perceives the limits of pleasure as unlimited and unlimited time is required to supply it. But the mind, having attained a reasoned understanding of the ultimate good of the flesh and its limits and having dissipated the fears concerning the time to come, supplies us with the complete life, and we have no further need of infinite time: but neither does the mind shun pleasure, nor, when circumstances begin to bring about the departure from life, does it approach its end as though it fell short in any way of the best life.

XXI. He who has learned the limits of life knows that that which removes the pain due to want and makes the whole of life complete is easy to obtain; so that there is no need of actions which involve competition.

XXII. We must consider both the real purpose and all the evidence of direct perception, to which we always refer the conclusions of opinion; otherwise, all will be full of doubt and confusion.

XXIII. If you fight against all sensations, you will have no standard by which to judge even those of them which you say are false.

XXIV. If you reject any single sensation and fail to distinguish between the conclusion of opinion as to the appearance awaiting confirmation and that which is actually given by the sensation or feeling, or each intuitive apprehension of the mind, you will confound all other sensations as well with the same

groundless opinion, so that you will reject every standard of judgement. And if among the mental images created by your opinion you affirm both that which awaits confirmation and that which does not, you will not escape error, since you will have preserved the whole cause of doubt in every judgement between what is right and what is wrong.

XXV. If on each occasion instead of referring your actions to the end of nature, you turn to some other nearer standard when you are making a choice or an avoidance, your actions will not be consistent with your principles.

XXVI. Of desires, all that do not lead to a sense of pain, if they are not satisfied, are not necessary, but involve a craving which is easily dispelled, when the object is hard to procure or they seem likely to produce harm.

XXVII. Of all the things which wisdom acquires to produce the blessedness of the complete life, far the greatest is the possession of friendship.

XXVIII. The same conviction which has given us confidence that there is nothing terrible that lasts forever or even for long, has also seen the protection of friendship most fully completed in the limited evils of this life.

XXIX. Among desires some are natural and necessary, some natural but not necessary, and others neither natural nor necessary, but due to idle imagination.

XXX. Wherever in the case of desires which are physical, but do not lead to a sense of pain, if they are not fulfilled, the effort is intense, such pleasures are due to idle imagination, and it is not owing to their own nature that they fail to be dispelled, but owing to the empty imaginings of the man.

XXXI. The justice which arises from nature is a pledge of mutual advantage to restrain men from harming one another and save them from being harmed.

XXXII. For all living things which have not been able to make compacts not to harm one another or be harmed, nothing ever is either just or unjust; and likewise too for all tribes of men which have been unable or unwilling to make compacts not to harm or be harmed.

XXXIII. Justice never is anything in itself, but in the dealings of men with one another in any place whatever and at any time it is a kind of compact not to harm or be harmed.

XXXIV. Injustice is not an evil in itself, but only in consequence of the fear which attaches to the apprehension of being unable to escape those appointed to punish such actions.

XXXV. It is not possible for one who acts in secret contravention of the terms of the compact not to harm or be harmed, to be confident that he will escape detection, even if at present he escapes a thousand times. For up to the time of death it cannot be certain that he will indeed escape.

XXXVI. In its general aspect justice is the same for all, for it is a kind of mutual advantage in the dealings of men with one another: but with reference to the individual peculiarities of a country or any other circumstances the same thing does not turn out to be just for all.

XXXVII. Among actions which are sanctioned as just by law, that which is proved on examination to be of advantage in the requirements of men's dealings with one another, has the guarantee of justice, whether it is the same for all or not. But if a man makes a law and it does not turn out to lead to advantage in men's dealings with each other, then it no longer has the essential nature of justice. And even if the advantage in the matter of justice shifts from one side to the other, but for a while accords with the general concept, it is none the less just for that period in the eyes of those who do not confound themselves with empty sounds but look to the actual facts.

XXXVIII. Where, provided the circumstances have not been altered, actions which were considered just, have been shown not to accord with the general concept in actual practice, then they are not just. But where, when circumstances have changed, the same actions which were sanctioned as just no longer lead to advantage, there they were just at the time when they were of advantage for the dealings of fellow-citizens with one another; but subsequently they are no longer just, when no longer of advantage.

XXXIX. The man who has best ordered the element of disquiet arising from external circumstances has made those things that he could akin to himself and the rest at least not alien: but with all to which he could not do even this, he has refrained from mixing, and has expelled from his life all which it was of advantage to treat thus.

XL. As many as possess the power to procure complete immunity from their neighbours, these also live most pleasantly with one another, since they have the most certain pledge of security, and after they have enjoyed the fullest intimacy, they do not lament the previous departure of a dead friend, as though he were to be pitied.

Chapter 5

EPICTETUS

Epictetus (c. 50–c. 130), born a Greek slave in Asia Minor, was freed sometime after the death of Nero, in 68. He along with all the philosophers was expelled from Rome by the Emperor Domitian in 90 and died in northern Greece about 130. He was known as a kindly man, humble and charitable, especially to children. He was crippled in slavery, which may have influenced his motto: "Bear and forbear." He embraced Stoicism and taught that we should submit to our fate as God's sacred gift and design. Epictetus did not publish anything, but his pupil Flavius Arrianus recorded his teachings, the most famous of which is the *Encheirideon* (a handbook).

Stoicism was a Greek school of philosophy founded in ca. 300 B.C. in Athens by Zeno of Citium and developed into the dominant philosophy of the Roman Empire. The word *stoa* from which "Stoic" derives is the Greek word for porch. Apparently Zeno lectured from the "painted porch," a public building in the Agora. The Stoics believed that we should resign ourselves to our fate, do our duty faithfully, and thereby acquire tranquillity of mind. The world is transient and unstable. We cannot change very much, but we can master our souls so that we attain tranquillity amidst the chaos all around us. Stoics were the first world citizens, "cosmopolitans," holding that a divine spark indwelt every human being. Chrysippus (c. 280–206 B.C.), referred to in the text, was the third leader of the Stoics and credited with over 700 treatises.

PRINCIPAL IDEAS

I. Religious Materialists: Everything was made up of matter (monists—one vs. many), including God. But there are degrees of condensation and rarefaction of matter (Aristotle's four elements). The soul in every man was a rarefied divine spark, which was manifest in reason (*logos*).

II. The Universe is a Vast Animal whose soul is God, a divine fire, the Universal *Logos*. We are mini-animals whose soul is a mini-god, possessing as it does sparks of the divine fire. Universe is a spherical plenum held together by tension, the more tension the more value. Accordingly, the world consists of four kinds of beings:

1. Least tension—mere material objects, rocks and sand
2. A little more tension—plants
3. Moderate tension (souls)—animals
4. High tension (mini-cosmos)—man (rational animals)

III. Universalism: The Stoics were the first cosmopolitans, believing that all men were brothers under one Father, God.

In the things are true which are said by the philosophers about the kinship between God and man, what else remains for men to do than what Socrates did Never in reply to the question, to what country you belong, say that you are an Athenian or a Corinthian, but that you are a citizen of the world. . . . He then who has observed with intelligence the administration of the world, and has learned that the greatest and supreme and the most comprehensive community is that which is composed of men and God, and that from God have descended the seeds not only to my father and grandfather, but to all beings which are generated on the earth and are produced, and particularly to rational beings—for these only are by their nature formed to have communion with God, being by means of reason conjoined with him—why should not such a man call himself a citizen of the world, why not a son of God, and why should he be afraid of anything which happens among men? Is kinship with Caesar or with any other of the powerful in Rome sufficient to enable us to live in safety, and above contempt and without any fear at all? and to have God for your maker and father and guardian, shall not this release us from sorrows and fears? (Epictetus, *Discourses* Bk I, 9)

IV. Virtuous Character. Like Aristotle the Stoics placed primary emphasis on moral character. They found Socrates, Zeno, and Diogenes prime examples of moral virtue. One of the most famous Stoics was the Roman Emperor Marcus Aurelius (121–180) who said, "Be like the headland, on which the billows dash themselves continually; but it stands fast, till about its base the boiling breakers are lulled to rest." The following is his *Dedication to Duty:*

Hour by hour resolve to do the task of the hour carefully, with unaffected dignity, affectionately, freely and justly. You can avoid distractions that might interfere with such performance if every act is done as though it were the last act of your life. Free yourself from random aims and curb any tendency to let the passions of emotion, hypocrisy, self-love and dissatisfaction with your allotted share cause you to ignore the commands of reason.

V. Attitude to Death and Suicide. Death is not to be feared but the idea is to be used to concentrate the mind, transforming our lives. Live every day as though it were your last. (Seneca A.D.[RC] 3–65):

Life has carried some men with the greatest rapidity to the harbor, the harbor they were bound to reach if they tarried on the way, while others it has fretted and harassed. To such a life, as you are aware, one should not always cling. *For mere living is not a good, but living well.* Accordingly, the wise man will live as long as he ought, not as long as he can. He will mark in what place, with whom, and how he is to conduct his existence, and what he is about to do. He always reflects concerning the quality, and not the quantity of his life. As soon as there are many events in his life that give him trouble and disturb his peace of mind, he sets himself free. And this privilege is his, not only when the crisis is upon him, but as soon as Fortune seems to be playing him false; then he looks about carefully and sees whether he ought, or ought not, to end his life on that account. . . . He does not regard death with fear, as if it were a great loss; for no man can lose very much when but a driblet remains. It is not a question of dying earlier or later, but of dying well or ill. And dying well means escape from the danger of living ill.

The wise person will accept the inevitability of all good things coming to an end, including life, and treating life as a glorious banquet: having enjoyed to the full but now coming to a close, he or she retires gracefully, grateful for all the good things experienced. Death becomes a way of saying thank you to life. As Epictetus said, "If the room is smoky, if only moderately, I will stay; if there is too much smoke, I will go. Remember this, keep firm hold on it, the door is always open."

FOR FURTHER READING

Inwood, Brad. *Ethics and Human Action in Early Stoicism.* (Clarendon Press, 1985).

Long, A. A. and D. N. Sedley, eds. *The Hellenistic Philosophers.* (Cambridge University Press, 1987).

Long, A. A. *The Hellenistic Philosophy: Stoics, Epicureans, Sceptics,* 2nd ed. (University of California Press, 1985).

Marcus Aurelius. *The Meditations,* trans. G. M. A. Grube. (Hackett Publishing Co., 1985).

Rist, John M., ed. *The Stoics.* (University of California Press, 1978).

Sandbach, F. H. *The Stoics.* (W. W. Norton, 1975).

Encheiridion

1. Some things are up to us, some are not up to us. Up to us are perception, intention, desire, aversion, and in sum, whatever are our own doings; not up to us are body, property, reputation, political office and in sum, whatever are not our own doings. And the things that are up to us are naturally free, unforbidding, unimpeding, while those not up to us are weak, slavish, forbidding, alien. Remember, then, that if you think naturally slavish things are free and that alien things are your own, you will be impeded, grieved, troubled, you will blame gods and men; but if you think that what is yours is yours and what is alien is alien, as it really is, nobody will ever compel you, nobody will forbid you, you will not blame anyone, you will not complain about anything, you will not do a single thing unwillingly, you will have no enemy, no one will hurt you; for you will not suffer anything harmful.

If you are aiming for such great things, remember that you must not be moderate in exerting yourself to attain them: you must avoid some things altogether and postpone others for the time being. For if you want both to accomplish these aims, and also to achieve eminence and riches, it may come about

that you will not get the latter because you were trying for the former, and certainly you will not get the former, which are the only things that produce freedom and wellbeing.

So take rigorous care to say to every menacing impression, "You are just an impression, not the real thing at all." Then test it and consider it according to your rules—first and foremost this: whether it belongs among the things that are up to us or to those not up to us. And if it is something not up to us, be ready to say "It is nothing to me."

2. Remember that the aim of desire is to get what arouses the desire, the aim of aversion is to avoid that to which you are averse; and he who fails to get what he desires is miserable, and so is he who gets what he is averse to. So then, if you are averse only to things contrary to nature that are up to you, you will not get anything to which you are averse; but if you are averse to sickness or death or poverty, you will be miserable. So take your aversion away from everything that is not up to you and transfer it to things contrary to nature that are up to you. But for the time being, destroy desire altogether; for if you desire something not up to you, necessarily you will be unfortunate; as for things that are up to us, and would be good to desire, none of them is yet within your grasp. But only make use of selection and rejection, and these lightly, discreetly, and tentatively.

3. As for every thing that delights your mind or is useful or beloved, remember to describe it as it really is, starting with the smallest thing. If you are fond of a pot, say "It is a pot that I am fond of." For then, if it breaks, you will not be upset. If you kiss your child or your wife, say that you are kissing a human being. Then if they die you will not be upset.

4. Whenever you are about to undertake some activity, remind yourself what kind of activity it is. If you are going out to bathe, picture to yourself what goes on in baths—the splashers, the elbow-jabbers, the foul-mouths, the thieves. You will undertake the activity with more security, if you declare right away "I want to bathe *and* to keep my own will in accord with nature." And so with every activity. Thus, if anything gets in the way of your bathing, you will be ready to say: "But I did not want this only, but also to keep my will in accord with nature; I will not keep it, if I am upset by what happens."

5. It is not things that upset people but rather ideas about things. For example, death is nothing terrible, else it would have seemed so even to Socrates; rather it is the idea that death is terrible that is terrible. So whenever we are frustrated or upset or grieved, let us not blame others, but ourselves—that is, our ideas. It is the act of a philosophically ignorant person to blame others for his own troubles. One who is beginning to learn blames himself. An educated person blames neither anyone else nor himself.

6. Do not pride yourself on superiority that is not your own. If a horse in its pride should say, "I am a fine horse," that could be tolerated. You however, when you boast "I have a fine horse," should realize that you are boasting about the excellence of a horse. What then is your own? The use of impressions. So, make use of your impressions in accord with nature, and then take pride; for your pride will be in a good thing that is your own.

7. When on a voyage the ship is anchored, you may go ashore to get fresh water, and on the way you may pick up a few shells and salad greens, but you have to keep your mind on the ship and continually turn around to look back and see whether the captain is summoning you; and if he summons, you must drop everything, or they will tie you up and dump you on board like a sheep. In life it is the

same: if, instead of a shell or a radish, you are given a wife or a child, fine; but if the captain summons, get back on board, leave them behind, don't turn around. If you are old, never go very far from the ship, or you may miss the summons.

8. Don't seek for things to happen as you wish, but wish for things to happen as they do, and you will get on well.

9. Illness is an impediment of the body, but not of the will, as long as the will itself does not so wish. Lameness is an impediment of the leg, not of the will. And say this to yourself of every accident that befalls you; for you will find it an impediment to something else, not to yourself.

10. Whatever occasion befalls you, remember to turn around and look into yourself to see what power you have to make use of it. If you see a handsome boy or a beautiful girl, you will find the relevant power to be self-control. If labor is heaped on you, endurance is what you need; if abuse, forbearance. And thus habituating yourself, you will not be carried away by impressions.

11. Never say about anything that you have "lost it," but that you have "given it back." Your child has died? It has been given back. Your wife has died? She has been given back. "I have been deprived of my estate." This too has been given back. "But the usurper is wicked." What concern is it of yours, through whom the gift was returned to the giver? For the time it is given to you, treat it as someone else's, as travellers do an inn.

12. If you want to make progress, shun these sorts of reasonings: "If I neglect my affairs, I shall have nothing to live on;" "if I don't punish my slave, he will be good for nothing." For it is better to attain freedom from sorrow and fear and then die of hunger than to live lavishly in vexation. It is better for your slave to be bad than for you to be unhappy. Begin with little things. A little oil has been spilled, a little wine has been swiped; say to yourself, "This is the price of peace, that of serenity." Nothing is gratis. When you call for your slave, consider that maybe he won't hear you, and even if he does he still won't do what you want him to do. But he is not so well off that your tranquillity should depend on him.

13. If you want to make progress, be content to appear stupid and foolish about externals, and don't wish to seem to know anything. And whenever you seem to be somebody to someone, distrust yourself. For be aware that it is not easy both to have your will in accordance with nature and to be on your guard about externals also, if you are to take care of the one it is absolutely necessary to neglect the other.

14. If you want your children and your wife and friends to live forever, you are a fool; for you want what is not up to you to be up to you, and what is not yours to be yours. Thus also if you want your slave not to do anything wrong, you are stupid; for you want badness not to be badness but something else. But if what you want is not to fail in getting what you desire, that you can bring about. So practise what you are capable of. Every person's master is the one who controls whether that person shall get what he wants and avoid what he doesn't want. Thus whoever wishes to be free should neither seek nor avoid anything that is up to others; otherwise he will necessarily be a slave.

15. Remember that you ought to conduct yourself as you do at a banquet. When something passed around reaches you, extend your hand and take it politely. If it is passing you by, don't grab. If it has not yet reached you, don't crave for it, but wait until it gets to you. Thus toward children, thus toward women, thus toward jobs, thus toward riches; and in due time you will be worthy to dine with the gods. But if you do not take even the things set out for you, but despise them, then not only will you be a banquet companion of the gods, you will even be a co-ruler. By thus acting, Diogenes and Heraclitus and like men came to be called divine, and deservedly.

16. Whenever you see someone weeping in grief because his child is going away or he has lost his property, be careful not to be misled by the impression that he is in a bad way because of external things, but be ready to say at once "It is not the circumstances that distress him (for someone else would not be distressed), but the idea he has about them." Don't, of course, hesitate to condole with him in words, and, if there is occasion, even to groan with him; but take care not to groan inwardly.

17. Remember that you are an actor in a drama such as the playwright wishes it to be. If he wants it short, it will be short; if long, long. If he wants you to play a beggar, play even that capably; or a lame man, or a ruler, or a private person. For this is yours, to play the assigned role well. Casting is the business of another.

18. If a raven croaks unsuspiciously, do not let the impression carry you away, but straightway draw a distinction and say: "This prophesies nothing for me, but either for my miserable body or my wretched property or my dubious reputation or my children or wife. But for *me* everything prophesies auspiciously, if I want it to; for, no matter what comes of this, it will be up to me to benefit from it."

19. You can be unbeatable if you never enter a contest in which it is not up to you who wins. Beware lest ever, seeing someone else preferred in honor or having great power or otherwise esteemed, you get carried away by impressions and deem him blessed. For since the essence of the good lies in the things up to us, neither jealousy nor envy has a place; and you yourself will not wish to be a praetor[1] or a senator or a consul, but a free man. There is but one way to this: contempt for things not up to us.

20. Remember that it is not the man who curses you or the man who hits you that insults you, but the idea you have of them as insulting. So, whenever someone irritates you, realize that it is your own opinion that has irritated you. First of all, try not to be carried away by impressions; if you succeed just once in gaining time and avoiding hastiness, you will easily control yourself.

21. Let death and exile and all dreadful appearances be before your eyes every day, and most of all, death; and you will never deem anything trivial, nor desire anything excessively.

22. If you are eager for philosophy, be prepared from the beginning to be ridiculed and sneered at by the mob, who will say things like "All of a sudden he has come back to us a philosopher!" and "Where did he get that high brow?" But don't be a highbrow; hold fast to what seems best for you, as one who has been assigned to this territory by the god. And remember this: if you stay with it, the ones who ridicule you at first will admire you afterwards; but if they get the better of you, it will be your lot to be laughed at twice.

23. If ever it happens that you turn to externals because you want to please someone, realize that you have lost your bearings. It suffices to *be* a philosopher in all things; but if you also want to *appear* to be one, appear so to yourself and that will be enough.

24. Don't let reflections like this upset you: "I shall live without honor, a complete nobody." For suppose not being honored is an evil: you cannot be subjected to evil by another, any more than to shamefulness. Is it your business to acquire power

1. Roman magistrate

or an invitation to a banquet? By no means. How then is this being without honor? How then will you be a complete nobody, when you ought to be somebody only with respect to those things that are up to you—the domain wherein it is given to you to be of the greatest worth? But your friends will get no help from you? What do you mean by help? They won't have a penny from you; nor will you make them Roman citizens. So who told you that these things are up to you, and not the business of others? Who can give to another things that he does not have himself? "Then get them," one says, "so that we can have them." If I can get them while preserving my self-respect and trustworthiness and high-mindedness, show me the way and I'll get them. But if you require me to be one who will lose my proper goods in order to produce worthless things for you,—just look, how partial and unfair you are. Which do you want more? Money, or a faithful and upright friend? Then you had better help me to acquire the characteristics of one and not require me to do the things that would ruin them.

"But my country, as far as its fate is up to me," one says, "will be helpless." Again, what kind of help do you mean? She will not get arcades or baths from you. So what? Neither does she get shoes from smiths nor weapons from shoemakers. It is enough if everyone fulfills his own task. If you make someone else into a faithful and upright citizen, have you done something for the state? "Yes." Then you yourself are not unhelpful if you are that one. "Then what status," one asks, "will I have in the city?" Whatever you are capable of, while conserving your faithfulness and uprightness. If in wishing to aid her you throw them away, what advantage will accrue to her when you have ended up shameless and faithless?

25. Has someone been honored above you at a feast or in form of address or in being invited to a conference? If these things are goods, you ought to rejoice that he succeeded in getting them; if they are evils, don't lament because you didn't get them. Remember that because you did not do the same things to succeed in getting things not up to you, you can not be considered worthy of getting an equal share. For how can one who does not hang around doorsteps be equal to one who does? One who does not march in the entourage, to one who does? One who does not praise, to one who does? So you would be unjust and immoderate if without paying the price for which these things are sold, you demanded them anyway. Well, how much does a head of lettuce sell for? An obol, maybe. Whoever lays down an obol gets his head of lettuce. You don't pay and you don't get one: don't suppose you are worse off than the buyer. For he has the lettuce, you have the obol you didn't spend.

The same thing applies here. You weren't invited to someone's banquet? You didn't pay the host the price he put on the dinner. It is sold for praise and service. So pay the charge, if it is to your advantage. But if you don't want to put it out and yet to get these things, you are greedy and stupid. So then you have nothing instead of the dinner? Oh yes, you have something: you didn't praise the fellow, which you didn't want to do; you didn't have to put up with his flunkies.

26. We can learn the will of nature by considering the matters about which we don't disagree with one another. For instance, when somebody else's miserable slave breaks a cup, you are ready right away to say "So it goes." But realize that when it is yours that gets broken, you ought to behave the same way you did when it was someone else's. Apply this to more important matters as well. Somebody else's child or wife has died; there is no one who would not say "That's life." But when his own child or wife dies, it is "Alas, woe is me!" We ought to remember what we feel when we hear the same thing about other people.

27. As a target is not set up for the purpose of being missed, so nothing in the world is intrinsically evil.

28. If someone were to hand over your body to just whomever happened along, you would be outraged. Why aren't you outraged at the fact that *you* turn over your own mind to whomever happens along—if he insults you and you let it upset and trouble you?

29. In every work examine the things that have to be done first and what is to follow, and only then get started on it. If you don't, you will go along eagerly at first, because you have given no consideration to what is coming next; later when difficulties appear the work will come to an ignoble halt. You want to win at Olympia? I do too, by the gods; for it is a fine thing. But look at what comes first, and what comes next, and then take on the work. You must keep discipline, diet, give up pastries, do the compulsory exercises at the set time in heat or in cold, never drink anything cold, take wine only with meals, completely submit yourself to your trainer as to your doctor, and then when the contest starts you have to wallow around in the mud, maybe dislocate your wrist or turn your ankle, swallow quantities of sand, perhaps sometimes be flogged,—and after all this you still lose. Taking it all into consideration, go ahead and be an athlete, if you still want to. Otherwise you will be turning from one thing to another like children, who now play wrestlers, now gladiators, now trumpeters, then tragic actors; you too would be now athlete, now gladiator, then orator, then philosopher, nothing with your whole soul; but like a monkey you mimic every sight that you see as one thing after another intrigues you. For you have never proceeded with something in accord with investigation, after looking at it from all sides; but just at random and out of frivolous enthusiasm.

Thus some people, when they have seen a philosopher and have heard someone speaking the way Euphrates speaks (but who can speak like him?), wish to philosophize themselves. Man, consider first what kind of business this is. And then learn what your own nature is; can you bear it? Do you want to be a pentathlete or a wrestler? Look at your arms, your thighs, learn about your hips. One man is naturally fitted for one thing, another for another. Do you suppose you can do these things and keep on eating and drinking and enthusing and sulking just as you do now? You will have to go without sleep, labor, leave home, be despised by a slave, have everyone laugh at you, get the worse in everything, in honors, in jobs, in lawsuits, in every trifle. Look these things over and decide whether you want to exchange them for tranquillity, freedom, and peace; if not, don't go ahead, don't be, like a child, now philosopher, afterwards tax collector, then orator, finally Caesar's procurator. These things do not go together. You ought to be one man, good or evil; you must cultivate either your own guiding principle or externals; that is, apply yourself either to the inner man or to outward things: assume either the role of philosopher or of layman.

30. What is proper for us to do is for the most part defined by our social relationships. He is your father: this means that it is for you to look after him, to defer to him in all things, to put up with his abuse and his beatings. "But he is a bad father." Did nature then assign you to a *good* father? No, just to a father. "My brother is wronging me." Then keep up your relationship toward him; don't look at what he may be doing, but at what *you* should do to keep your will in accord with nature. No other person will hurt you unless *you* will it; you will be hurt to the

extent that you think you are hurt. Thus if you will make a habit of contemplating social relationships, you will discover what it is fitting to do as a neighbor, as a citizen, as a consul.

31. Concerning piety toward the gods, know that this is the main thing: have right beliefs about them—that they exist, that they run the world well and justly; and you have been appointed to obey them and to resign yourself to whatever happens and to follow willingly because you are led by the best judgment. Thus you will never blame the gods nor accuse them of unconcern. However, this can never come about unless you withdraw yourself from things not up to us and place good and evil exclusively in the class of things up to us. Thus, if you consider anything else to be good or evil, inevitably, when you fail to get what you want and stumble into what you don't want, you will assign blame and hate those responsible. For it is natural for every creature to flee and avert itself from hurtful appearances and their causes, and on the other hand to go after and to admire the beneficial and their causes. So it is impossible for anyone who thinks he is being hurt to enjoy what he thinks is hurting him, just as enjoying harm itself is impossible. Consequently even a father is abused by his son, insofar as he does not give the child things that seem to be good; and Polyneices and Eteocles were made enemies of each other by the idea that having the tyranny would be a good thing. On this account also the farmer curses the gods, as do the sailor, the merchant, and those who have lost their wives and children. For wherever one's interest is, there also is one's piety. So, whoever concerns himself with desire and aversion as he ought, concerns himself in the same way with piety too. But libations and sacrifices and rites according to the traditions of the country are always appropriate, and they should be done with purity and not in a slovenly manner nor carelessly; neither stingily nor extravagantly.

32. When you go to a soothsayer, remember that you do not know *what* is going to happen—that is what you came to ask the seer about; but as to *how* it will be, you knew already before you arrived, since you are a philosopher. For if it is something not up to us, necessarily it will be neither good nor evil. So do not bring desire or aversion to the seer, nor approach him trembling, but recognizing that everything that will happen will be indifferent and nothing to you; whatever it may be, it will be possible to make good use of it; no one can prevent this. So approach the gods confidently, as your advisers; afterwards, when counsel has been given you, remember what counsellors you have adopted and whose advice you will be ignoring if, having heard them, you give no heed. Approach divination as Socrates thought proper: only about things where the inquiry exclusively concerns the facts of what is going to happen, and where neither reason nor any other art has resources for making the discovery. So, for example, if it is your duty to share the danger of your friend or your country, it is not right to ask a soothsayer whether you ought to share the danger. For if the diviner should tell you that the sacred omens are bad, it is clear that death or maiming of a limb of the body or exile is meant; reason chooses even so that you stand by your friend and your country, sharing the danger. Therefore give heed to the greater soothsayer, the Pythian Apollo, who expelled from his temple the man who did not come to the aid of his friend when he was being murdered.

33. Prescribe a certain character and type for yourself, and guard it both when you are by yourself and when you meet people. And be silent about most things, or chat only when necessary and about few matters. On rare occasions, when the time is ripe and you are called on to talk, talk—but not about banal topics; not about gladiators, or athletes, or horse races, or food and drink, such as you hear everywhere; and above all, not about blaming or praising or comparing people. If you can, lead the conversation around to something proper. But if you happen to be alone with strange people, be silent.

Laugh seldom and about few things and with restraint.

Totally abstain from taking oaths, if you can; if not, then refuse whenever circumstances allow.

Avoid celebrations, both public and private; but if the occasion calls you, be alert not to lapse into vulgarity. For know that if a companion is defiled, necessarily also one who keeps company with him will be defiled, even if he himself happens to be pure.

Partake of things having to do with the body only as far as bare need goes: such things as food, drink, clothing, housing, slaves. Dispense altogether with whatever has to do with reputation or luxury.

As to sex, be as pure as you can before marriage; but if you are aroused, indulge only to the extent that is customary. However, don't by any means be troublesome to those who do indulge, or censorious; and don't keep mentioning that you yourself can get along without it.

If someone tells you that somebody else is saying awful things about you, don't defend yourself against the accusations, but reply, "He must not know about the other faults that I have, if these are the only ones he mentioned."

It isn't necessary to attend shows for the most part. But if there is a proper occasion, do not appear to be more enthusiastic for anyone else than for yourself, that is, wish only that those things should happen that do happen and that only the winner should win; that way you will not be frustrated. Abstain altogether from shouting and ridiculing anyone or getting emotionally involved. And after the performance don't talk much about what happened, if it does not tend toward your improvement. For it would be evident from this that you were dazzled by the spectacle.

Don't attend authors' readings indiscriminately or eagerly; but if you are present, guard your decorum and dignity and at the same time be indulgent.

Whenever you are going to meet someone, especially one reputed to be important, consider what Socrates or Zeno would have done in the circumstances, and you will not be puzzled about how to use the occasion properly. When you are going to visit a powerful personage, propose to yourself that you will not find him at home, that you will be shut out, that the gates will be slammed in your face, that he will not notice you. And if nevertheless it is your duty to go, when you arrive bear with what happens and by no means say to yourself "It wasn't worth it." For it is unphilosophical to be troubled by externals.

In conversation avoid overmuch talk about your own deeds and dangers. For although it is pleasant for you to recall your own adventures, it may not be so for others to hear about what happened to you.

Also avoid raising laughter; for this is a slippery slope to vulgarity and at the same time sufficient to cancel the respect that others have for you. It is also dangerous to get into dirty talk. Whenever anything of this sort begins, if you get the opportunity, you might rebuke the person who starts it; or if not, make it clear by being silent or blushing and scowling that you are displeased by the talk.

34. When you receive an impression of a certain pleasure, be on your guard, just as you are with other impressions, lest you get carried away by it. Take your time with the thing, wait a while. Next call to mind both times—the time when you will enjoy the pleasure, and the time when, after enjoying it, you will change your mind and scold yourself; and set against these the thought of how, if you abstain, you will rejoice and praise yourself. But if it still seems to you to be the proper occasion to indulge, consider, lest you be overcome by the gentleness and sweetness of it and its seductiveness; set against it, how much better it will be to be conscious of yourself as having won this victory.

35. When you do something because you have recognized that it ought to be done, never go out of your way not to be seen doing it, not even if public opinion takes a different view of it. For if it isn't right for you to do, shun the deed itself; if it is right, why are you afraid of people who would be censuring you wrongly?

36. As the propositions "It is day" and "It is night" separately have truth values, but the conjunction of them has none, so also taking the bigger portion may be valid with respect to the body but invalid when the question is about what you must take care to do rightly when sharing a feast. So when you are dining with someone else, remember not only to look to which of the dishes set before you is good for your body, but also take care about what is seemly with regard to your host.

37. If you take on a role that is too much for you, you both disgrace yourself in it and neglect the one that you might have filled.

38. Just as in walking you pay attention not to step on a nail or to turn your ankle, pay attention not to hurt your ruling principle. And if we look out for this in all of our activities, we will take them on more securely.

39. For everyone the need of his body is the standard for possessions, as fitting the foot is for the shoe. So if you stop there, you will keep the measure; but if you go beyond, necessarily it will be like going over the edge of a cliff—just as in the case of shoes, if you depart from the foot standard, you will get into gilded shoes and then purple ones and on to studding with jewels; there is no limit, once you have gone beyond the measure.

40. Women, soon after they have reached the age of fourteen, are called "ladies" by men. Accordingly when they see how there is going to be nothing else for them but sleeping with men, they start in to adorn themselves and they put all their hopes in that. So it is worth thinking about: how they can be brought to sense that they are honored for no other reason than that they appear chaste and modest?

41. It is the sign of a weak mind to spend too much time on things having to do with the body, such as exercising a lot, eating a lot, drinking a lot, excreting, sex. Such things should be done incidentally; let all your attention be concentrated on your mind.

42. Whenever someone treats you badly or says bad things about you, remember that he does it or says it thinking that he is doing the right thing. Now it is not possible for him to adhere to *your* conception of the right, but only his own. Whence it follows that if he has a wrong view of things, he, being deceived, is the one who is hurt. For if someone believes that a true proposition is false, it is not the proposition that suffers but the deceived believer. If you consider these things you will deal gently with the slanderer. On each occasion just say, "So it seemed to him."

43. Every thing has two handles, one by which it may be borne, one by which it cannot be borne. If your brother has done wrong, don't grasp this by the "wrongdoing" handle—it can't be borne by that one—but by the "brother", the "brought-up-together" handle, and thereby you will be able to bear it.

44. These sorts of arguments are invalid: "I am richer than you are, therefore I am better than you"; "I am more eloquent than you are, therefore I am better than you". But these are valid: "I am richer than you are, therefore my possessions are better than yours"; "I am more eloquent than you are, therefore my speech is better than yours" *You*, however, are neither your possessions nor your speech.

45. Someone bathes hurriedly: do not say "badly," but "hurriedly." Someone drinks a lot of wine: do not say "badly," but "a lot." For before you know what idea motivated him, how do you know whether he did badly? Thus it will happen that in some cases you receive intuitively certain impressions, whereas in other cases you merely consent.[2]

46. Never refer to yourself as a philosopher or chatter much with laymen about philosophical principles, but do what the principles prescribe. For example, at a banquet do not talk about how one ought to eat, but eat as you ought. Remember that Socrates altogether eschewed ostentation. When people came to him who wanted him to introduce them to philosophers, he did so, being quite content to be over-

2. Text and translation of the last sentence are uncertain.

looked. And if an argument about some philosophical principle gets started among laymen, you should in most instances be silent; for there is great danger of straightway vomiting up what you have not digested. And if someone says to you that you know nothing, and you aren't hurt by the remark, you may then be sure that you are making a beginning at your task. Sheep brought to pasture don't show off to the shepherd how much they have eaten, but rather they digest their fodder internally and produce wool and milk on the outside. Likewise you should not show off your principles to laymen, but digest them and display the results.

47. When you have got adjusted to being frugal in supplying your body, do not brag about the fact. If you drink water, do not say every time you turn down wine that you drink only water. And if from time to time you want to train yourself to endure hardship, do it by yourself, not in front of people. Don't embrace statues;[3] but some time when you are terribly thirsty, take some cold water into your mouth and spit it out and don't tell anyone.

48. Position and character of a vulgar person: he never expects help or harm from himself, but only from outside. Position and character of a philosopher: he expects all help and harm to come from himself.

Marks of one making progress: he blames nobody, he praises nobody, he complains about nobody, he accuses nobody, he never speaks of himself as if he were anybody or knew anything. If he is impeded or frustrated he blames himself. And if someone praises him, he smiles to himself at the person giving the praise; but if he is blamed, he offers no defense. He comports himself as invalids do, taking care not to move a damaged limb before it has healed. He has purged himself of all desire; he has concentrated aversion solely on things that are against nature but up to us. He takes things as they come. If he appears stupid or ignorant, he doesn't care. In sum, he guards against himself as against an enemy lying in wait.

49. If someone brags because he understands the books of Chrysippus and can explain them, say to yourself: "If Chrysippus had not written unclearly, this fellow would have nothing to brag about."

But what is it that I want? To learn nature and to follow her. So I ask, Who is the interpreter? And hearing that it is Chrysippus, I go to him. But I do not comprehend the writings; so I ask for *their* interpreter. And so far there has been nothing to be proud of. But if I should find the interpreter, it will remain to make use of the precepts; this alone is what one might be proud of. But if I am dazzled by the interpretation itself, what else have I ended up as, than a grammarian instead of a philosopher?—except that it is Chrysippus rather than Homer who is being interpreted. Better, then, that whenever anyone says "Read Chrysippus to me," I should blush, because I can't exhibit deeds that match and accord with his words.

50. Whatever principles are set before you, follow them as laws, the dishonoring of which would be impious. But don't worry about what anyone says about you; for this is not at all up to you.

51. How much time will you take yet before you judge yourself worthy of the best, and never step over the bounds discriminated by reason? You have been apprised of the philosophical principles to which you ought to subscribe, and you have subscribed. So what sort of teacher are you still waiting for, that you put off your own reformation until he gets here? You are no longer a child, but a grown man. If now you take no care and loaf and always keep putting things off and set one day after another on which to start attending to your own affairs, you will lose yourself, making no progress but going on being a layman in life and in death. Right now, then, deem yourself worthy of living as an adult making progress. And let all that appears best to you be your inviolable law. And if some task is set for you, whether pleasant or glorious or inglorious, remember, that right now you are the contestant and here are the Olympic games, and there can't be any more delay, and that one day and one deed will determine whether progress is lost or saved. That is how Socrates became what he was: by attending in all things that he encountered to nothing other than reason. But you—even if you are not yet a Socrates, at least you ought to live as someone wishing to be like Socrates.

52. The primary and most essential topic in philosophy is that of the use of philosophical principles, for instance, not to lie. The secondary is that of proofs, for instance why one ought not to lie. Tertiary is of what gives certainty and consequence to the first two, for instance, why is this a proof? what indeed is a proof? implication? inconsistency? truth?

---

3. An allusion to Diogenes the Cynic, who in freezing weather stripped naked and threw his arms around a metal statue—in the marketplace of Athens, where people could see him.

falsity? The tertiary topic is required because of the secondary, the secondary because of the primary; but the one that is most necessary and that ought never to be neglected is the primary. But we turn them around: for we wrangle about the tertiary topics and bestow all our interest on them, while we altogether neglect the primary. And so we tell lies, and at the same time we are prepared to prove why lying is wrong.

53. On every occasion you ought to have the following ready for use:

> Lead thou me on, O Zeus, and Destiny,
> Wherever has been fixed by thy decree.
> I shall come willingly; though if I fall

> Into corruption,—no less, come I shall.
>
> —CLEANTHES

> Whoever yields with grace to what must be,
> We deem him wise: he knows divinity.
>
> —EURIPIDES

> Well, Crito, if so it pleases the gods,
>   let it be so.
>
> —SOCRATES

> Anytus and Meletus can kill me, but they cannot harm me.
>
> —SOCRATES

Chapter 6

SEXTUS EMPIRICUS

We do not know where Sextus Empiricus lived, but he did write in Greek and lived around the year 200. We know next to nothing about his life except that he was the compiler and historian of ancient Skepticism, especially the teachings of Pyrrho (360–270 B.C.) and the philosophy named after him, Pyrrhonism. Whereas the Academic Skeptics (the school originally founded by Plato) followed Socrates (who asserted that he knew only one thing—that he knew nothing) in claiming certainty about their lack of knowledge, the Pyrrhonists claimed that we could not even know that we knew nothing. For Sextus, "Skepticism is an ability to place in antithesis, in any manner whatever, appearances and judgments, and thus—because equality of force in the objects and arguments opposed—to come first of all to suspension of judgment and then to mental tranquillity."

Skeptics accept appearances, but not positive beliefs. Appearances of the way the world is are passive aspects of perceptions. One is forced, involuntarily, to see the world the way one does, but the skeptic *actively* refuses to draw conclusions from this regarding real existence. "While living undogmatically, we pay due respect to appearances."

Using a device called *tropes* (modes of balancing arguments), Skeptics called attention to the relativity and undecidability of beliefs and explanations. For every physical or nonphysical state of affairs there were innumerable possibilities for its explanation, and there is no reason to suppose that we can know which is the correct explanation. While they conceded similarities in some appearances, they doubted whether these similarities led to essential knowledge. "It appears to us that honey is sweet. This we concede, for we experience sweetness through sensation. We doubt, however, whether it is sweet by reason of its essence, which is not a question of the appearance, but of that which is asserted of the appearance." They pointed out that animals and humans perceived things differently and that among humans enormous differences existed in judgment, evaluation, taste, ability, and habits. "Different men take delight in different deeds" and "If fair and wise meant both the same to all, Dispute and strife would be no more."

Different philosophies and religions offer equally dogmatic accounts of the origin of life and the nature of reality. There is relativity of knowledge and custom, so that it is impossible to decide the truth on these matters—or any matter. This inherent undecidability leads to a state of confusion. Here the Skeptics advised withholding assent or dissent regarding any opinion. The term they coined for this suspension of judgment was *Epoche,* a state of purposefully refusing to have an opinion on metaphysical matters. It was not that they denied the gods or the soul, but they refused to assent either to their existence or nonexistence. They espoused a deliberate agnosticism. Doubt all! Maintain an inner *aphasia* (silence) on metaphysical matters! Doubt, thus characterized as the purgation or laxative of the soul, cleanses the soul of the excrescences that befoul it. Ultimately, the Skeptics thought and claimed to have reached *Ataraxia* (tranquillity or imperturbability of soul), their version of peace of mind.

FOR FURTHER READING:

Annas, Julia and Jonathan Barnes, eds. *Modes of Scepticism: Ancient Texts and Modern Interpretations*. (Cambridge University Press, 1985).

Barnes, Jonathan. *The Tolls of Scepticism.* (Cambridge University Press, 1990).

Buryeat, Myles, ed. *The Skeptical Tradition.* (University of California Press, 1983).

Frede, Michael. *Essays in Ancient Philosophy.* (University of Minnesota Press, 1987).

Long, A. A. *Hellenistic Philosophy: Stoics, Epicureans, Sceptics.* (University of California Press, 1985).

Stough, Charlotte. *Greek Skepticism: A Study in Epistemology.* (University of California Press, 1969).

Outlines of Pyrrhonism

BOOK 1 OF THREE

1. The Main Difference between the Philosophies

When people search for something, the likely outcome is that either they find it or, not finding it, they accept that it cannot be found, or they continue to search. So also in the case of what is sought in philosophy, I think, some people have claimed to have found the truth, others have asserted that it cannot be apprehended, and others are still searching. Those who think that they have found it are the Dogmatists, properly so called—for example, the followers of Aristotle and Epicurus, the Stoics, and certain others. The followers of Cleitomachus and Carneades, as well as other Academics, have asserted that it cannot be apprehended. The Skeptics continue to search. Hence it is with reason that the main types of philosophy are thought to be three in number: the Dogmatic, the Academic, and the Skeptic. Concerning the first two it will best become others to speak; but concerning the Skeptic Way we shall now give an outline account, stating in advance that as regards none of the things that we are about to say do we firmly maintain that matters are absolutely as stated, but in each instance we are simply reporting, like a chronicler, what now appears to us to be the case.

2. The Accounts of Skepticism

One account of the Skeptic philosophy is called "general"; the other, "specific". In the general account we set forth the characteristic traits of Skepticism, stating its basic idea, its origins, arguments, criterion and goal, as well as the modes of *epoche* [suspension of judgment], and how we take the Skeptic statements, and the distinction between Skepticism and the competing philosophies. In the specific account we state objections to each part of so-called "philosophy." Let us, then, first take up the general account, beginning the exposition with the various terms for the Skeptic Way.

3. The Nomenclature of the Skeptic Way

The Skeptic Way is called Zetetic ["questioning"] from its activity in questioning and inquiring, Ephectic ["suspensive"] from the *pathos* that arises concerning the subject of inquiry, Aporetic ["inclined to *aporiai*"] either, as some say, from its being puzzled and questioning about everything or from its being at a loss as to whether to assent or dissent, and Pyrrhonean because it appears to us that Pyrrho applied himself to Skepticism more vigorously and conspicuously than his predecessors did.

Reprinted from *Sextus Empiricus, Outlines of Pyrrhonism,* translated by Benson Mates (Oxford University Press, 1996) by permission.

4. What Skepticism Is

The Skeptic Way is a disposition to oppose phenomena and noumena to one another in any way whatever, with the result that, owing to the equipollence among the things and statements thus opposed, we are brought first to *epochē* and then to *ataraxia*. We do not apply the term "disposition" in any subtle sense, but simply as cognate with "to be disposed." At this point we are taking as phenomena the objects of sense perception, thus contrasting them with the noumena. The phrase "in any way whatever" can modify both the word "disposition" (so as to make us take that word in a plain sense, as we said) and the phrase "to oppose phenomena and noumena"; for since we oppose these in various ways—phenomena to phenomena, noumena to noumena, or *alternando* phenomena to noumena, we say "in any way whatever" in order to include all such oppositions. Or we can apply "in any way whatever" to "phenomena and noumena," in order that we may not have to inquire how the phenomena appear or the noumena are thought, but may take these terms in their plain senses. By "opposed" statements we simply mean inconsistent ones, not necessarily affirmative and negative. By "equipollence" we mean equality as regards credibility and the lack of it, that is, that no one of the inconsistent statements takes precedence over any other as being more credible. *Epochē* is a state of the intellect on account of which we neither deny nor affirm anything. *Ataraxia* is an untroubled and tranquil condition of the soul. In our remarks on the goal of Skepticism we shall come back to the question of how *ataraxia* enters the soul along with *epochē*.

5. The Skeptic

The definition of the Pyrrhonean philosopher is implicitly contained in that of the Skeptic Way: he is the person who has the aforementioned disposition.

6. The Origins of Skepticism

We say that the causal origin of the Skeptic Way is the hope of attaining *ataraxia*. Certain talented people, upset by anomaly in "the facts" and at a loss as to which of these "facts" deserve assent, endeavored to discover what is true in them and what is false, expecting that by settling this they would achieve *ataraxia*. But the main origin of Skepticism is the practice of opposing to each statement an equal statement; it seems to us that doing this brings an end to dogmatizing.

7. Does the Skeptic Dogmatize?

When we say that the Skeptic does not dogmatize we are not using the term "dogma" as some do, in its more common meaning, "something that one merely agrees to", for the Skeptic does give assent to the *pathē* that are forced upon him by a *phantasia*; for example, when feeling hot (or cold) he would not say "I seem not to be hot (or cold)." But when we assert that he does not dogmatize, we use "dogma" in the sense, which others give it, of assent to one of the non-evident matters investigated by the sciences. For the Pyrrhonist assents to nothing that is non-evident. Not even in putting forward the Skeptic slogans about nonevident things does he dogmatize—slogans like "Nothing more" or "I determine nothing" or any of the others of which we shall speak later. For the dogmatizer propounds as certainty the things about which he is said to be dogmatizing, but the Skeptic does not put forward these slogans as holding absolutely. He considers that, just as the "All things are false" slogan says that together with the other things it is itself false, as does the slogan "Nothing is true," so also the "Nothing more" slogan says that it itself is no more the case than its opposite, and thus it applies to itself along with the rest. We say the same of the other Skeptic slogans. So that since the dogmatizer is one who posits the content of his dogmas as being true, while the Skeptic presents his skeptical slogans as implicitly self-applicable, the Skeptic should not be said to dogmatize thereby. But the most important point is that in putting forward these slogans he is saying what seems to him to be the case and is reporting his *pathos* without belief, not firmly maintaining anything concerning what exists externally.

8. Does the Skeptic Have a System?

We proceed in the same way when asked whether the Skeptic has a system. If one defines a system as an attachment to a number of dogmas that agree with one another and with appearances, and defines a dogma as an assent to something non-evident, we shall say that the Skeptic does not have a system. But if one says that a system is a way of life that, in accordance with appearances, follows a certain rationale, where that rationale shows how it is possible to seem to live rightly ("rightly" being taken, not as referring only to virtue, but in a more ordinary sense) and tends to produce the disposition to suspend judgment, then we say that he does have a system. For we do follow a certain rationale that, in accord with appearances, points us toward a life in conformity with the customs of our country and its laws and institutions, and with our own particular *pathē*.

9. Does the Skeptic Theorize about Nature?

We reply in the same vein if asked whether the Skeptic needs to theorize about nature. On the one hand, if there is a question of making an assertion with firm confidence about any of the matters dogmatically treated in physical theory, we do not theorize; but, on the other hand, in the course of opposing to every statement an equal statement, and in connection with *ataraxia*, we do touch upon physical theory. This, too, is the way we approach the logical and ethical parts of so-called "philosophy."

10. Do the Skeptics Deny Appearances?

Those who claim that the Skeptics deny appearances seem to me not to have heard what we say. For, as we stated above, we do not reject the things that lead us involuntarily to assent in accord with a passively received *phantasia,* and these are appearances. And when we question whether the external object is such as it appears, we grant that it does appear, and we are not raising a question about the appearance but rather about what is said about the appearance; this is different from raising a question about the appearance itself. For example, the honey appears to us to be sweet. This we grant, for we sense the sweetness. But whether it *is* sweet we question insofar as this has to do with the [philosophical] theory, for that theory is not the appearance, but something said about the appearance. And even when we do present arguments in opposition to the appearances, we do not put these forward with the intention of denying the appearances but by way of pointing out the precipitancy of the Dogmatists; for if the theory is so deceptive as to all but snatch away the appearances from under our very eyes, should we not distrust it in regard to the non-evident, and thus avoid being led by it into precipitate judgments?

11. The Criterion of the Skeptic Way

That we hold to the appearances is obvious from what we say about the criterion of the Skeptic Way. The word "criterion" is used in two ways: first, for the criterion that is assumed in connection with belief about existence or nonexistence, and that we shall discuss in our objections; and second, for the criterion of action, by attention to which in the conduct of daily life we do some things and not others; it is of the latter that we are now speaking. Accordingly, we say that the criterion of the Skeptic Way is the appearance—in effect using that term here for the *phantasia*—for since this appearance lies in feeling and involuntary *pathos* it is not open to question. Thus nobody, I think, disputes about whether the external object appears this way or that, but rather about whether it is such as it appears to be.

Holding to the appearances, then, we live without beliefs but in accord with the ordinary regimen of life, since we cannot be wholly inactive. And this ordinary regimen of life seems to be fourfold: one part has to do with the guidance of nature, another with the compulsion of the *pathē,* another with the handing down of laws and customs, and a fourth with instruction in arts and crafts. Nature's guidance is that by which we are naturally capable of sensation and thought; compulsion of the *pathē* is that by which hunger drives us to food and thirst makes us drink; the handing down of customs and laws is that by which we accept that piety in the conduct of life is good and impiety bad; and instruction in arts and crafts is that by which we are not inactive in whichever of these we acquire. And we say all these things without belief.

12. What Is the Goal of Skepticism?

After these remarks, our next task is to explain the goal of the Skeptic Way. Now the goal or end is that for the sake of which everything is done or considered, while it, in turn, is not done or considered for the sake of anything else; or, it is the ultimate object of the desires. We always say that as regards belief the Skeptic's goal is *ataraxia,* and that as regards things that are unavoidable it is having moderate *pathē*. For when the Skeptic set out to philosophize with the aim of assessing his *phantasiai* —that is, of determining which are true and which are false so as to achieve *ataraxia*—he landed in a controversy between positions of equal strength, and, being unable to resolve it, he suspended judgment. But while he was thus suspending judgment there followed by chance the sought-after *ataraxia* as regards belief. For the person who believes that something is by nature good or bad is constantly upset; when he does not possess the things that seem to be good, he thinks he is being tormented by things that are by nature bad, and he chases after the things he supposes to be good; then, when he gets these, he falls into still more torments because of irrational and immoderate exultation, and, fearing any change, he does absolutely everything in order not to lose the things that seem to him good. But the person who takes no position as to what is by nature good or bad neither avoids nor pursues intensely. As a result, he achieves *ataraxia*.

Indeed, what happened to the Skeptic is just like what is told of Apelles the painter. For it is said that once upon a time, when he was painting a horse and wished to depict the horse's froth, he failed so completely that he gave up and threw his sponge at the picture—the sponge on which he used to wipe the paints from his brush—and that in striking the picture the sponge produced the desired effect. So, too, the Skeptics were hoping to achieve *ataraxia* by resolving the anomaly of phenomena and noumena, and, being unable to do this, they suspended judgment. But then, by chance as it were, when they were suspending judgment the *ataraxia* followed, as a shadow follows the body. We do not suppose, of course, that the Skeptic is wholly untroubled, but we do say that he is troubled only by things unavoidable. For we agree that sometimes he is cold and thirsty and has various feelings like those. But even in such cases, whereas ordinary people are affected by two circumstances—namely by the *pathē* themselves and not less by its seeming that these conditions are by nature bad—the Skeptic, by eliminating the additional belief that all these things are naturally bad, gets off more moderately here as well. Because of this we say that as regards belief the Skeptic's goal is *ataraxia*, but in regard to things unavoidable it is having moderate *pathē*. But some notable Skeptics have added "suspension of judgment during investigations" to these.

13. The General Modes of *Epochē*

Since we have been saying that *ataraxia* follows on suspending judgment about everything, the next thing would be to explain how we reach this suspension. Roughly speaking, one may say that it comes about through the opposition of things. We oppose phenomena to phenomena or noumena to noumena, or *alternando*. For instance, we oppose phenomena to phenomena when we say that the same tower appears round from a distance but square from close up; and noumena to noumena when, in reply to one who infers the existence of divine providence from the order of the heavenly bodies, we oppose the fact that often the good fare ill and the bad fare well, and deduce from this that divine providence does not exist; and noumena to phenomena, as when Anaxagoras argued, in opposition to snow's being white, that snow is frozen water and water is dark in color, and therefore snow is dark in color. Or, with a different concept of opposition, we sometimes oppose present things to present things, as in the foregoing examples, and sometimes present things to things past or to things future; for example, when somebody brings up an argument that we are not able to refute, we say to him: "Just as before the birth of the person who introduced the system which you follow, the argument supporting that system did not yet appear sound although it really was, so also it is possible that the opposite of the argument you now advance is really sound despite its not yet appearing so to us, and hence we should not yet assent to this argument that now seems so strong."

But in order that we may more accurately understand these oppositions, I shall set down the modes or arguments by means of which suspension of judgment is brought about, without, however, maintaining anything about their number or their force. For they may well be unsound, and there may be more than the ones I shall mention.

14. The Ten Modes

The older Skeptics, according to the usual account, have handed down some modes, ten in number, through which it seems that suspension of judgment is brought about, and which they also synonymously call "arguments" or "points." And these modes are as follows: first, there is the one based on the variety of animals; second, the one based on the differences among human beings; third, that based on the differences in constitution of the sense organs; fourth, on the circumstances; fifth, on positions, distances and locations; sixth, on admixtures; seventh, on the quantity and constitution of the external objects; eighth, on relativity; ninth, on the frequency or infrequency of occurrence; and tenth, on ways of life, customs and laws, mythic beliefs and dogmatic opinions. We adopt this order without prejudice.

Superordinate to these are three modes, one based on what does the judging, another based on what is judged, and a third based on both. The first four of the ten modes are subordinate to the mode based on what does the judging, for that is either an animal or a human being or a sense and is in some circumstance; the seventh and tenth modes are referred to the mode based on what is judged; and the fifth, sixth, eighth, and ninth are referred to the one that is based on both. These three in turn are referred to the relativity mode, making it the most generic, with the three as specific and the ten as subordinate. We offer the foregoing comments, as plausible, concerning their number; concerning their content, we say the following.

The first argument, as we were saying, is that according to which the same *phantasiai* do not arise from the same things because of the difference of animals. This we conclude from the difference in the ways animals are produced and from the variety in the structures of their bodies. As concerns the ways they are produced, some animals are produced without sexual union, and others from intercourse. And, of those produced without sexual union, some come from fire, like the tiny creatures that appear in ovens, some from stagnant water, like mosquitoes, some from wine that is turning, like gnats, some from earth, like [. . .], some from slime, like frogs, some from mud, like worms, some from donkeys, like dung-beetles, some from greens, like caterpillars, some from fruit, like the gall insects in the wild fig tree, some from rotting animals, like bees from bulls and wasps from horses. Of animals produced by intercourse, some, the majority, come from homogeneous parents, and others, like mules, from heterogeneous parents. Again, of animals in general, some are born viviparously, like human beings; others oviparously, like birds: and still others just as lumps of flesh, like bears. So one would expect these dissimilarities and differences of origin to result in great contrariety of *pathē*, contributing incompatibility, disharmony, and conflict.

However, it is the differences among the most important parts of the body, especially those naturally fitted for judging and sensing, that can produce the greatest conflict of the *phantasiai*. Thus, things that appear white to us are said to be yellow by people with jaundice, and reddish by those with bloodshot eyes. Since, then, some animals have yellow eyes, others bloodshot eyes, others white, and still others some other color, it is likely, I think, that their perception of colors will be different. Further, if we look long and fixedly at the sun and then stoop down to a book, the letters seem to us golden and moving around. Since, then, some animals have by nature a luster of the eyes and emit a fine and quick stream of light, so as even to be able to see at night, we should expect that external objects would not affect them and us in the same way. And illusionists, by treating lamp wicks with copper rust and cuttle fish ink, make the bystanders appear now copper-colored and now black, just by a slight sprinkling of the mixture. It is surely all the more reasonable that, since differing humors are mixed in the eyes of animals, these animals will have differing *phantasiai* of the external objects. Also, when we press the eyeball on one side, the forms, shapes and sizes of the things seen appear elongated and narrowed. So it is likely that those animals that have elongated and slanting pupils (e.g., goats, cats, and such) will in their *phantasiai* experience the external objects as different from and unlike what animals with round pupils take them to be. Mirrors, too, because of their differing construction, sometimes show the external objects as very short, when the mirror is concave, and sometimes as long and narrow, when it is convex. And some show the head of the reflected person at the bottom, and the feet at the top. Since, then, some of the organs of sight are bulging with convexity and others are quite concave, while still others are in a flat plane, it is likely that because of this the *phantasiai*, too, are various, and that dogs, fish, lions, human beings, and locusts do not see the same things as equal in size or similar in shape, but in each case what is seen depends on the imprint created by the eye that receives the appearance.

The same argument holds for the other senses as well. For how could one say, with regard to touch, that animals are similarly affected whether their surfaces consist of shell, flesh, needles, feathers, or scales? And, as regards hearing, how could one say that perceptions are alike in animals with a very narrow auditory canal and in those with a very wide one, or in those with hairy ears and those with ears that are hairless? Indeed, even we find our hearing affected one way when our ears are plugged and another way when we use them ordinarily. Smell, too, will differ according to the variety of animals. For if we ourselves are affected in one way when we have a cold with a lot of phlegm, and in another way when the parts about the head are filled with an excess of blood (in the latter case being repelled and feeling virtually assaulted by things that seem to others to smell sweet), then, since some animals are flabby and phlegmatic by nature, others very rich in blood, and still others have a predominant excess of yellow or black bile, it is reasonable to suppose that this makes odiferous things appear differently in each case. So, too, with the objects of taste, since some animals have rough and dry tongues and others very moist. And when in a fever we ourselves have relatively dry tongues, we consider the food offered to us to be earthy, bad tasting, and bitter, and we feel thus because of the differing strength of the humors said to be in us. Since, then, the animals too have differing organs of taste, with different humors predominating, they would get differing taste *phantasiai* of the external objects. For, just as the same food, when digested, becomes in one place a vein, in another an artery, in another a bone, and in still another a tendon, and so on, showing a differing disposition depending on the difference of the parts receiving it; and just as water, one and the same in form, when applied to trees becomes bark in one place, branch in another, and blossom in another and thus finally fig, pomegranate, and each of the other fruits; and just as one and the same breath of the musician, when blown into a flute becomes here a high note and there a low note, and the same stroke of the hand on the lyre produces here a bass sound and there a treble one; so, too, it is likely that the external objects are perceived differently depending on the differing makeups of the animals having the *phantasiai*.

But one can see this more clearly from the preferences and aversions of animals. Thus, perfume seems very pleasant to human beings but intolerable to dung beetles and bees, and the application of olive oil is beneficial to human beings but kills wasps and bees. And to human beings sea water is unpleasant and even poisonous to drink, while to fish it is most pleasant and potable. And pigs bathe more happily in the worst stinking mud than in clear and pure water. And, of animals, some eat grass and others eat bushes, some eat wood and others seeds or meat or milk, some like their food aged and others fresh, and some like it raw and others like it pre-

pared by cooking. And in general the things that are pleasant to some animals are unpleasant, repugnant and even poisonous to others. Thus, hemlock fattens quails and hyoscyamus fattens pigs, and pigs enjoy eating salamanders, as the deer enjoy eating poisonous creatures and swallows enjoy blister-beetles. Ants and mosquitoes, when swallowed by human beings, produce discomfort and stomach ache, whereas the she-bear, if she feels somehow weak, is strengthened by licking them up. The adder is stupefied by the mere touch of a branch of oak, and the bat by a leaf of the plane tree. The elephant fears the ram, the lion the rooster, sea-monsters the crackling of bursting beans, the tiger the sound of a drum. And it is possible to give further examples, but— that we may not seem more prolix than necessary— if the same things are unpleasant to some but pleasant to others, and if the pleasure and unpleasantness lie in the *phantasiai*, then differing animals receive different *phantasiai* from the external objects.

But if the same things do appear differently because of the difference of animals, then we shall be in a position to say how the external object looks to *us*, but we shall suspend judgment on how it is in nature. For we shall not be able to decide between our *phantasiai* and those of the other animals, since we are part of the dispute and thus are in need of someone to make the decision, rather than competent to pass judgment ourselves. Besides, we shall not be able to give preference, whether with or without proof, to our *phantasiai* over those of the non-rational animals. For in addition to the possibility of there being no such thing as a proof, as we shall point out, any purported proof will either be apparent or not apparent to us. And if, on the one hand, it is not apparent, then we shall not accept it with confidence. But if, on the other, it *is* apparent to us, then since what is apparent to animals is the very matter in question, and the proof is apparent to us animals, the proof itself will be in question as to whether, as apparent, it is true. But it is absurd to try to settle the matter in question by means of the matter in question, since the same thing will be both credible and not credible, which is impossible—credible insofar as tending to prove, not credible insofar as needing proof. Therefore, we shall not have a proof justifying us in preferring our own *phantasiai* to those of the so-called "non-rational" animals. If, therefore, the *phantasiai* differ because of the difference of animals, and it is impossible to decide between them, then it is necessary to suspend judgment concerning the external objects.

But for good measure we go on to match up the so-called "non-rational" animals with human beings as regards *phantasiai*. For, after our serious arguments, we do not consider it unseemly to poke a little fun at the Dogmatists, wrapped, as they are, in the fog of their discussions with themselves. We usually take the non-rational animals as a group when comparing them with human beings, but since in groping for an argument the Dogmatists say that the comparison is unfair, we shall for even more good measure carry our joking still further and base the argument on just one animal—the dog, if you will—which seems to be the humblest of all. For we shall find that even in this case the animals that are the subject of the argument are not inferior to ourselves as regards the credibility of the appearances.

So, then, the Dogmatists acknowledge that this animal differs from us in sensation; for it perceives more by the sense of smell than we do, being able by this sense to track wild animals that it cannot see, and with its eyes it sees them more quickly than we do, and its sense of hearing is more acute. Next let us consider reasoning. One kind of reasoning is internal, the other is expressed. Let us first look at the internal kind. This, according to those Dogmatists who at the moment are our chief opponents— namely, the Stoics—seems to involve the following: acceptance of the familiar and avoidance of the alien, knowledge of the arts related to this, possession of the virtues pertaining to one's proper nature and of those having to do with the *pathē*. Now then, the dog, the animal upon which as an example we decided to base the argument, chooses what is congenial to him and avoids the harmful, hunting for food and withdrawing before the raised whip. Furthermore, he has the art, namely hunting, to provide the congenial. Nor is he without virtue. For certainly if justice is giving to each according to his deserts, the dog, who fawns on and guards his family and benefactors but wards off strangers and malefactors, would not be lacking in justice. And if he has this virtue, then in view of the unity of the virtues he has them all, which the wise tell us is not the case with the majority of mankind. And we see him valiant and smart in his defending, to which Homer bears witness when he depicts Odysseus as unknown to all the people of the household but recognized by the dog Argus alone. The dog was not deceived by the physical changes in the man, nor had he lost his "apprehensive *phantasia*," which he clearly retained better than the human beings did. And according to

Chrysippus, who was certainly no friend of non-rational animals, the dog even shares in the celebrated Dialectic. In fact, this author says that the dog uses repeated applications of the fifth undemonstrated argument-schema when, arriving at a juncture of three paths, after sniffing at the two down which the quarry did not go, he rushes off on the third without stopping to sniff. For, says this ancient authority, the dog in effect reasons as follows: the animal either went this way or that way or the other; he did not go this way and he did not go that; therefore, he went the other. Furthermore, the dog is aware of and can deal with his own *pathē*. For when a thorn has got stuck in him, he hastens to remove it by rubbing his foot on the ground and by using his teeth. And when he has a wound anywhere he gently licks off the accumulated pus, since dirty wounds are hard to cure, while clean ones are easily healed. Indeed, he follows very well Hippocrates' prescription; since "immobility cures the foot," whenever his foot is injured he holds it up and keeps it undisturbed so far as possible. When he is troubled by humors that do not agree with him, he eats grass, and then regurgitates the uncongenial material along with it and gets well. Since, then, it is apparent that the animal upon which as an example we have rested the argument chooses what is congenial and avoids what is troublesome, and possesses the art of obtaining the congenial, and is aware of and able to deal with his own *pathē*, and furthermore is not without virtue—in which elements consists the perfection of internal reasoning—the dog would thus far be without deficiency. Which, I suppose, is why certain philosophers [the Cynics] have honored themselves with the name of this animal.

Concerning reasoning as expressed externally it is not necessary at present to inquire, for even some of the Dogmatists have deprecated it as counterproductive to the acquisition of virtue, and for this reason they used to practice silence during their schooling. And anyhow, supposing that a person is unable to speak, no one will infer that he is non-rational. But leaving these points aside, we certainly observe animals, the subject of our discussion, uttering quite human sounds—jays, for instance, and others. And letting this too pass, even if we do not understand the utterances of the so-called "non-rational" animals it is not at all improbable that they are conversing although we do not understand. For when we hear the talk of barbarians we do not understand that either, and it seems to us undifferentiated sound.

Moreover, we hear dogs making one sound when they are keeping people away and another when they are howling, and one sound when they are beaten and a different one when they are fawning. In general, if somebody were to study the matter he would find a great difference of sounds uttered by this and the other animals according to different circumstances, and so for that reason it may fairly be said that the so-called "non-rational" animals have their share of externally expressed reasoning. And if they are neither inferior to human beings in the acuteness of their senses nor in internal reasoning, nor, on top of that, in externally expressed reasoning, then as concerns *phantasiai* they are not less worthy of belief than we are. It is also possible to show this, I think, by basing the argument on each kind of non-rational animal. For instance, who would not say that birds excel in shrewdness and employ externally expressed reasoning? For they have knowledge not only of things present but also of the future, and by prophetic sounds or some other signs they reveal these things in advance to people who can understand them.

As I previously indicated, I have made this comparison for good measure, having sufficiently shown, I think, that we cannot prefer our own *phantasiai* to those of the non-rational animals. But if the non-rational animals are not less worthy of belief than we are when it comes to deciding about *phantasiai,* and the *phantasiai* differ depending on the variety of animals, then although I shall be able to say how each of the external objects appears to me, I shall be forced, for the reasons stated above, to suspend judgment as to how it is in nature.

Such, then, is the first mode of *epochē.* We said that the second was the one based on the differences among human beings. For even if it were granted, by way of supposition, that human beings are more to be believed than the non-rational animals, we shall find that even consideration of our own differences leads to suspension of judgment. For human beings are said to be composed of two elements, the soul and the body, and we differ from one another in respect to both of them. As regards the body, we differ in form and constitution. The body of a Scythian differs in form from that of an Indian, and the variation is produced, they say, by the differing relative strengths of the humors. Depending on this difference in relative strength of the humors there arise differing *phantasiai,* as we pointed out in the first mode. So, too, these humors

produce a great difference in the choice and avoidance of things external. Indians like some things and we like others, and liking different things is an indication of receiving differing *phantasiai* from the external objects. In consequence of our peculiarities of makeup, we differ in such a way that some of us digest beef better than rock fish or get diarrhea from the weak wine of Lesbos. There was, it is said, an old woman of Attica who safely drank thirty drams of hemlock, and Lysis took four drams of opium without trouble. And Demophon, who waited table for Alexander, used to shiver in the sun or the bath, but felt warm in the shade; the Argive Athenagoras felt no pain when stung by scorpions and venomous spiders; the Psyllaeans, as they are called, are not harmed when bitten by asps or other snakes; nor are the Egyptian Tentyritae harmed by crocodiles. Further, the Egyptians who live along the Astapous river opposite Lake Meroe safely eat scorpions, snakes, and the like. And Rufinus of Chalcis, when he drank hellebore, neither threw up nor suffered any laxative effect, but he took it and digested it as though it were something to which he was accustomed. Chrysermus the Herophilean, if he ever used pepper, risked a heart attack. And Soterichus the surgeon, whenever he smelled fried fish, got diarrhea. Andron the Argive was so immune to thirst that he even traveled through the Libyan desert without needing anything to drink. Tiberius Caesar could see in the dark, and Aristotle tells of a certain Thasian to whom it seemed that a human phantom was all the time leading him around.

Since there is so much variation among human beings as regards the body—and it suffices to mention only a few of the cases that the Dogmatists provide—it is likely that human beings will also differ among themselves as regards the soul. For the body is a kind of image of the soul, as indeed the art of Physiognomy shows. But the greatest indication of the vast and limitless difference in the intellect of human beings is the inconsistency of the various statements of the Dogmatists concerning what may be appropriately chosen, what avoided, and so on. The poets, too, have expressed themselves appropriately about these things. For Pindar says:

The crowns and trophies of his storm-foot steeds
Give joy to one; yet others find it joy
To dwell in gorgeous chambers gold-bedecked;
Some even take delight in voyaging

O'er ocean's billows in a speeding barque.

FRAG. 221 SNELL, AS TRANSLATED BY SIR J. E. SANDYS

And the poet says:

> One person delights in one activity, another
> in another.

ODYSSEY 14.228

Tragedy, too, is full of such things:

> If the same things were beautiful and wise for
>   everybody,
> There would be no disputatious strife among
>   mankind.

EURIPIDES, PHOENISSAE 499-500

And again,

> It is strange that the same thing should
> be pleasing to some mortals and
> hateful to others.

ANON., FRAY. 462 NAUCK

Since, then, choice and avoidance are in pleasure and displeasure, and pleasure and displeasure lie in sense and *phantasia,* when the same things are chosen by some people and avoided by others it is logical for us to infer that these people are not affected alike by the same things, since if they would alike have chosen and avoided the same things. But if the same things produce different affects depending on the difference of human beings, this too would reasonably lead to suspension of judgment and we would, perhaps, be able to say what each of the external objects appears to be, relative to each difference, but we would not be able to state what it is in nature. For we shall either have to give credence to all human beings or to some. But if to all, we shall be attempting impossibilities and accepting contradictory statements. And if to some, let the Dogmatists tell us to whom we should give assent. The Platonist will say "to Plato" and the Epicurean "to Epicurus," and the others analogously, and thus with their unsettled disputes they bring us again to suspension of judgment. Anyone who says that we ought to give assent to the majority view is making a childish proposal, for no one is able to approach the whole human race and by talking with them find out what pleases the majority. Indeed, there may be peoples of whom we know nothing but among whom attributes that are most rare among us are common, while the attributes most common among us are rare among them; so that, for example, most of them feel no pain when bitten by spiders, while a few, on rare occasions, do; and analogously with the other "idiosyncrasies" previously mentioned. Of necessity, therefore, suspension of judgment comes in again, via the differences of human beings.

While the Dogmatists egoistically claim that in deciding the facts preference ought to be given to themselves above all other human beings, we realize that this claim of theirs is inappropriate since they themselves are part of the dispute. And if, giving preference to themselves, they make a decision about the appearances, by entrusting the decision to themselves they beg the question before the deciding is begun. In any case, in order to arrive at suspension of judgment by an argument dealing with only one person—their Ideal Sage, for example, who is expert at interpreting dreams—we take up the third mode in the list.

This mode is the one that we say is based on the difference of the senses. That the senses differ from one another is obvious from the start. For instance, to the eye it seems that paintings have hollows and prominences, but not to the touch. And for some people honey seems pleasant to the tongue but unpleasant to the eye; consequently, it is impossible to say without qualification whether it is pleasant or unpleasant. And likewise in the case of perfume, for it pleases the sense of smell but displeases the taste. So too with spurge juice: since it is painful to the eyes but painless to all the rest of the body, we will not be able to say without qualification whether, insofar as its nature is concerned, it is painful or painless to bodies. And rain water is beneficial to the eyes, but it is rough on the wind pipe and lungs, as is olive oil despite its being soothing to the skin. The sting-ray, when it touches the extremities, produces numbness, but it can touch the rest of the body harmlessly. Hence we shall not be able to say how each of these things is in its nature, but only how it appears to be in each instance.

More examples can be given, but in order not to delay carrying out the purpose of our essay, the following point needs to be made. Each thing that appears to us in sensation seems to affect us as complex; for example, the apple seems smooth, fragrant, sweet, yellow. But it is not evident whether it really has these and only these qualities, or whether, having only one quality, it appears differently depending on the different constitutions of the sense organs, or again whether it has more qualities than are apparent but some of them do not affect us. That it has one quality could be argued on the basis of what we previously said about the food taken up by the body and the water taken up by the tree and the air breathed into flutes and pipes and similar instruments; for the apple, too, may be of one form but appear differently because of the difference of the sense organs through which it is perceived. And that the apple has more qualities than those that appear to us, we can reason as follows. Suppose that someone is born having the senses of touch, smell, and taste, but can neither hear nor see. Then he will assume that the origin of his perceptions is not something visible or audible, but that it has only those three types of quality which he is capable of perceiving. And it is possible that we, with only our five senses, perceive only those qualities of the apple that we are fitted to perceive, and that perhaps there are other qualities, affecting other sense organs which we lack and for which we consequently cannot perceive any corresponding objects.

But nature, someone may say, has made the senses exactly proportionate to the objects of sense. But what is this "nature", seeing that there is so much unresolved controversy among the Dogmatists concerning its very existence? For anyone who decides this question, that is, whether nature exists, will have no credibility with them if he is an ordinary person, while if he is a philosopher he will be part of the controversy and instead of being a judge will be subject to judgment himself. So that if it is possible that only those qualities exist in the apple which we seem to perceive, or that there are more than these, or again that there are not even the ones that affect us, what the apple is like will be nonevident to us. The same argument holds also in the case of the other objects of sense. And since the senses do not apprehend the external objects, the intellect is not capable of doing so either, so that this argument, too, seems conducive to suspension of judgment concerning the external objects.

In order that we shall be able to reach suspension of judgment when basing the argument on each single sense or even disregarding the senses, we take up further the fourth mode of *epochē*. This is the one described as "based on circumstances," where by "circumstances" we mean conditions. We say that it is concerned with being in a natural or unnatural condition, with being awake or asleep, with dependence on age, on being in motion or at rest, on hating or loving, on being in need or satisfied, on being drunk or sober, on predispositions, on being courageous or fearful, on being distressed or cheerful. Thus, things affect us in dissimilar ways depending on whether we are in a natural or unnatural condition, as when people who are delirious or possessed by a god seem to hear spirits but we do not. Similarly, those people often say that they perceive odors of storax or frankincense or some such thing, and much else, too, although we do not sense them. And the same water that seems to us to be lukewarm seems boiling hot when poured on an inflamed place. And the same coat appears tawny-orange to people with bloodshot eyes but not to me. Also, the same honey appears sweet to me but bitter to the jaundiced. Further, if someone says that an intermingling of certain humors produces, in persons who are in an unnatural condition, odd *phantasiai* of the external objects, it must be replied that since healthy people, too, have intermingled humors, it is possible that the external objects are in nature such as they appear to those persons who are said to be in an unnatural state, but that these humors are making the external objects appear to the healthy people to be other than they are. For to give the power of altering the external objects to some humors but not to others is arbitrary; since just as the healthy in a natural state have the nature of the healthy and in an unnatural state that of the sick, so too the sick in an unnatural state have the nature of the healthy and in a natural state that of the sick; so that credence should be given to these last, too, as being in a relatively natural state.

Different *phantasiai* come about, too, depending on whether we are asleep or awake. For when we are awake we do not imagine [*ou phantazometha*] what we imagine when we are asleep, nor when we are asleep do we imagine what we imagine when awake, so that whether the *phantasiai* are the case or are not the case is not absolute but relative, that is, relative to being asleep or awake. It is fair to say, then, that when asleep we see things that are not the case in the waking state, though not absolutely not the case. For they are the case in our sleep, just as what we see in our waking state is the case, though not in our sleep.

Depending on age, too, different *phantasiai* arise, since the same air seems cold to the aged but temperate to those who are in their prime, and the same color appears faint to older people but vivid to those in their prime, and likewise the same sound appears faint to the former but clearly audible to the latter. And people of differing ages are moved in different ways depending on their choices and aversions. For instance, children are interested in balls and hoops, but people in their prime prefer other things, and the elderly still others. From this we conclude that, also depending on differences of age, differing *phantasiai* arise from the same external objects.

Objects appear differently, too, depending on whether one is in motion or at rest. For things that we see as stationary when we are at rest seem to be moving when we are sailing by. Depending on liking and disliking, also: for some people are completely repelled by pork, while others eat it with the greatest of pleasure. Whence Menander, too, said:

> Look how his face appears now that he
>   has come to this—like an animal!
> It is acting justly that makes us fair.
>
>   FRAG. 518 KOCK

And many people who have ugly mistresses think them beautiful. Depending on hunger and satiety, too: since the same food seems very pleasant to the hungry but unpleasant to the sated. And depending on being drunk or sober: since things we consider shameful when we are sober appear to us not to be shameful when we are drunk. And depending on predispositions: since the same wine that appears sour to people who have previously eaten dates or figs seems sweet to those who have eaten nuts or chickpeas; and the vestibule of the bathhouse is warm to those entering from outside and cold to those leaving, if they have spent some time in it. And depending on being afraid or feeling courageous: since the same thing seems frightful and terrible to the timid but not at all so to the bold. And, finally, depending on being distressed or cheerful: since the same things that are annoying to people who are distressed are pleasant to those who are cheerful.

Since, therefore, there is so much anomaly depending on conditions, and human beings are in one condition at one time and another at another, how each external object appears to each person is easy to say, I suppose, but not how it is, since the anomaly is unresolved. For anyone resolving it is either in one of the aforementioned conditions or is in no condition at all. But to say that he is in no condition at all—for example, neither healthy nor sick, neither in motion nor at rest, nor of any particular age, and devoid of the other conditions as well—is completely absurd. But if he, being in some condition, makes a decision about the *phantasiai,* he will be part of the dispute and in other ways not a pure or fair judge of the external objects, because he has been contaminated by the conditions he is in. The waking person cannot compare the *phantasiai* of sleepers with those of people who are awake, nor can the healthy person compare those of the sick with those of the healthy. For we assent to things that are in the present and move us in the present, more than to things that are not in the present.

In another way, too, the anomaly of such *phantasiai* is unresolved. For anyone preferring one *phantasia* to another or one circumstance to another either does this without making a decision and without giving proof, or by making a decision and giving proof. But he will not do it without these means, for then he will not be credible, nor will he do it with them, either. For if he makes a decision about the *phantasiai,* he will certainly decide by means of a criterion. And certainly he will either say that this criterion is true or that it is false. But if he says that it is false, he will not be credible. And if he says that the criterion is true, either he will say this without proof or he will say it with proof. Again, if he says it without proof, he will not be credible; but if with proof, the proof will certainly need to be true if he is to be credible. When he affirms the truth of the proof which he is taking to establish the credibility of the criterion, will he have made a decision about this or not? If he has not made the decision, he will not be credible; and if he has made the decision, then it is obvious that he will say that he has decided by means of a criterion, in order that it may be maintained, and the criterion has need of a proof, in order that it may be shown to be true. And neither is it possible for a proof to be sound without the prior existence of a true criterion, nor for a criterion to be true without the previously confirmed proof. And thus the criterion and the proof fall into the circularity type of *aporia,* in which both are found not to be credible; for each, while it awaits the credibility of the other, is equally incredible with the other. Therefore, if nobody, with or without a proof and criterion, is able to give one *phantasia* preference over another, then the differing *phantasiai* that arise depending on the different conditions will be undecidable; so that this mode, too, leads to suspension of judgment concerning the nature of the external objects.

The fifth argument is that depending on positions, distances, and locations. For, depending on each of these, the same things appear different—for example, the same stoa viewed from either end appears tapering but from the middle completely symmetrical, and from afar the same boat appears small and stationary but from close up large and in motion, and the same tower appears round from afar but square from close up.

These depend on distances. But depending on locations: the same lamp-light appears dim in the sunshine but bright in the dark, and the same oar appears broken when it is in the water and straight when it is out, and the egg soft when it is in the bird but hard when it is in the air, and the ligure liquid in the lynx but hard in the air, and coral soft in the sea but hard in the air, and sound appears one way in a pipe, another in a flute, and still another when it is simply in the air.

And depending on positions: the same portrait appears smooth when tilted back, but when tilted forward a certain amount it seems to have depths and prominences. And the necks of pigeons appear different in color depending on the different angles of inclination.

Therefore, since everything apparent is viewed in some location and from some distance and in some position, each of which produces a great deal of variation in the *phantasiai*, as we have remarked above, we shall be forced also by this mode to have recourse to suspension of judgment. And anyone wishing to give preference to some of these *phantasiai* will be attempting the impossible. For if he makes his assertion simply and without proof, he will not be credible; whereas, supposing that he wishes to use a proof, if he says that the proof is false he will confute himself, while if he says that it is true he will need a proof of its being true, and again a proof of that, since it too must be true, and so on ad infinitum. But it is impossible to produce infinitely many proofs; and so he will not be able by means of a proof to give one *phantasia* preference over another. And if one cannot decide about the aforementioned *phantasiai* either with or without a proof, suspension of judgment results; for, I suppose, of any given thing we are able to say of what sort, relative to its particular position, distance, and place, it appears to be, but for the above reasons we cannot state of what sort it is in its nature.

The sixth mode is the one that depends on admixtures and according to which we conclude that, since none of the external objects affects us by itself but always in combination with something, it is perhaps possible to say what the mixture of the external object and that together with which it is observed is like, but we cannot do the same for the external object considered by itself. It is obvious from the start, I think, that none of the external objects affects us by itself, but always does so in combination with something, and that depending on this it is observed as different. Thus, our own complexion is seen as of one hue in warm air and as of another in cold air, and so we cannot say how our complexion is in nature, but only how it looks together with each of the two kinds of air. Further, the same sound appears one way in thin air and another in dense air, and spices are more pungent in the bathhouse and in the sun than in very cold air, and the body is light when immersed in water, but heavy in air.

In order to get away from just external admixtures: our eyes contain within themselves both membranes and liquids. Since things seen are not observed without these, they will not be accurately apprehended, for it is the mixture that we perceive, and because of this the jaundiced see everything yellow, while those with blood in the eyes see things as bloodred. And since the same sound appears of one quality in open places and of another in places that are narrow and winding, and of one quality in clear air and another in murky air, it is likely that we do not perceive the sound in and of itself; for the ears have narrow and winding passages and are contaminated by vaporous effluvia said to be conducted from places around the head. Moreover, since there are substances in the nostrils and in the areas of taste, we perceive the objects of taste and of smell together with these and not in and of themselves. Therefore, because of the admixtures the senses do not perceive precisely how the external objects are.

Nor does the intellect do so either, especially since its guides, the senses, go wrong; perhaps it too contributes some special admixture of its own to the reports of the senses; for we observe that there are humors situated around each of the places in which the Dogmatists suppose that the ruling part of the soul is located, whether the brain or the heart or whatever part of the animal anyone wants to put it in. And so by this mode also we see that, being unable to say anything about the nature of the external objects, we are forced to suspension of judgment.

The seventh mode, we said, is that depending on the quantity and constitution of the external objects, giving "constitution" its common meaning, namely, combination. It is obvious that by this mode, too, we are forced to suspend judgment about the nature of the objects. For example, shavings off a goat's horn appear white when observed by themselves and not in combination, but when they are combined in the substance of the horn they look black. And individual filings of a piece of silver appear black, but when united with the whole they affect us as white. And pieces of Taenarean marble look white when they are polished, but combined in the whole stone they appear yellow. And grains of sand when scattered appear rough, but when gathered together in a dune they affect our senses as soft. And helebore, taken when fine and light, tends to choke one, but not when coarse. And wine, when drunk in moderation, strengthens us, but when taken in excess, disables the body. And food, similarly, exhibits different powers depending on the amount; often, indeed, by being taken in too great quantity it brings the body down with indigestion and diarrhea. So here, too, we shall be able to say of what quality the shaving of horn is, and of what quality the combination of many shavings is, and the same for the particle of silver and the combination of many particles, and for the bit of Taenarean marble and the combination of many bits, and we can make relative statements in the case of the grains of sand and the helebore and the wine and the food, too, but we still cannot state the absolute nature of the things because of the anomaly of *phantasiai* depending on combination.

It seems that in general even beneficial things become harmful when they are used in immoderate quantities, and the things that seem hurtful when taken in excess are harmless in small quantities. The best indication of this point is what is observed in regard to the powers of medicines, in which the exact mixing of the simple drugs produces a compound that is beneficial, but the occasional slightest error in weighing, when overlooked, makes it not only not beneficial but even quite hurtful and often poisonous.

So the argument relating to quantities and constitutions muddles the existence of the external objects. Consequently this mode too may be expected to lead us around to suspension of judgment, for we are unable to say anything without qualification about the nature of the external objects.

The eighth mode is the one based on relativity, where we conclude that, since everything is in relation to something, we shall suspend judgment as to what things are in themselves and in their nature. But it must be noticed that here, as elsewhere, we use "are" for "appear to be," saying in effect "everything appears in relation to something." But this statement has two senses: first, as implying relation to what does the judging, for the object that exists externally and is judged appears in relation to what does the judging, and second, as implying relation to the things observed together with it, as, for example, what is on the right is in relation to what is on the left. And, indeed, we have taken into account earlier that everything is in relation to something: for example, as regards what does the judging, that each thing appears in relation to this or that animal or person or sense and in relation to such and such a circumstance; and as regards the things observed together with it, that each thing appears in relation to this or that admixture or manner or combination or quantity or position.

But it is also possible to prove by a special argument that everything is in relation to something, as follows. Do the things that are what they are by virtue of a difference differ from the things that are in relation to something, or not? If they do not differ, then they too are in relation to something; if they do differ, then, since whatever differs is in relation to something (for it is called what it is in relation to that from which it differs), the things that are what they are by virtue of a difference are in relation to something. And, according to the Dogmatists, of things that are, some are *summa genera*, others are *infimae species*, and others are genera and species. But all these are relative. Again, of things that are, some are pre-evident and others are non-evident, as they say; the appearances signify, and the non-evident things are signified by the appearances. For, according to them, "the appearances are a view of the non-evident." But what signifies and what is signified are relative. Therefore, everything is relative. Moreover, of things that are, some are similar and others are dissimilar, and some are equal and others are unequal; but these things are relative; therefore, everything is relative. And even the person who says that not all things are relative confirms the relativity of all things, for by the arguments he opposes to us he shows that the very relativity of all things is relative to us and not universal.

Now, when we have shown that all things are relative, the obvious result is that as concerns each external object we shall not be able to state how it is in its own nature and absolutely, but only how, in relation to something, it appears to be. It follows that we must suspend judgment about the nature of the objects.

In connection with the mode based on the constancy or infrequency of occurrence, which we say is the ninth in order, we consider such items as the following. The sun is certainly a much more marvelous thing than a comet. But since we see the sun all the time but the comet only infrequently, we marvel at the comet so much as even to suppose it a divine portent, but we do nothing like that for the sun. If, however, we thought of the sun as appearing infrequently and setting infrequently, and as illuminating everything all at once and then suddenly being eclipsed, we would find much to marvel at in the matter. And earthquakes are not equally troublesome to the person who is experiencing one for the first time and to the person who has become accustomed to them. And how marvelous is the sea to the person who sees it for the first time! And a beautiful human body that is seen suddenly and for the first time excites us more than if it were to become a customary sight. Things that are rare seem precious, but things that are familiar and easy to get do not. Indeed, if we thought of water as rare, how much more precious it would appear than all the things that do seem precious! And if we imagine gold simply scattered on the ground like stones, to whom do we think it would then be precious and worth hoarding away?

Since, then, the same things, depending on whether they occur frequently or infrequently, seem at one time marvelous or precious and at another time not, we infer that we shall perhaps be able to say how each of these appears when it occurs frequently or when it occurs infrequently, but that we shall not be able to state without qualification how each of the external objects is. And, accordingly, via this mode too we withhold assent as regards them.

The tenth mode, which is principally concerned with ethics, is the one depending on ways of life and on customs, laws, mythic beliefs, and dogmatic suppositions. A way of life is a chosen basis for living or for some particular action, adopted by one person or many—for example, by Diogenes or the Laconians. A law is a written agreement among the citizens, the violator of which is punished; a custom or common practice (for there is no difference) is the joint acceptance by a number of people of a certain

way of acting, where the violator is not in all cases punished; thus, there is a law against adultery, and for us it is a custom not to have intercourse with a woman in public. A mythic belief is the acceptance of things that are not the case and are fictional—such as, among others, the myths about Cronus—and in which many people place credence. And a dogmatic supposition is the acceptance of something that seems to be established by analogy or some kind of proof, such as that there are atomic elements of things, or homoeomeries [ultimate particles of matter], or *minima*, or other things.

And we oppose each of these items sometimes to itself and sometimes to each of the others. For example, we oppose custom to custom thus: some of the Ethiopians tattoo their babies, but we do not. And the Persians think it becoming to wear brightly colored garments that reach to the feet, but we consider it unbecoming; and whereas the Indians have intercourse with women in public, most others consider this shameful. We oppose law to law thus: among the Romans, he who gives up his patrimony does not pay his father's debts; but among the Rhodians he always pays them; and among the Tauri of Scythia there was a law that foreigners were to be sacrificed to Artemis, but with us it is forbidden to kill a human being at the temple. And we oppose a way of life to a way of life when we set Diogenes's way of life in opposition to that of Aristippus, or that of the Laconians to that of the Italians. We oppose a mythical belief to a mythical belief when in one place we say that according to myth Zeus is the father of men and gods, while in another we say that it is Oceanus, referring to the line:

Oceanus, the source of the gods, and Tethys,
   the mother.

ILIAD 14.201

And we oppose dogmatic opinions to one another when we say that some people assert that there is just one element and others that there are infinitely many, and that some assert that the soul is mortal and others that it is immortal, and that some assert that our affairs are arranged by divine providence while others assert that they are not.

We also oppose custom to the other items—to law, for example, when we say that among the Persians sodomy is customary but among the Romans it is prohibited by law; and with us adultery is prohibited, but among the Massagetae it is by custom treated as a matter of indifference, as Eudoxus of Cnidos reports in the first book of his *Travels*; and with us it is forbidden to have intercourse with one's mother, whereas with the Persians this sort of marriage is very much the custom. And among the Egyptians men marry their sisters, which for us is prohibited by law. Custom is opposed to way of life when, whereas the majority of men have intercourse with their wives in some place apart, Crates did it with Hipparchia in public; and Diogenes went around with shoulders bare, while we dress in the usual way. And custom is opposed to mythical belief, as when the myths say that Cronus ate his own children, it being customary among us to take care of children; and whereas with us it is customary to worship the gods as being good and immune from evil, they are presented by the poets as being wounded by and envious of one another. Custom is also opposed to dogmatic opinion when with us it is the custom to pray to the gods for good things, whereas Epicurus says that the divinity does not care about us; and when Aristippus thinks it a matter of indifference whether one wears women's clothing, while we think this shameful.

We oppose way of life to law when, though there is a law against striking a free and well-born man, the pancratiasts hit one another because of their way of life, and when, though homicide is forbidden, the gladiators kill one another for the same reason. Further, we oppose mythical belief to way of life when we point out that the myths say that Heracles in the house of Omphale "carded wool and endured slavery" and did these things which nobody would choose to do, even to a moderate degree, whereas Heracles's way of life was noble. We oppose way

of life to dogmatic supposition when athletes undertake an onerous way of life for the sake of glory, on the supposition that glory is good, while many philosophers dogmatize that it is an evil thing. And we oppose law to mythical belief when the poets present the gods as practicing adultery and sodomy, while with us the law prohibits doing these things; and we oppose law to dogmatic opinion when the Chrysippeans say that intercourse with mothers or sisters is a matter of indifference, while the law prohibits these things. Further, we oppose mythical belief to dogmatic supposition when the poets say that Zeus came down and had intercourse with mortal women, whereas this is deemed by the Dogmatists to be impossible; and the poet says that Zeus, because of grief over Sarpedon,

Let fall a shower of blood upon the earth,

ILIAD 16.459

while it is a dogma of the philosophers that the divinity is impassive; and when the philosophers reject the myth of the hippocentaurs, while offering us the hippocentaur as a paradigm of nonexistence.

For each of the foregoing oppositions it was possible to take many other examples, but in an outline these will suffice. At any rate, since by this mode, too, so many anomaly in "the facts" has been shown, we shall not be able to say how any external object or state of affairs is in its nature, but only how it appears in relation to a given way of life or law or custom, and so forth. And so because of this mode, too, we must suspend judgment about the nature of the external "facts." Thus, via all ten modes we end up with suspension of judgment.

Chapter 7
PLOTINUS

Plotinus (204–270), the last great Neo-Platonist, was born in Lykopolis, Egypt, in 204. He studied in Alexandria before traveling to Persia and India to learn Eastern wisdom, and then to Rome, where he established a school of philosophy. Hist most famous work is the *Enneads,* six groups of nine writings, from which our selection is taken. He died of leprosy.

As a Platonist he sought through mystical contemplation a supreme principle, the Good or One. The Good is infinite and overflows, producing the realm of the Intellect (*Nous*), the realm of Plato's Forms, which in turn overflows to produce the Divine Soul, the lowest of the emanations of the Good. The ascent of the soul to the highest goal demanded, not religious belief or ritual, but liberation from bodily needs (bodies are phantoms) and moral purity. One ascends upward through stages, first the realm of pure Soul, then the realm of the Intellect, and, finally, the Good or One. Plotinus thought his soul had ascended to the Good momentarily at various points in his later life.

Our selection describes the ascent of the soul to the Good.

Ennead

BEAUTY

1. Beauty addresses itself chiefly to sight; but there is a beauty for the hearing too, as in certain combinations of words and in all kinds of music, for melodies and cadences are beautiful; and minds that lift themselves above the realm of sense to a higher order are aware of beauty in the conduct of life, in actions, in character, in the pursuit of the intellect; and there is the beauty of the virtues. What loftier beauty there may be, yet, our argument will bring to light.

What, then, is it that gives comeliness to material forms and draws the ear to the sweetness perceived in sounds, and what is the secret of the beauty there is in all that derives from Soul?

Is there some One Principle from which all take their grace, or is there a beauty peculiar to the embodied and another for the bodiless? Finally, is beauty one or many, what would such a Principle be?

Consider that some things, material shapes for instance, are gracious not by anything inherent but by something communicated, while others are lovely of themselves, as, for example, Virtue.

The same bodies appear sometimes beautiful, sometimes not; so that there is a good deal between being body and being beautiful.

Plotinus, *The Six Enneads,* translated by Stephen MacKenna. Ennead I. 6 was first published in London in 1908 and then published with the entire *Enneads* by the Medici Society of London in 1917. I have made slight changes to the text.

What, then, is this something that shows itself in certain material forms? This is the natural beginning of our inquiry.

What is it that attracts the eyes of those to whom a beautiful object is presented, and calls them, lures them, toward it, and fills them with joy at the sight? If we possess ourselves of this, we have at once a standpoint for the wider survey.

Almost everyone declares that the symmetry of parts towards each other and towards a whole, with, besides, a certain charm of color, constitutes the beauty recognized by the eye, that in visible things, as indeed in all else, universally, the beautiful thing is essentially symmetrical, patterned.

But think what this means.

Only a compound can be beautiful, never anything devoid of parts; and only a whole; the several parts will have beauty, not in themselves, but only as working together to give a comely total. Yet beauty in an aggregate demands beauty in details; it cannot be constructed out of ugliness; its law must run throughout.

All the loveliness of colour and even the light of the sun being devoid of parts and so not beautiful by symmetry, must be ruled out of the realm of beauty. And how comes gold to be a beautiful thing? And lightning by night, and the stars, why are these so fair?

In sounds also the simple must be proscribed, though often in a whole noble composition each several tone is delicious in itself.

Again since the one face, constant in symmetry, appears sometimes fair and sometimes not, can we doubt that beauty is something more than symmetry, that symmetry itself owes its beauty to a remoter principle?

Turn to what is attractive in methods of life or in the expression of thought; are we to call in symmetry here? What symmetry is to be found in noble conduct, or excellent laws, in any form of mental pursuit?

What symmetry can there be in points of abstract thought?

The symmetry of being accordant with each other? but there may be accordance or entire identity where there is nothing but ugliness: the proposition that honesty is merely a generous artlessness chimes in the most perfect harmony with the proposition that morality means weakness of will; the accordance is complete.

Then again, all the virtues are a beauty of the soul,

a beauty authentic beyond any of these others; but how does symmetry enter here? The soul, it is true, is not a simple unity, but still its virtue cannot have the symmetry of size or of number: what standard of measurement could preside over the compromise or the coalescence of the soul's faculties or purpose?

Finally, how by this theory would there be beauty in the Intellectual-Principle, essentially the solitary?

2. Let us, then, go back to the source, and indicate at once the Principle that bestows beauty on material things.

Undoubtedly this Principle exists; it is something that is perceived at the first glance, something which the soul names as from an ancient knowledge and, recognizing, welcomes it, enters into unison with it.

But let the soul fall in with the Ugly and at once it shrinks within itself, denies the thing, turns away from it, not accordant, resenting it.

Our interpretation is that the soul—by the very truth of its nature, by its affiliation to the noblest Existents in the hierarchy of Being—when it sees anything of that kin, or any trace of that kinship, thrills with an immediate delight, takes its own to itself, and thus stirs anew to the sense of its nature and of all its affinity.

But, is there any such likeness between the loveliness of this world and the splendors in the Supreme? Such likeness in the particulars would make the two orders alike: but what is there in common between beauty here and beauty There?

We hold that all the loveliness of this world comes by participating in the Ideal Form.

Every shapeless thing whose kind admits of pattern and form, as long as it remains outside of Reason and Idea, is ugly by that very isolation from the Divine-Thought. And this is the Absolute Ugly: an ugly thing is something that has not been entirely mastered by pattern, that is by Reason, the Matter not yielding at all points and in all respects to the Ideal Form.

But where the Idea-Form has entered, it has grouped and coordinated what from a diversity of parts was to become a unity: it has rallied confusion into co-operation: it has made the sum one harmonious coherence: for the Idea is a unity and what it molds must come to unity as far as multiplicity may.

So beauty enthrones itself on what has been brought into unity, giving itself to the parts as to the sum: when it lights on some natural unity, a thing of like parts, then it gives itself to that whole. Thus, for an illustration, there is the beauty, conferred by craftsmanship, of all a house with all its parts, and the beauty which some natural quality may give to a single stone.

This, then, is how the material thing becomes beautiful—by participating in the thought that flows from the Divine.

3. And the soul includes a faculty peculiarly addressed to Beauty—a power incomparably certain in the appreciating of its own, never in doubt whenever any lovely thing presents itself for judgment.

Or perhaps the soul itself acts immediately, affirming the Beautiful where it finds something accordant with the Ideal Form within itself, using this Idea as a canon of accuracy in its decision.

But what accordance is there between the material and that which antedates all Matter?

On what principle does the architect, when he finds the house standing before him correspondent with his inner ideal of a house, pronounce it beautiful? Is it not that the house before him, the stones apart, is the inner idea stamped upon the mass of exterior matter, the indivisible exhibited in diversity?

So with the perceptive faculty: discerning in certain objects the Ideal Form which has bound and controlled shapeless matter, opposed in nature to Idea, seeing further stamped upon the common shapes some shape excellent above the common, it gathers into unity what still remains fragmentary, catches it up and carries it within, no longer a thing of parts, and presents it to the Ideal-Principle as something concordant and congenial, a natural friend: the joy here is like that of a good man who discerns in a youth the early signs of a virtue consonant with the achieved perfection within his own soul.

The beauty of colour is also the outcome of a unification; it derives from shape, from the conquest of the darkness inherent in Matter by the pouring in of light, the unembodied, which is a Rational-Principle and an Ideal Form.

Hence it is that Fire itself is splendid beyond all material bodies, holding the rank of Ideal-Principle to the other elements, proceeding ever upwards, the subtlest and sprightliest of all bodies, as very near to the unembodied; itself alone admitting no other, all the others penetrated by it: for they take warmth but this is never cold; it has colour primarily; they receive the Form of colour from it: hence the splendor of its light, the splendor that belongs to the Idea. And all that has resisted and is but uncertainly held by its light remains outside of beauty, as not having absorbed the plentitude of the Form of colour.

And harmonies unheard in sound create the harmonies we hear, and wake the soul to the consciousness of beauty, showing it the one essence in another kind: for the measures of our sensible music are not arbitrary but are determined by the Principle whose labor is to dominate Matter and bring pattern into being.

Thus far of the beauties of the realm of sense, images and shadow-pictures, fugitives that have entered into Matter—to adorn, and to ravish, where they are seen.

4. But there are earlier and loftier beauties than these. In the sense-bound life we are no longer granted to know them, but the soul, taking no help from the organs, sees and proclaims them. To the vision of these we must mount, leaving sense to its own low place.

As it is not for those to speak of the graceful forms of the material world who have never seen them or known their grace—men born blind, let us suppose—in the same way those must be silent upon the beauty of noble conduct and of learning and all that order who have never cared for such things, nor may those tell of the splendor of virtue who have never known the face of Justice and of Moral-Wisdom beautiful beyond the beauty of Evening and of Dawn.

Such vision is for those only who see with the Soul's sight—and at the vision, they will rejoice, and awe will fall upon them and a trouble deeper than all the rest could ever stir, for now they are moving in the realm of Truth.

This is the spirit that Beauty must ever induce, wonderment and a delicious trouble, longing and love and a trembling that is all delight. For the unseen all this may be felt as for the seen; and this the Souls feel for it, every soul in some degree, but those the more deeply that are the more truly apt to this higher love—just as all take delight in the beauty of the body but all are not stung as sharply, and those only that feel the keener wound are known as Lovers.

5. These Lovers, then, lovers of the beauty outside of sense, must be made to declare themselves.

What do you feel in the presence of the grace you discern in actions, in manners, in sound morality, in all the works and fruits of virtue, in the beauty of souls? When you see that you yourselves are beautiful within, what do you feel? What is this

Dionysian exultation that thrills through your being, this straining upwards of all your Soul, this longing to break away from the body and live sunken within the veritable self?

These are no other than the emotions of Souls under the spell of love.

But what is it that awakens all this passion? No shape, no colour, no grandeur of mass: all is for a Soul, something whose beauty rests upon no colour, for the moral wisdom the Soul enshrines and all the other colorless splendor of the virtues. It is that you find in yourself, or admire in another, loftiness of spirit; righteousness of life; disciplined purity; courage of the majestic face; gravity; modesty that goes fearless and tranquil and passionless; and, shining down upon all, the light of god-like Intellection.

All these noble qualities are to be reverenced and loved, no doubt, but what entitles them to be called beautiful?

They exist: they manifest themselves to us: anyone that sees them must admit that they have reality of Being; and is not Real-Being, really beautiful?

But we have not yet shown by what property in them they have wrought the Soul to loveliness: what is this grace, this splendor as of Light, resting upon all the virtues?

Let us take the contrary, the ugliness of the Soul, and set that against its beauty: to understand, at once, what this ugliness is and how it comes to appear in the Soul will certainly open our way before us.

Let us then suppose an ugly Soul, dissolute, unrighteous: teeming with all the lusts; torn by internal discord; beset by the fears of its cowardice and the envies of its pettiness; thinking, in the little thought it has, only of the perishable and the base; perverse in all its unclean pleasures; living the life of abandonment to bodily sensation and delighting in its deformity.

What must we think but that all this shame is something that has gathered about the Soul, some foreign bane outraging it, soiling it, so that, encumbered with all manner of turpitude, it has no longer a clean activity or a clean sensation, but commands only a life smoldering dully under the crust of evil; that, sunk in manifold death, it no longer sees what a Soul should see, may no longer rest in its own being, dragged ever as it is towards the outer, the lower, the darkness?

An unclean thing, I dare say; flickering hither and thither at the call of objects of sense, deeply infected with the taint of body, occupied always in Matter, and absorbing Matter into itself, in its commerce with the Ignoble it has trafficked away for an alien nature its own essential Idea.

If a man has been immersed in filth or daubed with mud his native comeliness disappears and all that is seen is the foul stuff besmearing him: his ugly condition is due to alien matter that has encrusted him, and if he is to win back his grace it must be his business to scour and purify himself and make himself what he was.

So, we may justly say, a Soul becomes ugly by something foisted upon it, by sinking itself into the alien, by a fall, a descent into body, into Matter. The dishonor of the Soul is in its ceasing to be clean and separate. Gold is degraded when it is mixed with earthly particles; if these be worked out, the gold with gold alone. And so the Soul; let it be but cleared of the desires that come by its too intimate converse with the body, emancipated from all the passions, purged of all that embodiment has thrust upon it, withdrawn, a solitary, to itself again—in that moment the ugliness that came only from the alien is stripped away.

6. For, as the ancient teaching was, moral discipline and courage and every virtue, not even excepting Wisdom itself, all is purification.

Hence the Mysteries with good reason adumbrate the immersion of the unpurified in filth, even in the Nether-World, since the unclean loves filth for its very filthiness, and swine foul of body find their joy in foulness.

What else is Sophrosune [Self-control], rightly socalled, but to take no part in the pleasures of the body, to break away from them as unclean and unworthy of the clean? So too, Courage is but being fearless of the death which is but the parting of the Soul from the body, an event which no one can dread whose delight is to be his unmingled self. And Magnanimity is but disregard for the lure of things here. And Wisdom is but the Act of the Intellectual-Principle withdrawn from the lower places and leading the Soul to the Above.

The Soul thus cleansed is all Idea and Reason, wholly free of body, intellectual, entirely of that divine order from which the wellspring of Beauty rises and all the race of Beauty.

Hence the Soul heightened to the Intellectual-Principle is beautiful to all its power. For Intellection and all that proceeds from Intellection are the Soul's beauty, a graciousness native to it and not foreign, for only with these is it truly Soul. And it is just to say that in the Soul's becoming a good and beautiful thing is its becoming like to God, for from the Divine comes all the Beauty and all the Good in beings.

We may even say that Beauty is the Authentic-Existence and Ugliness is the Principle contrary to Existence: and the Ugly is also the primal evil; therefore its contrary is at once good and beautiful, or is Good and Beauty: and hence the one method will discover to us the Beauty-Good and the Ugliness-Evil.

And Beauty, this Beauty which is also The Good, must be posed as The First: directly deriving from this First is the Intellectual-Principle which is preeminently the manifestation of Beauty; through the Intellectual-Principle Soul is beautiful. The beauty in things of a lower order—actions and pursuits for instance—comes by operation of the shaping Soul which is also the author of the beauty found in the world of sense. For the Soul, a divine thing, a fragment as it were of the Primal Beauty, makes beautiful to the fullness of their capacity all things whatsoever that it grasps and molds.

7. Therefore we must ascend again towards the Good, the desired of every Soul. Anyone that has seen This, knows what I intend when I say that it is beautiful. Even the desire of it is to be desired as a Good. To attain it is for those that will take the upward part, who will set all their forces towards it, who will divest themselves of all that we have put on in our descent: so, to those that approach the Holy Celebrations of the Mysteries, there are appointed purifications and the laying aside of the garments worn before, and the entry in nakedness—until, passing, on the upward way, all that is other than the God, each in the solitude of himself shall behold that solitary-dwelling Existence, the Apart, the Unmingled, the Pure, that from Which all things depend, for Which all look and live and act and know, the Source of Life and of Intellection and of Being.

And one that shall know this vision—with what passion of love shall he not be seized, with what pangs of desire, what longing to be molten into one with This, what wondering delight! If he that has never seen this Being must hunger for It as for all his welfare, he that has known must love and reverence It as the very Beauty; he will be flooded with awe and gladness, stricken by a salutary terror; he loves with a veritable love, with sharp desire; all other loves than this he must despise, and disdain all that once seemed fair.

This, indeed, is the mood even of those who, having witnessed the manifestation of Gods or Supernals, can never again feel the old delight in the comeliness of material forms: what then are we to think of one that contemplates Absolute Beauty in Its essential integrity, no accumulation of flesh and matter, no dweller on earth or in the heavens—so perfect Its purity—far above all such things in that they are non-essential, composite, not primal but descending from This?

Beholding this Being—the Choragos [Leader of the Chorus, ed.] of all Existence, the Self-Intent that ever gives forth and never takes—resting rapt, in the vision and possession of so lofty a loveliness, growing to Its likeness, what Beauty can the soul yet lack? For This, the Beauty supreme, the absolute, and the primal, fashions Its lovers to Beauty and makes them also worthy of love.

And for This, the sternest and the uttermost combat is set before the Souls; all our labor is for This, lest we be left without part in this noblest vision, which to attain is to be blessed in the blissful sight, which to fail is to fail utterly.

For not he that has failed of the joy that is in colour or in visible forms, not he that has failed of power or of honoring or of kingdom has failed, but only he that has failed of only This, for Whose winning he should renounce kingdoms and command over earth and ocean and sky, if only, spurning the world of sense from beneath his feet, and straining to This, he may see.

8. But what must we do? How lies the path? How come to vision of the inaccessible Beauty, dwelling as if in consecrated precincts, apart from the common ways where all may see, even the profane?

He that has the strength, let him arise and withdraw into himself, forgoing all that is known by the eyes, turning away for ever from the material beauty that once made his joy. When he perceives those shapes of grace that show in body, let him not pursue: he must know them for copies, vestiges, shadows, and hasten away towards That they tell of. For if anyone follow what is like a beautiful shape playing over water—is there not a myth telling in symbol of such a dupe, how he sank into the depths of the current and was swept away to nothingness? So too, one that is held by material beauty and will not break free shall be precipitated, not in body but in Soul, down to the dark depths loathed of the Intellective-Being, where, blind even in the Lower-

World, he shall have commerce only with shadows, there as here.

"Let us flee then to the beloved Fatherland:" this is the soundest counsel. But what is this flight? How are we to gain the open sea? For Odysseus is surely a parable to us when he commands the flight from the sorceries of Circe or Calypso—not content to linger for all the pleasure offered to his eyes and all the delight of sense filling his days.

The Fatherland to us is There whence we have come, and There is The Father.

What then is our course, what the manner of our flight? This is not a journey for the feet; the feet bring us only from land to land; nor need you think of coach or ship to carry you away; all this order of things you must set aside and refuse to see: you must close the eyes and call instead upon another vision which is to be waked within you, a vision, the birthright of all, which few turn to use.

9. And this inner vision, what is its operation?

Newly awakened it is all too feeble to bear the ultimate splendor. Therefore the Soul must be trained—to the habit of remarking, first, all noble pursuits, then the works of beauty produced not by the labor of the arts but by the virtue of men known for their goodness: lastly, you must search the souls of those that have shaped these beautiful forms.

But how are you to see into a virtuous soul and know its loveliness?

Withdraw into yourself and look. And if you do not find yourself beautiful yet, act as does the creator of a statue that is to be made beautiful: he cuts away here, he smoothes there, he makes this line lighter, this other purer, until a lovely face has grown upon his work. So do you also: cut away all that is excessive, straighten all that is crooked, bring light to all that is overcast, labor to make all one glow of beauty and never cease chiselling your statue, until there shall shine out on you from it the godlike splendor of virtue, until you shall see the perfect goodness surely established in the stainless shrine.

When you know that you have become this perfect work, when you are self-gathered in the purity of your being, nothing from without clinging to the authentic man, when you find yourself wholly true to your essential nature, wholly that only veritable Light which is not measured by space, not narrowed to any circumscribed form nor again diffused as a thing void of term, but ever unmeasurable as something greater than all measure and more than all quantity—when you perceive that you have grown to this, you are now become very vision: now call up all your confidence, strike forward yet a step—you need a guide no longer—strain and see.

This is the only eye that sees the might Beauty. If the eye that adventures the vision be dimmed by vice, or weak, and unable in its cowardly blenching to see the uttermost brightness, then it sees nothing even though another point to what lies plain to sight before it. To any vision must be brought an eye adapted to what is to be seen, and having some likeness to it. Never did eye see the sun unless it had first become sunlike, and never can the soul have vision of the First Beauty unless itself be beautiful.

Therefore, first let each become godlike and each beautiful who cares to see God and Beauty. So, mounting, the Soul will come first to the Intellectual-Principle and survey all the beautiful Ideas in the Supreme and will avow that this is Beauty, that the Ideas are Beauty. For by their efficacy comes all Beauty else, but the offspring and essence of the Intellectual-Being. What is beyond the Intellectual-Principle we affirm to be the nature of Good radiating Beauty before it. So that, treating the Intellectual-Kosmos as one, the first is Beautiful: if we make distinction there, the Realm of Ideas constitutes the Beauty of the Intellectual Sphere; and The Good, which lies beyond, is the Fountain at once and Principle of Beauty: the Primal Good and the Primal Beauty have the one dwelling-place and, thus, always, Beauty's seat is There.

PART II

THE MEDIEVAL PERIOD

Chapter 8
AUGUSTINE

Aurelius Augustinus (354–430), Bishop of Hippo (now Annaba, Algeria), is perhaps the most influential philosopher between Aristotle and Aquinas. As a pagan rhetoretician his career took him from his native Carthage in North Africa to Italy, first to Rome and then to Milan. After having been under the spell of the Manichaean religion, he became increasingly dissatisfied with its inability to answer philosophical problems. In 385 he was converted to Christianity and soon identified with a Neo-Platonic version of the faith. In 395 he became Bishop of Hippo. His numerous works include *On Free Will,* from which our first selection is taken, *Confessions,* from which our second selection is taken, and *The City of God,* in which he responds to the charge that Christianity is responsible for the fall of the Roman Empire under Alaric in 412 and in which he develops a Christian political philosophy.

ON FREE WILL

The chief ethical problem for Augustine is the problem of Evil. What is its definition, source, effect on human nature, and how is it to be remedied? Implicit in his thinking is Epicurus's puzzle: If God is willing to prevent evil and suffering but is unable to, then He is not omnipotent, and hence not worthy of worship. If God is able to prevent evil and suffering but unwilling, then He is not all good and still unworthy of worship. He defines evil as "the absence of good." Since existence is good (because it is created by God), evil is the negative element of existence, a privation of existence. It is compared to a disease and wound (i.e., absence of health) which cease to exist when the cure comes, "for the wound or disease is not a substance, but a defect in the fleshly substance."

The source or cause of evil is the will, the falling away from the unchangeable good (God) of a being made good but changeable. First, the angel Satan and all his followers fell from the high ideal, and then humanity, led by the first man, Adam, followed after. The angels and Adam were created with a will that permitted a free option between good and evil. They chose the latter and thereby limited the choice of all succeeding human beings. When the will ceases to adhere to what is above itself, its Source (God), and turns to what is lower (itself or created objects), it becomes evil, not because it itself is evil, but because of the improper valuing of things.

Evil's power over humans leads to ignorance of duty and lust *(libido)* for what is hurtful, which in turn lead to error and suffering, which lead to fear. Error also leads to a false evaluation of values and virtues, which alone explains human pride or foolish joy in earthly success and goods. From these basic evils flow all other forms of misery. A just God must punish evil.

The answer to Epicurus's puzzle is that free will is a good, necessary for doing good, but, as such, it can be directed to evil (through false valuations—created things over the Creator). So it is not God's fault that man sinned and that, consequently, moral evil exists. But he does intervene and save an elect, so that the fall turns out to be a good thing for the elect (a *felix culpa,* a happy fault).

In our second reading, "On Time and Eternity," Augustine reverentially ponders the paradoxes of time: "Provided that no one asks me, I know [what time is]. If I want to explain it, I do not know"; since the past no longer exists and the future is not yet, how can the time be measured? Normally we can only measure what exists, but only the fleeting present exists. But we cannot measure it, since it is past as soon as we attempt to measure it. Juxtaposed with temporal extension is God's eternity, which never changes.

FOR FURTHER READING

Armstrong, A. H. ed. *The Cambridge History of Later Greek and Early Medieval Philosophy.* (Cambridge University Press, 1967), ch 21-27.

Brown, Peter. *Augustine of Hippo.* (University of California Press, 1967).

Chadwick, Henry. *Augustine.* (Oxford University Press, 1986).

D'Arcy, M. C., ed. *Augustine: A Collection of Critical Essays.* (Meridian, 1957).

Kirwin, Christopher, *Augustine.* (Routledge, 1989).

Meagher, E. *An Introduction to Augustine.* (New York University Press, 1978).

Nash, Ronald. *The Light of the Mind: St. Augustine's Theory of Knowledge.* (University of Kentucky Press, 1969).

Gilson, Etienne. *The Christian Philosophy of Saint Augustine,* trans. L. Lynch. (Random House, 1960).

On Free Will

BOOK I

i. I. *Evodius.*—Tell me, pray, whether God be not the author of evil. *Augustine.*—I shall tell you, if you will make it clear what you mean by evil in your question. For we are wont to use the word evil in two senses: the evil a man has done, and the evil he has suffered. *Evodius.*—I want to know about both kinds of evil. *Augustine.*—If you know or believe that God is good (and we may not think otherwise) he cannot do evil. Again, if we confess that God is just (and to deny that is sacrilegious) he gives rewards to the good just as he gives punishments to the wicked, but of course these punishments are evil to those who suffer them. Hence if no one is penalized unjustly—and this we must believe, seeing we believe that the universe is governed by divine providence—God is not the author of the evil a man does though he is the author of the evil a man suffers.

Ev.—Is there then some other author of the kind of evil which we do not attribute to the action of God? *Aug.*—There certainly is, for we cannot say that it happens without an author. But if you ask who that is I cannot tell you. For there is no one single author. Every evil man is the author of his evil deeds. If you wonder how that is, consider what we have just said: evil deeds are punished by the justice of God. They would not be justly punished unless they were done voluntarily.

2. *Ev.*—I do not know whether anyone sins without being taught to do evil. If that is true I ask from whom have we learned to do wrong. *Aug.*—Is learning a good thing? *Ev.*—Who would venture to say it was a bad thing? *Aug.*—Perhaps it is neither good nor bad? *Ev.*—I think it is a good thing. *Aug.*—Quite right, at any rate if learning gives and stirs up knowledge, and if it is the only path to knowledge. Don't you agree that this is so? *Ev.*—I think that

Reprinted from *Augustine: Earlier Writings,* edited and translated by John H. S. Burleigh, 1953, used by permission of SCM Press and Westminster John Knox Press.

nothing but good is learned by education. *Aug.*— Yet possibly evil is also learned in this way, for learning [*disciplina*] is derived from the verb "to learn" *discere*. *Ev.*—How, then, are evils committed by a man if they are not learned? *Aug.*—Possibly because he turns away from learning and stands apart from it. However that may be, it is at least manifest that, since learning is good, evil cannot be learned. If it is learned, it must be a part of education, and education will not be good. But, as you yourself admit, it is good. Evil, therefore, is not learned, and it is vain to ask from whom we have learned to do evil. Or, if indeed evil is learned, that can only be in the sense that we learn to avoid deeds which ought not to be done. Hence to do evil is nothing but to stray away from education.

3. *Ev.*—I think there must be two kinds of education, one by which we learn to do well and one by which we learn to do evil. When you asked whether education was a good thing I replied that it was, because my enthusiasm for the good made me think of the education that teaches to do good. Now I have a suspicion that there is another kind, which I have no doubt is a bad thing. *Aug.*—At any rate you regard intelligence as entirely a good thing? *Ev.*—So good indeed that a man can have nothing better. I should never say that intelligence can possibly be evil. *Aug.*—If a man has been taught something but does not understand it, could you regard him as learned? *Ev.*—Certainly not. *Aug.*—If intelligence is entirely good and is the necessary result of learning, every one who learns does well and also arrives at intelligence, and so again does well. Whoever asks for the cause of our learning anything simply asks for the cause of our doing well. So do not look for any teacher of evil. If he is evil he is not a teacher. If he is a teacher he is not evil.

ii, 4. *Ev.*—Since you force me to agree that we are not taught to do evil, tell me the cause why we do evil. *Aug.*—That is a question that gave me great trouble when I was a young man. It wearied me and drove me into the arms of heretics. By that accident I was so afflicted and overwhelmed with such masses of vain fables that, had not my love of finding the truth obtained divine aid, I could never have found my way out or breathed the pure air of free inquiry. But I took the greatest pains to find deliverance from that quandary, so in discoursing with you I shall follow the order which led to my own deliverance. May God grant his aid, and give us to understand what we have first believed. The steps

are laid down by the prophet who says: "Unless ye believe ye shall not understand" (Isa. 7:9 LXX). We know well that we must hold fast to that. We believe that all things which exist are from one God; and yet God is not the author of sins. The difficulty for the mind is this. If sins originate with souls which God has created, and which therefore have their origin from God, how are sins not to be charged against God at least mediately?

5. *Ev.*—Now you have plainly stated the problem that was troubling my mind, and which impelled me to ask my question. *Aug.*—Have courage, and hold to your faith. You cannot do better than believe even when you do not know the reason for your faith. To think the best of God is the truest foundation of piety. And to think the best of God means to believe that he is omnipotent and absolutely unchangeable, that he is the Creator of all good things, being himself more excellent than them all; that he is the most just ruler of all that he has created; that he had no assistance in creating as if he were not sufficient in himself. Hence he created all things of nothing. One, however, he did not create, but begat, One equal to himself, whom we call the only Son of God, whom we endeavour to describe more fully when we call him the Power and Wisdom of God. By him he made all things which are made of nothing. Having stated these articles of our faith let us strive with God's help to reach understanding of the problem which you have raised, and in this fashion.

iii, 6. You ask for the cause of our doing evil. First we must discuss what doing evil is. Tell me what you think about this. If you cannot put the whole thing briefly in a few words, at least indicate your opinion by naming some evil deeds one by one. *Ev.*—Adultery, homicide, sacrilege. I need mention no more. To enumerate all the others neither time nor my memory would be sufficient. But no one doubts that those I have mentioned are examples of evil deeds. *Aug.*—Tell me now why you think adultery is evil. Is it because it is forbidden by law? *Ev.*— It is not evil because it is forbidden by law. It is forbidden by law because it is evil. *Aug.*—Suppose someone were to press us, stressing the delights of adultery and asking why it is evil and why we think it worthy of condemnation. Do you think that people who wanted not only to believe that adultery is evil but also to know the reason why it is so, would be driven to appeal to the authority of the law? You and I believe without the slightest hesitation that adultery is evil, and I declare that all peoples and nations must believe that too. But our present endeavour is to obtain intelligent knowledge and assurance of what we have accepted in faith. Give this matter your best consideration and tell me the reason why you know that adultery is evil. *Ev.*—I know it is evil because I should not wish it to be committed with my own wife. Whoever does to another what he would not have done to himself does evil. *Aug.*— Suppose someone offered his wife to another, being willing that she should be corrupted by him in return for a similar licence allowed him with the other's wife. Would he have done no evil? *Ev.*—Far from that. He would have done great evil. *Aug.*—And yet his sin does not come under your general rule, for he does not do what he would not have done to him. You must find another reason to prove that adultery is evil.

7. *Ev.*—I think it evil because I have often seen men condemned on this charge. *Aug.*—But are not men frequently condemned for righteous deeds? Without going to other books, think of scripture history which excels all other books because it has divine authority. If we decide that condemnation is a certain indication of evil-doing, what an evil opinion we must adopt of the apostles and martyrs, for they were all thought worthy of condemnation for their faith. If whatever is condemned is evil, it was evil in those days to believe in Christ and to confess the Christian faith. But if everything is not evil which is condemned you must find another reason for teaching that adultery is evil. *Ev.*—I have no reply to make.

8. *Aug.*—Possibly the evil thing in adultery is lust. So long as you look for the evil in the outward act you discover difficulties. But when you understand that the evil lies in lust it becomes clear that even if a man finds no opportunity to lie with the wife of another but shows that he desires to do so and would do it if he got the chance, he is no less guilty than if he were caught in the act. *Ev.*—Nothing is more manifest; and I now see that there is no need of lengthy argument to persuade me that the same is true of homicide, sacrilege and all other sins. For it is clear that lust alone dominates the whole realm of evil-doing.

BOOK II

i, I. *Evodius.*—Now explain to me, if it can be done, why God has given man free choice in will-

ing, for if he had not received that freedom he would not have been able to sin. *Augustine.*—You hold it to be certainly known that it is God who has given man this power which you think ought not to have been given. *Ev.*—My impression is that we learned in the earlier book both that we have free will, and that our sinning is due to it. *Aug.*—I too remember that that became manifest to us. But now my question was whether you know that God gave us this power which we clearly have and which is the cause of our sinning. *Ev.*—No one else could have done so, I think. For we derive our origin from him, and from him we merit punishment or reward according as we sin or act rightly. *Aug.*—Here is another thing I desire to know. Do you know this quite distinctly, or do you merely believe it, without knowing it, because you allow yourself to be influenced by authority? *Ev.*—Undoubtedly I was first brought to believe this on the ground of authority. But what can be more true than to say that every good thing is from God, that justice is entirely good, and that it is just that sinners should be punished and well-doers rewarded. Hence it follows that it is by God that sinners are made unhappy and well-doers happy.

2. *Aug.*—I am not objecting: but I ask the question: how do you know that we derive our origin from God? You have not explained this though you have explained how we merit punishment or reward at his hand. *Ev.*—If it is accepted that God punishes sins, as it must be if it is true that all justice has its source in him, this alone would prove that we derive our origin from him. No doubt it is the characteristic of goodness to confer benefits on strangers, but it is not similarly the mark of justice to punish sins in those who are not under its immediate jurisdiction. Hence it is clear that we belong to him because he is not only most kind in conferring benefits upon us, but also most just in his punishments. Moreover, from the statement I made and you accepted, that every good thing comes from God, it can be known that man also comes from God. For man, in so far as he is man, is good because he can live aright if he chooses to do so.

3. *Aug.*—Clearly if this is so, the problem you have posed is solved. If man is good, and if he would not be able to act rightly except by willing to do so, he ought to have free will because without it he would not be able to act rightly. Because he also sins through having free will, we are not to believe that God gave it to him for that purpose. It is, therefore, a sufficient reason why he ought to have been given

it, that without it man could not live aright. That it was given for this purpose can be understood from this fact. If anyone uses his free will in order to sin, God punishes him. That would be unjust unless the will was free not only to live aright but also to sin. How could he be justly punished who uses his will for the purpose for which it was given? Now when God punishes a sinner what else do you suppose he will say to him than "Why did you not use your free will for the purpose for which I gave it to you, that is, in order to do right?" Justice is praised as a good thing because it condemns sins and honours righteous actions. How could that be done if man had not free will? An action would be neither sinful nor righteous unless it were done voluntarily. For the same reason both punishment and reward would be unjust, if man did not have free will. But in punishing and in rewarding there must have been justice since justice is one of the good things which come from God. God, therefore, must have given and ought to have given man free will.

ii, 4. *Ev.*—I admit now that God has given us free will. But don't you think, pray, that, if it was given for the purpose of well-doing, it ought not to have been possible to convert it to sinful uses? Justice itself was given to man so that he might live rightly, and it is not possible for anyone to live an evil life by means of justice. So no one ought to be able to sin voluntarily if free will was given that we might live aright. *Aug.*—God will, I hope, give me ability to answer you, or rather will give you the ability to answer your own question. Truth, which is the best master of all, will inwardly teach us both alike. But I wish you would tell me this: I asked you whether you know with perfect certainty that God has given us free will and you replied that you did. Now if we allow that God gave it, ought we to say that he ought not to have given it? If it is uncertain whether he gave it, we rightly ask whether it was good that it was given. If then we find that it was good, we find also that it was given by him who bestows all good things on men. If, however, we find that it was not a good thing we know that it was not given by him whom it is impious to accuse. If it is certain that he has given it, we ought to confess that, however it was given, it was rightly given. We may not say that it ought not to have been given or that it ought to have been given in some other way. If he has given it his action cannot in any way be rightly blamed.

5. *Ev.*—I believe all that unshakably. Nevertheless, because I do not know it, let us inquire as if it

were all uncertain. I see that because it is uncertain whether free will was given that men might do right since by it we can also sin, another uncertainty arises, namely whether free will ought to have been given to us. If it is uncertain that it was given that we should act righteously, it is also uncertain that it ought to have been given at all. Hence it will also be uncertain whether it was God who gave it. If it is uncertain that it ought to have been given, it is uncertain that it was given by him whom it is impious to believe has given anything which ought not to have been given. *Aug.*—At any rate you are quite certain that God exists. *Ev.*—I firmly believe it, but I do not know it. *Aug.*—We read in Scripture: "The fool hath said in his heart: there is no God" (Ps. 52:18). If such a fool were to say to you there is no God, and would not believe as you do, but wanted to know whether what you believe is true, would you simply go away and leave him, or would you think it your duty somehow to try to persuade him that what you believe is true, especially if he were really eager to know and not merely to argue obstinately? *Ev.*—Your last proviso tells me what I ought to reply to him. However absurd he might be he would assuredly agree that one ought not to dispute with an insidious and obstinate opponent about anything at all, least of all about a matter so important. He would admit that, and try to get me to believe that his inquiry was made in all good faith, and that in this matter there was neither guile nor obstinacy in him. Then I would use an argument that ought to carry great weight with any fair-minded person. I should show him that, just as he wants his neighbour to believe him when he tells of the thoughts of his mind, which he of course knows, but which are quite concealed from his neighbour, so he ought to believe that God exists because that is taught in the books of great men who have left their testimony in writing that they lived with the Son of God, and because they have written that they saw things which could not have happened if there were no God. I should urge that he would be very foolish to blame me for believing them, when he wanted me to believe himself. And when he saw that he had no good ground for finding fault with me, he would find no reason for refusing to imitate my faith. *Aug.*—If you think the existence of God is sufficiently proved by the fact that we judge it not to be rash to believe the Scripture-writers, why don't you think we should similarly trust their authority in the matters we have begun to investigate as if they were uncertain or quite beyond our knowledge? So we should be spared much labour in investigation. *Ev.*—Yes. But we want to know and to understand what we believe.

6. *Aug.*—You remember the position we adopted at the beginning of our former discussion. We cannot deny that believing and knowing are different things, and that in matters of great importance, pertaining to divinity, we must first believe before we seek to know. Otherwise the words of the prophet would be vain, where he says: "Except ye believe ye shall not understand" (Isa. 7:9). Our Lord himself, both in his words and by his deeds, exhorted those whom he called to salvation first of all to believe. When he afterwards spoke of the gift that was to be given to believers he said, not: "This is life eternal that they may believe"; but: "This is life eternal that they may know thee, the only true God, and Jesus Christ whom thou hast sent" (John 17:3). To those who already believed he said: "Seek and ye shall find" (Matt. 7:7). He cannot be said to have found, who merely believes what he does not know. And no one is fit to find God, who does not first believe what he will afterwards learn to know. Wherefore, in obedience to the precepts of the Lord, let us press on in our inquiry. What we seek at his bidding we shall find, as far as that can be done in this life, and by people such as we are. And he himself will demonstrate it to us. We must believe that these things are perceived and possessed by people of superior character even while they dwell on earth, and certainly, more clearly and perfectly, by all the good and pious after this life. So we must hope it will be with us, and, despising earthly and human things, we must in every way desire and love heavenly things.

BOOK III

45. God owes nothing to any man, for he gives everything gratuitously. If anyone says God owes him something for his merits, God did not even owe him existence. Nothing could be owing to one who did not yet exist. And what merit is there in turning to him from whom you derive existence, that you may be made better by him from whom you derive existence? Why do you ask him for anything as if you were demanding repayment of a debt? If you were unwilling to turn to him, the loss would not be his but yours. For without him you would be noth-

ing, and from him you derive such existence as you have; but on condition that, unless you turn to him, you must pay him back the existence you have from him, and become, not indeed nothing, but miserable. All things owe him, first, their existence so far as they are natural things, and secondly, that they can become better if they wish, receiving additional gifts if they wish them and being what they ought to be. No man is guilty because he has not received this or that power. But because he does not do as he ought he is justly held guilty. Obligation arises if he has received free will and sufficient power.

46. No blame attaches to the Creator if any of his creatures does not do what he ought. Indeed, that the wrong-doer suffers as he ought redounds to the praise of the Creator. In the very act of blaming anyone for not doing as he ought, he is praised to whom the debt is owed. If you are praised for seeing what you ought to do, and you only see it in him who is unchangeable truth, how much more is he to be praised who has taught you what you ought to wish, has given you the power to do it, and has not allowed you to refuse to do it with impunity? If "oughtness" depends upon what has been given, and man has been so made that he sins by necessity, then he ought to sin. So when he sins he does what he ought. But it is wicked to speak like that. No man's nature compels him to sin, nor does any other nature. No man sins when he suffers what he does not wish. If he has to suffer justly he does not sin in suffering unwillingly. He sinned in that he did something voluntarily which involved him in suffering justly what he did not wish. If he suffers unjustly, where is the sin? There is no sin in suffering something unjustly but in doing something unjustly. So, if no one is compelled to sin either by his own nature or by another, it remains that he sins by his own will. If you want to attribute his sin to the Creator you will make the sinner guiltless because he has simply obeyed the laws of the Creator. If the sinner can be rightly defended he is not a sinner, and there is no sin to attribute to the Creator. Let us then praise the Creator whether or not the sinner can be defended. If he is justly defended he is no sinner and we can therefore praise the Creator. If he cannot be defended, he is a sinner so far as he turns away from the Creator. Therefore praise the Creator. I find, therefore, no way at all, and I assert that there is none to be found, by which our sins can be ascribed to the Creator. our God. I find that he is to be praised even for sins, not only because he punishes them, but also because sin arises only when a man departs from his truth.

Evodius.—I most gladly approve all you have said, and assent with all my heart to the truth that there is no way at all of rightly ascribing our sins to our Creator. xvii, 47. But I should like to know, if possible, why those beings do not sin whom God knew beforehand would not sin, and why those others do sin whom he foresaw would sin. I do not now think that God's foreknowledge compels the one to sin and the other not to sin. But if there were no cause rational creatures would not be divided into classes as they are: those who never sin, those who continually sin, and the intermediary class of those who sometimes sin and sometimes are turned towards well-doing. What is the reason for this division? I do not want you to reply that it is the will that does it. What I want to know is what cause lies behind willing. There must be some reason why one class never wills to sin, another never lacks the will to sin, and another sometimes wills to sin and at other times does not so will. For they are all alike in nature. I seem to see that there must be some cause for this three-fold classification of rational beings according to their wills, but what it is I do not know.

48. *Augustine.*—Since will is the cause of sin, you now ask what is the cause of will. If I could find one, are you not going to ask for the cause of the cause I have found? What limit will there be to your quest, what end to inquiry and explanation? You ought not to push your inquiry deeper, for you must beware of imagining that anything can be more truly said than that which is written: "Avarice is the root of all evils" (I Tim. 6:10), that is, wanting more than is sufficient. That is sufficient which is demanded by the need of preserving any particular creature. Avarice, in Greek *philarguria,* derives its name from *argentum* [silver], because among the ancients coins were made of silver or more frequently with an admixture of silver. But avarice must be understood as connected not only with silver and money but with everything which is immoderately desired, in every case where a man wants more than is sufficient. Such avarice is cupidity, and cupidity is an evil will. An evil will therefore, is the cause of all evils. If it were according to nature it would preserve nature and not be hostile to it, and so it would not be evil. The inference is that the root of all evils is not according to nature. That is sufficient answer to all who want to accuse nature. But you ask what is the cause of this root. How then will it be the root of all evils?

If it has a cause, that cause will be the root of evil. And if you find a cause, as I said, you will ask for a cause of that cause, and there will be no limit to your inquiry.

49. But what cause of willing can there be which is prior to willing? Either it is a will, in which case we have not got beyond the root of evil will. Or it is not a will, and in that case there is no sin in it. Either, then, will is itself the first cause of sin, or the first cause is without sin. Now sin is rightly imputed only to that which sins, nor is it rightly imputed unless it sins voluntarily. I do not know why you should want to inquire further, but here is a further point. If there is a cause of willing it is either just or unjust. If it is just, he who obeys it will not sin, if unjust he who does not obey it will not sin either.

xviii, 50. But it may perhaps be violent, and compel him against his will? Are we to repeat our reply over and over again? Remember how much we have spoken earlier about sin and free will. Perhaps it is difficult to commit everything to memory, but hold fast to this brief statement. Whatever be the cause of willing, if it cannot be resisted no sin results from yielding to it. If it can be resisted, and it is not yielded to, no sin results. Possibly it may deceive a man when he is off his guard? Let him then take care not to be deceived. Is the deception so great that he cannot possibly avoid it? In that case no sin results? No one commits sin in doing what there was no means of avoiding? Yes, indeed, sin does result, and that means he is able to be on his guard.

51. Nevertheless, some things are done in ignorance which are held to be wrong and worthy of correction, as we read in the divinely authoritative books. The apostle says: "I obtained mercy because I did it in ignorance" (I Tim. 1:13). And the prophet says: "Remember not the sins of my youth and of my ignorance" (Ps. 25:7). Wrong things are done by necessity when a man wills to do right and has not the power. For thus it is written: "The good that I would I do not, but the evil which I would not, that I do." Again: "To will is present with me; but how to perform that which is good I find not" (Rom. 7:18–19). And again: "The flesh lusteth against the spirit, and the spirit against the flesh; for these are contrary the one to the other, so that ye cannot do the things that ye would" (Gal. 5:17). These are the words of men emerging from deadly damnation. If this were a description of man's nature and not of the penalty of sin, his situation would not be sinful.

If man has not departed from the natural state in which he was created, and which could not be made better, he is doing what he ought even when he does evil. But now man might be good if he were different. Because he is what he now is, he is not good, nor is it in his power to become good, either because he does not see what he ought to be, or, seeing it, has not the power to be what he sees he ought to be. Who can doubt that his is a penal state? Every just penalty is the penalty of sin and is called punishment. If the penalty is unjust, there is no doubt that it is, in fact, penalty, but it has been imposed on man by some unjust power that lords it over him. But it is mad to have any doubt about the omnipotence or the justice of God. Therefore man's penalty is just and is recompense for sin. No unjust lord could have usurped dominion over man, as it were, without the knowledge of God. No one could have forced him in his weakness against his will either by terrorism or by actual affliction, so that man's punishment might be held to be unjust. It remains, therefore, that his punishment is just and comes to him because he is to be condemned.

52. It is not to be wondered at that man, through ignorance, has not the freedom of will to choose to do what he ought; or that he cannot see what he ought to do or fulfil it when he will, in face of carnal custom which, in a sense, has grown as strong, almost, as nature, because of the power of mortal succession. It is the most just penalty of sin that man should lose what he was unwilling to make a good use of, when he could have done so without difficulty if he had wished. It is just that he who, knowing what is right, does not do it should lose the capacity to to know what is right, and that he who had the power to do what is right and would not should lose the power to do it when he is willing. In fact there are for every sinful soul these two penal conditions, ignorance and difficulty. From ignorance springs disgraceful error, and from difficulty comes painful effort. To approve falsehood instead of truth so as to err in spite of himself, and not to be able to refrain from the works of lust because of the pain involved in breaking away from fleshly bonds: these do not belong to the nature of man as he was created. They are the penalty of man as condemned. When we speak of the freedom of the will to do right, we are speaking of the freedom wherein man was created.

xix, 53. Here comes in the question which men, who are ready to accuse anything for their sins ex-

cept themselves, are wont to cast up, murmuring amongst themselves. They say: If Adam and Eve sinned, what have we miserable creatures done to deserve to be born in the darkness of ignorance and in the toils of difficulty, that, in the first place, we should err not knowing what we ought to do, and, in the second place, that when the precepts of justice begin to be opened out to us, we should wish to obey them but by some necessity of carnal lust should not have the power? To them I reply: Keep quiet and stop murmuring against God. They might perhaps rightly complain if no man had ever been victorious over error and lust. And yet there is One present everywhere who, in many ways, by means of the creation that serves him as its Lord, calls back him who has gone astray, teaches him who believes, comforts him who has hope, exhorts the diligent, helps him who is trying and answers prayer. You are not held guilty because you are ignorant in spite of yourself, but because you neglect to seek the knowledge you do not possess. You are not held guilty because you do not use your wounded members but because you despise him who is willing to heal them. These are your own personal sins. To no man is it given to know how to seek to his advantage what to his disadvantage he does not know. He must humbly confess his weakness, so that as he seeks and makes his confession *he* may come to his aid who, in aiding, knows neither error nor difficulty.

54. All that a man does wrongfully in ignorance, and all that he cannot do rightly though he wishes, are called sins because they have their origin in the first sin of the will when it was free. These are its deserved consequences. We apply the name "tongue" not only to the member which we move in our mouth when we speak, but also to what follows from that motion, namely, words and language. Thus we speak of the Greek or the Latin tongue. So we apply the word "sin" not only to that which is properly called sin, that is, what is committed knowingly and with free will, but also to all that follows as the necessary punishment of that first sin. So we use the word "nature" in a double sense. Properly speaking, human nature means the blameless nature with which man was originally created. But we also use it in speaking of the nature with which we are born mortal, ignorant and subject to the flesh, which is really the penalty of sin. In this sense the apostle says: "We also were by nature children of wrath even as others" (Eph. 2:3).

xx, 55. As we are born from the first pair to a mortal life of ignorance and toil because they sinned and fell into a state of error, misery and death, so it most justly pleased the most high God, Governor of all things, to manifest from the beginning, from man's origin, his justice in exacting punishment, and in human history his mercy in remitting punishment. When the first man was condemned, happiness was not so completely taken from him that he lost also his fecundity. Though his offspring was carnal and mortal, yet in its own way it could contribute some glory and ornament to the earth. That he should beget children better than himself would not have been equitable. But if any of Adam's race should be willing to turn to God, and so overcome the punishment which had been merited by the original turning away from God, it was fitting not only that he should not be hindered but that he should also receive divine aid. In this way also the Creator showed how easily man might have retained, if he had so willed, the nature with which he was created, because his offspring had power to transcend that in which he was born.

56. Again, if only one soul was originally created, and the souls of all men since born derive their origin from it, who can say that he did not sin when the first man sinned? If however souls are created separately in individual men as they are born, it appears not to be unreasonable but rather most appropriate and in accordance with right order that the ill desert of an earlier soul should determine the nature of those which are created afterwards, and that by its goodness a soul later created should deserve to regain the state which the earlier one had lost. There would be nothing unworthy about it if the Creator had determined to show in this way that the soul so far excelled in dignity every corporeal creature that one soul could start from the position to which another had fallen. The sinful soul reached an estate of ignorance and toil, which is rightly called penalty, because before the penalty it had been better. Even if a soul, before it sinned and even before it was born, was given a nature like that which another acquired after a guilty life, it has no small good for which to give thanks to its Creator, for even in its inchoate beginning it is better than any body however perfect. These are no mean advantages, not only to be a soul and so naturally to excel all bodies, but also to have the power with the aid of the Creator to cultivate itself, and with pious care to acquire all the virtues by which it may be liberated both from

tormenting toil and from blinding ignorance. If that is so in the case of souls that are born, ignorance and toil will not be punishment for sin but a warning to improve themselves, and the beginning of their perfecting. It is no small thing to have been given, before there has been any merit gained by any good work, the natural power to discern that wisdom is to be preferred to error and tranquillity to toil, and to know that these good things are to be reached not simply by being born but by earnestly seeking them. But if the soul will not act in this way it will rightly be held guilty of sin for not making a good use of the power it has received. Though it is born in ignorance and toilsomeness there is no necessity for it to remain in that state. Indeed it could not exist were not Almighty God the Creator of such souls. For before he was loved he made them. In love he restores them. And being loved he perfects them. To souls which do not yet exist he gives existence; and to those who love him who gives them existence he gives happiness too.

57. If, on the other hand, souls pre-exist in some secret place and are sent out to quicken and rule the bodies of individuals when they are born, their mission is to govern well the body which is born under the penalty of the sin of the first man, that is, mortality. They are to discipline it with the virtues, and subject it to an orderly and legitimate servitude, so that in due order and in the due time men may attain the place of heavenly perfection. When they enter this life and submit to wearing mortal members these souls must also undergo forgetfulness of their former existence and the labours of their present existence, with consequent ignorance and toil which in the first man were a punishment involving mortality and completing the misery of the soul. But for these souls ignorance and toil are opportunities for ministering to the restoration of the integrity of the body. The flesh coming from a sinful stock causes this ignorance and toil to infect the souls sent to it. Only in this sense are they to be called sins, and the blame for them is to be ascribed neither to the souls nor to their Creator. For he has given them power to do good in difficult duties, and has provided for them the way of faith where oblivion had brought blindness. Also and above all, he has given them the insight which every soul possesses; that it must seek to know what to its disadvantage it does not know, and that it must persevere in burdensome duties and strive to overcome the difficulty of well-doing, and implore the Creator's aid in its efforts. By the law without and by direct address to the heart within, he has commanded that effort be made, and he has prepared the glory of the Blessed City for those who triumph over the devil, who with wicked persuasion overcame the first man and reduced him to his state of misery. That misery these souls undergo in lively faith in order to overcome the devil. No little glory is to be gained from the campaign to overcome the devil, waged by undergoing the punishment which he glories in having brought upon his victim, man. Whoever yields to love of the present life and takes no part in that campaign can by no means justly attribute the shame of his desertion to the command of his king. Rather the Lord of all will appoint his place with the devil, because he loved the base hire wherewith he bought his desertion.

58. But if souls existing in some place are not sent by the Lord God, but come of their own accord to inhabit bodies, it is easy to see that any ignorance or toil which is the consequence of their own choice cannot in any way be ascribed as blame to the Creator. He would be entirely without blame. If we accept the view that he himself sent souls, he did not take from them even in the state of ignorance and toil their freedom to ask and seek and endeavour, and was ever ready to give to those who ask, to demonstrate to those who seek and to open to those who knock. Similarly, on this other view, he would allow conquest over ignorance and difficulty on the part of earnest and rightminded souls to count as a crown of glory. He would not lay the ignorance or the difficulty to the charge of the negligent or of those who wished to defend their sins on the ground of their infirmity. But he would justly punish them because they would rather abide in ignorance and difficulty than reach truth and a life free from struggle by zeal in seeking and learning, and by humility in prayer and confession.

xxi, 59. Now there are these four opinions about the origin of the soul, viz., that it comes by propagation, that it is newly created with each individual who is born, that it exists somewhere beforehand and comes into the body of the newly-born either being divinely sent or gliding in of its own accord. None of these views may be rashly affirmed. Either that question, because of its obscurity and perplexity, has not been handled and illumined by catholic commentators on Holy Writ. Or, if it has been done, their writings have not come into our hands. God give us a true faith that will hold no false or unworthy opinion concerning the substance of the Cre-

ator. For by the path of piety we are wending our way towards him. If we hold any other opinion concerning him than the true one, our zeal will drive us not to beatitude but to vanity. There is no danger if we hold a wrong opinion about the creature, provided we do not hold it as if it were assured knowledge. We are not bidden to turn to the creature in order to be happy, but to the Creator himself. If we are persuaded to think otherwise of him than we ought to think or otherwise than what is true we are deceived by most deadly error. No man can reach the happy life by making for that which is not, or, if it does exist, does not make men happy.

60. That we may be able to enjoy and cleave to eternal truth in contemplation, a way out of temporalities has been prepared for our weakness, so that we may trust the past and the future so far as is sufficient for our journey towards eternal things. The discipline of faith is governed by the divine mercy, so that it may have supreme authority. Things present are perceived as transient so far as the creature is concerned. They consist in the mobility and mutability of body and soul. Of these things we cannot have any kind of knowledge unless they enter into our experience. If we are told on divine authority about the past or the future of any created thing we are to believe it without hesitation. No doubt some of this was past before we could have perceived it. Some of it has not yet reached our senses. Nevertheless we are to believe it, for it helps to strengthen our hope and call forth our love, inasmuch as it reminds us, through the ordered temporal series, that God does not neglect our liberation. If any error assumes the rôle of divine authority it is most reasonably refuted, if it is shown to hold or to affirm that there is any mutable form that is not the creation of God, or that there is any mutability in the substance of God; or if it contends that the substance of God is more or less than a Trinity. To understand that Trinity soberly and piously occupies all the watchful care of Christians, and that is the goal of every advance. Concerning the unity of the Trinity and the equality of persons and the properties of each, this is not the place to discourse. To relate some things which pertain to saving faith and which concern the Lord our God, Author and Maker and Governor of all things, may give useful support to a childlike incipient purpose to rise from earthly to heavenly things. That is easy to do and it has already been done by many. But to handle the whole question so as to bring all human intelligence into the light of clear reason, as far as possible in this life, does not seem an easy task for any man's eloquence or even for any man's thought, much less ours. It is therefore not to be lightly attempted. Let us go on with what we have begun, so far as we have the permission and the help of God. All that we are told of past events concerning the creation, and all that is foretold concerning the future is to be believed without hesitation, because it helps to commend pure religion by stimulating in us sincere love to God and our neighbour. It is to be defended against unbelievers, either by wearing down their unbelief with the weight of authority, or by showing them, as far as possible, first, that it is not foolish to believe it, and, secondly, that it is foolish not to believe it. But false doctrine, not about past or future events so much as about the present and above all about unchangeable things, must be convincingly refuted by clear reasoning, so far as it is granted to us.

61. Of course when we are thinking of the series of temporal things, expectation of things to come is more important than research into things past. In the divine books also past events are narrated, but they carry with them the forecast or promise or attestation of things to come. In fact no one pays much attention to temporal prosperity or adversity when they are past. All anxiety and care are bestowed on what is hoped for in the future. By some intimate and natural mechanism of the mind things which have happened to us, after they are past, are accounted, in any reckoning of felicity and misery, as if they had never happened. What disadvantage is it to me not to know when I began to be, when I know that I exist now and do not cease to hope that I shall continue to exist? I am not so interested in the past as to dread as deadly error any false opinion I may entertain as to what actually transpired. But as to my future I direct my course, guided by the mercy of my Maker. But if I have any false belief or opinion about my future, or about him with whom I am to be for ever, I must with all my might beware of that error. Otherwise I shall not make the necessary preparation, or I shall not be able to reach him who is the objective of my enterprise, because my outlook has been confused. If I were buying a garment it would be no disadvantage to me to have forgotten last winter, but it would be a disadvantage if I did not believe that cold weather was coming on. So it would be no disadvantage to my soul to forget anything that it may perhaps have endured, so long as it diligently observes and remembers all that may

warn it to make preparation for the future. For example, it will do no harm to a man who is sailing to Rome to forget from what shore he set sail, so long as he knows all the time whither he is directing his course. It will do him no good to remember the shore from which he began his voyage, if he has made some false calculation about the port of Rome and runs upon rocks. So it is no disadvantage to me not to remember the beginning of my life, so long as I know the end where I am to find rest. Nor would any memory or guess concerning life's commencement be of any advantage to me if, holding unworthy opinions of God who is the sole end of the soul's labours, I should run upon the reefs of error.

62. What I have said is not to be taken to mean that I forbid those who have the ability to inquire whether, according to the divinely inspired Scriptures, soul is propagated from soul, or whether souls are created separately for all animate beings; whether they are sent at the divine behest from some place where they abide to animate and rule the body, or whether they insinuate themselves of their own accord. Such inquiries and discussions are justifiable if reason demands them in order to answer some necessary question, or if leisure from more necessary matters is available. I spoke as I did rather that no one in so great a problem should rashly become angry with another because he will not yield to his opinion, having grounds for hesitation based perhaps on a broader culture; or even that no one who has clear and certain understanding of these matters from Scripture should suppose that another has lost all hope for the future because he does not remember the soul's origin in the past.

xxii, 63. However that may be, whether that question is to be passed over entirely or to be deferred for later consideration, there is no obstacle preventing us from answering the question with which we are dealing at present in such a way as to make clear that by the upright, just, unshaken and changeless majesty and substance of the Creator souls pay the penalty for their own sins. These sins, as we have explained at great length, are to be ascribed to nothing but to their own wills, and no further cause for sins is to be looked for.

64. If ignorance and moral difficulty are natural to man, it is from that condition that the soul begins to progress and to advance towards knowledge and tranquillity until it reaches the perfection of the happy life. If by its own will it neglects to advance by means of good studies and piety—for the capacity to do so is not denied to it—it justly falls into a still graver state of ignorance and struggle, which is now penal, and is ranked among inferior creatures according to the appropriate and fitting government of the universe. Natural ignorance and natural impotence are not reckoned to the soul as guilt. The guilt arises because it does not eagerly pursue knowledge, and does not give adequate attention to acquiring facility in doing right. It is natural for an infant not to know how to speak and not to be able to speak. But that ignorance and inability are not only blameless according to the rules of the teachers, but are also attractive and pleasing to human feeling. In this case there is no faulty failure to acquire the power of speaking, nor, if possessed, was it lost through any fault. If we supposed that happiness was to be found in eloquence and it was thought criminal to commit a fault in speaking, as it is thought criminal to commit a fault in action, no one would put the blame on our infancy, though as infants we began to acquire eloquence. But clearly one would be deservedly blamed if by perversity of will one either remained in the infantile condition or fell back into it. In the same way, if ignorance of the truth and difficulty in doing right are natural to man, and he has to begin to rise from that condition to the happiness of wisdom and tranquillity, no one rightly blames him for the natural condition from which he started. But if he refuses to progress, or voluntarily falls back from the path of progress, he will justly and deservedly pay the penalty.

65. But his Creator is to be praised on all counts. He gave him the power to rise from such beginnings to ability to attain the chief good. He renders aid as he advances. He completes and perfects his advance. And if he sins, that is, if he refuses to rise from these beginnings to perfection or if he falls back from any progress he may have made, he imposes on him a most just condemnation according to his deserts. The soul was not created evil because it was not given all that it had power to become. All corporeal things however perfect are far inferior to the soul's beginning, though anyone who takes a sane view of things judges that they, too, are to be praised in their own kind. That the soul does not know what it should do is due to its not yet having received that gift. It will receive it if it makes a good use of what it has received. It has received the power to seek diligently and piously if it will. That it cannot instantly fulfil the duty it recognizes as duty, means that that is another gift it has not yet received. Its higher part first

perceives the good it ought to do, but the slower and carnal part is not immediately brought over to that opinion. So by that very difficulty it is admonished to implore for its perfecting the aid of him whom it believes to be the author of its beginning. Hence he becomes dearer to it, because it has its existence not from its own resources but from his goodness, and by his mercy it is raised to happiness. The more it loves him from whom it derives its existence, the more surely it rests in him, and enjoys his eternity more fully. We do not rightly say of a young shoot of a tree that it is sterile, because several summers must pass before at the appointed time it reveals its fruitfulness. Why should not the Author of the soul be praised with due piety if he has given it so good a start that it may by zeal and progress reach the fruit of wisdom and justice, and has given it so much dignity as to put within its power the capacity to grow towards happiness if it will?

xxiii, 66. Against this reasoning, ignorant men are wont to repeat a calumny based upon the deaths of infants and certain bodily torments with which we often see them afflicted. They say: What need had the infant to be born if it was to die before it had acquired any merit in life? How is it to be reckoned in the future judgment, seeing that it cannot be put among the just since it performed no good works, nor among the evil because it never sinned? I reply: If you think of the all-embracing complexity of the universe, and the orderly connection of the whole creation throughout space and time, you will not believe that a man, whatsoever he may be, can be created superfluously. Why, not even the leaf of a tree is created superfluously. But it is idly superfluous to inquire about the merits of one who has done nothing to merit anything. There is no need to fear lest there be a life lived which is neither righteous nor sinful, nor that the judge will be able to pronounce sentence involving neither reward nor punishment.

67. At this point men are wont to ask what good the sacrament of Christ's Baptism can do to infants, seeing that many of them die after having been baptized but before they can know anything about it. In this case it is pious and right to believe that the infant is benefited by the faith of those who bring him to be consecrated. This is commended by the salutary authority of the Church, so that everyone may realize how beneficial to him is his faith, seeing that one man's faith can be made beneficial for another who has no faith of his own. The son of the widow of Nain could have had no advantage from any faith of his own, for, being dead, he had no faith. But his mother's faith procured him the benefit of being raised from the dead (Luke 7:11 ff.). How much more may the faith of another benefit an infant seeing that no faithlessness of its own can be imputed to it?

68. A greater complaint, and one with a show of pity about it, is often occasioned by the bodily torments which infants suffer, for by reason of their tender age they have committed no sins, at least if the souls which animate them have had no existence prior to their birth as human beings. People say: What evil have they done that they should suffer such things? As if innocence could have any merit before it has the power to do any hurt! Perhaps God is doing some good in correcting parents when their beloved children suffer pain and even death. Why should not such things happen? When they are past they will be for those who suffered them as if they never happened. And those on whose account they happened will be made better if they accept correction from temporal troubles and choose to live more righteously. Or, if they will not allow the sufferings of this life to turn their desire towards eternal life, they will be without excuse when they are punished at the last judgment. By the torments of their children parents have their hard hearts softened, their faith exercised and their tenderness proved. Who knows what good compensation God has reserved in the secrecy of his judgments for the children themselves who, though they have not had the chance of living righteously, at least have committed no sin and yet have suffered? Not for nothing does the Church commend for honour as martyrs the children who were slain by the orders of Herod when he sought to slay the Lord Jesus Christ.

69. These casuists, who ask questions of that kind not because they want to examine them seriously but because they are loquacious and want to ventilate them, are wont also to trouble the faith of the less learned by pointing to the pains and labours of animals. What evil, they say, have the animals deserved that they suffer such woes, or what good can they hope for in having such troubles imposed on them? They say that or feel like that because they have a perverted sense of values. They are not able to see what the chief good is, and they want to have everything just as they conceive the chief good to be. They can think of no chief good except fine bodies like the celestial bodies which are not subject to corruption. And so without any sense of order they demand

that the bodies of animals shall not suffer death or any corruption, as if forsooth they were not mortal, being lowly bodies, or were evil because celestial bodies are better. The pain which the animals suffer commends the vigour of the animal soul as admirable and praiseworthy after its own fashion. By animating and ruling the body of the animal it shows its desire for unity. For what is pain but a certain feeling that cannot bear division and corruption? Hence it is clearer than day that the animal soul is eager for unity in the whole body and is tenacious of unity. Neither gladly nor with indifference, but reluctantly and with obstinate resistance it meets bodily suffering which it is grieved to know destroys the unity and integrity of the body. We should never know what eagerness there is for unity in the inferior animal creation, were it not for the pain suffered by animals. And if we did not know that, we should not be made sufficiently aware that all things are framed by the supreme, sublime and ineffable unity of the Creator.

70. Indeed, if you give pious and diligent attention, every kind of creature which can come under the consideration of the human mind contributes to our instruction, speaking by its diverse movements and feelings as in so many diverse tongues, everywhere proclaiming and insisting that the Creator is to be recognized. There is no creature that feels pain or pleasure which does not by some sort of unity attain a beauty appropriate to its own kind, or some sort of stability of nature. There is no creature sensitive to pain or pleasure which does not, simply by avoiding pain and seeking pleasure, show that it avoids its own destruction and seeks unity. In rational souls all desire for knowledge, which is the delight of the rational nature, refers its acquisitions to unity, and, in avoiding error, avoids nothing so much as the confusion of incomprehensible ambiguity. Why is ambiguity so detestable save that it has no certain unity? Hence it is clear that all things, whether they offend or are offended, whether they delight or are delighted, proclaim or suggest the unity of the Creator. But if ignorance and moral difficulty from which we must set out on the rational life are not natural to souls, they must be undertaken as a duty or imposed as a punishment. I think we have said enough about these matters now.

xxiv, 71. What sort of creature the first man was when created is a more important question than how his posterity was propagated. People seem to pose a very acute question when they say: If the first man was created wise, why has he been seduced? If he was created foolish how is God to escape being held to be the author of vice, since folly is the greatest vice of all? As if human nature might not receive some intermediate quality which can be called neither folly nor wisdom! Man begins to be either foolish or wise, and one or other of these terms must necessarily be applied to him, as soon as it becomes possible for him to have wisdom or to neglect it. Then his will is guilty, for his folly is his own fault. No one is so foolish as to call an infant foolish, though it would be even more absurd to call it wise. An infant can be called neither foolish nor wise though it is already a human being. So it appears that human nature receives an intermediate condition which cannot be rightly called either folly or wisdom. Similarly, if anyone was animated by a soul disposed as men are who lack wisdom through negligence, nobody could rightly call him foolish, because he would owe his condition not to his own fault but to the nature with which he was endowed. Folly is not any kind of ignorance of things to be sought and avoided, but ignorance which is due to a man's own fault. We do not call an irrational animal foolish, because it has not received the power to be wise. Yet we often apply terms improperly where there is some similarity. Blindness is the greatest fault that eyes can have, yet it is not a fault in puppies, and is not properly called blindness.

72. If man was created such that, although he was not yet wise, he could at least receive a commandment which he ought to obey, it is not surprising that he could be seduced. Nor is it unjust that he pays the penalty for not obeying the commandment. Nor is his Creator the author of sins, for it was not yet a sin in man not to have wisdom, if that gift were not yet given him. But he had something that would enable him to attain what he did not have, provided he was willing to make a good use of it. It is one thing to be a rational being, another to be a wise man. Reason makes a man able to receive the precept to which he ought to be loyal, so that he may perform what is commanded. The rational nature grasps the precept, obedience to which brings wisdom. What nature contributes to the grasping of the precept, will contributes to obedience to it. As the merit of receiving the precept, so to speak, is to have a rational nature, so the merit of receiving wisdom is obedience to the precept. As soon as a man begins to have the power to receive the precept, he begins also to have the possibility of sinning. Before he becomes

wise he sins in one or other of two ways. Either he does not fit himself to receive the precept, or, receiving it, he does not obey it. The wise man sins if he turns away from wisdom. The precept does not come from him on whom it is laid, but from him who gives it; so wisdom, too, comes not from him who is illumined, but from him who gives the light. Why then should not the Creator of man be praised? Man is good, and better than the cattle because he is capable of receiving the precept; better still when he has received the precept; and still better when he has obeyed it; best of all when he is made happy by the eternal light of wisdom. Sin, or evil, consists in neglect to receive the precept or to obey it, or to hold fast the contemplation of wisdom. So we learn that, even although the first man had been created wise, it was nevertheless possible for him to be seduced. Because his sin was committed with his free will, a just penalty followed by divine law. As the apostle Paul says: "Saying they are wise they have become fools" (Rom. 1:22). It is pride that turns man away from wisdom, and folly is the consequence of turning away from wisdom. Folly is a kind of blindness, as he says: "Their foolish heart was darkened." Whence came this darkness, if not from turning away from the light of wisdom? And whence came the turning away, if not from the fact that man, whose good God is, willed to be his own good and so to substitute himself for God. Accordingly the Scriptures say: "Looking to myself, my soul is cast down" (Ps. 42:6. LXX). And again: "Taste and ye shall be as gods" (Gen. 3:5).

73. Some people are troubled by this question. Did folly cause the first man to depart from God, or did he become foolish by departing from God? If you answer that folly made him depart from wisdom, it will appear that he was foolish before he did so, so that folly is the cause of his doing so. If you reply that he became foolish by departing from wisdom, they ask whether he acted foolishly or wisely in departing. If wisely he did right and committed no sin. If foolishly there was folly already in him, they say, which made him depart from wisdom. For without folly he could do nothing foolishly. Clearly there is some middle state of transition from wisdom, to folly, which cannot be called either wisdom or folly; but it is not given to men to understand this except by way of contrast with both. No mortal becomes wise unless he passes from folly to wisdom. If there is folly in the actual transition it is not a good thing, but to say that would be mad. If there is wisdom in it, there must already be wisdom in a man before he makes the transition to wisdom. But that is equally absurd. Hence we learn that there is an intermediate state which may be said to be neither folly nor wisdom. In the same way when the first man passed from the citadel of wisdom to folly, the transition in itself was neither foolish nor wise. In the matter of sleeping and waking, to be asleep is not the same thing as to fall asleep, nor is to be awake the same thing as to awake. There is a transitional state between sleeping and waking as between folly and wisdom. But there is this difference. In the former case there is no intervention of will; in the latter the transition never takes place except by the action of the will. That is why the consequence is just retribution.

xxv, 74. But the will is not enticed to do anything except by something that has been perceived. It is in a man's power to take or reject this or that, but it is not in his power to control the things which will affect him when they are perceived. We must admit, therefore, that the mind is affected by perceptions both of superior things and of inferior things. Thus the rational creature may take from either what it will, and, according to its deserts in making the choice, it obtains as a consequence either misery or happiness. In the Garden of Eden the commandment of God came to man's attention from above. From beneath came the suggestion of the serpent. Neither the commandment of God nor the suggestion of the serpent was in man's power. But if he has reached the healthy state of wisdom he is freed from all the shackles of moral difficulty, and has freedom not to yield to the enticing suggestions of inferior things. How free he is we can infer from the fact that even fools overcome them as they pass on to wisdom, though of course they have the difficulty of trying to do without the deadly sweetness of the pernicious things to which they have been accustomed.

75. Here it may be asked, if man had impressions from both sides, from the commandment of God and from the suggestion of the serpent, whence did the devil receive the suggestion to follow impiety which brought him down from his abode on high. If there was nothing in his experience to affect him he would not have chosen to do what he did. If nothing had come into his mind he would not have directed his purpose to wickedness. Whence then did the thought come into his mind to attempt things which made of a good angel a devil? Whoever wills wills something. He cannot exercise will unless some hint

comes to him from outside through bodily sense, or some thought comes into his mind in some secret way. We must distinguish two kinds of experience. One proceeds from the will of another who uses persuasion, as, for example, when man sinned by consenting to the persuasion of the devil. The other kind springs from environment, mental and spiritual, or corporeal and sensational. The environment of the mind may be said to include the unchangeable Trinity, though the Trinity rather stands high above the mind. More properly the environment of the mind is, first of all, the mind itself which enables us to know that we live, and, secondly, the body which the mind governs, moving the appropriate limb to accomplish any action that may be required. The environment of the senses is corporeal objects of all kinds.

76. The mind is not sovereign wisdom, for that is unchangeable. Yet in contemplating sovereign wisdom the mutable mind may behold itself and in a fashion come to know itself. But that cannot be unless a distinction is made. The mind is not as God is, and yet, next to God, it can give us satisfaction. It is better when it forgets itself in love for the unchangeable God, or indeed utterly contemns itself in comparison with him. But if the mind, being immediately conscious of itself, takes pleasure in itself to the extent of perversely imitating God, wanting to enjoy its own power, the greater it wants to be the less it becomes. Pride is the beginning of all sin, and the beginning of man's pride is revolt from God (Eccl. 10:12–13). To the devil's pride was added malevolent envy, so that he persuaded man to show the same pride as had proved the devil's damnation. So man had imposed on him a penalty which was corrective rather than destructive. As the devil had offered himself to man as a pattern of pride to be imitated, so the Lord, who promises us eternal life, offered himself as a pattern of humility for our imitation. Now that the blood of Christ is shed for us, after unspeakable toils and miseries, let us cleave to our Liberator with such love, let us be so enraptured with his brightness, that nothing coming into our experience from the lower realms may rob us of our vision of the higher things. And if any suggestion springing from a desire for the inferior should deflect our purpose, the eternal damnation and torments of the devil will recall us to the true path.

77. Such is the beauty of justice, such the pleasure of the eternal light, that is, of unchangeable truth and wisdom, that, even if we could not abide

in it more than the space of a single day, for that day alone innumerable years of this life full of delights and abundance of temporal goods would be rightly and deservedly despised. Deep and unfeigned is the emotion expressed in these words: "One day in thy courts is better than thousands" (Ps. 84:10). These words can be understood in another sense. Thousands of days might be understood of mutable time, and by the expression "one day" changeless eternity might be denoted. I do not know whether I have omitted any point in replying, as God has deigned to give me the power, to your questions. Even if anything else occurs to you, moderation compels us now to bring this book to an end, and to take some rest after this disputation.

Time and Eternity

BOOK ELEVEN

The eternal Creator and the Creation in time. Augustine ties together his memory of his past life, his present experience, and his ardent desire to comprehend the mystery of creation. This leads him to the questions of the mode and time of creation. He ponders the mode of creation and shows that it was de nihilo and involved no alteration in the being of God. He then considers the question of the beginning of the world and time and shows that time and creation are cotemporal. But what is time? To this Augustine devotes a brilliant analysis of the subjectivity of time and the relation of all temporal process to the abiding eternity of God. From this, he prepares to turn to a detailed interpretation of Gen. 1:1, 2. [Translator's introduction]

Chapter I

1. Is it possible, O Lord, that, since thou art in eternity, thou art ignorant of what I am saying to thee? Or, dost thou see in time an event at the time it occurs? If not, then why am I recounting such a tale of things to thee? Certainly not in order to acquaint thee with them through me; but, instead, that through them I may stir up my own love and the love of my readers toward thee, so that all may say, "Great is the Lord and greatly to be praised." I have said this before and will say it again: "For love of thy love I do it." So also we pray—and yet Truth tells us, "Your Father knoweth what things you need before you ask him." Consequently, we lay bare our feelings before thee, that, through our confessing to thee our plight and thy mercies toward us, thou mayest go on to free us altogether, as thou hast already begun; and that we may cease to be wretched in ourselves and blessed in thee—since thou hast called us to be poor in spirit, meek, mourners, hungering and athirst for righteousness, merciful and pure in heart. Thus I have told thee many things, as I could find ability and will to do so, since it was thy will in the first place that I should confess to thee, O Lord my God—for "Thou art good and thy mercy endureth forever."

Chapter II

2. But how long would it take for the voice of my pen to tell enough of thy exhortations and of all thy terrors and comforts and leadings by which thou didst bring me to preach thy Word and to administer thy sacraments to thy people? And even if I could do this sufficiently, the drops of time are very precious to me and I have for a long time been burning with the desire to meditate on thy law, and to confess in thy presence my knowledge and ignorance of it—from the first streaks of thy light in my mind and the remaining darkness, until my weakness shall be swallowed up in thy strength. And I do not wish to see those hours drained into anything else which I can find free from the necessary care of the body, the exercise of the mind, and the service we owe to our fellow men— and what we give even if we do not owe it.

Reprinted from St. Augustine's *Confessions*, translated by A. Outler.

3. O Lord my God, hear my prayer and let thy mercy attend my longing. It does not burn for itself alone but longs as well to serve the cause of fraternal love. Thou seest in my heart that this is so. Let me offer the service of my mind and my tongue—and give me what I may in turn offer back to thee. For "I am needy and poor"; thou art rich to all who call upon thee—thou who, in thy freedom from care, carest for us. Trim away from my lips, inwardly and outwardly, all rashness and lying. Let thy Scriptures be my chaste delight. Let me not be deceived in them, nor deceive others from them. O Lord, hear and pity! O Lord my God, light of the blind, strength of the weak—and also the light of those who see and the strength of the strong—hearken to my soul and hear it crying from the depths. Unless thy ears attend us even in the depths, where should we go? To whom should we cry?

"Thine is the day and the night is thine as well." At thy bidding the moments fly by. Grant me in them, then, an interval for my meditations on the hidden things of thy law, nor close the door of thy law against us who knock. Thou hast not willed that the deep secrets of all those pages should have been written in vain. Those forests are not without their stags which keep retired within them, ranging and walking and feeding, lying down and ruminating. Perfect me, O Lord, and reveal their secrets to me. Behold, thy voice is my joy; thy voice surpasses in abundance of delights. Give me what I love, for I do love it. And this too is thy gift. Abandon not thy gifts and despise not thy "grass" which thirsts for thee. Let me confess to thee everything that I shall have found in thy books and "let me hear the voice of thy praise." Let me drink from thee and "consider the wondrous things out of thy law"—from the very beginning, when thou madest heaven and earth, and thenceforward to the everlasting reign of thy Holy City with thee.

4. O Lord, have mercy on me and hear my petition. For my prayer is not for earthly things, neither gold nor silver and precious stones, nor gorgeous apparel, nor honors and power, nor fleshly pleasures, nor of bodily necessities in this life of our pilgrimage: all of these things are "added" to those who seek thy Kingdom and thy righteousness.

Observe, O God, from whence comes my desire. The unrighteous have told me of delights but not such as those in thy law, O Lord. Behold, this is the spring of my desire. See, O Father, look and see—and approve! Let it be pleasing in thy mercy's sight that I should find favor with thee—that the secret things of thy Word may be opened to me when I knock. I beg this of thee by our Lord Jesus Christ, thy Son, the Man of thy right hand, the Son of Man; whom thou madest strong for thy purpose as Mediator between thee and us; through whom thou didst seek us when we were not seeking thee, but didst seek us so that we might seek thee; thy Word, through whom thou madest all things, and me among them; thy only Son, through whom thou hast called thy faithful people to adoption, and me among them. I beseech it of thee through him who sitteth at thy right hand and maketh intercession for us, "in whom are hid all treasures of wisdom and knowledge." It is he I seek in thy books. Moses wrote of him. He tells us so himself; the Truth tells us so.

Chapter III

5. Let me hear and understand how in the beginning thou madest heaven and earth. Moses wrote of this; he wrote and passed on—moving from thee to thee—and he is now no longer before me. If he were, I would lay hold on him and ask him and entreat him solemnly that in thy name he would open out these things to me, and I would lend my bodily ears to the sounds that came forth out of his mouth. If, however, he spoke in the Hebrew language, the sounds would beat on my senses in vain, and nothing would touch my mind; but if he spoke in Latin, I would understand what he said. But how should I then know whether what he said was true? If I knew even this much, would it be that I knew it from him? Indeed, within me, deep inside the chambers of my thought, Truth itself—neither Hebrew, nor Greek, nor Latin, nor barbarian, without any organs of voice and tongue, without the sound of syllables—would say, "He speaks the truth," and I should be assured by this. Then I would confidently say to that man of thine, "You speak the truth." However, since I cannot inquire of Moses, I beseech thee, O Truth, from whose fullness he spoke truth; I beseech thee, my God, forgive my sins, and as thou gavest thy servant the gift to speak these things, grant me also the gift to understand them.

Chapter IV

6. Look around; there are the heaven and the earth. They cry aloud that they were made, for they change and vary. Whatever there is that has not been made, and yet has being, has nothing in it that was not there before. This having something not already existent is what it means to be changed and varied. Heaven and earth thus speak plainly that they did not make themselves: "We are, because we have been made; we did not exist before we came to be so that we could have made ourselves!" And the voice with which they speak is simply their visible presence. It was thou, O Lord, who madest these things. Thou art beautiful; thus they are beautiful. Thou art good, thus they are good. Thou art; thus they are. But they are not as beautiful, nor as good, nor as truly real as thou their Creator art. Compared with thee, they are neither beautiful nor good, nor do they even exist. These things we know, thanks be to thee. Yet our knowledge is ignorance when it is compared with thy knowledge.

Chapter V

7. But how didst thou make the heaven and the earth, and what was the tool of such a mighty work as thine? For it was not like a human worker fashioning body from body, according to the fancy of his mind, able somehow or other to impose on it a form which the mind perceived in itself by its inner eye (yet how should even he be able to do this, if thou hadst not made that mind?). He imposes the form on something already existing and having some sort of being, such as clay, or stone or wood or gold or such like (and where would these things come from if thou hadst not furnished them?). For thou madest his body for the artisan, and thou madest the mind which directs the limbs; thou madest the matter from which he makes anything; thou didst create the capacity by which he understands his art and sees within his mind what he may do with the things before him; thou gavest him his bodily sense by which, as if he had an interpreter, he may communicate from mind to matter what he proposes to do and report back to his mind what has been done, that the mind may consult with the Truth which presideth over it as to whether what is done is well done.

All these things praise thee, the Creator of them all. But how didst thou make them? How, O God, didst thou make the heaven and earth? For truly, neither in heaven nor on earth didst thou make heaven and earth—nor in the air nor in the waters, since all of these also belong to the heaven and the earth. Nowhere in the whole world didst thou make the whole world, because there was no place where it could be made before it was made. And thou didst

not hold anything in thy hand from which to fashion the heaven and the earth, for where couldst thou have gotten what thou hadst not made in order to make something with it? Is there, indeed, anything at all except because thou art? Thus thou didst speak and they were made, and by thy Word thou didst make them all.

Chapter VI

8. But how didst thou speak? Was it in the same manner in which the voice came from the cloud saying, "This is my beloved Son"? For that voice sounded forth and died away; it began and ended. The syllables sounded and passed away, the second after the first, the third after the second, and thence in order, till the very last after all the rest; and silence after the last. From this it is clear and plain that it was the action of a creature, itself in time, which sounded that voice, obeying thy eternal will. And what these words were which were formed at that time the outer ear conveyed to the conscious mind, whose inner ear lay attentively open to thy eternal Word. But it compared those words which sounded in time with thy eternal word sounding in silence and said: "This is different; quite different! These words are far below me; they are not even real, for they fly away and pass, but the Word of my God remains above me forever." If, then, in words that sound and fade away thou didst say that heaven and earth should be made, and thus madest heaven and earth, then there was already some kind of corporeal creature before heaven and earth by whose motions in time that voice might have had its occurrence in time. But there was nothing corporeal before the heaven and the earth; or if there was, then it is certain that already, without a time-bound voice, thou hadst created whatever it was out of which thou didst make the time-bound voice by which thou didst say, "Let the heaven and the earth be made!" For whatever it was out of which such a voice was made simply did not exist at all until it was made by thee. Was it decreed by thy Word that a body might be made from which such words might come?

Chapter VII

9. Thou dost call us, then, to understand the Word—the God who is God with thee—which is spoken eternally and by which all things are spoken eternally. For what was first spoken was not fin-

ished, and then something else spoken until the whole series was spoken; but all things, at the same time and forever. For, otherwise, we should have time and change and not a true eternity, nor a true immortality.

This I know, O my God, and I give thanks. I know, I confess to thee, O Lord, and whoever is not ungrateful for certain truths knows and blesses thee along with me. We know, O Lord, this much we know: that in the same proportion as anything is not what it was, and is what it was not, in that very same proportion it passes away or comes to be. But there is nothing in thy Word that passes away or returns to its place; for it is truly immortal and eternal. And, therefore, unto the Word coeternal with thee, at the same time and always thou sayest all that thou sayest. And whatever thou sayest shall be made is made, and thou makest nothing otherwise than by speaking. Still, not all the things that thou dost make by speaking are made at the same time and always.

Chapter VIII

10. Why is this, I ask of thee, O Lord my God? I see it after a fashion, but I do not know how to express it, unless I say that everything that begins to be and then ceases to be begins and ceases when it is known in thy eternal Reason that it ought to begin or cease—in thy eternal Reason where nothing begins or ceases. And this is thy Word, which is also "the Beginning," because it also speaks to us. Thus, in the gospel, he spoke through the flesh; and this sounded in the outward ears of men so that it might be believed and sought for within, and so that it might be found in the eternal Truth, in which the good and only Master teacheth all his disciples. There, O Lord, I hear thy voice, the voice of one speaking to me, since he who teacheth us speaketh to us. But he that doth not teach us doth not really speak to us even when he speaketh. Yet who is it that teacheth us unless it be the Truth immutable? For even when we are instructed by means of the mutable creation, we are thereby led to the Truth immutable. There we learn truly as we stand and hear him, and we rejoice greatly "because of the bridegroom's voice," restoring us to the source whence our being comes. And therefore, unless the Beginning remained immutable, there would then not be a place to which we might return when we had wandered away. But when we return from error, it is through our gaining knowledge that we return. In

order for us to gain knowledge he teacheth us, since he is the Beginning, and speaketh to us.

Chapter IX

11. In this Beginning, O God, thou hast made heaven and earth—through thy Word, thy Son, thy Power, thy Wisdom, thy Truth: all wondrously speaking and wondrously creating. Who shall comprehend such things and who shall tell of it? What is it that shineth through me and striketh my heart without injury, so that I both shudder and burn? I shudder because I am unlike it; I burn because I am like it. It is Wisdom itself that shineth through me, clearing away my fog, which so readily overwhelms me so that I faint in it, in the darkness and burden of my punishment. For my strength is brought down in neediness, so that I cannot endure even my blessings until thou, O Lord, who hast been gracious to all my iniquities, also healest all my infirmities—for it is thou who "shalt redeem my life from corruption, and crown me with loving-kindness and tender mercy, and shalt satisfy my desire with good things so that my youth shall be renewed like the eagle's." For by this hope we are saved, and through patience we await thy promises. Let him that is able hear thee speaking to his inner mind. I will cry out with confidence because of thy own oracle, "How wonderful are thy works, O Lord; in wisdom thou hast made them all." And this Wisdom is the Beginning, and in that Beginning thou hast made heaven and earth.

Chapter X

12. Now, are not those still full of their old carnal nature who ask us: "What was God doing before he made heaven and earth? For if he was idle," they say, "and doing nothing, then why did he not continue in that state forever—doing nothing, as he had always done? If any new motion has arisen in God, and a new will to form a creature, which he had never before formed, how can that be a true eternity in which an act of will occurs that was not there before? For the will of God is not a created thing, but comes before the creation—and this is true because nothing could be created unless the will of the Creator came before it. The will of God, therefore, pertains to his very Essence. Yet if anything has arisen in the Essence of God that was not there before, then that Essence cannot truly be called eternal. But if it was the eternal will of God that the creation should come to be, why, then, is not the creation itself also from eternity?"

Chapter XI

13. Those who say these things do not yet understand thee, O Wisdom of God, O Light of souls. They do not yet understand how the things are made that are made by and in thee. They endeavor to comprehend eternal things, but their heart still flies about in the past and future motions of created things, and is still unstable. Who shall hold it and fix it so that it may come to rest for a little; and then, by degrees, glimpse the glory of that eternity which abides forever; and then, comparing eternity with the temporal process in which nothing abides, they may see that they are incommensurable? They would see that a long time does not become long, except from the many separate events that occur in its passage, which cannot be simultaneous. In the Eternal, on the other hand, nothing passes away, but the whole is simultaneously present. But no temporal process is wholly simultaneous. Therefore, let it see that all time past is forced to move on by the incoming future; that all the future follows from the past; and that all, past and future, is created and issues out of that which is forever present. Who will hold the heart of man that it may stand still and see how the eternity which always stands still is itself neither future nor past but expresses itself in the times that are future and past? Can my hand do this, or can the hand of my mouth bring about so difficult a thing even by persuasion?

Chapter XII

14. How, then, shall I respond to him who asks, "What was God doing before he made heaven and earth?" I do not answer, as a certain one is reported to have done facetiously (shrugging off the force of the question). "He was preparing hell," he said, "for those who pry too deep." It is one thing to see the answer; it is another to laugh at the questioner—and for myself I do not answer these things thus. More willingly would I have answered, "I do not know what I do not know," than cause one who asked a deep question to be ridiculed—and by such tactics gain praise for a worthless answer.

Rather, I say that thou, our God, art the Creator of every creature. And if in the term "heaven and earth" every creature is included, I make bold to say further: "Before God made heaven and earth, he did not make anything at all. For if he did, what did he make unless it were a creature?" I do indeed wish that I knew all that I desire to know to my profit as surely as I know that no creature was made before any creature was made.

Chapter XIII

15. But if the roving thought of someone should wander over the images of past time, and wonder that thou, the Almighty God, the All-creating and All-sustaining, the Architect of heaven and earth, didst for ages unnumbered abstain from so great a work before thou didst actually do it, let him awake and consider that he wonders at illusions. For in what temporal medium could the unnumbered ages that thou didst not make pass by, since thou art the Author and Creator of all the ages? Or what periods of time would those be that were not made by thee? Or how could they have already passed away if they had not already been? Since, therefore, thou art the Creator of all times, if there was any time before thou madest heaven and earth, why is it said that thou wast abstaining from working? For thou madest that very time itself, and periods could not pass by before thou madest the whole temporal procession. But if there was no time before heaven and earth, how, then, can it be asked, "What wast thou doing then?" For there was no "then" when there was no time.

16. Nor dost thou precede any given period of time by another period of time. Else thou wouldst not precede all periods of time. In the eminence of thy ever-present eternity, thou precedest all times past, and extendest beyond all future times, for they are still to come—and when they have come, they will be past. But "Thou art always the Selfsame and thy years shall have no end." Thy years neither go nor come; but ours both go and come in order that all separate moments may come to pass. All thy years stand together as one, since they are abiding. Nor do thy years past exclude the years to come because thy years do not pass away. All these years of ours shall be with thee, when all of them shall have ceased to be. Thy years are but a day, and thy day is not recurrent, but always today. Thy "today" yields not to tomorrow and does not follow yesterday. Thy "today" is eternity. Therefore, thou didst generate the Coeternal, to whom thou didst say, "This day I have begotten thee." Thou madest all

time and before all times thou art, and there was never a time when there was no time.

Chapter XIV

17. There was no time, therefore, when thou hadst not made anything, because thou hadst made time itself. And there are no times that are coeternal with thee, because thou dost abide forever; but if times should abide, they would not be times.

For what is time? Who can easily and briefly explain it? Who can even comprehend it in thought or put the answer into words? Yet is it not true that in conversation we refer to nothing more familiarly or knowingly than time? And surely we understand it when we speak of it; we understand it also when we hear another speak of it.

What, then, is time? If no one asks me, I know what it is. If I wish to explain it to him who asks me, I do not know. Yet I say with confidence that I know that if nothing passed away, there would be no past time; and if nothing were still coming, there would be no future time; and if there were nothing at all, there would be no present time.

But; then, how is it that there are the two times, past and future, when even the past is now no longer and the future is now not yet? But if the present were always present, and did not pass into past time, it obviously would not be time but eternity. If, then, time present—if it be time—comes into existence only because it passes into time past, how can we say that even this is, since the cause of its being is that it will cease to be? Thus, can we not truly say that time is only as it tends toward nonbeing?

Chapter XV

18. And yet we speak of a long time and a short time; but never speak this way except of time past and future. We call a hundred years ago, for example, a long time past. In like manner, we should call a hundred years hence a long time to come. But we call ten days ago a short time past; and ten days hence a short time to come. But in what sense is something long or short that is nonexistent? For the past is not now, and the future is not yet. Therefore, let us not say, "It is long"; instead, let us say of the past, "It was long," and of the future, "It will be long," And yet, O Lord, my Light, shall not thy truth make mockery of man even here? For that long time past: was it long when it was already past, or when

it was still present? For it might have been long when there was a period that could be long, but when it was past, it no longer was. In that case, that which was not at all could not be long. Let us not, therefore, say, "Time past was long," for we shall not discover what it was that was long because, since it is past, it no longer exists. Rather, let us say that "time present was long, because when it was present it was long." For then it had not yet passed on so as not to be, and therefore it still was in a state that could be called long. But after it passed, it ceased to be long simply because it ceased to be.

19. Let us, therefore, O human soul, see whether present time can be long, for it has been given you to feel and measure the periods of time. How, then, will you answer me?

Is a hundred years when present a long time? But, first, see whether a hundred years can be present at once. For if the first year in the century is current, then it is present time, and the other ninety and nine are still future. Therefore, they are not yet. But, then, if the second year is current, one year is already past, the second present, and all the rest are future. And thus, if we fix on any middle year of this century as present, those before it are past, those after it are future. Therefore, a hundred years cannot be present all at once.

Let us see, then, whether the year that is now current can be present. For if its first month is current, then the rest are future; if the second, the first is already past, and the remainder are not yet. Therefore, the current year is not present all at once. And if it is not present as a whole, then the year is not present. For it takes twelve months to make the year, from which each individual month which is current is itself present one at a time, but the rest are either past or future.

20. Thus it comes out that time present, which we found was the only time that could be called "long," has been cut down to the space of scarcely a single day. But let us examine even that, for one day is never present as a whole. For it is made up of twenty-four hours, divided between night and day. The first of these hours has the rest of them as future, and the last of them has the rest as past; but any of those between has those that preceded it as past and those that succeed it as future. And that one hour itself passes away in fleeting fractions. The part of it that has fled is past; what remains is still future. If any fraction of time be conceived that cannot now be divided even into the most minute momentary point, this alone is what we may call time present. But this flies so rapidly from future to past that it cannot be extended by any delay. For if it is extended, it is then divided into past and future. But the present has no extension whatever.

Where, therefore, is that time which we may call "long"? Is it future? Actually we do not say of the future, "It is long,'" for it has not yet come to be, so as to be long. Instead, we say, "It will be long." When will it be? For since it is future, it will not be long, for what may be long is not yet. It will be long only when it passes from the future which is not as yet, and will have begun to be present, so that there can be something that may be long. But in that case, time present cries aloud, in the words we have already heard, that it cannot be "long."

Chapter XVI

21. And yet, O Lord, we do perceive intervals of time, and we compare them with each other, and we say that some are longer and others are shorter. We even measure how much longer or shorter this time may be than that time. And we say that this time is twice as long, or three times as long, while this other time is only just as long as that other. But we measure the passage of time when we measure the intervals of perception. But who can measure times past which now are no longer, or times future which are not yet — unless perhaps someone will dare to say that what does not exist can be measured? Therefore, while time is passing, it can be perceived and measured; but when it is past, it cannot, since it is not.

Chapter XVII

22. I am seeking the truth, O Father; I am not affirming it. O my God, direct and rule me.

Who is there who will tell me that there are not three times—as we learned when boys and as we have also taught boys—time past, time present, and time future? Who can say that there is only time present because the other two do not exist? Or do they also exist; but when, from the future, time becomes present, it proceeds from some secret place; and when, from times present, it becomes past, it recedes into some secret place? For where have those men who have foretold the future seen the things foretold, if then they were not yet existing? For what does not exist cannot be seen. And those who tell of things past could not speak of them as if they were

true, if they did not see them in their minds. These things could in no way be discerned if they did not exist. There are therefore times present and times past.

Chapter XVIII

23. Give me leave, O Lord, to seek still further. O my Hope, let not my purpose be confounded. For if there are times past and future, I wish to know where they are. But if I have not yet succeeded in this, I still know that wherever they are, they are not there as future or past, but as present. For if they are there as future, they are there as "not yet"; if they are there as past, they are there as "no longer." Wherever they are and whatever they are they exist therefore only as present. Although we tell of past things as true, they are drawn out of the memory—not the things themselves, which have already passed, but words constructed from the images of the perceptions which were formed in the mind, like footprints in their passage through the senses. My childhood, for instance, which is no longer, still exists in time past, which does not now exist. But when I call to mind its image and speak of it, I see it in the present because it is still in my memory. Whether there is a similar explanation for the foretelling of future events—that is, of the images of things which are not yet seen as if they were already existing—I confess, O my God, I do not know. But this I certainly do know: that we generally think ahead about our future actions, and this premeditation is in time present; but that the action which we premeditate is not yet, because it is still future. When we shall have started the action and have begun to do what we were premeditating, then that action will be in time present, because then it is no longer in time future.

24. Whatever may be the manner of this secret foreseeing of future things, nothing can be seen except what exists. But what exists now is not future, but present. When, therefore, they say that future events are seen, it is not the events themselves, for they do not exist as yet (that is, they are still in time future), but perhaps, instead, their causes and their signs are seen, which already do exist. Therefore, to those already beholding these causes and signs, they are not future, but present, and from them future things are predicted because they are conceived in the mind. These conceptions, however, exist now, and those who predict those things see these conceptions before them in time present.

Let me take an example from the vast multitude and variety of such things. I see the dawn; I predict that the sun is about to rise. What I see is in time present, what I predict is in time future—not that the sun is future, for it already exists; but its rising is future, because it is not yet. Yet I could not predict even its rising, unless I had an image of it in my mind; as, indeed, I do even now as I speak. But that dawn which I see in the sky is not the rising of the sun (though it does precede it), nor is it a conception in my mind. These two are seen in time present, in order that the event which is in time future may be predicted.

Future events, therefore, are not yet. And if they are not yet, they do not exist. And if they do not exist, they cannot be seen at all, but they can be predicted from things present, which now are and are seen.

Chapter XIX

25. Now, therefore, O Ruler of thy creatures, what is the mode by which thou teachest souls those things which are still future? For thou hast taught thy prophets. How dost thou, to whom nothing is future, teach future things—or rather teach things present from the signs of things future? For what does not exist certainly cannot be taught. This way of thine is too far from my sight; it is too great for me, I cannot attain to it. But I shall be enabled by thee, when thou wilt grant it, O sweet Light of my secret eyes.

Chapter XX

26. But even now it is manifest and clear that there are neither times future nor times past. Thus it is not properly said that there are three times, past, present, and future. Perhaps it might be said rightly that there are three times: a time present of things past; a time present of things present; and a time present of things future. For these three do coexist somehow in the soul, for otherwise I could not see them. The time present of things past is memory; the time present of things present is direct experience; the time present of things future is expectation. If we are allowed to speak of these things so, I see three times, and I grant that there are three. Let it still be said, then, as our misapplied custom has it: "There are three times, past, present, and future." I shall not be troubled by it, nor argue, nor object—

always provided that what is said is understood, so that neither the future nor the past is said to exist now. There are but few things about which we speak properly—and many more about which we speak improperly—though we understand one another's meaning.

Chapter XXI

27. I have said, then, that we measure periods of time as they pass so that we can say that this time is twice as long as that one or that this is just as long as that, and so on for the other fractions of time which we can count by measuring.

So, then, as I was saying, we measure periods of time as they pass. And if anyone asks me, "How do you know this?", I can answer: "I know because we measure. We could not measure things that do not exist, and things past and future do not exist." But how do we measure present time since it has no extension? It is measured while it passes, but when it has passed it is not measured; for then there is nothing that could be measured. But whence, and how, and whither does it pass while it is being measured? Whence, but from the future? Which way, save through the present? Whither, but into the past? Therefore, from what is not yet, through what has no length, it passes into what is now no longer. But what do we measure, unless it is a time of some length? For we cannot speak of single, and double, and triple, and equal, and all the other ways in which we speak of time, except in terms of the length of the periods of time. But in what "length," then, do we measure passing time? Is it in the future, from which it passes over? But what does not yet exist cannot be measured. Or, is it in the present, through which it passes? But what has no length we cannot measure. Or is it in the past into which it passes? But what is no longer we cannot measure.

Chapter XXII

28. My soul burns ardently to understand this most intricate enigma. O Lord my God, O good Father, I beseech thee through Christ, do not close off these things, both the familiar and the obscure, from my desire. Do not bar it from entering into them; but let their light dawn by thy enlightening mercy, O Lord. Of whom shall I inquire about these things? And to whom shall I confess my ignorance of them with greater profit than to thee, to whom these stud-

ies of mine (ardently longing to understand thy Scriptures) are not a bore? Give me what I love, for I do love it; and this thou hast given me. O Father, who truly knowest how to give good gifts to thy children, give this to me. Grant it, since I have undertaken to understand it, and hard labor is my lot until thou openest it. I beseech thee, through Christ and in his name, the Holy of Holies, let no man interrupt me. "For I have believed, and therefore do I speak." This is my hope; for this I live: that I may contemplate the joys of my Lord. Behold, thou hast made my days grow old, and they pass away—and how I do not know.

We speak of this time and that time, and these times and those times: "How long ago since he said this?" "How long ago since he did this?" "How long ago since I saw that?" "This syllable is twice as long as that single short syllable." These words we say and hear, and we are understood and we understand. They are quite commonplace and ordinary, and still the meaning of these very same things lies deeply hid and its discovery is still to come.

Chapter XXIII

29. I once heard a learned man say that the motions of the sun, moon, and stars constituted time; and I did not agree. For why should not the motions of all bodies constitute time? What if the lights of heaven should cease, and a potter's wheel still turn round: would there be no time by which we might measure those rotations and say either that it turned at equal intervals, or, if it moved now more slowly and now more quickly, that some rotations were longer and others shorter? And while we were saying this, would we not also be speaking in time? Or would there not be in our words some syllables that were long and others short, because the first took a longer time to sound, and the others a shorter time? O God, grant men to see in a small thing the notions that are common to all things, both great and small. Both the stars and the lights of heaven are "for signs and seasons, and for days and years." This is doubtless the case, but just as I should not say that the circuit of that wooden wheel was a day, neither would that learned man say that there was, therefore, no time.

30. I thirst to know the power and the nature of time, by which we measure the motions of bodies, and say, for example, that this motion is twice as long as that. For I ask, since the word "day" refers not only to the length of time that the sun is above the earth (which separates day from night), but also refers to the sun's entire circuit from east all the way around to east—on account of which we can say, "So many days have passed" (the nights being included when we say, "So many days," and their lengths not counted separately)—since, then, the day is ended by the motion of the sun and by his passage from east to east, I ask whether the motion itself is the day, or whether the day is the period in which that motion is completed; or both? For if the sun's passage is the day, then there would be a day even if the sun should finish his course in as short a period as an hour. If the motion itself is the day, then it would not be a day if from one sunrise to another there were a period no longer than an hour. But the sun would have to go round twenty-four times to make just one day. If it is both, then that could not be called a day if the sun ran his entire course in the period of an hour; nor would it be a day if, while the sun stood still, as much time passed as the sun usually covered during his whole course, from morning to morning. I shall, therefore, not ask any more what it is that is called a day, but rather what time is, for it is by time that we measure the circuit of the sun, and would be able to say that it was finished in half the period of time that it customarily takes if it were completed in a period of only twelve hours. If, then, we compare these periods, we could call one of them a single and the other a double period, as if the sun might run his course from east to east sometimes in a single period and sometimes in a double period.

Let no man tell me, therefore, that the motions of the heavenly bodies constitute time. For when the sun stood still at the prayer of a certain man in order that he might gain his victory in battle, the sun stood still but time went on. For in as long a span of time as was sufficient the battle was fought and ended.

I see, then, that time is a certain kind of extension. But do I see it, or do I only seem to? Thou, O Light and Truth, wilt show me.

Chapter XXIV

31. Dost thou command that I should agree if anyone says that time is "the motion of a body"? Thou dost not so command. For I hear that no body is moved but in time; this thou tellest me. But that the motion of a body itself is time I do not hear; thou dost not say so. For when a body is moved, I measure by time how long it was moving from the time when it began to be moved until it stopped. And if I did not see when it began to be moved, and if it continued to move so that I could not see when it stopped, I could not measure the movement, except from the time when I began to see it until I stopped. But if I look at it for a long time, I can affirm only that the time is long but not how long it may be. This is because when we say, "How long?", we are speaking comparatively as: "This is as long as that," or, "This is twice as long as that"; or other such similar ratios. But if we were able to observe the point in space where and from which the body, which is moved, comes and the point to which it is moved; or if we can observe its parts moving as in a wheel, we can say how long the movement of the body took or the movement of its parts from this place to that. Since, therefore, the motion of a body is one thing, and the norm by which we measure how long it takes is another thing, we cannot see which of these two is to be called time. For, although a body is sometimes moved and sometimes stands still, we measure not only its motion but also its rest as well; and both by time! Thus we say, "It stood still as long as it moved," or, "It stood still twice or three times as long as it moved"—or any other ratio which our measuring has either determined or imagined, either roughly or precisely, according to our custom. Therefore, time is not the motion of a body.

Chapter XXV

32. And I confess to thee, O Lord, that I am still ignorant as to what time is. And again I confess to thee, O Lord, that I know that I am speaking all these things in time, and that I have already spoken of time a long time, and that "very long" is not long except when measured by the duration of time. How, then, do I know this, when I do not know what time is? Or, is it possible that I do not know how I can express what I do know? Alas for me! I do not even know the extent of my own ignorance. Behold, O my God, in thy presence I do not lie. As my heart is, so I speak. Thou shalt light my candle; thou, O Lord my God, wilt enlighten my darkness.

Chapter XXVI

33. Does not my soul most truly confess to thee that I do measure intervals of time? But what is it that I thus measure, O my God, and how is it that I do not know what I measure? I measure the motion of a body by time, but the time itself I do not measure. But, truly, could I measure the motion of a body—how long it takes, how long it is in motion from this place to that—unless I could measure the time in which it is moving?

How, then, do I measure this time itself? Do we measure a longer time by a shorter time, as we measure the length of a crossbeam in terms of cubits? Thus, we can say that the length of a long syllable is measured by the length of a short syllable and thus say that the long syllable is double. So also we measure the length of poems by the length of the lines, and the length of the line by the length of the feet, and the length of the feet by the length of the syllable, and the length of the long syllables by the length of the short ones. We do not measure by pages—for in that way we would measure space rather than time—but when we speak the words as they pass by we say: "It is a long stanza, because it is made up of so many verses; they are long verses because they consist of so many feet; they are long feet because they extend over so many syllables; this is a long syllable because it is twice the length of a short one."

But no certain measure of time is obtained this way; since it is possible that if a shorter verse is pronounced slowly, it may take up more time than a longer one if it is pronounced hurriedly. The same would hold for a stanza, or a foot, or a syllable. From this it appears to me that time is nothing other than extendedness; but extendedness of what I do not know. This is a marvel to me. The extendedness may be of the mind itself. For what is it I measure, I ask thee, O my God, when I say either, roughly, "This time is longer than that," or, more precisely, "This is twice as long as that." I know that I am measuring time. But I am not measuring the future, for it is not yet; and I am not measuring the present because it is extended by no length; and I am not measuring the past because it no longer is. What is it, therefore, that I am measuring? Is it time in its passage, but not time past [*praetereuntia tempora, non praeterita*]? This is what I have been saying.

Chapter XXVII

34. Press on, O my mind, and attend with all your power. God is our Helper: "it is he that hath made us and not we ourselves." Give heed where the truth begins to dawn. Suppose now that a bodily voice begins to sound, and continues to flow. We can measure it only while it is sounding, for when it has ceased to sound it will be already past and there will not be anything there that can be measured. Let us measure it exactly; and let us say how much it is. But while it is sounding, it cannot be measured except from the instant when it began to sound, down to the final moment when it left off. For we measure the time interval itself from some beginning point to some end. This is why a voice that has not yet ended cannot be measured, so that one could say how long or how briefly it will continue. Nor can it be said to be equal to another voice or single or double in comparison to it or anything like this. But when it is ended, it is no longer. How, therefore, may it be measured? And yet we measure times; not those which are not yet, nor those which no longer are, nor those which are stretched out by some delay, nor those which have no limit. Therefore, we measure neither times future nor times past, nor times present, nor times passing by; and yet we do measure times.

35. Deus Creator omnium [God, Creator of all things]: this verse of eight syllables alternates between short and long syllables. The four short ones—that is, the first, third, fifth, and seventh—are single in relation to the four long ones—that is, the second, fourth, sixth, and eighth. Each of the long ones is double the length of each of the short ones. I affirm this and report it, and common sense perceives that this indeed is the case. By common sense, then, I measure a long syllable by a short one, and I find that it is twice as long. But when one sounds after another, if the first be short and the latter long, how can I hold the short one and how can I apply it to the long one as a measure, so that I can discover that the long one is twice as long, when, in fact, the long one does not begin to sound until the short one leaves off sounding? That same long syllable I do not measure as present, since I cannot measure it until it is ended; but its ending is its passing away.

What is it, then, that I can measure? Where is the short syllable by which I measure? Where is the long one that I am measuring? Both have sounded, have flown away, have passed on, and are no longer. And still I measure, and I confidently answer—as far as a trained ear can be trusted—that this syllable is single and that syllable double. And I could not do this unless they both had passed and were ended. Therefore I do not measure them, for they do not exist any more. But I measure something in my memory which remains fixed.

36. It is in you, O mind of mine, that I measure the periods of time. Do not shout me down that it exists [objectively]; do not overwhelm yourself with the turbulent flood of your impressions. In you, as I have said, I measure the periods of time. I measure as time present the impression that things make on you as they pass by and what remains after they have passed by—I do not measure the things themselves which have passed by and left their impression on you. This is what I measure when I measure periods of time. Either, then, these are the periods of time or else I do not measure time at all.

What are we doing when we measure silence, and say that this silence has lasted as long as that voice lasts? Do we not project our thought to the measure of a sound, as if it were then sounding, so that we can say something concerning the intervals of silence in a given span of time? For, even when both the voice and the tongue are still, we review—in thought—poems and verses, and discourse of various kinds or various measures of motions, and we specify their time spans—how long this is in relation to that—just as if we were speaking them aloud. If anyone wishes to utter a prolonged sound, and if, in forethought, he has decided how long it should be, that man has already in silence gone through a span of time, and committed his sound to memory. Thus he begins to speak and his voice sounds until it reaches the predetermined end. It has truly sounded and will go on sounding. But what is already finished has already sounded and what remains will still sound. Thus it passes on, until the present intention carries the future over into the past. The past increases by the diminution of the future until by the consumption of all the future all is past.

Chapter XXVIII

37. But how is the future diminished or consumed when it does not yet exist? Or how does the past, which exists no longer, increase, unless it is that in the mind in which all this happens there are three functions? For the mind expects, it attends, and it remembers; so that what it expects passes into what it remembers by way of what it attends to. Who denies that future things do not exist as yet? But still there is already in the mind the expectation of things still future. And who denies that past things now exist no longer? Still there is in the mind the memory of things past. Who denies that time present has no length, since it passes away in a moment? Yet, our attention has a continuity and it is through this that what is present may proceed to become absent. Therefore, future time, which is nonexistent, is not long; but "a long future" is "a long expectation of the future." Nor is time past, which is now no longer, long; a "long past" is "a long memory of the past."

38. I am about to repeat a psalm that I know. Before I begin, my attention encompasses the whole, but once I have begun, as much of it as becomes past while I speak is still stretched out in my memory. The span of my action is divided between my memory, which contains what I have repeated, and my expectation, which contains what I am about to repeat. Yet my attention is continually present with me, and through it what was future is carried over so that it becomes past. The more this is done and repeated, the more the memory is enlarged—and expectation is shortened—until the whole expectation is exhausted. Then the whole action is ended and passed into memory. And what takes place in the entire psalm takes place also in each individual part of it and in each individual syllable. This also holds in the even longer action of which that psalm is only a portion. The same holds in the whole life of man, of which all the actions of men are parts. The same holds in the whole age of the sons of men, of which all the lives of men are parts.

Chapter XXIX

39. But "since thy loving-kindness is better than life itself," observe how my life is but a stretching out, and how thy right hand has upheld me in my Lord, the Son of Man, the Mediator between thee, the One, and us, the many—in so many ways and by so many means. Thus through him I may lay hold upon him in whom I am also laid hold upon; and I may be gathered up from my old way of life to follow that One and to forget that which is behind, no longer stretched out but now pulled together again—stretching forth not to what shall be and shall pass away but to those things that are before me. Not distractedly now, but intently, I follow on for the prize of my heavenly calling, where I may hear the sound of thy praise and contemplate thy delights, which neither come to be nor pass away.

But now my years are spent in mourning. And thou, O Lord, art my comfort, my eternal Father. But I have been torn between the times, the order of which I do not know, and my thoughts, even the inmost and deepest places of my soul, are mangled by various commotions until I shall flow together into thee purged and molten in the fire of thy love.

Chapter XXX

40. And I will be immovable and fixed in thee, and thy truth will be my mold. And I shall not have to endure the questions of those men who, as if in a morbid disease, thirst for more than they can hold and say, "What did God make before he made heaven and earth?" or, "How did it come into his mind to make something when he had never before made anything?" Grant them, O Lord, to consider well what they are saying; and grant them to see that where there is no time they cannot say "never." When, therefore, he is said "never to have made" something—what is this but to say that it was made in no time at all? Let them therefore see that there could be no time without a created world, and let them cease to speak vanity of this kind. Let them also be stretched out to those things which are before them, and understand that thou, the eternal Creator of all times, art before all times and that no times are coeternal with thee; nor is any creature, even if there is a creature "above time."

Chapter XXXI

41. O Lord my God, what a chasm there is in thy deep secret! How far short of it have the consequences of my sins cast me? Heal my eyes, that I may enjoy thy light. Surely, if there is a mind that so greatly abounds in knowledge and foreknowledge, to which all things past and future are as well known as one psalm is well known to me, that mind would be an exceeding marvel and altogether astonishing. For whatever is past and whatever is yet to come would be no more concealed from him than the past and future of that psalm were hidden from me when I was chanting it: how much of it had been sung from the beginning and what and how much still remained till the end. But far be it from thee, O Creator of the universe, and Creator of our souls and bodies—far be it from thee that thou shouldst merely know all things past and future. Far, far more wonderfully, and far more mysteriously thou knowest them. For it is not as the feelings of one singing familiar songs, or hearing a familiar song in which, because of his expectation of words still to come and

his remembrance of those that are past, his feelings are varied and his senses are divided. This is not the way that anything happens to thee, who art unchangeably eternal, that is, the truly eternal Creator of minds. As in the beginning thou knewest both the heaven and the earth without any change in thy knowledge, so thou didst make heaven and earth in their beginnings without any division in thy action. Let him who understands this confess to thee; and let him who does not understand also confess to thee! Oh, exalted as thou art, still the humble in heart are thy dwelling place! For thou liftest them who are cast down and they fall not for whom thou art the Most High.

Chapter 9

BOETHIUS

Boethius (ca. 480–525), Roman patrician, Consul of Rome, and minister to Ostrogoth King Theodoric, was known as "the last of the Roman philosophers and the first of the scholastic theologians." Next to Augustine he was the most influential thinker in the middle ages prior to Thomas of Aquinas. Until the thirteenth century Aristotle was known only through his translations. He set forth the famous definition of eternity as "perfect possession all at the same time of endless life" as well as the difference between conditional and simple necessity which Boethius discusses in our selection. Apparently a victim of political intrigue, Boethius was falsely accused of treason, tortured, imprisoned, and bludgeoned to death. While in prison he composed *The Consolation of Philosophy*, which Gibbon called "a golden volume not unworthy of the leisure of Plato or of Tully [Cicero]," from which the following selection is taken.

In *Consolation* Philosophy appears to Boethius as a woman of awe-inspiring beauty, "her eyes burning and keen beyond the usual power of ordinary mortals, whose color was full of life, and whose strength was still intact though she was so full of years that by no means would it be believed that she was of our generation." She then begins the process of applying spiritual medicine to Boethius's soul, leading him from his lonely despair to an understanding of and resignation to Providence. The healing process takes the form of a dialogue comparable to one of Plato's. In the last book of *Consolation,* Philosophy explains the meaning of chance and how free will can be reconciled with divine foreknowledge.

The Consolation of Philosophy

CHANCE, FREE WILL AND FOREKNOWLEDGE

1. Philosophy Discusses the Nature of Chance

Here Philosophy made an end and was steering the conversation to certain other matters when I interrupted her, "I am learning in fact what you stated in words a while ago: the question of Providence is bound up in many others. I would ask you whether you think that chance exists at all, and what you think it is."

She replied, "I am eager to fulfill my promise and to open for you the way which you may return home. But these things, though very useful to know, are nevertheless rather removed from our proposed path, and we must be careful lest you, wearied of side trips, be not strong enough to complete the main journey."

From *The Consolation of Philosophy*. Based on the translation of W. V. Cooper (London 1902).

"Have no fear about that," I said, "it will be satisfying to know these things in which I delight so much. At the same time, since every side of your argument has stood firm with unshaken credit, let there be nothing ambiguous about its sequel."

Then she said, "I will gratify you," and began to speak as follows: "If anyone define chance as the outcome of random motion produced by no sequence of causes, I am sure there is no such thing and consider it an empty, meaningless word, even if we refer by it to some actual event. For what place can be left for any random happening, seeing that God keeps everything in order? It is a true statement that nothing comes out of nothing. None of the ancients ever denied it, although they used it as a maxim of their natural philosophy with reference to material objects, not efficient causes. But if something were to arise from no cause, it would appear to have arisen out of nothing. Since this is impossible, then chance also, of the sort such as we just defined, cannot exist."

"Then," I asked, "Is there nothing which can justly be called chance or accident? Or is there something which, although unknown to common people, these words are fitting?"

"My philosopher, Aristotle," she replied, "defined it in his *Physics* briefly and close to the truth."

"In what way?" I asked.

"Whenever," she replied, "something is done with one intention but something else, other than what was intended, results from certain causes, that is called *chance*; as, for example, if a man, digging for the purpose of cultivating a field, finds a mass of buried gold. Such a thing is believed to have happened by chance, but not from nothing, for it has its own causes whose unforeseen and unexpected coincidence seems to have brought about a chance. For, had not the cultivator dug the ground and had not the depositor buried the money in that particular spot, the gold would not have been found. These then are the reasons for that profitable accident, which came about from the meeting and confluence of causes, not from the intention of the agents. For neither he who buried the gold nor he who worked the field intended that the gold should be found, but, as I said, it was a coincidence that the one happened to dig where the other had buried. Chance therefore may be defined as an unexpected result from the coincidence of certain causes in matter done for some other purpose. The order of the universe, advancing with inevitable sequence, brings about this coinci-

dence and confluence of causes. This order emanates from its source, which is Providence, and disposes all things in their proper time and place. . . .

2. Philosophy Asserts the Existence of Free Will

"I agree with what you say," said I, "but is there any place for free will in this series of cohering causes, or does the chain of Fate bind the very movements of our minds as well?"

"There is free will," she replied, "nor could there be any reasoning nature without it. For any being that, by its nature, can use reason has a power of discernment with which it can judge any thing. By itself, therefore, it distinguishes between objects to be shunned and objects to be desired. Now, everyone seeks what he judges to be desirable, and flees what he deems should be shunned. Wherefore all who have reason have also within themselves freedom of desiring and refusing. But I do not lay it down that this freedom is equal in all beings. Heavenly and divine substances have at hand an acute judgment, an uncorrupted will, and the power to effect their desires. Human souls must be the more free the more they maintain themselves in the contemplation of the divine mind, less free when their attention is distracted towards material things, and less free still when they are tied to their earthly members. Indeed, the last stage is mere slavery, wherein the spirit is delivered over to vices and has fallen away from the possession of its reason. For when the mind's eye turns from the light of the highest truth to what is lower and less lucid, it is soon dimmed by the clouds of ignorance and becomes turbid through ruinous passions; by yielding and consenting to these passions, men increase the slavery which they have brought upon themselves and become in a certain way captive through their own freedom. But all these things are known in the sight of that Providence which foresees all things from eternity and disposes each according to its own deserts as predestined."

3. Boethius Cannot Reconcile God's Foreknowledge with Human Free Will

"Behold," I said, "I am now more confused than ever."

"What is it," she asked, "although I already have an idea of what is troubling you?"

"There seems," I replied, "to be such incompatibility between the existence of God's universal foreknowledge and that of man's free will. For, if God foresees all things and can in no wise be mistaken, then that which His Providence foresees as going to happen must result necessarily. Wherefore, if from eternity He foreknows not only men's deeds but also their designs and wishes, there will be no free will; for there can neither be any deed done nor wish formed except such as the infallible Providence of God has foreseen. For, if matters could ever be so turned as to result otherwise than was foreseen, His foreknowledge of the future would never be certain but would rather be uncertain opinion, a thing which I deem impious to attribute to God. And, further, I cannot approve of that argument by which some men think they can solve this knotty problem: they say that a future event does not come to pass for the reason that Providence has foreseen it, but rather, on the contrary, since it is about to come to pass it cannot be hidden from divine Providence. In that way necessity is taken away from the events foreseen and attributed to the act of foreseeing, so that it is not necessary that what is forseen should actually happen but necessary that those things which are going to happen be also foreseen; as though, indeed, our problem was: What is the cause of what? Is God's foreknowledge the cause of the necessity of the future, or is the necessity of the future the cause of God's foreknowledge? Whereas we actually strive to prove this, that, howsoever this causal relation be ordered, the even of the things foreknown is necessary, even if foreknowledge itself does not seem to induce this necessity of the event into things to come.

"For, if a man is sitting, then the belief that he is sitting must be true and conversely, if the opinion that the man is sitting is true, then he must necessarily be sitting. There is therefore necessity in both cases: in the former the opinion must be true and in the latter the man must be sitting. However, he is not sitting because the opinion is true, but rather the opinion is true because his being seated preceded it.

"It is manifest that we should reason in like manner concerning Providence and future events. For, even if these are foreseen because they are about to happen, and do not happen because they are foreseen, it is nevertheless necessary both that what is about to happen should be foreseen by God and that what has been foreseen should happen as it was foreseen, and this last alone is enough to destroy free will. Yet how preposterous it is for us to say that the temporal event is the cause of eternal foreknowledge! Moreover, to hold that God foresees future things because they are about to happen is nothing else than to think that what has happened in the past is the cause of that highest Providence. Besides, just as when I really know that something exists it must needs exist, so also when I really know that something is about to come to pass it must needs come to pass. Thus it follows that the event of a thing foreknown is inevitable.

"Finally, if any one believes something which is actually not so, he has no knowledge but a fallacious opinion, a thing far removed from scientific truth. Wherefore, if any future thing is future in such a way that its event is not sure or necessary, how can it possibly be known beforehand that it will occur? For, just as knowledge itself is unmixed with falsity, so also that which is conceived by it cannot be otherwise than it is conceived. That is the reason why knowledge does not lie, because each matter must be just as knowledge understands it to be. What then? How does God foreknow uncertain future things? For, if He thinks they will inevitably happen while the possibility of their not happening exists, He is mistaken; and this is wicked to think or say. But if He judges these uncertain future events to be uncertain as they actually are, i.e., if He knows only that they may or may not occur, then one can hardly speak of fore*knowledge*, for He would know nothing certain and definite. Or wherein does it differ from that ridiculous prophecy of Tiresias in Horace's *Satires:*

Whatever I say shall either be or not be.

How, too, would God's Providence be better than man's opinion, if like mankind He judges uncertain those things whose events are uncertain? But if there can be nothing uncertain in that most certain Fount of all things, then those things which He has firmly foreknown as things which are going to happen will certainly happen. Wherefore there exists no liberty for human designs and actions. For the divine mind, foreseeing all things without the error of deception, restricts and binds each one of them to one single outcome.

"Once this has been admitted, it is plain what a destructive effect such an admission must have for all human affairs. In vain are rewards and punishments proposed for the good and the bad, for there are no free and voluntary actions of the mind to warrant them. And what we now judge most fair will prove to be most unfair in all respects, namely, to punish the wicked or reward the upright, since not their own will but the fixed necessity of the future forces them to do either good or evil. There will no longer be such things as virtues or vices but merely an indiscriminate mixture of merit and/or guilt. And nothing more criminal than this could be imagined: since the whole order of things proceeds from Providence and nothing is left to human designs, it follows that our vices as well as our virtues must be referred to the Author of all good things. Hence there is no reason to hope for or to pray against anything, for what could any man hope for or pray against when all that can be desired is merely a link in an inflexible chain of events? Thus there will be taken away that sole communication between God and man, namely, the right of prayer. . . .

4. Philosophy Tries to Show how Foreknowledge and Free Will May be Reconciled

Then Philosophy spoke, "This is an ancient complaint against Providence. Cicero argued against it when dealing with divination, and it is a matter about which you yourself have made long and frequent inquiries. But hitherto neither of you have developed it with sufficient diligence and precision. The reason why the solution of this problem has always remained hidden is the fact that the step-by-step process of human reasoning cannot attain to the act of simple insight which divine foreknowledge is. If our minds could somehow operate this latter way, there would be no doubt left at all. I will try to make this clear after I have explained your difficulties. Tell me why you reject the arguments of those who think that free will is not in any way hindered by foreknowledge, because they hold that foreknowledge is not the cause of the necessity in future things. Whence do *you* draw your evidence for the necessity of future things if not from the fact that things foreknown cannot but come to pass? If, then, as you yourself admitted a while back, foreknowledge imposes no necessity upon future things, what could possibly change voluntary acts into necessary ones? Let us assume for the sake of argument, so that you may see what follows, that there is no foreknowledge at all. Then, under the circumstances thus assumed, are the events resulting from free will bound by necessity?"

"Of course not."

"Now, let us assume that foreknowledge exists, but imposes no necessity upon things; then, I think, the same freedom of will shall be left, intact and absolute.

" 'But', you will say, 'although foreknowledge does not establish any necessity for the event of future things, yet foreknowledge is a sign that they will necessarily come to pass.' It would plainly follow that the event of future things would be necessary even if there were no foreknowledge. For a sign merely points at what is; it does not bring into being that which it points out. Wherefore it must first be proved that nothing happens but of necessity before it can be demonstrated that foreknowledge is a sign of this necessity. Otherwise, if there is no necessity, foreknowledge cannot be a sign of that which does not exist. . . . Now how can it possibly be that things which are foreseen as about to happen should not take place? For apparently we refuse to believe that those events whose occurrence Providence has foreseen might actually not occur; nevertheless we choose to believe that such events, even when they actually occur, did not have to happen by a necessity inherent in their nature—which fact you may easily gather from the following example:

"We see many things occur before our eyes, for instance, those things which charioteers are seen to do when they drive and turn their chariots, and in like manner other things. Does any necessity compel any one of these things to happen as it does?"

"By no means, for all skills would be of no effect if all things took place by compulsion."

"Therefore, since these things have no necessity for occurring at the moment they happen, they cannot, before they actually occur, happen with necessity in the future. Wherefore there are certain things about-to-come-to-pass whose occurrence is absolutely free from any necessity. For I believe no one would say that the things which are done in the present were not about-to-be-done in the past before they were done. Thus these foreknown events occur freely. Just as knowledge of present things imposes no necessity upon them while they are being done, so foreknowledge does not impose any necessity upon future things. 'But', you say, 'this itself is dubious, whether there can be any foreknowledge of those things which do not occur necessarily.' To you a 'foreknowledge of things which do not occur necessarily' implies a contradiction; you believe that if they are foreseen the necessity (of occurrence) follows, that without this necessity there can be no foreknowledge, that all knowledge is always knowledge of something certain, and that, if things which will not occur necessarily are foreknown as necessary, we are not dealing with the truth of knowledge but with the obscurity of opinion. For you believe that to judge anything as other than it is in fact is far removed from the integrity of true knowledge."

Philosophy Discusses the Various Grades of Cognition

"The cause of your error is that everyone believes that all the things he knows come to his knowledge solely through their own nature and through a force inherent in them. But the opposite is true. For everything which is known is comprehended not according to its own force but rather according to the faculty of those who comprehend it. Let me make this plain by a brief example: the roundness of a body is recognized by sight in one way, and by touch in another way. Sight, remaining at a distance, takes in the whole body at once with all its diverging radii, while touch, clinging and conjoined, as it were, to the sphere, comprehends the roundness of the body as it passes inch by inch over the actual circumference. Likewise sense, imagination, reason, and insight all behold a man differently. For sense considers his figure as it is impressed on his body, while imagination considers the figure by itself without the body. Reason goes further than this: by contemplating only the universal aspects it investigates the species itself, which is represented in particular specimens. Higher still is the view of insight: reaching beyond the sphere of the material universe it beholds with the pure vision of the mind the Idea of Man in its simplicity.

"Herein the chief point for consideration is this: the higher power of comprehension includes the lower, but the lower can never raise itself to the higher. For the senses are capable of comprehending nothing but matter; imagination cannot look upon universal species; reason cannot grasp the simple Idea; but insight seems to look down from above and, after having perceived the Idea, judges everything patterned after this Idea in the same way in which it comprehends the Idea itself, which can be known by no other faculty. For insight knows the universal grasped by reason, and the immaterial figure visualized by imagination, and the material object perceived by the senses, making use neither of reason nor of imagination nor of the senses but seeing with one grasp of the mind all things in their

Idea, so to speak. Reason, too, when it views a universal, makes no use of the imagination of the senses, and yet it comprehends the objects both of imagination and of sensation. For it is reason which defines a universal resulting from its own mode of conception like this: man is a two-footed, rational animal. Though this is a universal notion, everybody knows that what reason thus considers not by an act of the imagination or of the senses but by an act of rational conception is a thing accessible to imagination and sense. Likewise, although imagination takes its beginning of seeing and forming figures from the senses, still without their aid it surveys each sensible thing not with a sensory but with an imaginary faculty of distinguishing. Do you see, then, that in the act of knowing all subjects employ their own faculty rather than that of the objects known? And this is only reasonable for, since every judgement formed is an act of the person who judges, every man must of necessity perform his own operation with his own and not another's faculty. . . .

5. Philosophy Discusses the Difference Between Human Reason and Divine Insight

"If, with regard to perceiving physical objects, although the qualities projected from without affect the sensory organs and although the body's passive reception, preceding the mind's energetic action, calls forth to itself the mind's activity and arouses the hitherto quiescent ideas within; if, I repeat, with regard to perceiving physical objects, the mind does not passively receive impressions from said objects but of its own power judges the reception dependent on the body, how much less do those beings which are free from all affections of the body follow in their judgment external objects, but rather they release the independent actions of their minds. For this reason many different manners of cognition have fallen to widely different substances. The senses alone, destitute of any knowledge but their own, have fallen to those living beings which are incapable of motion, like the shellfish of the sea and other low forms of life which live by clinging to rocks; while imagination has fallen to animals with the power of motion, who seem to be affected by a desire to seek certain things and to avoid others. But reason belongs to the human race alone, just as insight is God's alone. . . .

"Suppose then that sensation and imagination oppose reasoning, saying that those universals which reason pretends to contemplate do not exist, arguing that what is comprehensible to the senses and imagination cannot be universal; that therefore either the judgment of reason is true and nothing comprehensible exists or (since reason knows full well that there are many objects comprehensible to the senses and imagination) the conceptions of reason are empty because it holds the individual thing comprehensible to the sense to be something universal. If reason were to respond that it does, indeed, perceive the objects of sense and imagination from a universal point of view; that sense and imagination, on the other hand, cannot aspire to knowledge of universals since their manner of cognition goes no further than bodies and figures; and that in matters of knowledge it is best to trust to the stronger and more nearly perfect judgment—if such a trial by debate occurred should not we, who have the power not only to reason but also to imagine and perceive with the sense, approve reason's cause rather than the others'? We are dealing with a similar situation when human reason supposes that the divine insight cannot contemplate future things except as it (the human reason) conceives them. For you argue thus: 'If there are some things which do not occur necessarily and certainly, then it cannot be known in advance with certainty that these things will actually occur; therefore there can be no foreknowledge of these things for, if we believe that they can be foreknown, then everything happens by necessity.' If we, however, who partake of reason, could also share that power of judgment which is proper to the divine mind, we would think it most fitting that, just as we have decided that the senses and imagination should yield to human reason, so the latter should submit itself to the divine mind. Let us therefore raise ourselves, if we can, to that height of the loftiest intelligence. For there reason will see what she cannot intuit on her own, i.e., how foreknowledge sees distinctly and certainly even those things which occur without necessity and how such foreknowledge is not mere opinion but rather the simplicity of the highest knowledge, unencumbered by any finite bounds. . . .

6. Philosophy Explains That God's Insight Views All Things in Their Eternal Design, while Human Reason Can See Them only from a Temporal Viewpoint

"Since then, as we have just now shown, everything that is known is apprehended not according to its own nature but according to that of the knower, let us examine now, so far as we lawfully may, what is the state of the divine substance, so that we may be able to learn also what its knowledge is. The common opinion, according to all men living, is that God is eternal. Let us therefore consider what eternity is, for this will make clear to us at the same time the divine nature and the divine knowledge. Now, eternity is the complete possession of an endless life enjoyed as one simultaneous whole; this will appear clearer from a comparison with temporal things. For whatever is living in time proceeds in the present from times past to times future; and nothing existing in time is so constituted as to embrace the whole span of its life at once, but it has not yet grasped tomorrow, while it has already lost yesterday. In this life of today you are living in no more than a fleeting, transitory moment. And so it is with everything that is subject to the condition of time: even if it should never have begun and would never cease to be—which Aristotle believed of the universe—even if its life were to be co-extensive with the infinity of time, yet it could not rightly be held to be eternal. For, even granted that it has an infinite lifetime, it does not embrace this life as a simultaneous whole; it does not now have a grasp of the future, which is yet to be lived through. What is rightly called eternal is that which grasps and possesses simultaneously the entire fullness of an unending life, a life which lacks nothing of the future and has lost nothing of the fleeting past. Such a being must necessarily always be its whole self, unchangingly present to itself, and the infinity of changing time must be as one present before him. Wherefore they are mistaken who, hearing that Plato thought this world had no beginning in time and would have no end, think that in this way the created universe is co-eternal with the Creator. For to pass step by step through an unending life, a process ascribed by Plato to the universe, is one thing; to embrace simultaneously the whole of an unending life in one present, an act manifestly peculiar to the divine mind, is quite another thing. And, further, God should not be regarded as older than His creations by any quantity of time but rather by the peculiar quality of simplicity in His nature. For the infinite motion of temporal things tries to imitate the ever present immobility of His life, does not succeed in copying or equalling it, sinks from immobility into motion, and falls from the simplicity of the present to the infinite stretch of future and past; and since it cannot possess its life completely and simultaneously it seems to emulate, by the very fact that it somehow exists forever without ceasing, what it cannot fully attain and express, clinging as it does to the so-called present of this short and fleeting moment, which, inasmuch as it bears a certain resemblance to that abiding present, makes those to whom it comes appear to exist. But, since this present could not be abiding, it took to the infinite journey through time, and so it has come to pass that, by journeying on, it continues that life the fullness of which it could not grasp by staying. Thus if we would apply proper epithets to these subjects we would say, following Plato, that God is eternal, while the universe is perpetual.

"Since, then, every judgment comprehends the objects of its thought according to its own nature, and since God has an ever present and eternal state, His knowledge also, surpassing every temporal movement, remains in the simplicity of its own present and, embracing infinite lengths of past and future, views with its own simple comprehension all things as if they were taking place in the present. If you will weigh the foresight with which God discerns all things, you will rightly esteem it to be the knowledge of a never fading instant rather than a foreknowledge of the 'future.' It should therefore rather be called *pro*vision than *pre*vision because, placed high above lowly things, it looks out over all as from the loftiest mountain top. Why then do you demand that those things which are translucent to the divine mind's light be necessary if not even men make necessary the things they see? Because you can see present things, does your sight impose upon them any necessity?"

"Surely not."

"Yet, if one may not unworthily compare the human present with the divine, just as you see certain things in this, your temporal present, so God sees all things in His eternal present. Wherefore this divine foreknowledge does not change the nature or properties of things: it sees things present to its contemplation just as they will turn out some time in the future. Neither is there any confusion in its judgments of things: with one glimpse of the mind it distinguishes what will happen necessarily and what will happen non-necessarily. For example, when you observe at the same time a man walking on the earth and the sun rising in the sky, although you see both sights simultaneously, nevertheless you distinguish between them and judge that the one is moving vol-

untarily, the other necessarily; in like manner the intuition of God looks down upon all things without at all disturbing their nature, yet they are present to Him and future in relation to time. Wherefore it is not opinion but knowledge grounded in truth when He knows that something will occur in the future and knows as well that it will not occur of necessity. If you say at this point that what God sees as about to happen cannot but happen and that what cannot but happen happens, and you pin me down to this definition of necessity, I will confess a matter of the firmest truth but one which scarcely any one save a contemplator of the divine can reach: i.e., I shall answer that one and the same future event is necessary with respect to God's knowledge of it but absolutely free and unrestrained when it is examined in its own nature.

"For there are two kinds of necessity. One is simple: for instance, it is necessary that all men are mortal. The other is conditional: for instance, if you really know that a man is walking, he must be walking. For what a man really knows cannot be otherwise than it is known to be. But the conditional kind of necessity by no means implies the simple kind, for the former is not based on the very nature of the thing called necessary but on the addition of an 'if.' For example, no necessity compels a man who is walking of his own accord to proceed, though it is necessary that, *if* he is walking, he should be proceeding. In the same way, if Providence sees any thing as present, that thing must be, though it has no necessity of its own nature; and, of course, God sees as present those future things which come to pass through free will. Therefore free acts, when referred to the divine intuition, become necessary in the conditional sense because God's knowledge provides that condition; on the other hand, viewed by themselves, they do not lose the perfect freedom of their nature. Without doubt, then, all things which God foreknows do come to pass, but certain of them proceed from free will. And these free acts, though they come to pass, do not by actually occurring lose their proper nature, because of which, before they come to pass, they could also not have come to pass. . . .

" 'But,' you will say, 'if it is within my power to change my mind I can make Providence void, for I may change what she foreknows.' To this I will answer that you can indeed change your mind but, since Providence truly sees in her present that you can change it, whether you will change it, and whither you may change it, you cannot avoid the divine foreknowledge any more than you can avoid the glance of an eye which is present, though you may by your free will turn yourself to various different actions. You will then say, 'Will the divine foreknowledge be altered by my own disposition, so that when I choose now one thing, now another, it too will seem to undergo alternations in its own cognition?' By no means; for the divine insight precedes the future and recalls it to the one present of its own proper cognition. It does not alternate, as you suppose, between this and that in its foreknowledge, but it is constantly preceding and grasping with one glance all mutations. This presence of comprehending and witnessing all things is not based on the actual occurrence of future events but on God's own peculiar simplicity—which fact also resolves that problem which you posed a little while ago when you said that it is shameful to maintain that our future acts are the cause of God's knowledge. For this power of knowledge to take cognizance, with one ever present glance, of all things has itself determined for each thing its mode of existence and owes nothing more to future things. Since this is so, mortal man's freedom of judgment remains inviolate and, because his will is free from any necessity, the laws which propose rewards and punishments are not unjust. God is the ever prescient spectator of all things, and the eternity of His vision, which is ever present, runs in unison with the future nature of our acts, dispensing rewards to the good, punishments to the evil. Hopes are not vainly put in God nor prayers vainly offered which, if they be right, must be effective. Therefore turn from vice, cultivate virtue, raise your heart to legitimate hope, direct humble prayers to the heavens. If you will only take notice and not dissemble, a great necessity for righteousness is laid upon you, since you live under the eyes of a Judge who discerns all."

Chapter 10

AVICENNA

Avicenna (Ibn Sina) (980–1037), Persian (Iranian) philosopher and physician, regarded as the greatest of the medieval Islamic philosophers, served as court physician for the Sultan of Bukhara. He was deeply influenced by Aristotle and still maintained a Muslim faith. He is best known for his distinction between essence and existence, in which the essences of existing things must be explained by their existing cause(s), whose reality is higher than the perceived essence. In the short selection he discusses the conflict between the philosophical and theological perspective.

Essay on the Secret of Destiny

In the name of God, the Merciful, the Compassionate.

Someone asked the eminent *shaykh* Abū 'Alī b. Sīnā (may God the Exalted have mercy on him) the meaning of the Sūfī saying, 'He who knows the secret of destiny is an atheist'. In reply he stated that this matter contains the utmost obscurity, and is one of those matters which may be set down only in enigmatic form and taught only in a hidden manner, on account of the corrupting effects its open declaration would have on the general public. The basic principle concerning it is found in a Tradition of the Prophet (God bless and safeguard him): 'Destiny is the secret of God; do not declare the secret of God'. In another Tradition, when a man questioned the Prince of the Believers, 'Alī (may God be pleased with him), he replied, 'Destiny is a deep sea; do not sail out on it'. Being asked again he replied, 'It is a stony path; do not walk on it'. Being asked once more he said, 'It is a hard ascent; do not undertake it'.[1]

The *shaykh* said: Know that the secret of destiny is based upon certain premises, such as [1] the world order, [2] the report[2] that there is Reward and Punishment, and [3] the affirmation of the resurrection of souls.

1. The first premiss is that you should know that in the world as a whole and in its parts, both upper and earthly, there is nothing which forms an exception to the facts that God is the cause of its being

---

1. These Traditions do not explain the meaning of the original saying, they merely reaffirm the prohibition.

2. 'Report' (*hadīth*) seems to hint that after-life Reward and Punishment in the usual sense are only traditional doctrines, not known by science. This view is confirmed below, and elsewhere, e.g. *Shifā': Ilāhiyyāt*, ed. I. Madkur, M. Y. Musa, S. Dunya, and S. Zayed, Cairo, 1960, IX, 7, pp. 414 ff.

Reprinted by permission from Avicenna, *Essay on the Secret of Destiny*, translated by George Hourani in *Bulletin of the School of Oriental and African Studies*, London, vol. 29, Pt. 1, 1996, pp. 31–33.

and origination and that God has knowledge of it, controls it, and wills its existence; it is all subject to His control, determination, knowledge, and will. This is a general and superficial account, although in these assertions we intend to describe it truly, not as the theologians understand it;[3] and it is possible to produce proofs and demonstrations of that. Thus, if it were not that this world is composed of elements which give rise to good and evil things in it and produce both righteousness and wickedness in its inhabitants, there would have been no completion of an order for the world. For if the world had contained nothing but pure righteousness, it would not have been this world but another one, and it would necessarily have had a composition different from the present composition; and likewise if it had contained nothing but sheer wickedness, it would not have been this world but another one. But whatever is composed in the present fashion and order contains both righteousness and wickedness.

2. The second premiss is that according to the ancients Reward is the occurrence of pleasure in the soul corresponding to the extent of its perfection, while Punishment is the occurrence of pain in the soul corresponding to the extent of its deficiency. So the soul's abiding in deficiency is its 'alienation from God the Exalted',[4] and this is 'the curse', 'the Penalty', [God's] 'wrath' and 'anger', and pain comes to it from that deficiency; while its perfection is what is meant by [God's] 'satisfaction' with it, its 'closeness' and 'nearness' and 'attachment'. This, then, and nothing else is the meaning of 'Reward' and 'Punishment' according to them.

3. The third premiss is that the resurrection is just the return of human souls to their own world; this is why God the Exalted has said, 'O tranquil soul, return to your Lord satisfied and satisfactory'.

These are summary statements, which need to be supported by their proper demonstrations.

a] Now, if these premises are established, we say that the apparent evils which befall this world are, on the principles of the Sage,[5] not purposed for the world—the good things alone are what is purposed,

the evil ones are a privation, while according to Plato both are purposed as well as willed; [b] and that the commanding and forbidding of acts to responsible beings, by revelation in the world, are just a stimulant to him of whom it was foreknown [by God] that there would occur in him [performance of] the commandments, or (in the case of a prohibition) a deterrent to him of whom it was foreknown that he would refrain from what is forbidden. Thus the commandment is a cause of the act's proceeding from him of whom it is foreknown that it will proceed, and the prohibition is a cause of intimidation to him who refrains from something bad because of it. Without the commandment the former would not have come to desire the act; without the prohibition the latter would not have been sacred. It is as if one were to imagine that it would have been possible for 100 per cent of wickedness to befall in the absence of any prohibition, and that with the presence of the prohibitions 50 per cent of wickedness has befallen, whereas without prohibitions 100 per cent would have befallen. Commandments must be judged in the same way: had there been no commandments nothing of righteousness would have befallen, but with the advent of the commandments 50 per cent of righteousness has occurred.

c] As for praise and blame, these have just two objects. One is to incite a doer of good to repeat the like act which is willed to proceed from him; the second is to scare the one from whom the act has occurred from repeating the like of it, and [ensure] that the one from whom that act has [not] occurred will abstain from doing what is not willed to proceed from him, though it is in his capacity to do it.

d] It is not admissible that Reward and Punishment should be such as the theologians suppose: chastisement of the fornicator, for example, by putting him in chains and shackles, burning him in the fire over and over again, and setting snakes and scorpions upon him. For this is the behaviour of one who wills to slake his wrath against his enemy, through injury or pain which he inflicts on him out of hostility against him; and that is impossible in the character of God the Exalted, for it is the act of one who wills that the very being who models himself on him should refrain from acts like his or be restrained from repeating such acts. And it is not to be imagined that after the resurrection there are obligations, commandments, and prohibitions for anyone, so that by witnessing Reward and Punish-

---

3. 'Truly', i.e. according to the Neoplatonic system of causal determination, not the voluntaristic conceptions of Muslim *kalām*, Mu'tazilite and other. Thus Ibn Sīnā's 'destiny' should not be called 'predestination'.

4. All the words put here within quotation marks are Islamic religious expressions which Ibn Sīnā is interpreting in his own way.

5. *al-hakīm*, the epithet of Aristotle.

ment they should be scared or refrain from what is proscribed to them and desire what is commanded to them. So it is false that Reward and Punishment are as they have imagined them.

e] As for the [system of] penalties ordained by the divine Law for those who commit transgressions, it has the same effect as the prohibitions in serving as a restraint upon him who abstains from transgression, whereas without it it is imaginable that the act might proceed from him. There may also be a gain to the one who is subject to penalty, in preventing him from further wickedness, because men must be bound by one of two bonds, either the bond of the divine Law or the bond of reason, that the order of the world may be completed. Do you not see that if anyone were let loose from both bonds the load of wickedness he would commit would be unbearable, and the order of the world's affairs would be upset by the dominance of him who is released from both bonds? But God is more knowing and wiser.

Chapter 11

ANSELM AND GAUNILO

St. Anselm (ca. 1033–1109) was Abbot of Bec and later Archbishop of Canterbury. He wrote several important treatises on theological subjects, including *Cur Deus Homo* (Why God Became Man). In this selection from his *Proslogium* he begins with the definition of God as "that than which nothing greater can be conceived." Today we might translate this as "the greatest possible being." From that definition Anselm proceeds to argue for the necessary existence of God, known as the *Ontological Argument* for the existence of God. Although a version of this argument can be found in Augustine, Anselm's rendition is more complete and better developed. He believes that God's existence is so certain that only a fool would doubt or deny it. Yet he desires understanding to fulfill his faith. The Ontological Argument is the product of this desire.

Anselm's contemporary, Gaunilo, a Benedictine monk, sets forth the first objection to Anselm's argument, centering on a delectable lost island, one that is more excellent than all lands. Since it is better that such a perfect island exists in reality than simply in the mind alone, this Isle of the Blest must necessarily exist.

Anselm's reply to Gaunilo is included in our readings.

FOR FURTHER READING:

Evans, G. R. *Anselm and Talking about God.* (Oxford University Press, 1978).
Harshorne, C. *Anselm's Discovery.* (Open Court, 1965).
Hick, John and Arthur McGill, eds. *The Many-Faced Arguments.* (Macmillan, 1967).
Hopkins, Jasper. *A Companion to the Study of St. Anselm.* (University of Minnesota Press, 1972).
Plantinga, Alvin, ed. *The Ontological Argument.* (Doubleday, 1965).
Southern, R. W. *Saint Anselm: A Portrait in a Landscape.* (Cambridge University Press, 1990).

Proslogium

ST. ANSELM'S PRESENTATION

Truly there is a God, although
  the fool hath said in his heart,
  There is no God.

And so, Lord, do thou, who dost give understanding and faith, give me, so far as thou knowest it to be profitable, to understand that thou art as we believe; and that thou art that which we believe. And, indeed, we believe that thou art a being than which nothing greater can be conceived. Or is there no such nature, since the fool hath said in his heart, there is no God? (Psalms xiii, I). But, at any rate, this very fool, when he hears of this being of which I speak—a being than which nothing greater can be conceived—understands what he hears, and what he understands is in his understanding; although he does not understand it to exist.

For, it is one thing for an object to be in the understanding, and another to understand that the object exists. When a painter first conceives of what he will afterwards perform, he has it in his understanding, but he does not yet understand it to be, because he has not yet performed it. But after he has made the painting, he both has it in his understanding, and he understands that it exists, because he has made it.

Hence, even the fool is convinced that something exists in the understanding, at least, than which nothing greater can be conceived. For, when he hears of this, he understands it. And whatever is understood, exists in the understanding. And assuredly that, than which nothing greater can be conceived, cannot exist in the understanding alone. For, suppose it exists in the understanding alone: then it can be conceived to exist in reality; which is greater.

Therefore, if that, than which nothing greater can be conceived, exists in the understanding alone, the very being, than which nothing greater can be conceived, is one, than which a greater can be conceived. But obviously this is impossible. Hence, there is no doubt that there exists a being, than which nothing greater can be conceived, and it exists both in the understanding and in reality.

God cannot be conceived not to exist.—God is that, than which nothing greater can be conceived.—That which can be conceived not to exist is not God.

And it assuredly exists so truly, that it cannot be conceived not to exist. For, it is possible to conceive of a being which cannot be conceived not to exist; and this is greater than one which can be conceived not to exist. Hence, if that, than which nothing greater can be conceived, can be conceived not to exist, it is not that, than which nothing greater can be conceived. But this is an irreconcilable contradiction. There is, then, so truly a being than which nothing greater can be conceived to exist, that it cannot even be conceived not to exist; and this being thou art, O Lord, our God.

So truly, therefore, dost thou exist, O Lord, my God, that thou canst not be conceived not to exist; and rightly. For, if a mind could conceive of a being better than thee, the creature would rise above the Creator; and this is most absurd. And, indeed, whatever else there is, except thee alone, can be conceived not to exist. To thee alone, therefore, it belongs to exist more truly than all other beings, and hence in a higher degree than all others. For, whatever else exists does not exist so truly, and hence in a less degree it belongs to it to exist. Why, then, has the fool said in his heart, there is no God (Psalms xiii, I), since it is so evident, to a rational mind, that thou dost exist in the highest degree of all? Why, except that he is dull and a fool?

How the fool has said in his heart what cannot be conceived.—A thing may be conceived in two ways: (1) when the word signifying it is conceived; (2) when the thing itself is understood. As far as the word goes, God can be conceived not to exist; in reality he cannot.

But how has the fool said in his heart what he could not conceive; or how is it that he could not conceive what he said in his heart? since it is the same to say in the heart, and to conceive.

But, if really, nay, since really, he both conceived,

Reprinted by permission from Open Court Trade & Academic Books, a division of Carus Publishing Company, Peru, IL, from *St. Anselm: Basic Writings*, translated by S. N. Deane.

because he said in his heart; and did not say in his heart, because he could not conceive; there is more than one way in which a thing is said in the heart or conceived. For, in one sense, an object is conceived, when the word signifying it is conceived; and in another, when the very entity, which the object is, is understood.

In the former sense, then, God can be conceived not to exist; but in the latter, not at all. For no one who understands what fire and water are can conceive fire to be water, in accordance with the nature of the facts themselves, although this is possible according to the words. So, then, no one who understands what God is can conceive that God does not exist; although he says these words in his heart, either without any or with some foreign, signification. For, God is that than which a greater cannot be conceived. And he who thoroughly understands this, assuredly understands that this being so truly exists, that not even in concept can it be non-existent. Therefore, he who understands that God so exists, cannot conceive that he does not exist.

I thank thee, gracious Lord, I thank thee; because what I formerly believed by thy bounty, I now so understand by thine illumination, that if I were unwilling to believe that thou dost exist, I should not be able not to understand this to be true.

Gaunilo's Criticism

IN BEHALF OF THE FOOL

For example: it is said that somewhere in the ocean is an island, which, because of the difficulty, or rather the impossibility, of discovering what does not exist, is called the lost island. And they say that this island has an inestimable wealth of all manner of riches and delicacies in greater abundance than is told of the Islands of the Blest; and that having no owner or inhabitant, it is more excellent than all other countries, which are inhabited by mankind, in the abundance with which it is stored.

Now if some one should tell me that there is such an island, I should easily understand his words, in which there is no difficulty. But suppose that he went on to say, as if by a logical inference: "You can no longer doubt that this island which is more excellent than all lands exists somewhere, since you have no doubt that it is in your understanding. And since it is more excellent not to be in the understanding alone, but to exist both in the understanding and in reality, for this reason it must exist. For if it does not exist, any land which really exists will be more excellent than it; and so the island already understood by you to be more excellent will not be more excellent."

If a man should try to prove to me by such reasoning that this island truly exists, and that its existence should no longer be doubted, either I should believe that he was jesting, or I know not which I ought to regard as the greater fool: myself, supposing that I should allow this proof; or him, if he should suppose that he had established with any certainty the existence of this island. For he ought to show first that the hypothetical excellence of this island exists as a real and indubitable fact, and in no wise as any unreal object, or one whose existence is uncertain, in my understanding.

St. Anselm's Rejoinder

APOLOGETIC

A criticism of Gaunilo's example, in which he tries to show that in this way the real existence of a lost island might be inferred from the fact of its being conceived.

But, you say, it is as if one should suppose an island in the ocean, which surpasses all lands in its fertility, and which, because of the difficulty, or rather the impossibility, of discovering what does not exist, is called a lost island; and should say that there can be no doubt that this island truly exists in reality, for this reason, that one who hears it described easily understands what he hears.

Now I promise confidently that if any man shall devise anything existing either in reality or in concept alone (except that than which a greater cannot be conceived) to which he can adapt the sequence of my reasoning, I will discover that thing, and will give him his lost island, not to be lost again.

But it now appears that this being than which a greater is inconceivable cannot be conceived not to be, because it exists on so assured a ground of truth; for otherwise it would not exist at all.

Hence, if any one says that he conceives this being not to exist, I say that at the time when he conceives of this either he conceives of a being than which a greater is inconceivable, or he does not conceive at all. If he does not conceive, he does not conceive of the non-existence of that of which he does not conceive. But if he does conceive, he certainly conceives of a being which cannot be even conceived not to exist. For if it could be conceived not to exist, it could be conceived to have a beginning and an end. But this is impossible.

He, then, who conceives of this being conceives of a being which cannot be even conceived not to exist; but he who conceives of this being does not conceive that it does not exist; else he conceives what is inconceivable. The nonexistence, then, of that than which a greater cannot be conceived is inconceivable.

Chapter 12

MOSES MAIMONIDES

The Jewish philosopher and physician Moses ben Maimon, or Maimonides, (1135–1204) was born in Cordova, Spain, and received training both in the biblical and rabbinic tradition and in philosophy, especially Aristotelian thought. In 1148 Muslim intolerance forced his family to migrate to North Africa, finally settling in Egypt, which was also Muslim but more tolerant, some seventeen years later (1165). There he gained renown not only as a rabbinic scholar and philosopher but also as a physician. He wrote commentaries on the Jewish law in Arabic and was considered the foremost Jewish scholar in the Medieval world. It was said of him "from Moses (the prophet) to Moses (ben Maimon) there had arisen no one like unto him."

His *Guide for the Perplexed*, written in Arabic in 1190, but soon translated into Hebrew and then into Latin, was addressed to Jews who were "perplexed" by the conflicting claims of philosophy and religion. His aim was to relieve the doubts by reconciling philosophy with religious faith. In our first selection from this work Maimonides shows the importance of the negative attributes of God. In the second selection he develops two Aristotelian arguments for the existence and unity of God, and in the third selection he argues for a version of divine Providence that is concerned with human beings but not animals.

FOR FURTHER READING:

Agus, J. *The Evolution of Jewish Thought*. (1959).
Goodman, Lenn, ed. *Rambam*. (1976)
Heschel, Abraham. *Maimonides*, tr. J. Neugroschel. (Farrar, Straus and Giroux, 1982).
Roth, Leon. *The Guide for the Perplexed*. (1949).
Twersky, I. *Maimonides Reader*. (Behrman).

Guide for the Perplexed

FROM PART I, CHAPTER 58: ON KNOWING GOD BY NEGATION

Know that the negative attributes of God are the true attributes: they do not include any incorrect notions or any deficiency whatever in reference to God, while positive attributes imply polytheism, and are inadequate, as we have already shown. It is now necessary to explain how negative expressions can in a certain sense be employed as attributes, and how they are distinguished from positive attributes. Then I shall show that we cannot describe the Creator by any means except by negative attributes. An attribute does not exclusively belong to the one object to which it is related; while qualifying one thing, it can also be employed to qualify other things, and is in that case not peculiar to that one thing. E.g., if you see an object from a distance, and on enquiring what it is, are told that it is a living being you have certainly learnt an attribute of the object seen, and although that attribute does not exclusively belong to the object perceived, it expresses that the object is not plant or a mineral. Again, if a man is in a certain house, and you know that something is in the house, but not exactly what, you ask what is in that house, and you are told, not a plant nor a mineral. You have thereby obtained some special knowledge of the thing; you have learnt that it is a living being, although you do not yet know what kind of a living being it is. The negative attributes have this in common with the positive, that they necessarily circumscribe the object to some extent, although such circumscription consists only in the exclusion of what otherwise would not be excluded. In the following point, however, the negative attributes are distinguished from the positive. The positive attributes, although not peculiar to one thing, describe a portion of what we desire to know, either some part of its essence or some of its accidents; the negative attributes, on the other hand, do not, as regards the essence of the thing which we desire to know, in any way tell us what it is, except it be indirectly, as had been shown in the instance given by us.

After this introduction, I would observe that,—as has already been shown—God's existence is absolute, that it includes no composition, as will be proved, and that we comprehend only the fact that He exists, not His essence. Consequently it is a false assumption to hold that He has any positive attribute; for He does not possess existence in addition to His essence, it therefore cannot be said that the one may be described as an attribute [of the other]; much less has He [in addition to His existence] a compound essence, consisting of two constituent elements to which the attribute could refer; still less has He accidents, which could be described by an attribute. Hence it is clear that He has no positive attribute whatever. The negative attributes, however, are those which are necessary to direct the mind to the truths which we must believe concerning God; for, on the one hand, they do not imply any plurality,

and on the other, they convey to man the highest possible knowledge of God; e.g., it has been established by proof that some being must exist besides those things which can be perceived by the senses, or apprehended by the mind; when we say of this being, that it exists, we mean that its non-existence is impossible. We then perceive that such a being is not, for instance, like the four elements, which are inanimate, and we therefore say that it is living, expressing thereby that it is not dead. We call such a being incorporeal, because we notice that it is unlike the heavens, which are living, but material. Seeing that it is also different from the intellect, which, though incorporeal and living, owes its existence to some cause, we say it is the first, expressing thereby that its existence is not due to any cause. We further notice, that the existence, that is the essence, of this being is not limited to its own existence; many existences emanate from it, and its influence is not like that of the fire in producing heat, or that of the sun in sending forth light, but consists in constantly giving them stability and order by well-established rule, as we shall show: we say, on that account, it has power, wisdom, and will, i.e., it is not feeble or ignorant, or hasty, and does not abandon its creatures; when we say that it is not feeble,we mean that its existence is capable of producing the existence of many other things; by saying that it is not ignorant, we mean "it perceives" or "it lives,"—for everything that perceives is living—by saying "it is not hasty, and does not abandon its creatures," we mean that all these creatures preserve a certain order and arrangement; they are not left to themselves; they are not produced aimlessly, but whatever condition they receive from that being is given with design and intention. We thus learn that there is no other being like unto God, and we say that He is One, i.e., there are not more Gods than one.

It has thus been shown that every attribute predicated of God either denotes the quality of an action, or—when the attribute is intended to convey some idea of the Divine Being itself, and not of His actions—the negation of the opposite. Even these negative attributes must not be formed and applied to God, except in the way in which, as you know, sometimes an attribute is negatived in reference to a thing, although that attribute can naturally never be applied to it in the same sense, as, e.g., we say, "This wall does not see." Those who read the present work are aware that, notwithstanding all the efforts of the mind, we can obtain no knowledge of the essence of the heavens—a revolving substance which has been measured by us in spans and cubits, and examined even as regards the proportions of the several spheres to each other and respecting most of their motions—although we know that they must consist of matter and form; but the matter not being the same as sublunary matter, we can only describe the heavens in terms expressing negative properties, but not in terms denoting positive qualities. Thus we say that the heavens are not light, not heavy, not passive and therefore not subject to impressions, and that they do not possess the sensations of taste and smell; or we use similar negative attributes. All this we do, because we do not know their substance. What, then, can be the result of our efforts, when we try to obtain a knowledge of a Being that is free from substance, that is most simple, whose existence is absolute, and not due to any cause, to whose perfect essence nothing can be superadded, and whose perfection consists, as we have shown, in the absence of all defects. All we understand is the fact that He exists, that He is a Being to whom none of His creatures is similar, who has nothing in common with them, who does not include plurality, who is never too feeble to produce other beings, and whose relation to the universe is that of a steersman to a boat; and even this is not a real relation, a real simile, but serves only to convey to us the idea that God rules the universe; that is, that He gives it duration, and preserves its necessary arrangement. This subject will be treated more fully. Praised be He! In the contemplation of His essence, our comprehension and knowledge prove insufficient; in the examination of His works, how they necessarily result from His will, our knowledge proves to be ignorance, and in the endeavour to extol Him in words, all our efforts in speech are mere weakness and failure!

FROM PART II, CHAPTER 1: ON THE EXISTENCE AND ONENESS OF GOD

This (third argument) is taken from the words of Aristotle, though he gives it in a different form. It runs as follows: There is no doubt that many things actually exist, as, e.g., things perceived with the senses. Now there are only three cases conceivable, viz., either all these things are without beginning and without end, or all of them have beginning and end, or some are with and some without beginning and

end. The first of these three cases is altogether inadmissible, since we clearly perceive objects which come into existence and are subsequently destroyed. The second case is likewise inadmissible, for if everything had but a temporary existence all things might be destroyed, and that which is enunciated of a whole class of things as possible is necessarily actual. All things must therefore come to an end, and then nothing would ever be in existence, for there would not exist any being to produce anything. Consequently nothing whatever would exist [if all things were transient]; but as we see things existing, and find ourselves in existence we conclude as follows:—Since there are undoubtedly beings of a temporary existence, there must also be an eternal being that is not subject to destruction, and whose existence is real, not merely possible.

It has been further argued that the existence of this being is necessary, either on account of itself alone or on account of some external force. In the latter case its existence and non-existence would be equally possible, because of its own properties, but its existence would be necessary on account of the external force. That force would then be the being that possesses absolute existence. It is therefore certain that there must be a being which has absolutely independent existence, and is the source of the existence of all things, whether transient or permanent, if, as Aristotle assumes, there is in existence such a thing, which is the effect of an eternal cause, and must therefore itself be eternal. This is a proof the correctness of which is not doubted, disputed, or rejected, except by those who have no knowledge of the method of proof. We further say that the existence of anything that has independent existence is not due to any cause, and that such a being does not include any plurality whatever; consequently it cannot be a body, nor a force residing in a body. It is now clear that there must be a being with absolutely independent existence, a being whose existence cannot be attributed to any external cause, and which does not include different elements; it cannot therefore be corporeal, or a force residing in a corporal object; this being is God.

It can easily be proved that absolutely independent existence cannot be attributed to two beings. For, if that were the case, absolutely independent existence would be a property added to the substance of both; neither of them would be absolutely independent on account of their essence, but only through a certain property, viz., that of this independent existence, which is common to both. It can besides be shown in many ways that independent existence cannot be reconciled with the principle of dualism by any means. It would make no difference, whether we imagine two beings of similar or of different properties. The reason for all this is to be sought in the absolute simplicity and in the utmost perfection of the essence of this being, which is the only member of its species, and does not depend on any cause whatever; this being has therefore nothing in common with other beings.

This (fourth argument) is likewise a well-known philosophical argument. We constantly see things passing from a state of potentiality to that of actuality, but in every such case there is for that transition of a thing an agent separate from it. It is likewise clear that the agent has also passed from potentiality to actuality. It has at first been potential, because it could not be actual, owing to some obstacle contained in itself, or on account of the absence of a certain relation between itself and the object of its action; it became an actual agent as soon as that relation was present. Whichever cause be assumed, an agent is again necessary to remove the obstacle or to create the relation. The same can be argued respecting this last-mentioned agent that creates the relation or removes the obstacle. This series of causes cannot go on *ad infinitum*; we must at last arrive at a cause of the transition of an object from the state of potentiality to that of actuality, which is constant, and admits of no potentiality whatever. In the essence of this cause nothing exists potentially, for if its essence included any possibility of existence it would not exist at all; it cannot be corporeal, but it must be spiritual; and the immaterial being that includes no possibility whatever, but exists actually by its own essence, is God. Since He is incorporeal, as has been demonstrated, it follows that He is One.

Even if we were to admit the Eternity of the Universe, we could by any of these methods prove the existence of God; that He is One and incorporeal and that He does not reside as a force in a corporeal object.

The following is likewise a correct method to prove the Incorporeality and the Unity of God: If there were two Gods, they would necessarily have one element in common by virtue of which they were Gods, and another element by which they were distinguished from each other and existed as two Gods, the distinguishing element would either be in

both different from the property common to both—in that case both of them would consist of different elements, and neither of them would be the First Cause, or have absolutely independent existence; but their existence would depend on certain causes—or the distinguishing element would only in one of them be different from the element common to both: then that being could not have absolute independence.

The principle laid down in the foregoing must be well understood; it is a high rampart erected round the Law, and able to resist all missiles directed against it. Aristotle, or rather his followers, may perhaps ask us how we know that the Universe has been created; and that other forces than those it has at present were acting in its Creation, since we hold that the properties of the Universe, as it exists at present, prove nothing as regards its creation? We reply, there is no necessity for this according to our plan; for we do not desire to prove the Creation, but only its possibility; and this possibility is not refuted by arguments based on the nature of the present Universe, which we do not dispute. When we have established the admissibility of our theory, we shall then show its superiority. In attempting to prove the inadmissibility of *creation from nothing*, the Aristotelians can therefore not derive any support from the nature of the Universe; they must resort to the notion our mind has formed of God. Their proofs include the three methods which I have mentioned above, and which are based on the notion conceived of God.

FROM PART III, CHAPTER 17: ON DIVINE PROVIDENCE

My opinion on this principle of Divine Providence I will now explain to you. In the principle which I now proceed to expound I do not rely on demonstrative proof, but on my conception of the spirit of the Divine Law, and the writings of the Prophets. The principle which I accept is far less open to objections, and is more reasonable than the opinions mentioned before. It is this: In the lower or sublunary portion of the Universe Divine Providence does not extend to the individual members of species except in the case of mankind. It is only in this species that the incidents in the existence of the individual beings, their good and evil fortunes, are the result of justice, in accordance with the words, "For all His ways are judgment." But I agree with Aristotle as regards all other living beings, and *a fortiori* as regards plants and all the rest of earthly creatures. For I do not believe that it is through the interference of Divine Providence that a certain leaf drops [from a tree], nor do I hold that when a certain spider catches a certain fly, that this is the direct result of a special decree and will of God in that moment; it is not by a particular Divine degree that the will of God in that moment; it is not by a particular Divine degree that the spittle of a certain person moved, fell on a certain gnat in a certain place, and killed it; nor is it by the direct will of God that a certain fish catches and swallows a certain worm on the surface of the water. In all these cases the action is, according to my opinion, entirely due to chance, as taught by Aristotle. Divine Providence is connected with Divine intellectual influence, and the same beings which are benefited by the latter so as to become intellectual, and to comprehend things comprehensible to rational beings, are also under the control of Divine Providence, which examines all their deeds in order to reward or punish them. It may be by mere chance that a ship goes down with all her contents, as in the above-mentioned instance, or the roof of a house falls upon those within; but its not due to chance, according to our view, that in the one instance the men went into the ship, or remained in the house in the other instance; it is due to the will of God, and is in accordance with the justice of His judgments, the method of which our mind is incapable of understanding.

I have been induced to accept this theory by the circumstance that I have not met in any of the prophetical books with a description of God's Providence otherwise than in relation to human beings. The prophets even express their surprise that God should take notice of man, who is too little and too unimportant to be worthy of the attention of the Creator; how, then, should other living creatures be considered as proper objects for Divine Providence! Comp. "What is man, that thou takest knowledge of him?" (Ps. 144, 3); "What is man, that thou art mindful of him?" (*ibid.* 8, 8). It is clearly expressed in many Scriptural passages that God provides for all men, and controls all their deeds—e.g., "He fashioneth their hearts alike, he considereth all their works" (*ibid.* 33, 15); "For thine eyes are open upon all the ways of the sons of men, to give every one according to his ways" (Jer. 32, 19). Again: "for his eyes are upon the ways of man, and he seeth all his

goings" (Job 32, 21). In the Law there occur instances of the fact that men are governed by God, and that their actions are examined by him. Comp. "In the day when I visit I will visit their sin upon them" (Exod. xxxii. 34); "I will even appoint over you terror" (Lev. xxvi. 16); "Whosoever hath sinned against me, him will I blot out of my book" (Exod. 32, 33); "The same soul will I destroy" (Lev. 23, 30); "I will even set my face against that soul" (*ibid.* 20, 6). There are many instances of this kind. All that is mentioned of the history of Abraham, Isaac, and Jacob is a perfect proof that Divine Providence extends to every man individually. But the condition of the individual beings of other living creatures is undoubtedly the same as has been stated by Aristotle. On that account it is allowed, even commanded, to kill animals; we are permitted to use them according to our pleasure.

The view that other living beings are only governed by Divine Providence in the way described by Aristotle, is supported by the words of the Prophet Habakkuk. When he perceived the victories of Nebuchadnezzer, and saw the multitude of those slain by him, he said, "O God, it is as if men were abandoned, neglected, and unprotected like fish and like worms of the earth." He thus shows that these classes are abandoned. This is expressed in the following passage: "And makest men as the fishes of the sea, as the creeping things, that have no ruler over them. They take up all of them with the angle," etc. (Hab. 1, 14, 15). The prophet then declares that such is not the case; for the events referred to are not the result of abandonment, forsaking, and absence of Providence, but are intended as a punishment for the people, who well deserved all that befell them. He therefore says: "O Lord, Thou hast ordained them for judgment, and O might God, Thou hast established them for correction" (*ibid.* ver. 12). Our opinion is not contradicted by Scriptural passages like the following: "He giveth to the beast his food" (Ps. 147, 9); "The young lions roar after their prey, and seek their meat from God" (*ibid.* 104, 21); "Thou openest thine hand, and satisfiest the desire of every living thing" (*ibid.* 145, 16); or by the saying of our Sages: "He sitteth and feedeth all, from the horns of the unicorns even unto the eggs of insects." There are many similar sayings extant in the writings of our Sages, but they imply nothing that is contrary to my view. All these passages refer to Providence in relation to species, and not to Providence in relation to individual animals. The acts of God are as it were enumerated; how He provides for every species the necessary food and the means of subsistence. This is clear and plain. Aristotle likewise holds that this kind of Providence is necessary, and is in actual existence. Alexander also notices that fact in the name of Aristotle, viz., that every species has its nourishment prepared for its individual members; otherwise the species would undoubtedly have perished. It does not require much consideration to understand this. There is a rule laid down by our Sages that it is directly prohibited in the Law to cause pain to an animal, and is based on the words: "Wherefore hast thou smitten thine ass?" etc. (Num. 22, 32). But the object of this rule is to make us perfect; that we should not assume cruel habits; and that we should not uselessly cause pain to others; that, on the contrary, we should be prepared to show pity and mercy to all living creatures, except when necessity demands the contrary: "When thy soul longeth to eat flesh," etc. (Deut. xii, 20). We should not kill animals for the purpose of practising cruelty, or for the purpose of play.

It cannot be objected to this theory, Why should God select mankind as the object of His special Providence, and not other living beings? For he who asks this question must also inquire, Why has man alone, of all species of animals, been endowed with intellect? The answer to this second question must be, according to the three afore-mentioned theories: It was the Will of God, it is the decree of His Wisdom, or it is in accordance with the laws of Nature. The same answers apply to the first question. Understand thoroughly my theory, that I do not ascribe to God ignorance of anything or any kind of weakness; I hold that Divine Providence is related and closely connected with the intellect, because Providence can only proceed from an intelligent being, from a being that is itself the most perfect Intellect. Those creatures, therefore, which receive part of that intellectual influence, will become subject to the action of Providence in the same proportion as they are acted upon by the Intellect. This theory is in accordance with reason and with the teaching of Scripture, whilst the other theories previously mentioned either exaggerate Divine Providence or detract from it. In the former case they lead to confusion and entire nonsense, and cause us to deny reason and to contradict that which is perceived with the senses. The latter case, viz., the theory that Divine Providence does not extend to man, and that there is no difference between man and other animals, implies very bad notions about God; it disturbs all social order, removes and destroys all the moral and intellectual virtues of man.

Chapter 13

THOMAS AQUINAS

The Roman Catholic Dominican monk Thomas Aquinas (1225–1274) is considered by many to be the greatest theologian in Western religion. He was born in Roccasecca near the Italian town of Aquino, the son of the Count Aquino. While at the University of Naples, much to the horror of his noble parents, he decided to join the Dominicans, a mendicant (begging) order, considered by many to be a hotbed of religious fanatics. His parents had him kidnapped and carried off to a family castle at Monte San Giovanni. His family both appealed to his family loyalty and threatened him with punishment in hope of persuading him to quit the habit of a monk. One night his brothers sent a prostitute to his cell to offer herself for his pleasure. Thomas leaped up, grabbed a brand from the fire and chased her from his room. From that time onward he avoided the sight and company of women, except where it was necessary. Neither his mother's tears, his brothers' threats, nor the lure of a prostitute were sufficient to strip him of his determination to live a celibate, mendicant life, dedicated to the Church. He was kept under house arrest for more than a year before he was allowed to rejoin his fellow monks. He went to the Dominican school at Cologne where from 1248 to 1252 he studied under the renowned scholar and theologian Albert the Great. It was there he studied Aristotle's work, which had recently become available in Latin translation. A large man, slow in movement, stubborn, deliberate, methodical, imperturbable, his fellow students thought him stupid and unkindly gave him the nickname, "Dumb Ox." His teacher, Albert the Great, however, saw great promise in the youth, and declared, "You call him a Dumb Ox; I tell you the Dumb Ox will bellow so loud his bellowing will fill the world."

In 1252 Albert declared that Thomas was ready for advanced studies in philosophy and theology and sent him to the University of Paris where he received his Mastership in 1256. During this time Thomas began teaching at the University of Paris and began developing an Aristotelian version of Catholic theology. His own writings are voluminous (over 8 million words of closely reasoned prose) and encyclopedic, dealing with questions of the problem of evil, truth, the nature of the soul, the existence and attributes of God, morality, and politics. He wrote two summations of theology: *On the Truth of the Catholic Faith against the Gentiles (Summa Contra Gentiles)*, which was a handbook for missionaries seeking to convert Muslims and others to the Christian faith, and *Summa Theologica (Summation of Theology)*. On December 6, 1273, he had a deeply religious experience, after which he ceased to write. He reported, "All that I have written seems to me like straw compared to what has now been revealed to me." He died four months later.

The five arguments given in our first selection from the *Summa Theologica* are a posteriori arguments, that is, based on premises that can be known only by means of experience of the world (for example, that there is a world, events have causes, and so forth). Put simply, their strategies are as follows: The first argument begins with the fact that there is change and argues that there must be an Unmoved Mover which originates all change (or motion) but itself is not changed or moved. The second argument is from causation and argues that there must be a first cause to explain the existence of cause. The third argument is from contingency. It argues that since there are dependent beings (e.g., humans), there must be an independent or necessary being on whom the dependent beings rely for their subsistence. The fourth argument is from excellence, and it argues that since there are degrees of excellence, there must be a perfect being from whence come all excellences. The final argument is from the harmony of things. There is a harmony of nature which calls for an explanation. The only sufficient explanation is that there is a divine designer who planned such harmony.

In our second selection from the Second Part of the *Summa Theologica* is Aquinas's classic treatise on Natural Law.

FOR FURTHER READING:

Aquinas, Thomas. *Basic Writings of St. Thomas Aquinas*, ed. Anton Pegis. (Random House 1945).

Aquinas, Thomas. *Summa Theologiciae*, ed. Thomas Gilby. (London, 1963–75), 60 vols.

Copleston, F. C. *Aquinas*. (Penguin Books, 1955).

Davies, Brian. *The Thought of Thomas Aquinas*. (Oxford University Press, 1992).

Gilson, Etienne. *The Christian Philosophy of St. Thomas Aquinas*. (Random House, 1956).

Kenny, Anthony. *Aquinas*. (Hill and Wang, 1980).

Kenny, Anthony, ed. *Aquinas: A Collection of Critical Essays*. (Anchor Doubleday, 1969).

Kenny, Anthony. *The Five Ways: St. Thomas Aquinas' Proofs of God's Existence*. (Routledge & Kegan Paul, 1969).

Kretzman, Norman and Eleonore Stump, eds. *The Cambridge Companion to Aquinas*. (Cambridge University Press, 1993).

Summa Theologica

QUESTION II. THE EXISTENCE OF GOD

FIRST ARTICLE. Whether the Existence of God Is Self-Evident?

We proceed thus to the First Article:—

Objection 1. It seems that the existence of God is self-evident. For those things are said to be self-evident to us the knowledge of which exists naturally in us, as we can see in regard to first principles. But a Damascene says, *the knowledge of God is naturally implanted in all.* Therefore the existence of God is self-evident.

Obj. 2. Further, those things are said to be self-evident which are known as soon as the terms are known, which the Philosopher says is true of the first principles of demonstration. Thus, when the nature of a whole and of a part is known, it is at once recognized that every whole is greater than its part, But as soon as the signification of the name *God* is understood, it is at once seen that God exists. For by this name is signified that thing than which nothing greater can be conceived. But that which exists actually and mentally is greater than that which exists only mentally. Therefore, since as soon as the name *God* is understood it exists mentally, it also follows that it exists actually. Therefore the proposition *God exists* is self-evident.

Obj. 3. Further, the existence of truth is self-evident. For whoever denies the existence of truth grants that truth does not exist: and, if truth does not exist, then the proposition *Truth does not exist* is

Reprinted by permission from Thomas Aquinas, *Basic Writings of Thomas Aquinas*, translated by A. Pegis (New York: Random House, 1945).

true: and if there is anything true, there must be truth. But God is truth itself: *I am the way, the truth, and the life (Jo.* xiv. 6). Therefore *God exists* is self-evident.

On the contrary, No one can mentally admit the opposite of what is self-evident, as the Philosopher states concerning the first principles of demonstration. But the opposite of the proposition *God is* can be mentally admitted: *The fool said in his heart, There is no God (Ps.* lii. I). Therefore, that God exists is not self-evident.

I answer that, A thing can be self-evident in either of two ways: on the one hand, self-evident in itself, though not to us; on the other, self-evident in itself, and to us. A proposition is self-evident because the predicate is included in the essence of the subject: e.g., Man is an animal, for animal is contained in the essence of man. If, therefore, the essence of the predicate and subject be known to all, the proposition will be self-evident to all; as is clear with regard to the first principles of demonstration, the terms of which are certain common notions that no one is ignorant of, such as being and non-being, whole and part, and the like. If, however, there are some to whom the essence of the predicate and subject is unknown, the proposition will be self-evident in itself, but not to those who do not know the meaning of the predicate and subject of the proposition. Therefore, it happens, as Boethius says, that there are some notions of the mind which are common and self-evident only to the learned, as that incorporeal substances are not in space. Therefore I say that this proposition, *God exists*, of itself is self-evident, for the predicate is the same as the subject, because God is His own existence as will be hereafter shown. Now because we do not know the essence of God, the proposition is not self-evident to us, but needs to be demonstrated by things that are more known to us, though less known in their nature—namely, by His effects.

Reply Obj. 1. To know that God exists in a general and confused way is implanted in us by nature, inasmuch as God is man's beatitude. For man naturally desires happiness, and what is naturally desired by man is naturally known by him. This, however, is not to know absolutely that God exists; just as to know that someone is approaching is not the same as to know that Peter is approaching, even though it is Peter who is approaching; for there are many who imagine that man's perfect good, which is happi-

ness, consists in riches, and others in pleasures, and others in something else.

Reply Obj. 2. Perhaps not everyone who hears this name *God* understands it to signify something than which nothing greater can be thought, seeing that some have believed God to be a body. Yet, granted that everyone understands that by this name *God* is signified something than which nothing greater can be thought, nevertheless, it does not therefore follow that he understands that what the name signifies exists actually, but only that it exists mentally. Nor can it be argued that it actually exists, unless it be admitted that there actually exists something than which nothing greater can be thought; and this precisely is not admitted by those who hold that God does not exist.

Reply Obj. 3. The existence of truth in general is self-evident, but the existence of a Primal Truth is not self-evident to us.

SECOND ARTICLE. Whether It Can Be Demonstrated that God Exists?

We proceed thus to the Second Article:—

Objection 1. It seems that the existence of God cannot be demonstrated. For it is an article of faith that God exists. But what is of faith cannot be demonstrated, because a demonstration produces scientific knowledge, whereas faith is of the unseen, as is clear from the Apostle (*Heb.* xi. I). Therefore it cannot be demonstrated that God exists.

Obj. 2. Further, essence is the middle term of demonstration. But we cannot know in what God's essence consists, but solely in what it does not consist, as Damascene says. Therefore we cannot demonstrate that God exists.

Obj. 3. Further, if the existence of God were demonstrated, this could only be from His effects. But His effects are not proportioned to Him, since He is infinite and His effects are finite, and between finite and infinite there is no proportion. Therefore, since a cause cannot be demonstrated by an effect not proportioned to it, it seems that the existence of God cannot be demonstrated.

On the contrary, The Apostle says: *The invisible things of Him are clearly seen, being understood by the things that are made (Rom.* i. 20). But this would not be unless the existence of God could be demonstrated through the things that are made; for the first thing we must know of anything is, whether it exists.

I answer that, Demonstration can be made in two ways: One is through the cause, and is called *propter quid,* and this is to argue from what is prior absolutely. The other is through the effect, and is called a demonstration *quia;* this is to argue from what is prior relatively only to us. When an effect is better known to us than its cause, from the effect we proceed to the knowledge of the cause. And from every effect the existence of its proper cause can be demonstrated, so long as its effects are better known to us; because, since every effect depends upon its cause, if the effect exists, the cause must pre-exist. Hence the existence of God, in so far as it is not self-evident to us, can be demonstrated from those of His effects which are known to us.

Reply Obj. 1. The existence of God and other like truths about God, which can be known by natural reason, are not articles of faith, but are preambles to the articles; for faith presupposes natural knowledge, even as grace presupposes nature and perfection the perfectible. Nevertheless, there is nothing to prevent a man, who cannot grasp a proof, from accepting, as a matter of faith, something which in itself is capable of being scientifically known and demonstrated.

Reply Obj. 2. When the existence of a cause is demonstrated from an effect, this effect takes the place of the definition of the cause in proving the cause's existence. This is especially the case in regard to God, because, in order to prove the existence of anything, it is necessary to accept as a middle term the meaning of the name, and not its essence, for the question of its essence follows on the question of its existence. Now the names given to God are derived from His effects, as will be later shown. Consequently, in demonstrating the existence of God from His effects, we may take for the middle term the meaning of the name *God.*

Reply Obj. 3. From effects not proportioned to the cause no perfect knowledge of that cause can be obtained. Yet from every effect the existence of the cause can be clearly demonstrated, and so we can demonstrate the existence of God from His effects; though from them we cannot know God perfectly as He is in His essence.

THIRD ARTICLE. Whether God Exists?

We proceed thus to the Third Article:—

Objection 1. It seems that God does not exist; because if one of two contraries be infinite, the other would be altogether destroyed. But the name God means that He is infinite goodness. If, therefore, God existed, there would be no evil discoverable; but there is evil in the world. Therefore God does not exist.

Obj. 2. Further, it is superfluous to suppose that what can be accounted for by a few principles has been produced by many. But it seems that everything we see in the world can be accounted for by other principles, supposing God did not exist. For all natural things can be reduced to one principle, which is nature; and all voluntary things can be reduced to one principle, which is human reason, or will. Therefore there is no need to suppose God's existence.

On the contrary, It is said in the person of God: *I am Who am* (Exod. iii. 14).

I answer that, The existence of God can be proved in five ways.

The first and more manifest way is the argument from motion. It is certain, and evident to our senses, that in the world some things are in motion. Now whatever is moved is moved by another, for nothing can be moved except it is in potentiality to that towards which it is moved; whereas a thing moves inasmuch as it is in act. For motion is nothing else than the reduction of something from potentiality to actuality. But nothing can be reduced from potentiality to actuality, except by something in a state of actuality. Thus that which is actually hot, as fire, makes wood, which is potentially hot, to be actually hot, and thereby moves and changes it. Now it is not possible that the same thing should be at once in actuality and potentiality in the same respect, but only in different respects. For what is actually hot cannot simultaneously be potentially hot; but it is simultaneously potentially cold. It is therefore impossible that in the same respect and in the same way a thing should be both mover and moved, i.e., that it should move itself. Therefore, whatever is moved must be moved by another. If that by which it is moved be itself moved, then this also must needs be moved by another, and that by another again. But this cannot go on to infinity, because then there would be no first mover, and, consequently, no other mover, seeing that subsequent movers move only inasmuch as they are moved by the first mover; as the staff moves only because it is moved by the hand. Therefore it is necessary to arrive at a first mover, moved by no other; and this everyone understands to be God.

The second way is from the nature of efficient

cause. In the world of sensible things we find there is an order of efficient causes. There is no case known (neither is it, indeed, possible) in which a thing is found to be the efficient cause of itself; for so it would be prior to itself, which is impossible. Now in efficient causes it is not possible to go on to infinity, because in all efficient causes following in order, the first is the cause of the intermediate cause, and the intermediate is the cause of the ultimate cause, whether the intermediate cause be several, or one only. Now to take away the cause is to take away the effect. Therefore, if there be no first cause among efficient causes, there will be no ultimate, nor any intermediate, cause. But if in efficient causes it is possible to go on to infinity, there will be no first efficient cause, neither will there be an ultimate effect, nor any intermediate efficient causes; all of which is plainly false. Therefore it is necessary to admit a first efficient cause, to which everyone gives the name of God.

The third way is taken from possibility and necessity, and runs thus. We find in nature things that are possible to be and not to be, since they are found to be generated, and to be corrupted, and consequently, it is possible for them to be and not to be. But it is impossible for these always to exist, for that which can not-be at some time is not. Therefore, if everything can not-be, then at one time there was nothing in existence. Now if this were true, even now there would be nothing in existence, because that which does not exist begins to exist only through something already existing. Therefore, if at one time nothing was in existence, it would have been impossible for anything to have begun to exist; and thus even now nothing would be in existence—which is absurd. Therefore, not all beings are merely possible, but there must exist something the existence of which is necessary. But every necessary thing either has its necessity caused by another, or not. Now it is impossible to go on to infinity in necessary things which have their necessity caused by another, as has been already proved in regard to efficient causes. Therefore we cannot but admit the existence of some being having of itself its own necessity, and not receiving it from another, but rather causing in others their necessity. This all men speak of as God.

The fourth way is taken from the gradation to be found in things. Among beings there are some more and some less good, true, noble, and the like. But more and less are predicated of different things according as they resemble in their different ways

something which is the maximum, as a thing is said to be hotter according as it more nearly resembles that which is hottest; so that there is something which is truest, something best, something noblest, and, consequently, something which is most being, for those things that are greatest in truth are greatest in being, as it is written in *Metaph.* ii. Now the maximum in any genus is the cause of all in that genus, as fire, which is the maximum of heat, is the cause of all hot things, as is said in the same book. Therefore there must also be something which is to all beings the cause of their being, goodness, and every other perfection; and this we call God.

The fifth way is taken from the governance of the world. We see that things which lack knowledge, such as natural bodies, act for an end, and this is evident from their acting always, or nearly always, in the same way, so as to obtain the best result. Hence it is plain that they achieve their end, not fortuitously, but designedly. Now whatever lacks knowledge cannot move towards an end, unless it be directed by some being endowed with knowledge and intelligence; as the arrow is directed by the archer. Therefore some intelligent being exists by whom all natural things are directed to their end; and this being we call God.

Reply Obj. 1. As Augustine says: *Since God is the highest good, He would not allow any evil to exist in His works, unless His omnipotence and goodness were such as to bring good even out of evil.* This is part of the infinite goodness of God, that He should allow evil to exist, and out of it produce good.

Reply Obj. 2. Since nature works for a determinate end under the direction of a higher agent, whatever is done by nature must be traced back to God as to its first cause. So likewise whatever is done voluntarily must be traced back to some higher cause other than human reason and will, since these can change and fail; for all things that are changeable and capable of defect must be traced back to an immovable and self-necessary first principle, as has been shown.

QUESTION XCII. OF THE EFFECTS OF LAW

FIRST ARTICLE. Whether an Effect of Law Is To Make Men Good?

We proceed thus to the First Article:—

Objection 1. It seems that it is not an effect of law to make men good. For men are good through virtue, since virtue, as stated in *Ethic*. ii. 6 is *that which makes its subject good*. But virtue is in man from God alone, because He it is Who *works it in us without us*, as we stated above in giving the definition of virtue. Therefore the law does not make men good.

Obj. 2. Further, Law does not profit a man unless he obeys it. But the very fact that a man obeys a law is due to his being good. Therefore in man goodness is presupposed to the law. Therefore the law does not make men good.

Obj. 3. Further, Law is ordained to the common good, as stated above. But some behave well in things regarding the community, who behave ill in things regarding themselves. Therefore it is not the business of the law to make men good.

Obj. 4. Further, some laws are tyrannical, as the Philosopher says. But a tyrant does not intend the good of his subjects, but considers only his own profit. Therefore law does not make men good.

On the contrary, The Philosopher says that the *intention of every lawgiver is to make good citizens*.

I answer that, As stated above, a law is nothing else than a dictate of reason in the ruler by whom his subjects are governed. Now the virtue of any subordinate thing consists in is being well subordinated to that by which it is regulated: thus we see that the virtue of the irascible and concupiscible faculties consists in their being obedient to reason; and accordingly *the virtue of every subject consists in his being well subjected to his ruler*, as the Philosopher says. But every law aims at being obeyed by those who are subject to it. Consequently it is evident that the proper effect of law is to lead its subjects to their proper virtue: and since virtue is that which makes its subject good, it follows that the proper effect of law is to make those to whom it is given, good, either simply or in some particular respect. For if the intention of the lawgiver is fixed on true good, which is the common good regulated according to Divine justice, it follows that the effect of the law is to make men good simply. If, however, the intention of the lawgiver is fixed on that which is not simply good, but useful or pleasurable to himself, or in opposition to Divine justice; then the law does not make men good simply, but in respect to that particular government. In this way good is found even in things that are bad of themselves: thus a man is called a good robber, because he works in a way that is adapted to his end.

Reply Obj. 1. Virtue is twofold, as explained above, viz., acquired and infused. Now the fact of being accustomed to an action contributes to both, but in different ways; for it causes the acquired virtue; while it disposes to infused virtue, and preserves and fosters it when it already exists. And since law is given for the purpose of directing human acts; as far as human acts conduce to virtue, so far does law make men good. Wherefore the Philosopher says in the second book of the *Politics* that *lawgivers make men good by habituating them to good works*.

Reply Obj. 2. It is not always through perfect goodness of virtue that one obeys the law, but sometimes it is through fear of punishment, and sometimes from the mere dictate of reason, which is a beginning of virtue, as stated above.

Reply Obj. 3. The goodness of any part is considered in comparison with the whole; hence Augustine says that *unseemly is the part that harmonizes not with the whole*. Since then every man is a part of the state, it is impossible that a man be good, unless he be well proportionate to the common good: nor can the whole be well consistent unless its parts be proportionate to it. Consequently the common good of the state cannot flourish, unless the citizens be virtuous, at least those whose business it is to govern. But it is enough for the good of the community, that the other citizens be so far virtuous that they obey the commands of their rulers. Hence the Philosopher says that *the virtue of a sovereign is the same as that of a good man, but the virtue of any common citizen is not the same as that of a good man*.

Reply Obj. 4. A tyrannical law, through not being according to reason, is not a law, absolutely speaking, but rather a perversion of law; and yet in so far as it is something in the nature of a law, it aims at the citizens being good. For all it has in the nature of a law consists in its being an ordinance made by a superior to his subjects, and aims at being obeyed by them, which is to make them good, not simply, but with respect to that particular government.

QUESTION XCIV. THE NATURAL LAW

FIRST ARTICLE. Whether the Natural Law Is a Habit?

We proceed thus to the First Article:—

Objection 1. It would seem that the natural law is a habit. For, as the Philosopher says, *there are three things in the soul, power, habit and passion*. But the natural law is not one of the soul's powers, nor is it one of the passions, as we may see by going through them one by one. Therefore the natural law is a habit.

Obj. 2. Further, Basil says that the *conscience or synderesis is the law of our mind*, which can apply only to the natural law. But *synderesis* is a habit, as was shown in the First Part. Therefore the natural law is a habit.

Obj. 3. Further, the natural law abides in man always, as will be shown further on. But man's reason, which the law regards, does not always think about the natural law. Therefore the natural law is not an act, but a habit.

On the contrary, Augustine says that *a habit is that whereby something is done when necessary.* But such is not the natural law, since it is in infants and in the damned who cannot act by it. Therefore the natural law is not a habit.

I answer that, A thing may be called a habit in two ways. First, properly and essentially, and thus the natural law is not a habit. For it has been stated above that the natural law is something appointed by reason, just as a proposition is a work of reason. Now that which a man does is not the same as that whereby he does it, for he makes a becoming speech by the habit of grammar. Since, then, a habit is that by which we act, a law cannot be a habit properly and essentially.

Secondly, the term habit may be applied to that which we hold by a habit. Thus *faith* may mean *that which we hold by faith.* Accordingly, since the precepts of the natural law are sometimes considered by reason actually, while sometimes they are in the reason only habitually, in this way the natural law may be called a habit. So, too, in speculative matters, the indemonstrable principles are not the habit itself whereby we hold these principles; they are rather the principles of which we possess the habit.

Reply Obj. 1. The Philosopher proposes there to discover the genus of virtue; and since it is evident that virtue is a principle of action, he mentions only those things which are principles of human acts, viz., powers, habits and passions. But there are other things in the soul besides these three: e.g., acts, as *to will* is in the one that wills; again, there are things known in the knower; moreover its own natural properties are in the soul, such as immortality and the like.

Reply Obj. 2. Synderesis is said to be the law of our intellect because it is a habit containing the precepts of the natural law, which are the first principles of human actions.

Reply Obj. 3. This argument proves that the natural law is held habitually; and this is granted.

To the argument advanced in the contrary sense we reply that sometimes a man is unable to make use of that which is in him habitually, because of some impediment. Thus, because of sleep, a man is unable to use the habit of science. In like manner, through the deficiency of his age, a child cannot use the habit of the understanding of principles, or the natural law, which is in him habitually.

SECOND ARTICLE. Whether the Natural Law Contains Several Precepts, or Only One?

We proceed thus to the Second Article:—

Objection 1. It would seem that the natural law contains, not several precepts, but only one. For law is a kind of precept, as was stated above. If therefore there were many precepts of the natural law, it would follow that there are also many natural laws.

Obj. 2. Further, the natural law is consequent upon human nature. But human nature, as a whole, is one, though, as to its parts, it is manifold. Therefore, either there is but one precept of the law of nature because of the unity of nature as a whole, or there are many by reason of the number of parts of human nature. The result would be that even things relating to the inclination of the concupiscible power would belong to the natural law.

Obj. 3. Further, law is something pertaining to reason, as was stated above. Now reason is but one in man. Therefore there is only one precept of the natural law.

On the contrary, The precepts of the natural law in man stand in relation to operable matters as first principles do to matters of demonstration. But there are several first indemonstrable principles. Therefore there are also several precepts of the natural law.

I answer that, As was stated above, the precepts of the natural law are to the practical reason what the first principles of demonstrations are to the speculative reason, because both are self-evident principles. Now a thing is said to be self-evident in two ways: first, in itself; secondly, in relation to us. Any proposition is said to be self-evident in itself, if its predicate is contained in the notion of the subject; even though it may happen that to one who does not know the definition of the subject, such a proposition is not self-evident. For instance, this proposition, *Man is a rational being*, is, in its very nature, self-evident, since he who says *man says a rational being*; and yet to one who does not know what a man is, this proposition is not self-evident. Hence it is that, as Boethius says, certain axioms or propositions are universally self-evident to all; and such are the propositions whose terms are known to all, as, *Every whole is greater than its part*, and, *Things equal to one and the same are equal to one another*. But some propositions are self-evident only to the wise, who understand the meaning of the terms of such propositions. Thus to one who understands that an angel is not a body, it is self-evident that an angel is not circumscriptively in a place. But this is not evident to the unlearned, for they cannot grasp it.

Now a certain order is to be found in those things that are apprehended by men. For that which first falls under apprehension is *being*, the understanding of which is included in all things whatsoever a man apprehends. Therefore the first indemonstrable principle is that *the same thing cannot be affirmed and denied at the same time*, which is based on the notion of *being* and *not-being*: and on this principle all others are based, as is stated in *Metaph.* iv. Now as *being* is the first thing that falls under the apprehension absolutely, so good is the first thing that falls under the apprehension of the practical reason, which is directed to action (since every agent acts for an end, which has the nature of good). Consequently, the first principle in the practical reason is one founded on the nature of good, viz., that *good is that which all things seek after*. Hence this is the first precept of law, that *good is to be done and promoted, and evil is to be avoided*. All other precepts of the natural law are based upon this; so that all the things which the practical reason naturally apprehends as man's good belong to the precepts of the natural law under the form of things to be done or avoided.

Since, however, good has the nature of an end, and evil, the nature of the contrary, hence it is that all those things to which man has a natural inclination are naturally apprehended by reason as being good, and consequently as objects of pursuit, and their contraries as evil, and objects of avoidance. Therefore, the order of the precepts of the natural law is according to the order of natural inclinations. For there is in man, first of all, an inclination to good in accordance with the nature which he has in common with all substances, inasmuch, namely, as every substance seeks the preservation of its own being, according to its nature; and by reason of this incli-

nation, whatever is a means of preserving human life, and of warding off its obstacles, belongs to the natural law. Secondly, there is in man an inclination to things that pertain to him more specially, according to that nature which he has in common with other animals; and in virtue of this inclination, those things are said to belong to the natural law *which nature has taught to all animals*, such as sexual intercourse, the education of offspring and so forth. Thirdly, there is in man an inclination to good according to the nature of his reason, which nature is proper to him. Thus man has a natural inclination to know the truth about God, as to live in society; and in this respect, whatever pertains to this inclination belongs to the natural law: e.g., to shun ignorance, to avoid offending those among whom one has to live, and other such things regarding the above inclination.

Reply Obj. 1. All these precepts of the law of nature have the character of one natural law, inasmuch as they flow from one first precept.

Reply Obj. 2. All the inclinations of any parts whatsoever of human nature, e.g., of the concupiscible and irascible parts, in so far as they are ruled by reason, belong to the natural law, and are reduced to one first precept, as was stated above. And thus the precepts of the natural law are many in themselves, but they are based on one common foundation.

Reply Obj. 3. Although reason is one in itself, yet it directs all things regarding man; so that whatever can be ruled by reason is contained under the law of reason.

FOURTH ARTICLE. Whether the Natural Law is the Same in All Men?

We proceed thus to the Fourth Article:—

Objection 1. It would seem that the natural law is not the same in all. For it is stated in the *Decretals* that *the natural law is that which is contained in the Law and the Gospel*. But this is not common to all men, because, as it is written (*Rom.* x. 16), *all do not obey the gospel*. Therefore the natural law is not the same in all men.

Obj. 2. Further, *Things which are according to the law are said to be just*, as is stated in *Ethics* v. But it is stated in the same book that nothing is so just for all as not to be subject to change in regard to some men. Therefore even the natural law is not the same in all men.

Obj. 3. Further, as was stated above, to the natural law belongs everything to which a man is inclined according to his nature. Now different men are naturally inclined to different things,—some to the desire of pleasures, others to the desire of honors, and other men to other things. Therefore, there is not one natural law for all.

On the contrary, Isidore says: *The natural law is common to all nations.*

I answer that, As we have stated above, to the natural law belong those things to which a man is inclined naturally; and among these it is proper to man to be inclined to act according to reason. Not it belongs to the reason to proceed from what is common to what is proper, as is stated in *Physics* i. The speculative reason, however, is differently situated, in this matter, from the practical reason. For, since the speculative reason is concerned chiefly with necessary things, which cannot be otherwise than they are, its proper conclusions, like the universal principles, contain the truth without fail. The practical reason, on the other hand, is concerned with contingent matters, which is the domain of human actions; and, consequently, although there is necessity in the common principles, the more we descend towards the particular, the more frequently we encounter defects. Accordingly, then, in speculative matters truth is the same in all men, both as to principles and as to conclusions; although the truth is not known to all as regards the conclusions, but only as regards the principles which are called *common notions.* But in matters of action, truth or practical rectitude is not the same for all as to what is particular, but only as to the common principles; and where there is the same rectitude in relation to particulars, it is not equally known to all.

It is therefore evident that, as regards the common principles whether of speculative or of practical reason, truth or rectitude is the same for all, and is equally known by all. But as to the proper conclusions of the speculative reason, the truth is the same for all, but it is not equally known to all. Thus, it is true for all that the three angles of a triangle are together equal to two right angles, although it is not known to all. But as to the proper conclusions of the practical reason, neither is the truth or rectitude the same for all, nor, where it is the same, is it equally known by all. Thus, it is right and true for all to act according to reason, and from this principle it follows, as a proper conclusion, that goods entrusted

to another should be restored to their owner. Now this is true for the majority of cases. But it may happen in a particular case that it would be injurious, and therefore unreasonable, to restore goods held in trust; for instance, if they are claimed for the purpose of fighting against one's country. And this principle will be found to fail the more, according as we descend further towards the particular, e.g., if one were to say that goods held in trust should be restored with such and such a guarantee, or in such and such a way; because the greater the number of conditions added, the greater the number of ways in which the principle may fail, so that it be not right to restore or not to restore.

Consequently, we must say that the natural law, as to the first common principles, is the same for all, both as to rectitude and as to knowledge. But as to certain more particular aspects, which are conclusions, as it were, of those common principles, it is the same for all in the majority of cases, both as to rectitude and as to knowledge; and yet in some few cases it may fail, both as to rectitude, by reason of certain obstacles (just as natures subject to generation and corruption fail in some few cases because of some obstacle), and as to knowledge, since in some the reason is perverted by passion, or evil habit, or an evil disposition of nature. Thus at one time theft, although it is expressly contrary to the natural law, was not considered wrong among the Germans, as Julius Caesar relates.

Reply Obj. 1. The meaning of the sentence quoted is not that whatever is contained in the Law and the Gospel belongs to the natural law, since they contain many things that are above nature; but that whatever belongs to the natural law is fully contained in them. Therefore Gratian, after saying that *the natural law is what is contained in the Law and the Gospel,* adds at once, by way of example, *by which everyone is commanded to do to others as he would be done by.*

Reply Obj. 2. The saying of the Philosopher is to be understood of things that are naturally just, not as common principles, but as conclusions drawn from them, having rectitude in the majority of cases, but failing in a few.

Reply Obj. 3. Just as in man reason rules and commands the other powers, so all the natural inclinations belonging to the other powers must needs be directed according to reason. Therefore it is universally right for all men that all their inclinations should be directed according to reason.

FIFTH ARTICLE. Whether the Natural Law Can Be Changed?

We proceed thus to the Fifth Article:—

Objection 1. It would seem that the natural law can be changed. For on *Ecclus.* xvii. 9 (*He gave them instructions, and the law of life*) the *Gloss* says: *He wished the law of the letter to be written, in order to correct the law of nature.* But that which is corrected is changed. Therefore the natural law can be changed.

Obj 2. Further, the slaying of the innocent, adultery and theft are against the natural law. But we find these things changed by God: as when God commanded Abraham to slay his innocent son (*Gen.* xii. 2); and when He ordered the Jews to borrow and purloin the vessels of the Egyptians (*Exod.* xii. 35); and when He commanded Osee to take to himself *a wife of fornications* (*Osee* i. 2). Therefore the natural law can be changed.

Obj. 3. Further, Isidore says that *the possession of all things in common, and universal freedom, are matters of natural law.* But these things are seen to be changed by human laws. Therefore it seems that the natural law is subject to change.

On the contrary, It is said in the *Decretals: The natural law dates from the creation of the rational creature. It does not vary according to time, but remains unchangeable.*

I answer that, A change in the natural law may be understood in two ways. First, by way of addition. In this sense, nothing hinders the natural law from being changed, since many things for the benefit of human life have been added over and above the natural law, both by the divine law and by human laws.

Secondly, a change in the natural law may be understood by way of subtraction, so that what previously was according to the natural law, ceases to be so. In this sense, the natural law is altogether unchangeable in its first principles. But in its secondary principles, which, as we have said, are certain detailed proximate conclusions drawn from the first principles, the natural law is not changed so that what it prescribes be not right in most cases. But it may be changed in some particular cases of rare occurrence, through some special causes hindering the observance of such precepts, as was stated above.

Reply Obj. 1. The written law is said to be given for the correction of the natural law, either because it supplies what was wanting to the natural law, or because the natural law was so perverted in the hearts of some men, as to certain matters, that they esteemed those things good which are naturally evil; which perversion stood in need of correction.

Reply Obj. 2. All men alike, both guilty and innocent, die the death of nature; which death of nature is inflicted by the power of God because of original sin, according to *1 Kings* ii. 6: *The Lord killeth and maketh alive.* Consequently, by the command of God, death can be inflicted on any man, guilty or innocent, without any injustice whatever.—In like manner, adultery is intercourse with another's wife; who is allotted to him by the law emanating from God. Consequently intercourse with any woman, by the command of God, is neither adultery nor fornication.—The same applies to theft, which is the taking of another's property. For whatever is taken by the command of God, to Whom all things belong, is not taken against the will of its owner, whereas it is in this that theft consists.—Nor is it only in human things that whatever is commanded by God is right; but also in natural things, whatever is done by God is, in some way, natural, as was stated in the First Part.

Reply Obj. 3. A thing is said to belong to the natural law in two ways. First, because nature inclines thereto: e.g., that one should not do harm to another. Secondly, because nature did not bring with it the contrary. Thus, we might say that for man to be naked is of the natural law, because nature did not give him clothes, but art invented them. In this sense, *the possession of all things in common and universal freedom* are said to be of the natural law, because, namely, the distinction of possessions and slavery were not brought in by nature, but devised by human reason for the benefit of human life. Accordingly, the law of nature was not changed in this respect, except by addition.

QUESTION XCV. HUMAN LAW

FIRST ARTICLE. Whether It Was Useful for Laws To Be Framed by Men?

We proceed thus to the First Article:—

Objection 1. It would seem that it was not useful for laws to be framed by men. For the purpose of every law is that man be made good thereby, as was stated above. But men are more to be induced to be good willingly by means of admonitions, than against their will, by means of laws. Therefore there was no need to frame laws.

Obj. 2. Further, As the Philosopher says, *men have recourse to a judge as to animate justice.* But animate justice is better than inanimate justice, which is contained in laws. Therefore it would have been better for the execution of justice to be entrusted to the decision of judges than to frame laws in addition.

Obj. 3. Further, every law is framed for the direction of human actions, as is evident from what has been stated above. But since human actions are about singulars, which are infinite in number, matters pertaining to the direction of human actions cannot be taken into sufficient consideration except by a wise man, who looks into each one of them. Therefore it would have been better for human acts to be directed by the judgment of wise men, than by the framing of laws. Therefore there was no need of human laws.

On the contrary, Isidore says: *Laws were made that in fear thereof human audacity might be held in check, that innocence might be safeguarded in the midst of wickedness, and that the dread of punishment might prevent the wicked from doing harm.* But these things are most necessary to mankind. Therefore it was necessary that human laws should be made.

I answer that, As we have stated above, man has a natural aptitude for virtue; but the perfection of virtue must be acquired by man by means of some kind of training. Thus we observe that a man is helped by diligence in his necessities, for instance, in food and clothing. Certain beginnings of these he has from nature, viz., his reason and his hands; but he has not the full complement, as other animals have, to whom nature has given sufficiently of clothing and food. Now it is difficult to see how man could suffice for himself in the matter of this training, since the perfection of virtue consists chiefly in withdrawing man from undue pleasures, to which above all man is inclined, and especially the young, who are more capable of being trained. Consequently a man needs to receive this training from another, whereby to arrive at the perfection of virtue. And as to those young people who are inclined to acts of virtue by their good natural disposition, or by custom, or rather by the gift of God, paternal training suffices, which is by admonitions. But since some are found to be dissolute and prone to vice, and not easily amenable to words, it was necessary for such to be restrained from evil by force and fear, in order that, at least, they might desist from evil-

doing, and leave others in peace, and that they themselves, by being habituated in this way, might be brought to do willingly what hitherto they did from fear, and thus become virtuous. Now this kind of training, which compels through fear of punishment, is the discipline of laws. Therefore, in order that man might have peace and virtue, it was necessary for laws to be framed; for, as the Philosopher says, *as man is the most noble of animals if he be perfect in virtue, so he is the lowest of all, if he be severed from law and justice.* For man can use his reason to devise means of satisfying his lusts and evil passions, which other animals are unable to do.

Reply Obj. 1. Men who are well disposed are led willingly to virtue by being admonished better than by coercion; but men whose disposition is evil are not led to virtue unless they are compelled.

Reply Obj. 2. As the Philosopher says, *it is better that all things be regulated by law, than left to be decided by judges.* And this for three reasons. First, because it is easier to find a few wise men competent to frame right laws, than to find the many who would be necessary to judge rightly of each single case.—Secondly, because those who make laws consider long beforehand what laws to make, whereas judgment on each single case has to be pronounced as soon as it arises; and it is easier for man to see what is right, by taking many instances into consideration, than by considering one solitary instance.—Thirdly, because law-givers judge universally and about future events, whereas those who sit in judgment judge of things present, towards which they are affected by love, hatred, or some kind of cupidity; and thus their judgment become perverted.

Since, then, the animated justice of the judge is not found in every man, and since it can be bent, therefore it was necessary, whenever possible, for the law to determine how to judge, and for very few matters to be left to the decision of men.

Reply Obj. 3. Certain individual facts which cannot be covered by the law *have necessarily to be committed to judges,* as the Philosopher says in the same passage: *e.g., concerning something that has happened or not happened,* and the like.

SECOND ARTICLE. Whether Every Human Law Is Derived from the Natural Law?

We proceed thus to the Second Article:—

Objection 1. It would seem that not every human law is derived from the natural law. For the Philosopher says that *the legal just is that which originally was a matter of indifference*. But those things which arise from the natural law are not matters of indifference. Therefore the enactments of human laws are not all derived from the natural law.

Obj. 2. Further, positive law is divided against natural law, as is stated by Isidore and the Philosopher. But those things which flow as conclusions from the common principles of the natural law belong to the natural law, as was stated above. Therefore that which is established by human law is not derived from the natural law.

Obj. 3. Further, the law of nature is the same for all, since the Philosopher says that *the natural just is that which is equally valid everywhere*. If therefore human laws were derived from the natural law, it would follow that they too are the same for all; which is clearly false.

Obj. 4. Further, it is possible to give a reason for things which are derived from the natural law. But *it is not possible to give the reason for all the legal enactments of the lawgivers*, as the Jurist says. Therefore not all human laws are derived from the natural law.

On the contrary, Tully says: *Things which emanated from nature, and were approved by custom, were sanctioned by fear and reverence for the laws.*

I answer that, As Augustine says, *that which is not just seems to be no law at all.* Hence the force of a law depends on the extent of its justice. Now in human affairs a thing is said to be just from being right, according to the rule of reason. But the first rule of reason is the law of nature, as is clear from what has been stated above. Consequently, every human law has just so much of the nature of law as it is derived from the law of nature. But if in any point it departs from the law of nature, it is no longer a law but a perversion of law.

But it must be noted that something may be derived from the natural law in two ways: first, as a conclusion from principles; secondly, by way of a determination of certain common notions. The first way is like to that by which, in the sciences, demonstrated conclusions are drawn from the principles; while the second is likened to that whereby, in the arts, common forms are determined to some particular. Thus, the craftsman needs to determine the common form of a house to the shape of this or that particular house. Some things are therefore derived from the common principles of the natural law by way of conclusions: e.g., that *one must not kill* may be derived as a conclusion from the principle that *one should do harm to no man*; while some are derived therefrom by way of determination: e.g., the law of nature has it that the evil-doer should be punished, but that he be punished in this or that way is a determination of the law of nature.

Accordingly, both modes of derivation are found in the human law. But those things which are derived in the first way are contained in human law, not as emanating therefrom exclusively, but as having some force from the natural law also. But those things which are derived in the second way have no other force than that of human law.

Reply Obj. 1. The Philosopher is speaking of those enactments which are by way of determination or specification of the precepts of the natural law.

Reply Obj. 2. This argument holds for those things that are derived from the natural law by way of conclusion.

Reply Obj. 3. The common principles of the natural law cannot be applied to all men in the same way because of the great variety of human affairs; and hence arises the diversity of positive laws among various people.

Reply Obj. 4. These words of the Jurist are to be understood as referring to the decisions of rulers in determining particular points of the natural law; and to these determinations the judgment of expert and prudent men is related as to its principles, in so far, namely, as they see at once what is the best thing to decide. Hence the Philosopher says that, in such matters, *we ought to pay as much attention to the undemonstrated sayings and opinions of persons who surpass us in experience, age and prudence, as to their demonstrations.*

Chapter 14

WILLIAM OF OCKHAM

William of Ockham was born in Ockham, England, around 1285. He joined the Franciscan order and studied at Oxford University. In 1324 he was accused of heresy and was denied a license to teach. He was involved in theological controversies and took refuge in Munich under the protection of Emperor Ludwig of Bavaria. He died in 1349.

Ockham is best known for the "Law of Parsimony" or "Ockham's Razor": "Entities are not to be multiplied beyond necessity." In other words, other things being equal, we should always adopt the simpler explanation.

Ockham applied this principle to the problem of universals and particulars. All there is are particular things or substances. The notion of universals is an unnecessary invention. There is no real universal apart from the particular thing. This position is called Nominalism as distinguished from Realism, the view that universals exist apart from individual substances. Ockham has been viewed as the founder of Nominalism. An early letter from the Nominalist masters of the University of Paris to King Louis XI in 1473 sets forth the Nominalist position.

> Those doctors are called Nominalists who do not multiply the things principally signified by terms in accordance with the multiplication of the terms. Realists, however, are those who contend on the contrary that things are multiplied according to the multiplicity of terms. For example, Nominalists say that divinity and wisdom are one and the same thing altogether, because everything which is in God, is God. But realists say that the divine wisdom is divided from divinity.
>
> Again, those are called Nominalists who show diligence and zeal in understanding all the properties of terms on which the truth and falsity of a sentence depends, and without which the perfect judgment of the truth and falsity of propositions cannot be made. These properties are: supposition, appellation, ampliation, restriction, exponible distribution. They especially understand obligations and the nature of the insoluble, the true foundation of dialectical arguments and their failure. Being instructed in these things, they easily understand concerning any given argumentation whether it is good or bad. But the realists neglect all these things, and they condemn them, saying, "We proceed to things, we have no concern for terms." Against them Master John Gerson said, "While you proceed to things, neglecting terms, you fall into complete ignorance of things themselves." This is in his treatise on the Magnificat; and he added that the said Realists involve themselves in inexplicable difficulties, since they seek difficulty where there is none, unless it is logical difficulty. (Translated by James J. Walsh from the text of Ehrle, *Der Sentenzenkommentater Peters von Candida* in *Philosophy in the Middle Ages*, eds. Arthur Hyman and James J. Walsh (Indianapolis: Hackett Publishing Co., 1973, p. 649f).

FOR FURTHER READING:

Boehner, P. *Collected Articles on Ockham*. (St. Bonaventure University Press, 1956).
Hyman, Arthur and James Walsh. *Philosophy in the Middle Ages*. (Hackett Publishing Co., 1973).
Moody, E. A. *The Logic of William of Ockham*. (New York, 1935).
Ockham. *Philosophical Writings*, ed. P. Boehner. (Nelson Philosophical Texts, 1957).

Summa Logicae

PART I

Chapter 14: On the Universal

It is not enough for the logician to have a merely general knowledge of terms; he needs a deep understanding of the concept of a term. Therefore, after discussing some general divisions among terms we should examine in detail the various headings under these divisions.

First, we should deal with terms of second intention and afterwards with terms of first intention. I have said that "universal," "genus," and "species" are examples of terms of second intention. We must discuss those terms of second intention which are called the five universals, but first we should consider the common term "universal." It is predicated of every universal and is opposed to the notion of a particular.

First, it should be noted that the term "particular" has two senses. In the first sense a particular is that which is one and not many. Those who hold that a universal is a certain quality residing in the mind which is predicable of many (not suppositing for itself, of course, but for the many of which it is predicated) must grant that, in this sense of the word, every universal is a particular. Just as a word, even if convention makes it common, is a particular, the intention of the soul signifying many is numerically one thing a particular; for although it signifies many things it is nonetheless one thing and not many.

In another sense of the word we use "particular" to mean that which is one and not many and which

cannot function as a sign of many. Taking "particular" in this sense no universal is a particular, since every universal is capable of signifying many and of being predicated of many. Thus, if we take the term "universal" to mean that which is not one in number, as many do, then, I want to say that nothing is a universal. One could, of course, abuse the expression and say that a population constitutes a single universal because it is not one but many. But that would be puerile.

Therefore, it ought to be said that every universal is one particular thing and that it is not a universal except in its signification, in its signifying many things. This is what Avicenna means to say in his commentary on the fifth book of the *Metaphysics*. He says, "One form in the intellect is related to many things, and in this respect it is a universal; for it is an intention of the intellect which has an invariant relationship to anything you choose." He then continues, "Although this form is a universal in its relationship to individuals, it is a particular in its relationship to the particular soul in which it resides; for it is just one form among many in the intellect." He means to say that a universal is an intention of a particular soul. Insofar as it can be predicated of many things not for itself but for these many, it is said to be a universal; but insofar as it is a particular form actually existing in the intellect, it is said to be a particular. Thus "particular" is predicated of a universal in the first sense but not in the second. In the same way we say that the sun is a universal cause and, nevertheless, that it is really and truly a particular or individual cause. For the sun is said to be a universal cause because it is the cause of many things (i.e., every object that is generable and corruptible), but it is said to be a particular cause because it is one cause and not many. In the same way the intention of the soul is said to be a universal because it is a sign predicable of many things, but it is said to be a particular because it is one thing and not many.

But it should be noted that there are two kinds of universals. Some things are universal by nature; that is, by nature they are signs predicable of many in the same way that the smoke is by nature a sign of fire; weeping, a sign of grief; and laughter, a sign of internal joy. The intention of the soul, of course, is a universal by nature. Thus, no substance outside the soul, nor any accident outside the soul is a universal of this sort. It is of this kind of universal that I shall speak in the following chapters.

Other things are universals by convention. Thus, a spoken word, which is numerically one quality, is a universal; it is a sign conventionally appointed for the signification of many things. Thus, since the word is said to be common, it can be called a universal. But notice it is not by nature, but only by convention, that this label applies.

Chapter 15: That the Universal Is Not a Thing Outside the Mind

But it is not enough just to state one's position; one must defend it by philosophical arguments. Therefore, I shall set forth some arguments for my view, and then corroborate it by an appeal to the authorities.

That no universal is a substance existing outside the mind can be proved in a number of ways:

No universal is a particular substance, numerically one; for if this were the case, then it would follow that Socrates is a universal; for there is no good reason why one substance should be a universal rather than another. Therefore no particular substance is a universal; every substance is numerically one and a particular. For every substance is either one thing and not many or it is many things. Now, if a substance is one thing and not many, then it is numerically one; for that is what we mean by "numerically one." But if, on the other hand, some substance is several things, it is either several particular things or several universal things. If the first alternative is chosen, then it follows that some substance would be several particular substances; and consequently that some substance would be several men. But although the universal would be distinguished from a single particular, it would not be distinguished from several particulars. If, however, some substance were to be several universal entities, I take one of those universal entities and ask, "Is it many things or is it one and not many?" If the second is the case then it follows that the thing is particular. If the first is the case then I ask, "Is it several particular things or several universal things?" Thus, either an infinite regress will follow or it will be granted that no substance is a universal in a way that would be incompatible with its also being a particular. From this it follows that no substance is a universal.

Again, if some universal were to be one substance existing in particular substances, yet distinct from them, it would follow that it could exist without them; for everything that is naturally prior to something else can, by God's power, exist without that thing; but the consequence is absurd.

Again, if the view in question were true, no individual would be able to be created. Something of the individual would pre-exist it, for the whole individual would not take its existence from nothing if the universal which is in it were already in something else. For the same reason it would follow that God could not annihilate an individual substance without destroying the other individuals of the same kind. If He were to annihilate some individual, he would destroy the whole which is essentially that individual and, consequently, He would destroy the universal which is in that thing and in others of the same essence. Consequently, other things of the same essence would not remain, for they could not continue to exist without the universal which constitutes a part of them.

Again, such a universal could not be construed as something completely extrinsic to the essence of an individual; therefore, it would belong to the essence of the individual; and consequently, an individual would be composed of universals, so that the individual would not be any more a particular than a universal.

Again, it follows that something of the essence of Christ would be miserable and damned, since that common nature really existing in Christ would be damned in the damned individual; for surely that essence is also in Judas. But this is absurd.

Many other arguments could be brought forth, but in the interests of brevity, I shall dispense with them. Instead, I shall corroborate my account by an appeal to authorities. First, in the seventh book of the *Metaphysics*, Aristotle is treating the question of whether a universal is a substance. He shows that no universal is a substance. Thus, he says, "it is impossible that substance be something that can be predicated universally."

Again, in the tenth book of the *Metaphysics*, he says, "Thus, if, as we argued in the discussions on substance and being, no universal can be a substance, it is not possible that a universal be a substance in the sense of a one over and against the many."

From these remarks it is clear that, in Aristotle's view, although universals can supposit for substances, no universal is a substance.

Again, the Commentator in his forty-fourth comment on the seventh book of the *Metaphysics* says, "In the individual, the only substance is the particular form and matter out of which the individual is composed."

Again, in the forty-fifth comment, he says, "Let us say, therefore, that it is impossible that one of those things we call universals be the substance of anything, although they do express the substances of things."

And, again, in the forty-seventh comment, "It is impossible that they (universals) be parts of substances existing of and by themselves."

Again, in the second comment on the eighth book of the *Metaphysics*, he says, "No universal is either a substance or a genus."

Again, in the sixth comment on the tenth book, he says, "Since universals are not substances, it is clear that the common notion of being is not a substance existing outside the mind."

Using these and many other authorities, the general point emerges: no universal is a substance regardless of the viewpoint from which we consider the matter. Thus, the viewpoint from which we consider the matter is irrelevant to the question of whether something is a substance. Nevertheless, the meaning of a term is relevant to the question of whether the expression "substance" can be predicated of the term. Thus, if the term "dog" in the proposition "The dog is an animal" is used to stand for the barking animal, the proposition is true; but if it is used for the celestial body which goes by that name, the proposition is false. But it is impossible that one and the same thing should be a substance from one viewpoint and not a substance from another.

Therefore, it ought to be granted that no univer-

sal is a substance regardless of how it is considered. On the contrary, every universal is an intention of the mind which, on the most probable account, is identical with the act of understanding. Thus, it is said that the act of understanding by which I grasp men is a natural sign of men in the same way that weeping is a natural sign of grief. It is a natural sign such that it can stand for men in mental propositions in the same way that a spoken word can stand for things in spoken propositions.

That the universal is an intention of the soul is clearly expressed by Avicenna in the fifth book of the *Metaphysics*, in which he comments, "I say, therefore, that there are three senses of 'universal.' For we say that something is a universal if (like 'man') it is actually predicated of many things; and we also call an intention a universal if it could be predicated of many." Then follows the remark, "An intention is also called a universal if there is nothing inconceivable in its being predicated of many."

From these remarks it is clear that the universal is an intention of the soul capable of being predicated of many. The claim can be corroborated by argument. For every one agrees that a universal is something predicable of many, but only an intention of the soul or a conventional sign is predicated. No substance is ever predicated of anything. Therefore, only an intention of the soul or a conventional sign is a universal; but I am not here using the term "universal" for conventional signs, but only for signs that are universals by nature. That substance is not capable of functioning as predicate is clear; for if it were, it would follow that a proposition would be composed of particular substances; and, consequently, the subject would be in Rome and the predicate in England which is absurd.

Furthermore, propositions occur only in the mind, in speech, or in writing; therefore, their parts can exist only in the mind, in speech, and in writing. Particular substances, however, cannot themselves exist in the mind, in speech, or in writing. Thus, no proposition can be composed of particular substances. Propositions are, however, composed of universals; therefore, universals cannot conceivably be substances.

Chapter 16: Against Scotus' Account of the Universal

It may be clear to many that a universal is not a substance outside the mind which exists in, but is distinct from, particulars. Nevertheless, some want to claim that the universal is, in some way, outside the soul and in particulars; and while they do not want to say that a universal is really distinct from particulars, they say that it is formally distinct from particulars. Thus, they say that in Socrates there is human nature which is contracted to Socrates by an individual difference which is not really, but only formally, distinct from that nature. Thus, while there are not two things, one is not formally the other.

I do not find this view tenable:

First, in creatures there can never be any distinction outside the mind unless there are distinct things; if, therefore, there is any distinction between the nature and the difference, it is necessary that they really be distinct things. I prove my premise by the following syllogism: the nature is not formally distinct from itself; this individual difference is formally distinct from this nature; therefore, this individual difference is not this nature.

Again, the same entity is not both common and proper, but in their view the individual difference is proper and the universal is common; therefore, no universal is identical with an individual difference.

Again, opposites cannot be attributed to one and the same created thing, but *common* and *proper* are opposites; therefore, the same thing is not both common and proper. Nevertheless, that conclusion would follow if an individual difference and a common nature were the same thing.

Again, if a common nature were the same thing as an individual difference, there would be as many common natures as there are individual differences; and, consequently, none of those natures would be common, but each would be peculiar to the difference with which it is identical.

Again, whenever one thing is distinct from another it is distinguished from that thing either of and by itself or by something intrinsic to itself. Now, the humanity of Socrates is something different from the humanity of Plato; therefore, they are distinguished of and by themselves and not by differences that are added to them.

Again, according to Aristotle things differing in species also differ in number, but the nature of a man and the nature of a donkey differ in species of and by themselves; therefore, they are numerically distinguished of and by themselves; therefore, each of them is numerically one of and by itself.

Again, that which cannot belong to many cannot be predicated of many; but such a nature, if it really

is the same thing as the individual difference, cannot belong to many since it cannot belong to any other particular. Thus, it cannot be predicable of many; but, then, it cannot be a universal.

Again, take an individual difference and the nature which it contracts. Either the difference between these two things is greater or less than the difference between two particulars. It is not greater because they do not differ really; particulars, however, do differ really. But neither is it less because then they would admit of one and the same definition, since two particulars, can admit of the same definition. Consequently, if one of them is, by itself, one in number, the other will also be.

Again, either the nature is the individual difference or it is not. If it is the difference I argue as follows: this individual difference is proper and not common; this individual difference is this nature; therefore this nature is proper and not common, but that is what I set out to prove. Likewise, I argue as follows: the individual difference is not formally distinct from the individual difference; the individual difference is the nature; therefore, the nature is not formally distinct from the individual difference. But if it be said that the individual difference is not the nature, my point has been proved; for it follows that if the individual difference is not the nature, the individual difference is not really the nature; for from the opposite of the consequent follows the opposite of the antecedent. Thus, if it is true that the individual difference really is the nature, then the individual difference is the nature. The inference is valid, for from a determinable taken with its determination (where the determination does not detract from or diminish the determinable) one can infer the determinable taken by itself; but "really" does not express a determination that detracts or diminishes. Therefore, it follows that if the individual difference is really the nature, the individual difference is the nature.

Therefore, one should grant that in created things there is no such thing as a formal distinction. All things which are distinct in creatures are really distinct and, therefore, different things. In regard to creatures modes of argument like the following ought never be denied; this is *A*; this is *B*; therefore, *B* is *A*; and this is not *A*; this is *B*; therefore, *B* is not *A*. Likewise, one ought never deny that, as regards creatures, there are distinct things where contradictory notions hold. The only exception would be the case where contradictory notions hold true because of some syncategorematic element or similar determination, but in the same present case this is not so.

Therefore, we ought to say with the philosophers that in a particular substance there is nothing substantial except the particular form, the particular matter, or the composite of the two. And, therefore, no one ought to think that in Socrates there is a humanity or a human nature which is distinct from Socrates and to which there is added an individual difference which contracts that nature. The only thing in Socrates which can be construed as substantial is that particular matter, this particular form, or the composite of the two. And, therefore, every essence and quiddity and whatever belongs to substance, if it is really outside the soul, is just matter, form, or the composite of these or, following the doctrine of the Peripatetics, a separated and immaterial substance.

CPSIA information can be obtained
at www.ICGtesting.com
Printed in the USA
BVHW061825210722
642708BV00002B/6

9 780195 116458